ISRAEL
ORIENTAL
STUDIES
XX

ISRAEL
ORIENTAL
STUDIES

XX

SEMITIC LINGUISTICS: THE STATE OF THE ART
AT THE TURN OF THE TWENTY-FIRST CENTURY

EDITED BY

Shlomo Izre'el

EISENBRAUNS
2002

The paper in this book meets the guidelines for permanence and durability of the Committee on Production Guidelines for Book Longevity of the Council on Library Resources.

ISRAEL ORIENTAL STUDIES
Annual Publication of the Lester and Sally Entin Faculty of Humanities
Tel-Aviv University

Editor: Shlomo Izre'el
Associate Editor: David J. Wasserstein
Technical Editor: Baruch Podolsky
Editorial Board: Ilai Alon, Joel L. Kraemer, Anson F. Rainey, Shlomo Raz, Uri Rubin, Joseph Sadan, Itamar Singer
Executive Editor: Edna Liftman

Library of Congress Cataloging-in-Publication Data

LC card number 72-955546

LC card number 72-955546

ISSN 0334–4401
ISBN 1–57506–059–0

Typeset in Israel: Graphit Press Ltd., Jerusalem
Printed and bound in the United States of America

This volume of *Israel Oriental Studies* is dedicated

to the memory of

Professor Shlomo Raz (1936–1999)

CONTENTS

PREFACE

A turn of a century is a good pretext to sum up and look ahead. Yet the raison d'être of this volume is, I admit, something I have always felt was needed: to define what lies behind the term "Semitic linguistics". In other words, in more general terms: to try to define where Semitic linguistics stands in relationship to "linguistics". When I took over the position of editor of *Israel Oriental Studies*, I thought that I might now have a proper stage for discussion of this issue. *IOS*, which had built its reputation — among other fields — also in Semitic linguistics, was the right place to do so. The year in which volume 20 was scheduled to be published was also my last year as editor of *IOS*, and coincided with the turn of the century. It thus seemed the right time to materialize this plan.

The year 2000 marked not only the turn of a century, but also the turn of a millennium. This is not merely a nice point in time for such an evaluation, but a real occasion for celebration: not only can Semitic linguistics celebrate a century of research, but a millennium (in fact, more than a millennium) of linguistic learning. While this volume aims at presenting a century of learning, this learning has a long tradition of Semitic studies to lean on, and thus, the past century is only the latest period in a long tradition of study and research, as well as a most significant period. In any case, volume 20 of *Israel Oriental Studies* seemed a good opportunity for a loud and outspoken presentation of our field, and thus a statement on the state of the art of Semitic linguistics on its own and its implications for the general study of language.

Semitic linguistics — or, I should perhaps say, the study of Semitic languages — has always been associated with philology rather than linguistics, with the decipherment of dead languages rather than the study of modern living languages, and with diachronic and comparative linguistics rather than synchronic analyses of languages. While languages and language families are the main concern of Semitic linguistics in general, I thought it would be preferable to adopt a different point of view, and to present our interest in the various languages in this family from a variety of angles.

The volume comprises seven sections, each dealing with a different aspect of Semitic linguistics. It opens with a section on methodological issues, then goes on to overviews of what has been done in linguistic

7

study within the Semitic sphere. Then follows a section consisting of two supplementary discussions that go beyond the Semitic sphere, viz., into Egyptian and the Hamito-Semitic phylum. The two following sections are devoted to linguistic domains that have not really gained the status of distinct disciplines in Semitic linguistics, as they have in general linguistics: language contact and dialectology. The sixth section goes beyond the pure study of language that is established and commonplace in Semitic linguistics, to explore either the relationship of language to other disciplines or some new ways of studying texts. Finally, some space is devoted to reviewing recently published books that are of general interest to Semitic linguistics and are inherently related to the subject matter of this volume: Hetzron's *The Semitic Languages*, a collection of language descriptions; Lipiński's *Semitic Languages: Outline of a Comparative Grammar*, Bennett's textbook, *Comparative Semitic Linguistics: A Manual*, and the first volume of Takács's *Etymological Dictionary of Egyptian*. The general aim of this volume is to convey the achievements, the drawbacks and the desiderata in the wide and diverse field of Semitic linguistics, i.e., to emphasize progress, conservatism and current gaps in research. Some desiderata can be called upon before even starting to read this collection of papers. Some of these are gaps in this very collection of studies, caused by poor organization or lack of efficiency in getting the right people to fill them. Others are gaps inherent in the specifics of Semitic studies or the specifics of fields of interest in linguistics as such. Just a few examples of these gaps are geographical linguistics as a more general and comprehensive issue than that which is presented here; the period between the ancient world and the modern world; sociolinguistics; psycholinguistics and cognitive sciences.

As a first step toward the publication of this volume, a preparatory symposium was held at Tel Aviv University in January 1999 under the auspices of the rector of Tel Aviv University. This provided an opportunity for contributors to the volume, many of whom are involved in large research projects, to offer oral presentations on the areas being investigated and discuss matters of mutual interest. Special emphasis was placed on pinpointing desiderata and making suggestions for future research and possible international cooperation. The symposium was the basis upon which the written contributions and the setup of this *IOS* volume eventually emerged. Prior presentations and discussions of topics and matters of mutual interest thus resulted in a more coherent statement for the published volume. This volume appears some three years after the conference, due to unexpected delays, for which I should apologize. Some authors have updated their papers to some extent. Still, it must be remembered that most of what is presented here reflects the state of the art in Semitic linguistics just before the turn of the century.

Scholars of high repute from the major study centers of Semitic linguistics and related disciplines worldwide were invited to take part in this project. We have been honored by the participation of David L. Appleyard, Anna Belova, Yaacov Choueka, Peter Daniels, Jo Ann Hackett, Uri Horesh, John Huehnergard, Otto Jastrow, Olga Kapeliuk, Stephen Kaufman, Geoffrey Khan, Joseph L. Malone, Michael P. O'Connor, Marie-Claude Simeone-Senelle, Ruth Berman, Edward L. Greenstein, Gideon Goldenberg, Baruch Podolsky, Victor Porkhomovsky, Dorit Ravid, Helmut Satzinger, Rainer Voigt, and Bruce Zuckerman.

Our esteemed colleague, Shlomo Raz, who was also invited to take an active part in the project, enjoyed the conference in person, but was unable to prepare a lecture. Shlomo, a dear friend and a great supporter, on both personal and academic levels, and an enthusiastic promoter of this very project, passed away on the twelfth of April 1999. It is with deep sorrow and much yearning that I dedicate this volume to him.

ACKNOWLEDGMENTS

The very first step I took before attempting any organizational procedures was to approach my teacher and colleague, whom I have always regarded as my linguistic father, Gideon Goldenberg. Gideon has advised me in matters of shape and personae, and I thank him for his teaching and continuing support over decades. Marcelo Dascal, then dean of The Lester and Sally Entin Faculty of Humanities at Tel Aviv University, always gave special attention to linguistics in general and Semitic linguistics in particular. I thank him for his constant support. Special thanks are due to Uri Horesh for his invaluable assistance in the phase of preparations and during the symposium. I further thank the dean, the rector, the president of Tel Aviv University, and The Chaim Rosenberg School of Jewish Studies, for granting funds for convening the symposium and for the publication of this volume.

It is a special pleasure to acknowledge the financial support for the symposium of external donors: The Austrian Embassy in Tel Aviv and its cultural attaché, Ulf Hausbrandt; The British Council and Sonia Feldman of its Visits Department; The Deutsche Forschungsgemeinschaft in Bonn, through the recommendation of the German Embassy in Tel Aviv and Ronald Münch, head of its Cultural Department; Rachel and Oded E'dan; Meir Lipshes, President of Omnitec Eichut; and Zvi Zorfati and Sons. I wish to acknowledge further grants by The Lucius N. Littauer Foundation and by The Irene Young Endowment Fund for Scientific Publications for the publication of this *IOS* volume.

Baruch Podolsky and Edna Liftman have been an immeasurable academic and administrative comfort in sustaining *IOS* volumes during many years of publication. The editorial board of *IOS* has furnished solid backing and a source of inspiration and good advice during all these years.

Last, but definitely not least, I wish to thank all the distinguished colleagues who accepted the invitation to take part in this project.

Shlomo Izre'el   Tel Aviv, October 2001

Methodologies

INTRODUCTION

WITH SOME NOTES ON THE RUSSIAN SCHOOL OF SEMITIC LINGUISTICS

The first section of this volume deals with methodologies in studying Semitic linguistics. Gideon Goldenberg was entrusted with the issue of the interrelationship between Semitic linguistics and the general study of language, a subject that he had been dealing with for some time. Goldenberg's studies show deep appreciation of the fact that Semitic linguistics is a branch of linguistics and that research in Semitic studies can contribute a great deal to the general study of language (see his recently published Collected Papers, Goldenberg 1998; further Goldenberg 1997; Goldenberg forthcoming). In his paper, Goldenberg speaks of genealogical studies with historical, areal and cultural connections, preaching the need to acquire a profound knowledge of languages not only to study their relationship with other languages, but also for the sake of synchronic analyses, and, of course, for enhancing theoretical observations on language. With this in mind, he touches briefly upon some relevant points in the comparative method, and goes on to explore various linguistic concepts and terms where the study of Semitic languages can contribute to better understanding of linguistic features and processes.

This volume on Semitic linguistics in the twentieth century was to include two reports on individual schools of Semitic studies that can be singled out as not being part of the mainstream of this field. These are the Chomskian school and the Russian school. As duly recognized in the diverse papers in this volume, and as a brief survey of the bibliographical lists attached to them or to other collective or individual publications (e.g., Hetzron 1997) will show, most of the work done in Semitic linguistics belongs to a different stream from what might be regarded as the mainstream of general linguistics of the second half of the twentieth century, namely, the Chomskian School. Chomsky himself started his linguistic exploration on a Semitic language (Modern Hebrew; Chomsky 1979, a publication of his MA thesis from 1951). Still, research in the formative years of generative linguistics was centered on English. Extensive research in Semitic languages in this school started much later.

It is to this trend in Semitic linguistics that Joseph L. Malone has devoted his paper. Malone, finding himself overwhelmed by the task of writing a comprehensive survey of "what might count as Chomsky-inspired", bases his survey on materials drawn from "his attic study". This was not a bad

13

idea, since, being himself a follower of the Chomskian School (Malone 1985, 1989, 1993, 1995 and 1999 are representative works), the author could pinpoint the most significant encounters between Semitic languages and this school of thought. After a brief survey of the origins of generative linguistics and its expansion, Malone discusses the work of five scholars who had something to offer to Semitic linguistics from a different direction, using Chomskian-inspired thought or techniques. Malone mentions the explication of internal flexion as "the most impressive contribution of Chomskian linguistics to Semitic morphophonology", which is tied to the name of John McCarthy. McCarthy's line of thinking has since gained wide attention. More recently, new trends in the Chomskian School have attracted other followers, and much work is being done in these areas. For example, a conference held in Fez (Morocco), in March 1999, issued a call in these very words:

> Chamito-semitic languages have generally been associated with descriptive and diachronic linguistics. They have been described and analyzed at the phonological, morphosyntactic and semantic levels by functional, structural and generative schools of linguistics. **Today most Chamito-semitic studies are inspired by the generative trend** (my emphasis, Sh.I.). However, in the light of the new developments in the Minimalist Theory, Chamito-semitic languages have been overlooked. The aim of this conference is to discuss new researches in the syntax of Chamito-semitic languages within the framework of the latest approaches in generative syntax. The ultimate goal is to establish the parameters of these languages and bring changes and improvements to the Minimalist Theory on the basis of empirical data.
>
> New data and comparative studies are encouraged in order to strengthen or disconfirm the principles of minimalism and UG.

What this call shows, I believe, is that there is a gap, both academic and social, between schools of study, which very rarely allows for mutual fertilization. As shown by Malone, this was not necessarily the case in earlier times, when, e.g., an appendix presenting "Generative Statements" seemed not at all odd in a structural grammar of Akkadian (Reiner 1966: 128–136). Moreover, there are many points of convergence between paths taken by linguists on both sides of the barrier, in spite of their different points of departure (cf. Goldenberg 1994: §22). Much of the work done in Semitic linguistics today has integrated concepts and techniques of the Chomskian school. In recent years, however, this gap has been growing deeper, and the introduction of new concepts and new terminologies makes bridging it almost impossible.

In contrast to Chomskian-inspired Semitic studies, the Russian school of Semitic studies constitutes a different branch of Semitic linguistics, not because of a deliberate choice made by its members, but due to the scientific isolation imposed on them by twentieth century politics. The political situation also entailed the almost sole use of Russian — a language usually not accessible to Western scholars — in publications. The fall of the iron curtain toward the end of that century has made possible the realization of Belova and Porkhomovsky's wish that such a presentation will be the last one needed in conferences in Semitic linguistics. The period around the turn of the century already shows promising signs of renewed ties and scientific cooperation between Russian Semitists and the West, as works by Russian scholars have found ways to integrate into the global effort of Semitic linguistics (some references to Russian and C.I.S. scholars from recent years in this volume will prove this statement).

Unfortunately, our initial desire to have a written report on the Russian school of Semitic linguistics in the twentieth century could not be realized. Instead, I would like to summarize the main points raised in Belova and Porkhomovsky's oral presentation at the 1999 symposium.[1]

Before the twentieth century, Semitic studies in Russia were mostly focused on Arabic studies, influenced by the importation of German scholars who had Arabic as their main subject of interest. This focus on Arabic — in contrast to Western European scholarship, which focused mainly on Hebrew, was enhanced by the existence of a large Muslim population in the Russian Empire during the 17th and 18h centuries that had Arabic as its cultural language. This focused interest on Arabic has had its influence on Semitic studies in Russia also in the twentieth century. Another major factor that has had an impact on Semitic studies in Russia is the presence of rich collections of Oriental manuscripts, both Arabic and Hebrew, notably by Karaites, in St. Petersburg.

During the beginning and middle of the twentieth century, the Russian school of Semitic linguistics showed special interest in studying Semitic root and stem structure. This morphological domain was dealt with in a very different approach from that of the Neo-Grammarians. This trend in Semitic studies had been influenced by the work of N. Ya. Marr, leader of the so-called sociological approach in Soviet linguistics, who specialized in Caucasian studies. Marr regarded standard genetic comparative linguistics as methodologically problematic, and his alternative methodological attitude has become ideologically compelling for his followers. Basically, Marr has developed

---

[1] The lecture was given by Victor Porkhomovky. Anna Belova could not be present in the symposium. I thank Baruch Podolsky and Gideon Goldenberg who helped with finding references for works mentioned in this lecture.

a theory of historical evolvement of human languages through their written form, which is, obviously, a major handicap, since human language had emerged in the world a long time before the first script appeared in history.[2] This theoretical trend was part and parcel of Soviet Semitists trying to explain the emergence of human language through the structure of the Semitic root. Still, the research conducted with this attitude to the study of Semitic roots and stem formation is interesting. The scholars worth mentioning in this respect are Grande, Yushmanov, Maizel, Starinin, and Gazov-Ginzberg. Grande was a traditional Semitic and Arabic scholar whose work, although published in the sixth and seventh decades of the century (Grande 1963, 1972), still follows the work of Carl Brockelmann and reflects the scholarship of the first half of the twentieth century. Yushmanov is a key figure in the Russian school of Semitic and Hamito-Semitic studies in the pre-WWII period; he published a series of short grammatical descriptions of Semitic and Hamitic languages (e.g., Yushmanov 1936, 1937, 1938, 1985), some of which remained unpublished until recently (Yushmanov 1998). These descriptions contain penetrating observations on the respective linguistic structures reached by other scholars only after decades. Yushmanov's views on the structure of the Semitic root are expressed in a 1927 paper, published in Yushmanov 1998: 126–190. Solomon Maizel is mostly known for his work on Semitic roots (Maizel 1983), published posthumously by his grandson, a Semitic scholar on his own, Alexander Militarev (see Podolsky's paper, p. 213). Starinin is a specialist in Ethio-Semitic languages (cf. Starinin 1963). Gazov-Ginsberg (1965) introduced a further step in this direction by proposing the development of roots — Semitic and other — from the imitation of natural sounds, to be followed by actual word derivation.

While the described trend of study may look quite outdated to most, Belova and Porkhomovsky pointed out that a similar approach had become quite popular toward the end of the century among European scholars outside the Russian sphere. They mentioned in this connection two

---

[2] Gideon Goldenberg has kindly supplied some further details on the work and influence of Marr: Nikolaj Jakovlevich Marr (1865–1934 [or 1935]) was the notorious Russian linguist of Georgian origin who claimed that languages of the same social class belonged together, by which theory he wished to show that linguistics agrees with Marxism. He accordingly connected the Georgian language with other "socially-similar" languages in a Japhetic family. When in the 1930s he became vice-president of the Academy of Sciences of the U.S.S.R., he managed to impose his ideas on Russian linguists, who were not allowed to reject his theory and hold other ideas, like genetic classification. Marr's remained the dominating theory until an article (by Vinogradov, they say) was published signed by Joseph Stalin, which refuted that theory and instructed all linguists to go back to a more acceptable methodology. Marr's selected works were published in a set of four volumes (Marr 1933–37).

recent publications: Murtonen's comparative work on Hebrew (Murtonen 1986–1990), where the Comparative Lexicon (Part One) has been processed using a similar methodology; and George Bohas' recent work on Arabic lexicography (1997), which is closely related to Yushmanov's work. This new trend of study shows that the Russian school of Semitic linguistics has not been totally concentric in the twentieth century, and that it deserves a further look.

One other major aspect of Russian Semitic studies has been dialectology. This trend emerged after two new Central-Asian Arabic dialects were discovered by an ethnographic expedition and described by Vinnikov and by G. Tsereteli (some information on these dialects with references will be found in Jastrow's paper on Arabic Dialectology, pp. 347–363). In contrast to some who say that these dialects are now extinct, the authors bring forth new information that may confirm that some speakers of these dialects or related dialects still exist. In addition, there are published and still-unpublished works on Arabic dialects by Russian scholars (e.g., a comprehensive and ambitious dictionary of Egyptian Arabic by Sharbatov). As for Neo-Aramaic, the authors mention the work done by Soviet scholars in the 1930s, when Neo-Aramaic in the Soviet Union was given a literary status, a status that was later denied it. This denial entailed the persecution of scholars involved in this project during Stalinist times (as is the case with Marogulov, the author of a Neo-Aramaic textbook, Marogulov 1976[=1935]). Still, publications from that period still exist and may serve as useful material for the study of Neo-Aramaic dialects of the area. In this connection, the name of Konstantin Tsereteli should be mentioned, a specialist in classical Syriac, but mostly known — also in the West — for his work on Neo-Aramaic dialects (e.g., Tsereteli 1958).

As a final comment, the authors mentioned the work of Diakonoff, who is probably the best known Russian Semitist of the twentieth century, and whose fame has exceeded the borders of the Soviet Union. Having studied with Riftin, a specialist in northern Semitic languages and Assyriology, this was the starting point for Diakonoff as well. The authors especially stressed Diakonoff's wisdom in integrating the study of spoken, contemporary African dialects into Assyriology. This methodology of a broadened look at ancient languages has made it possible for Diakonoff to integrate the study of Semitic languages within a larger framework of Hamito-Semitic (Afroasiatic, Afrasian) comparative linguistics. A comparison between Diakonoff's two major comparative linguistic reconstructions (Diakonoff 1965, 1988) will serve well in seeing the development and enrichment of this field. I would refer the reader to

Voigt's paper (pp. 265–290) for further evaluation of Diakonoff's work and influence.

One last paper dealing strictly with methodological issues discusses the study of partially documented languages. Semitic languages are attested from many geographical regions and go back to remote times. Some languages and dialects are attested in only a handful of inscriptions. Documents written in those languages can wear diverse shapes. They are written in a variety of script types, which exhibit a continuum going from logographic and syllabic to alphabetical, some of them have not been designed for the language that uses them. These and other issues are dealt with by Jo Ann Hackett, who takes Ugaritic and other Northwest Semitic texts as her test case. Since this is a methodological essay, one can draw analogies and conclusions with regard to the study of partially documented language elsewhere in the Semitic realm as well, and even beyond.

As Hackett justly states, it was the nineteenth century that saw the greatest advances in the study of epigraphic Semitic languages. Still, many new discoveries have been made in the twentieth century, and new ways of studying epigraphic materials have been developed, both technological and intellectual, leaning on the great advances in linguistic study. Hackett surveys all these advances, devoting prominent space to linguistics. She further anticipates Zuckerman's paper (pp. 481–497) by mentioning some modern technologies that enable us to have better access to written materials, as well as new ways of dealing with texts, like computerized concordances, dictionaries, and other electronic tools (cf. pp. 436–438 [Choueka] below). Hackett ends her paper by summarizing all these new developments and pointing out some desiderata. I absolutely endorse Hackett's "most heartfelt" desideratum, viz. the need for greater professionalism in the study of partially documented Semitic languages.

REFERENCES

Bohas, Georges. 1997. *Matrices, étymons, racines: éléments d'une théorie lexicologique du vocabulaire arabe*. (Orbis. Supplementa, 8.) Leuven.

Chomsky, Noam. 1979. *Morphophonemics of Modern Hebrew*. (Outstanding Dissertations in Linguistics, 12.) New York and London.

Diakonoff, Igor M. 1965. *Семито-хамитские языки* [Hamito-Semitic Languages]. Moscow.

Diakonoff, Igor M. 1988. *Afrasian Languages*. Moscow. (A Revised edition of Diakonoff 1965.)

Gazov-Ginzberg, A. M.. 1965. *Был ли язык изобразителен в своих истоках?* [Is Language Imitative by Origin? (Evidence from common Semitic stock of roots)]. Moscow.

Goldenberg, Gideon. 1994. Principles of Semitic Word-Structure. In: Gideon Goldenberg and Shlomo Raz (eds.). *Semitic and Cushitic Studies*. Wiesbaden. 29–64. [= Goldenberg 1998: 10–45.]

Goldenberg, Gideon. 1997. Conservative and Innovative Features in Semitic Languages. In: *Afroasiatica Neapolitana*. (Studi Africanistici: Serie Etiopica, 6.) Napoli. 3–21.

Goldenberg, Gideon. 1998. *Studies in Semitic Linguistics: Selected Writings*. Jerusalem.

Goldenberg, Gideon. Forthcoming. Word-Structure, Morphological Analysis, the Semitic Languages and Beyond. *Proceedings of the 10th Meeting of Hamito-Semitic (Afroasiatic) Linguistics, Università degli Studi di Firenze (17–21 April 2001)*.

Grande, B. M. 1963. *Курс арабской грамматики в сравнительно-историческом освещении* [A Course of Arabic Grammar in Historical-Comparative Light]. Moscow.

Grande, B. M. 1972. *Введение в сравнительное изучение семитских языков* [Introduction to Comparative Study of Semitic Languages]. Moscow.

Hetzron, Robert (ed.). 1997. *The Semitic Languages*. London.

Maizel, S.S. 1983. *Пути развития корневого фонда семитских языков* [Ways of Development of Semitic Roots]. Moscow.

Malone, Joseph L. 1985. Classical Mandaic Radical Metathesis, Radical Assimilation, and the Devil's Advocate. *General Linguistics* 25: 92–122.

Malone, Joseph L. 1989. Geminates, the Obligatory Contour Principle, and Tier Conflation: The Case of Tiberian Hebrew. *General Linguistics* 29: 112–130.

Malone, Joseph L. 1993. *Tiberian Hebrew Phonology*. Winona Lake, Indiana.

Malone, Joseph L. 1995. La circonscription prosodique en Mandéen classique. *Langues Orientales Anciennes: Philologie et Linguistique* 5–6: 233–257.

Malone, Joseph L. 1999. Metathesis and Antiwedging in Classical Mandaic. *General Linguistics* 36: 227–255.

Marogulov, Q.I. 1976. *Grammaire néo-syriaque pour écoles d'adultes (dialecte d'Urmia)*. Paris. (Originally published in Neo-Aramaic, Moscow 1935).

Marr, N.Ya. 1933–1937. *Избранные работы* [Selected Works]. Four volumes. Leningrad.

Murtonen, A. 1986–1990. *Hebrew in its West Semitic Setting: A Comparative Survey of Non-Masoretic Hebrew Dialects and Traditions.* (Studies in Semitic Languages and Linguistics, 13–16.) Leiden.

Reiner, Erica. 1966. *A Linguistic Analysis of Akkadian.* (Janua Linguarum, Series Practica, 21.) The Hague.

Starinin, V.P. 1963. *Структура семитского слова* [The Structure of the Semitic Word]. Moscow.

Tsereteli, K. 1958. *Хрестоматия современного ассирийского языка со словарем* [A Reader of the Modern Assyrian Language with a Dictionary]. Tbilisi. (2nd ed. 1980.)

Yushmanov, N.V. 1936. *Строй амхарского языка* [The structure of Amharic]. Leningrad.

Yushmanov, N.V. 1937. *Строй языка хауса* [The structure of Hausa]. Leningrad.

Yushmanov, N.V. 1938. *Строй арабского языка* [The structure of Arabic]. Leningrad.

Yushmanov, N.V. 1985. *Грамматика литературного арабского языка* [Grammar of Literary Arabic]. 2nd ed., Moscow.

Yushmanov, N.V. 1998. *Избранные труды. Работы по общей фонетике, семитологии и арабской классической морфологии* [Selected Words. Papers in general phonetics, Semitic studies and morphology of Classical Arabic]. Edited by V.S. Khrakovsky and A.G. Belova. Moscow.

SEMITIC LINGUISTICS AND THE GENERAL STUDY OF LANGUAGE

GIDEON GOLDENBERG

1. LINGUISTIC STUDY OF GENEALOGICALLY RELATED LANGUAGES

Semitic Linguistics and the General Study of Language was the subject of two talks of mine about a decade ago.[1] I do not intend to repeat what has already been said in those lectures, but one section I shall have to plagiarize (viz. the formal plural-marking of conjoined nominal complexes) in order to connect it to an issue which is at present being generally discussed.

The fact that some languages show evidence of being genetically related is a sufficient reason to make the examination of that relation an important facet of their linguistic study, and, needless to say, in the comparative inquiry for the sake of historical reconstruction and genetic-genealogical classification, it is language-families that naturally define the special fields of research. Since the history of languages, which necessarily turns into genetic classification (Baudouin *General Remarks* 70–71), is an important branch of linguistic science, even if not as central as it used to be considered in the nineteenth century, some methodological comments on Comparative Semitics are not out of place in a discussion on Semitic linguistics and the general study of language. It might, however, be questioned in what sense the special study of a genealogically related group of languages is relevant to linguistic methodology beyond the comparative, since the structure of each tongue is equally and independently important for the general science of language and for the typology of human speech-forms.

Notwithstanding, the investigation of language families is in my opinion of great relevance to any linguistic study. At the end of the twentieth century we ought to have learnt that the perception of the history of languages, their changes and processes is practically inseparable from their synchronic analysis, despite some persuasions formerly prevalent. Linguistic studies will be doomed to be banal without vast and

[1]   See GG *Contribution of Semitic Languages* and GG *Semitics and Linguistics*.

21

profound knowledge of each language which one investigates, without comprehensive and intimate familiarity with its geographical-historical and cultural background. Procuring such knowledge of a language with its niceties and intricacies would inescapably involve the study of its historical, genealogical, areal and cultural connexions. These introductory notes may suffice for justifying the title of the present paper, which should not, however, be taken as necessarily connecting Semitic collectively in each point made which is of general linguistic interest.

Since no form of general linguistics is thinkable, which is prior to the analysis of human tongues, special studies ought naturally to be the foundation of theoretical generalizations rather than the other way round. It is consequently not for applying general theories to Semitic that we need to keep constant connexion with the science of language, but rather for putting those theories to the test, for watchfully examining alternative methodologies, also for seeing linguistic phenomena in Semitic languages in broader perspective, and lend the deeper insights thus gained to the study of linguistic typology and to the general study of language.

For the general study of any linguistic subject, it is the ideal to have data from all relevant language types on earth. This was, e.g., what the old masters of general linguistics, like Wilhelm von Humboldt and Hans Conon von der Gabelentz, had in mind and tried to accomplish, the former, inter alia, in his study on the dual (Humboldt *Dualis*) and the latter in his monograph on the passive (Gabelentz *Passivum*). So also nowadays, this practice is mostly attempted in many typological studies of various sections of linguistics. The authors of those old treatises had reasonable command of the many languages which they used, sufficient for being able to refer directly to the best standard grammars available at their time without needing interlinear morpheme-deciphering glosses. I strongly recommend to stick to that practice. Because of the difficulty, or practical incapability, of treating all language-types at one time, the ambition to achieve universal comprehensiveness should better be restrained rather than bring out cross-linguistic studies based on unsolid grounds. Expert information on thoroughly-studied languages of various stocks is still greatly deficient in the general literature. Alan Gardiner wrote in 1932 that "such information as Egyptian can yield to throw light upon the nature of speech is due not so much to its antiquity as to the difference of its structure from that of the languages most frequently studied by writers on general linguistics" (Gardiner *Speech and Language* 4–5). During the 20th century, casual reference to diverse speech-forms has become rather common; reliable evidence adduced from the better-studied languages, like those of the Semitic family, old and new, is all the more indispensable.

Semitic linguistics, which originally developed from Biblical philology, was lucky in attracting outstanding scholars, who not only represented most estimably the science of language of their time, but also left excellent grammars and special studies of long-lasting value, thoughtfully devised and richly documented. Many studies, however, relating to Semitic languages refrain from original linguistic thought, either reposing on achievements of the past, or — which is by no means better — embracing servilely whatever theory is in vogue.

At the end of the 20th century we find writings seeking refuge in textbook-form with pedagogical orientation, also collections of abridged surveys, often avoiding scholarly discussion and withholding bibliographical references; we even find in a recent *Outline of a Comparative Grammar of Semitic* the rather strange statement that "Semitics is more wonderful than linguistics!" (Lipiński *Comparative Grammar* 18). But there is also a flow of linguistically significant studies of various phenomena in some Semitic languages.

2. SEMITIC LANGUAGES AND THE COMPARATIVE METHOD

In the present essay I would not try to make any material contribution to Comparative Semitics, nor to evaluate the state of the art in this field of study at the end of its first millennium, but just make a few general comments on the application of the genetic-genealogical method and the historical model on which it is based to the groupings and subgroupings of Hamito-Semitic languages. Scholars cannot be blamed for being fascinated by the mysteries of human origins concealed in the reconstructible history of languages. In fact, Leibniz, who made occasional use of the terms Semitic and Hamitic for genetic classification of languages as early as 1710, was really interested in using linguistic data for reconstructing unrecorded historical circumstances (Leibniz *De Originibus Gentium* 4–5). Being thus fascinated, Semitists (among others) were always very enthusiastic about the division and genealogical interrelations of Semitic languages, especially of those little known. The great Ewald classified Akkadian as a separate branch of Semitic in 1871, when Assyriology was in its infancy (Ewald *Geschichtliche Folge* 179 — the whole of his division was practically identical with that of Nöldeke's); Gurage played an important role in Reinisch's disposition of Hamito-Semitic in 1909, when it was hardly known at all; when Ugaritic was discovered, its mapping within the Semitic family took much energy which could probably be better used for studying the language itself; discussions regarding the position of Eblaite could be found in the

literature before a single document written in the language was exposed
to the scholarly world; also much of the linguistic literature about Cushitic
or Chadic languages concentrates on their genealogical relations.

As to the principles of the comparative method, we all may agree
that "genetic models of linguistic relatedness and areal models of mutual
linguistic influence are complementary rather than competitive" (Faber
Subgrouping 3), but the necessary distinction between common material
inheritance and structural analogy is not universally applicable with
sufficient clarity, and comparative studies, even overviews, introductions
or summaries, dealing with the classification of Semitic languages cannot
follow the genetic model without qualification. The ideal conditions for
reconstruction based on the genetic model are rather rarely found in
languages upon earth. (**1**) The most desirable condition is the availability of
chronological depth of data, which would enable the examination of some
of the historical reconstructions against attested facts. Semitic languages
and Egyptian well meet this requirement so far as they are attested. Other
branches of Hamito-Semitic fall far behind. (**2**) Another requisite for safely
applying the comparative method is a meaningful diversity, discontiguity,
separation and distance of the languages compared. As defined by Antoine
Meillet, "la définition de la parenté de langues ne s'applique donc qu'à de
grands groupes, nettement distincts les uns des autres, non à des parlers
distingués par de simples nuances" (Meillet *Linguistique* I 88). Disregarding
the Euro-centric claim for superiority, we may find the following comment
which Henry Sweet made at the beginning of the century being still
pertinent: "There are, indeed, [he says] many reasons why the Aryan
languages should take a prominent part in general comparative philology.
They are not only themselves the most important family of languages
on the earth, but they also have the advantage of being easily accessible
in varied literary documents of various periods, besides showing great
variety of structure. In the latter respect they have the advantage over the
Semitic languages, which resemble each other so closely as to be little more
than dialects [...]. Hence, although the foundations of comparative Semitic
grammar were laid as early — or earlier — than those of comparative
Aryan grammar, the Semitic languages have had much less influence on the
general development of the science" (Sweet *Affinity* 64). We need not care
about influence, but be cognizant of the limits of the comparative method,
especially in employing it for classifying closely related dialects spoken in
adjacent regions.[2]

---

2   The considered claim that for achieving optimal results genetic models of linguistic
     relatedness require diversity, discontiguity, separation and distance of the languages
     compared, and that genetic-genealogical comparison would not safely apply "à des
     parler distingué par de simples nuances," just means that in the investigation of

In such circumstances, as is well known, "a special precaution ought to be taken against using synchronical phonetic criteria in dividing languages" (Hetzron *Ethiopian Semitic* 11), as "the boundaries between different phonological features often do not coincide with the boundaries between languages or language families" (Jakobson *Phonology* 232), but even inflexional paradigms, by far the safest criteria for genetic grouping, may fail to secure clear and reliable genealogical mapping of closely related tongues.

Thus, e.g., those Arabic dialects of the Yemen with Perfect subject markers in –*k*– for 1st & 2nd sg. and 2nd pl. are still forms of Arabic, even though the generalization of –*t*– in those afformatives is regarded as a distinctive mark of Central Semitic, to which Arabic is said to belong, as against the South Semitic –*k*–.

It is now commonly accepted that a sound principle of genetic classification is grounding common ancestry on shared innovations, which requires previous judgement as to which common features are to be regarded as shared innovations and which are retentions or typological parallels. In principle we might ask whether the form of the 1st plural pronoun with final –*a* — (*ʔǎ*)*naḥnā*, *əḥna*, *nəḥna*, *ḥəna*, also *nḥa* &c., and perhaps *əñ̃ña* — is not a shared innovation common to Aramaic, colloquial (but not Classical) Arabic and South Semitic; it looks, after all, less unreasonable than involving forms of the definite article in Semitic subgrouping, or syntactical features that do not share specific commonly-inherited morphemes.

Two methodological recommendations will largely be accepted and have clearly been formulated by John Huehnergard, viz. (1) to apply the "developmental approach", understanding that "sound historical linguistic

closely related adjacent dialects, it should be taken into account that genetically inherited forms and characteristics may be blurred by the interference of areal and other features developed through contacts of parallel processes or plurilinear evolution. The genetic model and the methods of Comparative Linguistics have recently been rejected altogether by Lutz Edzard (see Edzard *Polygenesis*), whose counterproposal assumes polygenetic creation of "language family" from "chaos", where an undetermined number of languages in the initial stage would form gradually a "family" through processes of convergence and subsequent entropy of linguistic features. This "alternative model of linguistic evolution" has been applied to Semitic languages, with great attention paid to various features of Arabic dialects and to difficulties in the genetic explanation of some phenomena within Semitic, but injudiciously avoiding any reference, e.g., to the inflexional systems of Arabic, Turkish and Persian, which according to proposed model might have been expected to form a "family". A model assuming "language centres" formed from "chaos" to become a "family" could also have given good chances to Hungarian and German, or to Welsh and English to form such "families" via convergence and entropy of linguistic features, or specify some conditions for such processes.

method" requires "complete descriptions of the intermediate nodes" prior to making any larger comparisons, and (2) "to consider the larger language family of which Semitic is a member", viz. Hamito-Semitic (Huehnergard *New Directions* 260–263). Both of these suggestions would practically be called for and should earnestly be followed, though from the viewpoint of rigorous method they are conspicuously incompatible.

Also word origins, the history and distribution of vocabulary, as well as lexical and semantic changes, well deserve to be examined in the comparative context and the methods of their treatment desperately need thorough revision. I would not discuss here exercises in reconstruction of biradical etyma in Hamito-Semitic and beyond, which raise serious doubts.

3. GENERAL-LINGUISTIC STUDIES AND SEMITIC LANGUAGES

As already mentioned, Semitic languages, primarily Hebrew, Arabic, Syriac and Ethiopic, were commonly figuring in typological and general studies for illustrating constructions and ways of expression. Mid-century and later innovations in linguistics have not, however, produced great grammars of Semitic (or any other) languages based on current theoretical grounds. At the turn of the century, developments in the conception and practice of linguistic research seem to have been spreading, with the return from intuition to scientific investigation, and from speculation to data-based study with much higher requirements of profounder familiarity with the niceties of structure, variation of usage, attested textual evidence written and spoken, and processes of contact and change.

It is impossible and useless to try to evaluate individual references to Semitic languages in discussions of general-linguistic theoretical issues. Some of them are rather revealing, many of them just marginally recall some commonly-known phenomena of Hebrew or Arabic, most of them are not based on actually attested evidence, and nearly all of them show total unacquaintance with the extensive grammatical literature on the relevant languages [this is in fact the greatest drawback of linguistics in late twentieth century]. An auspicious development, however, has been recently observable of scholars who being immersed in some theoretical issues of phonology got strongly interested in Gurage dialects in all their aspects and were totally and successfully absorbed in this fascinating field of study, meeting the high requirements of familiarity with the subtleties of those tongues and with relevant previous research.[3]

---

[3] Some results of such fruitful studies originally motivated by purely theoretical interest will be found, e.g., in *Essays on Gurage* (1996).

4. SOME LINGUISTIC CONCEPTS AND TERMS IN SEMITICS AND ELSEWHERE

As scholars specialized in a branch of linguistic research we shall wish to examine, carefully and critically, the findings, recognitions, accomplishments, insights, theories, methods and technical terms developed in other branches of the language sciences, or born in general speculations generated by pure inspiration. On the occasion of the present symposium I shall mostly try to examine only a few concepts and terms, some of them chosen at random, against the background of Semitic languages and their investigation.

PHONOLOGY

The analysis of phonemes by the examination of the presence or absence of a list of distinctive features, as mainly developed by Roman Jakobson, was one of the most significant innovations in mid-century phonology.[4] This method, however, had its problems. In particular it was questioned whether the distinctive features as defined ought necessarily to be either positively present (+) or absolutely absent (–), or inapplicable (0), also whether the list of features were not somewhat arbitrary. The phonological analysis of Arabic raised questions as to how to represent "emphatic" in the system of distinctive features.[5] Two central problems of Semitic phonology are consonant-gemination and vowel-length in those tongues which show these distinctions or their reflexes. I made some comments on the linguistic treatment of these issues a few years ago and would not repeat them today.[6]

A central problem of gemination in Semitic languages is the tension between stem-derivational gemination and tense-marking gemination and the difficulty in accommodating both of them in the same form. Recent theoretical discussion of gemination, though based on the evidence of some Semitic languages, has unfortunately failed to take notice of the two independent levels of thematic gemination, and thus went all wrong. Familiarity with Semitistic literature could here as elsewhere be of great help and significant consequence.

---

[4] The idea of dyadic distinctive features as the ultimate components of phonemes was mainly developed in Jakobson & Halle *Phonology and Phonetics* and subsequent writings.

[5] Following Haim Blanc's dissertation on North Palestinian Arabic (Blanc *Druzes*), Jakobson found it necessary to provide various clarifications as to the representation of *tafxīm* in the list of distinctive features; see Jakobson *Mufaxxama*, cf. McCawley *Traits phonologiques*, Halle & alii *Introduction* 2–3.

[6] See GG *Word-Structure* §§ 22–23.

NOMINAL SENTENCE / VERB

At present, when the pure nominal sentence is again recognized widely and unquestionably as a basic genuine construction (or *the* basic genuine construction) in many languages of various stocks,[7] it is difficult to believe that just a few decades ago it was unthoughtfully held by many linguists that the core of any sentence must constitute of a Noun Phrase and a Verb Phrase, usually written in abbreviation as NP and VP. Nominal sentences on the surface were said to result from the deletion of the verbal constituent, in this case the verbal copula; i.e. they were regarded as a special case of ellipsis. In fact, the Noun Phrase + Verb Phrase formula, which directly continues the Western school-grammar tradition, besides misconstruing the nominal sentence, fails to conceive the complex structure of the conjugated verb-form, where a pronominal subject, predicative attribute and predicational bond are incorporated, that is to say that the finite verb would rather be analysed as being deeply a nominal sentence rather than the nominal predicate as involving a deleted copular verb-form. The right understanding of verb-structure and nominal sentence was not unknown in linguistic literature and it was repeatedly expounded in many language-specific and general-linguistic writings, and anyway, Semitic-orientated syntax (or grammar based on most other languages) could never have fallen that deep. The need for a copula with non-verbal predicates has developed in some Neo-Semitic languages, where the copular paradigm, however, is not necessarily identical with the verbal. Such development marks a basic syntactical revolution.[8]

GERUND

The Latin term gerund (*gerundium*) has been figuring harmlessly in the grammatical treatment of quite a few languages. There is, however, some difficulty in employing this term outside Latin, arising from the divergent meanings that "gerund" has taken in English as against other languages. Being originally a verbal substantive coming in an oblique case only, "gerund" has been employed for verbal substantive generally (also as subject) in English grammatical terminology, but exclusively for deverbal adverbials elsewhere, as in grammars of Romance languages, owing to the extended use of the ablative gerund in Post-Classical Latin and later developments, where it is reported to have largely supplanted the present

---

[7]   See specially Cohen *Verbalisation*, Cohen *Phrase nominale*, Hodge *Nominal Sentence*.
[8]   The historical significance of this process has been reiterated in GG *Conservative and Innovative* 14 (§6) and elsewhere.

participle in its adverbial functions. "Gerund" has also been commonly used for verbal adverbs in grammars of other languages, for what in the French terminology of Damourette & Pichon was termed affonctif verbal, for the Russian *деепричастие*, also for the Turkish *rabıt sıygası* or *ulaç [-e, -erek, -ip, -ince &c.]*. To Ethiopic, "gerund" was introduced in the Latin version of Praetorius' short grammar and in Bezold's second edition of Dillmann's, then commonly adopted in grammars of other Ethiopian languages, though the Ethiopian gerund is not an absolutivum, but an inflected adverbative. Since in Gurage, clause-chaining is mostly marked by finite verb-form + *-m* rather than by a verbal adverbial, but West-Gurage still has a verbal adverbial form in *-(y)tä* (though limited in use), Polotsky suggested to preserve the term "gerund" for the morphological category and to borrow from Turkic linguistics the term "converb" for the non-final complex of verb + *-m*. He further noted that in English, *gerundium* was normally called "gerund" (whereas "gerundive" in the same sense is a Gallicism, replicating the French *gérondif*). Here no little confusion was caused in Semitistic literature, mainly by Hetzron, who regarded "converb" as just a more modern term for "gerund", and mentioned "gerund" as a Gallicism. "Converb" has actually become common in linguistic parlance indistinctively referring to any adverbial, or apparently adverbial, form or construction which includes, or is derived from, a verb.[9] Also, confusion between "gerund" and the (present) "participle" (in its adverbial functions) is everywhere in linguistic literature (not connected to the terminology in which all non-finite forms of the verb were called "participials"[10]). In English, the *-ing* form in the phrasal tenses is now often regarded as participial, despite history, meaning and parallels in many languages, all of which point to adverbial gerund-phrases. The constructions in question are made of an auxiliary with an adverbial complex of preposition+verbal substantive. In English as well, *he was coming* is mostly the continuation of *he was on coming*, shortened to *he was a-coming*, and then dropping the preposition altogether. Basically it is the same construction as the Turkish *gelmekteydi*, or the Neo-Aramaic *bitəjivə* (U.) or *wēle bītāya* (Ẓ.), or the similar expressions in Amharic or French or other languages. The only reason that I mention here these forms, in which there is nothing new or unknown, is because by losing the preposition Neo-Aramaic is shown to be the closest parallel to the English: In Early Neo-Aramaic we witness the beginning of this process (cf. Ẓ. *hwi ʿāhıt dāyım b-mṣalōye*

---

[9] See, *e.g.* Haspelmath *Converb*, esp. 45–46.
[10] "Die Partizipialien, unter denen wir die Partizipien, Infinitive, Gerundien und Supine begreifen" (Becker *Organism* 514).

"be always praying" as against *wēwa mar·ōye ·irwe* "he was grazing his sheep", Sabar *Homilies* 149:5 & 157:12 resp.; Az. *qjamet ~ qjámlet* "you are rising", *kwaša wela* "she was descending", *šatójle ~ šatúle* "he is drinking", *šato ~ šata welax* "you[f.sg] were drinking"). In the dialect of Zakho the *b–* is always omitted before *m–*, and in the Jewish dialect of Azerbaijan it is never there. Since in Neo-Aramaic there was no merger of the forms of verbal noun (infinitive) and participle, there was no distortion in construing those phrasal tense-forms similar to that found in English. Some linguists might wish to refrain altogether from analysing the surface constituents of phrasal tense-forms, let alone the inner structure of fused forms, and prefer the branching of speculated features. Such method, however, will not be very revealing and leaves untouched the most significant question of verb-structure, viz. the actual constitution of verbal forms and compounds, which is a rather central issue in the investigation of the structural universality and typological diversity of languages.

AGREEMENT AND APPOSITION

In the present paper, may I just repeat without discussing it in detail the conception of agreement as an appositive repetition. This view, again, is not new, and it came up repeatedly in linguistic discussion in various contexts. The often-mentioned agreement between subject and verb involves the pronominal person-marker that is incorporated in the conjugated verb-form and is the term representing the subject directly and independently in the predicative bond inherent in the verb; there can be a subject-noun in apposition to it, but not necessarily.[11] The agreement between substantive and co-referential adjective similarly entails apposition of the substantive and the pronominal head inherent by definition in the adjective form. So far there is nothing special that should call for considering agreement in the present context. There are, however, some problems relating to agreement, which have been imperfectly treated in the linguistic literature, and for which some Semitic languages can well provide instructive examples. We shall need also to consider such constructions in the next (and last) chapter. These occur, e.g., in Amharic when different conjoined nouns or pronouns are collectively to be marked for number, where not only "horse + horse" would be referred to as "horses", i.e.

---

[11] "*Volat avis* ne signifie pas «l'oiseau vole», mais «il vole, (scil.) l'oiseau». La forme *volat...* inclut la notion grammaticale de sujet" (Benveniste *Personne dans le verbe* 231). It is categorically implausible to posit in languages with verb-inflexion an independent personal pronoun with which the verb-form is made to agree in person and number, after which agreement the original pronoun is deleted.

"horse"[plural], but also "husband + wife" would formally be marked as plural, ("husband + wife")[plural], usually in agreement with a plural verb. On another occasion I have discussed some forms of actualizing such formal mark of the plural when referring to a complex of conjoined non-identical nouns or pronouns, which could be represented as put in brackets, viz. (A+B)[pl], as observed in Amharic, Arabic and some other languages.[12] I am returning in brief to this topic here, as it is a typical example of a linguistic phenomenon of general interest which familiarity with the subtleties of some languages of our stock as of others may greatly elucidate. I have suggested that the formal marking of plural observed of such (A+B)[pl] might be described as actualized (1) out of the brackets, (2) through the brackets, (3) by opening the brackets, (4) by the omission from the brackets, and (5) by breaking the brackets (or portrayed otherwise).

(1) Plural marker affixed *outside* the brackets, to mark the conjoined complex as a whole, is observed in Amharic. It will physically stick to the last noun (the B) of the syntagm: (A+B)[pl] will look like A+B[pl], but in any possible sense it is not to B, but to (A+B) that the plural suffix belongs: (*bal-ənna məšt)-očč* "the husband-and-wife[pl]", (*and wänd ləǧ-ənna and set ləǧ)-očč näbbärut* "he had one-boy-and-one-girl[pl]".

(2) We may present as plural-marking *through* the brackets the construction known in many languages, which was thought to represent elliptic dual (or plural) with a complementary word, or to be the product of contamination between two incongruous structures, or to be a syllepsis, or attraction. It is the actualization of ("I" [1st sg. pron]+X)[pl] as "we + X",[13] where the plurality that refers to the bracketed syntagm as a whole moves, as it were, through the brackets, to be actually marked on the first conjoined word, like in Russian the ubiquitous *мы с тобой* ("I with you")[pl] → "I[pl] with you" → "we with you"; French *nous deux Jean* ("I [and] Jean")[du] → "I[du] [and] Jean" → "the two of us [and] Jean"; Neo-Aramaic *əxnən ammux* ("I with you")[pl] → "I[pl] with you" → "we with you". The first component can also be the pronominal person-marker in a verb-form or a possessive suffix, as in the Amharic *kärsu gar ənnəggänaññallän* ("I-meet with him")[pl] → "I-meet[pl] with him" → "we-meet with him"; Turkish *onunla ahbaplığımız* ("*my* friendship with *her*")[pl] → "my[pl] friendship with her" → "our friendship with her". It can be learnt from the Amharic that the explanation of such constructions as plural/dual with a complementary word cannot be sustained, at least not as a general explanation for all cases.

(3) We can speak of marking formally the plurality of (A+B)[pl], or

---

12 See mainly GG *Semitics and Linguistics* 110–113 (§3, ג).

13 The "+" will here represent "and" or "with" or 0. See GG *Congruence and Comitative*.

duality of $(A+B)^{du}$, by opening the brackets, if we visualize it, for the sake of easy presentation, as an algebraic expression where /^{pl}/, or /^{du}/, is the multiplier. The result will be $A^{pl} + B^{pl}$, or $A^{du} + B^{du}$, i.e. expressing the conception of a pair of nouns by using both nouns in the dual or plural. Such conjoining, as was also recorded in ancient Indo-European, will be recognized in the Arabic *al-mašriqāni wa-l-magribāni* or *al-mašāriq wa-l-magārib* "East$^{du/pl}$ and West$^{du/pl}$", i.e. the whole world.

(4) The conception of a pair of commonly-associated nouns by the use of only one of them in the dual form can be described as involving omission from the brackets, as if it were $(A+B)^{du} \rightarrow (A)^{du}$ or $(B)^{du}$, as also implied in the term "elliptic dual", by which such constructions were commonly named. Among the Semitic languages, elliptic dual is known in Classical Arabic, conventionally termed *al-mutannà 'alà l-taglīb* "dualis a potiori", and plentifully attested in locutions like the well-known *al-qamarāni* "the two moons" = "the sun and the moon", *al-'Umarāni* "the two 'Umars" = "'Abū Bakr and 'Umar", *al-Furatāni* "the two Euphrates-rivers" = "the Euphrates and the Tigris", *al-mašriqāni* "the two Easts" = "the East and the West" &c.

(5) The last type that I have mentioned of plural-marking of a non-uniform complex, viz. by breaking the brackets or so, mostly refers to some problems of verbs having to agree with conjoined subjects of different persons. A repeated discussion of this type can here be omitted.

These manners of formally marking a complex are also pertinent for marking syntagms other than those of conjoined nominals, and also for grammatical categories other than the plural, and this brings us to the next chapter.

SUFFIXAUFNAHME

The last general subject which I should like to examine in the light of Semitic is really a story of the century, and therefore especially suitable for the present symposium. It is about the phenomenon defined as Suffixaufnahme, not unknown in the beginning of the twentieth century, when it was so named by the renowned typologist Franz Nikolaus Finck. It recently became the latest hit of linguistic discussion, after being the topic of a special symposium in 1991, followed by the publication of a collective volume, *Double Case*, in 1995, and subsequently treated in articles, reviews and linguistic conferences from the general-linguistic, language-specific and cross-linguistic angles. The term Suffixaufnahme even found its way to the style sheet of *Linguistic Typology* with an instruction not to print it in italics. The phenomenon so named was mainly referring to adnominal possessive constructions where the possessor, besides its genitive case-marker (or its analytic equivalent), was also made to agree in case with the nominal head. Hence the term Suffixaufnahme and the title *Double Case*. Such constructions were first noticed in Old Georgian, like *gwam-isa krist-es-isa* "of the body of Christ" (F. Bopp ap. Plank *Suffixaufnahme* 3), where the genitive case-ending is suffixed twice to the last noun, the former identifying the possessive relation with the head and the latter marking an agreement with the head noun, itself in the genitive in this case; Finck adduced the following Georgian example: *ra t'urp'a p'rinvelia, c'amoiʒaxa ert'-ma bavšv-t'a-gan-ma* "What wonderful bird it is, exclaimed one of the children", where the ergative suffix *–ma* as in *ert'-ma* "one" is also repeated in the attributive phrase *bavšv-t'a-gan-ma* "of the children" (Finck *Haupttypen* 141–142, cf. Plank *Suffixaufnahme* 7). Such constructions with Suffixaufnahme, which in the mid-1970s "seemed [so it was claimed] too inconspicuous for anybody to notice much", have repeatedly been said to be "not widespread", "ostensibly marginal" (Plank in the Preface to *Double Case* v–vi), marked by "oddity" and "cross-linguistic rarity" (Moravcsik *Suffixaufnahme* 479, 482) and by "the anomaly of th[eir] pattern" (Plank in the Preface to *Double Case* ibid.), "a rare and seemingly marginal phenomenon" (Plank *Suffixaufnahme* 3) based on "little-known data from little-known languages" (Haspelmath *Review* 417), "dealing with languages that most linguists haven't even heard of" (ibid. 421). In fact it comes out to be attested in Sumerian, Hurrian, Urartian, Basque, and in Kartvelian, Cushitic, Indian and Australian languages, and also elsewhere.

It has been found that the markers involved are not always **suffixes**, that Aufnahme is not in all instances the exactly ideal term, that the categories indicated are not only cases, that the presence of a head nominal or its case marking here is not indispensable, and consequently that Suffixaufnahme was not necessarily required for the purpose of syntactical agreement. The core of the construction in question has been defined as having "distinct syntactic case relations of the same nominal [...] signalled by distinct case markers on that constituent" (Moravcsik *Suffixaufnahme* 482). This in fact was a challenge to current linguistic theory, which claimed (rightly, I must say) that for one nominal or noun phrase to be assigned more than one case was constitutionally unattainable and practically unknown in natural languages, and this mostly raised the renewed interest in examining Suffixaufnahme.

In the various contributions to the 1995 *Double Case* volume, edited by Frans Plank, especially as summed up there admirably in Edith A. Moravcsik's Epilogue, the distinct syntactical functions of the contiguous case markers are defined, differentiating the internal case from the external case explaining that "the former is a relation marker, indicating the

kind of relation that obtains between that nominal and another; the latter is a relatedness marker, identifying the **terms** of the relation through agreement" (Moravcsik *Suffixaufnahme* 458). Three main variant constructions of double-case involving an attribute nominal and a head nominal are discerned, and can be represented as follows, the internal case being indicated in lower superscript and the external case in higher superscript:

AttrNom$^{case^{case}}$	HeadNom^{case}	(Suffixaufnahme proper)
AttrNom$^{case^{case}}$	HeadNom	("Suffixhäufung")
AttrNom$^{case^{case}}$		("hypostasis")

The parallel constructions with the attribute *following* the head are here omitted (see Moravcsik *Suffixaufnahme* 453). In construing this type of attribution-complexes, showing that two or more accumulated case markers[14] do not actually refer to the same constituent, three theories have been suggested, viz. (1) the Phrase-Marking Theory, (2) the Pronoun, or Appositive, Theory, and (3) the Adjective Theory (see mainly Moravcsik *Suffixaufnahme* 479–481). According to the Phrase-Marking Theory, the internal case is assigned to the attributive nominal, but the external case marks the entire phrase, although actually attached to the attributive constituent. The Pronoun, or Appositive, Theory assigns the external case to a pronoun intimately built in the attributive constituent, appositively representing the head nominal. The Adjective Theory regards the internal case as an adjectivizing derivational affix, so that the attributive constituent is defined as an adjective and not as a case-marked nominal; there is consequently no internal case here, and no double case, but a natural and common agreement of an adjective to its head.

I fail to find any basic difference between the "three theories". We might say that all of them are impeccable, but more precisely all of them are one, not pertaining specifically and distinctively to the phenomenon in question. The definition of phrases and clauses by the simple forms to which they are syntactically equivalent has long become a commonplace of linguistic analysis. In fact, to speak of embedded clauses, e.g., without defining the form-class of their simple equivalents, is meaningless or non-analysis. This simple truth has long become the basis of linguistic method and grammatical terminology; thus we speak of substantive forms, substantive phrases and substantive clauses, or of an adjective form, adjective phrases (genitive constructions) and adjective clauses (alias relative clauses). In inflected languages, adjective-forms, like their syntactically equivalent phrases and clauses, imply or subsume

---

[14] 'Cases' are understood in this paper in the conceptual sense of the term, whether their exponents are morphological or syntactical.

a pronominal head; they are constitutionally self-contained and do not depend on a head substantive, which in any case would be appositive to the direct pronominal head of the attributive constituent. Case markers applied to adjective-forms will always be assigned to the adjective, which is an attributive complex, as a whole, and directly refer to its subsumed pronominal head, and in no way will it belong directly to a dependent constituent within this complex-form. If adjectivals, whether adjective-forms or «adjectifs syntaxiques» (Benveniste *Phrase relative* 222), are complexes, syntactically equivalent and structurally analogous, their "external case" does always belong to the phrase as a whole and refers directly to the appositive head nominals. In other words, *all* attributive expressions are complex, imply or contain a pronominal head and are in this sense adjectives. Neither of these properties, which were suggested as theories for explaining Suffixaufnahme, belongs specifically to the main problem encountered in that construction-type, which is mainly the difficulty of accepting morphological suffixes attached to syntactic complexes. This problem is not special to Suffixaufnahme; we have seen the same difficulty in plural (or dual) marking of conjoined nominals. Nor is it restricted to inflexional categories of case or number or gender. From the evidence of Neo-Ethiopian languages we may learn that the real typological peculiarity which is also seen in the typical cases of Suffixaufnahme lies in the question how far the logic of syntactical transpositions[15] of adjectivization or substantivization can be stretched to go beyond the limits of morphology and subject syntactical constructions to morphological inflexion and derivation. In some Neo-Ethiopian Semitic languages, the treatment of syntactical adjectivizations and substantivizations as if they were morphological units is in some cases unusually consistent. Such nominalizations in Amharic and in Harari will be found capable of assuming post-nominal suffixes, and even susceptible of entering, as bases, into further noun-derivation.

In Amharic, the article (here represented by the f.sg. def.art.-*itu*), and the nominal plural-marker –*očč*, may equally be applied to plain nouns and to paraphrased nouns whether phrases (genitive) or clauses (relative), for instance:

Adjective	"Genitive"	"Relative"
*dägg-**itu** nəgəst*	*yäne-y**itu** gäräd*	*käbet yalläčč-**itu** set*
"the good queen"	"my maid"	"the woman who is at home"
*addis-**očč**-u särratäññočč*	*yäne-**očč**-u gärädočč*	*yämmannawq-äw-**očč***
"the new workers"	"my maids"	"we who do not know"

---

[15] Or "conversion", or (Fr.) "translation", or "transference", or "transformation", or "Überführung", or "Verwandlung", &c. See GG *Nominalization* 170–171 = 343–344, fn. 1, for a bibliographical note concerning the relevant terminology.

təlləq-očč-u	*yäAksum-očč-u nägästat*	*yä-hed-očč*
"the big (ones)"	"the Kings of Aksum"	"those who went"

And in Harari (pl.suff. *-āč*):

Adjective	"Genitive"	"Relative"
rāgāč indōčāč	*tōyāč ūgāč*	*zisäma'āč usu'āč*
"old women"	"the streets of	"people who have heard"
	the neighbourhood"	

There, also the possessive sufix, whether as a possessive-relational expression or as the exponent of the definite article, will be suffixed to syntactical nominalizations the same as to plain nominals: *gār-zo* "his house, the house", *gidīr-zo* "the big one(s), the adult(s)", *zi-gädära-zo* "the biggest"; [*bäǧīḥ usu'* "many people", *abzaḥ usu'* "most people"], *abzaḥ-zo*, *yibäzḥi-zo* "the / its majority", *yansi-zo* "lesser (of it)", *yansi-ziyu* "a few of them".

Of even greater importance for the understanding of the grammatical status of subordinate phrases and clauses are some forms of syntactical substantivization of genitive syntagms in Amharic, and of relative clauses in Harari:

yäňňa-nnät-əh qärrä "your (of-us)-ness is finished", "you are no longer ours".

Substantivization of "Relative" in Harari is marked morphologically by the suffixation of the abstract-derivational *–nät* to the clause: *zi-ḥārti-nät-u yūqal* "he knows [the] (that-she-went)-ness[acc]", "he knows that she went" (see Leslau *Gleanings* 157a-b, GG Harari 435, §9).

The importance of such forms goes far beyond the special constructions in those examples: From such instances in which adjectivization and substantivization are fully transparent, one can better understand the adjectival and substantival nature of embedded phrases and clauses where it is less transparent. Syntactically transposed phrases and clauses are susceptible not only of inflexion, which could be labelled "phrase marking", but also of further morphological derivation, which takes complex syntagms as morpheme-equivalents. The general-linguistic lesson to be learnt from such examples of maximal transparency is that the time-honoured treatment of embedding as *ta'wīl*, or transposition, reposes, as put by Meillet, on linguistic facts as organized from the point of view of language itself.[16] And by the way, substantive clauses have had various names, among them "content clause" had gained some popularity. The worst term that has been employed in this realm is "complementizer",

---

[16] "... pour ordonner les faits linguistiques au point de vue de la langue même" (Meillet *Linguistique* I, p. viii).

a complete misnomer which does not tell what is most important, viz. the formal category that it makes, while what it does tell is incorrect. At the turn of the century, when central interest and unprecedented activity in the extensive investigation of language diversity and typological bridges marks general linguistic study, and when special studies on some Semitic languages, and especially the study of Neo-Semitic dialectology has had remarkable achievements, features of the variegated Semitic languages attract notice, and may play an important role in the language sciences if based on high level of proficiency, worthy field-work, rich documentation and familiarity with the grammatical literature.

I have tried to detect in this paper a few points in which the evidence of some Semitic languages is of general interest. It was not much, but still touched upon some problems of method and comparison, a few terms and categories, agreement and apposition, and the treatment of syntactic complexes as bases in morphological processes.

BIBLIOGRAPHICAL INDICATIONS AND ABBREVIATIONS

Az. — the Jewish Neo-Aramaic dialect of Persian Azerbaijan.

Baudouin *General Remarks* — Jan Baudouin de Courtenay. 1877. Некоторые общие замечания о языковедении и языке, ap. *Бодуэн де Куртенэ: Избранные труды по общему языкознанию*. 1963, Москва, I: 47–77.

Becker *Organism* — Karl Ferdinand Becker. 1841. *Organism der Sprache*. Zweite neubearbeitete Ausgabe. Frankfurt am Main.

Benveniste *Personne dans le verbe* — Émile Benveniste. 1946. Structure des relations de personne dans le verbe. *Bulletin de la Société de linguistique de Paris* 43 fasc. 1, ap. Émile Benveniste, 1966. *Problèmes de linguistique générale* [I], 225–236.

Benveniste *Phrase relative* — Émile Benveniste. 1957–58. La phrase relative, problème de syntaxe générale. *Bulletin de la Société de Linguistique de Paris* 53, ap. Émile Benveniste, 1966. *Problèmes de linguistique générale* [I], 208–222.

Blanc *Druzes* — Haim Blanc. 1953. *Studies in North Palestinian Arabic*: Inquiries among the Druzes of Western Galilee and Mt. Carmel. [The Israel Oriental Society — Oriental Notes and Studies No. 4] Jerusalem.

Cohen *Phrase nominale* — David Cohen. 1984. *La phrase nominale et l'évolution du système verbal sémitique. Études de syntaxe historique*. [Collection linguistique publiée par la Société de linguistique de Paris, 71] Paris.

Cohen *Verbalisation* — David Cohen. 1957. Phrase nominale et Verbalisation en sémitique. *Mélanges linguistiques offerts à Émile Benveniste.* Paris, 87–98.

Double Case — Double Case: Agreement by Suffixaufnahme. 1995. Edited by Frans Plank. New York, Oxford.

Edzard *Polygenesis* — Lutz Edzard. 1998. *Polygenesis, Convergence, and Entropy : An Alternative Model of Linguistic Evolution Applied to Semitic Linguistics.* Wiesbaden.

Essays on Gurage — Essays on Gurage Language and Culture Dedicated to Wolf Leslau on the occasion of his 90th Birthday November 14th 1996. 1996. Edited by Grover Hudson. Wiesbaden.

Ewald *Geschichtliche Folge* — Heinrich Ewald. 1871. Abhandlung über die geschichtliche Folge der semitischen Sprachen. Dritte sprachwissenschaftliche Abhandlung. *Abhandlungen der Königlichen Gesellschaft der Wissenschaften zu Göttingen* 15: 157–219.

Faber *Subgrouping* — Alice Faber. 1997. Genetic Subgrouping of the Semitic Languages. *The Semitic Languages.* Edited by Robert Hetzron. New York, 3–15.

Finck *Haupttypen* — Franz Nikolaus Finck. 1910. *Die Haupttypen des Sprachbaus* [Aus Natur und Geisteswelt 268]. Leipzig.

Gabelentz *Passivum* — Hans Conon von der Gabelentz. 1860. Über das Passivum. Eine sprachvergleichende Abhandlung. *Abhandlungen der Königlich Sächsischen Gesellschaft der Wissenschaften* [Leipzig] 8: 451–546.

Gardiner *Speech and Language* — Alan H. Gardiner. 1932. *The Theory of Speech and Language.* Oxford.

GG *Congruence and Comitative* — Gideon Goldenberg. 1978. Congruence and Comitative and a Problem of Linguistic Typology. *Quaderni di Semitistica* 5 = Atti del Secondo Congresso Internazionale di Linguistica Camito-Semitica (Firenze, 16–19 aprile 1974) raccolti da Pelio Fronzaroli. Firenze, 133–147. Reprinted in *Studies in Semitic Linguistics*: Selected Writings by Gideon Goldenberg. 1998. Jerusalem, 123–137.

GG *Conservative and Innovative* — Gideon Goldenberg. 1997. Conservative and Innovative Features in Semitic Languages. *Afroasiatica Neapolitana* [Istituto Universitario Orientale: Studi Africanistici, Serie Etiopica 6] : Papers from the 8th Italian Meeting of Afroasiatic (Hamito-Semitic) Linguistics, ed. Alessandro Bausi & Mauro Tosco. Napoli, 3–21.

GG *Contribution of Semitic Languages* — Gideon Goldenberg. 1987–1988. The Contribution of Semitic Languages to

Linguistic Thinking. *Jaarbericht van het Vooraziatisch-Egyptisch Genootschap Ex Oriente Lux* 30: 107–115. Leiden. Reprinted in *Studies in Semitic Linguistics*: Selected Writings by Gideon Goldenberg. 1998. Jerusalem, 1–9.

GG *Harari* — Gideon Goldenberg. 1998. Notes on Harari. *Studies in Semitic Linguistics*: Selected Writings by Gideon Goldenberg. Jerusalem, 427–438 [Extracts translated from "On New Texts in the Language of Harar" [in Hebrew], *Lĕšonénu* 32 (1967–68) 247–263].

GG *Nominalization* — Gideon Goldenberg. 1983. Nominalization in Amharic and Harari : Adjectivization. *Ethiopian Studies* Dedicated to Wolf Leslau on the occasion of his seventy-fifth birthday, edited by S. Segert & A. J. E. Bodrogligeti. Wiesbaden, 170–193. Reprinted in *Studies in Semitic Linguistics*: Selected Writings by Gideon Goldenberg. 1998. Jerusalem, 343–366.

GG *Semitics and Linguistics* — Gideon Goldenberg. 1993. The Semitic Languages and the Science of Language [in Hebrew], in: *Moises Starosta Memorial Lectures*. First Series. Edited by Joseph Geiger. Jerusalem, 99–126.

GG *Word-Structure* — Gideon Goldenberg. 1994. Principles of Semitic Word-Structure. *Semitic and Cushitic Studies*, ed. G. Goldenberg and Sh. Raz. Wiesbaden, 29–64. Reprinted in *Studies in Semitic Linguistics*: Selected Writings by Gideon Goldenberg. 1998. Jerusalem, 10–45.

Halle & alii *Introduction* — Morris Halle, Hagit Borer and Youssef Aoun. 1981. Introduction. *Theoretical Issues in the Grammar of Semitic Languages*, edited by Hagit Borer and Youssef Aoun [MIT Working Papers in Linguistics, vol. 3], 1–20.

Haspelmath *Converb* — Martin Haspelmath. 1995. The Converb as a Cross-Linguistically Valid Category. *Converbs in Cross-Linguistic Perspective*: Structure and Meaning of Adverbial Verb Forms — Adverbial Participles, Gerunds . Edited by Martin Haspelmath & Ekkehard König [Empirical Approaches to Language Typology, 13]. Berlin–New York, 1–55.

Haspelmath *Review* — Martin Haspelmath. 1997. Review of *Double Case. Linguistics* 35: 417–421.

Hetzron *Ethiopian Semitic* — Robert Hetzron. 1972. *Ethiopian Semitic*: Studies in Classification. (Journal of Semitic Studies. Monograph No. 2). Manchester.

Hodge *Nominal Sentence* — Carleton T. Hodge. 1975. The Nominal Sentence in Semitic. *Afroasiatic Linguistics* 2/4 = II 69–75.

Huehnergard *New Directions* — John Huehnergard. 1996. New Directions in the Study of Semitic Languages. *The Study of the Ancient Near East in the Twenty-First Century*: The William Foxwell Albright Centennial Conference, edited by Jerrold S. Cooper and Glenn M. Schwartz. Winona Lake, 251–272.

Humboldt *Dualis* — Wilhelm von Humboldt. 1827. Über den Dualis, ap. Wilhelm von Humboldt, *Werke* in fünf Bänden, hrsg. Andreas Flinter u. Klaus Gill. 5. Aufl. III: Schriften zur Sprachphilosophie. Stuttgart 1979, 113–143.

Jakobson *Mufaxxama* — Roman Jakobson. 1957. Mufaxxama: The 'Emphatic' Phonemes in Arabic. Reprinted in Roman Jakobson, *Selected Writings* I. 'S-Gravenhage 1962, 510–522.

Jakobson *Phonology* — Roman Jakobson. 1932. Phoneme and Phonology. Reprinted in Roman Jakobson, *Selected Writings* I. 'S-Gravenhage 1962, 231–233.

Jakobson & Halle *Phonology and Phonetics* — Roman Jakobson & Morris Halle. 1971. *Fundamentals of Language*. Second, revised edition [Janua Linguarum, Series Minor 1] The Hague. Part I: Phonology and Phonetics, 11–66. Reprinted in Roman Jakobson, *Selected Writings* I 'S-Gravenhage 1962, 464–504.

Leibniz *De Originibus Gentium* — G(odefridi) G(uilielmi) L(eibnitii) Brevis designatio meditationum de Originibus Gentium, ductis potissimum ex indicio linguarum. *Miscellanea Berolinensia ad incrementum scientiarum*, ex scriptis Societati Regiæ Scientiarum exhibitis edita (Berlin 1710) 1–16.

Leslau *Gleanings* — Wolf Leslau. 1965. Gleanings in Harari Grammar I. *Journal of the American Oriental Society* 85: 153–159.

Lipiński *Comparative Grammar* — Edward Lipiński. 1997. *Semitic Languages*: Outline of a Comparative Grammar [Orientalia Lovanensia Analecta 80]. Leuven.

McCawley *Traits phonologiques* — James D. McCawley. 1967. Le rôle d'un système de traits phonologiques dans une théorie du langage. *Langages* 8: 112–123.

Meillet *Linguistique* — Antoine Meillet. 1921–1936. *Linguistique historique et linguistique générale*. 2 vols. Paris.

Moravcsik *Suffixaufnahme* — Edith A. Moravcsik. 1995. Summing up Suffixaufnahme. In *Double Case* 451–484.

Plank *Suffixaufnahme* — Frans Plank. 1995. (Re-)Introducing Suffixaufnahme. In *Double Case* 3–110.

Sabar *Homilies* — Yona Sabar. 1984. *Homilies in the Neo-Aramaic of the Kurdistani Jews on the Parashot Wayḥi, Beshallaḥ and Yitro*. Edition, Hebrew Translation and Introduction [in Hebrew]. Jerusalem.

Sweet *Affinity* — Henry Sweet. 1900–1901. Linguistic Affinity. *Otia Marseiana* 2: 113–126, ap. *Collected Papers of Henry Sweet,* arranged by H. C. Wyld. Oxford 1913, 56–71.

U. — the Christian Neo-Aramaic dialect of Urmia; standard literary Neo-Syriac.

Z. — the Jewish Neo-Aramaic dialect of Zakho.

THE CHOMSKIAN SCHOOL AND SEMITIC LINGUISTICS

JOSEPH L. MALONE

[0. PREAMBLE

The very first spade work for this paper convinced me of the impossibility of what I had at first hoped to develop. This would have been something like a comprehensive annotated bibliography of Chomsky-inspired work on Semitic languages, under a liberal interpretation of what might count as Chomsky-inspired, to the tune of a running historico-philosophical commentary. Even assuming it might be in my power to bring it off, such a project would have taken years of time and at least a volume of space.

So instead I decided to toss the sheets to the wind and proceed in an unabashedly helterskelter way, winnowing materials solely from the haphazard supplies of my private attic study, and hoping that the results might turn out to be at least dimly representative of the ideal implicit in the original pie-in-the-sky conception.

I don't know to what extent I've succeeded, but I do know that, unwillingly if wittingly, I'm going to get a large number of excellent Semitists mad at me for not citing their work. To these innocent victims of my circumstances I can only say, no hard feelings, don't take it personally, I know where you're coming from, I've been there too (often, believe me)...]

1. ORIGINS

In the spirit of what work in the "Chomskian school" should best be interpreted as meaning, I think it fair to say that such work, at least in syntax, antedated Noam Chomsky's own publications, appearing publicly first in the writings of Chomsky's teacher, Zellig Harris. Harris, one of the true giants of American structuralism, actually invented transformational grammar merely as a tool for pushing structural analysis beyond morphology into syntax. Moreover, since Harris included Hebrew among his languages of analysis from the earliest times, it is probably accurate to say that the first publications relevant to the title of this paper were such as Harris 1954, or even the virtual Bible of structuralism, Harris 1951, where his work on "morphemic long components" to the tune of Hebrew morphology and syntax prefigures what several years later would come to be called "agreement transformations" (1951: 314–24).

While Chomsky's syntactic ideas thus owe much of their essence to Harris, it seems likely that the origins of Chomsky's orientation in phonology should rather be traced back to the general pursuit of **morphophonemics** by many structuralist luminaries of the late 40's. To be sure, Harris himself figured squarely among them; but Harris's own work in morphophonemics distinguished him less from his contemporaries than did his work on morphosyntax, preeminently because of his budding ideas on transformational grammar. In any event, Chomsky's master's thesis (1951) bids fair to be the earliest Chomskian contribution to Semitic phonology. And though as the years rolled on, what was to become "generative phonology" got more and more associated with Chomsky's MIT colleague Morris Halle, the merism of Chomsky's early master's thesis and his later revolutionary collaboration with Halle on *The Sound Pattern of English* (1968) is warrant enough for me to consider work on generative phonology just as Chomskian as work on generative syntax for what follows in this essay.

2. GROWTH

How could one obtain an evolutionary profile of the growth of Semitic linguistics à la Chomsky over the years? One way I struck upon was to examine the pages of *Linguistic Inquiry*, the linguistics house organ of Chomsky's MIT, from its inaugural issue in 1970 up through the latest issue while drafting this paper, 29:3 of 1998.

All in all, 40-odd pieces, whether fullblown articles, discussion papers, or squibs, have used one or more Semitic languages as objects of analysis or at least illustration. In about half of these, Semitic languages were the sole or primary analytic focus, while in the other half Semitic languages were a minority component. And roughly half of the 40-odd papers dealt primarily with syntax (a tad more than half), while roughly half again focused on phonology.

In the early days of *Linguistic Inquiry*, Hebrew was the prime target of research, while in recent years that primacy has shifted to Arabic. Spoken forms of both languages have predominated, though there has been attention to classical forms as well: Biblical (Tiberian) Hebrew on the one hand, and Standard Literary Arabic on the other. Colloquial forms of Arabic covered have rung the changes: Bedouin Hijazi, Cairene/Egyptian, Damascene, Harga Oasis, Iraqi, Lebanese, Maltese, Moroccan, Palestinian/Levantine, Sudanese, Tunisian.

Only two pieces have dealt with Semitic languages other than Arabic or Hebrew: McCarthy 1986 (Akkadian and the Ethiopic languages Amharic, Chaha, Ennemor) and Bohas 1990 (the Aramaic language Syriac as well as Proto-Semitic).

Earliest and latest Semitic-relevant *Linguistic Inquiry* pieces both deal with Hebrew (Sampson 1973, Idsardi 1998), while the second and penultimate focus on Arabic (Brame 1974, McCarthy 1997). Curiously, all are phonological, the most recent pair taking antithetic positions on cutting-edge Optimality Theory (McCarthy pro, Idsardi contra).

3. OVERVIEW

There are, of course, a plethora of Chomsky-school works in Semitica outside the pages of *Linguistic Inquiry*. Just a sprinkling will be mentioned here, with an eye to variation in subject matter and type of publication (or other dissemination). To keep things manageable, I will limit the core of the discussion to Hebrew, noting however that it would be just as easy to do the same with Arabic. At the end of the section, we'll return briefly to some languages other than these two giants.

To begin with, there are a number of important dissertations. Two dealing with Hebrew morphophonology (in the widest sense) are Prince 1975 on the ancient language (the bellwether of several MIT works dealing with Biblical (Tiberian) Hebrew, all despite considerable general merits given to questionable notions about the original pronunciation of the vowels, see Garr 1990 for discussion) and Bat-El 1989 on the modern (Israeli) language (some of her concerns overlap those of Bolozky 1980). Another dissertation, arguably the most important of all, will be discussed in §4.5 below.

Diachronic studies are represented by Givón 1974 and Faber 1986. The former deals with syntax and the latter with phonology, and in fact the vast majority of all Chomsky-school Semitica is devoted to one or both of these areas. Eminent exceptions, dealing with orthography and prosodic structure, are Aronoff 1985 and Dresher 1994.

Then there are book-length treatments. Two are Berman 1978 (fine vintage) and Shlonsky 1997 (cutting-edge enough to use in part the framework of Chomsky's Minimalist Theory).

When we travel beyond Hebrew and Arabic, we find little quantity but we do find quality. The lamented genius Robert Hetzron did not work consistently in Chomskian frames, but he did so sometimes, and much of that work was devoted to Ethiopic (e.g. 1970, 1972). And fine work in Aramaic is being pursued by, among others, (e.g. Bohas §2 above), Hoberman in both modern and premodern languages, notably dialects of Syriac (e.g. 1988, 1992–93) and Garr in the classical tongues (e.g. 1986).

We will return to minority Semitic languages shortly, in a few subsections of §4.

4. SCRUTINY

This final substantive section will be given over to an examination of selected works by five scholars. These specific choices have been made in large part to illustrate what I perceive to be various important qualities of Chomsky-school linguistics, and in minor part just for the sake of variety in language and linguistic subdiscipline. For want of other criteria, the five scholars are presented in alphabetical order.

4.1. BORER 1986

In their section on the (Biblical) Hebrew preposition $?\acute{e}\theta$ ~ $?\varepsilon\theta$-, Waltke & O'Connor (1990: 177–83) note that in addition to its canonical function as an accusative marker, as in (1), this formative likewise occasionally appears under other conditions which resist general formulation. They list several representative examples under the rubric "elsewhere" (182–3), from which a pair are reproduced here in (2):

(1) *wayyɔ́ɔśɛm šɔ́ɔm ?ɛθ-hɔɔ?ɔɔðɔ́ɔm* (Genesis 2:8)
    "and (God) placed Adam there" (Waltke & O'Connor 1990: 179;
    lit. "and-put there *?ɛθ*-the-Adam")

(2) a. *wǎ?ɛθ-habbarzél nɔɔfɔ́ɔl ?ɛl-hammɔɔyim* (2 Kings 6:5)
      "and the iron (axhead) fell into the water"
      (lit. "and-*?ɛθ*-the-iron fell to-the-water")

   b. *wayyiwwɔɔléð lahǎnóox ?ɛθ-ʕiirɔ́ɔð* (Genesis 4:18)
      "and Irad was born to Henoch"
      (lit. "and-was-born to-Henoch *?ɛθ*-Irad")

Despite their explicit recognition that cases like (2) have sometimes been considered as "ergative, in which the morphological marking of the subject of an intransitive verb [including the passive — JLM] is the same as the direct object of a transitive verb" (1990: 178), a view which might succeed in providing a unitary explanation for the like of (1–2), Waltke & O'Connor nevertheless conclude that "ergative theory should be rejected because it does not account for the wide use of ʔéθ ~ ʔɛθ- in other constructions in Biblical Hebrew" (1990: 179), by which they presumably have in mind other cases listed under their "elsewhere" rubric not apparently unifiable with (1–2).

It strikes me that several of their "elsewhere" cases might turn out to be unifiable with (1–2) after all. But even granting that ʔéθ ~ ʔɛθ- may end up showing a certain amount of irreducible polysemy or homonymy (note in particular comitative ʔɛθ "with", Waltke & O'Connor 1990: 195), I think that an adequate explication of what Waltke & O'Connor call the ergative hypothesis might go a long way toward explaining the behavior of this morpheme. And I think that the groundwork for just such an explanation may be provided in Borer 1986, very much in the Chomskian vein.

The gist of Borer's hypothesis, based on colloquial Modern Hebrew data quite similar to (1–2) (1986: 385), is that there are circumstances under which the functional element Agr and a verb may so to speak compete for Case-marking an argument. For a language with the general typology of Modern Hebrew (and granting the possibility of necessary adjustments for Biblical Hebrew), the set-up is provided by these simplified schemata (cf. Borer's (13) (1986: 379)):

(3) a.   X Agr V Y
    b.   X V+Agr Y

If in (3a) X is an NP subject, V a transitive verb, and Y an NP object, Agr Case-marks X as nominative while V Case-marks Y as accusative. If the language also inflects its verbs for subject-agreement features, as does Hebrew, Agr then adjoins to V as in (3b). In fact, such adjunction may take place even if X is the null pronoun **pro**, in which case the result is a sentence where identification of the subject wholly devolves upon the inflection of the verb. This is essentially the situation in Biblical example (1), where X is null (**pro**), V+Agr is *wayyɔ́ɔśɛm* (placed + 3rd m sg), and Y is ʔɛθ-hɔɔʔɔɔðɔ́ɔm with ʔɛθ- marking the accusative function.

Crucially now, Borer proposes that in some languages, Hebrew included, passive and ergative verbs are optional Case-assigners. Since well-formedness normally requires passives and ergatives to be monadic verbs, X in (3b) will be absent. Then in the unmarked scenario V will select the negative option, allowing Agr to Case-mark the NP Y as nominative. But in the marked scenario V will select the positive option and Case-mark Y as accusative, which is the situation found in the example of (2).

Assuming its empirical adequacy, an admirable feature of Borer's proposal is the degree to which it smoothly integrates with other facets of the language. It is elegant, simple, and requires but minimal stipulation.

4.2. GREENSTEIN 1974, 1980

The science of linguistics has always supplied tools at the service of the language arts and technologies, and the Chomskian brand of linguistic science is no exception. In fact, the generally rigorous and comprehensive nature of the Chomskian enterprise makes it particularly well suited for the provision of such tools.

A case in point is the work of Edward Greenstein on syntactic parallelism in the belles lettres of the ancient Northwest Semitic languages. In this enterprise Greenstein has found transformational grammar to be greatly useful in explicating various patterns — and perhaps even especially in accounting for what have been taken to be deviations from conventionally recognized patterns, by showing that when viewed transformationally many of these nexuses are not deviations after all. In this regard note the Ugaritic couplet <*adnh yšt mṣb mznm / umh kp mznm*> "her father set the stand of the balances / her mother the trays of the balances" (NK 33–34). If, Greenstein argues, (1974: 90), one analyzes this couplet as having undergone a transformational rule of **gapping**, this couplet can be seen as instantiating word-for-word symmetry after all, on the underlying level; cf. (4), where the bold-face form represents the gapped verb restored underlyingly (loosely, assuming morphological decomposition of the subject prefix <*t*–> etc.):

(4) <*adnh yšt mṣb mznm*>
     her-father set stand of-the-balances
     <*umh **tšt** kp mznm*>
     her-mother set trays of-the-balances

Greenstein's wide-reaching applications of up-to-date linguistic techniques to problems of classical Semitic philology take him to generative phonology no less than to generative syntax. Thus he offers a solution to a long-standing paradox in Akkadian morphophonology with the simple expedient of a **minor rule**, whereby pronominal /š/ is replaced by /s/ when immediately following a dental or a sibilant (1980). With the leisure of hindsight in the wake of Greenstein's proposal, the difficulty tacitly investing the traditional paradox was the unwarranted assumption that the pronominal morphemic segment in question was invariably /š/. For on this assumption, it was puzzling indeed why a form like /*uppiš-ši*/ "treat her!" should end up being pronounced [uppissi], as if the geminate /šš/ had for some reason transmogrified to [ss]. On Greenstein's view, of course, the minor rule will already have operated to give /*uppiš-si*/ before the rules proper of the phonology have a chance to apply: and when they do, the group /šs/ will straightforwardly assimilate regressively to [ss], as

do other groups in any number of unproblematic cases, e.g. /ḥitsas/ →
[ḥissas] "pay heed!".

4.3. JOHANNESSEN 1996

Wright (1898) spends several pages (188–90) cataloguing the grabbag of
verb-subject agreement in (Classical) Arabic, among them (294):

(5) [if] the preceding verb has several subjects, it may be
a. put in the plural, as in
jiʔnaa ʔanaa waʔanta "thou and I are come";

or it may agree in number and gender with the

b. nearest subjects, as
wayusnid haaruunu wabanuuhu ʔaydiyahum ʕalaa raʔsihi
"and Aaron and his sons shall lay their hands upon his
head"

where in the first case (5a) the verb *jiʔnaa* is inflected as 1 pl in agreement
with the phrasally plural subject *ʔanaa waʔanta* lit. "I and-thou",while
in the second case (5b) the verb *(wa)yusnid* is inflected as 3 m sg in
agreement with the first conjunct of the subject, *haaruunu* "Aaron".

Using data from Lebanese Arabic, Johannessen (1996) provides a
Chomsky-style account of such patterning. The gist of his proposal is
that Universal Grammar makes available two types of coordination:
balanced and unbalanced (1996: 668–73, importantly with note 8).
In balanced coordination, each conjunct contributes features to the
overarching coordination on an equal footing; this is instantiated in
(5a), where the [–plural] feature of *ʔanaa* "I" and the [–plural] feature of
ʔanta "thou" unite to [+plural] as marked by the suffix *-naa* "we" (the 1
pl set subsuming also 2nd person members as nearly universally). While
the Chomskian school certainly has no claim to monopoly over such an
account of balanced coordination, Johannessen's approach to unbalanced
coordination, instantiated in (5b), is consummately Chomskian. According
to Johannessen, in such cases coordination subsumes the participating
conjuncts as specifier and complement of an overarching Conjunction
Phrase (CoP), the choice of which conjunct is mapped into specifier
position and which into complement position depending on the typological
issue of whether the language is head-initial or head-final. In a head-initial
language like Arabic, the first conjunct maps to specifier, so that the
coordinate subject of (5b) would look like this (simplified):

(6)   CoP

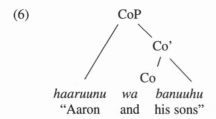

haaruunu   wa   banuuhu
"Aaron   and   his sons"

Johannessen now appeals to the most recent incarnation of Chomskian syntax, Minimalist Theory, to propose that "the only relevant relation between elements in the CoP be specifier-head agreement" (1996: 669), the mechanics of which would have it that the features of the specifier [[–plural] *haaruunu* in (6)] invest the head (*wa–*) and thence percolate up the tree to CoP, while the "conjunct in the complement position [here [+plural] *banuuhu*] takes no part in agreement and offers no syntactic features to the CoP itself" (loc. cit.).

A particularly cheering prediction, I think, is that most of the dozen or so other agreement patterns described in Wright (1898: 288–99) also seem in principle susceptible to Johannessen's analysis, modulo a handful of additional rather straightforward assumptions.

4.4. LOWENSTAMM 1991

In the early of the Chomskian era the complaint was often heard that not enough attention, or even no attention at all, was paid to antecedent or contemporary linguistic approaches of distinct stripes. However it is my impression that in recent decades workers in the Chomskian paradigm appear to be becoming more receptive of other approaches; if not always explicitly, then at least by dint of showing de facto similarities in theory and method. To the extent that this impression is well founded, I suspect that we are often witnessing the salubrious phenomenon of **scientific convergence**: the pursuit of similar analytic goals in initially dissimilar ways gradually becomes more homogeneous; and this is salubrious in that it most frequently means that both approaches are on the right track.

A good example of such convergence is Lowenstamm's (1991) proposal for the synchronic structure of the Ethiopic Semitic vowel system, as well as for its diachronic evolution from Proto-Semitic. Though the approach he brings to bear is the altogether neo-generative, hence Chomskian, theory of "charm phonology" codeveloped with Jonathan Kaye (cf. Kaye and Lowenstamm 1985), both form and substance of his analysis bring strongly to mind the best of both American structural phonology (e.g.

Hockett 1955, Hoenigswald 1960) and European functional phonology (notably Martinet 1964).

A striking feature of Lowenstamm's analysis is the degree to which it is "automated", in that what appears to be a complex of changes is taken to be the result of a series of mini-changes triggered by one or two simple mutations. (Such automation has long been a goal in generative phonology, from Chomsky & Halle's **marking conventions** (1968) down through work in Optimality Theory (e.g. Kirchner 1996); and, under an earlier sun, was a prime ideal of Martinet 1964). As a case in point, Lowenstamm explicates the evolution of Ethiopic vowels from Proto-Semitic as involving one primary and one secondary mutation. The primary mutation is **dechromatization of short vowels** (modeled as nuclear delinking (1991: 9–10, esp. (18) and (21)). Had the consequences remained unadulterated, all short vowels would have imploded to the colorless "cold" vowel [ɨ]. But a secondary mutation is taken to have intervened, a "role-reversal" (1991: 11) switching the structural priority of features within the reflex of Proto-Semitic *a* allowing this segment, alone of the original short vowels, to survive.

4.5. McCARTHY 1979, 1981

Perhaps the most impressive contribution of Chomskian linguistics to Semitic morphophonology is the explication of **internal flexion**, the Semitic-particular special case of what Sapir (1921) called "symbolic-fusional morphology" in the form of largely consonantal root morphemes composing with largely vocalic scheme morphemes. The earliest publicly disseminated full articulation of this explanation is probably John McCarthy's MIT dissertation (1979), subsequently digested and developed in McCarthy 1981.

In gist, this explication proceeds by dispersing the interaction of roots and schemes into the coordinated association of three quasi-independent **autosegmental tiers**, two so-called **melodic** tiers each anchorable onto a so-called **skeletal** tier. While the melodic tiers accommodate the root and scheme morphemes, the skeletal tier regulates the mutual association of root and scheme, i.e., what at times is traditionally called their interdigitation. Take the Classical Mandaic (Eastern Aramaic) verb *haššeß* "he thought". Traditionally, this word would be said to manifest the interdigitation of the root √hšß (lexically/phonologically √hšb) "think" with the intensive past tense scheme *CaCCeC*, whereby the first schematic *a* (1∫a) is interdigitated between the first radical *h* (1√h) and the second radical *š* (2√š), similarly 2∫e between 2√š and 3√ß, and whereby 2√š is geminated. In autosegmental terms, the situation may be displayed as in (7), in which connection it may be noted how one-to-two association between root and skeleton captures the geminate nature of šš:

(7)   root tier   ḥ   š   ß
       skeletal tier   C   V   C   C   V   C
       scheme tier   a   e

This relatively straightforward modeling of the traditional notions of root and scheme proves salutary for the reconciliation of classical (originally Arab) Semitistic morphophonology with general (universal) linguistics, and in the process provides some relatively simple answers to some traditionally puzzling or vexing questions. Thus it is well known that the classical Aramaic languages show a predilection for lowering short vowels to *a* immediately preceding a low consonant (viz. the gutturals along with *r*, whose apical trilling induces lowering of the tongue body). And yet the precise conditions for this lowering are tricky to formulate in standard phonology. Note for example *šaddar* "he sent", vis-à-vis *haššeß* "he thought" displayed in (7). Since both verbs belong to the same conjugational type, one would presumably account for *šaddar* ≠ §*šadder* (§ for illformedness) in terms of *e* lowering to *a* / _*r*. But why doesn't one have such lowering in *nerkaß* "he'll ride" ≠ §*narkaß*; cf. identiconjugational *neθbar* "he'll break"? Or in *berxii* "he blessed it" ≠ §*barxii*; cf. *keðßii* "he wrote it"? For similar discrepancies in other Aramaic languages appeal has sometimes been made to stress differences, on the assumption that lowering might be restricted to stressed syllables. Assuming the classical Aramaic stress pattern for Classical Mandaic, these forms might in fact be so accomodated: *šaddár, nerkáß, berxíi*. And even if the penultimate stress pattern typical of Modern Mandaic held as early as the classical language (*šáddar, nérkaß, bérxii*), one could still claim that the lowering preceded the stress retraction. Yes, but what then of forms like *šaddartollii* "ye sent to me"? Why isn't this rather §*šaddertollii*, with canonically expected 2∫e as in *haššeßton* "ye thought" (or nonattested but unimpeachable *haššeßtollii* "ye thought of me")? Whether *šaddartollii* was accentuated *šaddartollíi* or *šaddartóllii*, in neither case was the 2∫ stressed, and yet the *e* has lowered to *a*. Well, this behavior can be captured if phonological theory can convey the traditional Semitistic condition of "immediately preceding a low 3√" (לֹ גרונית). Given autosegmentsl modeling, this is in fact easily achieved — "immediately preceding a skeleton-final C associated with [+low]":

(8)

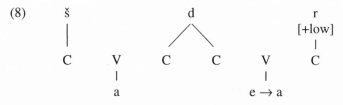

Structurally, this characterization of "low 3√" as skeleton-final is not affected by addition of the suffix complex *–tollii* (< *—/tonn-lii/*), which resides on a distinct tier; and the *r*'s of forms like *nerkaβ* and *berxii* are correctly identified as being other than skeleton-final (skeleton-initial and skeleton-medial respectively).

5. ENVOI

In the early days of the Chomskian school, it was sometimes quipped that this new brand of linguistic research must be guided by the tacit delusion that all languages are but notational variants of English, given the dominance of English as focus of the devotees' research. Now however, nearly half a century later, such quips are no longer heard, and Chomskian work has truly become universal, extending its pale to virtually every language family on earth. And the Semitic family, that of Chomsky's forebears, is no exception — a cheering fact for linguists and Semitists alike.

REFERENCES

Aronoff, Mark. 1985. Orthography and linguistic theory: the syntactic basis of Masoretic Hebrew punctuation. *Language* 61:28–72.

Bat-El, Outi. 1989. *Phonology and Word Structure in Modern Hebrew.* UCLA Ph.D. Dissertation.

Berman, Ruth A. 1978. *Modern Hebrew Structure.* Tel Aviv University.

Bohas, Georges. 1990. A diachronic effect of the OCP. *LI* 21:298–301.

Bolozki, Shmuel. 1980. On the monophonematic interpretation of Modern Hebrew affricates. *LI* 11:793–9.

Borer, Hagit. 1986. I-subjects. *LI* 17:375–416.

Brame, M.K. 1974. The cycle in phonology: stress in Palestinian, Maltese, and Spanish. *LI* 5:39–60.

Chomsky, Noam. 1951 [1979]. *The Morphophonemics of Modern Hebrew.* University of Pennsylvania Masters Thesis [New York].

Chomsky, Noam & Morris Halle. 1968. *The Sound Pattern of English.* New York.

Dresher, Bezalel Elan. 1994. The prosodic basis of the Tiberian Hebrew system of accents. *Language* 70:1–52.

Faber, Alice. 1986. On the origin and development of Hebrew spirantization. *Mediterranean Language Review* 2:117–37.

Garr, W. Randall. 1986. Attenuation in the Aramaic verbal system. MS, Department of Religious Studies, University of California at Santa Barbara.

Garr, W. Randall. 1990. Interpreting orthography. In: B. Halpern et al., eds. *The Hebrew Bible and its Interpreters.* Winona Lake, 53–80.

Givón, Talmy. 1974. Verb complements and relative clauses: a diachronic case study in Biblical Hebrew. *Afroasiatic Linguistics* 1:4.

Greenstein, Edward L. 1974. Two variations of grammatical parallelism in Canaanite poetry and their psycholinguistic background. *Journal of the Ancient Near Eastern Society of Columbia University* 6:87–105.

Greenstein, Edward L. 1980. The assimilation of dentals and sibilants with pronominal *š* in Akkadian. *Journal of the Ancient Near Eastern Society of Columbia University* 12:51–64.

Harris, Zellig S. 1951 [1961]. *Structural Linguistics.* Chicago.

Harris, Zellig S. 1954. Transfer grammar. *International Journal of American Linguistics* 20:259–70.

Hetzron, Robert. 1970. Toward an Amharic case grammar. *Studies in African Linguistics* 1:301–54.

Hetzron, Robert. 1972. The shape of a rule and diachrony. *Bulletin of the School of Oriental and African Studies* 35:451–75.

Hoberman, Robert D. 1988. Emphasis harmony in a Modern Aramaic dialect. *Language* 64:1–26.

Hoberman, Robert D. 1992–93. Local spreading. *Journal of Afroasiatic Languages* 3:226–54.

Hockett, Charles F. 1955. *A Manual of Phonology.* Baltimore.

Hoenigswald, Henry. 1960. *Language Change and Linguistic Reconstruction.* Chicago.

Idsardi, William J. 1998. Tiberian Hebrew spirantization and phonological derivations. *LI* 29:37–73.

Johannessen, Janne Bondi. 1996. Partial agreement and coordination. *LI* 27:661–76.

Kaye, Jonathan D. & Jean Lowenstamm. 1985. The internal structure of phonological elements: a theory of charm and government. *Phonology Yearbook* 2:305–28.

Kirchner, Robert. 1996. Synchronic chains in Optimality Theory. *LI* 27:341–50.

Lowenstamm, Jean. 1991. Vowel length and centralization in two branches of Semitic. *Semitic Studies in Honor of Wolf Leslau*, ed. Alan S. Kaye. Wiesbaden.

Martinet, André. 1964. *Économie des changements phonétiques*. Berne.

McCarthy, John. 1979. *Formal Problems in Semitic Phonology and Morphology*. MIT Ph.D. dissertation.

McCarthy, John. 1981. A prosodic theory of nonconcatenative morphology. *LI* 12:373–418.

McCarthy, John. 1986. OCP effects: gemination and antigemination. *LI* 17:207–63.

McCarthy, John. 1997. Process-specific constraints in Optimality Theory. *LI* 28:231–51.

Prince, Alan S. 1975. *The Phonology and Morphology of Tiberian Hebrew*. MIT Ph.D. dissertation.

Sampson, Geoffrey. 1973. Duration in Hebrew consonants. *LI* 4:101–4.

Sapir, Edward. 1921. *Language*. New York.

Shlonsky, Ur. 1997. *Clause Structure and Word Order in Hebrew and Arabic*. New York & Oxford.

Waltke, B. & M. O'Connor. 1990. *An Introduction to Biblical Hebrew Syntax*. Winona Lake.

Wright, W. 1898 [1967]. *A Grammar of the Arabic Language*. Vol. II, 3rd edition. Cambridge.

THE STUDY OF PARTIALLY DOCUMENTED LANGUAGES

JO ANN HACKETT

I have been asked to write about "partially documented languages," that is, languages about which our knowledge is incomplete: we may not have enough material written in the language to allow us to understand its grammar completely, or we may have only the consonants of the language, not uncommon in ancient Semitic writing. The 20th century has been a remarkable one for partially documented languages, and not just in Semitics, or even mainly in Semitics: one thinks immediately of Linear B, of course, and the Indus Valley and Mayan remains where much progress has been made, or of Hieroglyphic Luwian, the decipherment of which depended in large part on its bilingual with another partially documented language, Phoenician.

I have left out of this paper epigraphic Hebrew and Aramaic, since we do have quite a bit of evidence about both from later texts, so that the study of, say, Ugaritic is a very different animal. It will be obvious, however, that the general statements I make about other epigraphic languages also often apply to Hebrew and Aramaic. I will be limiting my discussion to the languages and dialects I know best, which are Northwest Semitic and more specifically Phoenician and Ugaritic; but I believe the issues that need to be discussed here in the study of partially documented languages can be brought out with this corpus as well as any other.

I am also leaving out any discussion of the many contributions to our understanding of the writing systems these languages employ, but in many such languages, the writing system must be deciphered before any other progress can take place, and that decipherment is in large part a linguistically-based process. (An exception to the writing-system exclusion is O'Connor 1983, which should be noted because it certainly draws its insights about Semitics from more general linguistics.)

And finally, I have limited the scope of my discussion even more by concentrating on work within Semitics that has put general linguistics to use to make major progress. That is to say, I have left out a lot of very insightful work in interpretation of these languages, or in the significance of an inscription or corpus within ancient society or on our understanding of history, because the insights were not linguistic or did not advance our use of linguistics to read these languages. Donner and Röllig 1971–76 and the recent volumes of Renz 1995 (Hebrew only) are two of the more obvious omissions, as is Watson and Wyatt 1999 in the field of Ugaritic studies.

In many ways, it was the nineteenth century that saw the greatest advances in the study of epigraphic Semitic languages; already in the seventeenth century, in fact, scholars were publishing books and articles about Northwest Semitic inscriptions, and articles by Barthélemy and Swinton in the mid-eighteenth are generally credited with making the first serious progress toward an understanding of how the Phoenician alphabet and language worked (Barthélemy 1764; Swinton 1764a,b). The nineteenth century saw the advances of Gesenius, whose *Scripturae linguaeque phoeniciae monumenta* saw the light in 1837. He edited, published, and commented upon everything he could find up to his day, and used other Semitic languages to explain difficulties in his texts. His discussions are both philological and paleographic, since the very readings of many of the texts he had access to were still being established. (Otto Eissfeldt published a delightful article in 1947, translating a letter from Gesenius to a colleague in Paris, that provides a look at this very process.) And Schröder's grammar of Phoenician, published in 1869, is remarkably modern, as is William Wright's *Lectures on the Comparative Grammar of the Semitic Languages*, published by Robertson Smith in 1890.

By 1900, the scholarly world knew quite a few inscriptions already. The first part of *CIS* I was published in 1881[1] and Lidzbarski's *Handbuch der nordsemitischen Epigraphik* in 1898.[2] In Phoenician, thousands of Carthaginian inscriptions came to light in the last half of the nineteenth century; there were several discussions already of the Eshmunazor inscription (e.g., Dietrich 1855; Salisbury 1856; Schlottmann 1868) and many hundreds of publications on several colonial Phoenician inscriptions as well. The Moabite Stone was published in the second half of the century (e.g., Clermont-Ganneau 1870; 1875; 1887; Nöldeke 1870;

---

[1] *Corpus Inscriptionum Semiticarum.* The second came out from 1890–1907 and the third from 1916–62. *CIS* I was continued in *RES, Répertoire d'épigraphie sémitique,* I (1900–05), II (1907–14), III (1916–18), and IV (1919–20).

[2] The *Handbuch* has a remarkable bibliography of early epigraphic works. Lidzbarski continued to provide commentaries for newly-found and already-known inscriptions even after the Handbuch had appeared, and that work is compiled in his three-volume *Ephemeris für semitische Epigraphik.* Javier Teixidor's *Bulletin d'épigraphie sémitique* (1984) is an updated compilation of the author's bibliographic essays in the journal *Syria,* from 1967–79.

Smend and Socin 1886), as were the Hebrew Siloam tunnel inscription (Schick 1880; Guthe 1882) and the Sam'alian texts from Zincirli (von Luschan 1893). The Moabite language was understood to be different from Hebrew, though not much, and the two were seen to be related to Phoenician. Some of the early work on Moabite sounds quite modern as well, such as Christian Ginsburg's 1871 discussion of the light shed on biblical orthographic practices by the Moabite stone as opposed to the Phoenician inscriptions he knew. For instance:

> Very remarkable is the uniform use of *He* (ה) in the Moabite Stone to express the final O. ....Compare בה *in him* with Hebrew בּוֹ (line 7); [בְּנֹה *his son* with Hebrew בְּנוֹ] (line 6).... The light, therefore, which the orthography of the Moabite Stone throws upon the orthography of the Massoretic text, is...that in this respect the Moabite dialect fully harmonises with the Massoretic system, and entirely differs from the Phoenician; that the *scriptio plena* was used very sparingly in the middle of words both in the Moabite and in Hebrew; that the latter extended the use of it in the course of time, when the language was more developed, and that in Hebrew, as in the Moabite, ה *he* was originally and uniformly used to express O at the end of the word, and that this consonant was afterwards supplanted by *Vav.* .....
> In the forms which mark the gender of Nouns, the feminine singular ending is simply the original ת- as in Phoenician..., and not ה-ָ as in Hebrew. ...A very remarkable feature in so early a document is the form of the plural masculine -ֹן instead of -ֹם both in the Nouns and Numerals,....since it has hitherto been supposed that it is an Aramaic termination, which has crept into Hebrew at a later period of the language (pp. 25–27).

Obviously, the dating of inscriptions was much more of a problem a century ago than today because of the paucity of comparative material. But there was already an understanding of the importance of comparing little-known scripts and languages with better-known. So, by the beginning of the 20th century, the groundwork for our understanding of epigraphic Northwest Semitic languages was already laid. What the twentieth century has added falls into several categories: the amount of material available to us has increased and is still increasing; there have been great advances in linguistic method in this century; and we now have technology that is changing both the access that we have to texts and our ease of dealing with them.

Let me turn first of all to archaeology, to the great deal of excavation that has revealed more and more material: Byblian Phoenician, more Phoenician and Punic from around the Mediterranean, Ammonite inscriptions, Edomite, and Old Aramaic, and of course Ugaritic. Each provenanced and well-dated addition to a corpus of texts allows us to confirm or alter our typology of the scripts the texts are written in and of their orthography, and these help us understand morphology and syntax better. With luck we increase the known vocabulary items as well.

The twentieth century has seen not only an increase in archaeological excavation, but also a honing of archaeological method, so that we are much more likely to know the context of an inscription that comes from a legal dig, and in fact to know a great deal more about the inscription: date; function perhaps; where the clay of the ostracon or tablet originated; whether it was part of an archive or was buried in a private house; whether it was written by a professional scribe; and so on. Unfortunately, the twentieth century has also seen enough of a market for antiquities that forgeries have become more common, and modern technology makes them easier to make and probably harder to uncover.[3]

As was mentioned earlier, the twentieth century has also seen more sophisticated linguistic methods for dealing with partially documented languages, and since I am emphasizing methods and tools for approaching such languages, I will review here a very limited and no doubt idiosyncratic selection of items that have appeared in the last century. I have tried to document advances in our linguistic understanding of texts in these languages, and in how they in turn contribute to our linguistic understanding of Semitics in general. Hence the dual focus in this survey on vocalization of languages in unvocalized scripts and, at the other end, classification of languages and dialects.

It is in the comparative and historical study of languages that general linguistics has made the most impact on Semitics in the 20th century. The first volume of Brockelmann's *Grundriss* appeared in 1908, and many of the basic explanations still taught in courses on comparative Semitic linguistics were already present in that book. Even in the nineteenth century there was already a kind of comparative work going on — words in Phoenician inscriptions or in the Mesha Stela might be explained with reference to Biblical Hebrew, for instance — but it is really only in the 20th century that serious diachronic comparative and reconstructive work has been done in Semitic languages, following by a few decades the same kind of study of Indo-European languages.

Zellig Harris's *Grammar of the Phoenician Language* (1936) and *Development of the Canaanite Dialects* (1939), nicely subtitled *An Investigation in Linguistic History*, were also landmark books. The

---

[3]   Note the recent *IEJ* article about the possibility that the Moussaieff ostraca (in Hebrew) were forged (Eph'al and Naveh 1998).

discussions of regular sound changes, for example, in both these books depend on reconstructing *expected* forms in order to understand unexpected forms, especially in languages like Phoenician where vocalization is generally lacking. That is, how do you explain sound changes in the vocalic system of a language written without vowels? The linguist must use several resources. One is words transmitted in languages that *are* vocalized, such as Phoenician words written out in Greek or Latin letters or in syllabic cuneiform. Another is historical and comparative linguistics, studies that allow us to reconstruct what we can reasonably expect to see in the vowel system of an unvocalized language, based on evidence from vocalized cognate languages. (To continue with Phoenician, we reconstruct, based on all sorts of vocalized Hebrew, Aramaic, and Ugaritic evidence, what we would expect a given Phoenician word to look like.) A knowledge of phonological processes that operate generally in the world's languages will allow the linguist to spell out reasonable steps that take reconstructed forms (produced on the basis of vocalized cognate languages) to the vocalized Phoenician words we have identified in Greek or Latin script.

Take, for instance, Joshua Fox's recent discussion of vowel shifts in Phoenician in *JNES* (1996). He finds a consistent chain of vowel shifts, especially noticeable in transcriptions of Phoenician, that move from [a] up the back of the oral cavity to the back rounded [u], and all the way over to a front vowel, [ü] or [i]. Fox points out that this direction of vowel shifts is well established in general linguistics and in many language families, so we do not hesitate to accept the possibility in Phoenician.

Richard S. Tomback's *A Comparative Semitic Lexicon of the Phoenician and Punic Languages* (1978) is based on an understanding of the importance of cognates in reconstruction and provides many data for such reconstruction, as do the dictionaries by Jean and Hoftijzer, *Dictionnaire des inscriptions sémitiques de l'Ouest* (1960–65), and the update, Hoftijzer and Jongeling, *Dictionary of the North-west Semitic Inscriptions* (1995). Mention should be made at this point of Friedrich's *Phönizisch-punische Grammatik* (1951), the 1970 revision by Friedrich and Röllig, and the new 3rd edition, revised by M. G. Amadasi Guzzo (1999), although they are much more attuned to providing transliterations of Phoenician words into classical, vocalized languages — and provide a wealth of such material — than they are in exploring the linguistic arguments to be deduced from those transliterations.

Sabatino Moscati's 1969 *An Introduction to the Comparative Grammar of the Semitic Languages: Phonology and Morphology* (with A. Spitaler, E. Ullendorff, and W. von Soden) was an assembling of a mass of material, using vocabulary and methods from general linguistics. They describe their goals this way: "Within the limits of time and space already described, the present study aims at a reconstruction of the earliest phonological and morphological units (Proto-Semitic...) as well as their historical development in the principal languages of the group" (p. 5). Although the volume does use words and phrases like "phoneme" and "conditioned phonetic change," more examples within their reconstructions would have been helpful (and more on the process of reconstruction in each case), as would a final systematization of their reconstructions. It is not clear, in fact, who their audience was to be. Some explanations at the beginning of the book are of rather common concepts, but a term like "aspect" is used in the discussion of the verb, enclosed in quotation marks, but not explained. Perhaps their unconscious audience was general linguists, and the book would then be one of a very few examples of our field's attempting to make an impact on general linguistics, rather than the other way around.

W. F. Albright championed comparative and historical method for understanding partially documented languages, and its use is scattered throughout his work, producing, for instance, in the area this paper is addressing, his 1947 *JAOS* article on the Phoenician inscriptions from Byblos. Even those cases where new data have forced a revision of Albright's conclusions are a testament to his method: much of Albright's enduring legacy was the insistence on the creation of systems that could accommodate new information, rather than any particular conclusion. Cross and Freedman's *Early Hebrew Orthography* (1952) goes farther and reconstructs forms for unvocalized Hebrew, Phoenician, Moabite, and Aramaic inscriptions based on their knowledge of earlier and later Northwest Semitic languages, such as the Canaanite glosses in the Amarna letters. William Moran, another Albright student, was working precisely on these Amarna materials, and other sources of evidence for Northwest Semitic, at the same time at Johns Hopkins University (Moran 1961).

Anson Rainey is the scholar most identified with continuing the Amarna Canaanite work, and his four-volume *Canaanite in the Amarna Tablets: a linguistic analysis of the mixed dialect used by the scribes from Canaan* (Rainey 1996a) lays out the evidence in detail. Shlomo Izre'el's work on Amarna, like the forthcoming "Some Methodological Requisites for the Study of the Amarna Jargon" (Izre'el forthc.) with its explanation of the workings of the verbal system of Amarna Akkadian, is very helpful to the scholar trying to use what we know of Canaanite from Amarna. His insistence that we understand Amarna Akkadian as a mixed language or "fused language" and apply to these ancient texts modern linguistic tools for dealing with such spoken languages is a great aid in reconstruction of later, less well understood languages.

Cross and Freedman (1951), Charles Krahmalkov (1970; 1972; 1974; 1993), John Huehnergard (1991a), and Maria Giulia Amadasi Guzzo (1997; 1999) have published a string of articles over almost 50 years analyzing the pronominal suffixes in Phoenician and Punic. I mention these because they work together as a set on such similar topics, and these varied authors, too, utilize the process I outlined above: given what we think on historical and comparative grounds these suffixes began as in Northwest Semitic, and using established sound changes such as reduction of diphthongs, nasalization, and so on, we can explain what the texts present us with, in the consonantal orthography of Phoenician. Less well known is Thomas O. Lambdin's "The Junctural Origin of the West Semitic Definite Article" (1971). Lambdin offers a more technically linguistic argument than most, but in the category of application of general linguistics to understanding less well-known languages it finds a very useful place. His discussion of the article in Phoenician is the best attempt I know of to find some order in what first appears to be a haphazard writing of the definite article, even in texts from a time period where its use should be standard.

Ugaritic is the Northwest Semitic language whose understanding has most been affected by comparative linguistics. In Cyrus Gordon's *Ugaritic Grammar* (1940) and its successors, comparative and historical methods are evident on every page, used for instance to explain the verbal system and the vocabulary, and to reconstruct the morphology of nouns and pronouns;[4] but there have been many more smaller works over the decades that have been essentially linguistic and have furthered our understanding of the language. H. L. Ginsberg argued that of the three *aleph*s in Ugaritic, *ʔi* was used to denote syllable-closing *aleph* (Ginsberg 1933; 1936; Ginsberg and Maisler 1934).[5] The only way one can make such an argument, of course, is to know where to expect *aleph* at the end of a syllable, and the only way to know that is to figure it out using comparative and historical linguistics. (See Verreet 1988 for an extension of the use of *aleph* to determine verbal morphology and then syntax.)

One of the recent advances in our knowledge of Ugaritic came with John Huehnergard's 1987 book, *Ugaritic Vocabulary in Syllabic Transcription*, which utilizes a broad range of linguistic skills to reconstruct the pronunciation and meaning of several hundred Ugaritic words based on polyglot texts and glosses, and on other indications of Ugaritic words in Akkadian texts written at Ugarit. Huehnergard, further, analyzes the

---

[4]   For the influence of H. L. Ginsberg on Gordon's work see W. F. Albright's comments in his review of another Gordon work, *Before the Bible* (Albright 1964: 191).

[5]   David Marcus came to the same conclusion (1968), and more recently Josef Tropper (1990) has suggested a slightly more complicated system than Ginsberg-Marcus.

forms he has found, and the phonological and morphological results of that analysis — conditioned sound changes that seem to be operating, for instance — can then be extended to the language as a whole, and Ugaritic starts to sound like a real language.

Another large linguistic field that has made major advances in Semitics in the twentieth century is that of classification and dialectology. Robert Hetzron's 1974 article, "La division des langues sémitiques," has often been cited as a watershed in this field.[6] Instead of the older division of Brockelmann where Semitic languages are divided into Northeast, Northwest, and South Semitic, which has been used in one form or another for most of the 20th century, Hetzron proposed first a division between Akkadian (East Semitic) and everything else (West Semitic), then divided West Semitic into Central and South Semitic. Hetzron has been followed most notably by Rainer Voigt and John Huehnergard, in several articles each (Voigt 1987; 1998; Huehnergard 1991b; 1992; 1995a,b; see also his contribution to this volume), and Alice Faber (Faber 1980; 1997).

Within Northwest Semitic we have W. Randall Garr's 1985 *Dialect Geography of Syria-Palestine, 1000–586 B.C.E.*, a book no epigrapher can live without. Not only does Garr provide all the evidence available to him and demonstrate his reconstructions, but he amasses all this evidence in the service of an attempt at real dialect geography, grouping features together on the basis of shared isoglosses and giving us a few maps of isoglosses, enough to serve as illustration of what could be done using maps.

There have been other interesting discussions of classification in the 20th century, usually dealing with only one corpus. The confusion over Ugaritic's classification, specifically whether it is one of the Canaanite languages, is still with us, although the group of Hetzron-Voigt-Huehnergard-Faber, each in their own way, separates Ugaritic and Canaanite. (But cf. Tropper 1994; Isaksson 1989–90.) Earlier, Albrecht Goetze among others also argued against the classification of Ugaritic as Canaanite (1941), although his own solution, to group it with Amorite, has not been followed; and Anson Rainey (1963; 1996b) has vociferously opposed the classification of Ugaritic as Canaanite and Ugarit as part of Canaan.

The question of the dialects of the plaster text from Deir 'Allā and of the Sam'alian inscriptions has occupied several of us over the years (for Sam'alian, Tropper 1993 gives a summary of the debate, as does Cross and Freedman 1952; Dion 1974; 1978 are essential), and the debate has usually centered on how to assign new inscriptions to the general categories of

---

[6] Hetzron himself said that he began his systematization with earlier suggestions by V. Christian (1919–20) and O. Rössler (1950).

Canaanite or Aramaic (for Deir 'Allā, e.g., Hoftijzer in Hoftijzer and van der Kooij 1976; Caquot and Lemaire 1977; Fitzmyer 1978; Greenfield 1980; 1991; McCarter 1980; Hackett 1984a,b; Garr 1985), with one scholar going so far as to pronounce Deir 'Allā spoken proto-Aramaic (Weippert 1991, 179–80 and n. 108). To my mind, the breakthroughs in these discussions have come, not with further investigations of the texts in question, but rather with current discussions of classification itself. In particular, John Huehnergard and Josef Tropper have refined the discussion of shared innovations that we identify as the hallmarks of proto-Aramaic (Huehnergard 1991b; 1995b; Tropper 1993), and Huehnergard has suggested that neither Deir 'Allā nor Sam'alian can be seen to participate in the major defining innovations of Aramaic, *or* of Canaanite, and more importantly *need* not. We need not work with a Northwest Semitic that divides into Ugaritic, Canaanite, and Aramaic and nothing more, but rather, any given dialect can be simply another form of Northwest Semitic.[7]

Beyond more documentation and advances in linguistics, the twentieth century has given us new technologies, and one of the still-developing areas for working with less-understood languages is the use of computers. Richard Whitaker's *Concordance of the Ugaritic Literature* (1972), prepared on computer, was and still is a terrific tool for Ugaritic studies. More recently, the project in Madrid under J.-L. Cunchillos' leadership (Banco de Datos Filológicos Semíticos Noroccidentales at the Laboratorio de Hermeneumática in the Philology Institute of the Consejo Superior de Investigaciones Científicas) has produced both a compact disk and hard-copy version of a Ugaritic data base and dictionary (Cunchillos and Vita 1993; 1995; Cunchillos et al. 1996).[8] The compact disk allows for morphological analysis, concordance work, and possibilities for reconstructing damaged portions of texts, some of which information is also available at the web site of the Hermeneumática project (http://www.labherm.filol.csic.es/Sapanu97/PaginaWeb/1ConsultaBD.html). The Edinburgh Ras Shamra Project also has an interesting web site — http://www.ed.ac.uk/~ugarit/home.htm — as does the West Semitic Research Project — http://www.usc.edu/dept/LAS/wsrp/scholarly_site/. Links to dozens of sites of interest to scholars of the Near East can be found at ABZU: http://www.oi.uchicago.edu/OI/DEPT/RA/ABZU/ABZU.HTML.

---

7   Because of the use of *ḥd* for 'one', Huehnergard (1995b) sees Deir 'Allā breaking off from Northwest Semitic along with Aramaic, but then still not participating in the usual defining features of Aramaic.

8   Much new work on Ugaritic has been coming out of Spain; note also del Olmo Lete and Sanmartín 1996.

Elsewhere in Ugaritic and other Northwest Semitic epigraphic languages, the West Semitic Research Project, under Bruce Zuckerman's guidance, has opened up a new world, first with high-resolution photographs painstakingly made of epigraphic finds housed all over the world, and now with the extension of that technology to compact disks that we can all use on our personal computers (see his contribution to this volume). That day has not quite come, since the undertaking is huge, but we are getting closer each year. And Zuckerman has succeeded in training not a few people to follow in his footsteps.

Let me try to summarize how we have learned to deal with partially documented languages, and then ask what general conclusions we can draw and what we should be emphasizing for the future. First, it is obvious that our understanding of such languages is advanced much more quickly when we have an analog, that is, when we can compare these languages to one that has more complete documentation that helps us to fill in the gaps in our knowledge. Languages written in an unknown script and whose linguistic affinity is not known are almost impossible to decipher, as Peter Daniels points out in his chapter on decipherment (Daniels 1996, basing himself on Gelb's 1973 discussion). If, however, we have a way to deal with the script, we turn to phonology and morphology and, based on orthography and the comparative materials available, attempt to reconstruct. The use of linguistic comparison and reconstruction is our most powerful tool, where the comparative material is available.

It is very helpful if we know everything we can about the context of the finds we are trying to read. Does archaeology provide a date? Is the context cultic or royal, ritual or administrative or epistolary? If we know enough about other languages from the same family, or the same time period, or the same location, we might be able to suggest formulaic phrases or structures, such as looking for repeated patterns that could be "Darius the great king" in suspected Old Persian (Daniels 1996, 145–46). We also ask whether there is any art related to any of our linguistic evidence that might suggest a context or suggest divine names, for instance, that we should be looking for. In most cases, these are still just the beginning stages of understanding any partially documented language. In order to help us understand the semantics and syntax of a given language, we need to be able to recognize patterns in usage. Comparative work can also be useful here, as when we realize how much the body of Ugaritic letters or administrative texts follows Akkadian models. If the language in question is well-enough documented, we need to work within the language to find all the usages of a given problematic vocabulary or syntactic item, categorize them in terms of find-spot and genre, then attempt to find an explanation that covers each case. We have done very little of this so far, at least in the languages I deal with, but computerization will make this task much easier, until we reach the point of diminishing returns (that is, entering and properly coding our texts might take longer than the results would justify).

The decipherment of Linear B and continuing work on Linear A are instructive here. It is worth noting that some breakthroughs have come in that process through the careful indexing and analysis of groupings of signs that might be identified, for instance, as inflectional endings — obviously a task for computers. It is also worth noting that the identification of Linear B as a form of Greek could be made because comparative and historical linguists had already reconstructed early forms of Greek; Linear B forms could be seen to be related to those *reconstructed* forms (Daniels 1996, 153). To understand these languages with "not enough documentation," then, a scholar needs imagination, but imagination that is well trained: a thorough grounding in comparative and historical linguistics; an understanding of the specific place and time the texts come from so that analogs might suggest themselves; a broader study of writing and society, again so that analogs might be obvious.[9]

Finally, let me turn to some desiderata for the twenty-first century. At the top of anyone's wish list must be more text finds; we need more documentation. Another clear desideratum is the "simple" compiling of our materials for these languages onto searchable disks. We all have our own lists and data bases, but we need easier access to as much information as other scholars are willing to share.[10]

My most heartfelt desideratum is a professionalization of the study of partially documented languages, and here again I am particularly thinking of the languages I study. One reason for this need is that so many people who *do* epigraphy were never *trained* to do epigraphy. Many of us in the field of Northwest Semitics also study Hebrew Bible, or at least the Bible is the reason there is so much interest in the study of Semitic languages related to Hebrew, including the partially documented ones. Bible scholars are in the awkward situation that almost everything that could possibly be said about the Bible has already been said many times over, so they/we need to find something new to contribute. One method is to look at old materials in a new way, from a new angle — a necessity over time, that should not, however, degenerate into simply

---

9   For example, if scholars have seen enough ancient receipts, it is easier for them to postulate that a given unknown text is also a receipt if it seems to be a list of pictures and numbers, or a list of words with repeated category markers plus numbers.

10   The compilations by G. Davies (1991) and Aufrecht (1989) are admirable, but the impetus could and should be extended to as many partially documented languages and dialects as is practical and distributed on searchable disks that can be updated. This is perhaps the work of the more computer-literate generations following mine.

casting doubt on every well-known datum and reinventing the wheel. Another tried and true method is to keep an eye out for discoveries in archaeology, or newly-publicized material culture or inscriptions, and see whether something can be made of them in relation to the specific text one is studying. Very many people know Hebrew for a variety of reasons, but most have no real linguistic training; instead they have just enough ancient Hebrew to think they can read anything similar that they come across. Then they discover the Canaanite shift, and all of a sudden we have $\bar{a}$'s becoming $\bar{o}$'s all over the place. I would go so far as to say, in fact, that the majority of what is written about epigraphic Northwest Semitic languages and dialects is the work of amateurs. It gets published because many editors know no more than these authors, and because the publish-or-perish ethic has produced so many new venues. The result of these combined factors — desperation to find something new to say, to find *something* to publish; inadequate knowledge of biblical Hebrew and of Aramaic; lack of linguistic training; venues and editors who have no training in judging the quality of this kind of work — can be more clutter than valuable ideas. It would take all of one's time simply to explain what is wrong with such work, and in general one simply ignores it, unless it rises to the level of the "Hellenistic" Siloam tunnel inscription (Davies and Rogerson 1996; cf. Hendel 1996; Hackett et al. 1997) or the *bêt dāwīd* discussion of the lack of a word divider that was such a waste of time and paper (P. Davies 1994a,b; Lemche 1994; cf. Rainey 1994; Rendsburg 1995).

It sometimes seems that there are two very different types of scholars in our field. One sees chaos everywhere and rather enjoys that chaos because it means just about anything can be seen as a valid suggestion (hunting for cognates can be really quite imaginative); training is unnecessary, typologies fail, and so anything clever that one comes up with is just as good as something clever that someone else comes up with. The other kind of scholar sees patterns, consistency, order, and finds the excitement in scholarship in discovering this order, in piecing it together from evidence, in keeping good records of where things fit. These are the people who may not always know the one right answer, but they believe it is clear that there are such things as wrong answers. They know these wrong answers when they see them, and they jettison their own theories when the evidence accumulates against those theories. One scholar looks at a row of 50 *aleph*s or *mem*s or *zayin*s or at pottery assemblages and sees that the dated ones change in certain ways over time and sees, too, that the others could be fitted nicely into that pattern.[11] Another scholar

---

[11]   See the recent defense of typology in Cross 1982.

looks at a row of 50 *aleph*s and sees 50 individual scribes with individual handwriting and no pattern that is absolutely dependable and foolproof. One scholar sees order and another sees none at all. Surely comparative and historical linguistics is about finding order, and not simply throwing up our hands and being satisfied with the chaos. My survey of the influence of linguistics on this field in the twentieth century should have made clear that many features we take for granted about these partially documented languages are not at all self-evident, but have in fact been earned over decades and centuries by the judicious use of rigorous linguistic methods. These features must be adjusted when the evidence changes, but if they stand and are useful, it is only because someone figured it out rigorously, looking for patterns instead of reveling in lack of pattern.

We must not impose order where it does not exist, of course, but my final desideratum for the influence that general linguistics might have on our study of less well-understood languages within Semitics is that we will keep insisting on the kind of rigor that linguistic study teaches, and not allow our fields to be diverted from the progress we have already made, before we get the opportunity to enjoy what the future will bring.

BIBLIOGRAPHY

Albright, William Foxwell. 1947. The Phoenician Inscriptions of the Tenth Century B.C. from Byblus. *JAOS* 67: 153–60.

Albright, William Foxwell. 1964. Review of Cyrus Gordon, *Before the Bible*. *Interpretation* 18: 191–98.

Amadasi Guzzo, Maria Giulia. 1997. L'accompli à la 3e personne du féminin singulier et le pronom suffixe à l'accusatif de la 3e personne du singulier: note de grammaire phénicienne. In Beate Pongratz-Leisten, Hartmut Kühne, and Paolo Xella, ed. *Ana šadî Labnāni lū allik: Festschrift für Wolfgang Röllig*. Neukirchen-Vluyn. 1–9.

Amadasi Guzzo, Maria Giulia. 1999. Plural Feminine Personal Suffix Pronouns in Phoenician. *EI* 26 (Cross volume): 46*–51*.

Aufrecht, Walter E. 1989. *A Corpus of Ammonite Inscriptions*. Ancient Near Eastern Texts and Studies 4. Lewiston, N.Y.

Barthélemy, Abbé. 1764. Reflexions sur quelques monuments phéniciens, et sur les alphabets qui en résultent. *Mémoires de littérature, tirés des registres de l'Académie Royale des Inscriptions et Belles-Lettres* 30: 405–21.

Brockelmann, Carl. 1908–13. *Grundriss der vergleichenden Grammatik der semitischen Sprachen*. Berlin.

Caquot, André, and André Lemaire. 1977. Les textes araméens de Deir 'Alla. *Syria* 54: 189–208.

Christian, V. 1919–20. Akkader und Südaraber als ältere Semitenschichte. *Anthropos* 14–15: 729–39.

Clermont-Ganneau, Charles. 1870. *La stèle de Dhiban ou stèle de Mesa.* Paris (= *Revue archéologique* 11 [1870] 184–207, 357–86).

Clermont-Ganneau, Charles. 1875. La Stèle de Mesa. *Revue critique d'histoire et de litterature* 37, Sept. 11, 1875: 166–74.

Clermont-Ganneau, Charles. 1887. *La Stèle de Mésa.* Paris.

Corpus Inscriptionum Semiticarum (CIS). Pars Prima, Inscriptiones Phoeniciae. 1881–. Paris.

Cross, Frank Moore. 1982. Alphabets and Pots: Reflections on Typological Method in the Dating of Human Artifacts. *Maarav* 3/2: 121–36.

Cross, Frank Moore, Jr., and David Noel Freedman. 1951. The Pronominal Suffixes of the Third Person Singular in Phoenician. *JNES* 10: 228–30.

Cross, Frank Moore, Jr., and David Noel Freedman. 1952. *Early Hebrew Orthography: A Study of the Epigraphic Evidence.* American Oriental Series 36. New Haven.

Cunchillos, J.-L., and J.-P. Vita, ed. 1993. *Banco de datos filológicos semíticos noroccidentales: I. Textos ugaríticos.* Madrid.

Cunchillos, J.-L., and J.-P. Vita, ed. 1995. *Concordancia de palabras ugaríticas en morfología desplegada.* 3 vols. Madrid — Zaragoza.

Cunchillos, J.-L. et al., ed. 1996. *Generador de segmentaciones restituciones y concordancias*, Banco de datos filológicos semíticos noroccidentales, Primera parte: Datos ugaríticos, III, (CD-ROM version of *Textos ugaríticos* and *Concordancia de palabras ugaríticas*, with additions and corrections). Madrid.

Daniels, Peter T. 1996. Methods of Decipherment. In Peter T. Daniels and William Bright, ed. *The World's Writing Systems.* New York. 141–59.

Davies, G. I. 1991. *Ancient Hebrew Inscriptions: Corpus and Concordance.* Cambridge.

Davies, Philip R. 1994a. Bytdwd and Swkt Dwyd: A Comparison. *JSOT* 64: 23–24.

Davies, Philip R. 1994b. "House of David" Built on Sand. *BAR* 20/4: 54–55.

Davies, Philip, and John Rogerson. 1996. Was the Siloam Tunnel Built by Hezekiah? *BA* 59: 138–49.

Dietrich, Franz E. C. 1855. *Zwei sidonische Inschriften, eine griechische aus christlicher Zeit und eine altphönizische Königsinschrift.* Marburg.

Dion, Paul-E. 1974. *La langue de Ya'udi: description et classement de l'ancien parler de Zencirli dans le cadre des langues sémitiques du nord-ouest.* Waterloo, Ont.

Dion, Paul-E. 1978. The Language Spoken in Ancient Sam'al. *JNES* 37: 115–18.

Donner, Herbert, and Wolfgang Röllig. 1971–76. *Kanaanäische und aramäische Inschriften.* 3rd ed. 3 vols. Wiesbaden.

Eissfeldt, Otto. 1947. The Beginnings of Phoenician Epigraphy according to a Letter Written by Wilhelm Gesenius in 1835. *PEQ* 79: 68–86.

Eph'al, Israel, and Joseph Naveh. 1998. Remarks on the Recently Published Moussaieff Ostraca. *IEJ* 48: 269–73.

Faber, Alice. 1980. *Genetic Subgrouping of Semitic Languages.* Ph.D. dissertation, University of Texas.

Faber, Alice. 1997. Genetic Subgrouping of the Semitic Languages. In Robert Hetzron, ed. *The Semitic Languages.* London and New York. 3–15.

Fitzmyer, Joseph. 1978. Review of Hoftijzer and van der Kooij 1976. *CBQ* 40: 93–95.

Fox, Joshua. 1996. A Sequence of Vowel Shifts in Phoenician and Other Languages. *JNES* 55: 37–47.

Friedrich, Johannes. 1951. *Phönizisch-punische Grammatik.* Analecta Orientalia 32. Rome.

Friedrich, Johannes, and Wolfgang Röllig. 1970. *Phönizisch-punische Grammatik.* 2nd ed. Analecta Orientalia 36. Rome.

Friedrich, Johannes, and Wolfgang Röllig. 1999. *Phönizisch-punische Grammatik.* 3rd ed. revised by Maria Giulia Amadasi Guzzo. Analecta Orientalia 55. Rome.

Garr, W. Randall. 1985. *Dialect Geography of Syria-Palestine, 1000–586 B.C.E.* Philadelphia.

Gelb, Ignace J. 1973. Written Records and Decipherment. In Thomas A. Sebeok, ed. *Current Trends in Linguistics,* vol. 11. The Hague. 253–84.

Gesenius, Wilhelm. 1837. *Scripturae linguaeque phoeniciae monumenta.* Lipsiae.

Ginsberg, H. L. 1933. Responses and Notes. *Tarbiz* 4: 380–90, esp. 381–83 [Hebrew].

Ginsberg, H. L. 1936. The Rebellion and Death of Ba'lu. *Or.* 5: 161–98.

Ginsberg, H. L., and B. Maisler. 1934. Semitised Hurrians in Syria and Palestine. *JPOS* 14: 243–67, esp. p. 250.

Ginsburg, Christian. 1871. *The Moabite Stone.* 2nd ed. London.

Goetze, Albrecht. 1941. Is Ugaritic a Canaanite Dialect? *Language* 17: 127–38.

Gordon, Cyrus H. 1940. *Ugaritic Grammar*. Rome.

Gordon, Cyrus H. 1965. *Ugaritic Textbook*. Analecta Orientalia 38. Rome.

Greenfield, Jonas C. 1980. Review of Hoftijzer and van der Kooij 1976. *JSS* 25: 248–52.

Greenfield, Jonas C. 1991. Philological Observations on the Deir 'Alla Inscription. In Hoftijzer and van der Kooij 1991. 109–20.

Guthe, H. 1882. Die Siloahinschrift. *ZDMG* 36: 725–50.

Hackett, Jo Ann. 1984a. *The Balaam Text from Tell Deir 'Allā*. Chico, Calif.

Hackett, Jo Ann. 1984b. The Dialect of the Plaster Text from Tell Deir 'Alla. *Or.* 53: 57–65.

Hackett, Jo Ann, Frank Moore Cross, P. Kyle McCarter, Jr., Ada Yardeni, André Lemaire, Esther Eshel, Avi Hurvitz. 1997. Defusing Pseudo-Scholarship. *BAR* 23/2: 41–50, 68.

Harris, Zellig. 1936. *A Grammar of the Phoenician Language*. American Oriental Series 8. New Haven.

Harris, Zellig. 1939. *Development of the Canaanite Dialects*. American Oriental Series 16. New Haven.

Hendel, Ronald. 1996. The Date of the Siloam Inscription: A Rejoinder to Rogerson and Davies. *BA* 59: 233–37.

Hetzron, Robert. 1974. La division des langues sémitiques. In A. Caquot and D. Cohen, ed. *Actes du premier Congrès international de linguistique sémitique et chamito-sémitique, Paris 16–19 juillet 1969*. The Hague/Paris. 181–94.

Hoftijzer, J., and K. Jongeling. 1995. *Dictionary of the North-West Semitic Inscriptions*. 2 vols. Handbuch der Orientalistik 21. Leiden.

Hoftijzer, J., and G. van der Kooij. 1976. *Aramaic Texts from Deir 'Alla*. Leiden.

Hoftijzer, J., and G. van der Kooij, ed. 1991. *The Balaam Text from Deir 'Alla Re-evaluated*. Proceedings of the International Symposium held at Leiden 21–24 August 1989. Leiden.

Huehnergard, John. 1987. *Ugaritic Vocabulary in Syllabic Transcription*. Harvard Semitic Studies 32. Atlanta.

Huehnergard, John. 1991a. The Development of the Third Person Suffixes in Phoenician. *Maarav* 7: 183–94.

Huehnergard, John. 1991b. Remarks on the Classification of the Northwest Semitic Languages. In Hoftijzer and van der Kooij 1991. 282–93.

Huehnergard, John. 1992. Languages: Introductory Survey. In David Noel Freedman, ed. *The Anchor Bible Dictionary*. New York. 4.155–70.

Huehnergard, John. 1995a. Semitic Languages. In Jack M. Sasson, ed. *Civilizations of the Ancient Near East*. New York. 4.2117–34.

Huehnergard, John. 1995b [1998]. What Is Aramaic? *ARAM* 7: 261–82.

Isaksson, Bo. 1989–90. The Position of Ugaritic Among the Semitic Languages. *Orientalia Suecana* 38–39: 54–70.

Izre'el, Shlomo. forthcoming. Some Methodological Requisites for the Study of the Amarna Jargon: Notes on the Essence of That Language. In Barry J. Beitzel and Gordon D. Young, ed. *Amarna in Retrospect: A Centennial Celebration.* Winona Lake, Ind.

Jean, Charles F., and Jacob Hoftijzer. 1960–65. *Dictionnaire des inscriptions sémitiques de l'Ouest.* Leiden.

Krahmalkov, Charles R. 1970. Studies in Phoenician and Punic Grammar. *JSS* 15: 181–88.

Krahmalkov, Charles R. 1972. Comments on the Vocalization of the Suffix Pronoun of the Third Feminine Singular in Phoenician and Punic. *JSS* 17: 68–75.

Krahmalkov, Charles R. 1974. The Object Pronouns of the Third Person of Phoenician and Punic. *RSF* 2: 39–43.

Krahmalkov, Charles R. 1993. The Third Feminine Plural Possessive Pronoun in Phoenician-Punic. *JNES* 52: 37–41.

Lambdin, Thomas O. 1971. The Junctural Origin of the West Semitic Definite Article. In Hans Goedicke, ed. *Near Eastern Studies in Honor of William Foxwell Albright.* Baltimore. 315–33.

Lemche, Niels Peter. 1994. Did Biran Kill David? The Bible in the Light of Archaeology. *JSOT* 64: 3–22.

Lidzbarski, Mark. 1898. *Handbuch der nordsemitischen Epigraphik.* I. Text. II. Tafeln. Weimar.

Lidzbarski, Mark. 1900–1915. *Ephemeris für semitische Epigraphik.* 3 vols. Giessen.

Luschan, F. von. 1893. *Ausgrabungen in Sendschirli 1.* Mittheilungen aus den Orientalischen Sammlungen 11. Berlin.

Marcus, David. 1968. The Three Alephs in Ugaritic. *JANES* 1: 50–60.

McCarter, P. Kyle, Jr. 1980. The Balaam Texts from Deir 'Allā: The First Combination. *BASOR* 239: 49–60.

Moran, William L. 1961. The Hebrew Language in Its Northwest Semitic Background. In G. Ernest Wright, ed. *The Bible and the Ancient Near East: Essays in Honor of William Foxwell Albright.* Garden City, N.Y. 54–72.

Moscati, Sabatino. 1969. *An Introduction to the Comparative Grammar of the Semitic Languages: Phonology and Morphology.* Porta Linguarum Orientalium NS 6. Wiesbaden.

Nöldeke, Theodor. 1870. *Die Inschrift des Königs Mesa von Moab.* Kiel.

O'Connor, Michael Patrick. 1983. Writing Systems, Native Speaker Analyses, and the Earliest Stages of Northwest Semitic Orthography. In C. L. Meyers and M. O'Connor, ed. *The Word of the Lord Shall Go Forth: Essays in Honor of David Noel Freedman in Celebration of His Sixtieth Birthday.* Winona Lake, Ind., 439–65.

Olmo Lete, G. del and J. Sanmartín. 1996–2000. *Diccionario de la lengua ugarítica.* 2 vols. Aula Orientalis Supplement 7–8. Barcelona.

Rainey, Anson F. 1963. A Canaanite at Ugarit. *IEJ* 13: 343–45.

Rainey, Anson F. 1994. The "House of David" and the House of the Deconstructionists. *BAR* 20/6: 47.

Rainey, Anson F. 1996a. *Canaanite in the Amarna Tablets: A Linguistic Analysis of the Mixed Dialect Used by the Scribes from Canaan.* 4 vols. Leiden.

Rainey, Anson F. 1996b. Who is a Canaanite: A Review of the Textual Evidence. *BASOR* 304: 1–15.

Rendsburg, Gary. 1995. On the Writing ביתדוד in the Aramaic Inscription from Tel Dan. *IEJ* 45: 22–25.

Renz, Johannes. 1995. *Die althebräischen Inschriften.* Handbuch der althebräischen Epigraphik, vols. I, II/1. Darmstadt.

Répertoire d'épigraphie sémitique (RES). 1900–. Paris.

Rössler, Otto. 1950. Verbalbau und Verbalflexion in den semitohamitischen Sprachen: Vorstudien zu einer vergleichenden semitohamitischen Grammatik. *ZDMG* 100: 461–514. Translated by Y. Arbeitman as The Structure and Inflection of the Verb in the Semito-Hamitic Languages: Preliminary Studies for a Comparative Semito-Hamitic Grammar. In Y. Arbeitman and A. R. Bomhard, ed. *Bono Homini Donum: Essays in Historical Linguistics in Memory of J. Alexander Kerns.* Amsterdam, 1981. 679–748.

Salisbury, Edward E. 1856. Phoenician Inscription of Sidon. *JAOS* 5: 227–59.

Schick, C. 1880. Phoenician Inscription in the Pool of Siloam. *Palestine Exploration Fund Quarterly Statement*: 238–39.

Schlottmann, Konstantin. 1868. *Die Inschrift Eschmunazars, Königs der Sidonier.* Halle.

Schröder, Paul. 1869. *Die phönizische Sprache.* Halle.

Smend, Rudolf, and Albert Socin. 1886. *Die Inschrift des Königs Mesa von Moab.* Freiburg.

Swinton, John. 1764a. Some remarks upon the first Part of M. l'Abbé Barthélemy's Memoir on the Phoenician Letters, relative to a Phoenician Inscription in the Island of Malta. *Philosophical Transactions* 54: 119–36.

Swinton, John. 1764b. Farther Remarks upon M. l'Abbé Barthélemy's Memoir on the Phoenician Letters, containing his Reflections on certain Phoenician Monuments, and the Alphabets resulting from them. *Philosophical Transactions* 54: 393–438.

Teixidor, Javier. 1984. *Bulletin d'épigraphie sémitique (1964–1980)*. Paris.

Tomback, Richard S. 1978. *A Comparative Semitic Lexicon of the Phoenician and Punic Languages*. Society of Biblical Literature Dissertation Series 32. Missoula, Mont.

Tropper, Josef. 1990. Silbenschließendes Aleph im Ugaritischen. *Ugarit-Forschungen* 22: 359–69.

Tropper, Josef. 1993. *Die Inschriften von Zincirli*. ALASP 6. München.

Tropper, Josef. 1994. Is Ugaritic a Canaanite Language? In G. J. Brooke et al., ed. *Ugarit and the Bible*. Münster, 343–53.

Verreet, E. 1988. *Modi ugaritici: eine morpho-syntaktische Abhandlung über das Modalsystem im Ugaritischen*. Orientalia Lovaniensia Analecta 27. Leuven.

Voigt, Rainer M. 1987. The Classification of Central Semitic. *JSS* 32: 1–21.

Voigt, Rainer M. 1998. Der Artikel im Semitischen. *JSS* 43: 221–58.

Watson, Wilfred G. E., and Nicolas Wyatt, ed. 1999. *Handbook of Ugaritic Studies*. Handbuch der Orientalistik 39. Leiden.

Weippert, Manfred. 1991. The Balaam Text from Deir 'Allā and the study of the Old Testament. In Hoftijzer and van der Kooij 1991. 151–84.

Whitaker, Richard E. 1972. *A Concordance of the Ugaritic Literature*. Cambridge, Ma.

Wright, William. 1890. *Lectures on the Comparative Grammar of the Semitic Languages, from the papers of the late William Wright*. William Robertson Smith, ed. Cambridge.

Overviews

INTRODUCTION

WITH SOME NOTES ON THE STUDY OF TENSE AND ASPECT SYSTEMS

The second section of this volume presents overviews of the progress of several important issues in Semitic studies. Traditionally, the study of Semitic languages has been engaged mostly with morphology, since Semitic morphology is complex and interesting. The roots of this interest go far back in time, in fact to the Middle Ages. Still, the discoveries of new Semitic languages during the nineteenth and twentieth centuries gave philologists the opportunity to publish more and more texts for the benefit of historical and cultural studies. The genetic proximity of the newly discovered languages to already known Semitic tongues enabled these philological studies to be carried out with relative ease. Against this background, comparative studies flourished, and it was possible for new texts to be published with no comprehensive linguistic research needed to support them. I believe it is not really necessary to set a clear point of time for evaluating the study of Semitic morphology. Similarly, it seems superfluous to evaluate phonological studies, although the significant changes of the Prague structural school have enormously enhanced the use of advanced concepts in the study of both phonology and morphology in twentieth century Semitic studies. All these innovations have become part and parcel of Semitic linguistics at this time. Phonology and morphology are so much of the core of Semitic studies, that any endeavor in trying to deal with the state of the art in the methodologies used for these aspects is doomed to result in a rather hackneyed presentation. In fact, phonology and morphology have been mentioned more than once and dealt with in various papers in this volume: those by Goldenberg, Huehnergard, Voigt, Jastrow, Simeone-Senelle, and others. The state of the art in the study of the phonological systems of Semitic languages is represented in the comprehensive collection edited by Kaye (1997). The second section of our volume includes four topics: the study of writing, comparative linguistics, syntax and lexicography. Newly established areas of exploration will be investigated in the sixth section in a paper by Edward L. Greenstein.

The study of writing in the twentieth century is presented by Peter T. Daniels. Daniels, a student of Igance J. Gelb, the founder of the study of writing as a separate field of research, is himself an eminent grammatologist, and has published a plethora of studies and reviews in this field. Daniels shows in his paper how "from the first decipherment to the first theoretical discussion of writing to the latest investigations of the nature of literacy, the nature of writing, and the workings of the brain in the reading process, Semitists and Semitic scripts are in the forefront." The first part of Daniels' paper opens with introductory discussions of the study of decipherment, the study of epigraphy, and histories of writing. Then follows a detailed evaluation of theories of writing: typology, evolution, and transfer of scripts involving their changes and innovations. Among the desiderata, Daniels calls for a comprehensive paleography of cuneiform and regional studies of cuneiform writing, and suggests advancing from the epigraphic treatment of West Semitic scripts toward a wider investigation of the social and cultural aspects of writing.

Phonology and morphology, while not represented in themselves by individual papers for the reasons mentioned above, still form the basic factors in the study of the genetic relationships among languages. John Huehnergard surveys the great achievements of comparative Semitic linguistics from the end of the nineteenth century until the publication of three general books on Semitic studies (Hetzron 1997, Lipiński 1997 and Bennett 1998), marking the end of a century of studies in this field (see the reviews of the three respective books, below, in the last section of our volume). Huehnergard compares developments in the field with those of general linguistics, and goes on to specific, mainly phonological and morphological, topics that were central during the last century, leading his discussion to the study of classification and reconstruction. He ends this section of his paper by stating desiderata in comparative studies, suggesting both tools and lacunae to be filled in specific areas. The paper concludes with some remarks on the scant contribution of comparative Semitic linguistics to general and theoretical comparative linguistics.

One relatively neglected area of Semitic studies is syntax. While the Chomskian School has a deep interest in syntactic structure, the mainstream in twentieth-century Semitic linguistics seems not to invest much interest in syntax. As an illustrative curiosity, I presented at the conference my second-hand personal copy of Brockelmann's *Grundriss der vergleichenden Grammatik der semitischen Sprachen* (1908, 1913). The first volume looks as if its previous owner made good use of it, while the volume on syntax (much smaller than the first!) hardly seems used at all... Geoffrey Khan's paper is illuminating in this respect, since much of his paper deals with Semitic studies prior to the twentieth century. Khan tries to show that much of the understanding of syntax goes back to medieval times and the insights of the ancient Arabic grammarians. When Khan's paper does get back to the twentieth century, he sees that the major developments discussed are not really syntactic, at least not in the strict sense of the term, but cases in which syntax becomes entangled with several different domains, such as TMA analysis, narrative analysis and discourse grammar.

TMA, i.e., the study of tense, mood and aspect systems, has always been a major point of discussion and interest in Semitic linguistics, in the study of both individual languages and genetic and areal features. The core ancient Semitic languages attest to morphological marking of TMA features, either in internal patterning or in affixes (in the Central Semitic languages). The few morphological oppositions marking TMA categories and the complex ways the various forms functioned syntactically have made analyses difficult, so much so that even for a language as well-researched as Biblical Hebrew, a recent evaluation of the state of the art in its TMA analysis has been titled *The Enigma of the Hebrew Verbal System* (McFall 1982). As I will mention later, in my review of Hetzron's *The Semitic Languages* (pp. 501–510 [TMA]), tradition shows its persistence, especially in the terms used for describing TMA systems, and old concepts, backed by persistent terminology, make the reevaluation of studies in this linguistic field especially problematic. A paper on the study of TMA systems in the twentieth century was presented at the conference by Uri Horesh, who used the contributions in Hetzron's book to compare attitudes and evaluate the state of the art. Points of view and terminology being so confused here, it is perhaps not surprising that this paper has not matured into a published statement. Most recently, new insights from work in general linguistics have started to find their way into studies of Semitic languages (e.g., Hoberman 1989; Hatav 1997), and one finds more and more updated terminology in modern studies (e.g., Streck 1995; some contributions in Hetzron 1997), but this is not the rule. As pointed out by Horesh, we may all know what certain forms in the languages that we study look or sound like; we may be extensively familiar with the morphological nature of given structures; we can often cite by heart the very spectrum of, say, verb conjugations in the language of our choice (or in a broader variety thereof within the Semitic language family); but we may name these phenomena arbitrarily, at times even thoughtlessly, make it more subtle; e.g., "just using accepted traditional terms" or the like, disregarding the ramifications that the terminology is likely to have for the substantial comprehension of the relations between form and function.

Horesh has concluded his paper listing the following desiderata:

○ Clear definitions of the categories with which we are dealing, based on current research in the world's languages.

○ Large scale corpora for prompting the inclusion of all relevant

categories and subcategories. It is crucial that we have the statistical stability to assure that all possible forms are indeed detected and analyzed.
o Strengthening the theoretical apparatus to support our finds.
o A reexamination of existing accounts for TMA in the various languages, in order to draw a precise picture, with special attention to formerly neglected components (e.g., modality).

It will be inferred that TMA examination is inherently a trait of a single system, and should be studied accordingly. Comparative and historical studies can benefit from such evaluations after they have been established for the individual languages and periods. After all, like any other linguistic system, TMA systems also change over time. A final desideratum would then arise, suggesting the incorporation of solid data and evaluations from Semitic languages in cross-linguistic typological studies. Those found today are far less than satisfactory when one comes to evaluate the data from Semitic languages (e.g., Dahl 1985).

The fourth contribution in this section is an overview of European dictionaries of Biblical Hebrew in the twentieth century, which Michael Patrick O'Connor takes as a convenient methodological test case. O'Connor establishes three "tasks" that he finds basic to lexicography. The first task is a delimitation of the material studied. The two other tasks are more linguistically-oriented: the structural segregation of units and the provision and arrangement of relevant information. Following the discussion of these tasks and a short survey of the major European lexica of Biblical Hebrew, O'Connor evaluates the lexica of Biblical Hebrew in relation to the three tasks discussed. While future dictionaries will be electronic, thus enabling more sophisticated handling and applications, still, O'Connor maintains, "the basic questions of how dictionaries are to be assembled will be those that have emerged in the twentieth century." One further lesson that one may gain from reading O'Connor's paper is that thorough historiographical research can serve us well in our endeavor to improve our learning and our methodologies, when dealing with the lexicography of dead as well as of living languages. Knowing the history of research entails understanding its gains and pitfalls. This lesson can further be broadened to include not only lexicography, but also all other domains of Semitic linguistics.

In this connection I would like to comment on one point raised in passing by O'Connor. When stating his primary concern as European scholarship in Biblical Hebrew lexicography, O'Connor refers to Michael Sokoloff, who mentioned "that there is no Modern Hebrew dictionary of Biblical or ancient Hebrew". He then states that "this apparent gap is worth studying". While I agree with the basics of this claim as well as with the need to study the circumstances behind this "apparent gap", I would like to mention that the gap is not total: There have been several endeavors to fill it. Let me mention two of these endeavors. In 1961 a new edition of Joshua Steinberg's Biblical Hebrew lexicon *mišpaṭ haʔurim* "The Decision of the Urim" (titled after Numbers 27:22), which had been published in Vilnius in 1899. The Israeli edition was meant to update Steinberg's lexicon and present it in contemporary Hebrew. This new edition was titled *millon hatt∂nak* "Bible Dictionary" (Steinberg 1961) and was published in many reprints, which shows the great need for such a lexicon, at least at that time. Avraham Even-Shoshan, who is known as the author of the standard Hebrew dictionary *hammillon heḥadaš* (second edition, 1966), published between 1977 and 1980 a concordance of Biblical Hebrew. It may be worthwhile to cite Even-Shoshan's reasoning for the publication of this concordance for the Israeli public, as it may serve as a clue regarding the question of the apparent gap in Biblical Hebrew lexicographical tools in Modern Hebrew:

Indeed, the educated layman who loves the Bible will apparently find sufficient the Hebrew dictionary he has at home: In case he needs to tackle a linguistic problem, he goes to the dictionary and finds, without any obstacle, an answer, general or more elaborate. So why would he need a concordance? (Even-Shoshan 1977: I: vii; my translation).

Indeed, each entry in Even-Shoshan's *hammillon heḥadaš*, as in other dictionaries of Modern Hebrew, presents meanings separated into periods of attestation. The underlying reason for this tradition can be said to be self-evident, given the history of the Hebrew language. Still, this very history, from the point of view of lexicography, is worthy of study, as is the more general question of linguistic attitudes in Israel, linguistic education and education in general, and many other related issues. Needless to say, all these dictionaries, including Steinberg's *millon hatt∂nak*, are not aimed at the scholarly community but designed for the use of the general public.

At the end of this section, a selected list of dictionaries of Semitic languages is furnished by Baruch Podolsky, thus complementing O'Connor's study.

REFERENCES

Bennett, Patrick R. 1998. *Comparative Semitic Linguistics: A Manual.* Winona Lake, Indiana.
Brockelmann, Carl. 1908, 1913. *Grundriss der vergleichenden Grammatik der semitischen Sprachen.* Two volumes. Berlin.
Dahl, Östen. 1985. *Tense and Aspect Systems.* Oxford.

Even-Shoshan, Avraham. 1977–1980. *qonqordancya ḥadaša letanak̲*. [A New Concordance of the Bible]. Three volumes. Jerusalem.

Even-Shoshan, Avraham. 1966–1970. *hammillon heḥadaš* [The New Dictionary]. Seven volumes. Second edition. Jerusalem.

Hatav, Galia. 1997. *The Semantics of Aspect and Modality: Evidence from English and Biblical Hebrew.* (Studies in Language Companion Series, 34.) Amsterdam.

Hetzron, Robert (ed.). 1997. *The Semitic Languages.* London.

Hoberman, Robert D. 1989. *The Syntax and Semantics of Verb Morphology in Modern Aramaic: A Jewish Dialect of Iraqi Kurdistan.* (American oriental Series, 69.) New Haven, Connecticut.

Kaye, Alan S. (ed.). 1997. *Phonologies of Asia and Africa (Including the Caucasus).* Two volumes. Winona Lake, Indiana.

Lipiński, Edward. 1997. *Semitic Languages: Outline of a Comparative Grammar.* (Orientalia Lovaniensia Analecta, 80.) Leuven.

McFall, Leslie. 1982. *The Enigma of the Hebrew Verbal System.* Sheffield.

Steinberg, Joshua. 1961. *millon hattənak̲: šivrit vʔaramit.* [Bible Dictionary: Hebrew and Aramaic]. Tel-Aviv.

Streck, Michael P. 1995. *Zahl und Zeit: Grammatik der Numeralia und des Verbalsystems im Spätbabylonischen.* (Cuneiform Mornographs, 5.) Groningen.

THE STUDY OF WRITING
IN THE TWENTIETH CENTURY:
SEMITIC STUDIES
INTERACTING WITH NON-SEMITIC

PETER T. DANIELS

INTRODUCTION

The question put to me was, How has the study of Semitic writing systems influenced the study of writing systems in general? And the most appropriate reply is, How not? From the first decipherment to the first theoretical discussion of writing to the latest investigations of the nature of literacy, the nature of writing, and the workings of the brain in the reading process, Semitists and Semitic scripts are in the forefront. In these remarks I focus on a few individuals and topics that either have received little notice or especially illustrate the interaction of the study of Semitic writing and non-Semitic writing. To adequately emphasize the significance of Semitic in this story, I must considerably transcend the temporal boundary of the turn of the twentieth century.

I also need to limit the territory covered in these remarks: I gloss over decipherments, because I have treated them in several other fora (Daniels 1995, 1996); I have little to say about epigraphy, both because I know little about it, and because Giovanni Garbini's *Storia e problemi dell'epigrafia semitica* (1979) has surveyed the field briefly but with a wealth of early references.

My main interest is the theory of writing systems, and there indeed is where the most interaction between Semitic studies and other fields has taken place.

THE STUDY OF DECIPHERMENT

As regards decipherment, I will remark only that it seems to me that if the methodologies followed by Edward Hincks in deciphering cuneiform, between 1846 and 1852, had been adequately publicized — if the glory

85

had not gone all to H. C. Rawlinson, and if George Rawlinson in his
biography (1898) and Wallis Budge in his chronicle of Assyriology (1925)
had not been bent on promoting Rawlinson's claim to the decipherment, to
the disparagement of all other contributors, despite Rawlinson's inability
to explain to either of them, or to anyone else, how he had done it
— if Hincks's work had been known in the later part of the 19th
century (Daniels 1994), his methods and accomplishment could have
been emulated by Americanists studying the Mayan inscriptions, and
they could have been read much sooner than the full century later with
Knorozov's initial breakthrough in 1952. For the decipherment of Mayan
glyphs involved all the same steps that Hincks had passed through; but
each one had to be arrived at independently, rather than by observation
and analogy with the prior achievement (Daniels 1993).

THE STUDY OF EPIGRAPHY

As for epigraphy, my two observations also predate the century
under consideration. I always stress that the decipherment of Semitic
scripts, or any other, was absolutely predicated on the availability of
accurate reproductions of the inscriptions; Barthélemy's decipherment
of Palmyrene followed immediately upon the publication of faithful
engravings (Daniels 1988). It is a nice coincidence that one of the
pioneers in cuneiform studies, Fox Talbot, was also a pioneer in the
science of photography. But his two interests did not intersect.

Much more important was a pair of scholars who were active at the
turn of the twentieth century: Julius Euting (1839–1913; Lyall 1913) and
Mark Lidzbarski. Euting is perhaps not quite so forgotten as Hincks, at
least by those who consult the fine print in the front matter of the classic
works of Semitic philology. An almost exact contemporary of Theodor
Nöldeke (1836–1931), and for many years his colleague as the librarian
at Strassbourg, Euting should be remembered today as the delineator of
most of the painstaking script tables that grace those classic grammars.
A complete list would be difficult to compile. The earliest example I
have found is in the Mandaic grammar of Nöldeke himself, from 1875;
and this is quite fitting, for the earliest work of Julius Euting's that I
have located is a Mandaic edition from 1867. But Euting is important
for more than his productivity. If we consult the table of scripts in
Schröder's Phoenician grammar, of 1869 (pp. 112–115),[1] we find an at
best indifferently written chart: several of the Hebrew letters acting as keys

[1]   All these images were provided by the Semitics librarian at the Catholic University of
America, Monica J. Blanchard, via Prof. M. O'Connor.

in the margin are omitted, and the letterforms are written, it appears, with a flexible steel-pointed pen, with inappropriate thick and thin strokes — even if the shapes are accurately reproduced, and one can only be suspicious, the over-all impression is highly misleading. This plate is unsigned, and I could find no attribution in the preface, so we might assign it to Schröder himself. But turning to Euting's work in Nöldeke's Mandaic, or far more impressively to his own *Semitische Schrifttafel,* of 1877 (pp. 116–117), which includes no fewer than 57 columns of alphabets extracted from inscriptions, what Isaac Taylor called "admirable" in 1883 (1: 279), in Euting's tables we find a combination of art, craft, and science that set a standard that is still emulated today. But Euting's work not only looked forward: he was also among the last in a line of explorer-epigraphers (such as le Comte de Vogüé 1868ff.) who went on extended journeys through wilderness lands, discovering and copying inscriptions: in the fifth decade of his life, he traveled Arabia in 1883, the Sinai in 1889, and Zinjirli in 1890. He published volumes of Punic inscriptions in 1883, Nabatean in 1885, North Arabic in 1889, and Sinaitic in 1891. He provided illustrations for, among doubtless others, Horn's Sassanid inscriptions, Hübschmann's Pehlevi in 1878, Nöldeke's Syriac in 1880, and Zimmern's *Vergleichende Grammatik* in 1898. He wrote a guidebook to his home region in Germany, and published a two-volume travel diary of his Arabian expedition. But nearly everyone reading these words probably owns a copy of one of Euting's works; for his is the facsimile of the Siloam tunnel inscription included in Gesenius–Kautzsch–Cowley's *Hebrew Grammar* (Kautzsch 1910).

The Table of Alphabets in that volume, however, is not Euting's work: it is by an epigrapher of another generation, Mark Lidzbarski (1868–1928), whose first great work, along with Zimmern's *Grammatik,* ushered in the past century of Semitic studies in 1898: the *Handbuch der nordsemitischen Epigraphik.* Its bibliography to that date seems absolutely complete; it incorporates paleography, grammar, lexicon, and editions of all the major and many lesser inscriptions known to the time. Over the next decade and a half he regularly produced fascicles of his *Ephemeris für semitische Epigraphik* (1900–15), wherein he expanded his attention to South Semitic questions as well. Subsequently he devoted his attention fully to Mandaic studies, of which he was the leading exponent before Lady Drower and Rudolf Macuch. A most curious statement appears in René Dussaud's obituary (1929): he says that the mother tongue of Lidzbarski (born in Plock, Poland, in 1868) was Hebrew! Both the *Handbuch* and the *Ephemeris* remain indispensable today.

A bridge to the modern era is provided by another pair of scholars, again near-exact contemporaries, whose students are among today's revered senior colleagues: W. F. Albright (1891–1971) and G. R. Driver (1892–1975). Both these jacks-of-all-trades included influential publications on writing among their extensive œuvres: for Albright we may name monographs on Egyptian "group writing" (1934), the Nash papyrus (1937), and Proto-Sinaitic inscriptions (1966); for Driver above all the volume *Semitic Writing*, a supremely disorganized compilation of a vast amount of material, originally from 1948, with extensive supplementary notes of 1976. Time has not been terribly kind to any of these works. Albright's are marked by sometimes unjustifiable confidence and a willingness to step well beyond paths that seem to be marked out by evidence; Driver appears not to notice how impossibly complicated the results of his chains of inferences and suppositions sometimes become. The last dozen or so pages of his text, on the origins and ordering of the Semitic letters, are breathtaking in their complexity and ultimate overall implausibility. And so I come, in a roundabout fashion, to my own particular interest: the theory of writing.

HISTORIES OF WRITING

A survey of the past century of writing studies can begin with a hundred-year-old benchmark: the second edition of Isaac Taylor's *The Alphabet*, which was published in 1899. Unlike comparable volumes today, this one combined chronicle and description with theory and abstraction. We may take up these two aspects of Canon Taylor's work separately, after a few words of biography (Anon. 1912): He graduated from Trinity College, Cambridge, in 1853, and was ordained in 1857; assigned to poor parishes, he made a great success of charitable work but was compelled to retire by an attack of typhoid fever. Eventually he was made canon of York and was able to devote himself to the intellectual pursuits appropriate to his distinguished ancestry. He was among the first to apply German philological scholarship to Anglo-Saxon place names, and investigated Etruscan and runes. He gained some notoriety through his favorable attitude toward Islam. The first edition of his *Alphabet* was the result of at least eight years of work, and it was a new thing.

A bit over a hundred years ago, the first general surveys of writing systems were compiled. The last "premodern" one was by Faulmann (1880a,b), and the first "scientific" one that still merits — and rewards — consulting was by Taylor. Neither of these authors is known as a Semitist; but Taylor's two volumes are dedicated respectively to "Semitic" and "Aryan" alphabets. In both departments, of course, much material was not yet known; for Semitic, his oldest monuments were the Moabite Stone,

the Siloam inscription, and the Nineveh lion weights. For Greek, he relied
on an inscription from Abu Simbel mentioning Psammetichus (Jeffery
1961: 358 no. 48), the earliest reliably datable one available. He was very
much in touch with the latest publications, and eager to incorporate their
findings; his version of de Rougé's Egyptian Hieratic origin of the Semitic
script is as convoluted in its way as Driver's Hieroglyphic account a half-
century later (but a quarter of the forty pages devoted to it deal with
"its difficulties"). Of Korean, he knows nothing — this syllabographic
alphabet was not to be described in a European journal until 1912 (Gale
1912) — and his information on the scripts of India is severely limited:
he barely mentions the principles of indicating vowels (2: 303 n. 1), and
he appears unaware of the indication of consonant clusters by means of
ligatures involving reduced forms of consonant letters. Nonetheless he
has studied the shapes of the letters of many local Indian varieties, as
they had been made available, and his deduction as to the source of the
Indian scripts (whose overall common ancestry was well established) may
represent several similar passages. After easily dismissing the suggestions
of Greek and indigenous origin (2: 306–9), Taylor focuses on the three
Semitic possibilities:

> India, prior to the third century B.C., had been in commercial or
> political connection with Phœnicia, Babylonia, and Arabia: from
> any one of these regions the art of alphabetic writing might have
> been transmitted.
> 1. Benfey's conjecture that it came direct from the Phœnicians is
> open to fatal objections. The trade of the Phœnicians with India,
> which commenced in the time of Solomon, ceased as early as
> the year 800 B.C. If the alphabet had been communicated at this
> early period a variety of Indian scripts would in all probability
> have sprung up during the long interval which elapsed before the
> time of Asoka, whereas, in the 3rd century B.C. a uniform alphabet
> prevailed over a vast Indian area. ... A further difficulty ... is the
> want of any appreciable resemblance between the Asoka characters
> and the early Phœnician types.
> 2. Dr. Burnell's hypothesis of a Babylonian or Persian origin for the
> Asoka alphabet is open to a similar objection. The ancient Iranian
> alphabet belonged to the Aramean type, in which the loops of the
> letters had been opened, whereas in the Asoka alphabet they are
> closed. ...
> 3. There remains only one possible source, the ancient alphabet
> of Arabia Felix. [fn.: This solution was suggested by Weber, a
> quarter of a century ago, at a time when so little was known of

South Semitic Epigraphy as to make an absolute determination impossible. ...] The transmission of the Semitic alphabet could only have been effected through some nation which was in commercial or political contact with India prior to the expedition of Alexander. ... (2: 312–14)

... and so on for ten more pages, followed by several more on the possible date of transmission.

The preceding argument was based on some information, and more has since come to light that certainly would have led Taylor to modify his conclusions. The following case, though, is quite spectacular: In his brief, but by no means negligible, discussion of the Inner Asian alphabets (which properly find their place in volume 1, within the Aramean chapter), Taylor writes:

It will be noticed that it is not always from the so-called Nestorian letters that the Uighur and Mongolian forms can be most readily derived. This can easily be accounted for. Since the distinctive peculiarities of the Nestorian writing were not developed before the 9th century A.D. it is plain that the Mongolian alphabets must have been derived from some earlier type. Hence the Estrangelo and Syro-Palestinian alphabets of the 6th and 7th centuries frequently supply better prototypes for the Mongolian forms than the more recent Nestorian characters. In some cases the nearest analogues are found in the alphabet of the Mendaïtes [i.e. Mandeans]. Klaproth even went so far as to refer the origin of the Mongolian alphabet to the Mendaïte rather than to the Nestorian script. It is more probable that the analogies between the two alphabets are due to the Manichæans, who, like the Nestorians, had fled from persecution into Persia. (1: 310–11)

This is in fact exactly right; it reflects Canon Taylor's sensitivity to the place of religion in the spread of writing (and also reflects the aforementioned openmindedness toward the non-Christian). What arouses our awestruck admiration, however, is the simple fact that not the slightest hint of any Manichean script had yet been discovered — this was announced by F. W. K. Müller on February 18, 1904, 28 months to the day after Taylor died. Indeed, Müller considered the Manichean script actually to be a form of Estrangelo, and it was Lidzbarski some years later (1916) who awarded it its distinct status.

Taylor's chronicle of alphabet history is distinguished from all comparable works in its discussion of theoretical matters: both innovations in the matter of script typology, to be taken up later, and an overarching organizing viewpoint of the nature of script development. Though it is adumbrated here and there in the text of the book, and the Preface refers (1: v) to "the gradual recognition of those fundamental principles of Palæographic Science which are set forth in the concluding chapter of this book," not until that last chapter, coyly called "The Epilogue," is it revealed that "[o]f these principles the most important is the doctrine of Evolution[—]the scientific revolution, of which Darwin has been the greatest apostle" (2: 363). In 1883 it might still have been a bit daring for a churchman to proclaim such allegiance; but he provides ten pages of analogies to natural selection, environmental pressure, and so on.

In the realm of comprehensive histories of writing, Taylor apparently held the field alone for more than 50 years. The next full survey that I am aware of is Hans Jensen's, which first appeared in 1935 and was revised twenty years later and again after another decade; its English translation of 1969 remains the fullest source of philological bibliography to that time.

What Faulmann (Taylor, by the way, calls his book "wholly popular and uncritical" [1: v]), Taylor, and Jensen have in common is that they were not specialists in Semitic philology. But soon their genre was to be completely taken over by Semitists: in one decade at mid-century, David Diringer (1948), James-Germain Février (1948), and Marcel Cohen (1958) published worldwide script overviews, followed later by that of Johannes Friedrich (1966, which actually can be taken as the most convenient, compact reference source). Diringer's is most readable, but very inadequately documented, and between the first edition of 1948 and the third of 1968 the only difference I have been able to find is the purely practical one that the illustrations were separated into a second volume. Février has the fewest illustrations but, I find, the soundest judgments, and Cohen is difficult to use because its organizing principles are, to say the least, obscure; I. J. Gelb, who in the 1960s campaigned against Marxist interpretations of ancient economies, notes in his review that

> the respect in which ... Cohen's work differs completely from all its predecessors ... is his attempt to explain the use and evolution of writing in the light of the historical process of evolution of society and its economy. Observing with keen and sensitive eyes the socio-economic background of the area whose writing he is discussing, Cohen tries at every step to link the two together and bring out and evaluate the reasons why certain socio-economic conditions provoked or may have provoked the rise and evolution of a certain form of writing. Therein probably lies the most original contribution of Cohen's great work. (1962: 207)

I am sorry to say that Florian Coulmas's *Blackwell Encyclopedia of*

Writing Systems (1996) is a great disappointment. Its strengths are in its many entries on the social aspects of writing, but it is riddled with factual mistakes — scarcely one article on a Semitic or cuneiform topic is completely error-free.[2]

Two compilations bracket this era that are edited by Semitists and have different orientations from those just mentioned: *Notices sur les caractères étrangers*, created for the International Congress of Orientalists in Paris in 1924 and revised for the 1948 one, is intended for the use of compositors faced with setting type in exotic languages (Fossey 1924, 1948); *The World's Writing Systems* (Daniels and Bright 1996) is meant to provide information on the ways writing systems represent language, and there is certainly no intent or claim of historical thoroughness.[3] Not to be overlooked is *Studium Generale*, a journal "for the unity of science" edited in Berlin, four numbers of which from 1965 and 1967 comprise a fairly complete survey of writing in nineteen chapters;[4] Iranian, Japanese, and Korean are the most serious omissions. Only about a third of the massive German/English encyclopedia *Schrift und Schriftlichkeit* (Günther et al. 1994–96) specifically concerns scripts, and a limited number are considered by several authors from several points of view, rather than attempting worldwide coverage (see below).

For completeness I should acknowledge that some handsomely illustrated volumes exist whose purpose is decoration more than edification (Daniels 2000b). Doubtless they can be found in many languages, so it may be pointless to name those that have come to my attention; regrettably to this category must be assigned Albertine Gaur's

---

[2]   This may be exemplified from "Arabic alphabet": "One of the major Semitic scripts descended from the Aramaic and the Nabataean alphabets." ["and"?] "A little circle above a consonant letter (*sukūn*) is sometimes used to show doubling of a consonant, that is, the absence of a vowel." [*Sukūn* does not mark doubling of a consonant.] From "Gelb, Ignace J.": "(1907–)" [Gelb died in 1985]. From "Syriac scripts": "V[owel] pointing on the Hebrew model" [Syriac vocalization systems predate Hebrew vocalization systems by several centuries].

[3]   The articles in *The World's Writing Systems* that ought to be brought to the attention of Semitists are as follows: Piotr Michalowski, Jerrold S. Cooper, and Gene B. Gragg, "Mesopotamian Cuneiform" (33–72); M. O'Connor, "Epigraphic Semitic Scripts" (88–119); Richard L. Goerwitz, "The Jewish Scripts" (487–98); Peter T. Daniels and Robert D. Hoberman, "Aramaic Scripts for Aramaic Languages" (499–514); Thomas Bauer, "Arabic Writing" (559–68); Getatchew Haile, "Ethiopic Writing" (569–76); Benjamin Hary and Howard I. Aronson, "Adaptations of Hebrew Script" (727–42); and Alan S. Kaye, "Adaptations of Arabic Script" (743–62).

[4]   The articles in *Studium Generale* that ought to be brought to the attention of Semitists are as follows: Wolfgang Röllig, "Die Keilschrift und die Anfänge der Alphabetschrift" (18: 729–42) and Hans-Rudolf Singer, "Die arabische Schrift: Ihre Herkunft und ihre Entwicklung" (18: 769–78).

History of Writing (1992), though it is illustrated (almost exclusively) from the collections of the British Museum, where she was Deputy Keeper of Oriental Manuscripts and then transmogrified to Deputy Director, Oriental Collection, British Library — one of the more egregious errors is the miscounting of Ethiopic consonants as 27 (100).

THEORIES OF WRITING

TYPOLOGY

From descriptions of writing systems, I turn to theories of writing systems. Here, it seems safe to say, the pioneering essay was indeed created by a Semitist — the Assyriologist, my teacher, I. J. Gelb. His stated aim in *A Study of Writing* (1952) was "to lay a foundation for a new science of writing ... [which] attempts to establish general principles governing the use and evolution of writing on a comparative-typological basis. The importance of this study [he writes] lies in its being the first systematic presentation of the history and evolution of writing as based on these principles" (v).

Certainly Gelb's most important hypothesis is the Principle of Uniform Development, to be discussed later; first I will consider the antecedents of Gelb's well-known ternary typology of word-syllabic, syllabic, and alphabetic writing. Something like it is found in various popular accounts of the alphabet that appeared earlier in the century. Special importance accrues once again to Isaac Taylor, because as far as I have been able to find, he in 1883 was the first to use a tripartite typology of word writing, syllable writing, and sound writing:

> Writing began with IDEOGRAMS, which afterwards developed into PHONOGRAMS.
> IDEOGRAMS may be defined to be pictures intended to represent either things or thoughts. There are two kinds of Ideograms; (1) Pictures, or actual representations of objects; (2) Pictorial symbols, which are used to suggest abstract ideas.
> PHONOGRAMS may be defined as the graphic symbols of sounds. They have usually arisen out of conventionalized Ideograms, which have been taken to represent sounds instead of things. Phonograms are of three kinds; (1) Verbal signs, which stand for entire words; (2) Syllabic signs, which stand for the articulations of which words are composed; (3) Alphabetic signs, or letters, which represent the elementary sounds into which the syllable can be resolved.

The development of alphabetic writing proceeds regularly through these five stages. (1: 5–6)

He does not view this as a theoretical statement, nor does he claim originality; but neither does he acknowledge any prior source. E. B. Tylor, the founder of anthropology, alludes only to picture-writing and sound-writing (1881: 169) (and also fails to notice what is now taken as a rather significant development: "The original Phoenician alphabet was weak in vowels. ... The Phoenician alphabet did not altogether suit the writers of Greek and Latin, who altered some letters and made new ones in order to write their language more perfectly" [178]).

Later, fairly scholarly treatments include versions of Taylor's scheme. Edward Clodd (a "banker and author," he prolifically wrote popular books on science and religion; Haynes 1937) reckoned Taylor's book "necessarily charged with a mass of technical detail which is stiff reading even for the student of graphiology" (1900: 5) and deficient in not adequately treating the pre-alphabetic stages of writing and in its second edition not noticing such discoveries as the Proto-Sinaitic and Minoan materials. Thus more than half of Clodd's *Story of the Alphabet* is devoted to non-alphabets. Regarding the alphabets of India, "Those who care to pursue a subject yielding to few in dryness will find it summarised in the tenth chapter" of Taylor's *Alphabet* (192). Clodd presents a version of Taylor's classification that is a development from it; but as with all the authors before Gelb, the outline almost ritually included in an opening chapter is thenceforth ignored:

A survey of the long period which this development covers shows four well-marked stages, although in these, as in aught else appertaining to man's history, there are no true lines of division. The making of these, like the apparent lines of longitude and latitude of the cartographer, is justified by their convenience. These stages are:—

(*a*) The MNEMONIC, or memory-aiding, when some tangible object is used as a message, or for record, between people at a distance, and also for the purpose of accrediting the messenger. As will be seen, it borders on the *symbolic*; indeed, it anticipates that stage.

(*b*) The PICTORIAL, in which a picture of the thing is given, whereby at a glance it tells its own story.

(*c*) The IDEOGRAPHIC, in which the picture becomes representative, *i.e.* is converted into a *symbol*.

(*d*) The PHONETIC, in which the picture becomes a phonogram, or sound-representing sign. The phonogram may be—(1) *verbal, i.e.*

a sound-sign for a whole word; (2) *syllabic, i.e.* a sound-sign for syllables; or (3) *alphabetic*, a sound-sign for each letter.

To recapitulate stages (*b*), (*c*), and (*d*):—

In stage (*b*) the sign as eye-picture suggests the thing;

In stage (*c*) the sign as eye-picture suggests the name;

In stage (*d*) the sign as eye-picture suggests the sound;

and it is in the passage from (*c*) to (*d*), whereby constant signs are chosen to stand for constant sounds, that the progress of the human race was assured, because only thereby was the preservation of all that is of abiding value made possible. (35–36)

On William A. Mason, I have found no information; I suspect he is American rather than British. His version of the classification is as follows:

I. Pictographic or iconographic writing.
    (a) Mnemonic devices antecedent to pictography.
    (b) Disconnected and fragmentary pictures.
    (c) Connected stories, songs or epics.
II. Ideographic or hieroglyphic picture-writing.
III. Phonetic writing.
    (a) Syllabic symbols or signs.
    (b) Alphabetic characters. (1920: 50)

The explanation is confused; the writing of South and Inner Asia goes completely unmentioned.

The Welsh Classicist Alfred C. Moorhouse's *Triumph of the Alphabet* (1953) was considered significant enough to be reviewed alongside Gelb's *Study of Writing* by Wolf Leslau in the journal *Word* (1955), and rightly so — as appears even in his classification summary, he is sensitive to the relation between writing and language, a question that seems to have eluded previous writers:

(1) Picture-writing: a synoptic view of a scene or event, as seen or imagined by the artist

(2) Pictograms: separation of the different items in the picture, and portrayal by means of a number of distinct signs, each standing directly for the object shown

(3) Ideograms: as in (2), except that here the connection between the object shown in the sign, and the idea portrayed, is indirect, working by suggestion

In all stages (1) to (3) the writing is independent of language, as in our traffic signs (the picture of a gate to warn of a level crossing, for instance).

(4) Phonograms: the sign stands for a sound, and so is bound up with the language. Signs are of three sorts, being the equivalent (*a*) of an indefinite number of sounds, and especially of the whole of a word (mono- or polysyllabic); (*b*) of one sound only, the syllable; (*c*) in the alphabet, of either a vowel sound, or of a consonant that is not properly a sound by itself.

Between stage (1) and the rest there is a big gap, since it is only in retrospect that we can see that picture-writing is a system of writing at all. (22)

I am troubled, though, by his finding *two* big gaps — between (1) and (2) and between (3) and (4). Unfortunately, he seems to have done so because he has assigned cuneiform and Chinese to category (3), mistakenly supposing "the writing is independent of language."

Now we come back, of course, to the first, the seminal book dedicated to theory rather than chronicle: I. J. Gelb's *Study of Writing*. His version of the typology is summarized as follows:

No Writing: *Pictures*

Forerunners of Writing: *Semasiography*

   1. Descriptive-Representational Device

   2. Identifying-Mnemonic Device

Full Writing: *Phonography*

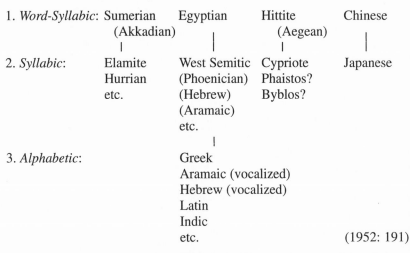

1. *Word-Syllabic*:	Sumerian (Akkadian)	Egyptian	Hittite (Aegean)	Chinese
2. *Syllabic*:	Elamite Hurrian etc.	West Semitic (Phoenician) (Hebrew) (Aramaic) etc.	Cypriote Phaistos? Byblos?	Japanese
3. *Alphabetic*:		Greek Aramaic (vocalized) Hebrew (vocalized) Latin Indic etc.		(1952: 191)

There is one major but easily overlooked difference between this scheme and all its predecessors: the substitution of "word-syllabic" for "verbal" or "word" writing. Gelb was apparently the first to point out that no logographic script is purely so; every one incorporates a method of recording syllables devoid of semantic associations. ("Word-syllabic" instead of "logosyllabic" reflects Gelb's mild case of linguistic chauvinism — in his descriptive grammars he also insisted on "B-stem" for 'basic' rather than "G-stem" for *Grundstamm.*) This important observation paved the way for John DeFrancis's assertion of the ultimately phonological basis of even Chinese writing (1989).

Another important observation by DeFrancis is that none of the so-called "forerunners of writing" (to use Gelb's label for them) in fact "fore-ran" writing — that is, we know of no example of a writing system developing out of something that came before (even when pictograms are used that might stand for individual words). DeFrancis's insistence on the necessarily phonological basis of writing, to which I fully subscribe, has led to a seemingly endless exchange with Geoffrey Sampson, the first linguist into the lists since Gelb with a general book on writing (1985), who insists that even international signage conventions must be included in studies of writing. (The semiotician and gadfly Roy Harris seems to cast his net considerably wider, but consistently declines to provide a characterization of what he thinks should be covered, e.g. 1996.)

EVOLUTION

DeFrancis did not have the work of Denise Schmandt-Besserat on Near Eastern "tokens" before him when he wrote, but it now seems that her claims went well beyond the evidence; and it is clear that her claims have changed over the years, though she seems not to acknowledge this, especially since her earlier articles were not revised when they were reprinted in her book (1992); and in the paperback epitome of that book (1997), the preface says that nothing has been altered in the abridgment. Paul Zimansky's reanalysis of her database is definitive (1993). What we must give Schmandt-Besserat credit for is illuminating the origin of Mesopotamian numerical notation: it is very true that the step from six pictures of sheep to one picture of a sheep accompanied by a sign for six — whether it be a group of six tally-marks or a single mark with the meaning '6' — is a giant step. A comprehensive survey of prehistoric examples of visual communication, by the way, is available in a Bochum semiotics dissertation by Heinz Markus Röhr (1994). He seems to want to find a connection between Ice Age cave paintings or squiggles on pebbles and later writing, but offers no suggestions as to what the relation might be; his summary of writing systems suffers, as so often, from omission or misunderstanding of crucial South and Inner Asian cases.

Thus setting aside the "forerunners" of writing, we may return to Gelb's typology of "full writing." As befitted his aim of establishing general principles, he went beyond his version of the typology to enounce the Principle of Uniform Development, which postulates that the "evolution" of writing must proceed through exactly three stages in order. All alphabets develop from syllabaries, and all syllabaries develop from logographies, and the only possible starting-point for such a chain is logography. The Latin tag "natura non facit saltus" 'nature does not make leaps' that Gelb applies (201) is found also in Taylor's Epilogue on evolution, but that was probably not Gelb's source, since there it is in the singular and identified as "the axiom of Leibnitz" (2: 363); too, Gelb's use of "evolution" is colloquial and metaphoric, while Taylor's is serious and literal.

It is the Principle of Uniform Development, and not any inherent properties of them, that forced Gelb to claim that West Semitic scripts are "syllabaries with indeterminate vowel," a description that has infiltrated general linguistics books and even history books unexamined. It is this principle that leads him to gloss over the scripts of Ethiopia and India and to misrepresent Korean. It was my dissatisfaction with that characterization of West Semitic and with his treatment of Ethiopic that led me to realize that we cannot be content with a mere three types of phonography; five are needed for the scripts in Gelb's list and a sixth to adequately cover Korean and a number of other recent scripts. Gelb was right to firmly separate the West Semitic consonantary from the Greek alphabet, denying the latter label to the former (for which I thereupon suggested the Arabic word *abjad*); but he was not right to lump it together with the prior syllabaries. Similarly, he was right to firmly separate the Ethiopic signary (which denotes syllables) from the prior syllabaries, denying the latter label to the former (for which I thereupon suggested the Ethiopic word *abugida*); but he was not right to lump it together with the alphabet.[5]

An immediate consequence of recognizing the distinction between syllabary and abugida was an insight into the origin of writing. Necessarily turning to languages and scripts that are completely unrelated to Semitic, I noticed that whenever a script was invented in modern times by someone who could not write or even read some language (I call that "unsophisticated"), that invented script is a simple Consonant–Vowel syllabary. There are at least a dozen examples, and Alfred Schmitt, originally a Classical philologist, did the principal work on them (1980).

---

[5]   W. C. Watt (1998: 120–25), in an ostensible review article on *The World's Writing Systems*, accuses me of perpetuating Gelb's alphabetolatry through this typology. I am at a loss to see how such an interpretation can be put on what I wrote there, or in the fuller version in Daniels 1992.

On the other hand, when someone who is sophisticated in writing devises a new script for a language, the new script might be an adaptation of an existing one, or, more interestingly, it is an alphabet or an abugida. The linguistically unsophisticated person analyzes into syllables (Daniels 1992). Awareness of segments is, as Alice Faber (1992) calls it, an "Epiphenomenon" of segmental writing.

This identification of two kinds of script creation suggests that the original origins of writing in Sumer, China, and Yucatan (and presumably Indus Valley) involved syllables. Further, it suggested that the other great leap in the development of writing was the invention of the West Semitic consonantary or abjad, not the Greek invention of the vowels. I can summarize the two suggestions in turn.

As regards the origin of writing, an anecdote may be in order. In the spring of 1984, a small symposium on "The Language of Writing in the Mayan Region" was held at the University of Chicago (Hanks and Rice 1989). I saw a small advertisement for it, excused myself from the Assyrian Dictionary office, and crossed Woodlawn Avenue to attend the morning session. There, for the first time, I learned that decipherment of the Maya glyphs as a phonetic — more precisely, a logosyllabic — script was well under way. I rushed back to Jay Gelb's office, startling him with this news, and importuning him to come to the afternoon session. Eventually he turned up, but by the time he appeared, the papers had moved on to archeological matters, and as far as I know he went to the grave continuing to believe what appears on page 56 of *A Study of Writing*:

> The best proof that the Maya writing is not a phonetic system results from the plain fact that it is still undeciphered. This conclusion is inescapable if we remember the most important principle in the theory of decipherment: *A phonetic writing can and ultimately must be deciphered if the underlying language is known.* Since the languages of the Mayas are still used to-day, and therefore well known, our inability to understand the Maya system means that it does not represent phonetic writing.

He overlooked the other possibility: at the time of his writing, we hadn't tried hard enough. In fact, the key contributions to the decipherment of Maya glyphs appeared at the same time as his first edition (Knorozov 1952) and just before the expanded reprint (Berlin 1958, Proskouriakoff 1960).

I then had a third example of the origin of writing to compare with the two certain ones we had already known: Sumerian and Chinese. It might have been simply a coincidence that Sumerian and Chinese are both monosyllabically organized. But when it turned out that the third example *also* involved a language with monosyllabic roots, I was able to put this together with the observation about unsophisticated modern script creation, to suggest that the act of making a sign for a word — a pictogram — was *also* the act of representing a single syllable; and a representation of a single syllable could also be used to represent an identical or similar-sounding syllable that was a completely different word, one for which a pictogram could perhaps not so easily be devised. This is the rebus principle, on which all the word-syllabic writing systems are built. The invention of writing would thus seem to be practically inevitable, given the right sort of language and a culture or society sufficiently complex to find a use for it.

It must always be kept in mind that writing has never been invented for the purpose of recording narratives or of transmitting messages across a distance; bards and envoys suffice everywhere for that. Writing happens when administrators need to keep accounts of commodities and people when producers and consumers of ordinary goods are no longer in direct contact — that is, some degree of urbanism is a necessary condition for writing. Calendrical records and divine communications soon follow. These are all things not amenable to the usual sort of linguistic interaction.

This is an appropriate point to bring in the so-called Toronto School of literacy studies.[6] It goes back to Marshall McLuhan, and in some respects seems not to have progressed in a scholarly sense beyond his proto-pop-psychology initiatives. Its leading exponent these days is David Olson (1994) — in fact Gelb's survey article in the *Encyclopædia Britannica* (1974) was replaced by Olson's (1988), and Diringer's on the alphabet was rewritten by him (Diringer and Olson 1988) — and in some crucial ways Olson relies on an earlier Torontan, Eric Havelock. Havelock specialized in Plato; and he decided that "true literacy" did not exist before the Greek philosophers. Even though he knew the Bible and the Mesopotamian literature only in translation (and the latter, apparently, only in Speiser's archaizing translations in *ANET* [1950]), he made these assessments:

> A stark contrast appeared between the sheer richness of Greek orality as transcribed and the caution of its competitors. A wealth of detail and depth of psychological feeling contrasted with an economy of vocabulary and a cautious restriction of sentiment which seemed to be specific properties of all Near Eastern and Hebrew literature. (1986: 9)
>
> Selfhood and the soul, when expressed in Greek, conjure up

---

6   A thorough and useful survey of many aspects of the study of written language is
     Jahandarie 1999.

convictions which in the West have been powerfully reinforced by two thousand years of Christianity (though it is worth notice that the same conceptions seem to be lacking in the Old Testament). (120f.)

Havelock makes no attempt at explaining why the Greek innovation of vowels should have been responsible for this flowering of intellectual or spiritual achievement.

Another Torontan, in work that is apparently well known to psychologists or neuroscientists (to judge by the number of times de Kerckhove and Lumsden 1988 has been borrowed from the NYU library), but which I learned of only from many references in Röhr's survey, offered a hypothesis. Derrick de Kerckhove, whose title at the time was Co-Director of The McLuhan Program in Culture and Technology and Professor of French, made the largely legitimate observation that scripts without explicit indication of vowels are written leftward, "while all vocalic alphabets are written to the right" (10). He also claims that "another surprising discovery is that fewer than 10 of over 200 world syllabaries are written to the left" (ibid.). Unfortunately, nowhere is a list, or even a reference to a list, of these 209 syllabaries given. De Kerckhove decided that this kind of lateralization of script relates to brain lateralization, and that brain lateralization relates to cognitive style; he convened two conferences and two workshops in Toronto and Paris in 1982, 1983, and 1985 that resulted in an amazing hodgepodge of a book, which includes an excerpt from Naveh 1987, a surprisingly ill-informed essay by Claude Hagège, and several useful chapters on aspects of neurolinguistics. But only de Kerckhove himself seems to pursue the directional hypothesis, unconvincingly. It has been refuted in a book by Herbert Brekle[7] (1994: 40–46), summarized in his long and brilliant contribution to *Schrift und Schriftlichkeit*, "Die Buchstabenformen westlicher Alphabetschriften in ihrer historischen Entwicklung" (pp. 171–204). Brekle's main interest is in how the physical act of writing affects the appearance of the characters in a signary and their diachronic development, a topic adumbrated in my first journal article (Daniels 1984).

A word now on the contents of this encyclopedia: aside from separate, and widely separated, sections on history of writing, literate cultures, and linguistic aspects of writing systems, which have been the traditional subject matter of the study of writing, there are substantial sections devoted to general aspects, material and formal aspects, functional aspects, social aspects, psychological aspects, and the acquisition of literacy —

I.   Allgemeine Aspekte von Schrift und Schriftlichkeit/General

---

[7]   To whom I am grateful for the gift of a copy of this already out-of-print work.

— subjects that have been divided among semioticians, sociologists, psychologists, and educators at the least,[8] and attention to which is the great strength of Florian Coulmas's textbook (1989), which tends to be weak on the facts of writing systems. A remarkably acute discussion of the political significance of official scripts is found in a world-wide-ranging essay in Toynbee's *Study of History* (1954).

This string of digressions has led away from the first of my two suggestions stimulated by the recognition of additional basic types of writing system, which concerned the origin of writing. The second suggestion concerns the isolation of the segment and the innovation of alphabetic writing. When we recognize that the Greek adaptation of the Phoenician laryngeals as vowel letters was accidental and virtually inevitable, we must acknowledge that the second great achievement

---

[8]   The other articles in *Schrift und Schriftlichkeit* that ought to be brought to the attention of Semitists are as follows: M. Krebernik and H. J. Nissen, "Die sumerisch-akkadische Keilschrift" (274–88); J. Tropper, "Die nordwestsemitischen Schriften" (297–306); W. Müller, "Die altsüdarabische Schrift" (307–12); V. Wilbertz, "Die arabische Schrift" (312–16); E. Hammerschmidt, "Die äthiopische Schrift" (317–21); H. Haarmann, "Entstehung und Verbreitung von Alphabetschriften" (329–47); C. Wilcke, "Die Keilschriftkulturen des Vorderen Orients" (491–503); W. Röllig, "Die nordwestsemitischen Schriftkulturen" (503–10); A. Schimmel, "Die arabische Schriftkultur" (525–36 [there is also a section on Arabic calligraphy, 248–52, in C. Scheffler's "Kalligraphie," 228–55); K. Wedekind, "Alphabetisierung und Literalität in Äthiopien" (814–24); H. H. Biesterfeldt, "Lese- und Schreibunterricht im arabischen Sprachraum" (1299–1309); T. Bauer, "Das arabische Schriftsystem" (1433–36); and T. Bauer, "Die schriftliche Sprache im Arabischen" (1483–90). Clearly the coverage is selective rather than comprehensive.

in the development of writing was in fact the provision of the 27-letter consonantal abjad: this was a stupendous accomplishment, since it required an insight that seems all but unique: the recognition that the usual stretches of speech perception, syllables, could be decomposed into what we know as consonants and vowels (that is, segments). I am willing to recognize that Egypt's writing system underlies the West Semitic system somehow (though I am not willing to concede that the specific finds known as Proto-Sinaitic are in the direct lineage; newly discovered inscriptions from Wadi el-Hol, Egypt, may further illuminate this question), because it was Egyptians who saw Mesopotamian scribes in action and got the idea of recording speech; it was Egyptians who, in puzzling out how to do it, realized that they could record words without specifying the vowels (I think Alfred Schmitt's explanation [1952] is the most successful — recall that he had studied contemporary script invention, but cf. Daniels 1999); it was the Egyptians who came up with a handful of monoconsonantal signs scattered among their biconsonantal, triconsonantal, and logographic ones; but it was *not* the Egyptians who realized that a mere couple of dozen signs could be used to write everything. And the lack of correspondence between sound and shape between hieroglyphs and Proto-Canaanite shows that West Semitic is not simply an adaptation of Egyptian writing, but an adoption of an Egyptian writing *principle*.

I hope that it is by now uncontroversial to state that the invention of vowel letters by the Greeks was not a stroke of genius — Aryan genius, no less — but an accident of the phonemic structure of Phoenician versus Greek. And I hope further that it will not be claimed that Greek, being Indo-European, "needed" to write the vowels where Semitic languages did not (Daniels to appear). And I am also sure that it was Phoenician and not Aramaic writing that gave rise to the Greek alphabet (Daniels 2000c). In order to justify my last four or so assertions, I will summarize a finding that emerged from studying the progress of writing across Inner Asia (Daniels 2000a).

TRANSFER

There is not room here to lay out the evidence and the arguments. There seem to have been three prongs of advance of Aramaic-based scripts eastward into Asia.

(1) The Achaemenid empire invented its own script, the Old Persian cuneiform, but only for monumental use, not for everyday use. Its successor empires, the Sassanian and Parthian, used a cumbersome-seeming script that we call Pahlavi: in its fullest development, it abounded

in Aramaeograms or "heterograms" (like "etc." or "i.e." or "viz." in English, which are pronounced "and so on" or "that is" or "namely") — the changeover from Aramaic to Iranian recordkeeping can be traced in the record: at no point was there a reorganization of the bureaucracy; eventually, the scribes were writing in Iranian but still using Aramaic orthography for purely Iranian words (Henning 1958, Skjærvø 1995).

(2) Beginning with the aforementioned Manichean origin of the sequence Sogdian–Uyghur– Mongolian–Manchu, etc., the Aramaic script travelled gradually to the Pacific, changing slightly at each remove, but in its essence unaltered until the present, with even the revival of traditional vertical Mongolian upon the demise of the communist regime in Mongolia (Skjærvø 1996, Kara 1996).

(3) Some forms of Semitic underlie both Indian scripts, what we call Kharoṣṭhi and Brahmi.[9] However, in India the basic consonantal letters were provided with obligatory vowel indicators — an inherent unmarked vowel (usually /a/), and appendages to denote the other vowels or word-final vowellessness; word-internal vowellessness is indicated by joining sequences of consonants into ligatures, and these ligatures combine syllable-final with syllable-initial consonants. Of all the civilizations so far mentioned, only in India was there a preexisting grammatical tradition — and an elaborate one at that.

But India is not the only example of a script's inner structure changing when it is adapted for a language with a grammatical tradition. As Buddhism and its scholar-missionaries spread across South and Southeast Asia, so did Indian scripts, with the same internal structure — simplified, to be sure, for Austronesian languages like Javanese, with smaller phoneme inventories and few consonant clusters. However, in Tibet, when a Brahmi-based script was adapted to an isolating language, the internal structure changed somewhat: vowel indication is on the same principle, but syllable structure is clearly marked: only a few consonants enter into ligatures — most are written on the line — but every syllable boundary is marked by a dot at the right shoulder of the rightmost consonant letter. And Tibet possessed a grammatical tradition. An adaptation of Tibetan script for (primarily) the Mongolian language ordered by Kubla Khan again changes language-type (to agglutinative), but in the absence of a Mongolian grammatical tradition, the hPags pa script is somewhat clumsier. In turn, the Korean alphabet (but so much more than an alphabet!) is influenced by hPags pa; but there was a Korean grammatical tradition, and Korean writing may be the most sophisticated of all (Kim-Renaud 1997).

---

[9] P. Kyle McCarter [1995] says he has identified the form of Semitic writing underlying Brahmi — remember Taylor deduced that it had to be South Arabian — yet I have been unable to see his manuscript.

There is one other important Asian script type innovation, and that is the Avestan script, which both does away with the mergers in shape found in Pahlavi and adopts vowel letters. This cannot be attributed to an indigenous grammatical tradition, but it does reflect the crisis of the imminent loss of oral tradition of the Zoroastrian scriptures — since the language was apparently already close to incomprehensible — and familiarity with Greek writing.

The lessons of studying script innovation across Asia can be applied to earlier instances of script transfer. Major changes happen in the presence of a grammatical tradition — that is, where the practice of linguistic introspection already existed — or on the occasion of a brusque, i.e. not gradual — script introduction. Thus I suggest that if Egyptian scribes had carefully studied Sumerian writing, hieroglyphics would probably have been a logosyllabary rather than a logoconsonantary. If West Semitic scribes had gone to Egyptian scribal school, they would not have been content with applying but one of the principles of Egyptian writing to their language, since mastering a logographic script represents a considerably larger investment of resources than mastering a phonographic script (compare what happened in Japan, where the scribes *did* learn how Chinese is written: a pair of syllabaries emerged from a restricted set of Chinese characters, well illustrated in *SuS* 387–90). If Greek scribes had learned to write from Aramaean scribes, they would have learned to write long vowels with *matres lectionis* and that short vowels can safely be omitted (even Mandaic, which is supposed to have developed the *matres* into effectively a full alphabet, does not explicitly notate every vowel) and would not have mistakenly taken the Phoenician laryngeals as denoting vowels. And if the writing of vowels for Indo-European languages was so essential, then the Iranian scribes would have had to come up with some means of notating them using the resources of Pahlavi.

In these remarks I have had to omit any number of topics that are of particular interest within the study of Semitic writing (such as letter order and script direction), while I have tried to present those where non-Semitic data and general theory are particularly relevant. It is a sad duty to have to note that familiarity with the facts of Semitic writing is often gravely lacking in those who write more general treatments. I hope that when Semitists held their near-monopoly on general surveys, they presented the more exotic material accurately. It must be recognized that Gelb's *Study of Writing* includes misstatements, some of them major, about other areas. I can point out a legion of mistakes on Semitic in recent work by Olson, de Kerckhove, DeFrancis, and Coulmas, in some cases with repercussions for their theoretical claims.

But I would rather end with desiderata. The twentieth century began with monumental works by Mark Lidzbarski and Isaac Taylor, which both summed up the previous century of work on West Semitic and general writing systems and laid the foundation for the next century. The paleography of Arabic, Hebrew/Aramaic, and Ethiopic have received due attention (Gruendler 1993 with refs., Birnbaum 1954–71, Naveh 1970, Pirenne 1963, Uhlig 1988), and even South Arabian paleography and (perhaps less satisfactorily) epigraphy (Ryckmans, Müller, and Abdallah 1994, Pirenne 1956). Middle Aramaic epigraphy, which may appear to be the neglected stepchild, has also had a careful treatment, which remains unfortunately unpublished: a few years ago Alexander Klugkist kindly sent me the last spare copy of his dissertation (1982b), but he went from Semitic studies into librarianship — like Julius Euting — and was not planning to return to the work to update and release it beyond two articles derived from it (1982a, 1986). At the beginning of the twenty-first century, we still have no comprehensive paleography of cuneiform — and barely a start on regionally and temporally restricted studies (e.g. Biggs 1973 — in the Gelb Festschrift). We do not know much about all those non-epigraphic "aspects" of Semitic writing under which *Schrift und Schriftlichkeit* is organized. We need to know more about what was going on in the minds and hands of ancient scribes as well as modern ones. When our descendants look back from the turn of the twenty-second century, I hope — I trust — they will find that some of our work will still reward study a hundred years hence.

REFERENCES

Albright, W. F. 1934. *The Vocalization of the Egyptian Syllabic Orthography.* American Oriental Series 5. New Haven.

Albright, W. F. 1937. A Biblical Fragment from the Maccabean Age: The Nash Papyrus. *Journal of Bibilical Literature* 56: 145–76.

Albright, W. F. 1966. *The Proto-Sinaitic Inscriptions and Their Decipherment.* Harvard Theological Studies 22. Cambridge.

Anon. 1912. Isaac Taylor (1829–1901). In *Dictionary of National Biography 1901–1911.* N.p.: Oxford University Press. 3: 485–86.

Berlin, Heinrich. 1958. El glifo "emblema" en las inscripciones mayas. *Journal de la Société des Américanistes* 47: 111–19.

Biggs, Robert D. 1973. On Regional Cuneiform Handwritings in Third Millennium Mesopotamia. *Orientalia* 42: 39–46.

Birnbaum, Solomon A. 1954–71. *The Hebrew Scripts.* 2 vols. Vol. 1, Leiden, 1971; vol. 2, London, 1954–57.

Brekle, Herbert E. 1994. *Die Antiqualinie von ca. −1500 bis ca. +1500:*

Untersuchungen zur Morphogenese des westlichen Alphabets auf kognitivistischer Basis. Münster.

Budge, E. A. Wallis. 1925. *The Rise and Progress of Assyriology*. London.

Clodd, Edward. 1900. *The Story of the Alphabet*. New York, 1904.

Cohen, Marcel. 1958. *La grande invention de l'écriture et son évolution*. 3 vols. Paris.

Coulmas, Florian. 1989. *The Writing Systems of the World*. Oxford.

Coulmas, Florian. 1996. *The Blackwell Encyclopedia of Writing Systems*. Oxford.

Daniels, Peter T. 1984. A Calligraphic Approach to Aramaic Paleography. *Journal of Near Eastern Studies* 43: 55–68.

Daniels, Peter T. 1988. "Shewing of Hard Sentences and Dissolving of Doubts": The First Decipherment. *Journal of the American Oriental Society* 108: 418–36.

Daniels, Peter T. 1992. The Syllabic Origin of Writing and the Segmental Origin of the Alphabet. In P. Downing, S. Lima, & M. Noonan (eds.). *The Linguistics of Literacy*. Amsterdam, 83–110.

Daniels, Peter T. 1993. Breaking the Maya Code and Cracking Cuneatics. Paper presented at the meeting of the International Linguistic Association, New York, April.

Daniels, Peter T. 1994. Edward Hincks's Decipherment of Mesopotamian Cuneiform. In Kevin J. Cathcart (ed.). *The Edward Hincks Bicentenary Lectures*. Dublin, 30–57.

Daniels, Peter T. 1995. The Decipherment of Near Eastern Scripts. In Jack M. Sasson et al. (eds.). *Civilizations of the Ancient Near East*. New York, 81–93.

Daniels, Peter T. 1996. Methods of Decipherment. In Peter T. Daniels & William Bright (eds.). *The World's Writing Systems*. New York, 141–59.

Daniels, Peter T. 1999. A Study of Origins. Paper presented at conference on the Origins of Writing, University of Pennsylvania Museum, Philadelphia.

Daniels, Peter T. 2000a. On Writing Syllables: Three Episodes of Script Transfer. *Studies in the Linguistic Sciences* (Urbana) 30: 73–86.

Daniels, Peter T. 2000b. Review article on popular books on writing. *Sino-Platonic Papers* 98, "Reviews VIII." 47–57.

Daniels, Peter T. 2000c. Syllables, Consonants, and Vowels in West Semitic Writing. *Lingua Posnaniensis* 42: 43–55.

Daniels, Peter T. to appear. Script Typology Inside and Outside Afroasiatic. In M. Lionel Bender et al. (eds.). Diakonoff Memorial Volume. [Incorporates papers presented at 1999 meeting of the American Oriental Society and 2000 NACAL.]

Daniels, Peter T. & William Bright (eds.). 1996. *The World's Writing Systems*. New York.

DeFrancis, John. 1989. *Visible Speech: The Diverse Oneness of Writing Systems*. Honolulu.

de Kerckhove, Derrick & Charles J. Lumsden (eds.). 1988. *The Alphabet and the Brain: The Lateralization of Writing*. Berlin.

de Vogüé, M. 1868ff. *Syrie centrale. Inscriptions sémitiques*.

Diringer, David. 1948. *The Alphabet: A Key to the History of Mankind*. New York. 3rd ed., 2 vols., 1968.

Diringer, David & David R. Olson. 1988. Writing: Alphabetic Writing. *Encyclopædia Britannica* 15th ed. revised Macropædia 30: 1040–49.

Driver, G. R. 1976. *Semitic Writing*. Schweich Lectures 1944, 3d ed. prepared by S. A. Hopkins. London.

Dussaud, René. 1929. Mark Lidzbarski (1868–1928). *Syria* 10: 112–14.

Euting, Julius. 1877. *Semitische Schrifttafel*. Strassbourg. [Repr. in *Outlines of Hebrew Grammar* by Gustavus Bickell, revised by the author, and annotated by the translator Samuel Ives Curtiss, Jr. Leipzig 1877].

Euting, Julius. 1883. *Sammlung der carthagischen Inschriften*. Strassbourg.

Euting, Julius. 1885. *Nabatäische Inschriften aus Arabien*. Berlin.

Euting, Julius. 1889. *Epigraphische Denkmäler aus Arabien*, by D. H. Müller. Vienna.

Euting, Julius. 1891. *Sinaitische Inschriften*. Berlin.

Faber, Alice. 1992. Phonemic Segmentation as Epiphenomenon: Evidence from the History of Alphabetic Writing. In P. Downing, S. Lima, & M. Noonan (eds.). *The Linguistics of Literacy*. Amsterdam, 111–34.

Faulmann, Karl. 1880a. *Das Buch der Schrift enthaltend die Schriftzeichen und Alphabete aller Zeiten und aller Völker des Erdkreises*, 2d ed. Vienna. Repr. Augsburg, 1995.

Faulmann, Karl. 1880b. *Illustrierte Geschichte der Schrift: Popular-wissenschaftliche Darstellung der Entstehung der Schrift der Sprache und der Zahlen sowie der Schriftsysteme aller Völker der Erde*. Vienna. Repr. with Afterword by Eva-Maria Hanebutt-Benz & Dirk H. Veldhuis, Nördlingen, 1989.

Février, James-G. 1948. *Histoire de l'écriture*. Paris. 2nd ed., 1959.

Fossey, Charles, ed. 1924. *Notices sur les caractères étrangers*. Paris. 2nd ed., 1948.

Friedrich, Johannes. 1966. *Geschichte der Schrift*. Heidelberg.

Gale, J. S. 1912. The Korean Alphabet. *Transactions of the Korea Branch of the Royal Asiatic Society* 4/1: 13–61.

Garbini, Giovanni. 1979. *Storia e problemi dell'epigrafia semitica*. Annali dell'Istituto Orientale di Napoli Supp. 19.

Gaur, Albertine. 1992. *A History of Writing*. 2nd ed. London & New York.

Gelb, I. J. 1952. *A Study of Writing*. Chicago. 2nd ed., 1963.

Gelb, I. J. 1962. Review of Cohen 1958. *Language* 38: 206–13.

Gelb, I. J. 1974. Writing, Forms of. *Encyclopædia Britannica* 15th ed. Macropædia 19: 1033–45.

Gruendler, Beatrice. 1993. *The Development of the Arabic Scripts*. Harvard Semitic Studies 43. Atlanta.

Günther, Hartmut, Otto Ludwig, et al. (eds.). 1994–96. *Schrift und Schriflichkeit/Writing and Its Use*. 2 vols. Berlin.

Hanks, William F. & Rice, Don S. (eds.). 1989. *Word and Image in Maya Culture: Explorations in Language, Writing, and Representation*. Salt Lake City.

Harris, Roy. 1996. *Signs of Writing*. London.

Havelock, Eric A. 1986. *The Muse Learns to Write*. New Haven.

Haynes, E. S. P. 1937. Edward Clodd (1840–1930). *Dictionary of National Biography 1922–1930*. London, 190–92.

Henning, W. B. 1958. Mitteliranisch. *Handbuch der Orientalistik 1/4/1 Iranistik*. Leiden, 20–130.

Jahandarie, Khosrow. 1999. *Spoken and Written Discourse: A Multidisciplinary Perspective*. Stanford, Conn.

Jeffrey, Lilian H. 1961. *The Local Scripts of Archaic Greece*. Oxford.

Jensen, Hans. 1969. *Sign, Symbol and Script*. 3rd ed., trans. George Unwin. London, New York.

Kara, György. 1996. Aramaic Scripts for Altaic Languages. In Daniels & Bright 1996: 536–58.

Kautzsch, Emil. 1910. *Gesenius' Hebrew Grammar*, trans. A. E. Cowley. Oxford.

Kim-Renaud, Young-Key (ed.). 1997. *The Korean Alphabet*. Honolulu.

Klugkist, Alexander C. 1982a. The Importance of the Palmyrene Script for Our Knowledge of the Development of the Late Aramaic Scripts. In Michael Sokoloff (ed.). *Arameans, Aramaic and the Aramaic Literary Tradition*. Bar Ilan, 57–74.

Klugkist, Alexander C. 1982b. Midden-aramese schriften in Syrië, Mesopotamië, Persië en aangrenzende gebieden. Doctoral dissertation, University of Groningen.

Klugkist, Alexander C. 1986. The Origin of the Mandaic Script. In H. L. Vanstiphout, K. Jongeling, F. Leemhuis, and G. J. Reinink (eds.). *Scripta Signa Vocis: Studies about Scripts, Scriptures, Scribes and*

Languages in the Near East, Presented to J. H. Hospers by His Pupils, Colleagues and Friends. Groningen, 111–20.

Knorozov, Yuri V. 1952. Drevnjaja pis'mennost' Tsentral'noi Ameriki [Ancient writing of Central America]. *Sovetskaja Etnografia* 1952/3.

Leslau, Wolf. 1950–55. Reviews of Diringer 1948, Février 1948, Gelb 1952, Moorhouse 1953. *Word* 6: 89–90, 90–91; 11: 280–82, 282–83.

Lidzbarski, Mark. 1898. *Handbuch der nordsemitischen Epigraphik.* 2 vols. Weimar.

Lidzbarski, Mark. 1900–15. *Ephemeris für semitische Epigraphik.* 3 vols. Giessen.

Lidzbarski, Mark. 1916. Die Herkunft der manichäischen Schrift. *Sitzungsberichte der Deutschen Akademie der Wissenschaften* 1213–22.

Lyall, C. J. 1913. Julius Euting (1839–1913). *Journal of the Royal Asiatic Society* 505–10.

Mason, William A. 1920. *A History of the Art of Writing.* New York.

McCarter, P. Kyle. 1995. [Abstract for American Oriental Society meeting, Salt Lake City, withdrawn due to illness].

Moorhouse, Alfred C. 1953. *The Triumph of the Alphabet: A History of Writing.* New York.

Müller, F. W. K. 1904. Handschriften-Reste in Estrangelo-Schrift aus Turfan, Chinesisch-Turkistan. Part 1, *Sitzungsberichte der Deutschen Akademie der Wissenschaften zu Berlin* 348–52; part 2, *Abhandlungen der Deutschen Akademie der Wissenschaften zu Berlin* 1904/2.

Naveh, Joseph. 1970. *The Development of the Aramaic Script.* Israel Academy of Sciences and Humanities, Proceedings 5/1. Jerusalem.

Naveh, Joseph. 1987. *Early History of the Alphabet.* Jerusalem.

Nöldeke, Theodor. 1875. *Mandäische Grammatik.* Halle.

Olson, David R. 1988. Writing: The Nature and Origin of Writing. *Encyclopædia Britannica* 15th ed. revised *Macropædia* 30: 1025–34.

Olson, David R. 1994. *The World on Paper: The Conceptual and Cognitive Implications of Writing and Reading.* Cambridge.

Pirenne, Jacqueline. 1956. *Paléographie des inscriptions sud-arabes,* vol. 1. Verhandelingen van de Koninklijke Vlaamse Academie voor Wetenschappen, Letteren en Schone Kunsten van België, Klasse der Letteren 26. Brussels.

Pirenne, Jacqueline. 1963. Aux origines de la graphie syriaque. *Syria* 40: 101–37.

Proskouriakoff, Tatiana. 1960. Historical Implications of a Pattern of Dates at Piedras Negras. *American Antiquity* 25: 454–75.

Rawlinson, George. 1898. *A Memoir of Major-General Sir Henry Creswicke Rawlinson.* London.

Röhr, Heinz Markus. 1994. *Writing: Its Evolution and Relation to Speech.* Bochum.

Ryckmans, Jacques, Walter Müller, & Yusuf M. Abdallah. 1994. *Textes du Yémen antique inscrits sur bois.* Louvain.

Sampson, Geoffrey. 1985. *Writing Systems.* London, Stanford.

Schmandt-Besserat, Denise. 1992. *Before Writing.* 2 vols. Austin.

Schmandt-Besserat, Denise. 1997. *How Writing Came About.* Austin.

Schmitt, Alfred. 1952. *Der Buchstabe H* [i.e. Eta] *im Griechischen.* Orbis Antiquus 6.

Schmitt, Alfred. 1980. *Entstehung und Entwicklung der Schrift.* Wiesbaden.

Schröder, Paul. 1869. *Phönizische Grammatik.* Halle.

Skjærvø, Prods Oktor. 1995 [pub. 1997]. Aramaic in Iran. *Aram* 7: 283–318.

Skjærvø, P. Oktor. 1996. Aramaic Scripts for Iranian Languages. In Daniels & Bright 1996: 515–35.

Speiser, E. A. 1950. Akkadian Myths and Epics. In James B. Pritchard (ed.). *Ancient Near Eastern Texts Relating to the Old Testament.* 3rd ed. 1969. Princeton, 60–119.

Studium Generale: Zeitschrift für die Einheit der Wissenschaften 18/12 (1965), 20/7–9 (1967).

Taylor, Isaac. 1883. *The Alphabet.* 2 vols. London. New ed., 1899.

Toynbee, Arnold J. 1954. Official Languages and Scripts. In *A Study of History* (VI.C.II.(d).1, vol. 7, pp. 239–55), referring to Lingue Franche (V.C.I.(d).6.(γ), vol. 5, pp. 483–527, 1939) and Archaism in Language and Literature (V.C.i.(d).8.(γ), vol. 6, pp. 62–83, 1939) N.p.: Oxford University Press.

Tylor, Edward B. 1881. *Anthropology: An Introduction to the Study of Man and Civilization.* New York.

Uhlig, Siegbert. 1988. *Äthiopische Paläographie.* Äthiopistische Forschungen 28. Stuttgart.

Watt, W. C. 1998. The Old-fashioned Way. *Semiotica* 122: 99–138.

Zimansky, Paul. 1993. Review of Schmandt-Besserat 1992. *Journal of Field Archaeology* 20: 513–17.

		Egyptian, Ebers.			Phenician									
		Hieroglyph	Hieratic		Mêša on. 830 B.C.	Sidon.1 Eshmun. IV. Sec.	Gebûl IV Sec.?	Sardin. Nor. i. Thurr. i.	Cyprus			Malta No. i.5.	Marseilles	Carthage (N? 108,195,P.241,356) prior to 150 B.C.
			12+13 Dynasty	late					Cr.t.32.37	Idal.1-3. 380 B.C.	Idal.5. 25½ B.C.			
א	1	(a)ʼā												
ב	2	b												
ג	3	g												
ד	4	d												
ה	5	h												
ו	6	u,v												
ז	7	ʼẓ												
ח	8	ch												
ט	9	ṭ												
י	10	i,j												
כ	11	k,k												
ל	12	l												
מ	13	m												
נ	14	n												
ס	15	s												
ע	16	ʼā												
פ	17	p												
צ	18	t(z)												
ק	19	q												
ר	20	r												
ש	21	š												
ת	22	t(u)												
		1. Column	2.	3.	4.	5.	6.	7.	8.	9.	10.	11.	12.	13.

		Modern Punic.			Aramaic						
Athens	Spain Statue of Harpocr. see.th Caria y Rivero.	Mauret. Numid. Carth . Sardin . 2!! Cent .B.C-3Cent. A.D.	Assyr. Weights Lion from Abydes. 8-6 Cent.	Aram. Seals & Gems 7-3t Cent B.C. Coins 4 Cent.	Carp.	Serap. 1Cent. AD.	Papyri P.Berol. Louvre. P.Vatic. Taurin. Blacas 3-4.See.a.Chr. 1		Palmyr. I See a.Ch IISee.p.Ch	Nabat. I-IV Sec. p.Chr.	Pehlevi. Chald.Sass. anc.to Thomas
14.	15.	16.	17.	18.	19.	20.	21.	22.	23.	24.	25.	26.

	Syriac		Arabic		Mand.	Old Hebr. Seals & Gems	Coins acc. to Madden.	Samaritan	U. T. Quad.	Rabb. pottery from Babylon	Grave stones from 'Ade
estr.	Modern Nestor.	Palest.Syr. acc.Land.u. P.Petersbg.	Kufi	Naskhi		↑ 8-5 cent. B.C?	2. Sec. a, Ch- 135 p. Chr.	Lapid. prior to 527 p. Ch.	Jerus. t.Sp.u. Rabv. Rersim 3.Sec. p. Chr.	5. Sec.	7. Sec.	AD. 717	AD.

| 27. | 28. | 29. | 30. | 31. | 32 | 33. | 34. | 35. | 36. | 37. | 38. | 39. |

Mss.								Berberic (Libyan) acc. to J.Halévy		South Semitic				Hebr.
Adai Br.Mus. Ar.Or 51. AD.1189	Current XII.XIII.Sec.	Lapidar. Strassbg XII.Sec. or earlier	Rashi	Female German	Spanish Levantine	Cursive Germ.Pal	Cursive K'att el-brawāt Algiers · Morocco	right to left Thugga	from bottom to top	Himyar.	Old Ethiopia	Geez	Harra	with Tagin
אא	צ	אא	ħ	וו	ﻟ	אא ﬞ	hﬞײַ · ﬗ	—	١	ḥ̣ħ	λ	λ	א
בב	בֿ	בֿב	ב	ב	כ	2ב̃	ﬞ · בﬞ	⊙ロ	⊙ロ	Π	Π	ᴒ	ב
גגג	ג	ג	ג	ג	ﬞ	גﬞ	ﬞ · ﬞ	←	Ⲙﬞⲱ	⅃	⅂	ﬞ	ג
דד	ד	ד	ד	ד	ﬞ	ﬞ	ﬞﬞﬞ · ﬞﬞ	Π	⊏⊐	ﬞ̣Ḥ̣	ΧΧ	ﬞ	ד
ההה	ה	ההה	ה	ﬞ	ﬞ	ﬞ	ﬞﬞ · ﬞﬞ	≡	Ч	Υ	U	Υ	ה
ווו	ﬞ	ﬞווו	ﬞ	ﬞ	ﬞ	ﬞ	ﬞ · ﬞ	=	‖ḤṬ⅃	⊕	▽⊕	⊕	ו
ﬞז	ﬞ	ﬞﬞﬞ	ﬞ	ﬞ	ﬞ	ﬞ	ﬞﬞ · ﬞﬞ	⫿	⫿	Χ		H	ז
חחח	ﬞ	ﬞﬞ	ﬞ	ﬞ	ﬞ	ﬞﬞ	ﬞ	‖‖‖	ﬞ	Ψ	ﬞ	ﬞ	ﬞ
ﬞ	ﬞ	ﬞ	ﬞ	ﬞ	ﬞ	ﬞ	ﬞﬞ	→	→	⫿ﬞ	ﬞ	ﬞ	ﬞ
ﬞ	ﬞ	ﬞﬞﬞ	ﬞ	ﬞ	ﬞ	ﬞﬞ	ﬞﬞ	Z	Z⋀S	ﬞ	ΥΡ	ﬞ	ﬞ
ﬞﬞ	ﬞﬞ		ﬞﬞ	ﬞﬞ	ﬞﬞ	ﬞ	ﬞﬞ · ﬞﬞ	⫘⫘	ﬞ	ﬞ	ﬞ	ﬞ	ﬞ
ﬞﬞﬞ	ﬞ	ﬞﬞﬞ	ﬞ	ﬞ	ﬞ	ﬞﬞ	ﬞﬞ	‖	=	ﬞ	Λ	Λ	ﬞ
ﬞﬞ	ﬞﬞ	ﬞﬞﬞ	ﬞﬞ	ﬞﬞ	ﬞﬞ	ﬞﬞ	ﬞﬞﬞ	⅃	⊔	ﬞ	ﬞ	ﬞ	ﬞ
ﬞﬞ	ﬞﬞ	ﬞﬞﬞ	ﬞ	ﬞ	ﬞ	ﬞ	ﬞﬞ	⎮	—	ﬞ	ﬞ	ﬞ	ﬞ
ﬞﬞﬞ	ﬞ		ﬞ	ﬞ	ﬞﬞ	o	ﬞﬞ	⊏	Π	ﬞ	ﬞ	ﬞ	ﬞ
ﬞﬞ	ﬞﬞ	ﬞﬞ	ﬞ	ﬞ	ﬞ	ﬞﬞ	ﬞﬞ	≡÷	‖‖⫶	∘∘ﬞ	∇	U	∘
ﬞﬞﬞﬞ	ﬞ		ﬞﬞ	ﬞﬞﬞ	ﬞﬞ	ﬞﬞﬞ	ﬞﬞﬞ	Χ	⋈	◇◇	44	ﬞ	ﬞ
ﬞﬞﬞﬞ	ﬞﬞ	ﬞﬞﬞ	ﬞﬞﬞ	ﬞ	ﬞ	ﬞﬞﬞ	ﬞﬞﬞ	Χ8	Χ8Χ	ﬞΘ	ΛΘΧΘ	ΛΘ	ﬞ
ﬞﬞ	ﬞ	ﬞﬞﬞ	ﬞ	ﬞ	ﬞ	ﬞﬞ	ﬞﬞ	≡	◇◇	◇◇	ﬞ	ﬞ	ﬞ
ﬞﬞ	ﬞ	ﬞﬞﬞ	ﬞ	ﬞ	ﬞ	ﬞﬞ	ﬞﬞ	∘ロ	∘ロ	ﬞﬞ	⌐	⌐	ﬞ
ﬞﬞﬞ	ﬞ	ﬞﬞﬞ	ﬞ	ﬞ	ﬞ	ﬞﬞ	ﬞﬞ	≷	WH	ﬞﬞ	Ш	Ш	ﬞﬞ
ﬞﬞﬞ	ﬞ	ﬞﬞﬞ	ﬞ	ﬞ	ﬞ	ﬞﬞ	ﬞﬞ	+Χ⧖	+Χﬞ	Χⱦ̣Χ	┼	┼	χﬞ
42.	43.	44.	45.	46.	47.	48.	49. · 50.	51.	52.	53.	54.	55.	56.

DAS PHÖNIZISCHE ALFABET.

Taf. B

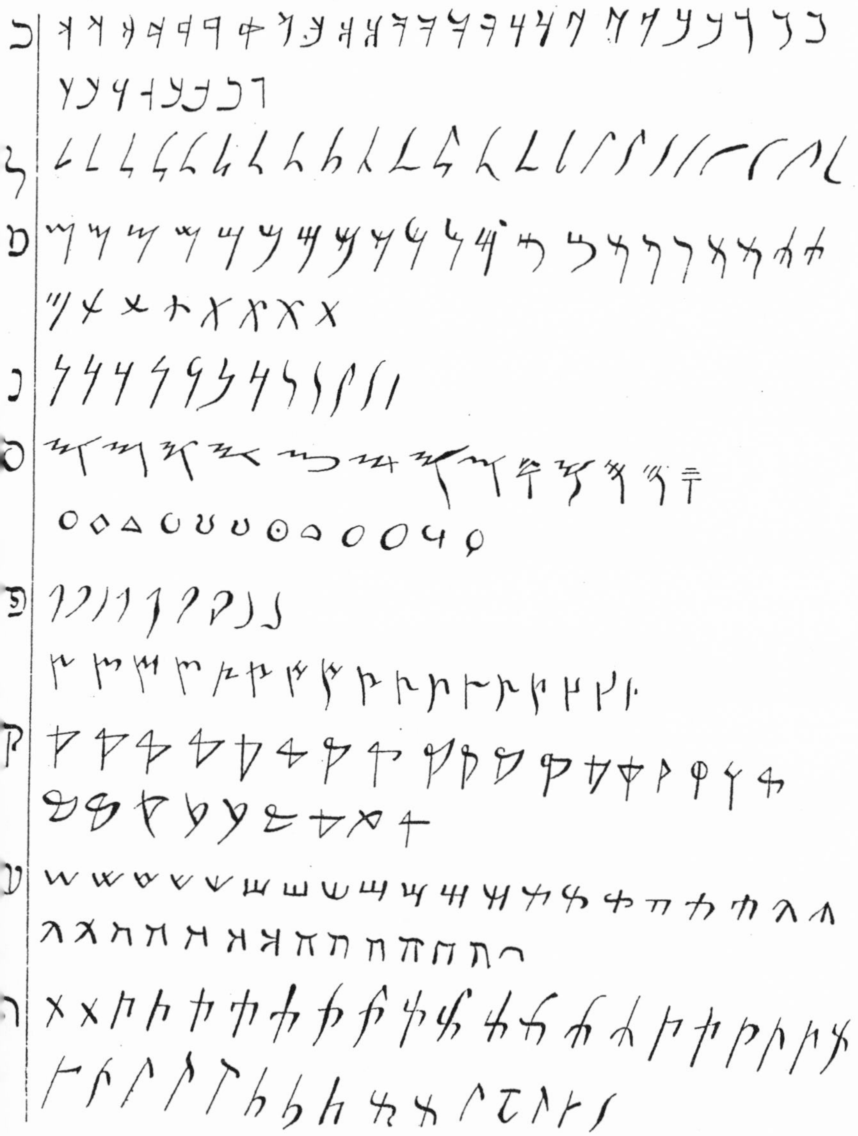

COMPARATIVE SEMITIC LINGUISTICS

JOHN HUEHNERGARD

I. FINS DE SIÈCLE

The nineteenth century closed with the appearance of three introductions to the field of comparative Semitic linguistics. In 1890, William Wright's still-useful *Lectures on the Comparative Grammar of the Semitic Languages* were given posthumous printed form (Wright 1890). In 1897, O. Lindberg published the first of what were planned as several volumes under the title *Vergleichende Grammatik der semitischen Sprachen*, although the subsequent volumes never appeared (Lindberg 1897). And the following year, 1898, Heinrich Zimmern brought out a fine book with the same title as Lindberg's (Zimmern 1898). These were not the earliest such general works; already in 1855 Ernest Renan had published the first edition of his *Histoire générale et système comparé des langues sémitiques*, which would go through several more editions over the next two decades, by which time it was quite out of date in terms of both its approach and its data (Renan 1855 et seq.).

The twentieth century now likewise draws to a close with the appearance of three new volumes on general Semitic, each of them quite different from the other. The lamented Robert Hetzron's final offering was a volume he edited, entitled simply *The Semitic Languages* (Hetzron ed. 1997), a superb collection of descriptions, by recognized experts, of each of the languages or dialect groups in the family, both ancient and modern. Edward Lipiński has published a large book, *Semitic Languages: Outline of a Comparative Grammar* (Lipiński 1997), about which more in a moment. And Patrick R. Bennett has produced a manual for students with the title *Comparative Semitic Linguistics*, a very useful introduction to the methodologies of historical and comparative linguistics and to the Semitic languages and their basic phonologies and morphologies, complete with many helpful exercises (Bennett 1998). (It is telling that such a manual was prepared by a comparative linguist who has worked primarily not in Semitics, but rather in Niger-Congo.)

In some ways, Lipiński 1997 is the most intriguing of these three new books. With its extensive store of data, it seems to aspire, at least in part, to replace another work, one that has overshadowed all others for most

119

of the 20th century. I refer of course to Carl Brockelmann's *Grundriss*, the first volume of which appeared in 1908 and the second in 1913. The *Grundriss* truly represented the state of the art at the beginning of the 20th century; it was a monumental effort to catalogue and organize all the evidence then available on the Semitic languages and to digest the best nineteenth-century scholarship in Semitic linguistics, scholarship by the likes of Barth, de Lagarde, Gesenius, Haupt, Hommel, König, Müller, Philippi, Praetorius, and, most prominently, Nöldeke.

Like the volumes published at the end of the nineteenth century, those that have appeared in the last two years are attempts at summing up or taking stock of the field and at presenting it, especially to non-specialists, in a digestible fashion. They are also a good measure of the health of the field. It was only some twenty years ago that Moshe Goshen-Gottstein published what he called a "premature obituary" of comparative Semitics (Goshen-Gottstein 1979). Nearly two decades before that, Edward Ullendorff had lamented what he considered the demise of the general Semitist in an age of ever-increasing specialization (Ullendorff 1961: 26), and H. J. Polotsky had expressed his concern over centrifugal tendencies — such as the interest of scholars in individual languages solely as tools to understand the literatures and histories of the ancient world — that seemed to him to be acting against comparative Semitic linguistics (Polotsky 1964: 102; see also Ullendorff 1970: 263). Fortunately, these tendencies have waned; the obituary was indeed premature. The last decade or so has seen the publication of many important new works in the field: to mention only those that have appeared in monograph form: Geoffrey Khan on extraposition and related issues in Semitic syntax (Khan 1988); Rainer Voigt on weak roots and biradicalism (Voigt 1988); Jan Retsö on the derived stems (Retsö 1989); Josef Tropper on the Ugaritic and Semitic causative (Tropper 1990); N. J. C. Kouwenberg on gemination in the Akkadian verb, a book from which all Semitists can profit (Kouwenberg 1997); David Testen on the Arabic particle *la-* and related Semitic particles (Testen 1998); and Robert Ratcliffe on the broken plural (Ratcliffe 1998b). A fine 1996 Harvard dissertation on Semitic noun patterns, by Joshua Fox, will also be published soon (Fox forthc.). But perhaps the best gauge of the vitality of comparative Semitic linguistics is the two-volume collection of papers in the 1991 Wolf Leslau Festschrift, which contains well over a hundred articles on all aspects of Semitic linguistics, many of them comparative (Kaye 1991).

There are, obviously, many workers in the field these days. And unlike the situation in the nineteenth century and for much of the twentieth, when much of the work on comparative Semitics was done by scholars with little formal linguistic training, as a sideline of their main fields of interest (such as Biblical studies, Assyriology, Islamwissenschaft, and the like), today there are many Semitists who are well trained in general comparative and historical linguistics and for whom Semitic linguistics is their main field of research, as the present volume of papers so clearly demonstrates.

II. MODERN LINGUISTICS AND COMPARATIVE SEMITIC LINGUISTICS

One often reads in the summaries of Semitic scholarship that have appeared in the second half of the 20th century that Semitists have been slow to adopt the methods and approaches of their Indo-Europeanist cousins, and that comparative Semitic linguistics has lagged behind comparative Indo-European linguistics. A number of historical factors brought about that state of affairs. Comparative linguistics began with the study of the languages of Europe, and the spectacular success of the comparative method, first applied to the reconstruction of Proto-Indo-European — one of the greatest achievements of nineteenth-century scholarship — meant that the first university chairs in linguistics were chairs in Indo-European. Semitists, preoccupied with other concerns such as theology and biblical history, did not jump on the linguistic bandwagon with alacrity or enthusiasm. By the time they did, linguistics was enshrined as Indo-European linguistics, while Semitists interested in comparative linguistics had to continue being professors of other subjects. Thus, the major theoretical and methodological advances continued to be made by those who could focus all their energies on linguistics.

The second linguistic revolution, the beginning of modern linguistics, was also brought about by a comparative Indo-Europeanist, Saussure, a revolution that for a time placed comparative work in the shadows (Saussure 1916). The Saussurian revolution has also brought about, over the course of the 20th century, extraordinary advances in our understanding of the phenomenon of human language. And again, Semitics lagged behind, in part for the same reason as before, namely, a dearth of scholars who could afford to be engaged in the subject full time. It is notable in this regard that the second volume of Brockelmann's *Grundriss*, the presentation of all that was known about the Semitic languages at the beginning of the 20th century, was published just three years before Saussure's students published the revolutionary *Cours de linguistique général*. With the encyclopedic *Grundriss* in hand, many Semitists seemed content to let the next several decades of general linguistics unfold without them. There were, however, noteworthy exceptions, such as

Frank Blake (1917–53, 1920), Jean Cantineau (1932, 1937, 1949, 1950a, 1950b, 1951–52), V. Christian (1919–20, 1924, 1926, 1927, 1944), and especially Marcel Cohen. But Cohen, in keeping with the times, was more interested in the descriptive and structural study of modern languages than in comparative study and the dead ones (M. Cohen 1931, 1936, 1939). So too were most of the scholars working with Semitic languages who were able to keep up with contemporary developments in linguistics. What happened for a time, then, was the rise of what might almost be considered two "camps" of Semitists: those using the methods of modern linguistics to study the modern languages, which had received scant attention previously, and the philologists working on the ancient languages who did not have the time to keep up with the rapidly changing developments in linguistics.[1]

In the 1930's, then, Marcel Cohen produced a number of masterly studies of the modern Semitic languages of Ethiopia; he was soon joined in this endeavor by equally impressive studies in the '30's and '40's by H. J. Polotsky (1938) and Wolf Leslau (1939a, 1939b, 1939c, 1941, 1945, 1948), the latter also producing a lexicon of Soqotri (Leslau 1938).

In addition to revitalizing the study of modern Semitic languages, Cohen was also at the forefront in a second area of research that began to flourish at that time: following by a decade an important work by Franz Graf Calice comparing Egyptian and Semitic vocabulary (Calice 1936), Cohen published his groundbreaking comparative essay on the vocabulary and phonology of Afro-Asiatic, or as it was then called, Hamito-Semitic (M. Cohen 1947). This was followed three years later by Otto Rössler's equally important study of Afro-Asiatic verbal morphology (Rössler 1950). Around the same time, H. J. Polotsky was beginning to bring out his revolutionary work on Coptic (Polotsky 1944). It seems fair to say that the works of these scholars in modern Semitic languages and in the larger Afro-Asiatic family not only broadened but actually revitalized the study of comparative Semitic linguistics. Moreover, their work was firmly grounded in contemporary linguistic theory, which slowly began to infiltrate more traditional Semitic language study as well.

There remained, however, scholars who shied away from comparative study, not least in the field of Assyriology. One prominent school of Assyriologists, led by Benno Landsberger, explicitly rejected the study of Akkadian within the framework of Semitic linguistics (Landsberger

---

[1]   We should note, however, that a few books on the Semitic languages in general did appear over the years, most of them, naturally, heavily dependent on Brockelmann. A few were innovative, such as Bergsträsser 1928 and Gray 1934, but most were fairly traditional in their presentation: O'Leary 1923; Dhorme 1930; Kramers 1949; Rinaldi 1954. More recent presentations are Garbini 1972, ²1984 and Garbini–Durand 1994.

1926); this school produced a number of excellent works, such as Erica Reiner's *Linguistic Analysis of Akkadian* (1966), Giorgio Buccellati's recent *Structural Grammar of Babylonian* (1996), and, of course, the *Chicago Assyrian Dictionary* (Oppenheim et al., ed., 1956–). Others, however, including Albrecht Goetze and I. J. Gelb, whose linguistic credentials were quite respectable, and more traditional philologists like Landsberger's student Wolfram von Soden, continued to refer to comparative Semitics in their work; so too have other prominent Assyriologists such as D. O. Edzard and Burkhardt Kienast (e.g., Goetze 1936, 1946a, 1946b, 1947a, 1947b, 1958; Gelb 1961, 1969; von Soden 1952 et seq., 1965–81; Edzard 1965, 1973; Kienast 1957, 1961a, 1961b, 1967).

Much of the scholarship of the first six decades of the 20th century was summarized in the 1964 work, *An Introduction to the Comparative Grammar of the Semitic Languages*, by four leading scholars, Sabatino Moscati, Anton Spitaler, Edward Ullendorff, and Wolfram von Soden, under the general editorship of Moscati. Designed as an introductory work, it is necessarily rather superficial, but this relatively short, easily digestible presentation has remained the most commonly-used introduction ever since its first publication.

It was noted above that the methodology of nineteenth-century comparative linguistics had worked remarkably well for what it was intended to do, namely, determine the features common to all of the members of a family and describe the structure of their common ancestor. The Saussurian revolution did not bring about tremendous changes in that methodology, but rather various refinements, most of which have also found their way, sooner or later, into comparative Semitic linguistics. Thus, for example, phonemic analysis and distinctive feature analysis have greatly facilitated the comparison of phonological systems among related languages. The very process of sound change, one of the two main engines of language change, has been studied in minute detail, both as more of the world's languages have been described and as the histories of well-studied languages have become better known. The subtle and irregular workings of analogy, the other basic force in language change, has continued to be analyzed in detail, perhaps most famously by Jerzy Kuryłowicz in his article on the nature of analogical processes (Kuryłowicz 1945–49); with a better understanding of analogical processes historical linguists are freed from the tyranny of exceptionless sound rules in their explanation of change in language, and many studies in Semitic linguistics could be cited in which analogy is invoked to account for a development or a seemingly irregular correspondence between languages. The fields of dialect geography, dialectology, and language contact, too, have added much-needed subtlety and explanatory power to the description of genetic relationships and language history; here, mention should be made especially of W. Randall Garr's *Dialect Geography of Syria-Palestine* (1985).

More narrowly within the purview of comparative linguistics, the criterion of shared innovations has been consistently identified as the pre-eminent factor in the determination of common linguistic ancestry, something that is unfortunately still not recognized by many Semitists.[2] This criterion was explored in detail and refined by Robert Hetzron in a fundamental essay, in which he also propounded another principle, that of archaic heterogeneity (Hetzron 1976).

But for the most part, Semitists, like Indo-Europeanists, continue to use the comparative method as worked out in large part already in the nineteenth century. We have not found it necessary to come up with radically new methodologies to continue the successful reconstruction of the family (Lieberman 1990: 573).

III. TWENTIETH-CENTURY THEMES AND ISSUES

We turn now to a review of some of the major themes and issues in comparative Semitic linguistics that have occupied scholars over the course of the 20th century. This must obviously be an incomplete list, and necessarily somewhat subjective, not only in the choice but also in the categorization of the issues.

One significant achievement of comparative Semitics in the last two decades has been a reanalysis of the phonetics of the Semitic consonant system. The catalyst for this was Richard Steiner's monograph arguing the case for lateral consonants in Proto-Semitic (Steiner 1977). Other work by Steiner and by Alice Faber and Rainer Voigt, *inter alia*, has resulted in a new understanding of the earliest Semitic consonant grid and its development in the descendant languages (e.g., Steiner 1982, 1987, 1991; Faber 1981, 1984, 1985, 1986, 1989, 1990; Voigt 1979, 1981, 1988–89, 1992, 1994a, 1994b). Among the more significant conclusions are the following: that the Proto-Semitic "emphatic" consonants were probably glottalic or ejective, as they still are in Ethiopian Semitic and the Modern South Arabian languages, rather than pharyngealized, as they are in Arabic; that Proto-Semitic had a triad of lateral consonants, voiced

---

[2]   It is disappointing that a number of scholars continue to use glottochronology and lexicostatistics as the basis of their internal classifications of Semitic. As noted by R. M. W. Dixon (1997: 35–37), the use of lexicostatistics to infer genetic relationships has been discredited for decades.

*l, voiceless * ɬ (a fricative-lateral, also transliterated as *ś, the Hebrew reflex of which is ś, and the Arabic š), and an emphatic * ɬ̣ (or *ṣ́, phonetically [ɬ']); that the triad of consonants that are usually thought of as dental or alveolar fricatives were more likely to have been affricates, i.e., voiceless *s, voiced *z, and emphatic *ṣ were actually [ᵗs], [ᵈz], and [ᵗs'], respectively; and that the most common of the Semitic sibilants, corresponding to Hebrew, Aramaic, and (Babylonian) Akkadian š, and to Arabic and Ethiopic s, should probably be reconstructed to Proto-Semitic as [s] rather than as [š].

Another topic that Semitists have worked on with profit in the 20th century is the morphological structure of the languages. Among the many studies are those by Karel Petráček in the early 1960's, Igor Diakonoff in the 1970's, and John McCarthy (on non-concatenative morphology) in the 1980's, as well as Gideon Goldenberg's insightful recent paper entitled "Principles of Semitic Word-Structure" (Petráček 1960–64; Diakonoff 1970, 1975; McCarthy 1979, 1981, 1984, 1986; McCarthy and Prince 1990; Goldenberg 1994). Mention was made above of a forthcoming monograph by Joshua Fox, *Semitic Noun Patterns*; while its coverage is not as detailed as that in Barth's *Nominalbildung* of a century ago (Barth 1889, ²1894), Fox's study supersedes the latter in methodology and results. Proceeding on the basis of a standard subgrouping of the Semitic languages, Fox examines both nouns that are associated with verbal roots and what he terms "isolated nouns," that is, nouns that are not primarily associated with a verbal root (see Fox 1998). One of his most significant conclusions is that while individual isolated nouns can be reconstructed back to intermediate proto-languages, and often to Proto-Semitic, nominal forms associated with verbal roots usually cannot be reconstructed back very far. For such forms, only the patterns, not individual words, are reconstructible above one or two nodes of subgrouping. This means that we must reckon with speakers' constant reanalysis and reformation of deverbal nouns on the basis of perceived patterns of morphological and semantic interrelationship.

The history of the Semitic verbal system seemed opaque to many scholars at the beginning of the 20th century, and as late as 1982 there appeared a book titled *The Enigma of the Hebrew Verbal System* (McFall 1982). But here, in my opinion, is another area in which Semitists can claim to have solved many, if not all, of the outstanding problems. It is now generally accepted (see, e.g., Polotsky 1964: 110) that the Proto-Semitic system is to be reconstructed to resemble that found in Akkadian, that is, with one form, *yaqtul*, marked for perfective aspect and another, *yaqattal*, either imperfective or simply unmarked. (Whether the aspectual — in addition to the derivational — use of the Akkadian *t*-form "Perfect," *iptaras*, is an Akkadian innovation or an inheritance of a Proto-Semitic feature is a question that requires further study; see most recently Voigt 1987a.) In addition there is a verbal adjective which could be inflected for person in a verbless clause, as in **s¹alim-nŭ* 'we are well'. The latter became a finite, perfective, active verb, *qatala*, after Akkadian had hived off the common trunk; the details of that process have yet to be explained satisfactorily, in my view. Active *qatala* replaced the earlier *yaqtul*, which was then relegated to secondary uses, in a nice illustration of Kuryłowicz's fourth law of analogy (Kuryłowicz 1945–49: 30–31), and is still found in such secondary uses in all of the classical languages. In Central Semitic, the early *yaqattal* form was replaced by *yaqtulu*, a form that seems to have been marked originally as a non-main clause verb (see Hamori 1973).

The derived stems have also been the subject of many studies over the past century, and again we can, I think, report progress. It now seems fairly clear that we need to reconstruct only a single causative form for the proto-language, marked with a sibilant that was probably related originally to the third person pronoun (e.g., Rundgren 1955; differently, however, Retsö 1987). In West Semitic, except for a few outliers in south Arabia, the sibilant became *h* in a simple and typologically common sound change (Bravmann 1969; Voigt 1987b). While the causative *s*-stem is found throughout Afro-Asiatic, the stem with doubled middle radical seems to be a Proto-Semitic innovation. There have been numerous attempts to account for the polysemy of the D-stem, but although the proposal made by Goetze in 1942 held sway for many years, neither it nor others offered a satisfactory explanation (see Kaufman 1996: 280–82). The recent monograph by Kouwenberg on gemination in Akkadian (1997), however, is a major step forward. Employing recent linguistic discussions of transitivity and of iconicity, he offers a persuasive explanation for the transitivizing and pluralic signification of the stem. Along the way, he presents a compelling elucidation of the origin of the Akkadian *tan* forms, rightly arguing that the *n* of the imperfective forms (such as Gtn *iptanarras*) emerged through metanalysis, historically morphological doubling being reinterpreted by speakers as the result of assimilation. Important work has also been done on the *t*-stems and on the *n*-stem (see, e.g., Diem 1982; Voigt 1987a; Lieberman 1986).

The study of the Proto-Semitic lexicon and the society and culture reflected in that lexicon has been significantly advanced, most notably by Pelio Fronzaroli (1964–71, 1974, 1975; see also Fronzaroli ed. 1973) and I. M. Diakonoff 1981, 1998.

There have also been substantial gains in the study of the larger genetic unit to which Semitic belongs, Afro-Asiatic. (See the paper by R. Voigt in the present volume.) The gains have been both in the description of many more languages and in the understanding of the several subfamilies. These have had at least some impact on comparative Semitic studies, although not as much as might have been expected (but see, for example, the studies of Brugnatelli, Castellino, Diakonoff, Dolgopolsky, Greenberg, Hetzron, Pennacchietti, Petráček, Rössler, Sasse, Voigt, and Zaborski). It may be hoped that comparative Afro-Asiatic linguistics will play a larger role in Semitics in the future.

But the most important gains in Semitic linguistics over the course of the 20th century have been in the raw data with which comparativists work, namely, the languages themselves. The twentieth century has seen the discovery of two ancient languages, Ugaritic and Eblaite. It has also seen the description of many modern languages. The modern South Arabian languages were first described in detail at the beginning of the 20th century following the recording of texts by an Austrian expedition to the area. But the transcriptions of these were pre-phonemic and difficult for subsequent linguists to use with confidence. Wolf Leslau was virtually alone in writing about these important languages until T. M. Johnstone began recording and describing new data in the late 1960's and the 1970's, followed by Simeone-Senelle and Lonnet in the 1980's and 1990's, so that we are now in a much better position to integrate them into our comparative analysis of the Semitic family (see the paper of Simeone-Senelle in the present volume). In addition to the MSA languages, a large number of Ethiopian Semitic languages have been expertly investigated and described, especially by Marcel Cohen in the 1930's and by Leslau since the 1940's. Many modern Aramaic languages have also received modern treatments in the last few decades, as have the Arabic colloquial dialects. And, of course, there is the whole phenomenon of Modern Hebrew. (See the papers on modern Semitic languages in the present volume.) Clearly we have come a long way from Renan's curious claim that "Il n'y a pas de langues néo-sémitiques" (Renan 1863 [1855]: 429).[3]

These discoveries and descriptions are the primary grist for the comparativist's mill, including those of the modern languages and dialects. The modern South Arabian languages are the only representatives of an entire sub-branch (on the importance of which see Porkhomovsky 1997 as well as the papers of Appleyard and Simeone-Senelle in the present volume). The modern South Ethiopic languages such as Amharic represent a separate branch of Ethiopian Semitic that is not attested in

---

[3] Renan's claim followed directly from his belief that the Semitic languages were essentially immutable; see Olender 1992 [1989]: 54.

an ancient form. As for the other modern varieties of Semitic, although it is a truism in comparative linguistics that the earliest attested form of a language is more important for reconstruction than its modern descendants, nevertheless it is also well known that modern languages often preserve archaic features; further, they are invaluable for illustrating the typology of linguistic change within a family (see, e.g., Blau 1969, 1985). I have, for example, found studies of Amharic phonology and root structure to be very illuminating in my work on Akkadian, which like Amharic lost its guttural consonants, prompting significant rearrangement of the root patterns (see especially the fine monograph of Podolsky 1991).

IV. CLASSIFICATION AND RECONSTRUCTION

The rediscovery of a hitherto-unknown language, or a new description of a previously-little studied one, inevitably prompts a reappraisal of the classification of the family to which it belongs, and that is naturally true of Semitic comparative study as well. The classification system now espoused by many Semitists, inspired by the work of Robert Hetzron (e.g., 1972, 1974, 1976), places Arabic as a member of Central Semitic, the most innovating of the subgroups of Semitic, and this in turn has contributed to the slow drift away from the nearly-universal tendency a century ago to consider Arabic as all but equivalent to Proto-Semitic.[4] In Hetzron's classification, the family first divides into East versus West Semitic, East Semitic comprising only Akkadian and Eblaite; West Semitic in turn consists of the Ethiopian branch, the Modern South Arabian branch (the last two usually being subsumed under the label South Semitic), and the Central branch, which includes both Arabic and the Northwest Semitic languages. The main isogloss that characterizes Central Semitic is the innovative imperfective *yaqtulu*, which replaces the earlier *yaqattal*.

Hetzron's classification has taken some hits over the years, but the basic framework still stands. The main innovative feature by which he grouped Arabic and Canaanite together over against Aramaic, for example, has been shown to have been present in the earliest Aramaic as well (Huehnergard 1987a). Voigt (1987c) suggested that the Old South Arabian languages should be classified within Central Semitic. The

---

[4]   Note, for example, the statement of Nöldeke 1911 [1887]: 619a: "A comparative grammar of the Semitic languages must of course be based upon Arabic." It should be noted, however, that Zimmern's 1898 comparative grammar, which was mentioned at the beginning of this paper, represented an early effort to counteract the reigning Arabo-centric bias in comparative Semitic studies, by giving more weight to Akkadian; Zimmern was, after all, an Assyriologist.

evidence he offered was slim, but his suggestion was recently confirmed when a leading scholar of Old South Arabian, Norbert Nebes, showed that most of those languages do not have the old *yaqattal* form (Nebes 1994). This fact casts serious doubt on the usual assumption that among those languages was the ancestor of both the modern South Arabian languages and Ethiopian Semitic (see Porkhomovsky 1997: 222). I have suggested elsewhere, however (Huehnergard 1992: 158b), that the key may well lie with the one Old South Arabian language that Nebes was not able to consider, because of lack of evidence, namely, Hadramitic. It is Hadramitic inscriptions that are found in the area where the modern South Arabian languages are spoken. More important are a few linguistic features that Hadramitic shares with the modern languages, such as the preposition *h* and, more significantly, the third person pronouns, which in Hadramitic show s^1 (*s*, the cognate of Hebrew *šin*) in the masculine and s^3 (*ś*, the cognate of Hebrew *samek*) in the feminine, and which must be reconstructed identically in Proto-MSA.

In another challenge to Hetzron's classification, Robert Ratcliffe, in a lengthy recent article (Ratcliffe 1998a), has mustered an impressive amount of evidence to argue that the patterns and distribution of the broken plurals found in (North) Arabic, South Arabian, and (North) Ethiopic must reflect a common ancestor. It is possible, however, to propose a set of developments that takes Ratcliffe's arguments into account and yet preserves the existence of Central Semitic, which is, as was noted above, so well established on the basis of other isoglosses; these developments may be outlined as follows: (1) Common Semitic inherited from Common Afro-Asiatic a small number of broken plural formations, including, for example, *a*-insertion (Greenberg 1955); (2) East Semitic (Akkadian and Eblaite) lost these formations and the use of broken plurals in general, with a few exceptions (for which see Huehnergard 1987b); (3) in West Semitic the system of broken plurals was expanded and their use extended along the lines suggested in Ratcliffe's study, and Proto-Central Semitic, including Arabic and Old South Arabian, would by definition have participated in this expansion; and, finally, (4) in Proto-Northwest Semitic the system was greatly reduced, as had happened earlier in East Semitic, although in Northwest Semitic, *a*-insertion to mark the plural of nouns of the pattern *qVtl* was preserved (along with the addition of an external ending).[5] Thus, the non-use of the broken plurals (for the most part) in East Semitic and in Northwest Semitic should perhaps be seen as the result

---

[5] One wonders whether vestigial broken plurals are reflected in the **ʔaqtal* pattern of some of the early Northwest(?) Semitic names of cities along the eastern Mediterranean coast, such as **ʔak θapu* (Achshaph) and **ʔaθqalānu* (Ashkelon), attested already in early-second millennium Egyptian execration texts.

of two parallel, but independent, losses of a system that was inherited from Common Semitic. (Another independent loss of the system also occurred in South Ethiopic.)

Classification and subgrouping of language families are among the most important of the comparativist's tasks, and this obtains in our field, too; yet there has been a consistent denigration of this type of work among Semitists, as in the following statement: "Classification is harmless, unobjectionable, and at times even useful if limited to describing present-day habitat and the prevailing geographical circumstances, but it becomes positively dangerous, i. e. obscuring rather than illuminating, if meant to explain genetic connexions" (Ullendorff 1961:30; see also idem 1970: 264). Such a negative assessment of classification is without parallel in comparative work in other language families, and should, I believe, be rejected. The main goal of comparative linguistics is to explain the genetic relationships and histories of related languages. Linguistic history is no less real than archaeological history or the history revealed in texts; like archaeology, in fact, it provides evidence for the *pre*-history of peoples (see Avanzini 1991: 108). Indeed, classification and subgrouping should inform comparative work and historical reconstruction, for these activities are inextricably intertwined. We should not, to cite a simple example, compare the Aramaic feminine plural ending -*ān* with the Ethiopic masculine plural ending -*ān* unless we can show either that the two languages inherited the ending from common Semitic or that they inherited it from a common intermediate ancestor and thus are part of a common subgroup. In other words, classification is not simply a mind game. It makes claims about cultural history. Therefore it is important whether, for example, Ugaritic is part of the Canaanite subgroup, and whether Eblaite is closely related to Akkadian or part of the western branch of the family. As a number of recent publications have shown, whether the Old South Arabian languages can still be considered to have shared an immediate common ancestor with Ethiopian Semitic and the modern South Arabian tongues (see above) is a crucial factor in shaping our understanding of early South Arabian and Ethiopian cultural history in the larger sense (see, e.g., Rodgers 1991; Avanzini 1991; Appleyard 1996).

This leads me to another point, or rather, to a set of interrelated desiderata. One of the things that is strikingly absent from most monographic treatments of comparative Semitic, and from many *Einzeluntersuchungen* as well, is an effort at reconstruction (see Goshen-Gottstein 1991: 564). There is little Proto-Semitic in Brockelmann's *Grundriss* (1908–13) or in Moscati's *Introduction* (1964). Nor is there much reconstruction of the proto-language in Lipiński's new volume

(1997), which despite its subtitle, *Outline of a Comparative Grammar*, strikes one as neither an outline nor comparative; indeed, one is reminded of a comment made by Gene Schramm concerning Brockelmann's *Grundriss*: "a vast compilation of virtually all the data available ... with practically no comparative reconstruction at all" (Schramm 1970: 260; see also Goshen-Gottstein 1991: 566).

One of the most noticeable differences between the recent book on the Semitic languages edited by Hetzron and its equally recent counterparts in the same series on Indo-European, Romance, Germanic, and Celtic, is the lack of a chapter on the proto-language, like the superb fifty-page chapter by Calvert Watkins, "Proto-Indo-European: Comparison and Reconstruction," in the Indo-European volume (Giacalone Ramat and Ramat, ed., 1998), where, I might add, there are two other introductory chapters on Common Indo-European: "The Indo-Europeans: Origins and Culture" by Enrico Campanile, and "The Indo-European Linguistic Family: Genetic and Typological Perspectives" by Bernard Comrie. It is not clear to me why Semitists do not engage in reconstruction more readily, why we do not present descriptions of our conceptions of Proto-Semitic. If nothing else, such descriptions at least summarize our assumptions, views, and starting points. Gotthelf Bergsträsser did this in clear and insightful fashion in the first chapter of his *Introduction to the Semitic Languages*, one of many reasons why that book is still worth reading (Bergsträsser 1928). I. J. Gelb in the preface of his *Sequential Reconstruction of Proto-Akkadian* said that he "could have used the term 'Proto-Semitic' in the title" (Gelb 1969: xi); Jerzy Kuryłowicz in his brilliant — if sometimes obscure — monograph on apophony and related issues (1961, [2]1973),[6] essentially proceeded from a tacit reconstruction of common Semitic, as did Hetzron in his volume on *Ethiopian Semitic* (1972). I recently offered a very brief, schematic description of my conception of the proto-language in an encyclopedia article (Huehnergard 1995). But there are not many other such descriptions (apart from the relatively straightforward presentations of the common Semitic inventory of consonants), and nothing like Watkins's essay on Indo-European cited above. More endeavors of this type would be helpful, both for clarifying where we stand and for use as jumping-off points for further discussion. (Monograph-length and abridged essays along these lines will be offered in Huehnergard forthc. a, forthc. b.)

In order to reconstruct a proto-language, it is essential to start lower down on the family tree, with adequate reconstructions of the various

---

[6]   Note the comment of G. Schramm (1970: 260) on the first edition of this work: "the only monograph dealing with comparative Semitic studies that can be termed a truly great contribution was produced not by a Semitist at all, but by an Indo-Europeanist."

genetic subgroups that constitute the family as a whole. Here we return to the issue of classification and subgrouping. Classification should be the first factor in our reconstruction of Proto-Semitic and thus of early Semitic linguistic history. Indo-Europeanists may occasionally compare a feature of, say, Bulgarian with a feature of German, but this is usually shorthand for the more common practice of comparing features of a reconstructed common Slavic and a reconstructed common Germanic. Likewise Semitists should be working toward, for example, reconstructions of Proto-Canaanite and Proto-Aramaic, and only then toward Proto-Northwest Semitic (see, e.g., Blau 1968, 1978), and then toward Proto-Central Semitic, and next Proto-West Semitic; and it is only a reconstructed Proto-West Semitic that can legitimately be compared with Akkadian, or, more precisely, with a reconstructed Proto-Akkadian or, if Eblaite is to be considered a separate language (as I believe), a reconstructed Proto-East Semitic. This is important: for purposes of reconstruction, features of Akkadian and Eblaite, which are the sole members of East Semitic, are in a real sense equal in weight to the cognate features found in all the other languages, all of which constitute merely one coordinate West Semitic branch on the same node as East Semitic. A well-known and generally accepted example of this principle is the function of the suffix-conjugation: a conjugated adjective in Akkadian but an active, perfective verb everywhere else, and yet most Semitists now agree that it is the Akkadian that preserves the more original function (see above, under III). But the examples could be multiplied. A trivial phonological example is root meaning 'heavy', which appears as *kbt* in Akkadian but as *kbd* everywhere else; which of these is the original must be decided, if it can be decided, not by the number of languages on either side of the ledger but rather by considerations of the typology of sound change and of the tendencies and constraints in the formation of Semitic roots. Less trivial is the Proto-Semitic status of features such as dative pronouns, the *t*-form "perfect" tense, the *-u* ending of *yaqtulu*, word order, and many others.

The usual complaint of those who see little value in classification is that the choice of isoglosses on which subgroupings are based is subjective or even arbitrary. But there are ways to check such tendencies. Theories should, in theory, be testable, and I would suggest that a few "thought experiments" can and should be devised to test our proposed classifications. As with many theoretical frameworks in the physical sciences, especially in fields such as particle physics and cosmology, it may be impossible ever to prove conclusively that a proposal is true, but it should be possible to prove that it is not true; it should be falsifiable. Now, subgroupings make implicit claims about what we should find in a given group, and these can be investigated. An example is Fox's study of noun patterns, which was mentioned earlier (Fox forthc.). Nothing in Fox's investigation ran counter to the standard Hetzronian classification; this is not a proof, but the classification was also heuristically useful. The latter point is significant: besides being falsifiable, a good theory should also explain more data than its competitors. As another example we might consider certain types of weak verbs. Geminate verbs, for instance, are essentially regular in Akkadian and in classical Ethiopic, but they exhibit a consistent set of paradigmatic divergences from the sound verb in Arabic, Aramaic, Hebrew, and Ugaritic that is most economically explained as due to shared ancestry, namely, a common Central Semitic forebear. (Geminate verbs in Sabaean also pattern in this way, a further indication that Sabaean is to be grouped with Central Semitic.) The paradigms of the so-called hollow verbs, verbs with medial *w* or *y*, in Arabic, Aramaic, and Hebrew are also most easily accounted for by assuming a common ancestor in which the paradigm was essentially that found in Arabic, as in **qāma* ~ **qumtŭ*. Hebrew and Aramaic then exhibit a shared innovation that supports the traditional subgrouping of those languages in a Northwest Semitic branch, namely, the leveling of the vowel quality of the third person forms, to **qāma* ~ **qamtŭ*. When Canaanite and Aramaic split off from common Northwest Semitic, each then underwent a second leveling of these forms, a leveling of vowel length throughout the paradigm, long vowels in Aramaic **qāma* ~ **qāmtŭ* and short vowels in Canaanite **qama* ~ **qamtĭ*. Again, such reconstructions do not prove that a particular subgrouping is correct, but they can suggest that a given subgrouping explains the evidence of the languages more economically and more fully than a competing subgrouping does.

V. DESIDERATA

The comparativist needs good research tools — reliable grammars, dictionaries, and text editions of the relevant languages — and over the last few decades the comparative Semitist's toolbox has become richly stocked with excellent materials for many of the languages, both ancient and modern. It is still fairly easy to come up with a long wish list, however. Among the most pressing needs, I would single out the following: full descriptions of the modern South Arabian languages, and, after that, a comparative grammar of the group; a lexicon of the remaining Old South Arabian language that still lacks one, Hadramitic; a comprehensive Aramaic lexicon, and a comparative Aramaic grammar; a complete etymological dictionary of classical Arabic; a new grammar of Old Akkadian; and, of course, a complete etymological dictionary of Semitic (so also Hospers 1966: 151). I mention a new grammar of Old Akkadian as a desideratum for the comparativist because, compared with Old Babylonian (the form of Akkadian usually cited in comparative studies), Old Akkadian is less influenced by Sumerian (as is Old Assyrian, for that matter).

Beyond such basic research tools there are other desiderata. A historical grammar of Akkadian would be very helpful, as would new historical grammars of classical Hebrew and classical Ethiopic. Historical and comparative studies of aspects of Semitic syntax continue to be few and far between (so also Hospers 1966: 151), though in addition to Khan (1988; see also 1984) we may note several very insightful papers by Meïr Bravmann (see the collection of articles in Bravmann 1977), Gideon Goldenberg (1971, 1977, 1978, 1987, 1989, 1995), and Amikam Gai (1983, 1984, 1995), as well as two recent, superbly instructive studies by Orin Gensler (1997, 1998), one on preposition-hopping, the other on verbs with two object suffixes. Historical and comparative syntax is admittedly a slippery undertaking,[7] but there is little doubt that much more good work could be done in this area.

Semitic linguistics would also profit, as indicated above, from more work involving reconstruction, at the level of intermediate nodes, such as Proto-Central Semitic, or Proto-Ethiopian Semitic, as well as at the Proto-Semitic level. Such work can be extremely profitable; if carried out beyond the simple level of the phonology, it often throws up unexpected and revealing stumbling blocks.[8]

At several points in this paper reference has been made to comparative Indo-European studies; I am certain that there is still much that we can learn from that field, if only because there are so many more workers in it, and they have been at it longer. But as a number of Semitists have pointed out over the years, Indo-European is much bigger and more diverse than Semitic. Indeed Afro-Asiatic is more analogous to Indo-European, while Semitic, in certain important ways, is more like some of the subbranches of the latter, such as Germanic, Romance, and Slavic (so already, e.g., Nöldeke 1890 [1887]: 641 = 1887 [German]: 2). In

---

[7] Although this was not, interestingly, the opinion of Nöldeke (1911 [1887]: 619a): "It would probably be easier to give a comparative presentment of Semitic syntax than of Semitic phonetics and the theory of Semitic forms."

[8] I have, moreover, found it to be a useful way to teach historical linguistics; in my course on the historical grammar of classical Hebrew, I regularly have the students take forms, and eventually entire biblical verses, back to the Proto-Northwest Semitic level, both to illustrate the methodology involved and to discover what problems appear.

such relatively tightknit genetic units, which cover a smaller geographical region and in which there has been constant contact among the descendant languages, mutual linguistic influence and borrowing over the centuries may be commonplace (see Thomason and Kaufman 1988; Nichols 1992). We could, I suspect, learn a great deal from the research that has been done and continues to be done in comparative Romance or comparative Germanic studies (e.g., Posner 1996). Of course, we need not confine ourselves in this respect to Indo-European subfamilies; similar situations and issues of comparative study and historical reconstruction present themselves in most relatively small genetic units, such as subgroups of Algonkian or Bantu, or many others. We could, in other words, profit from paying more attention to current theoretical issues in comparative and historical linguistics. Even within Semitic, obviously, we can learn by studying the interactions among the modern Ethiopian languages, the modern colloquial Arabic speech forms, and the interplay between Arabic and the Modern South Arabian languages.

VI. THE CONTRIBUTION OF COMPARATIVE SEMITIC LINGUISTICS

The impact of comparative Semitics on general and theoretical comparative linguistics has thus far been modest at best. A few contributions and potential contributions can be noted, however.

An important contribution to general comparative linguistics was made by Robert Hetzron in the influential article mentioned earlier, titled "Two Principles of Genetic Classification" (Hetzron 1976).

Another contribution of Semitics has been in the discussion of diglossia, the situation in which a language has a formal or prestige variety spoken by an elite, that differs significantly from other, colloquial varieties. The phenomenon of diglossia was brought to prominence by Charles Ferguson, who used Arabic as his case study, and diglossic situations in many languages are now commonly studied by sociolinguists (Ferguson 1959). The significance of diglossic situations for historical and comparative linguistics lies in part in that forms of the prestige variety often penetrate the colloquial, in a type of dialect mixing that naturally plays havoc with otherwise straightforward linguistic development. Diglossia in Biblical Hebrew has recently been investigated, especially by Gary Rendsburg in a 1990 monograph. It is entirely likely that much of post-Achaemenid Aramaic reflects the influence of the Imperial dialect. And the use of archaic and archaizing forms in post-Old Babylonian Akkadian texts might also be considered a type of diglossia, the study of which would be intriguing.

Joshua Blau has pointed out the significance of parallel development among the languages in a family (e.g., Blau 1977, 1980, 1985).

In the realm of comparative phonology, the likelihood that Proto-Semitic is to be reconstructed with glottalic rather than pharyngealized emphatics has actually had some impact on Indo-European studies; at least, it has contributed to the debate over whether common Indo-European, too, had glottalic phonemes.

A potential contribution of comparative Semitics to general linguistics may lie in the long recorded history of some of the Semitic languages, two and a half millennia for Akkadian, nearly three millennia for Aramaic, for example. Indo-European of course also boasts a few languages with similar time depths, such as Indic, Iranian, and Greek; Chinese has been recorded for even longer than Aramaic; and Egyptian holds the recorded record, at roughly four millennia. Thus, Semitic is not the only family with a long history; but it is one of the few, and it might well be used to investigate the types of changes that languages may undergo over very long periods, as Leo Depuydt (1997) has recently done with Egyptian.

BIBLIOGRAPHY

Appleyard, David L. 1996. Ethiopian Semitic and South Arabian: Towards a Re-examination of a Relationship. In S. Izre'el and S. Raz, ed. *Israel Oriental Studies* 16 (*Studies in Modern Semitic Languages*): 203–28.

Arnold, W. 1993. Zur Position des Hóbyót in den neusüdarabischen Sprachen. *ZAL* 25: 17–24.

Avanzini, Alessandra. 1991. Linguistic Data and Historical Reconstruction: Between Semitic and Epigraphic South Arabian. In Kaye 1991. 107–18.

Barth, Jacob. 1889. *Die Nominalbildung in den semitischen Sprachen.* Leipzig. [2]1894. Reprint Hildesheim.

Baumstark, A., Carl Brockelmann, et al. 1953–54. *Semitistik.* Handbuch der Orientalistik, 1, part 3. Leiden / Köln.

Bennett, Patrick R. 1998. *Comparative Semitic Linguistics: A Manual.* Winona Lake, Indiana.

Bergsträsser, Gotthelf. 1928. *Einführung in die semitischen Sprachen: Sprachproben und grammatische Skizzen.* München. Reprint Ismaning 1989. Translated, with Notes and Bibliography and an Appendix on the Scripts, by Peter T. Daniels, as *Introduction to the Semitic Languages. Text Specimens and Grammatical Sketches.* Winona Lake, Indiana, 1983.

Blake, Frank R. 1917–53. Studies in Semitic Grammar. I. *JAOS* 35 (1917): 375–85; II. *JAOS* 62 (1942): 109–18; III. *JAOS* 65 (1945): 111–16; IV. *JAOS* 66 (1946): 212–18; V. *JAOS* 73 (1953): 7–16.

Blake, Frank R. 1920. Congeneric Assimilation as a Cause of the Development of New Roots in Semitic. In *Studies in Honor of Maurice Bloomfield by a Group of His Students*. New Haven, 35–48.

Blau, Joshua. 1968. Some Difficulties in the Reconstruction of «Proto-Hebrew» and «Proto-Canaanite». In Matthew Black and Georg Fohrer, ed., *In Memoriam Paul Kahle*. Berlin, 29–43.

Blau, Joshua. 1969. Some Problems of the Formation of the Old Semitic Languages in the Light of Arabic Dialects. In *Proceedings of the International Conference on Semitic Studies, held in Jerusalem, 19–23 July 1969*. Jerusalem, 38–44.

Blau, Joshua. 1977. *An Adverbial Construction in Hebrew and Arabic: Sentence Adverbials in Frontal Position Separated from the Rest of the Sentence*. Jerusalem.

Blau, Joshua. 1978. Hebrew and North West Semitic: Reflections on the Classification of the Semitic Languages. *HAR* 2: 21–44.

Blau, Joshua. 1980. The Parallel Development of the Feminine Ending *–at* in Semitic Languages. *HUCA* 51: 17–28.

Blau, Joshua. 1985. On some Arabic Dialectal Features Paralleled by Hebrew and Aramaic. *JQR* 76: 5–12.

Bravmann, Meïr M. 1969. The Semitic Causative-Prefix *š/sa*. *Le Muséon* 82: 517–22. Reprinted in Bravmann 1977: 200–5.

Bravmann, Meïr M. 1977. *Studies in Semitic Philology*. Leiden.

Brockelmann, Carl. 1906. *Semitische Sprachwissenschaft*. ²1916. Berlin / Leipzig.

Brockelmann, Carl. 1908–13. *Grundriss der vergleichenden Grammatik der semitischen Sprachen*. 2 vol. Berlin.

Brockelmann, Carl. 1908. *Kurzgefasste vergleichende Grammatik der semitischen Sprachen. Elemente der Laut- und Formenlehre*. Berlin. Translated by W. Marçais and M. Cohen as *Précis de linguistique sémitique*. Paris 1910.

Brugnatelli, Vermondo. 1982. *Questioni di morfologia e sintassi dei numeri cardinali semitici*. (Pubblicazioni della Facoltà di Lettere e Filosofia dell'Università di Milano, 93, Sezione a Cura dell'Istituto di Glottologia, 7.) Firenze.

Buccellati, Giorgio. 1996. *A Structural Grammar of Babylonian*. Wiesbaden.

Calice, Franz Graf. 1936. *Grundlagen der ägyptisch-semitischen Wortvergleichung*. (WZKM Beiheft, 1.) Vienna.

Cantineau, J. 1932. Accadien et sudarabique. *BSL* 33: 175–204.

Cantineau, J. 1937. Une alternance quantitative dans des pronoms suffixes sémitiques. *BSL* 38: 148–64.

Cantineau, J. 1949. La voyelle de secours *i* dans les langues sémitiques. *Semitica* 2: 50–67.

Cantineau, J. 1950a. À propos des sons *g, k, q* dans les langues sémitiques. *BSL* 46: v–xxvii.

Cantineau, J. 1950b. La notion de «schème» et son altération dans diverses langues sémitiques. *Semitica* 3: 73–83.

Cantineau, J. 1951–52. Le consonantisme du sémitique. *Semitica* 4: 79–94.

Castellino, G. R. 1962. *The Akkadian Personal Pronouns and Verbal System in the Light of Semitic and Hamitic.* Leiden.

Castellino, G. R. 1978. The Case System of Cushitic in Relation to Semitic. In Pelio Fronzaroli, ed. *Atti del secondo congresso internazionale di linguistica camito-semitica, Firenze, 16–19 aprile 1974.* Florence, 31–42.

Christian, V. 1919–20. Akkader und Südaraber als ältere Semitenschichte. *Anthropos* 14–15: 729–39.

Christian, V. 1924. Die deiktischen Elemente in den semitischen Sprachen nach Herkunft, Anwendung und Verwandtschaft untersucht. *WZKM* 31: 137–92.

Christian, V. 1926. Zur inneren Passivbildung im Semitischen. *WZKM* 34: 263–70.

Christian, V. 1927. Das Wesen der semitischen Tempora. *ZDMG* 81: 232–58.

Christian, V. 1944. Die Stellung des Mehri innerhalb der semitischen Sprachen. *Sitzungsberichte der Kaiserlichen Akademie der Wissenschaften*, Phil.-hist. Kl. I, 222/3.

Cohen, David. 1984. *La phrase nominale et l'évolution du système verbal en sémitique.* Paris/Leuven.

Cohen, David. 1989. *L'aspect verbal.* Paris.

Cohen, Marcel. 1924. *Le système verbal sémitique et l'expression du temps.* Publications de l'École des Langues Orientales Vivantes, 5/11. Paris.

Cohen, Marcel. 1929. Verbes déponents internes (ou verbes adhérents) en sémitique. *Mémoires de la Société de Linguistique de Paris* 23: 225–48.

Cohen, Marcel. 1931. *Études d'éthiopien méridional.* (Collection d'ouvrages orientaux.) Paris.

Cohen, Marcel. 1936. *Traité de langue amharique (Abyssinie).* 2nd ed. (Travaux et mémoires de l'Institut d'Ethnologie, 24.) Paris.

Cohen, Marcel. 1939. *Nouvelles études d'éthiopien méridional.* (Bibliothèque de l'École des Hautes Études, Sciences historiques et philologiques, 275.) Paris.

Cohen, Marcel. 1947. *Essai comparatif sur le vocabulaire et la phonétique du chamito-sémitique.* (Bibliothèque de l'École des Hautes Études, Sciences historiques et philologiques, 291.) Paris.

Depuydt, Leo. 1997. Four Thousand Years of Evolution: On a Law of Historical Change in Ancient Egyptian. *JNES* 56: 21–35.

Dhorme, Edouard. 1930. *Langues et écritures sémitiques.* Paris.

Diakonoff, I. M. 1965. *Semito-Hamitic Languages: An Essay in Classification.* Moscow.

Diakonoff, I. M. 1970. Problems of Root Structure in Proto-Semitic. *ArOr* 38: 453–80.

Diakonoff, I. M. 1975. On Root Structure in Proto-Semitic. In James and Theodora Bynon, ed. *Hamito-Semitica.* The Hague / Paris, 133–53.

Diakonoff, I. M. 1981. Earliest Semites in Asia: Agriculture and Animal Husbandry According to Linguistic Data (VIIIth–IVth Millennia B.C.). *Altorientalische Forschungen* 8: 23–74.

Diakonoff, I. M. 1988. *Afrasian Languages.* Moscow.

Diakonoff, I. M. 1998. The Earliest Semitic Society: Linguistic Data. *JSS* 43: 209–19.

Diem, Werner. 1982. Die Entwicklung des Derivationsmorphems der *t*-Stämme im Semitischen. *ZDMG* 132: 29–84.

Dixon, R. M. W. 1997. *The Rise and Fall of Languages.* Cambridge.

Dolgopolsky, Aharon B. 1983. Semitic and East Cushitic: Sound Correspondences and Cognate Sets. In S. Segert and A.J.E. Bodrogligeti, eds. *Ethiopian Studies Dedicated to Wolf Leslau on the Occasion of His Seventy-fifth Birthday.* Wiesbaden, 123–42.

Dolgopolsky, Aharon B. 1984. Semitic and East Cushitic: Word-initial Laryngeals. In Taddese Beyene, ed. *Proceedings of the Eighth International Conference of Ethiopian Studies, University of Addis Ababa, 1984.* Addis Ababa, 1.629–37.

Dolgopolsky, Aharon B. 1987. South Cushitic Lateral Consonants as Compared to Semitic and East Cushitic. In H. Jungraithmayr and W. W. Müller, ed. *Proceedings of the Fourth International Hamito-Semitic Congress, Marburg, 20–22 September, 1983.* (Current Issues in Linguistic Theory, 44.) Amsterdam / Philadelphia, 195–214.

Dolgopolsky, Aharon B. 1990. On Chadic Correspondences of Semitic *š. In H. G. Mukarovsky, ed. *Proceedings of the Fifth International Hamito-Semitic Congress 1987.* 2 vol. (Veröffentlichungen der

Institut für Afrikanistik und Ägyptologie der Universität Wien, 56–57. Beiträge zur Afrikanistik, 40–41.) Wien. Vol. 1, 213–25.

Edzard, D. O. 1965. Die Stämme des altbabylonischen Verbums in ihrem Oppositionssystem. In H. Güterbock and T. Jacobsen, ed. *Studies in Honor of Benno Landsberger on His Seventy-fifth Birthday April 21, 1965.* (Assyriological Studies, 16.) Chicago, 111–20.

Edzard, D. O. 1973. Die Modi beim älteren akkadischen Verbum. *Or.* 42 (I. J. Gelb Volume): 121–41.

Faber, Alice. 1981. Phonetic Reconstruction. *Glossa* 15: 233–62.

Faber, Alice. 1984. Semitic Sibilants in an Afro-Asiatic Context. *JSS* 29: 189–224.

Faber, Alice. 1985. Akkadian Evidence for Proto-Semitic Affricates. *JCS* 37: 101–7.

Faber, Alice. 1986. On the Actuation of a Sound Change: A Semitic Case Study. *Diachronica* 3: 163–84.

Faber, Alice. 1989. On the Nature of Proto-Semitic *l. JAOS* 109: 33–36.

Faber, Alice. 1990. Interpretation of Orthographic Forms. In Philip Baldi, ed. *Linguistic Change and Reconstruction Methodology.* (Trends in Linguistics, Studies and Monographs, 45.) Berlin / New York, 619–37.

Ferguson, Charles A. 1959. Diglossia. *Word* 15: 325–40.

Fleisch, Henri. 1947. *Introduction à l'étude des langues sémitiques: Éléments de bibliographie.* Paris.

Fox, Joshua. 1998. Isolated Nouns in the Semitic Languages. *ZAH* 11: 1–31.

Fox, Joshua. Forthc. *Semitic Noun Patterns.* (Harvard Semitic Studies.) Winona Lake, Indiana.

Fronzaroli, Pelio. 1964–71. Studi sul lessico commune semitico. *RANL* 19 (1964): 155–72 (I), 243–80 (II); 20 (1965): 135–50 (III), 246–69 (IV); 23 (1968): 267–303 (V); 24 (1969): 285–320 (VI); 26 (1971): 603–42 (VII).

Fronzaroli, Pelio, ed. 1973. *Studies on Semitic Lexicography.* (Quaderni di Semitistica, 2.) Florence.

Fronzaroli, Pelio. 1975. On the Common Semitic Lexicon and its Ecological and Cultural Background. In James and Theodora Bynon, ed. *Hamito-Semitica.* The Hague / Paris, 43–53.

Fronzaroli, Pelio. 1974. Réflexions sur la paléontologie linguistique. In A. Caquot and D. Cohen, ed. *Actes du premier Congrès international de linguistique sémitique et chamito-sémitique, Paris 16–19 juillet 1969.* The Hague / Paris, 173–80.

Gai, Amikam. 1983. Embedded Non-Sentence Nexuses in Semitic Languages. *ZDMG* 133: 18–23.

Gai, Amikam. 1984. Predicative State and Inflection of the Nominal Predicate in Akkadian and Syriac. *AAL* 9: 72.

Gai, Amikam. 1995. The Category "Adjective" in Semitic Languages. *JSS* 40: 1–9.

Garbini, G. 1972. *Le lingue semitiche. Studi di storia linguistica.* (Istituto Universitario Orientale, Dipartimento di Studi Asiatici, Series Minor, 24.) Naples. ²1984.

Garbini, G. and Olivier Durand. 1994. *Introduzione alle lingue semitiche.* Brescia.

Garr, W. Randall. 1985. *Dialect Geography of Syria-Palestine, 1000–586, B.C.E.* Philadelphia.

Gelb, I. J. 1961. *Old Akkadian Writing and Grammar.* 2nd ed. (Materials for the Assyrian Dictionary, 2.) Chicago.

Gelb, I. J. 1969. *Sequential Reconstruction of Proto-Akkadian.* (Assyriological Studies, 18.) Chicago.

Gensler, Orin D. 1997. Mari Akkadian Iš "to, for" and Preposition-Hopping in the Light of Comparative Semitic Syntax. *Or.* 66: 129–56.

Gensler, Orin D. 1998. Verbs with Two Object Suffixes: A Semitic Archaism in its Afroasiatic Context. *Diachronica* 15: 231–84.

Giacalone Ramat, Anna and Paolo Ramat, ed. 1998. *The Indo-European Languages.* London.

Goetze, Albrecht. 1936. The *t*-form of the Old Babylonian Verb. *JAOS* 56: 297–334.

Goetze, Albrecht. 1942. The So-called Intensive of the Semitic Languages. *JAOS* 62: 1–8.

Goetze, Albrecht. 1946a. Number Idioms in Old Babylonian. *JNES* 5: 185–202.

Goetze, Albrecht. 1946b. Sequence of Two Short Syllables in Akkadian. *Or.* 15: 233–38.

Goetze, Albrecht. 1947a. The Akkadian Dialects of the Old-Babylonian Mathematical Texts. In O. Neugebauer and A. Sachs. *Mathematical Cuneiform Texts.* (American Oriental Series, 29.) New Haven, 146–51.

Goetze, Albrecht. 1947b. The Akkadian Passive. *JCS* 1: 50–59.

Goetze, Albrecht. 1958. The Sibilants of Old Babylonian. *RA* 52: 137–49.

Goldenberg, Gideon. 1971. Tautological Infinitive. *IOS* 1: 36–85. Reprinted in Goldenberg 1998: 66–115.

Goldenberg, Gideon. 1977. Imperfectly-Transformed Cleft Sentences. *Proceedings of the Sixth World Congress of Jewish Studies.* Jerusalem, 1.117–33. Reprinted in Goldenberg 1998: 116–22.

Goldenberg, Gideon. 1978. Congruence and Comitative and a Problem of Linguistic Typology. In Pelio Fronzaroli, ed. *Atti del secondo congresso internazionale di linguistica camito-semitica, Firenze, 16–19 aprile 1974*. Florence, 133–47. Reprinted in Goldenberg 1998: 123–37.

Goldenberg, Gideon. 1987. Syntactic Relations and Typology in Semitic Languages. In *Following Polotsky's Teachings: Lectures in Honour of H. J. Polotsky on the Occasion of his Gvurot*. Jerusalem, 7–18. Reprinted in Goldenberg 1998: 138–47.

Goldenberg, Gideon. 1989. The Contribution of Semitic Languages to Linguistic Thinking. *JEOL* 30: 107–15. Reprinted in Goldenberg 1998: 1–9.

Goldenberg, Gideon. 1994. Principles of Semitic Word-Structure. In G. Goldenberg and S. Raz, eds. *Semitic and Cushitic Studies*. Wiesbaden, 29–64. Reprinted in Goldenberg 1998: 10–45.

Goldenberg, Gideon. 1995. Attribution in Semitic Languages. *Langues Orientales Anciennes: Philologie et Linguistique* 5–6: 1–20. Reprinted in Goldenberg 1998: 46–65.

Goldenberg, Gideon. 1998. *Studies in Semitic Linguistics: Selected Writings*. Jerusalem.

Goshen-Gottstein, M. H. 1979. Comparative Semitics: a Premature Obituary. In Abraham I. Katsh and Leon Nemoy, eds. *Essays on the Occasion of the Seventieth Anniversary of the Dropsie University (1909–79)*. Philadelphia, 141–50.

Goshen-Gottstein, M. H. 1991. The Present State of Comparative Semitic Linguistics. In Kaye 1991. 558–69.

Gray, Louis H. 1934. *Introduction to Semitic Comparative Linguistics*. New York. Reprint Amsterdam 1971.

Greenberg, Joseph H. 1952. The Afro-Asiatic (Hamito-Semitic) Present. *JAOS* 72: 1–9.

Greenberg, Joseph H. 1953. A Reply. *JAOS* 73: 167–68.

Greenberg, Joseph H. 1955. Internal *a*-plurals in Afroasiatic (Hamito-Semitic). In J. Lukas, ed. *Afrikanistische Studien*. Berlin, 198–204.

Hamori, Andras. 1973. A Note on *yaqtulu* in East and West Semitic. *ArOr* 41: 319–24.

Hayward, K. M., R. J. Hayward, and Sālim Bakhīt al-Tabūki. 1988. Vowels in Jibbāli Verbs. *BSOAS* 51: 240–50.

Hetzron, Robert. 1967. Agaw Numerals and Incongruence in Semitic. *JSS* 12: 169–97.

Hetzron, Robert. 1972. *Ethiopian Semitic: Studies in Classification*. (JSS Monograph, 2.) Manchester.

Hetzron, Robert. 1974. La division des langues sémitiques. In A. Caquot and D. Cohen, ed. *Actes du premier Congrès international de linguistique sémitique et chamito-sémitique, Paris 16–19 juillet 1969.* The Hague / Paris, 181–94.

Hetzron, Robert. 1976. Two Principles of Genetic Reconstruction. *Lingua* 38: 89–108.

Hetzron, Robert. 1987. Afroasiatic Languages. In Bernard Comrie, ed. *The World's Major Languages.* New York, 645–53.

Hetzron, Robert, ed. 1997. *The Semitic Languages.* London / New York.

Hospers, J. H. 1966. A Hundred Years of Semitic Comparative Linguistics. In *Studia biblica et semitica Theodoro Christiano Vriezen dedicata.* Wageningen, 138–51.

Huehnergard, John. 1987a. The Feminine Plural Jussive in Old Aramaic. *ZDMG* 137: 266–77.

Huehnergard, John. 1987b. Three Notes on Akkadian Morphology. In David M. Golomb, ed. *Working With No Data: Semitic and Egyptian Studies Presented to Thomas O. Lambdin.* Winona Lake, Indiana, 181–93.

Huehnergard, John. 1992. Languages: Introductory Survey. In David Noel Freedman, ed. *The Anchor Bible Dictionary.* New York, 4.155–70.

Huehnergard, John. 1995. Semitic Languages. In Jack M. Sasson, ed. *Civilizations of the Ancient Near East.* New York, 4.2117–34.

Huehnergard, John. Forthc. a. The Afroasiatic and Semitic Languages. In Roger D. Woodard, ed. *The Cambridge Encyclopedia of the World's Ancient Languages.* Cambridge.

Huehnergard, John. Forthc. b. *Comparative and Historical Semitic Grammar.* London.

Kaye, Alan S., ed. 1991. *Semitic Studies in Honor of Wolf Leslau on the Occasion of His Eighty-fifth Birthday.* 2 vol. Wiesbaden.

Khan, Geoffrey A. 1984. Object Markers and Agreement Pronouns in Semitic Languages. *BSOAS* 47: 468–500.

Khan, Geoffrey A. 1988. *Studies in Semitic Syntax.* (London Oriental Studies, 38.) Oxford.

Kienast, Burkhardt. 1957. Verbalformen mit Reduplikation im Akkadischen. *Or.* 26: 44–50.

Kienast, Burkhardt. 1961a. Satzeinleitendes *mā* im älteren Akkadischen. *ZA* 54: 90–99.

Kienast, Burkhardt. 1961b. Weiteres zum R-Stamm des Akkadischen. *JCS* 15: 59–61.

Kienast, Burkhardt. 1967. Zu den Vokalklassen beim akkadischen Verbum. In *Heidelberger Studien zum Alten Orient: Adam Falkenstein zum 17. September 1966.* Wiesbaden, 63–85.

Kouwenberg, N. J. C. 1997. *Gemination in the Akkadian Verb.* (Studia Semitica Neerlandica.) Assen.

Kramers, J. H. 1949. *De semietische Talen*. Leiden.

Kuryłowicz, Jerzy. 1945–49. La nature des procès dites "analogiques". *Acta Linguistica* 5: 121–38.

Kuryłowicz, Jerzy. 1961. *L'apophonie en sémitique*. Wrocław / Warszawa / Kraków / 's-Gravenhage. Revised edition *Studies in Semitic Grammar and Metrics*. London 1973.

Landsberger, Benno. 1926. Die Eigenbegrifflichkeit der babylonischen Welt. *Islamica* 2: 355–72. Translated by T. Jacobsen, B. Foster, and H. von Siebenthal as *The Conceptual Autonomy of the Babylonian World*. Introduction by T. Jacobsen. (Monographs of the Ancient Near East, 1/4.) Malibu 1976.

Leslau, Wolf. 1939a. Essai de reconstitution des désinences verbales du Tigrigna (éthiopien septentrional). *RES* 1939: 70–99.

Leslau, Wolf. 1939b. Le thème verbal fréquentatif dans les langues éthiopiennes. *RES* 1939: 15–31.

Leslau, Wolf. 1939c. Observations sur quelques dialectes du Tigrigna. *Journal Asiatique* 231: 61–115.

Leslau, Wolf. 1941. *Documents tigrigna (éthiopien septentrional). Grammaire et textes*. (Collection de la Société de Linguistique de Paris, 48.) Paris.

Leslau, Wolf. 1945. *Short Grammar of Tigre*. New Haven. Originally "The Verb in Tigre," *JAOS* 65 (1945): 1–26 and "Grammatical Sketches in Tigre," *JAOS* 65 (1945): 164–203.

Leslau, Wolf. 1948. Le problème de la gémination du verb tchaha (gouragué). *Word* 4: 42–47.

Lieberman, Stephen J. 1986. The Afro-Asiatic Background of the Semitic N-Stem: Toward the Origins of the Semitic and Afro-Asiatic Verb. *BiOr* 43: 577–628.

Lieberman, Stephen J. 1990. Summary Report: Linguistic Change and Reconstruction in the Afro-Asiatic Languages. In Philip Baldi, ed. *Linguistic Change and Reconstruction Methodology*. (Trends in Linguistics, Studies and Monographs, 45.) Berlin / New York, 565–75.

Lindberg, O. E. 1897. *Vergleichende Grammatik der semitischen Sprachen*, vol. 1. *Lautlehre*, A. *Konsonantismus*. Göteborg. (Only vol. 1 appeared.)

Lipiński, Edward. 1997. *Semitic Languages: Outline of a Comparative Grammar*. (Orientalia Lovaniensia Analecta, 80.) Leuven.

McCarthy, John J. 1979. *Formal Problems in Semitic Phonology and Morphology*. PhD Dissertation, Massachusetts Institute of Technology. Published New York 1985.

McCarthy, John J. 1981. A Prosodic Theory of Nonconcatenative Morphology. *Linguistic Inquiry* 12: 373–418.

McCarthy, John J. 1984. Speech Disguise and Phonological Representation in Amharic. In H. van der Hulst and N. Smith, ed. *Advances in Nonlinear Phonology.* Dordrecht, 305–12.

McCarthy, John J. 1986. Lexical Phonology and Nonconcatenative Morphology in the History of Chaha. *Revue Québécoise de Linguistique* 16: 209–28.

McCarthy, John J. and Alan S. Prince. 1990. Foot and Word in Prosodic Morphology: The Arabic Broken Plural. *Natural Language and Linguistic Theory* 8: 209–83.

McFall, Leslie. 1982. *The Enigma of the Hebrew Verbal System.* Sheffield.

Moscati, Sabatino, ed. 1964. *An Introduction to the Comparative Grammar of the Semitic Languages: Phonology and Morphology.* Wiesbaden.

Müller, W. W. 1993. Zum Wortschatz des neusüdarabischen Mehri. *ZAL* 25: 225–32.

Naumkin, V. V. and V. Ja. Porchomovskij. 1981. *Očerki po etnolingvistike Sokotry.* Moskva.

Nebes, Norbert. 1994. Zur Form der Imperfektbasis des unvermehrten Grundstammes im Altsüdarabischen. In W. Heinrichs and G. Schoeler, eds. *Festschrift Ewald Wagner zum 65. Geburtstag,* vol. 1: *Semitische Studien unter besonderer Berücksichtigung der Südsemitistik.* Beirut / Stuttgart, 59–81.

Nichols, Johanna. 1992. *Linguistic Diversity in Space and Time.* Chicago / London.

Nöldeke, Theodor. 1887. Semitic Languages. *Encyclopaedia Britannica,* 9th ed. London 1875–89. American reprint Chicago 1890. 21.641–56. Original German, with revisions and additions, *Die semitischen Sprachen: Eine Skizze.* Leipzig 1887. ²Leipzig 1899. Revised English, *Encyclopaedia Britannica,* 11th ed. London 1911 24.617–30.

Nöldeke, Theodor. 1904. *Beiträge zur semitischen Sprachwissenschaft.* Strassburg.

Nöldeke, Theodor. 1910. *Neue Beiträge zur semitischen Sprachwissenschaft.* Strassburg.

O'Leary, de Lacy. 1923. *Comparative Grammar of the Semitic Languages.* London. Reprint Amsterdam 1969.

Oldender, Maurice. 1989. *Les langues du paradis: Aryens et Sémites: un couple providentiel.* Paris. Translated by Arthur Goldhammer as *The Languages of Paradise: Race, Religion, and Philology in the Nineteenth Century.* Cambridge, Mass. 1992.

Oppenheim, A. L., et al., ed. 1956–. *The Assyrian Dictionary of the Oriental Institute of the University of Chicago.* Glückstadt.

Pennacchietti, F. A. 1974. Le classe degli aggettivi denotativi nelle lingue semitiche e nelle lingue berbere. In A. Caquot and D. Cohen, eds. *Actes du premier Congrès international de linguistique sémitique et chamito-sémitique, Paris 16–19 juillet 1969.* The Hague / Paris, 30–39.

Petráček, Karel. 1960–64. Die innere Flexion in den semitischen Sprachen. *ArOr* 28 (1960): 547–606; 29 (1961): 513–45; 30 (1962): 361–408; 31 (1963): 577–624; 32 (1964): 185–222.

Podolsky, Baruch. 1991. *Historical Phonetics of Amharic.* Tel-Aviv.

Polotsky, H. J. 1938. Études de grammaire gouragué. *BSL* 39: 137–75.

Polotsky, H. J. 1944. *Études de syntaxe copte.* Cairo.

Polotsky, H. J. 1964. Semitics. In E. A. Speiser, ed. *The World History of the Jewish People*, vol. 1: *Dawn of Civilization.* London, 99–111, 357–58.

Porkhomovsky, Victor. 1997. Modern South Arabian Languages from a Semitic and Hamito-Semitic Perspective. *Proceedings of the Seminar for Arabian Studies* 27: 219–23.

Posner, Rebecca. 1996. *The Romance Languages.* (Cambridge Language Surveys.) Cambridge.

Ratcliffe, Robert R. 1998a. Defining Morphological Isoglosses: The "Broken" Plural and Semitic Subclassification. *JNES* 57: 81–123.

Ratcliffe, Robert R. 1998b. *The Broken Plural Problem in Arabic and Comparative Semitic: Allomorphy and Analogy in Non-concatenative Morphology.* (Current Issues in Linguistic Theory, 168.) Amsterdam.

Reiner, Erica. 1966. *A Linguistic Analysis of Akkadian.* (Janua Linguarum, series practica, 21.) The Hague / Paris.

Renan, Ernest. 1855. *Histoire générale et système comparé des langues sémitiques.* Paris. [2]1858, [3]1863, [4]1863, [5]1878.

Rendsburg, Gary A. 1990. *Diglossia in Ancient Hebrew.* (American Oriental Series, 72.) New Haven.

Retsö, Jan. 1987. Copula and Double Pronominal Objects in Some Semitic Languages. *ZDMG* 137: 219–45.

Retsö, Jan. 1989. *Diathesis in the Semitic Languages: A Comparative Morphological Study.* (Studies in Semitic Languages and Linguistics, 14.) Leiden.

Rinaldi, Giovanni. 1954. *Le lingue semitiche: Introduzione generale storica e bibliografica.* Torino / Rome.

Rodgers, Jonathan. 1991. The Subgrouping of the South Semitic Languages. In Kaye 1991. 1323–36.

Rössler, Otto. 1950. Verbalbau und Verbalflexion in den semitohamitischen Sprachen: Vorstudien zu einer vergleichenden semitohamitischen Grammatik. *ZDMG* 100: 461–514. Translated by Y. Arbeitman as The Structure and Inflection of the Verb in the Semito-Hamitic Languages: Preliminary Studies for a Comparative Semito-Hamitic Grammar. In Y. Arbeitman and A. R. Bomhard, eds. *Bono Homini Donum: Essays in Historical Linguistics in Memory of J. Alexander Kerns*. Amsterdam, 1981, 679–748.

Rössler, Otto. 1951. Akkadisches und libysches Verbum, I, II. *Or.* 20: 101–7, 366–73.

Rössler, Otto. 1952. Der semitische Charakter der libyschen Sprache. *ZA* 50: 121–50.

Rössler, Otto. 1964. Libysch-Hamitisch-Semitisch. *Oriens* 17: 199–216.

Rössler, Otto. 1983. Äthiopisch und Hamitisch. In Stanislav Segert and András J. E. Bodrogligeti, eds. *Ethiopian Studies Dedicated to Wolf Leslau on the Occasion of His Seventy-fifth Birthday*. Wiesbaden.

Rundgren, Frithiof. 1955. *Über Bildungen mit s/š– und n-t– Demonstrativen im Semitischen*. Uppsala.

Rundgren, Frithiof. 1959. *Intensiv und Aspektkorrelation*. Uppsala, Wiesbaden.

Rundgren, Frithiof. 1960. Das aspektuelle Charakter des altsemitischen Injunktivs. *OrSuec* 9: 75–101.

Rundgren, Frithiof. 1963a. Das Verbalpräfix *yu–* im Semitischen und die Entstehung der faktitiv-kausativischen Bedeutung des D-Stammes. *OrSuec* 12: 98–114.

Rundgren, Frithiof. 1963b. *Erneuerung des Verbalaspekts im Semitischen*. Uppsala.

Rundgren, Frithiof. 1964. Ablaut und Apothematismus im Semitischen. *OrSuec* 18: 48–83.

Rundgren, Frithiof. 1980. Principia linguistica semitica. *OrSuec* 29: 32–102.

Sasse, Hans-Jürgen. 1980. Ostkuschitische und semitische Verbalklassen. In Werner Diem and Stefan Wild, eds. *Studien aus Arabistik und Semitistik Anton Spitaler zum siebzigsten Geburtstag von seinen Schülern überreicht*. Wiesbaden, 153–74.

Sasse, Hans-Jürgen 1981. Afroasiatisch. In B. Heine, et al., ed. *Die Sprachen Afrikas*. Hamburg, 129–48.

Sasse, Hans-Jürgen. 1981. Die semitischen Sprachen. In B. Heine, et al., ed. *Die Sprachen Afrikas*. Hamburg, 225–38.

Sasse, Hans-Jürgen. 1984. Case in Cushitic, Semitic and Berber. In James Bynon, ed. *Current Progress in Afro-Asiatic Linguistics: Papers* of the Third International Hamito-Semitic Congress. Amsterdam / Philadelphia, 111-26.

Saussure, Ferdinand de. 1916. *Cours de linguistique générale*. Publié par Charles Bally et Albert Sechehay, avec la collaboration de Albert Riedlinger. Lausanne / Paris. ²1922. Édition critique préparée par Tullio de Mauro. Paris 1972.

Schramm, Gene M. 1970. The Semitic Languages: An Overview. In Thomas A. Sebeok, ed. *Current Trends in Linguistics*, vol. 6: *Linguistics in South West Asia and North Africa*. The Hague / Paris, 257-60.

Soden, Wolfram von. 1952. *Grundriss der akkadischen Grammatik*. (Analecta Orientalia, 33, 47.) Rome, ²1969, ³1995 (with W. Mayer).

Soden, Wolfram von. 1965-81. *Akkadisches Handwörterbuch*. 3 vol. Wiesbaden.

Steiner, Richard C. 1977. *The Case for Fricative-Laterals in Proto-Semitic*. (American Oriental Series, 59.) New Haven.

Steiner, Richard C. 1982. *Affricated Ṣade in the Semitic Languages*. (The American Academy for Jewish Research Monograph Series, 3.) New York.

Steiner, Richard C. 1987. *Lulav versus *lu/law*: A Note on the Conditioning of *aw > ū in Hebrew and Aramaic. *JAOS* 107: 121-22.

Steiner, Richard C. 1991. Addenda to *The Case for Fricative-Laterals in Proto-Semitic*. In Kaye 1991. 1499-1513.

Swiggers, P. A. 1981. Phonological Analysis of the Ḥarsūsi Consonants. *Arabica* 28: 358-61.

Testen, David. 1998. *Parallels in Semitic Linguistics: the Development of Arabic la– and Related Semitic Particles*. (Studies in Semitic Languages and Linguistics, 26.) Leiden.

Thomason, Sarah Grey and Terrence Kaufman. 1988. *Language Contact, Creolization, and Genetic Linguistics*. Berkeley.

Tropper, Josef. 1990. *Der ugaritische Kausativstamm und die Kausativbildungen des Semitischen: Eine morphologisch-semantische Unversuchung zum Š-Stamm und zu den umstrittenen nichtsibilantischen Kausativstämmen des Ugaritischen*. (Abhandlungen zur Literatur Alt-Syrien-Palästinas, 2.) Münster.

Ullendorff, Edward. 1961. Comparative Semitics. In G. Levi della Vida, ed. *Linguistica semitica: presente e futuro*. (Studi Semitici, 4.) Rome, 13-32.

Ullendorff, Edward. 1970. Comparative Semitics. In Thomas A. Sebeok, ed. *Current Trends in Linguistics*, vol. 6: *Linguistics in South West Asia and North Africa*. The Hague / Paris, 261-73.

Voigt, Rainer M. 1979. Die Laterale im Semitischen. *WdO* 10: 93–114.

Voigt, Rainer M. 1981. Inkompatibilitäten und Diskrepanzen in der Sprache und das erste phonologische Inkompatibilitätsgesetz des Semitischen. *WdO* 12: 136–72.

Voigt, Rainer M. 1987a. Derivatives und flektives *t* im Semitohamitischen. In H. Jungraithmayr and W. W. Müller, eds. *Proceedings of the Fourth International Hamito-Semitic Congress*. Amsterdam / Philadelphia, 85–107.

Voigt, Rainer M. 1987b. Die Personalpronomina der 3. Personen im Semitischen. *WdO* 18: 49–63.

Voigt, Rainer M. 1987c. The Classification of Central Semitic. *JSS* 32: 1–21.

Voigt, Rainer M. 1988. *Die infirmen Verbaltypen des Arabischen und das Biradikalismus-Problem*. Wiesbaden / Stuttgart.

Voigt, Rainer M. 1988–89. The Development of the Old Ethiopic Consonantal System. In Taddese Beyene, ed. *Proceedings of the Eighth International Conference of Ethiopian Studies, University of Addis Ababa, 1984*. Addis Ababa, 633–47.

Voigt, Rainer M. 1992. Die Lateralreihe /*š ṣ ź*/ im Semitischen. *ZDMG* 142: 37–52.

Voigt, Rainer M. 1994a. Der Lautwandel *s*¹ > *h* in wurzellosen Morphemen des Alt- und Neusüdarabischen. In G. Goldenberg and S. Raz, eds. *Semitic and Cushitic Studies*. Wiesbaden, 19–28.

Voigt, Rainer M. 1994b. Die Entsprechung der ursemitischen Interdentale im Altäthiopischen. In W. Heinrichs and G. Schoeler, eds. *Festschrift Ewald Wagner zum 65. Geburtstag*, vol. 1: *Semitische Studien unter besonderer Berücksichtigung der Südsemitistik*. Beirut / Stuttgart, 102–17.

Voigt, Rainer M. 1998. Der Artikel im Semitischen. *JSS* 43: 221–58.

Wagner, Ewald. 1993. Gedanken zum Verb des Mehri aufgrund der neuen Materialien von Johnstone. *ZAL* 25: 316–39.

Wright, William. 1890. *Lectures on the Comparative Grammar of the Semitic Languages with a General Survey of the Semitic Languages and their Diffusion and of the Semitic Alphabet, Origin and Writing*. Edited with a Preface and Additional Notes by William Robertson Smith. Cambridge. Reprint Amsterdam 1981.

Zaborski, Andrzej. 1969. Root-Determinatives and the Problem of Biconsonantal Roots in Semitic. *Folia Orientalia* 11: 307–13.

Zaborski, Andrzej. 1978. Some Internal Plurals in Cushitic. In Pelio Fronzaroli, ed. *Atti del secondo congresso internazionale di linguistica camito-semitica, Firenze, 16–19 aprile 1974*. Florence, 369–78.

Zaborski, Andrzej. 1991. Biconsonantal Roots and Triconsonantal Root Variation in Semitic: Solutions and Prospects. In Kaye 1991. 1675–1703.

Zaborski, Andrzej. 1994. Archaic Semitic in the Light of Hamito-Semitic. *ZAH* 7: 234–44.

Zaborski, Andrzej. 1995. First Person Pronouns in Arabic in the Light of Arabic and Hamito-Semitic Dialectology. *Studia Orientalia 75 (Dialectologia Arabica: A Collection of Articles in Honour of the Sixtieth Birthday of Professor Heikki Palva)*: 289–94.

Zaborski, Andrzej. 1996. Problems of an "Introduction" to Afroasiatic/Hamitosemitic Linguistics. *Sprawozdania z Posiedzeń Komisji Naukowych* 39: 103–6.

Zimmern, Heinrich. 1898. *Vergleichende Grammatik der semitischen Sprachen. Elemente der Laut- und Formenlehre.* Berlin.

THE STUDY OF SEMITIC SYNTAX

GEOFFREY KHAN

In the short space of this paper, I shall not attempt to present a systematic survey of all work on the syntax of the Semitic languages. I shall restrict myself to discussing various general features that have characterized the study of Semitic syntax at various periods. A large proportion of my remarks will concern recent developments in the discipline and the possible directions it may take in the future.

The general trends in recent research on Semitic syntax cannot be fully assessed without viewing them against the background of the history of grammatical thought. I believe that it is important to consider the developments that have taken place in a broad historical perspective from the beginnings of grammatical studies of Semitic languages in the Middle Ages until the present day. This is because, in my opinion, some aspects of the general approach and purpose of recent studies in Semitic syntax exhibit parallels to those of the earliest grammatical studies. In certain respects, studies of the syntax of Semitic languages at the end of this millennium have come full circle and are closer in spirit to the earliest grammatical inquiries at the beginning of the millennium than ever before. I do not wish to argue, of course, that modern studies in Semitic syntax are not offering anything new or that they do not represent progress in our understanding. The point that I wish to make is that there are parallels in general perspective and purpose between the approach to syntax in the earliest and most recent periods and that recognition of these parallels may help us to assess the directions in which the discipline is moving. For this reason I think it is helpful to go beyond a consideration of the work achieved in the 20th century and devote some space to the development of the discipline in earlier periods.

It may be argued that some of the earliest syntactic statements regarding Semitic languages are descriptions of the relationship between words and larger components of speech that occur in works concerned with the transmission and exegesis of the Holy Scriptures. The Scriptures of Eastern Christianity, Judaism and Islam, which were in Syriac, Hebrew and Arabic respectively, were transmitted from an early period in both a written tradition and also a reading tradition. The reading traditions were originally passed on orally, at least in the case of the Syriac and

Hebrew Scriptures, until a graphic notation was developed to represent them in manuscripts. The Syriac and Hebrew reading traditions included not only the way that the consonants and vowels were pronounced but also expressions of the connection between syntactic components and even the function of syntactic components. This was expressed by a system of pauses and pitch changes in the recitation of the texts. Technical terminology was developed to express the interpretation of these features of the reading traditions. The earliest examples of this are found in the Syriac tradition, where we find already before the 7th century A.D. terms such as *pāsoqā* "breaking-off", *samkā* "support", *rahṭā* "running", *mša'lānā* "interrogative" (Segal 1953:64).

In the Jewish tradition, some of the earliest analyses of the relation between syntactic components are interpretations of the relationships in meaning that are reflected by the pauses and connections expressed in the biblical reading tradition. This is found, for example, in a Hebrew grammatical text know as the *Diqduq* that was written in the tenth century by the Karaite Jew Joseph ben Noah. Although written down in the second half of the tenth century, the text represents a tradition of grammatical exposition that existed in earlier generations. This text is not a systematic grammatical treatise but has the form of a commentary on the Bible that discusses grammatical and exegetical issues in the Biblical text (cf. Khan 1998 and 1999). There is no fully developed theory of syntactic categories and syntactic relations. Divisions and connections expressed by the reading tradition, however, are considered to reflect divisions and connections in meaning between words and larger components. The examination of relations between components often goes beyond what we would now term the level of the sentence. The approach can be seen as the explanation of linguistic structure by the application of rhetorical exegesis. Some aspects of Joseph ben Noah's analysis of relations in meaning between components can indeed be traced back to hermeneutical principles that were developed in the earlier Rabbinic tradition (cf. Khan 2000). It is important to take into consideration that the primary purpose of the early Hebrew grammatical text of Joseph ben Noah was not to present a description of the Hebrew language but rather to elucidate the text of Scripture by an examination of its grammatical structure. His presentation was not intended to comprehend all the structures of the language. He formulates some general rules, but is particularly concerned with the analysis of individual constructions that require elucidation. As far as the relationship between components is concerned, each construction tends to be treated separately and interpreted according to its individual context.

The earliest form of syntactic analysis of Arabic is likewise found in exegetical texts. These are commentaries on the Quran from the first two centuries of Islam (7th–8th centuries A.D.). They do not present a full taxonomy of syntactic structures, but discuss various aspects of the relationship in meaning between words and larger components, sometimes above the level of the sentence (cf. Versteegh 1993). As is the case with the Hebrew grammatical text of Joseph ben Noaḥ, these early Quran commentaries are primarily concerned with the elucidation of the text of Scripture rather than the analysis of language. By the third century of Islam (9th century A.D.), the study of Arabic grammar as an independent discipline had been established. This developed mainly in the so-called Basran school of Arabic grammar, the framework of whose teachings was set by the grammarian Sībawayhi. Within this new discipline of Arabic grammar, a considerable amount of attention was given to syntax. The primary purpose of the discipline was no longer the elucidation of a text but rather the study of the structure of the language as a dynamic system of expression. It took account not only of what is attested in a given text but also the potential expression of the language. As a result of this, the focus was on the language structure itself more than on the context in which it was used. The scope of analysis, moreover, became restricted as a general rule to the level of the sentence. The study of language in the context of its use continued, however, in works on Arabic rhetoric (*al-balāġa*), which became a separate discipline from that of grammar. This discipline was principally concerned with the relation between thought and expression, which included a study of sentence structure and the appropriate context of its use.

A tradition of studying language as an independent discipline was also developed for Hebrew by Jewish scholars in the Middle Ages. This seems to have developed mainly under the influence of the Arabic grammatical tradition.

With a few exceptions, however, syntax did not preoccupy the Hebrew grammarians to the same extent as the Arabic grammarians. This applied especially to the Hebrew grammarians of Spain, through which the tradition of Hebrew grammar was transmitted to Christian Europe. One grammarian who applied Arabic syntactic theory extensively to Hebrew was the Karaite Abū al-Faraj Hārūn (first half of the eleventh century), who was the pupil of Joseph ben Noaḥ in Jerusalem. His grammatical works were known by some scholars in Spain, but they did not appear to have had much influence and knowledge of them was not transmitted to Christian Europe at a later period (Bacher 1895). The Spanish grammarian Jonah ibn Janaḥ devoted five chapters of his Hebrew grammar book *Kitāb al-Luma'* ("The book of coloured flowerbeds") to aspects of rhetoric, some of which could be considered to belong to syntax, such as inversion of word order. By the late Middle Ages, however, the vestiges of the medieval tradition of Hebrew grammar in Europe were restricted to phonology and morphology. In 1523 the Jewish scholar Abraham de Balmes published a Hebrew grammar (*Miqneh Avram*) that used the taxonomy of grammatical categories that was currently used for the description of Latin. Much of this taxonomy had its roots in the writings of the Classical Latin grammarians, such as Priscian. This included a long chapter with a comprehensive treatment on syntax. It applied contemporary syntactic concepts such as *compositio et regimen*, which included features like the combination of nouns and verbs and the agreement between subject and predicate. At this period Christian scholars of Europe began to write grammars of Hebrew and Arabic. They drew to some extent on the medieval Oriental traditions, but followed the Latin tradition of grammatical taxonomy in the organization of their grammars. As a general rule, however, these early Christian grammars of Hebrew and Arabic were concerned mainly with morphology rather than syntax. This is clear from the works of the leading Christian grammarians of Arabic and Hebrew, such as the Arabic grammar of Thomas Erpenius (Leiden 1613), which contained only eight pages of syntax, and the Hebrew grammar of Johannes Reuchlin (*De rudimentis Hebraicis*, 1506) and those of Sebastian Muenster (e.g. *Epitome Hebraicae grammaticae*, 1537 and *Institutiones Grammaticae in Hebraeam Linguam*, 1524), which contained no syntax at all. In the Latin tradition, the discipline of rhetoric was completely separate from that of grammar.

The syntax of Semitic languages received more attention from European scholars in the 19th century. This is shown, for example, by the thorough treatment of Arabic syntax in the *Grammaire Arabe* of Antoine Silvestre de Sacy, which first appeared in 1810. This was based both on the contemporary taxonomy of syntax as used for Latin and also on the syntactic taxonomy of the native Arab grammarians. Thorough treatments of syntax are also found in the works of other 19th century scholars. We may mention, by way of illustration, the grammars of Ewald (Hebrew and Arabic), Gesenius, Bötcher, König (Hebrew), Nöldeke (Syriac, Mandaean), Dillmann (Ethiopic), Praetorius (Amharic) and Wright (Arabic). Syntax was also treated independently from the rest of the grammar, as is the case, for example, in Reckendorf's exposition of Arabic syntax (1895–1898). The taxonomy of these treatments of syntax was essentially similar, namely one based on the Latin tradition with some modifications derived from the medieval Arabic tradition. There was also a general consensus about the boundaries of the study of syntax, namely the level of the sentence. It should be noted, however, that the taxonomy in the 19th century tended to be driven more by the data than in some works of earlier centuries, in which Semitic syntactic constructions were often forced, inappropriately, into the Procrustean bed of Latin categories.

The influence of the native Arabic tradition of grammar is, of course, most conspicuous in grammars of Arabic that were written in Europe in the 19th century. This is particularly clear in the grammar of W. Wright (first edition 1862), which is ultimately based on an earlier grammar of C.P. Caspari (1848). It had been recognized already by Silvestre de Sacy, however, that a "scientific" presentation of the syntax of Arabic must distinguish between the tradition of the native Arabic grammarians and the views concerning language that were current in contemporary European linguistic thought. This is shown by the fact that Silvestre de Sacy in his treatment of Arabic syntax places his description that is based on the Arabic grammarians in a separate section from the description that is based on contemporary general linguistics. By the end of the 19th century, many European scholars had moved away almost completely from the framework of the medieval Arabic grammarians in their descriptions of Arabic syntax. This is the case, for example, with the works of Reckendorf (1898) and Nöldeke (1886).

The same basic framework for syntactic description continued to be used in many Semitic grammars throughout the 20th century, including the grammars of the recently discovered Semitic languages such as Akkadian and Ugaritic. Separate volumes devoted entirely to systematic treatments of syntax have also continued to be produced. We may mention, by way of illustration, the *Arabische Syntax* of Reckendorf (1921), which was a sequel to his work *Die syntaktischen Verhältnisse des Arabischen* (1895–98), and also other syntaxes of Arabic and its dialects such as Feghali (1928), Blau (1960) and Cantarino (1974–75), Watson (1993). Various volumes have been devoted to systematic treatments of Biblical Hebrew syntax, e.g. Davidson (1901, recently reworked by Gibson 1994), Brockelmann (1956), Williams (1976) and Waltke and O'Connor (1990). Note also Schlesinger (1928) on Babylonian Aramaic.

This framework of "traditional grammar," as it has now come to be known, consists of the identification of syntactic categories and their arrangement in an organized scheme of presentation. This approach to syntactic description, accordingly, has been termed "category and arrangement". It has proved to be a successful way of presenting the attested syntactic structures in a language, as is shown by the fact that many of the descriptions of Semitic syntax that were made at the end of the 19th and during the first half of the 20th century are still widely consulted today.

The traditional category and arrangement presentation of syntax is concerned primarily with the classification of syntactic structure. The meaning and function of the various syntactic structures were, nonetheless, given considerable attention. It was recognized that certain syntactic structures had a variety of different functions. Although the limit of structural analysis was the sentence, one finds in some of the Semitic grammars from the end of 19th or the first half of the 20th century some consideration of the surrounding discourse context in order to elucidate the function of the structure. This is seen, for example, in the description of syntax by Brockelmann in the second volume of his *Grundriss der vergleichenden Grammatik der semitischen Sprachen.* The placement of the subject before the verb in those languages that have the predominant order verb-subject is said to occur "at the beginning of narratives" (*Grundriss* II, 171–172). The semantic relations between clauses that are not marked explicity by syntactic subordination are also discussed by Brockelmann. In his description of co-ordinated clauses ("beigeordnete Sätze") he refers to relations such as "contrast" ("Gegensatz"), "motivation" ("Begründung"), "elucidation" ("Erläuterung"), "purpose" ("Absicht") (*Grundriss* II, 471–499). A separate section (*Grundriss* II, 501–506) is devoted to "circumstantial clauses" largely on functional rather than structural grounds and some classification is made of the various different contexts in which such clauses are used.

The function of some syntactic structures was also sought in psychological notions of language. Some of these may seem impressionistic today. Ewald (1879:152–158), for example, in his treatment of Hebrew syntax, explains the placement of a subject in initial position in a circumstantial clause as a means of presenting us with "a harmonious and placid picture of something continuous." Inversion of the usual word order, he claims, may also be used to impart a "tinge of juvenile restlessness and vivacity" (English translation by James Kennedy) to the clause and thus place "emphasis" on one of the elements. It should be noted, however, that similar impressionistic notions of "emphasis" have continued to be used to explain inversions of word order throughout the 20th century.

At the end of the 19th century, psychological theories of language, such as the concept of psychological starting point or "psychological subject" were used to explain word order in Semitic languages. These notions were developed by G. von der Gabelentz (1869:378) and subsequently also by W. Wundt (1900–20) and were applied also to Indo-European languages at this period (see Khan 1988:xxx). One finds the influence of these notions in the works of Brockelmann and Reckendorf and also in works on Semitic syntax written later in the century, such Bloch (1946) and Bravmann (1953).

A thorough treatment of syntactic function is also found in studies of the Semitic verbal system that were made in the 19th century, especially that of Hebrew which received particular attention. Detailed investigations of the function of the Hebrew verbs led scholars to recognize many of the functional complexities exhibited by the various verbal forms. A major contribution was made in this respect by S.R. Driver in his *Treatise on the Use of the Tenses in Hebrew* (1874), in which he identified features of meaning that we would now term aspect and mood, as well as pragmatic features of the use of verbs, such as the performative perfect.

Another approach that was taken to explain certain aspects of the syntax of Semitic languages was the consideration of rhythmic structure. Ehelolf (1916), for example, in his analysis of Akkadian word order, demonstrated that constituents tended to be ordered according to their length, with the longer one being placed after the shorter ones. This was inspired by Behagel's "Gesetz der wachsenden Glieder", which was one of the laws that he formulated for Germanic word order (1909). This "endweighting" principle was later identified in the syntax of other Semitic languages, e.g. in Arabic by Beeston (1970:110) and in Hebrew by Friedman (1971).

The increasing interest in comparative-historical grammar of the Semitic languages that arose in the second half of the 19th century was concerned primarily with phonology and morphology. Some treatments of Semitic syntax, nevertheless, considered comparative-historical issues. The classic case of this was the second volume of Brockelmann's *Grundriss der vergleichenden Grammatik der semitischen Sprachen*, which was devoted entirely to syntax. Brockelmann recognized, however, that syntax was not amenable to a comparative-historical treatment in the same way as phonology and morphology. The main body of the work is a presentation of a traditional taxonomy of syntactic categories illustrated by examples from a variety of Semitic languages. His stated aim, nonetheless, was not typological comparison, but rather the distinction between historically primitive syntactic structures and those that are later developments (*Grundriss* II, p.3.). His comparative approach, therefore, corresponded in spirit to the genealogical framework of the first volume of the Grundriss, which was concerned with phonology and morphology. He was primarily concerned with syntactic structures in the attested languages that would cast light on the primitive syntactic structures of Semitic. For this reason his comparative syntax did not direct much attention to the syntax of some of the "peripheral" Semitic languages that are heavily influenced by that of non-Semitic languages with which they are in contact.

A number of monographs on specific topics of Semitic syntax that were concerned primarily with a comparative-historical approach were also published in the 20th century. Particular interest was shown in the historical development of the Semitic verbal system (see McFall 1982 for a survey of published works). The historical development of various other aspects of syntax has also attracted interest, especially within the corpus of the Hebrew Bible. Some examples of works on the historical syntax of Hebrew are A. Kropat (1909) and E. Kuhr (1929). We may mention here also the work of Bravmann (1953) on cleft sentences and Semitic word order and D. Cohen (1984) on the development of the nominal sentence and the verbal system in the Semitic languages.

The comparison of the syntax of the newly discovered languages such as Akkadian and Ugaritic with that of other Semitic languages has led to some important advances. This certainly applies to a number of aspects of Hebrew syntax, such as the function of some prepositions and particles, which has been clarified by comparison with the function of cognate elements in Ugaritic.

By the middle of the 20th century, a synchronic structuralist analysis of language was favoured in the mainstream of general linguistics. The ideal of most structuralists was to concentrate on the classification of linguistic units on the basis of their distribution in a synchronic segment of language. This took attention away from the full range of functions performed by the syntactic structures. It was taxonomy by category and arrangement in its extreme form. It, nevertheless, had the advantage of introducing objectivity in syntactic description and breaking away from the preconceived Latin based taxonomy. It also avoided introspective psychological explanations. This structuralist distributional approach to syntax has been adopted by I. Garbell (1965) in her description of the Neo-Aramaic dialect of the Jews of Azerbaijan. It has also inspired a number of studies in Semitic syntax, mainly in North West Semitic and Biblical Hebrew, which strive for objectivity by an exhaustive examination of the distribution of phenomena in a fixed corpus. These include such works as those of F. Andersen (1970) on the Biblical Hebrew verbless clause, J. Hoftijzer (1965) on the particle *'et* in Biblical Hebrew and Contini (1982) on the verbless clause in North West Semitic. We should also mention in this connection the work of W. Richter and his school on Hebrew grammar, which adheres to a strict distributional methodology, cf. for example the comprehensive grammar by Richter (1978–80) and the monograph by Gross (1987), which treats an individual topic of syntax (extraposition). Entire monographs have been devoted to an exhaustive analysis of the syntax of the noun, such as Michel (1977) and Kapeliuk (1994).

The shift towards a synchronic analysis of language has also given rise to "contrastive" comparisons between languages rather than comparisons for the sake of establishing historical developments. Some studies of this nature have involved Semitic languages (e.g. Ennaji 1985, Werner

1995 and Shlonsky 1997). In some cases the contrastive studies are concerned with dialectal variation in the syntax of a Semitic language (e.g. Hayes 1985 on the Western Akkadian dialects and Folmer 1995 on the dialects of Aramaic in the Achaemenid period). We should also note here that, following the move away from diachronic studies of language in structuralist linguistics, many treatments of the Semitic verbal system since the middle of the 20th century have focused on the synchronic function of the verbal forms rather than on their historical background. A number of these studies offer detailed analyses of temporal, modal and aspectual dimensions of the verbal system, as did S.R. Driver before the comparative-historical approach became the fashion. This applies to some recent work on the verbal system of individual Semitic languages, e.g. Nebes (1982) for Arabic, Verreet (1988) for Ugaritic and Hoberman (1989) for Neo-Aramaic.

The development of transformational grammar by N. Chomsky put syntax in the centre of attention in general linguistics. The transformational model of grammar offered a theory that was intended to explain the form of syntactic structures. It was based on the assumption that the fundamental descriptive taxonomy of syntax was known. It was claimed, moreover, that the transformational rules were of universal application to human language in general. Much of the attention of the transformationalists was on the theory of language acquisition. A number of attempts were made to apply some type of transformational analysis to a Semitic language. See the contribution of J. Malone in this volume for a detailed discussion of the application of Chomskyan theories to Semitic languages. Some monographs that treat syntax of Arabic in this framework are Khrakovskii (1973), Wise (1975), Al-Khuli (1979), Bakir (1980), Al-Waer (1987) and Fehri (1993). Some examples of studies in Hebrew are Ornan (1969), Cole (1976) and Berman (1978). Shlonsky (1997) treats both Arabic and Hebrew in this framework. This model of linguistic theory, however, was designed primarily to explore the potential of language structure, often by appealing to highly artificial sentences, rather than describe and explain attested linguistic structures. It was generally concerned, moreover, with a limited range of constructions and not a complete taxonomy.

Following the work of J.H. Greenberg (1966), much attention has been given in general linguistics to the comparison of the syntax of languages to establish typological universals. The contention of this school of thought has been that certain features of syntax typically co-occur with or 'imply' other features. Languages in which the dominant order of clause components is Verb-Subject-Object, for example, have been found "with overwhelming more-than-chance frequency" to have the adjective after the noun (Greenberg's Universal number 17). It has been argued that languages that exhibit an inconsistency with the normal typological tendencies are in a process of historical change in some features of their syntax. This approach, therefore, was seen as an important tool for comparative-historical syntax. It has received relatively little attention, however, among scholars working on Semitic languages. In general, consideration of Semitic languages in this framework has been restricted to general linguists with a knowledge of one or more Semitic language. Some attention has been given to Semitic languages, mainly Hebrew, by the general linguist T. Givon (e.g. 1977). One should note also the work of A. Faber (1980), who used the theory of typological tendencies in word order to study historical change in Semitic syntax.

In general linguistics over the last two decades, there has been an increasing interest in the study of syntax within the context in which it is used. In contrast to transformational grammar, which regarded syntax as an autonomous component of language, independent of the level of meaning, it is now widely recognized that many aspects of syntactic structure are determined by features of the context of communication. The study of syntax within the context in which it is used belongs to a discipline that is generally referred to as discourse analysis or text linguistics, the former being the normal term used by North American linguists and their followers and the latter being the more usual term that is used in continental Europe. The study of language in context, however, includes not only the adjacent discourse (i.e. the linguistic context), but also such features as the presuppositions of the speaker/writer with regard to the knowledge of the hearer/reader and the type of act of communication, or "speech act", that the speaker/writer intends to perform. The focus of this type of approach is on the communicative function of language structure rather than rules governing the potential limits of structure, which preoccupied the transformational grammarians. For this reason the term "functional grammar" is sometimes applied to the discipline.

The growth of interest in discourse analysis has led to a more descriptive study of attested syntactic data than was the case with transformational grammar. In recent years an increasing number of studies in Semitic syntax have been made with this approach. There is by no means a general consensus concerning the scope and methodology of discourse analysis. As we have seen, there is indeed no agreement concerning the name of the discipline. Applications of discourse analysis to Semitic languages have followed various approaches. Some are based on a methodology developed by Joseph Grimes (1975) and Robert Longacre (cf. for example 1976 and 1996), which is ultimately founded on the tagmemic analysis of language proposed by Kenneth and Evelyn Pike (1983). According to this approach, language can be segmented at levels higher than the sentence, such as paragraphs and episodes, and each segment has a specific function in relation to other segments. Longacre himself has applied this framework to an analysis of Biblical Hebrew (1989). Some other analyses of Biblical Hebrew syntax following a similar methodology are Andersen (1974), Eskhult (1990) and Dawson (1994). Khan (1988) has used some aspects of this methodology in the analysis also of other Semitic languages.

Some studies on Semitic syntax are based on the theories of the German linguist Harald Weinrich (1977), which overlaps to some extent with the concepts of the tagmemic school, but puts greater emphasis on features such as the attitude and perspective that are adopted by the speaker. The theories of Weinrich have acted as the basis of the work of a number of Hebraists, e.g. H. Schneider (1982), A. Niccacci (1990) and Talstra (1978, 1982, 1983, 1982).

Some work on Semitic syntax has adopted a functional approach to syntax that is concerned with the presuppositions of the speaker/writer and the interaction between the information structure of a clause and its syntactic ordering. This approach has been developed particularly among the Prague school (cf. Firbas 1992) and by M.A.K. Halliday (Halliday and Hasan 1976 and Halliday 1985), S.C. Dik (1978, 1980, 1989) and K. Lambrecht (1994). The issues that are examined include the identification of the topic of the clause and whether items in a clause convey new information or information that is assumed by the speaker/writer to be recoverable from the context. Goldenberg (1971), (1977) and (1990), for example, has used notions concerning the information structure of the clause to explain the use of the "tautological infinitive" and the syntax of the clause in Semitic languages. The study of "emphasis" in Biblical Hebrew by Muraoka (1985) uses some concepts that fall under this head. Gianto (1990) makes a functional study of the ordering of clause components in the Akkadian of Byblos on the basis of information structure. Kapeliuk (1994) elucidates the use of the definite article in Amharic by examining the information structure of the clauses. Murre-van den Berg (1995) uses this framework for Neo-Aramaic and Abdul-Raof (1998) for Arabic. Some of the work of Givon on "topic continuity" is based on this approach, see especially the volume edited by him (1983), which contains studies of topic continuity in Biblical Hebrew narrative (Fox) and Amharic narrative (Gasser). A number of recent studies of Biblical Hebrew word order have used similar functional approaches.

It should be noted that, whereas these discourse orientated approaches mark a radical change from structuralist and Chomskyan approaches to syntax, many elements of functional analysis with which they are concerned can be found already in traditional treatments of Semitic syntax. The modern study of information structure, for example, has its roots in the psychological theories of language that were developed in the 19th century, such as the notion of psychological subject. As we have seen, these notions were already applied to Semitic languages by scholars such as Brockelmann and Reckendorf. The study of the functional relationship between clauses, which is integral to the tagmemic approach, moreover, can be found in embryonic form in traditional treatments of "coordinated sentences".

It is beyond the scope of this paper to survey all the recent work on Semitic syntax that has adopted a discourse orientated approach. I intend here to restrict myself to a number of general observations. The study of syntax from a discourse perspective seeks general principles in a language but, due to the nature of the discipline, is restricted to a limited corpus of texts. The traditional taxonomic treatments of Semitic syntax have generally aimed at a comprehensive description of structures that occur in the attested language as a whole, or at least in a wide range of literary texts of different genres. In the traditional approach, the language itself, abstracted from the texts in which it occurs, is the main object of investigation. In the discourse approach to syntax, the language is no longer the only focus of attention but is regarded as a component of a text or act of communication. For this reason, in many discourse orientated approaches to syntax each text has to be treated individually and it is not practical to present analyses that involve a wide range of texts. Many recent studies of Semitic syntax in the context of discourse are indeed restricted to syntactic structures that occur in one single text. The focus of such studies is no longer exclusively the syntax itself but rather it is the analysis of the text from the perspective of syntax. Indeed, discourse approaches to syntax show that many uses of syntax cannot be reduced to general linguistic rules but reflect the personal touch of the writer/speaker in the presentation of the message. For this reason, many syntactic structures in a text must be given individual treatment in the context in which they occur.

Given my preceding remarks, it is significant to note that a very large proportion of recent studies of Semitic syntax from a discourse perspective are devoted to Biblical Hebrew. Several surveys have been published recently of work on the syntax of Biblical Hebrew in the framework of discourse analysis. The reader is referred to these for further bibliographical references. These include Dawson (1994), Eskhult (1994–1995) and Merwe (1997). Note also the volume edited by Bergen (1994).

The discourse analysis of syntax has been adopted by many biblical scholars as a means to elucidate the text of Scripture, which is, of course, one of the primary aims of biblical studies. This development in biblical analysis has been facilitated by the current movement away from historical criticism and the increasing tendency to treat the biblical text in its attested form as a literary unity worthy of synchronic analysis into its constituent components. Discourse treatments of the syntax of Biblical Hebrew are closely allied to works on literary analysis and rhetorical criticism, which have appeared in abundance in recent years. The principal concern of these types of work is the study of the literary artistry of the text and the motivation for its structure. The reader is referred to the bibliographical survey of rhetorical criticism of the Bible by Watson and Hauser (1994).

Scholars have not had the same motivation to apply discourse analysis to texts in other Semitic languages. The reason, it seems, is that there is not so much interest to undertake a minute analysis and exegesis of these texts. Discourse orientated studies of other Semitic languages tend to focus on the ordering of clause components as a reflection of the information structure of the clause rather than on a suprasentential analysis of the structure of discourse. Some studies of the syntax of Semitic languages other than Hebrew that take into account the structure of discourse are Belova (1985), in which a form of discourse analysis is applied to the syntax of Arabic, and Khan (1988), where the syntax of a variety of Semitic languages is studied in the context of the structure of discourse.

There is nothing special about Biblical Hebrew as a language that makes it more amenable to a discourse analysis of its syntax than other Semitic languages. In fact, some of the methodologies of discourse analysis are more easily applied to living spoken languages. This is especially the case with regard to the information structure of clauses and also the functional relation between clauses, which are often signalled explicitly by stress and intonation in spoken languages.

Another point of difference between the traditional taxonomic approach to Semitic syntax and the discourse approach is that in the traditional approach there was far more consensus and objectivity concerning the assessment of the data. The taxonomic approach was concerned primarily with the classification of observable syntactic structures. The discourse approach is concerned to a greater extent with function and meaning. This necessitates a greater degree of interpretation and exegesis, which opens up the possibility of differences of opinion.

In the traditional approach, moreover, there was far more consensus concerning the method of treating the data. When a Semitist of the 19th century such as Nöldeke arranged the taxonomy of syntactic data in one of his grammars, he felt no need to justify his approach or explain most of his terminology and concepts. He is unlikely, moreover, to have had any doubt concerning the boundaries of his syntactic description. The wide ranges of different discourse approaches to syntax that are found in the literature reflect the fact that there is no consensus either with the method of treating data or with the limits of the investigation. Some discourse treatments of syntax carry the elucidation of the data beyond the language structure into fields such as cognitive psychology and sociology.

At the beginning of my paper I proposed that in some respects the study of Semitic syntax has come full circle and taken on some features of the earliest treatments of Semitic syntax in the Middle Ages. My intention is that in the early medieval works and in many recent discourse studies of syntax, the focus is primarily on the analysis of the text rather than the language system. This has meant that, in many of the recent treatments of Biblical Hebrew syntax at least, the partitions between the study of syntax, rhetorical criticism and exegesis have fallen away and syntax, rhetoric and exegesis are treated as a single discipline, as was the case in the early period of Hebrew and Arabic grammatical thought.

I should like to conclude by making a few comments on some desiderata for the future of studies in Semitic syntax.

One may infer from my preceding remarks that there is a crisis of purpose in the study of Semitic syntax as to whether one should focus on the language or on the text. I believe that this should be regarded as a broadening of purpose rather than a crisis. There is no reason why in future the syntax of a Semitic language should not be studied at two levels, that of its structure and that of its communicative function. The structural analysis could conform to the traditional type of taxonomy whereas the functional analysis would take into account discourse context. The analysis of syntax in its discourse context, however, would have to be restricted, for practical purposes, to a small text corpus and possibly even a single text. It should be pointed out that important work is still being done by applying a traditional taxonomic approach to Semitic syntax. I should like to mention, for example, the brilliant study of Syriac sentence structure of G. Goldenberg (1983), which clarifies many aspects of this area of syntax by offering a more elaborate category and arrangement taxonomy of the data than is offered by the standard grammars of the language. Some recent work on Semitic syntax has indeed combined to some extent a traditional taxonomy with a functional approach. This is the case, for example, with the excellent syntax of Hebrew by B.K. Waltke and M. O'Connor (1990), which incorporates some of the insights gained from the study of the function of syntax in discourse.

It has been remarked that the extension of syntactic analysis to the study of the function of syntax in discourse has blurred the boundaries of syntax. An investigator of syntax is likely to be in doubt as to how far the analysis should be carried. I believe an important consideration in this regard is the readership at which a grammatical description is aimed. Elementary pedagogical grammars of Semitic languages generally do not contain a detailed treatment of syntax. In most university courses nowadays, the time spent by students on elementary language courses in Semitic languages is quite limited and more time is devoted to the reading of texts. For practical purposes, therefore, lengthy treatments of syntax in a pedagogical context should be separated from elementary grammars. Even at a more advanced level, a student may wish to have an overview of syntactic structures in the language as a whole. For such purposes, the traditional descriptive taxonomy would still be the most suitable method of presentation.

At the level of research publications consideration of the purpose of the work influences the extent to which syntax is treated. Investigators making grammatical descriptions of a language or dialect who are aiming primarily at a comparative study may regard it as a priority to focus on phonology and morphology. A detailed treatment of syntax is more appropriate to an independent, synchronic approach to the language, especially the treatment of syntax within discourse, in which the perspective is limited to individual texts. Ideally, perhaps, a reference grammar of a language should serve the needs both of the comparativist and also of investigators interested in the details of syntactic structures and functions.

As I remarked above, there is no consensus over the methodology of investigating the function of syntax or the limits of the investigation. This, I believe, is a more serious problem. It is an obstacle to investigators who wish to undertake such research on the Semitic languages. A consequence of the lack of consensus is that studies following one particular methodology may have a relatively limited appeal. A solution to this problem may be to take an eclectic approach, as far as this is feasible. In a similar vein, since the analysis of the function of syntax in literary texts is often open to various interpretations, one should avoid taking too dogmatic an approach and remain open to various alternative opinions.

A further point that one needs to take into consideration is the background of literary texts. As I have remarked, the rapid growth in works on the discourse analysis of Biblical Hebrew syntax has been facilitated in part by the fact that historical criticism of the Bible has fallen from favour among many scholars and that the text as we have it is treated synchronically as a literary unity. This attitude to the Biblical text, or indeed to any literary text, should not blind the investigator to the fact that some syntactic aspects of the text are readily explicable by studying the historical, literary and cultural background of the text rather than the internal structure of the text itself.

Finally, as I have indicated above, some of the problems of interpretation of the function of syntax disappear when one studies a language in its spoken form. The information structure of clauses and the semantic connection between clauses, both of which can generally be established in written texts only with a certain degree of subjective interpretation, are objectively signalled by stress and intonation patterns in a spoken language. I would like to express the hope, therefore, that future treatments of the spoken Semitic languages do not neglect the study of syntax and that investigators of the spoken languages recognize the insights that can be gained by applying a discourse approach to syntax. In many respects spoken languages are more suitable for discourse analysis than ancient literary texts.

REFERENCES

Abdul-Raof, H. 1998. *Subject, Theme and Agent in Modern Standard Arabic*. Richmond.

Al-Khuli, M.A. 1979. *A Contrastive Transformational Grammar: Arabic and English*. Studies in Semitic languages and linguistics 10. Leiden.

Al-Waer, M. 1987. *Toward a Modern and Realistic Sentential Theory of Basic Structures in Standard Arabic*. Damascus.

Andersen, F.I. 1974. *The Sentence in Biblical Hebrew*. Janua Linguarum, Series Practica 231. The Hague.

Andersen, F.I. 1970. *The Hebrew Verbless Clause in the Pentateuch*. Journal of Biblical Literature Monograph 14, Nashville.

Bacher, W. 1895. Le grammairien anonyme de Jérusalem et son livre. *Revue des Etudes Juives* XXX: 232–256.

Bakir, M.J. 1980. *Aspects of Clause Structure in Arabic: A study of word order variation in Literary Arabic*. Bloomington.

Beeston, A.F.L. 1970. *The Arabic Language Today*. London.

Behagel, O. 1909. Beziehungen zwischen Umfang und Reihenfolge von Satzgliedern. *Indogermanische Forschungen* 25: 110–142.

Belova, A.G. 1985. *Sintaksis pis'mennykh tekstov arabskogo yazyka*. Moscow.

Bergen, R.D. (ed.). 1994. *Biblical Hebrew and Discourse Linguistics*. Dallas.

Berman, R.A. 1978. *Modern Hebrew Structure*. Tel-Aviv.

Blau, J. 1960. *Syntax des palästinensichen Bauerndialektes von Bir-Zet, auf Grund der "Volkerzählungen aus Palästina"*. Beiträge zur Sprach- und Kulturgeschichte des Orients 13. Walldorf, Hessen.

Bloch, A. 1946. *Vers und Sprache im Altarabischen: metrische und syntaktische Untersuchungen.* Acta Tropica Supplementum 5. Basel.

Böttcher, F. 1866–1868. *Ausführliches Lehrbuch der hebräischen Sprache.* 2 vols. Leipzig.

Bravmann, M.M. 1953. *Studies in Arabic and General Syntax.* Publications de l'Institut d'Archéologie Orientale du Caire, Textes arabes et islamiques, XI. Cairo.

Brockelmann, C. 1913. *Grundriss der vergleichenden Grammatik der semitischen Sprachen.* II. Band: Syntax. Berlin.

Brockelmann, C. 1956. *Hebräische Syntax.* Neukirchen.

Cantarino, V. 1974–1975. *Syntax of Modern Arabic Prose.* Asian Studies Research Institute. Oriental series 4. Bloomington.

Caspari, C.P. 1848. *Grammatica Arabica in usum scholarum academicarum.* Accedit Brevis Chrestomathia ex codd. mscr. concinnata. Lipsiae.

Cohen, D. 1984. *La phrase nominale et l'évolution du système verbal en sémitique: Étude de syntaxe historique.* Leuven.

Cole, P. (ed.). 1976. *Studies in Modern Hebrew Syntax and Semantics: the transformational-generative approach.* North Holland linguistic series 32. Amsterdam.

Contini, R. 1982. *Tipologia della frase nominale nel semitico nordoccidentale del I millennio.* Pisa.

Davidson, A.B. 1901. *Hebrew Syntax.* 3rd edition. Edinburgh.

Dawson, D.A. 1994. *Text-linguistics and Biblical Hebrew.* Journal for the Study of the Old Testament Supplement Series 177. Sheffield.

Dillmann, A. 1857. *Grammatik der aethiopischen Sprache.* Leipzig.

Driver, S.R. 1874. *A Treatise on the Use of the Tenses in Hebrew and Some Other Syntactical Questions.* Oxford.

Ehelolf, H. 1916. *Ein Wortfolgeprinzip im Assyrisch-Babylonischen.* Leipzig.

Ennaji, M. 1985. *Contrastive Syntax: English, Moroccan Arabic and Berber Complex Sentences.* Würzbug.

Eskhult, M. 1990. *Studies in Verbal Aspect and Narrative Technique in Biblical Hebrew Prose.* Acta Universitatis Uppsaliensis. Studia Semitica Uppsaliensia 12. Uppsala.

Eskhult, M. 1994–1995. The Old Testament and textlinguistics. *Orientalia Suecana* 43: 93–103.

Ewald, G.H.A. 1831–1833. *Grammatica critica linguae Arabicae*: cum brevi metrorum doctrina. Lipsiae.

Ewald, G.H.A. 1879. *Syntax of the Hebrew Language of the Old Testament* (translated from the 8th German edition of *Ausführliches Lehrbuch der hebräischen Sprache des Alten Bundes* by James Kennedy). Edinburgh.

Faber, A. 1980. *Genetic Subgroupings of the Semitic Languages*. Ph.D. thesis, University of Texas at Austin. Ann Arbor, Mich.

Feghali, M.T. 1928. *Syntaxe des parlers arabes actuels du Liban*. Bibliothèque de l'Ecole des Langues Orientales Vivantes 9. Paris.

Fehri, A.F. 1993. *Issues in the Structure of Arabic Clauses and Words*. Dordrecht/London.

Firbas, J. 1992. *Functional Sentence Perspective in Written and Spoken Communication*. Cambridge.

Folmer, M.L. 1995. *The Aramaic Language in the Achaemenid Period: A study in linguistic variation*. Orientalia Lovaniensia analecta 68. Leuven.

Friedman, S.Y. 1971. Kol qaşar qodem. *Lešonénu* 35/2: 117–129, 35/3–4: 192–206.

Gabelentz, G. von der. 1869. Ideen zu einer vergleichenden Syntax. *Zeitschrift für Völkerpsychologie und Sprachwissenschaft* 6: 376–384.

Garbell, I. 1965. *The Jewish Neo-Aramaic Dialect of Persian Azerbaijan*: Linguistic analysis and folkloristic texts. Janua Linguarum, Series Practica 3. The Hague.

Gesenius, W. 1813. *Hebräische Grammatik*. Halle.

Gianto, A. 1990. *Word Order Variation in the Akkadian of Byblos*. Studia Pohl 15. Rome.

Gibson, J.C.L. 1994. *Davidson's Introductory Hebrew Grammar: Syntax*. Edinburgh.

Givon, T. 1977. The drift from VSO to SVO in Biblical Hebrew: The pragmatics of tense-aspect. In Li, C.N. (ed.). *Mechanisms of Syntactic Change*. Austin, 181–254.

Givon, T. 1983. *Topic Continuity in Discourse: A Quantitative Cross-language Study*. Typological Studies in Language 3. Amsterdam.

Goldenberg, G. 1971. Tautological infinitive. *Israel Oriental Studies* I: 36–85.

Goldenberg, G. 1977. Imperfectly-transformed cleft sentences. *Proceedings of the Sixth World Congress of Jewish Studies*, Jerusalem, vol. I: 127–33.

Goldenberg, G. 1983. On Syriac sentence-structure. In M. Sokoloff (ed.). *Aramaeans, Aramaic and the Aramaic Literary Tradition*. Ramat Gan, 97–140.

Goldenberg, G. 1990. On some niceties of Syriac syntax. In R. Lavenant (ed.). *V Symposium Syriacum, 1988: Katholieke Universiteit, Leuven,*

29–31 août, 1988. Orientalia Christiana Analecta 236. Rome, 335–344.

Greenberg, J.H. Some universals of grammar with particular reference to the 'order of meaningful elements'. In J.H. Greenberg (ed.). *Universals of Language.* Cambridge, Mass., 73–113.

Grimes, J. 1975. *The Thread of Discourse.* Janua linguarum. Series minor 207. The Hague.

Gross, W. 1987. *Die Pendenskonstruktion im biblischen Hebräisch.* Arbeiten zu Text und Sprache im Alten Testament 27. St. Ottilien.

Gross, W. 1996. *Die Satzteilfolge im Verbalsatz alttestamentlicher Prosa.* Tübingen.

Halliday, M.A.K. and Hassan, R. 1976. *Cohesion in English.* London.

Halliday, M.A.K. 1985. *Introduction to Functional Grammar.* London.

Hayes, J.L. 1985. *Dialectical Variation in the Syntax of Coordination and Subordination in Western Akkadian of the el-Amarna Period.* Ph.D. thesis, University of California, Los Angeles 1984. Ann Arbor, Mich.

Hoberman, R.D. 1989. *The Syntax and Semantics of Verb Morphology in Modern Aramaic: a Jewish dialect of Iraqi Kurdistan.* American Oriental Series 69. New Haven.

Kapeliuk, O. 1994. *Syntax of the Noun in Amharic.* Äthiopistische Forschungen 37. Wiesbaden.

Khan, G. 1988. *Studies in Semitic Syntax.* London Oriental Series 38. Oxford.

Khan, G. 1998. The book of Hebrew Grammar by the Karaite Joseph ben Noaḥ. *Journal of Semitic Studies* 43: 265–286.

Khan, G. 1999. The Karaite tradition of Hebrew grammatical thought. In W. Horbury (ed.). *Hebrew Study from Ezra to Ben-Yehudah.* Edinburgh.

Khan, G. 2000. *The Early Karaite Tradition of Hebrew Grammatical Thought: Including a Critical Edition, Translation and Analysis of the Diqduq of 'Abū Ya ʿqūb Yūsuf ibn Nūḥ on the Hagiographa.* Leiden.

Khrakovskii, V.S. 1973. *Ocherki po obshchemu i arabskomu sintaksisu.* Moscow.

Kinberg, N. 1991. "Clause" and "sentence" in *Maʿnā al-Qur'ān* by al-Farrā': A study of the term *kalām*. In *Proceedings of the Colloquium on Arabic Grammar*, ed. by Kinga Dévényi and Tamás Iványi. Budapest, 239–246.

König, E. 1881–1897. *Historisch-kritisches Lehrgebäude der hebräischen Sprache.* 2 vols in 3, Leipzig (vol. 2.2, 1897, is devoted to syntax).

Kropat, A. 1909. *Die Syntax des Autors der Chronik verglichen mit seiner*

Quellen: Ein Beitrag zur historischen Syntax des Hebräischen. Beiheft zur Zeitschrift für die Alttestamentliche Wissenschaft 16. Giessen.

Kuhr, E. 1929. *Die Ausdrucksmittel der Konjunktionslosen Hypotaxe in der ältesten hebräischen Prosa: Ein Beitrag zur historischen Syntax des Hebräischen.* Beiträge zur Semitischen Philologie und Linguistik, Heft 7. Leipzig.

Lambrecht, K. 1994. *Information Structure and Sentence Form: Topic, focus, and the mental representations of discourse referents.* Cambridge.

Longacre, R.E. 1976. *An Anatomy of Speech Notions.* Lisse.

Longacre, R.E. 1989. *Joseph: A story of Divine Providence.* A text-theoretical and text-linguistic analysis of Genesis 37 and 39–48. Winona Lake.

Longacre, R.E. 1996. *The Grammar of Discourse.* New York — London, second edition.

McFall, L. 1982. *The Enigma of the Hebrew Verbal System: Solutions from Ewald to the present.* Sheffield.

Merwe, C.H.J. 1997. An overview of Hebrew narrative syntax. In E. Van Wolde (ed.). *Narrative Syntax and the Hebrew Bible: Papers of the Tilburg conference 1996.* Biblical Interpretation Series 29. Leiden, 1–20.

Michel, D. 1977. *Grundlegung einer hebräischen Syntax.* Neukirchen-Vluyn.

Muraoka, T. 1985. *Emphatic Words and Structures in Biblical Hebrew.* Jerusalem.

Murre-van den Berg, H.L. 1995. *From a Spoken to a Written Language: The introduction and development of Literary Urmia Aramaic in the nineteenth century.* Ph.D. thesis, University of Leiden.

Nebes, N. 1982. *Funktionsanalyse von kāna yaf'alu: ein Beitrag zur Verbalsyntax des Althocharabischen mit besonderer Berücksichtigung der Tempus-und Aspektproblematik.* Studien zur Sprachwissenschaft 1. Hildesheim.

Niccacci, A. 1990. *The Syntax of the Verb in Classical Hebrew Prose.* Translated by W.G.E. Watson from *Sintassi del verbo ebraico nella prosa biblica classica*, 1986, JSOTS 86, Sheffield.

Nöldeke, T. 1875. *Mandäische Grammatik.* Halle.

Nöldeke, T. 1886. *Zur Grammatik des klassischen Arabisch.* Denkschr. der k. Akademie des Wiss. in Wien, phil.-hist. Kl. XLV. Wien.

Nöldeke, T. 1880. *Kurzgefasste syrische Grammatik;* mit einer Schrifttafel von Julius Euting. Leipzig.

Ornan, U. 1969. *Hammišpaṭ happašuṭ.* Jerusalem.

Pike, K.L. and Pike, E.G. 1983. *Text and Tagmeme.* London.

Praetorius, F. 1879. *Die Amharische Sprache.* Halle.

Reckendorf, H. 1895-1898. *Die syntaktischen Verhältnisse des Arabischen.* Leiden.

Reckendorf, H. 1921. *Arabische Syntax.* Heidelberg.

Reiner, E. 1966. *A Linguistic Analysis of Akkadian.* The Hague.

Richter, W. 1978-80. *Grundlagen einer althebräischen Grammatik.* 3 vols. St. Ottilien.

Schlesinger, M. 1928. *Satzlehre der aramäischen Sprache des babylonischen Talmuds.* Leipzig.

Schneider, W. 1982. *Grammatik des biblischen Hebräisch.* Munich.

Segal, J.B. 1953. *The Diacritical Point and the Accents in Syriac.* London.

Shlonsky, U. 1997. *Clause Structure and Word Order in Hebrew and Arabic.* Oxford.

Silvestre de Sacy, A.I. 1810. *Grammaire arabe à l'usage des élèves de l'école speciale des langues orientales vivantes.* 2 vols. Paris.

Talmon, R. (1988). "*Al-kalām mā kāna muktafiyan bi-nafsihi wa-huwa ğumla*": A study in the history of sentence concept and the Sībawaihian legacy in Arabic grammar: *Zeitschrift der Deutschen Morgenländischen Gesellschaft* 138: 74-98.

Talstra, E. 1978. Text grammar and Hebrew Bible. I. Elements of a theory. *Bibliotheca Orientalis* 35: 169-174.

Talstra, E. 1982. Text grammar and Hebrew Bible. II. Syntax and semantics. *Bibliotheca Orientalis* 39: 26-38.

Talstra, E. 1992. Text grammar and Hebrew Bible: The viewpoint of Wolfgang Schneider. *Journal of Translation and Textlinguistics* 5(4): 269-297.

Verreet, E. 1988. *Modi Ugaritici: eine morpho-syntaktische Abhandlung über das Modalsystem im Ugaritischen.* Orientalia Lovaniensia analecta 27. Leuven.

Versteegh, C.H.M. 1993. *Arabic Grammar and Qur'ānic Exegesis in Early Islam.* Leiden.

Waltke, B.K. and O'Connor, M. 1990. *An Introduction to Biblical Hebrew Syntax.* Winona Lake.

Watson, D. and Hauser, A.J. 1994. *Rhetorical Criticism of the Bible.* Leiden.

Watson, J.C.E. 1993. *A Syntax of Ṣan'ani Arabic.* Semitica Viva 13. Wiesbaden.

Weinrich, H. 1977. *Tempus, Besprochene und erzählte Welt.* 3rd edition. Sprache und Literatur 16. Stuttgart.

Werner, J. 1995. *Emphatische Syntax: zur Funktionalität oraler Syntagmen; eine komparative Studie am Beispiel des Bairischen und des Iraq-Arabischen mit einer einführenden Diskussion der relevanten Termini.* Tübinger Beiträge zur Linguistik 414. Tübingen.

Williams, R.J. 1976. *Hebrew Syntax: An Outline.* 2nd edition. Toronto.

Wise, H. 1975. *A Transformational Grammar of Spoken Egyptian Arabic.* Philological Society (Great Britain) Publications 26. Oxford.

Wright, W. 1862. *A Grammar of the Arabic Language.* London.

Wundt, W. 1900–20. *Völkerpsychologie: Eine Untersuchung der Entwicklungsgesetze von Sprache, Mythus und Sitte.* Leipzig.

SEMITIC LEXICOGRAPHY: EUROPEAN DICTIONARIES OF BIBLICAL HEBREW IN THE TWENTIETH CENTURY

M. O'CONNOR

1. INTRODUCTION

The relationship between general linguistics and Semitic linguistics has been complex ever since the two disciplines struggled into existence.* A survey of questions relating to the lexicography of the most widely studied of the classical Semitic languages, Biblical Hebrew, may shed light on some of the twists and turns in the broader relationship. The role of lexicography in the two fields has been radically different. Dictionary making has never occupied the limelight in general linguistics, although it is the oldest and most rigorous of the "applied" linguistic subdisciplines. Lexica play a greater role in the study of written languages than in general linguistics, so that, insofar as Semitics has shown a philological turn, lexica have been a major occupation. Wilhelm Gesenius (1786–1842), a major forebear of modern Semitics, was both a grammarian and a lexicographer, and so have been Carl Brockelmann, Jean Cantineau, I. J. Gelb, and Wolfram von Soden. In our time the combination is found in the work of, for example, Erica Reiner and Jacob Hoftijzer.

Semitic lexicography is a slow-moving field, but it moves more rapidly than other branches of Semitic linguistics. It is through lexica that one can best trace developments and reassessments over the span of the twentieth century. Thus lexicography is a useful index of growth in the field as a whole. Lexica are also important in themselves, the category of linguistic reference tool most often found in the hands of non-linguists, for better or worse.[1] After some comments on lexicography, general and Semitic, I devote the bulk of my attention to Hebrew as it existed up to approximately

---

* This paper was presented at the "Conference on Semitic Linguistics: The State of the Art at the Turn of the Twenty-First Century," held at Tel Aviv University in January 1999. I wish to thank the organizers for inviting me and my fellow conferees for their comments. I owe a debt as well to two members of the audience, Aron Dolgopolsky and Michael Sokoloff, for their remarks.

[1] For a survey of "The Lexicography of the ancient Near Eastern Languages," see *Studi epigrafici e linguistici* 12 (1995). For a survey of Semitic lexicography, see Fronzaroli

the turn of the eras. I am primarily concerned with European scholarship, but it is worth noting, as Michael Sokoloff reminds me, that there is no Modern Hebrew dictionary of Biblical or ancient Hebrew; this apparent gap is worthy of study.

Linguistics has its theoretical and applied sides. At least notionally, theoretical linguistics presents a substructure of assumptions and arguments to undergird its every move, while applied linguistics is more oriented to language-based tasks. To take an example remote from the present subject, the development of speech therapy for a stroke victim is an applied matter; the neuro- and psycholinguistic bases for the therapy are theoretical issues (Menn et al. 1995). The theory is disputed, but that does not mean that the therapy cannot be developed; it means rather that the therapy does not follow from the theory in a straightforward way but has to be elaborated in other terms, the terms of what works or seems to work. If the therapy works well enough, it may provide insights or hints for the theory: such is the lumbering way science operates.

In the matter of the "lexicon," there is a similar distinction between theoretical and applied fields (see Ilson 1992; Mel'čuk and Sproat 1992). Producing an actual lexicon, a reference work to be used, is a matter of applied or practical linguistics. This task is entirely different from the theoretical description of the mental faculty "the lexicon," one of the faculties that make up the ability to speak, listen, and otherwise use language. There are various claims that have been made in theoretical linguistics concerning the lexicon, but the claims do not add up to a single description. The claims are of two types. The first and larger set of claims concerns the articulation of the mental lexicon with the other components of the grammar. Linguists often use the language of partitioning: such and such a feature "belongs in" the lexicon, as opposed to "belonging" in the phonology, morphology, or syntax. The second and smaller set of claims concerns the shape of the lexicon itself; this is a smaller set because it is difficult to describe a mental faculty that operates simultaneously in terms of phonology, morphology, and syntax, as well as semantics. The equation of the linguistic study of semantics with the linguistic study of the lexicon, popular as it seems to be, is fallacious. Semantics is only a small though

(1973). For surveys of Biblical Hebrew lexicography, see Barr (1973, 1992), Muraoka (1995c). In particular, for the work of the European Science Foundation Workshop on the Semantics of Classical Hebrew (directed by J. Hoftijzer), now the Semantics of Ancient Hebrew Database (directed by T. Muraoka), see reports in *Zeitschrift für Althebraistik* 6 (1993):1–127 and 7 (1994):3–50, under Hoftijzer's editorship, and Muraoka (1998). On other aspects of the relationship between linguistics and the study of extinct Semitic languages, see Buccellati (1996:viii–x).

important part of the linguistic consideration of the lexicon; the problem of polysemy and homonymy has been amply discussed recently.[2]

Lexicography is a matter of applied linguistics rather than of theoretical linguistics; the theory behind lexicography is sometimes called lexicology, but I shall not use that distinction. Lexicography is committed to describing language already at work, in parallel with other areas of applied linguistics: first- and second-language teaching, speech therapy, language policy studies, and so on. Scholarship in these areas is a matter of what works. Lexicography seeks to guide and describe the production of books that people actually use.

Three tasks are basic to lexicography, and the Semitic languages present special features related to each of these tasks. These are (a) the delimitation of the material studied (What is this a lexicon of?), (b) the structural segregation of units (What are the working units of the lexicon?), and (c) the delimitation and arrangement of relevant information (What is the lexicon going to provide the user with concerning each of the working units?).

2. THE FIRST TASK: DELIMITATION

The first task, the delimitation of the material studied, is the point at which lexicographer and user most clearly betray their reasons for making and consulting the lexicon. It is also the point at which historical dimensions may be relevant, whether in plain or encrypted form. Also relevant to the delimitation of the material is the quantity of the sources and, especially in the case of ancient and medieval sources, various facets of their character.

The millennium-long history of Semitic lexicography illustrates these points. The material of the earliest Semitic lexica is scripture. The motive for lexicographic study is the need to understand scripture as authoritative and canonical; the motivation, though not the methodology, of the earliest lexicography is exegetical. The basic delimitation of the material studied is not performed by the lexicographers, poor drudges that they are, but in a different dimension, in a non-linguistic way. The autonomy that some lexicographers claim for their work is a dubious quality at best, but it is irrelevant to the medieval lexicography of Arabic and Hebrew.[3]

The facts of quantity and history can both be relevant to the

---

2   On semantics, see Barr (1961, 1993), and Sawyer (1967); Clark (1992) provides further bibliography and discussion. On polysemy and homonymy, see Barr (1993) again, Hospers (1993), and Kedar-Kopfstein (1994).

3   For recent work on medieval Semitic lexicography, for Hebrew, see Muraoka and Shavitsky (1991); for the Syriac tradition, little studied, see Balzaretti (1997).

delimitation behind scriptural lexicography. Just as there are two primary scriptures in the classical Semitic languages, so there are two models of lexicographical delimitation. The first model is provided by the earliest Hebrew lexicographic work: it is in part because the Tanakh is a large body of material that it can be studied on its own; additional Hebrew material is not consistently adduced by the medievals. The second model is provided by the earliest Arabic lexicography: the Quran is a small body of material that seems to cry out for external illumination. There are in the technical literature of lexicography studies of corpus size in relation to the adequacy of the resulting lexicon (i.e., How many hundred thousand words do you need before you get multiple attestations of nearly everything?). We need not take up these studies here; the earliest Arab grammarians anticipated these studies and felt that to understand the language of the Quran other sources were needed. This Arabic model has an explicit historical dimension: the external illumination that the lexicographers of the Quran felt they needed was sought in *earlier* materials. It also has a cultural-geographical dimension, since external illumination was sought in *culturally remote* materials; this point is more relevant to features of language other than the lexicon. Since the Prophet Muḥammad lived in the Age of Ignorance, his language could best be studied in terms of the poetry and proverbs of that time; failing relevant sources there, his language (again, grammar perhaps more than lexicon) could best be studied in terms of the speech of Arabians remote from the urban centers of Islam.

Thus, the earliest Arabic lexicographic studies have a historical dimension: they turn to material contemporary with and earlier than the Prophet. One assumption behind this procedure can be made explicit: material later than the Prophet is not used at least in part because it is assumed to reflect knowledge of the Quran, whether in oral or written form. The Quran, when it was disseminated, changed the language of the Arabs to a scriptural language, the language of Islam: this and similar developments may be called the scriptural turn. Before the Prophet, the Arabs were a people devoted to various uses of language; after the rise of Islam the Quran took on a special place among those uses. The role of writing in early Islam cannot be denied, but I am not, I think, merely talking about the role of written scripture; after all, the Quran is a small enough book to be memorized, and it is regularly memorized.

Another feature of the first, delimiting task of Semitic lexicography is implicit here: the ranking of materials. In lexicography a corpus is not only studied but subdivided and its parts rank-ordered in various senses. For example, the poetry of the Age of Ignorance is primarily studied in order to illuminate the Quran; the reverse process is secondary. The task of delimiting the material studied includes to some extent the task of ranking the material, arranging it in some constellation that reflects how the dictionary is intended to be used and ultimately an understanding of how the corpus or language itself works.[4]

Such a sense of rank can be found in lexica that are not scripturally based. Both the Akkadian dictionaries, *AHw* and *CAD*, are grounded in a model of the history of Akkadian, though that model is not an explicit part of either. The model has both historical and geographical dimensions; material from the Mesopotamian heartland and from the Old Babylonian period is favored (as it is in the grammars, though there it is *explicitly* favored, see, e.g., Huehnergard 1997:xxvi–xxvii).

The historical dimension of the delimitation of material thus appears in both the scriptural context of Arabic and (to a lesser extent) the non-scriptural context of Akkadian. The historical dimension is not inevitable: the earliest lexica of Hebrew do not obviously have such a dimension. But it should come as no surprise to find a historical dimension encoding itself in another form, and what other form should history take for a scriptural mindset than scripture itself? If the three sectors of the Tanakh are taken as being of different degrees of importance, as they generally are in Judaism, then a historical dimension may have begun to insert itself, insofar as the Torah presents itself as older than the Prophets and the Writings. It is also noteworthy that the bulk of biblical scholarship regards at least parts of the Torah as older than at least parts of the other sections.

A related aspect of corpus delimitation involves distinguishing central materials and genuine outliers of various sorts, which tend to fall together. The distance from central materials to materials that differ in various minor respects is a matter of increments; but there are often materials that are still further out, where distances cannot be measured stepwise but reflect chasms not easily mapped. In the Bible, Qoheleth is an outlier on many different measures that otherwise have nothing in common (see, e.g., Isaksson 1987, Schoors 1991, Seow 1997); this is commonly associated with a late date for the book (as by those just cited), though such has been questioned (see, e.g., Hurvitz 1995a:3, 10). Outliers may be the linguistic

---

[4] For examples of the scriptural turn in Late Second Temple Period Hebrew, see Skehan's discussion (1970) of the role of the Song of the Well, Num 21:17–18, of the Song of Moses, especially Deut 32:7–9, and, more surprisingly, of Qoh 12:11, in the "Praise of the Ancestors" section of Ben Sira, especially Sir 44:2–5; and the treatment in Morrison (1997), following Schiffman (1982) and Newsom (1985:313–14), of the 'sound of divine stillness' in the Songs of the Sabbath Sacrifice (4Q405 fragments 20 ii-21–22 lines 7–8, Newsom 1985:303), arising from Elijah's experience on Mount Horeb, 1 Kgs 19:12.

equivalent of historically or geographically distant material but need not be.

Thus a variety of considerations is relevant to the first task of Semitic lexicography, the definition of the corpus. Questions of scripture and related areas of authority and social structure pertain; so do questions of history and geography. And the problem of size also appears. There is one further set of questions that can only be alluded to, those related to translation: some Qumran texts represent translations;[5] the earliest literature in Syriac and Coptic is translational, as is much of medieval Arabic and Hebrew literature. Does translational literature belong to the corpus of a language in the same way that literature composed in the language does? The question, although often addressed in specific contexts (extending also to the Old Greek translation of the Tanakh) remains to be broadly formulated and studied.

3. THE SECOND TASK: SEGREGATION

The second and third tasks of lexicography are, in contrast to the first, more clearly linguistic. The second is the structural segregation of the units of the lexicon. The analysis that is applied to the language material can be of various sorts with various results. In Semitic lexicography there are three possible modes of analysis, and each of these can be presented in different ways.

The first mode of analysis involves *the word*, as that term is ordinarily understood, with the relevant inflectional variations gathered under a single heading. Words with the same consonantal skeleton are usually given in the order verbs first, then nouns, and among these, simple nouns and then nouns with various prefixes and suffixes. Identical words are ordered in terms of frequency or according to a logical schema. One difficulty here concerns the various verbal nouns, which belong to the verb in reflecting different types of nominalizations and adjectivizations of the verb. Generally the infinitives, verbal nouns of action or state, are grouped with the verb, as are the derived participles. Often the stative participle or verbal adjective associated with the simple stem, though it is quite regular in formation, is listed as a separate word because its existence and meaning are less predictable than those of other verbal nouns. The other simple-stem participles are generally listed as part of

---

5   Qumran translation from Hebrew to Aramaic is well known in, e.g., 11QtgJob, Sokoloff
     1974; translation from Aramaic to Hebrew may be found in the Hebrew Tobit text,
     4QTob[e], Fitzmyer 1995.

the verb entry, even in the cases where the simple-stem finite forms do not occur.

The second mode of analysis involves the *root*, the abstract consonantal skeleton and associated sense that underlies much of the Semitic vocabulary. In the mode familiar from most European dictionaries of Hebrew and Aramaic, all the words belonging to one root are grouped together, followed by all the words belonging to the other(s). The ordering of the roots is usually based on frequency or a logical schema. Root structure analysis is retained in vestigial form even in one of the Akkadian dictionaries, though Akkadian root structure is often obscure due to distinctive Akkadian phonology. Von Soden's guides to roots at the beginning of most letters of the *AHw* are a far cry from a root-based dictionary, but they preserve the historical memory of such works and they are useful. Analysis of vocabulary for roots is often difficult in the West Semitic languages, and discussions of the difficulty are often themselves confused. It seems plausible to align the root with the verb, but in much of the vocabulary in which the root is apparent there is no corresponding verb. In considering this vocabulary, one is tempted to ask, Do we suppose that the root had some meaningful existence in the language because of vocabulary "derived" in some sense from the root? Tempting as the question is, it is the wrong question, since the arrangement of the lexicon is not designed as a map of the mental lexicon; entering a root in a dictionary does not involve a claim that the root existed, but merely that the analytical procedure of extracting roots from the vocabulary, which often does reflect the association of root, verb, and other words, is useful for the producer and user of the lexicon. A major problem with a root-based arrangement is posed by words which have no root structure that can be predictably assigned by the user. These words, often grammatical function words, then have to be tucked in around the edges of the root structure, with predictable results: frustration for the experienced user and great frustration for the student.

The third mode of analysis involves the *root-shape*, the abstract consonantal skeleton of one or more roots. Arabic lexicography began with this mode of analysis and has for the most part retained it: all the words with a common root-shape are kept together and presented in a fixed order, from simple-stem forms through derived-stem forms through nouns with a monosyllabic base and their feminines, nouns with a disyllabic base and their feminines, and ending with nouns with prefixes and suffixes.[6]

---

[6] Root-shape analysis is found in all the European Arabic dictionaries known to me with one exception. The French dictionary founded by Régis Blachère (Blachère et al. 1967–), now known as *Al-Kāmil* and working on its fifth letter, distinguishes roots: "Il

Working with the root-shape does reflect aspects of the dynamics of readerly activity in encountering an unfamiliar term. Despite the view occasionally expressed that this mode of arrangement reflects a limitation of analysis, it is a thoroughly readerly convention: a reader who looks up an unfamiliar word based on a root-shape analysis and follows the grid of patterns used in the dictionary will find the word based on its morphology. The convention is based on the fact, not surprising but perhaps worth mentioning, that people often use a dictionary to look up words they are not familiar with. There is a limitation reflected in this Arabic method, but not, I think, of linguistics but of typography. In a manuscript dictionary, it would be difficult to distinguish various levels of analysis that modern typography can easily separate visually. Because the visual coordination of the elements of the dictionary works well, the separation of groups of words based on roots with the same shape but different meanings becomes manageable and has become standard in most European dictionaries of Hebrew and Aramaic.

The difference between roots and root-shapes seems straightforward enough, and the earliest comments indicating that a given root-shape comprehends several different roots appear in the work of Ibn Fāris (d. 1004; Fleisch 1971)[7] and thus go back to the moment around the turn of the last millennium when native Semitic lexicography saw its greatest achievements.

Despite this major difference between most Arabic lexica and most modern dictionaries of other Semitic languages, it has led to some confusion among Hebraists, in several different ways. Let me mention two cases of confusion. For the first, consider the common view that Biblical Hebrew had two verbs *'ny* for verbal activity; one of these *'ny* roots means 'to reply, answer', though it is possible that the root does not at base designate a verbal activity, while the other means 'to sing', cognate to Arabic *ġny* II 'to sing' (so most recently Barr 1994:39). KB 3 (*HALAT/HALOT*) recognizes that the second is "not

est cependant apparu comme indispensable d'introduire des divisions dans les racines homophones," I.viii. The rival German product, Ullmann (1970–), claims to work on the root principle ("Die Worter sind nach dem Wurzelprinzip angeordnet," I.xix), but is actually based on root-shapes: "Homonyme Wurzel sind entgegen den Forderungen, die Johann Fuck und Wolfram von Soden erhoben haben, nicht getrennt. Einer Trennung stehen erhebliche sachliche Schwierigkeiten entgegen, zumal semantische Kriterien oftmals nicht gegenüber, um zu entscheiden, welcher Wurzel ein bestimmtes Wort zugeordnet werden muss" (I.xx). Writing in 1884, Steingass seems embarrassed to admit the fact: "It is true... sometimes different roots or their derivatives are thrown together under the same heading," Steingass 1987:vi.

[7]   As my colleague Richard M. Frank informs me.

always clearly distinguishable from" the first (*HALOT* 2.854b), and the Madrid dictionary does not record the 'sing' root ("There is no reason to suppose a different root" [from the 'answer' root'], Madrid 577b). The question of whether there are one or two verbal activity roots need not concern us. Rather, I am concerned with the argumentation about the matter. In a recent discussion, a Hebraist, not offering a pretense of familiarity with Arabic (Clines 1998c:629), cited a European dictionary of Classical Arabic (Steingass 1884/1987) and alleged that because the sense for *ġny* in Form I, 'to be free from want, have no need', is quite different from 'to sing' and because the 'sing' sense occurs further down in the entry, under Form II, the 'sing' sense must be quite "specialized" and thus secondary and thus not relevant for comparative work. This scholar is reading a (European) dictionary of Classical Arabic, organized by root-shapes, as if it were a (European) dictionary of Biblical Hebrew, organized by roots. The Arabic dictionary groups together different roots, one meaning 'to be free from want' and another meaning 'to sing', under a common root-shape (see Lane 2302); no inferences about "specialization" can legitimately be made. For another case of confusion, consider the Arabic root-shape *ḥlq* and its treatment by a scholar whose chief burden is the vexed issue of methodology and the use of Arabic lexica in the study of Biblical Hebrew. He writes of the various meanings associated with the root-shape, "The primary meaning of the Arabic root has to do with roundness and the shape of a circle. ... A further sense ... is related to the idea of shaving and the removal of hair. This may be connected to the primary sense through the circular movements of the sharp object which produce a smooth, round surface" (Kaltner 1996:25). Here, Arabic dictionaries (based on root-shapes) are being read as if they were based on roots. The crude search for a unifying *Grundbedeutung* exemplified here, the search to tie together every word and sense into a tidy bundle, is archaic even for single words; in this case the treatment distorts the evidence (see Lane 628–30). Thus, the distinction between roots and root-shapes is worth rehearsing.

The questions attendant on the second task of Semitic lexicography, the structural segregation of units, are more strictly linguistic than those considered in connection with the first task. A Semitic dictionary can use one level of analysis, the word, or two levels of analysis, the root or root-shape and then the word. The root method is on the whole more common. A root-shape dictionary, such as most Arabic lexica are, avoids the problem of distinguishing different roots of the same shape. In all these matters, there is a linguistic analysis going on, and the linguistic reality of its results is open to question. Consider the listing as a lemma of the 3ms perfective form of a verb that is attested only in the 1cs imperfective: there is an analysis involved that bases itself on attested facts and goes beyond them. Now consider listing as a lemma a root with no verb attached for three nouns with the same consonantal skeleton and related meanings: here too is an analysis based on attested facts and going beyond them. It is reasonable to draw a line between the two types of analysis, but it is wrong to insist, as is sometimes done, that they have nothing in common.

4. THE THIRD TASK: INFORMATION

The third task of lexicography involves the provision and arrangement of relevant information: What is the lexicon going to provide the user with for each of the working units, what does a speaker or reader (in the judgment of the dictionary makers) need to know? Under this heading are all the issues familiar from the great English-language dictionary wars of our own time (see, e.g., Green 1996:440–68; Crystal 1995:170–87). We may begin by rehearsing some of these. First, there have been the etymology battles: to what extent is it necessary or useful for a reader to know the origin and meaning of a word in earlier stages of a language or in a language from which it was borrowed? Traditionally etymology has played a role in the lexicography of modern languages, but especially since the Second World War it has been judged, with some reason, that that role was exaggerated, and etymology has been assigned a more subsidiary role or no role at all. Second, there have been the usage battles: to what extent is a dictionary licensed to prescribe "proper usage"? More recent modern-language dictionaries have tended to move away from doing such duty. Third, there have been the definition battles: in shaping a string of words as a definition, is it more important to describe explicitly the meaning of a word (as in most monolingual dictionaries) or to provide one or more translational equivalents (as in most older bilingual dictionaries)? This last set of arguments has generally been resolved in favor of the first alternative, on the view that there is no principled difference between mono- and bilingual dictionaries (Chadwick 1996).

In lexica of extinct Semitic languages these issues are also relevant, though in somewhat different forms. The information a lexicon provides can be partitioned under three headings: (1) the *morphological* (including the citation and linguistic description of forms), (2) the *definition proper and semantic and syntactic analysis*, and (3) the *philological data*, a term I shall use to cover all the data not derived from the linguistically immediate context of occurrence. The first heading involves the presentation of morphological data: what forms are attested and in what relationship to the system of the morphology of the language? Such data can be often key to the writing of the definition, since the morphology may supply clues to the working of a word, notably in terms of the stem or form (Hebrew *binyan*) system. The second heading extends from the translational term or phrase outward to the immediate linguistic environment in which the lemma occurs.

The last heading, the philological, brings together groups of data often wrongly, in my view, separated from one another. One subheading of it covers (3a) various *registers and categories of usage*. Another treats (3b) data internal to the language but *not involving the immediate linguistic contexts of the occurrences under study*: what words does the lemma occur in the vicinity of, in association with, or in contrast to? This subheading includes the data provided by verse "parallelism," "synonymy," and "antonymy": all of these rubrics have been objected to on linguistic and literary grounds (Berlin 1985, Cloete 1989, Cooper 1987, O'Connor 1980, 1993, 1997), but the usefulness of the data is not thereby ruled out (for a nuanced statement, see Barr 1993:9). An accepted model for the use of such data is wanting.

Here too belongs (3c) the *so-called etymological data*, which is generally the slab of Comparative Semitic data in, say, a Biblical Hebrew dictionary that furnishes the meanings of a given root or word in Arabic, Aramaic, Akkadian, and rarely Ethiopic. The "etymological" label is misleading. There are, to be sure, Biblical Hebrew words that are loans or *Wanderwörter* that have true etymologies. Much of the so-called etymological data in Hebrew dictionaries is, however, not truly etymological but comparative.

The category of material related to usage (3a) is most richly exemplified by the enormous fund of data provided by the Mesopotamian lexical lists, a guide to coordinating in particular Sumerian and Akkadian usage, translational practice, and writing systems (Civil 1994, Reiner 1994). If the headings of "Comparative Semitic" and "lexical list" data are grouped together as philological data, as I am proposing, then we can be clearer about the best-known difference between the two Akkadian dictionaries. *AHw* and *CAD* do not differ in so absolute a manner as is often suggested. Rather they present different selections of philological data: the *CAD* uses only the native philological information, while von Soden provides both the native information and largely Comparative Semitic data. Thus both dictionaries have a philological base.

Consideration of this point concerning Akkadian, which has no ongoing literary tradition, reminds us that there is a greater range of philological data relevant to Hebrew dictionary-making than simply the etymological data. The tradition of translation of Hebrew material into other languages is as venerable and as difficult to use as the Mesopotamian lexical-list materials. Some of these translations involve movement into unrelated languages (as Sumerian is unrelated to Akkadian), and the translation of the Tanakh into Greek here takes pride of place. The translations into other Semitic languages, chiefly various forms of Aramaic, are also important. This enormous fund of material has never been registered in dictionaries of Biblical Hebrew, but it is not unfair to say that it has been lurking offstage all along. As people using the dictionaries have known less and less about these translations — after all, the last major polyglot Bible, the London Polyglot edited by Brian Walton, was produced in the mid-seventeenth century — their role in dictionary making has sometimes been forgotten.

The use of the ancient versions has always been difficult and perhaps is more difficult today than in the past. Consider only the Old Greek (Septuagint): in order to grasp how the translation was made, it is necessary to consider the understanding of the individual Hebrew (or Aramaic) words implicit at each point *along with* questions of the Hebrew text being represented *and* the cultural needs and religious sensitivities of the audience being addressed. The textual and cultural-religious problems do not constitute an impenetrable veil separating us from the Old Greek at every point. Most of the time we can look at the Greek text and see an approach to the Hebrew that is preserved in the Masoretic text. The claims of the Septuagint on our attention are enormous: the translators intended to represent the Hebrew text before them and they intended their Greek to be meaningful. These goals are too close to our own for us to ignore them. (See Hanhart 1994, Muraoka 1995b, Tov 1997.)

In the early history of Hebrew lexicography it is the Semitic versions and more broadly the Semitic languages Aramaic and Arabic that played a role (Greenstein 1984:220–23). Indeed the comparison of these three languages, particularly associated with Yehuda ibn Qurayš, represents the advent of comparative-historical linguistics as well as "the most exciting linguistic discovery of medieval Hebrew scholarship" (Goldenberg 1998:4); John Elwolde's revisionist description of such scholarship misses the mark (Elwolde 1995). Hebrew excursions into neighboring languages are comparable in some sense to the Arab grammarians' excursions into the pre-Islamic poetry; both movements represent attempts to expand the range of study, in both cases in response to actual difficulties.

The amount of philological data relevant to Hebrew dictionary-making is thus enormous. There is no generally accepted model for its overall assessment, and the failure of attempts earlier in the last century to create a model may have led to a sense that any model is doomed to fail. It is certainly true that in the last century practitioners of the analysis of such data have often been inclined to heap up information without an explicit model of argumentation and that the information itself, particularly as it involved the Arabic lexicon, was often open to question.[8]

Such failures do not, however, answer the underlying need, which is for a plausible approach to argumentation; only a considered approach can lead to the goal of formatting the philological data in a dictionary.

The shift in fashion away from the sort of philology I have in mind has led to various results. The most alarming is the simple abandonment of such argumentation altogether. Let me mention one apparently orphaned proposal, involving a passage in Chronicles and a pair of well-known Semitic words, not in order to argue for the correctness of the proposal involved, but to highlight the kind of case I have in mind. The passage concerns the ugly death of Jehoram of Judah, a fate not alluded to by the author of Kings (2 Kings 8:24).

> Yhwh smote him [Jehoram of Judah] in his innards with a sickness with no cure. Time went on, and just as the end of the second year went out his innards went out because of his sickness, and he died of his vile diseases. His people made no fire (*śərĕpâ*) for him like the fires for his forebears. He was thirty-two when he became king, and he reigned eight years in Jerusalem; he departed (*wayyélek*) *bəlō' ḥemdâ*, and they buried him in the City of David but not in the royal tombs. (2 Chr 21:18b–20)

That the verb *hlk* here refers to the mode of death is accepted by most scholars, although Jerome seems to take it as referring to Jehoram's mode of life, *ambulavit*; his translation of *bəlō' ḥemdâ* as *non recte* 'not properly' certainly fits the Chronicler's evaluation of this king but cannot be defended otherwise. Thus we are dealing with death.

The common BHeb root *ḥmd* 'to desire, covet' could be the source for the term *ḥemdâ*, elsewhere used with the plain sense 'desire' (so, e.g., BDB), but that meaning is hard to make sense of here. The text, after all, seems not to say that he *lived* 'with no desire', i.e., perhaps 'as no one desired' (so BDB s.v.), but that he *died* that way. The phrase is sometimes translated as if it referred to what people thought of the king, e.g., "He departed with no-one's regret" (NRSV, cf. RSV), "he departed unloved" (NAB), but it is not obvious that the text can mean that.[9] Thus the relevance of the common BHeb root may be doubted.

---

[8] Kaltner (1996) demonstrates this for the Arabic; his survey of European Arabic dictionaries omits the two ongoing projects, Blachère et al. (1967–) and Ullmann et al. (1970–).

[9] It is also not obvious that the Syriac, which reads a form of *rgā* 'to desire', can mean, as BHS has it, "[et abiit] non desideratus" 'and he went undesired'.

It seems that the common Arabic root *hamida yahmadu hamd* 'to praise, commend' may be relevant, in line with the Old Greek's rendering, *kai eporeúthē en ouk epaínō*. The use of *épainos* 'praise, approval' for BHeb *hemdâ* is unique. Elsewhere the Hebrew word is rendered by the expected terms related to 'desire', *epithumētós* 'desired' (8 times), *epithumía* 'yearning' (twice), and *epithúmēma* 'yearning' (once), or by terms referring to desirability, *eklektós* 'chosen' (4 times), *kállos* 'beauty' (once), and *hōraîos* 'beautiful' (once) (Muraoka 1998:52). Contrariwise, the Greek *épainos* 'praise' is used in the Septuagint to render Hebrew *tehillâ* three times in the Psalter; it also occurs once to render *hādār* in the psalm in 1 Chronicles 16 (at 16:27), though not in the parallel passage in Psalm 96, where *hōraiótēs* is used. The cognate verb *epainéō* 'to praise' renders Hebrew *hll* and *šbh* both in the D stem. Thus the rendering *en ouk epaínō* for *balō' hemdâ* seems to suggest that *hmd* 'to desire' is not involved in 2 Chr 21:20, and the Arabic suggests that Hebrew had a word *hemdâ* 'praise'.

This bit of philology contains no great surprises, and it is also no surprise to find that such a view lies behind several recent translations. The NJPS version translates here "he departed unpraised," with a note: "Following Septuagint; cf. Arabic *hamada* 'praise'." The NEB and the REB similarly have "his passing went unsung," and the NJB has "he passed away unlamented." The hand of Jonas Greenfield may be suspected behind the NJPS version, and that of G. R. Driver behind the NEB and the REB; I have not located articles by either scholar dealing with this point, nor can I suggest a source for the NJB rendering.

The matter is worth mentioning here because, although this understanding of Hebrew *hemdâ* is clear in several translations, it is not to be found in recent dictionaries or commentaries. Sara Japhet (1993:817) reports these 'unpraised' translations as if they were equivalent to the 'to no one's regret' translations despite the clear note to the contrary in NJPS; she also cites Sh. Abramson's suggestion (Abramson 1987–88:381–82), with Rabbinic parallels, that *hemdâ* here has the sense of 'heat, fire' and refers to the burial practice of fire cited in 2 Chr 21:19. Whatever the merits of the Rabbinic solution, it should be noted that the "Arabic" solution, though found in several recent translations, goes unrecorded in recent lexical works (*HALOT*, *ThWAT*, *TDOT*, and the Madrid and Sheffield dictionaries). It is possible that the matter has been aired in full and the Arabic solution definitively refuted, but that seems unlikely. Rather, it seems that the endeavor of philological assessment has been given up. A proposed solution to a real problem in the text has thus been abandoned. This orphaning of products of twentieth-century comparative philology is at least in part a byproduct of unfortunate shifts in scholarly fashion.

In Andersen's resonant formulation, "Even if much of [the comparative] work [on BHeb] has been done badly ... the remedy for bad work is not no work but good work" (Andersen 1995a:56–57).

The last feature of this third task is the arrangement of the data: the lexicographer can put the data together in a variety of ways, with philology at the beginning or the end, standard combinations mixed in with the rarely attested phrases and idioms or separated out, and so on. The various meaning entries can be written independently of the superstructure of the entire article or they can be written to make sense only within it.

5. THE MAJOR EUROPEAN LEXICA OF BIBLICAL HEBREW

There have been half-a-dozen or so major European lexica of Biblical Hebrew produced in the 20th century. They have appeared in pairs, and they neatly span the century: BDB (Brown, Driver, and Briggs 1907) and Buhl (Gesenius-Buhl 1915) produced early in the century, Koehler-Baumgartner (1953, KB 1) and Zorell (1954) at the midpoint, and the Madrid and Sheffield dictionaries in the 1990s (Madrid, Sheffield). The revision of Koehler-Baumgartner (KB 3, *HALAT*, *HALOT*) is so extensive that it may be counted as a separate work.[10]

The earliest of these is the English-language lexicon of Brown, Driver, and Briggs. Although dated 1907, it is a product of the 19th century, as its subtitle reveals: "Based on the lexicon of William [sic] Gesenius as translated by Edward Robinson." Though it is European in spirit, it is not a purely European product, since Francis Brown and Charles Augustus Briggs were Americans, as was Edward Robinson; indeed, all three taught at the Union Theological Seminary in the City of New York. The seventeenth edition of Gesenius' work, prepared by Frants Buhl, is comparable to BDB. Buhl did the thirteenth and following revisions, and by the seventeenth he freely admits that a new book or two is needed. As revisions of work begun by Gesenius, BDB and the Buhl dictionary reach back to the earliest stages of the scientific study of Hebrew, although they also reflect the great upheavals of nineteenth-century exploration as well as the steady progress of biblical studies.[11] These dictionaries of the Gesenius tradition emerged from the Protestant matrix of European biblical scholarship. I refer to the ideological backgrounds of the various lexica

---

10 I omit the lexicon of Phillipe Reymond (1991), which, though not a translation of *HALAT*, reflects Reymond's collaboration on that project.

11 It may be mentioned in passing that a revival of the Gesenius tradition of lexicography was undertaken some years ago; the first volume appeared under the editorship of Rudolf Meyer and Herbert Donner (1987); after foundering following Meyer's death

here in part because they are facets of the intellectual pedigree of the works in question and in part because the Sheffield dictionary claims its secular origin as a peculiar point of pride. In fact, apart from the status of Sirach, the religious backgrounds of the other lexicographers has had little discernible effect on their work and no serious scholar has ever alleged otherwise.

The next two major lexica are those of the mid-century. Both derive from German-speaking Europe, reflecting the two sides of German-speaking Christianity. The *Lexicon in Veteris Testamenti libros* of the Swiss scholars Ludwig Koehler and Walter Baumgartner of 1953 is the Protestant product, and indeed Koehler's preface to the Hebrew part ends with a prayer, although Baumgartner's preface to the Aramaic does not. Despite the Latin title, Koehler-Baumgartner is written in German and a sort of English; in this respect it looks forward to later developments. The *Lexicon Hebraicum Veteris Testamenti* of Franciscus Zorell, S.J., which appeared a year later, is the Catholic product. Here the Latin title goes with a Latin text, produced in Rome by a member of the staff of the Pontifical Biblical Institute, sponsored by the Society of Jesus. Zorell's teaching responsibilities included Armenian and Georgian, important languages for the Christian Near East. Because it is written in Latin, Zorell's lexicon has been unjustly neglected; as Francis I. Andersen recently noted, it is "always worth consulting" (1995a:51). Zorell had originally intended to include Aramaic in his lexicon; he died before the Hebrew portion was completed — the Pole Ludovicus Semkowski finished it from Zorell's notes — and Zorell seems not to have written any of the Aramaic. The companion lexicon to Zorell is that of Ernestus Vogt, S.J., *Lexicon linguae Aramaicae Veteris Testamenti documentis antiquis illustratum* of 1971, an independent work, although it, too, is in Latin and is unjustly neglected. Zorell unintentionally anticipated one of the later developments in the lexicography of ancient Hebrew by separating off the Aramaic material. Baumgartner's work on the Biblical Aramaic is so much more detailed than that of Koehler on the Hebrew that it, too, takes on a different character.

Lexicography is a rough business, and Zorell is not the only lexicographer of Biblical Hebrew who died in the saddle. Ludwig Koehler died before the revision of the work he initiated got very far — the second, 1958 edition differs from the first only by a group of supplements — and the work of the revision fell to Baumgartner, who got the process well underway before he, too, died on the job. KB 3 (*HALAT* in the German edition, Koehler, Baumgartner et al. 1967–1996, *HALOT* in the English

in 1991, the project seems to have been revived: the second part of a projected five appeared in 1995.

edition, Koehler, Baumgartner et al. 1994–2000) is a thorough revision but remains grounded in the mid-century conceptions of the first edition. It is a European product, in fact, largely Swiss, but it reflects the collaboration of Christians and Jews, of German-speaking Europeans and Israelis. The names of E. Y. Kutscher on the title page of the first, 1967 volume and of Ze'ev Ben-Ḥayyim on the third, 1983 volume are among the great signs of a shift in the life of the field of biblical studies. In a history of the Koehler-Baumgartner lexicon, there would be much to say of why those Jews were chosen and how they were involved, but it is signally important to recognize that Jews were involved. The first American effort to include both Jews and Christians in a comparably significant collaborative work was the Anchor Bible, begun in 1964; the first two volumes were E. A. Speiser's *Genesis* and Bo Reicke's *James, Peter, and Jude* (both 1964). Much has been made of the pioneering work in bringing together Jewish and Christian scholars of the Tanakh undertaken by the editors, W. F. Albright and D. N. Freedman. I think that it is important to recall the comparable European gesture of Walter Baumgartner and the significance of Switzerland and perhaps especially Basel, in coming to some terms with the hatred evident in the Second World War and the resulting destruction of European Jewry.

The notion of revision was not confined to Koehler-Baumgartner: there were also plans to revise Brown, Driver, and Briggs, plans that never came to fruition. These plans are the source of numerous articles by G. R. Driver and James Barr and of a complete but never-to-be-published manuscript of Driver's student D. Winton Thomas (cited in the Sheffield lexicon; see Sheffield II.11, cf. I.13). The full story of this project remains to be written.

So far we have four or five dictionaries: Buhl and Brown, Driver, and Briggs; Koehler-Baumgartner 1 and Zorell; and, arguably a separate product, Koehler-Baumgartner 3. A pair from the beginning of the century, a pair from the mid-century, and one spanning the second half of the century. The languages so far are the scholarly languages of Europe, Latin, German, and English; the absence of French is striking. There were no major original European lexica of Biblical Hebrew between the early 1950s and the 1990s.

There are two products of the 1990s, of the end of the century. The greatest surprise here is that there is a new language represented, Spanish. The Madrid *Diccionario bíblico hebreo-español*, edited by the late Luís Alonso Schökel, although it has not been widely heralded in the English-speaking world, is as fresh a product as the first Koehler-Baumgartner and Zorell. Like Zorell and Vogt, Alonso Schökel was a member of the Society of Jesus and of the faculty of the Pontifical Biblical Institute.

His dictionary is written, not in Latin, like Zorell's and Vogt's, but in Spanish, the second-most important language of world Christianity. (For background presentations, see Alonso Schökel 1988, 1991a, 1991b.)

The other product of the current decade is the Sheffield *Dictionary of Classical Hebrew*, which began to appear in 1993 and in 1998, with the publication of its fourth volume, reached the half-way point.[12] This, too, presents a new thing, a dictionary produced under the auspices of a research university in a secular academic setting. Though the staff of the dictionary is largely Protestant, there are Catholics and Jews included, in a designedly non-religious enterprise. The editor is David J. A. Clines, the consulting editors are Philip R. Davies and John W. Rogerson and latterly J. Cheryl Exum, and the executive editor is John Elwolde; the best-known member of the staff (those who do the actual entry writing) is W. G. E. Watson. The Sheffield dictionary is a British product, "published under the auspices of The Society for Old Testament Study" and with a largely British "editorial board of reference" and staff of "research associates."

The stamp of David J. A. Clines on the work as a whole is notable. It would be unfair to consider such a large product only in terms of Clines's well-known agenda for biblical studies, since it is rather "a corporate project" (Sheffield I.11), but my comments here will focus on Clines's shaping role. It is also worth noting that Clines himself has provided numerous, different forms of that agenda. The intellectual biography that he supplies for himself in the introduction to his collected essays (Clines 1998a:I.xv–xx) is, for example, different from the one supplied in an essay reprinted therein, "Varieties of Indeterminacy" and dated only three years earlier (Clines 1998d). The unacquainted reader needs to keep in mind that Clines idiosyncratically offers scholarly rigor or toughness in his books and scholarly vigor or exuberance in his essays. The author of an essay on "Psalm 2 and the MLF (Moabite Liberation Front)" (1995b) is also the author of a sober commentary on Job (Clines 1989). The Clinesian maxim for biblical studies, "Everything begins in religion and ends in politics" (1998d:135), is relevant for understanding the Sheffield lexicon, but one's views of Clines's work should not determine the assessment of the dictionary.

Both of the dictionaries of the 1990s reflect encounters with modern linguistic study. Notions of polysemy and undifferentiated breadth of meaning; of semantic fields; of the syntactic frameworks in which words occur; the categories of words they co-occur with; of idiomaticity, zero

---

[12] Major discussions are Andersen (1995a) and Muraoka (1995a); for comparisons with the on-going Hebrew-English lexicon of the Old Testament based on semantic domains, in process in South Africa, see de Regt (1997).

functors, and context — all of these are introduced and put to use in the dictionaries.

Before we take up the tasks presented in the first half of the paper, let me say a word about these dictionaries as physical products. About the chief such issue, readability, I can be brief: all of these dictionaries are readable, though only BDB represents a real triumph of typography: it is a book that makes typography work for the reader in every way.

About the second "physical" point, usability, more needs to be said. The dictionaries are all complete dictionaries of Biblical Hebrew, i.e., one could read the Hebrew portions of the Tanakh using all of them. Nonetheless, they are not all shaped the same. Four of the lexica are one-volume dictionaries: BDB, KB 1, Zorell, and Madrid. Indeed BDB and KB 1 include Biblical Aramaic in the same volume. None of these four books is easy to use physically, but each is manageable; again the supremacy of the Oxford University Press has to be recognized: the sewing of my 1950s reprint of BDB is better than the binding of any of these other books. KB 1 is the thickest and has the smallest layout or footprint, although recent, cheap reprints of BDB are similarly squat. Madrid is the thinnest and tallest. Madrid is two inches thick, KB 1 three inches thick. So much for the one-volume works: two of the lexica, *HALAT/HALOT* and Sheffield, go a great distance beyond this limit. *HALAT* in the German format is under five inches thick, while *HALOT* in English is a good deal larger, seven inches, a little over. Sheffield, half-way completed, is already just over six inches thick, and when completed will be thicker than the average human foot is long. In terms of the space on one's desk, if I look at the two dictionaries of the 1990s, I am bound to report that one can have Madrid plus a good Spanish-English dictionary for the space of three of the four Sheffield volumes; people with good Spanish can save even more space with Madrid. I mention this because the achievement of a dictionary is ultimately a function of its utility on the desk, not on the shelf.

6. THE LEXICA OF BIBLICAL HEBREW IN RELATION TO THE THREE TASKS

In considering the three tasks that I described earlier, it is the second, the segregation of the units, that is mostly simply treated. Buhl and BDB at the beginning of the century used two levels of analysis, the root and the word. In this task of assigning every word a root they continued the millennial labor of reconciling the typologically more advanced morphology of Biblical Hebrew to the conservative morphology of Classical Arabic.

That is, they continued the labors most signally engaged in by Yehuda Hayyuj (d. ca. 1000) and Jonah ibn Janaḥ (d. ca. 1030). In the Oxford of S.R. Driver's time, the move away from the root model had already begun. The *Thesaurus Syriacus* of Robert Payne Smith (1879–1901) is a root-and-word dictionary, but *A Compendious Syriac Dictionary* of Jesse Payne Smith, his daughter, published in 1903, drops the root arrangement and uses only one level of analysis, the word. She was a pioneer of Semitic lexicography: although Buhl and Brown, Driver, and Briggs resisted her innovation, the dictionaries of Biblical Hebrew from the 1950s and later have followed her lead. Nevertheless, it is not unusual to find in reviews of recent lexica complaints about word rather than root ordering (e.g., Beyer 1992:196–97 on Sokoloff 1990). The word-based dictionary is dominant: the labors of Hayyuj and Ibn Janaḥ are still relevant to the study of Biblical Hebrew but not to the arrangement of the lexicon.

The other two tasks of lexicography require more attention, since the corpus of study and the corpus from which philological data are drawn must be defined in terms of one another. That is, roughly, if a word is part of the corpus, it goes in one place, while if it is part of philological data, it goes in another place. The corpus of study for all the dictionaries save the Sheffield is basically the Tanakh. Modest nuancing is required in the matter of Sirach. The Book of Ecclesiasticus or the Wisdom of Jesus ben Sira survives complete only in Greek and derivative forms. Late in the nineteenth century, Hebrew texts of Sirach were found in the geniza materials from the syngagogue of Old Cairo; since Sirach was so well known, they entered immediately into the mainstream of study. By 1907, Brown, Driver, and Briggs were able to refer to substantial work on Sirach by ten scholars (1907:viii). These fragments have been augmented since by other materials, most notably an ancient text, the Masada text, Manuscript M. The lexica done under Protestant auspices, BDB and Koehler-Baumgartner 1 and 3, have treated Sirach as part of post-biblical Hebrew. The lexica done under Catholic auspices, Zorell and Madrid, have treated Sirach as part of Biblical Hebrew (Madrid 7). Sheffield, operating on a non-religious basis, includes Sirach in its corpus of study. This difference in the definition of the corpus is in itself a relatively minor matter, since Sirach is, in comparison to the Tanakh, small, though it is a good deal bigger than many of us wish it was.

Another small body of material claims attention as well: the inscriptions that can be defined in the narrow sense as Hebrew, that is, the inscriptions with a date within the desired range and either a Palestinian provenance or some linguistic feature characteristic of Hebrew and not of the other South and Central Canaanite dialects. For all the lexica treated here except for the Sheffield dictionary, the inscriptions are part of the philological background; they are often cited where appropriate by BDB, Buhl, Zorell, and Koehler-Baumgartner 1 and 3, though omitted by Alonso Schökel, who cites no such material.[13] In Sheffield the inscriptions are a portion of the corpus of study.

A third body of material is no small matter: it is the material from Qumran and the other Dead Sea sites, and its bulk is considerable. The publication of the Zorell and Koehler-Baumgartner dictionaries in the earlier 1950s were notable events, but the really big news involving ancient Hebrew was the material from the Judean desert. During the 1990s materials discovered in the late 1940s and 1950s have finally seen the light of day, complementing materials made available more promptly.

The question of the corpus of study for an ancient Hebrew dictionary was a minor matter even as recently as 1990, but no longer. One or another canonical decision controlled the study of "ancient Hebrew" up until recently; Sirach and inscriptional materials could be incorporated into a dictionary of Biblical Hebrew one way or another without unbalancing the core of the material. The recent Qumran publications have changed that. David Clines and his team are the first group of lexicographers to confront the changed situation and make decisions about it (see Elwolde 1997). They have decided to denominate their object of study "Classical Hebrew" and to include under that heading the Hebrew Bible, Sirach, the Dead Sea Scrolls, and the inscriptions down to 200 C.E., which they take as pre-Rabbinic ancient Hebrew. The bulk of the nonbiblical material is still limited: "The non-biblical texts are in extent about 15% of the size of the Hebrew Bible" (Sheffield I.14). I believe that the decision was wrong headed on the grounds of historical linguistics and of lexicographic procedure.

On historical grounds, I believe that it would be advisable to separate Biblical Hebrew and Ben Sira, undatable literary texts preserved in a manuscript tradition, from the inscriptions and from the Dead Sea Scrolls, which are to varying degrees archeologically datable. Such a separation does not require a dating for the biblical material, but only a separation of it from material that can be dated on other grounds. A similar position has been advocated in slightly different terms by Elisha Qimron: "Since DSS Hebrew and that of the Bar-Kokhba letters are the only dialects whose

---

13   For example: in the Siloam Inscription (*KAI* 189; Renz 1995:I.178–89), there are words also found in the Tanakh, e.g., *ḥṣbm* 'hewers' lines 1?, 4, 6, cited under *ḥṣb* 'to hew' in BDB, Buhl, Zorell [in the article!], and KB 3; biblical words that are difficult to parse, e.g., *qr'* lines 2–3, cited under *qr'* 'to encounter' by BDB but now usually taken as *qr'* 'to call', *KAI* 2.186, Smelik (1991:70), Renz (1995:I.187); and non-biblical words from biblically attested roots, e.g., *nqbh* 'breakthrough' line 1 *bis*, cited under *nqb* 'to pierce' in BDB, Buhl, Zorell, KB 1, and KB 3.

time and place are known, we should try to classify the other types of Hebrew by comparing them to these two dialects" (Qimron 1992:360, cf. 1995; for another formulation, see Andersen 1995a:55).[14]

The argument is not that Biblical Hebrew stopped in, say, the year 200 B.C.E., and that a distinct dialect, Late Second Temple Period Hebrew, started the next year, but rather that most Late Second Temple Period texts can be dated "late," while much of the Bible can be dated earlier but cannot be dated with certainty. If only in the case of Daniel, the Hebrew of the Late Second Temple Period was used in the Bible. If the distribution outlined here were taken as a basis of study, the range of inscriptions could be adjusted to align with the larger corpora: Iron II period-texts and texts from the early Imperial Age (Neo-Babylonian, Persian, the first Macedonian century) could be set with Biblical Hebrew, and later Macedonian and Roman inscriptional texts with the Late Second Temple Period Hebrew. (The aim here is not to suggest how a dictionary of "ancient" or "classic" Hebrew should be done, but simply to suggest alternatives to Sheffield's approach.)

The other historical basis for such a separation is what I earlier referred to as the scriptural turn of the Hebrew of Qumran and Ben Sira, the exegetical impulse manifest in these texts. Certainly the biblical text has echoes and allusions within it: "The Hebrew we encounter in the Bible was a literary language and, as such, marked both by a large store of equivalent ways of expression and by a tradition that retained such semantic material rather longer than a purely colloquial language might do. As users of a literary language learn it from existing literary works, words and phrases can also reappear after having lain dormant for a time" (Rabin 1982:172). True as this is of the Bible, it is overwhelmingly more true of Qumranic Hebrew and Ben Sira; thus Elwolde's summary of the Sheffield's team's findings is arguable but misleading: "We were struck by the small quantity of new vocabulary at Qumran, or, put another way, the high degree of continuity between the vocabulary of the Bible and that of the scrolls" (1997:48–49). The Hebrew of the Late Second Temple Period is in deeper and more various ways a scriptural language, a language full of quotations and paraphrases; the continuity is a complex matter (Morag 1996).

---

[14] The linguistic history of first-millennium Hebrew can be to some extent reconstructed from the biblical text, as many have long argued, and such a reconstruction has long been implicit in my own work. The Sheffield project reflects a tendency to overlook and misunderstand such argumentation, a tendency discussed by Andersen (1995a:52–54) and manifest also in, e.g., P. R. Davies (1992), aptly criticized by Hurvitz (1997). See also Barr (1973, 1993, 1994), Hurvitz (1982, 1995a, 1995b), and Hoftijzer (1995:92–93).

This point about the scriptural quality of much of the Dead Sea Scroll language leads to the second objection I bring against the Sheffield notion of "Classical Hebrew," the objection of lexicographic procedure. The objection here is a practical matter: the texts of the Hebrew inscriptions, the Dead Sea Scrolls, and Ben Sira are much less thoroughly controlled and understood than the biblical text. Their inclusion on the same level of comprehension is simply not warranted; in many cases the Dead Sea Scroll texts in particular have barely begun to be discussed by scholars. Sheffield has rushed to judgment. It is true that any student who can read Deuteronomy can also read the Temple Scroll; indeed, he might have an easier time with the Temple Scroll. But the crucial work of reading the Temple Scroll is figuring out exactly how it differs from Deuteronomy, and for that work a knowledge of Deuteronomy itself is needed. The demands only grow greater with the more technical halachic literature and greater still with the abundant poetic literature. The newness of the Qumran material, whether published in the 1950s or the 1990s, mitigates against its being incorporated into a lexicon of a much better known form of the language. Qimron has demonstrated that the task of understanding how difficult words and constructions "were understood by the DSS themselves" is primary (1995:296, see also Sarfatti 1995); such understanding must precede evaluation (cf., e.g., Qimron 1995:313–14). This objection is purely historical on our end of the matter: in twenty-five years the situation will have changed and the bringing together of biblical and Qumranic vocabulary will be not merely a different task, but also a different sort of task.

The kinds of control that are needed in lexicographic work vary depending on the source material, but the Sheffield dictionary has to an alarming degree leveled the sources and thereby distorted the evidence. Though it does show restorations of letters, it shows no marks of uncertainty for any readings in any of its non-biblical texts and does not indicate the existence of problems in a text. G. I. Davies states clearly that the Cambridge corpus of Hebrew inscriptions "is in no way regarded by us [the editorial team] as a substitute for a fully critical publications of the texts. ... Reference to other editions of the texts remains necessary" (Davies et al. 1991:xii–xiii). Yet Sheffield uses the corpus in a way that begs to be called "religious." An example may be useful.

Lachish Letter 5 is a notoriously difficult text. This letter may contain several cases of the substantive *ṭb* 'good(ness)'. In the first case, in the greeting of the letter, the reading of *ṭb* is unclear but non-controversial: **line 1** *yšmʿ* [*yhwh ʾt ʾd*]*ny* **line 2** [*šmʿt š*]*lm wṭb* [*ʾt*] **line 3** [*kym*] *ʾt ky*[*m*] (Davies et al. 1991:3), "May YHWH let my lord hear tidings of health and prosperity right now!" A nearly identical benediction occurs in, e.g.,

Lachish Letter 4.1–2 (Davies et al. 1991:2); in Lachish Letter 8.1–2 the comparable phrase is more damaged (Davies et al. 1991:4); this last is wrongly reported in Sheffield as *ṭb šm['t]*, with the words reversed, due to the demons of Hebrew-English word processing (Sheffield III.355a).

After the greeting Lachish Letter 5 continues with difficulties: the sender of this (as of other Lachish letters) is exercised: documents have been sent and are herewith returned, evidently in anger. A wish, perhaps seasonal, follows: **line 7** *yr'k y* **line 8** *hwh*, "May YHWH make you see ...." What follows, presumably the object of the verb, is difficult to read. Röllig leaves the following letters as blanks (*KAI* 195), though he cites in his commentary the proposal of Henri Michaud to read as the object of the verb *hqšr* (*KAI* II.196) 'conspiracy'. Lemaire in preparing his volume for the Littératures anciennes du Proche-Orient series reread the text and provided a translation but as that series does not accommodate texts did not specify his reading (Lemaire 1977:117). It is not, however, in doubt: Lemaire read *hqṣr . bṭb*, rendering "[May YHWH make you see] the harvest *in joy.*" Pardee et al. confirmed this reading in their edition of the Hebrew letters (1982:96), providing detailed references to the published photographs and explaining how Lemaire's reading accounts for the surviving traces admirably (1982:97). Lindenberger (1994:115) takes the words similarly and so does Smelik in his translation of the Hebrew epigraphic texts, the English version of which was prepared by G. I. Davies: "May YHWH let you see *the harvest in good fortune*" (Smelik 1991:128). Renz (1995:I.424) goes so far as to say that *qṣr* seems relatively clear.

It is possible to accept only part of Lemaire's reading of Lachish Letter 5.8. In terms of the letter as a whole, the reference to the harvest may comport with the last line's mention of *zr' lmlk* 'royal grain'; the phrase *bṭb* has no such support elsewhere in the letter. G. I. Davies and the Cambridge team, in fact, take over the 'harvest' part of Lemaire's reading but not the reference to prosperity or fortune (so also, roughly, Hoftijzer and Jongeling 1995 s.v. *qšr* 2 'conspiracy'). Davies provides 'conspiracy' as an alternative, but omits the last word of Lemaire's line 8: **line 7** *yr'k y* **line 8** *hwh h̊qṣr* {**or** h̊q[š]r̊} *b*[   ].[15] Thus the student consulting the handbooks of Lemaire, Pardee et al., Lindenberger, Smelik, and Renz would be led to expect an occurrence of *ṭb* in Lachish Letter 5:8, but because Davies, defensibly on epigraphic grounds, omits the reading, the student who looks in the Sheffield dictionary will be disappointed or, more likely, confused and frustrated. The editor's claim that "We certainly do not have

---

[15] The interpretation of the first word on line 9 — if it is *hym* does it mean 'today' or 'in this season'? — remains difficult; see Renz (1995:I.423).

time to linger over every debatable point" (Sheffield IV.8) will provide the student a cold comfort. I do not wish to defend Lemaire's reading but rather to insist that the text of Lachish Letter 5 is uncertain enough and Lemaire's 1977 reading is in wide enough circulation to require the kind of presentation that Sheffield makes no room for.

Comparable issues about uncertain and disputed readings arise throughout the inscriptional corpus. It is important to note that they have various sources: the material state of the surface of the inscriptions, problems about the shape of the inscriptions, and problems in identifying the letter forms. The problems of overall text shape and of letter forms do not arise so acutely in the Dead Sea material: the general format of the texts is known and the letter forms are stable. The Ben Sira manuscripts present a different problem of control, relating to the date. The ancient manuscript, the M or Masada manuscript, presents a unitary text of undoubted date. The medieval manuscripts are not so simple (pace Sheffield I.30). There are considerable variations between the A and C texts, and there are variants within the B text. Since the Hebrew Ben Sira was not a canonical text, it is conceivable that it was rewritten and revised at various points in its history, extending even into the medieval period. The Sheffield dictionary takes no account of these variations, reporting all of Ben Sira as Hebrew (and that is correct) of the pre-200 C.E. period (and that is disputed). It "has no time" for the details of readings on which it claims to be based.

With so many difficulties attendant on using the larger corpus, which were familiar to the Sheffield team, why did they decide to use or attempt to use "the evidence of all the extant texts" (Sheffield I.7, cf. 13)? It has generally been assumed that the answer is obvious. The extra-biblical material furnishes further scientific data: the Sheffield dictionary wishes to comport itself as a scientific project, unrestrained by the dead hand of the religious traditions of Christianity and Judaism. It has gone beyond religion to attain the level of science; there are names for such aspirations, and the most common these days is probably "the Enlightenment project," but the one I would like to point to is rather "modernity." Part of the essence of modernity is to have left behind particularities associated with local beliefs and customs and to have moved to a higher plane of discourse governed by reason. Linguistics is a scientific enterprise, and including the extra-biblical material can be seen as a scientific task. There is much to be said in favor of such claims in principle. Michael Sokoloff, both in his already published lexicon of Jewish Palestinian Aramaic (1990) and in his forthcoming lexicon of Jewish Babylonian Aramaic, combined (a) the great rabbinic corpora of Talmud and late targums, (b) inscriptions and amulets, (c) papyri and manuscripts discovered in the last century, mostly in the Cairo Geniza, and (d) grammatical terms from the Masoretic traditions. The total effect of Sokoloff (1990) is, however, different from that of the Sheffield dictionary (see also Sokoloff 1994).

David Clines is not attracted to a scientistic rhetoric of modern scholarship. For Clines, modernity is best understood in neo-Marxian or materialist terms. He speaks frankly of his own enterprise in such terms: "The preparation of a Hebrew dictionary... sets research in a social and economic context" (Sheffield I.7). His description of the enlarged corpus is similarly colored by the language of various theoretical positions that are alien to linguistics. The positions are variously those of materialist and cultural criticism and New Historicism (see, e.g., Bauerlein 1997, Leitch 1993, McCanles 1993).

The key term here for Clines (and not, I suspect, for the other members of the team) is "privilege." In the preface to the first volume, he writes, "Unlike all previous dictionaries of ancient Hebrew, this work does not restrict itself to, or privilege in any way, those ancient Hebrew texts found in the Hebrew Bible" (Sheffield I.7). Again, "there is no reason to privilege" comparative evidence (Sheffield I.18; cf. Clines 1995a:72, 74). Yet again, Sheffield is "a dictionary of the classical language as a whole, in which the language of the Bible is not privileged over that of the non-biblical texts" (Sheffield I.24).[16] I point this out primarily as evidence of how distant Clines's own thinking is from that of linguists.[17] The set of this dictionary is not so much linguistics as it is cultural criticism that has read up on linguistics. Linguistic principles are here narrowed to a small set of ideas and corresponding mechanical operations: focus on the use of words, close attention to more common words, no cognate evidence, no differentiation of metaphorical and figurative usage (Sheffield I.15–16, 19). The impulse is as determined by something like exegetical needs as any eleventh-century Jewish or Muslim work.

It would be easy to provide a 1990s description of these quasi-exegetical needs: "The goal of Clines the cultural critic is to complexify and problematize a site of power so as to find inscribed within it and indeed so as to inscribe within his reading of it the aesthetic impulse repressively commodified by the social orders." That sentence (created here for the

---

[16]   Bauerlein (1997) discusses the engagé critical theory of the 1990s under the heading
        of representational criticism, pp. 7–11; although he does not single out the term
        "privilege" for examination, he provides several examples of the approach I have in
        mind, e.g., pp. 26, 29, 33.

[17]   Note this, from Bauerlein's hostile discussion of manifesto of cultural studies: "How
        might a scholar use both phonemic analysis and deconstruction in a single inquiry
        when deconstructionist arguments call into question the basic premises of phonetics?"
        (1997:34).

sake of argument) makes good sense in the current field of literary theory, but frankly I cannot imagine a linguist believing that it meant anything relevant to linguistics. It is an ungainly pile of 1990s theory jargon. In order to understand Clines, it may help to quote an example of 1970s theory, from the great Cambridge critic Raymond Williams: "[The] 'aesthetic' response is an affirmation ... of certain human meanings and values which a dominant social system reduced and even tried to exclude. Its history is ... a protest against the forcing of experience into instrumentality ('utility'), and of all things into commodities. This must be remembered even as we add, necessarily, that this form of protest ... led almost inevitably to new kinds of privileged instrumentality and specialized commodity" (Williams 1977:151). Williams here presents a British appropriation of the Western Marxian tradition chiefly associated with the Italian theorist Antonio Gramsci. This tradition protests against the controlling power or hegemony of certain ideological positions; it is privilege that often supports hegemony.

What is privileged is what has been socially and ideologically made use of, as, for example, by synagogue and church; Clines's goal is to move decisively away from assigning any special role to a text that has been so used. In theological terms, some would say that Clines should be searching for Williams's great good thing, "the multiplicity of writing" (Williams 1977) and ultimately culture, not outside the Tanakh but inside it; in Gramsci's terms, privilege is not always complicitous with hegemony.[18]

Before leaving the topic of Clines's take on the Bible as an element in the background of the Sheffield dictionary, it may be useful to say a word about canon, a term avoided in the introductory material. For much of the 1970s and 1980s the canon was seen among literary theorists as the great wicked thing: that is, the literary canon, the texts that make up the various curricula of classes in modern literature. It was the canon that excluded marginal voices, those of women, blacks, and Asians, and so on. There was much truth to this, and reforms have long since taken place. Lurking behind this discussion was the suspicion that anything called "canon" was probably a bad thing because that term originated (or at least gained importance) in a religious setting. At least some literary theorists have come to see that for various reasons the biblical and literary canons were always different phenomena (Guillory 1995:239). The most salient difference here is that the literary canon lacks the exegetical impulse; it does not reveal the scriptural turn. The literature from Qumran is committed to using and reusing the language of the Tanakh in a way

---

[18] For more discussion of literature as a "privileged" discursive practice among other discursive practices of culture, see Eagleton (1983:205-7).

that is simply not found across a literary canon, from, say, Shakespeare to Wallace Stevens. There is much allusion, much reuse and reworking, at various points within a literary canon, but it lacks the characteristic intensity found in the Hodayot or the Temple Scroll.

So much for Clines the modernist. The attendant questions about culture and discourse are significant questions; they are not, however, linguistic questions, for better or worse. What of Clines the post-modernist and the post-modernist claims floated at various points in the introductory materials of the dictionary? Post-modernist features (or quasi-features), such as the destabilized signifier and instability of reference, are casually alluded to in the introductory material, but these are even less relevant to a linguistic enterprise (e.g., Sheffield I.26, II.10). The fact that such notions reflect the linguistic turn of much twentieth-century thought does not make them part of or even potentially comfortable with the discipline of linguistics. I will not pursue the point, since I am not convinced that the dictionary (or Clines) is post-modernist.

Let us return to Hebrew lexica. The corpus of study and the philological background are, I said earlier, mutually defined. I have sketched basic facts about the corpus in these major lexica, and let me now sketch basic facts about the definitions and the philological background, both of which show the same pattern across the century.

The definitions and other elements of the semantic analysis show an increase in orderliness. The material in Buhl and BDB is abundant but sometimes seems put together with a pitchfork. The lexica of mid-century tend to be more schematic in logical or developmental terms, often alien to the material of study. Thus Zorell and KB 1 set out material according to a format that they believe accounts for the origins, growth, and use of the word over time. This often results in supposed "primitive" meanings that are rarely attested appearing first in the entry, ahead of common but supposedly more developed meanings. It would be misleading to see such approaches as historical, since in many cases they involve an anthropology or sociology that has no historical grounding at all, while in other cases the schema of the entry is only tangentially related to historical notions. Both the lexica of the 1990s give priority to frequency as the central criterion for the arrangement of the meanings, though both recognize the utility of other factors as well.[19] The Sheffield dictionary provides full citations for a variety of syntactic patterns, and Takamitsu Muraoka in his review notes that it is often serviceable as a database where deficient as a dictionary. Whether a boundary between dictionaries and concordances in

---

[19]   These points can easily be illustrated by the entries for *'élep*, to which must now be added the evidence adduced by Malamat (1995). The problems created for rare words by the focus of frequency are outlined by Andersen (1995a:61–63).

electronic formats needs to be drawn will only emerge as such electronic sources become available.

The pattern regarding philological data across the century has also been uniform. BDB and Buhl present a good chunk of Comparative Semitic material and include a great deal of other philological data. The dictionaries of mid-century include less overall, but what is given shows more careful consideration and preparation. Both KB 1 and Zorell include some Comparative Semitic data; KB 1 tends to include more, and Zorell tends to be more relevant and specific in his citations. The most important change between them and Buhl was the discovery of Ugaritic: this is well represented in Koehler-Baumgartner 1 and almost not at all in Zorell. An interesting feature of Zorell's lexicon is his putting the Comparative Semitic data at the end of the entry. Such an arrangement is found sporadically in nineteenth-century European dictionaries of Hebrew (e.g., Tregelles 1882), but dictionaries of English did not begin doing that, as a way of deemphasizing such data, for several decades.

Both the dictionaries of the 1990s include only language-internal philological data. They approach the exclusion of other such data in different ways. Alonso Schökel's exclusion of what he calls etymological, historical, and comparative information is presented as a matter of principle, i.e., the compilers' principle, not a principle attributed to others unknown (as Clines seems to do). This has resulted in a tremendous freeing up of space. Alonso Schökel allows that, although it is not cited, such data has been used in preparing the dictionary: "Nonetheless, the comparative study of related languages has value in itself and can perform two services for the Hebrew-Spanish dictionary. First, it allows us to distinguish two homophonous roots in Hebrew, because they are distinct in other languages. Second, in cases of difficult or unknown meaning, the information from related languages can aid in proposing reasonable conjectures" (Madrid 8). By excluding this information, the Madrid dictionary achieves a usable shape.

The Sheffield exclusion of non-Hebrew philological data is harder to make out.[20] The Introduction states, "Unlike previous dictionaries, the Dictionary of Classical Hebrew has a theoretical base in modern linguistics" (Sheffield I.14, cf. 25), where the term "modern" evidently means post-World War II. Earlier dictionaries had bases in the linguistics of their own time; the suggestion that the historical-comparative linguistics of the nineteenth and early twentieth centuries is not "modern" is simply unfair. In the long view of the history of linguistics, at least as much happened in

---

[20] The contrast of Elwolde (1995) and Johnstone (1995) on Robertson Smith's work is instructive.

the nineteenth century as in the twentieth century. In any case, Clines here attributes the basis for his work to another scholarly discipline, almost as if to say that he has no responsibility for the captious behavior of those wily linguists. As Francis I. Andersen and Takamitsu Muraoka have shown in their reviews of the first volume of the dictionary (Andersen 1995a, Muraoka 1995a), this is a misrepresentation of modern linguistics. At the same time, Andersen may err in concluding that the Sheffield team explicitly rules out the use of all data that they do not report; the introductory material is not, I think, clear on this point (see especially Sheffield I.10, 16–18). It is also worth noting that Clines, who elsewhere displays a missionary zeal for spreading the word about the reading that underlies his scholarly work (e.g., Clines 1990:21–22), is mum, both in the prefatory material of the dictionary and in the papers he has written in connection with the project (most of them conveniently reprinted in Clines 1998a; note also Clines 1992 and 1995a). No representative textbooks or handbooks of modern linguistics are cited, not even for the "beginner in Hebrew," who is part of the target audience (Sheffield I.15); no models of dictionaries done well or ill are referred to.

The Introduction continues, "This theoretical base [in modern linguistics] comes to expression primarily in the overriding concern in this dictionary for the *uses* of words in the language ...; we subscribe to the dictum that the meaning of a word is its use in the language" (Sheffield I.14). There can be no possibility that this means that, say, BDB or Zorell does not show an "overriding concern" for "the uses of words in the language." The suggestion rather is that the etymological data might have misled BDB or Zorell, particularly with regard to what the Introduction calls "the regular and normal uses" (I.14) of the words. There are no examples cited, and users do not report that BDB or Zorell presents a picture of "the regular and normal uses" that is distorted, whether on etymological or other grounds. It is certainly true that "a search for origins is not an appropriate way of inquiring after meaning" (Sheffield I.25), but here Clines is misled by the term "etymological" rather than the material in question. (See rather, e.g., Margain 1995.)

A practical matter concerning the Sheffield dictionary requires explanation. Starting in Volume II it records (and marks with a *star) words alleged to exist in Biblical Hebrew on the basis of comparative philological study; in the text of the dictionary no reasoning behind the suggestions is provided, though references are furnished in the bibliography at the end of the volume (contrast Sheffield I.16–17). Thus after the entry on the verb *dbr* I 'to speak' (Sheffield II.387–96), there is an entry for *dbr* II Piel 'to destroy' (II.396); in the bibliography for this item (II.623) there is a parenthetical notation ("cf. Akk. *dabāru* overthrow") and then references to studies by Israel Eitan, G. R. Driver, D. Winton Thomas, and J. A. Emerton. In many cases the parenthetical notation of the Comparative Semitic evidence is omitted. In the case of this verb, the dictionary entry notes one relevant piece of internal evidence: 2 Chr 22:10 has *dbr* Piel where 2 Kgs 11:1 has *'bd* Piel. In general, these "star" entries are guides rather than full presentations; in some cases there are cross-references to the entry for the better known word (i.e., read this occurrence as **dbr* VI word *unless* it is taken as **dbr* I). This change in policy means that Volumes II and following are arranged differently than Volume I, which is problematic in itself; there are other policy changes as well in Volumes II (Sheffield II.13–14) and III (III.10). The description of the "'new' word" policy, under the heading "Philological Proposals" claims, "From this volume [i.e., II] onward ... we intend to include also the 'new' words that have been recognized or proposed (rightly or wrongly) in the scholarly literature" (Sheffield II.9, cf. 9–12). This has been found by some reviewers to be unclear, since in terms of words that are new to the study of ancient Hebrew, Volume I was full of words found at Qumran and not in the Tanakh. I suspect that the quotation marks around "new" are intended as mocking scare quotes, but the passage was found "puzzling" by J.A. Fitzmyer, not a man easily puzzled and one moreover well disposed toward the dictionary, which he calls "a remarkable achievement" (Fitzmyer 1998).

Let me summarize these remarks on the role of non-Hebrew/ non-internal philological data. The pattern has been decreasing use over the century; the 1990s dictionaries drop such information altogether. In practical terms, by the bang-for-the-buck criterion, these two dictionaries differ radically: the Madrid dictionary has little philological data but it is a workable volume; the Sheffield dictionary has little philological data and it will sprawl all over your desk. I believe that dropping the bulk of the philological material distorts the picture of Biblical Hebrew. It may be that the excesses of G. R. Driver and Mitchell Dahood are to be blamed for the negative view often taken nowadays of comparative argumentation, but the neglect of such argumentation has had a deleterious effect.

Although I use all these books regularly, I was surprised to realize the extent to which Zorell and KB 1 on the one hand and on the other Sheffield and Madrid were alike in treating major problems. There is no question of collaboration or consultation. Rather, the points of agreement reflect the general state of European thinking about these issues. The 1990s lexica have, I think, gone too far in searching for a stripped-down approach that may be linguistic in impulse, though not necessarily in method or result. The Madrid dictionary has the advantage that the product is stripped down as well. The Sheffield dictionary, with its pinched sense of the linguistic enterprise, is bloated in contrast to any other European dictionary of Biblical Hebrew.

The future of lexicographic work, general and Semitic, will be electronic in one way or another, but the basic questions of how dictionaries are to be assembled will be those that have emerged in the twentieth century. The amount of material to be sifted and incorporated into a given dictionary has to remain within bounds set down by the work's users, linguistically trained, linguistically eager, and linguistically naive. For Semitists, the ways in which that sifting takes place will develop across the field of Semitic linguistics, as it interacts with the disciplines it seeks to serve and shape, readers of texts, students of history and culture. The tendency to downplay the role of Semitics in shaping and presenting Biblical Hebrew lexica will have to be confronted in its complex background; that confrontation will, it seems, be held over for another generation.

ABBREVIATIONS

AHw	von Soden 1965–1981
BDB	Brown, Driver, and Briggs 1907
Buhl	[Gesenius-]Buhl 1915
CAD	Gelb et al. 1956–
HALAT	[Koehler-]Baumgartner et al. 1967–96
HALOT	[Koehler-]Baumgartner et al. 1994–2000
KAI	Donner and Röllig 1968–1973
KB 1	Koehler-Baumgartner 1953
KB 3	*HALAT, HALOT*
Lane	Lane 1863–1893
Madrid	Alonso Schökel et al. 1994
NEB	New English Bible (1970)
NJB	New Jerusalem Bible (1985)
NJPS	New Jewish Publication Society (1985)
NRSV	New Revised Standard Version (1990)
REB	Revised English Bible (1989)
RSV	Revised Standard Version (1952)
Sheffield	Clines et al. 1993–
TDOT	Botterweck et al. 1977–
ThWAT	Botterweck et al. 1970–

REFERENCES

Abramson, Shraga. 1987–88. Bamiqra'ot. *Beth Miqra* 33:380–82.

Alonso Schökel, Luís. 1988. El diccionario bíblico hebreo-español. *Sefarad* 48:373–89.

—. 1991a. Sobre diccionarios bilingües. In W. Gross et al. (eds.). *Text, Methode und Grammatik: Wolfgang Richter zum 65. Geburtstag.* St. Ottilien, 1–10.

—. 1991b. The Diccionario bíblico Hebreo-español (*DBHE*). *Zeitschrift für Althebraistik* 4:76–84.

Alonso Schökel, Luís, et al. 1994. *Diccionario bíblico hebreo-español.* Madrid.

Andersen, Francis I. 1995a. Review article, *Dictionary of Classical Hebrew*, Vol. 1. *Australian Biblical Review* 43:50–71.

—. 1995b. Rejoinder to Clines's Comments on Andersen, Review article, *Dictionary of Classical Hebrew*, Vol. 1. *Australian Biblical Review* 43:74–75.

Balzaretti, Claudio. 1997. Ancient Treatises on Syriac Homonyms. *Oriens Christianus* 81:73–81.

Barr, James. 1961. *The Semantics of Biblical Language.* Oxford.

—. 1973. Hebrew Lexicography. In P. Fronzaroli (ed.). *Studies on Semitic Lexicography.* Quaderni di Semitistica 2. Florence, 103–26.

—. 1992. Hebrew Lexicography: Informal Thoughts. In W. R. Bodine (ed.). *Linguistics and Biblical Hebrew.* Winona Lake, 137–51.

—. 1993. Scope and Problems in the Semantics of Classical Hebrew. *Zeitschrift für Althebraistik* 6:3–14.

—. 1994. Three Interrelated Factors in the Semantic Study of Ancient Hebrew. *Zeitschrift für Althebraistik* 7:33–44.

Bauerlein, Mark. 1997. *Literary Criticism: An Autopsy.* Critical Authors & Issues. Philadelphia.

Berlin, Adele. 1985. *The Dynamics of Biblical Parallelism.* Bloomington, Indiana.

Beyer, Kurt. 1992. Review, Sokoloff 1990. *Abr-Nahrain* 30:195–201.

Blachère, R., Ch. Pellat, M. Chouémi, and C. Denizeau. 1967–. *Al-Kāmil. Dictionnaire Arabe-français-anglais (Langue Classique et Moderne).* Paris.

Botterweck, G. J., H. Ringgren, H.-J. Fabry, eds. 1970–. *Theologisches Wörterbuch zum Alten Testament.* Stuttgart.

—. 1977–. *Theological Dictionary of the Old Testament.* Trans. David E. Green et al. Grand Rapids, Michigan.

Brown, Francis, S. R. Driver, and Charles A. Briggs. 1907. *A Hebrew and English Lexicon of the Old Testament with an Appendix Containing the Biblical Aramaic. Based on the Lexicon of William Gesenius as Translated by Edward Robinson.* Oxford. Corrected ed., 1955.

Buccellati, Giorgio. 1996. *A Structural Grammar of Babylonian.* Wiesbaden.

Chadwick, John. 1996. *Lexicographica Graeca: Contributions to the Lexicography of Ancient Greek.* Oxford.

Civil, Miguel. 1994. Linguistics in the Ancient Near East: Sumerian. In G. Lepschy (ed.). *History of Linguistics. Vol. I: The Eastern Traditions of Linguistics.* Longman Linguistics Library. London, 76–87.

Clark, Gordon R. 1992. *ḥesed* — A Study of a Lexical Field. *Abr-Nahrain* 30:34–54.

Clines, David J. A. 1989. *Job 1–20.* Word Bible Commentary 17. Dallas.

—. 1990. *What Does Eve Do to Help? and Other Readerly Questions to the Old Testament.* JSOT Supplement 94. Sheffield.

—. 1992. The New Dictionary of Classical Hebrew. In K.-D. Schunk and M. Augustin (eds.). *Goldene Äpfel im Silbernen Schalen. Collected Communications to the XIIIth Congress of the International Organization for the Study of the Old Testament, Leuven 1989.* Beiträge zur Erforschung des Alten Testament und des antiken Judentums 20. Frankfurt, 169–79.

—. 1995a. Comments on Andersen, Review article, *Dictionary of Classical Hebrew*, Vol. 1. *Australian Biblical Review* 43:72–74.

—. 1995b. Psalm 2 and the MLF (Moabite Liberation Front). In M.D. Carroll R. et al. (eds.). *The Bible in Human Society: Essays in Honour of John Rogerson.* JSOT Supplement 200. Sheffield, 158–185.

—. 1998a. *On the Way to the Postmodern: Old Testament Essays, 1967–1998.* 2 vols. JSOT Supplement 292–293. Sheffield.

—. 1998b. The Dictionary of Classical Hebrew. In Clines 1998a:602–11. Originally 1990.

—. 1998c. Philology and Power. In Clines 1998a:613–30. Originally 1995.

—. 1998d. Varieties of Indeterminacy. In Clines 1998a:126–37. Originally 1995.

—. 1998e. Was There an *'bl* II 'to Dry' in Classical Hebrew? In Clines 1998a:585–94. Originally 1992.

Clines, David J. A., John Elwolde et al., eds. 1993–. *Dictionary of Classical Hebrew.* Sheffield Vol. I 1993, II 1995, III 1996, IV 1998, V 2001.

Cloete, W. T. W. 1989. The Colometry of Hebrew Verse. *Journal of Northwest Semitic Languages* 15:15–29.

Cooper, Alan. 1987. On Reading Biblical Poetry. *Maarav* 4:221–41.

Crystal, David. 1995. *The Cambridge Encyclopedia of the English Language*. Cambridge.

Davies, G. I., et al. 1991. *Ancient Hebrew Inscriptions: Corpus and Concordance*. Cambridge.

Davies, Philip R. 1992. *In Search of 'Ancient Israel'*. JSOT Supplement 148. Sheffield.

de Regt, L. J. 1997. Multiple Meanings and Semantic Domains. *Zeitschrift für Althebraistik* 10:63–75.

Donner, H., and W. Röllig. 1968–1973. *Kanaanäische und Aramäische Inschriften*. 3 vols. Wiesbaden.

Eagleton, Terry. 1983. *Literary Theory: An Introduction*. Minneapolis.

Elwolde, J. F. 1995. The Use of Arabic in Hebrew Lexicography: Whence?, Whither?, and Why? In W. Johnstone (ed.). *William Robertson Smith: Essays in Reassessment*. JSOT Supplement 189. Sheffield, 368–75.

—. 1997. Developments in Hebrew Vocabulary Between Bible and Mishnah. In T. Muraoka and J.F. Elwode (eds.). *The Hebrew of the Dead Sea Scrolls and Ben Sira. Proceedings of a Symposium Held at Leiden University 11–14 December 1995*. Studies on the Texts of the Desert of Judah 26. Leiden, 17–55.

Fitzmyer, Joseph A. 1995. The Aramaic and Hebrew Fragments of Tobit from Qumran Cave 4. *Catholic Biblical Quarterly* 57:655–75.

—. 1998. Review of Sheffield II. *Journal of the American Oriental Society* 118:437–39.

Fleisch, H. 1971. Ibn Fāris. In *Encyclopedia of Islam*. 2d ed. Leiden, 3.764–65.

Fronzaroli, P., ed. 1973. *Studies on Semitic Lexicography*. Quaderni di Semitistica 2. Florence.

Gelb, I.J., et al. 1956–. *The Assyrian Dictionary*. Chicago.

[Gesenius, Wilhelm] — Frants Buhl. 1915. *Hebräisches und Aramäisches Handwörterbuch über das Alte Testament*. 16th ed. Leipzig.

Goldenberg, Gideon. 1998. *Studies in Semitic Linguistics: Selected Writings*. Jerusalem.

Green, Jonathon. 1996. *Chasing the Sun: Dictionary Makers and the Dictionaries They Made*. New York.

Greenstein, E. L. 1984. Medieval Bible Commentaries. In B. W. Holtz (ed.). *Back to the Sources: Reading the Classic Jewish Texts*. New York, 213–59.

Guillory, John. 1995. Canon. In F. Lentricchia and T. McLaughlin (eds.). *Critical Terms for Literary Study*. 2d ed. Chicago, 233–49.

Hanhart, Robert. 1994. Die Übersetzung der Septuaginta im Licht ihr Vorgegebener und auf ihr Gründender Tradition. In S.E. Balentine and J. Barton (eds.). *Language, Theology, and the Bible: Essays in Honour of James Barr.* Oxford, 81–112.

Hoftijzer, J. 1995. The Present and Future of the Dictionary of the Northwest-Semitic Epigraphy. *Studi Epigrafici e Linguistici* 12 [*The Lexicography of the Ancient Near Eastern Languages*]:85–103.

Hoftijzer, J., K. Jongeling, et al. 1995. *Dictionary of the Northwest Semitic Inscriptions.* Handbuch der Orientalistik 1.21. Leiden.

Hospers, J. H. 1993. Polysemy and Homonymy. *Zeitschrift für Althebraistik* 6:114–23.

Huehnergard, John. 1997. *A Grammar of Akkadian.* Harvard Semitic Studies 45. Atlanta.

Hurvitz, Avi. 1982. *A Linguistic Study of the Relationship Between the Priestly Source and the Book of Ezekiel: A New Approach to an Old Problem.* Cahiers de la Revue biblique 20. Paris.

—. 1995a. Continuity and Innovation in Biblical Hebrew — The Case of 'Semantic Change' in Post-exilic Writings. In T. Muraoka (ed.). *Studies in Ancient Hebrew Semantics.* Abr-Nahrain Supplement 4. Louvain, 1–10.

—. 1995b. Terms and Epithets Relating to the Jerusalem Temple Compound in the Books of Chronicles: The Linguistic Aspect. In D. P. Wright et al. (eds.). *Pomegranates and Golden Bells: Studies in Biblical, Jewish, and Near Eastern Ritual, Law, and Literature in Honor of Jacob Milgrom.* Winona Lake, Indiana, 165–83.

—. 1997. The Historical Quest for 'Ancient Israel' and the Linguistic Evidence of the Hebrew Bible: Some Methodological Observations. *Vetus Testamentum* 47:301–15.

Ilson, Robert. 1992. Lexicography. In W. Bright (ed.). *International Encyclopedia of Linguistics.* New York, 2.330–32.

Isaksson, Bo. 1987. *Studies in the Language of Qoheleth with Special Emphasis on the Verbal System.* Acta Universitatis Upsaliensis. Studia Semitica Upsaliensia 10. Stockholm.

Japhet, Sara. 1993. *I & II Chronicles.* Old Testament Library. Louisville, Kentucky.

Johnstone, William. 1995. The Legacy of William Robertson Smith: Reading the Hebrew Bible with Arabic-sensitized Eyes. In W. Johnstone (ed.). *William Robertson Smith: Essays in Reassessment.* JSOT Supplement 189. Sheffield, 390–97.

Kaltner, John. 1996. *The Use of Arabic in Biblical Hebrew Lexicography.* Catholic Biblical Quarterly Monograph Series 28. Washington, D.C.

Kedar-Kopfstein, Benjamin. 1994. On the Decoding of Polysemantic Lexemes in Biblical Hebrew. *Zeitschrift für Althebraistik* 7:17–25.

Koehler, Ludwig, and Walter Baumgartner. 1953. *Lexicon in Veteris Testamenti Libros*. 1st ed. Leiden.
——. 1958. *Lexicon in Veteris Testamenti Libros*. 2d ed. Leiden.
[Koehler, Ludwig], Walter Baumgartner, and Johann Jakob Stamm et al. 1967–96. *Hebräisches und Aramäisches Lexikon zum Alten Testament*. 3d edition. Leiden.
[Koehler, Ludwig,] Walter Baumgartner, and Johann Jakob Stamm et al. 1994–2000. *Hebrew and Aramaic Lexicon of the Old Testament*. 3d edition. Trans. M.E.J. Richardson et al. Leiden.
Lane, Edward. 1863–93. *An Arabic-English Lexicon*. London.
Leitch, Vincent B. 1993. Cultural Criticism. In A. Preminger, T. V. F. Brogan et al. (eds.). *The New Princeton Encyclopedia of Poetry and Poetics*. Princeton, 262–64.
Lemaire, André. 1977. *Inscriptions hébraïques. Tome I. Les ostraca*. Littératures anciennes de Proche-Orient 9. Paris.
Lindenberger, James M. 1994. *Ancient Aramaic and Hebrew Letters*. SBL Writings from the Ancient World 4. Atlanta.
McCanles, Michael. 1993. Historicism. In A. Preminger and T. V. F. Brogan et al. (eds.). *The New Princeton Encyclopedia of Poetry and Poetics*. Princeton, 529–33.
Malamat, Abraham. 1995. A Recently Discovered Word for 'clan' in Mari and its Hebrew Cognate. In Z. Zevit et al. (eds.). *Solving Riddles and Untying Knots: Biblical, Epigraphic, and Semitic Studies in Honor of Jonas C. Greenfield*. Winona Lake, Indiana, 177–79.
Margain, Jean. 1995. Sémantique hébraïque: L'apport des targums. In T. Muraoka (ed.). *Studies in Ancient Hebrew Semantics*. Abr-Nahrain Supplement 4. Louvain, 11–17.
Mel'čuk, Igor, and Richard Sproat. 1992. Lexicon. In W. Bright (ed.). *International Encyclopedia of Linguistics*. New York, 2.332-35.
Menn, Lise, M. O'Connor, Loraine K. Obler, and Audrey Holland. 1995. *Non-fluent Aphasia in a Multilingual World*. Studies in Speech Pathology and Clinical Linguistics 5. Amsterdam.
Meyer, Rudolf, and Herbert Donner, with U. Rüterswörden. 1987–. *Wilhelm Gesenius: Hebräisches und Aramäisches Handwörterbuch über das Alte Testament*. Berlin.
Morag, Shelomo. 1996. Some Notes (following Elisha Qimron's Paper, 'The Biblical Lexicon in the Light of the Dead Sea Scrolls'). *Dead Sea Discoveries* 3:152–56.
Morrison, Craig E. 1997. Handing on the Mantle: The Transmission of the Elijah Cycle in the Biblical Versions. In K. J. Egan and C. E. Morrison (eds.). *Master of the Sacred Page: Essays and Articles in Honor of Roland E. Murphy*. Washington, D.C., 109–29.

Muraoka, T. 1995a. A New Dictionary of Classical Hebrew. In T. Muraoka (ed.). *Studies in Ancient Hebrew Semantics.* Abr-Nahrain Supplement 4. Louvain, 87–101.

—. 1995b. The Semantics of the LXX and Its Role in Clarifying Ancient Hebrew Semantics. In T. Muraoka (ed.). *Studies in Ancient Hebrew Semantics.* Abr-Nahrain Supplement 4. Louvain, 19–32.

—. 1998. *Hebrew/Aramaic Index to the Septuagint.* Grand Rapids, Michigan.

Muraoka, T., ed. 1995c. *Studies in Ancient Hebrew Semantics.* Abr-Nahrain Supplement 4. Louvain.

—, ed. 1998. *Semantics of Ancient Hebrew.* Abr-Nahrain Supplement 6. Louvain.

Muraoka, T., and Z. Shavitsky. 1991. Abraham Ibn Ezra's Biblical Hebrew Lexicon: The Minor Prophets: II. *Abr Nahrain* 29:106–28.

Newsom, Carol. 1985. *Songs of the Sabbath Sacrifice. A Critical Edition.* Harvard Semitic Studies 27. Atlanta, Georgia.

O'Connor, M. 1980. *Hebrew Verse Structure.* Winona Lake, Indiana. 2nd printing, 1997.

—. 1993. Parallelism. In Alex Preminger and T. V. F. Brogan et al. (eds.). *The New Princeton Encyclopedia of Poetry and Poetics.* Princeton, 877–79.

—. 1997. The Contours of Hebrew Verse: An Afterword. In *Hebrew Verse Structure.* Supplement to 2d printing. Winona Lake, Indiana, 631–61.

Pardee, Dennis, with J. David Whitehead, Paul E. Dion, and S.D. Sperling. 1982. *Handbook of Ancient Hebrew Letters.* Chico, California.

Payne Smith, J. 1903. *A Compendious Syriac Dictionary.* Oxford: Clarendon. Rpt. Winona Lake, Indiana, 1998.

Payne Smith, R. et al., eds. 1879–1901. *Thesaurus Syriacus.* Oxford.

Qimron, Elisha. 1992. Observations on the History of Early Hebrew (1000 B.C.E–200 C.E.) in Light of the Dead Sea Documents. In D. Dimant and U. Rappaport (eds.). *The Dead Sea Scrolls: Forty Years of Research.* Studies in the Texts of the Desert of Judah 10. Leiden, 349–61.

—. 1995. The Biblical Lexicon in Light of the Dead Sea Scrolls. *Dead Sea Discoveries* 2:295–329.

Rabin, Chaim. 1982. Discourse Analysis and the Dating of Deuteronomy. In J. A. Emerton and S. C. Reif (eds.). *Interpreting the Hebrew Bible: Essays in Honour of E. I. J. Rosenthal.* Cambridge, 171–77.

Reiner, Erica. 1994. Linguistics in the Ancient Near East: Akkadian. In G. Lepschy (ed.). *History of Linguistics. Vol. I: The Eastern Traditions of Linguistics.* Longman Linguistics Library. London, 87–96.

Reymond, Phillipe. 1991. *Dictionnaire d'hébreu et d'araméen bibliques.* Paris.

Renz, Johannes. 1995. *Handbuch der althebräischen Epigraphik. I. Die Althebräische Inschriften 1: Text und Kommentar.* Darmstadt.

Sarfatti, Gad B. 1995. Mishnaic Vocabulary and Mishnaic Literature as Tools for the Study of Biblical Semantics. In T. Muraoka (ed.). *Studies in Ancient Hebrew Semantics.* Abr-Nahrain Supplement 4. Louvain, 33–48.

Sawyer, J. F. A. 1967. Root-meanings in Hebrew. *Journal of Semitic Studies* 12:37–50.

Schiffman, Lawrence H. 1982. Merkavah Speculation at Qumran: The 4Q Serekh Shirot 'Olat Ha-Shabbat. In J. Reinharz et al. (eds.). *Mystics, Philosophers, and Politicians: Essays in Jewish Intellectual History in Honor of Alexander Altmann.* Duke Monographs in Medieval and Renaissance Studies 5. Durham, North Carolina, 15–47.

Schoors, A. 1992. *The Preacher Sought to Find Pleasing Words.* Orientalia Lovaniensia Analecta 41. Leuven.

Seow, C. L. 1997. *Ecclesiastes.* Anchor Bible 18C. New York.

Skehan, Patrick W. 1970. Staves, and Nails, and Scribal Slips (Ben Sira 44:2–5). *Bulletin of the American Schools of Oriental Research* 200:66–71.

Smelik, Klaas A. D. 1991. *Writings from Ancient Israel: A Handbook of Historical and Religious Documents.* Trans. G. I. Davies. Louisville.

Sokoloff, Michael. 1974. *The Targum to Job from Qumran Cave XI.* Ramat-Gan.

—. 1990. *A Dictionary of Jewish Palestinian Aramaic of the Byzantine Period.* Ramat-Gan.

—. 1994. Jewish Babylonian Aramaic and Syriac: Mutual Elucidation. In R. Lavenant (ed.). *VI Symposium Syriacum 1992. University of Cambridge, Faculty of Divinity, 30 August–2 September 1992.* Orientalia Christiana Analecta 247. Roma, 401–8.

—. Forthcoming. *A Dictionary of Jewish Babylonian Aramaic.* Ramat-Gan.

Steingass, F. 1987. *A Learner's Arabic-English Dictionary.* London. Originally *The Student's Arabic-English Dictionary,* 1884.

Tov, Emanuel. 1997. *The Text-critical Use of the Septuaginta in Biblical Research.* 2d ed. Jerusalem Biblical Studies 8. Jerusalem.

Tregelles, S. P. 1882. *Gesenius' Hebrew and Chaldee Lexicon to the Old Testament Scripture.* New York.

Ullmann, Manfred et al. 1970–. *Wörterbuch der klassischen arabischen Sprache.* Wiesbaden.

Vogt, Ernestus. 1971. *Lexicon linguae aramaicae Veteris Testamenti documentis antiquis illustratum*. Roma.

von Soden, Wolfram. 1965–1981. *Akkadisches Handwörterbuch*. Wiesbaden.

Williams, Raymond. 1976. *Keywords: A Vocabulary of Culture and Society*. New York.

——. 1977. *Marxism and Literature*. Oxford.

——. 1983. *Keywords: A Vocabulary of Culture and Society*. Rev. ed. New York.

Zorell, Franciscus. 1954. *Lexicon hebraicum Veteris Testamenti*. Roma.

A SELECTED LIST OF
DICTIONARIES OF SEMITIC LANGUAGES

BARUCH PODOLSKY

The list is divided into sections according to languages or language groups.

GENERAL AND MULTILINGUAL

Cohen, D. 1970–. *Dictionnaire de racines sémitiques ou attestées dans les langues sémitiques*. La Haye. [not finished]

Diakonoff, Igor M. (head of team), Anna G. Belova, Alexander Ju. Militarev, Victor Ja. Porkhomovsky. 1994–97. Historical Comparative Vocabulary of Afrasian. *St. Petersburg Journal of African Studies* 2: 5–28, 3: 5–26, 4: 7–38, 5: 4–32, 6: 12–35 [to be continued]. [This is an English version, corrected and expanded, of the Vocabulary originally published in Russian in several instalments in *Pis'mennyje pamjatniki i problemy kul'tury narodov Vostoka*, Moscow 1981, 1982, 1986.]

Leslau, W. 1991. *Comparative Dictionary of Ge'ez*. Wiesbaden [with comparisons to all Semitic languages].

Militarev, A. and L. Kogan. 2000. *Semitic Etymological Dictionary*. Vol. I: Anatomy of Man and Animals. Münster.

Orel, V.E., Stolbova, O.V. 1995. *Hamito-Semitic Etymological Dictionary: Materials for a Reconstruction*. Leiden [hardly useful for a Semitist; mostly comparisons of various Chadic, Omotic, Egyptian words, often unsubstantiated].

AKKADIAN

CAD. 1956–. *The Assyrian Dictionary of the Oriental Institute of the University of Chicago*. Chicago. [By 2000 includes the letters A-N, R, S, Ṣ, Š, Z]

Soden, W. von. 1959–81. *Akkadisches Handwörterbuch*. Wiesbaden [with Semitic etymologies].

ARABIC

Blachère, R., Ch. Pellat, M. Chouémi, and C. Denizeau, C. 1967–. *Al-Kāmil. Dictionnaire arabe-français-anglais (langue classique et moderne)*. Paris.
Dozy, R. 1881. *Supplément aux dictionnaires arabes*. 2 vols. Leiden [reprint 1927].
Kazimirski, A. de Biberstein. 1846–60. *Dictionnaire arabe-français*. 2 vols. Paris [reprint 1875, 1960].
Lane, E.W. 1863–93. *Maddu-l-Kamoos. An Arabic-English Lexicon*. In 8 parts. London [reprinted in Beirut 1968].
Lisān al-'Arab, by Ibn Manzur, Beirut [several reprints].
Muḥīṭ al-Muḥīṭ, by al-Bustani, 2 vols. 1867–70, Beirut.
Tāǧ al-'Arūs, by al-Zubaydi, various editions.
Ullmann, Manfred et al. 1970–. *Wörterbuch der klassischen arabischen Sprache*. Wiesbaden.
Wehr, H. 1952. *Arabisches Wörterbuch für dir Schriftsprache der Gegenwart*. Wiesbaden [several reprints].
Wehr, H. 1961. *A Dictionary of Modern Written Arabic*. Wiesbaden [English translation of the preceding item, edited by J. Milton Cowan; several reprints].

ARABIC DIALECTS

EGYPT

Badawi, El-Said, Hinds, Martin. 1986. *A Dictionary of Egyptian Arabic*. Beirut.
Spiro, S. 1895. *An Arabic-English Dictionary of the Colloquial Arabic of Egypt*. Beirut [new impression 1973].

LEVANT

Barthélemy, A. 1935. *Dictionnaire Arabe-Français*. Dialectes de Syrie: Alep, Damas, Liban, Jérusalem. Paris.
Denizeau, C. 1960. *Dictionnaire des parlers arabes de Syrie, Liban et Palestine* (Supplément au *Dictionnaire arabe-français* de A. Barthélemy). Paris.

Frahya, A. 1973. *A Dictionary of Non-Classical Vocables in the Spoken Arabic of Lebanon*. Beirut.

El-Massarani, M., V.S. Segal'. 1978. *Arabsko-russkij slovar' sirijskogo dialekta* (Arabic-Russian dictionary of the Syrian dialect). Moscow.

Stowasser, K. and Moukhtar Ani. 1964. *A Dictionary of Syrian Arabic (Dialect of Damascus)*. English-Arabic. Washington D.C.

IRAQ

Woodhead, D.R., Wayne Beene. 1967. *A Dictionary of Iraqi Arabic*. Washington D.C.

NORTH AFRICA

Beaussier, M. 1958. *Dictionnaire pratique arabe-français contenant tous les mots employés dans l'arabe parlé en Algérie et en Tunisie*. [4th edition] Alger.

Boris, G. 1958. *Lexique du parler arabe des Marazig*. Paris.

Fox, Th., Mohammed Abu-Talib. 1966. *A Dictionary of Moroccan Arabic: Arabic-English*. Ed. by R.S. Harris. Washington, D.C.

Marçais, W., Abderrahmân Guîga. 1958–61. *Textes arabes de Takroûna*. II. Glossaire, tomes 1–8. Paris.

Taine-Cheikh, C. 1988–1990. *Lexique ḥassāniya-français*. 6 vols. Paris.

Taine-Cheikh, C. 1990. *Lexique français-ḥassāniya*. Nouakchott.

OTHER AFRICAN

Jullien de Pomerol, P. 1999. *Dictionnaire arabe tchadien-français*. Paris.

Kaye, A.S. 1982–86. *Dictionary of Nigerian Arabic*. 2 vols. Malibu.

Roth-Laly, A. 1969–1972. *Lexique des parlers arabes tchado-soudanais*. Paris.

ANDALUSIA

Corriente, F. 1988. *El léxico árabe Andalusí según P. de Alcalá*. Madrid.

Corriente, F. 1997. *A Dictionary of Andalusi Arabic*. Leiden.

YEMEN

Landberg. 1920–42. *Glossaire Datînois*. 3 tomes. Leiden.

Piamenta, M. 1990. *Dictionary of Post-classical Yemeni Arabic*. 2 vols. Leiden.

CENTRAL ASIA

Vinnikov, I.N. 1962. *Slovar' dialekta buxarskix arabov*. Moscow-Leningrad [a dictionary of the dialect of Bukharan Arabic].

MALTESE

Barbera, D.G. 1940. *Dizionario Maltese-Arabo-Italiano*. 4 vols. Beyrouth.

GE'EZ

Dillmann, A. 1865. *Lexicon linguae aethiopicae*. Lipsiae [reprint New York 1955] [contains numerous examples of usage; retains its value in spite of Leslau's new dictionaries].

Grébaut, S. 1952. *Supplément au Lexicon linguae aethiopicae de August Dillmann (1865) et édition du lexique de Juste d'Urbin (1850–1855)*. Paris.

Da Maggiora, G. 1953. *Vocabolario etiopico-italiano-latino*. Asmara [translation of Dillmann's *Lexicon*].

Leslau, W. 1989. *Concise Dictionary of Ge'ez (Classical Ethiopic)*. Wiesbaden.

Leslau, W. 1991. *Comparative Dictionary of Ge'ez*. Wiesbaden [with comparisons to all Semitic languages].

AMHARIC

Amsalu Aklilu, G.P. Mosback. 1973. *English-Amharic Dictionary*. Addis Ababa.

Gankin, E.B. 1965. *Russko-amxarskij slovar'*. Moscow [Russian-Amharic dictionary].

Gankin, E.B. 1969. *Amxarsko-russkij slovar'*. Moscow [Amharic-Russian dictionary].

Leslau, W. 1976. *Concise Amharic Dictionary*. Wiesbaden.

Kane, T.L. 1990. *Amharic-English Dictionary*. 2 vols. Wiesbaden.

TIGRINYA

Bassano, F. da. 1918. *Vocabolario tigray-italiano e repertorio italiano-tigray*. Roma.

Coulbeaux, P.S., Schreiber, J. 1915. *Dictionnaire de la langue tigraï.* Wien.

English-Tigrinya-Arabic Dictionary. Rome 1985.

Dictionnaire Tigrigna-Français-Tigrigna. Paris 1990.

TIGRE

Littmann, E., Höfner, M. 1962. *Wörterbuch der Tigre-Sprache.* Tigre-Deutsch-Englisch. Wiesbaden.

OTHER ETHIOSEMITIC

Gutt, Eeva & Hussein Mohammed. 1997. *Silt'e-Amharic-English Dictionary (with Concise Grammar by Ernst-August Gutt).* Addis Ababa.

Leslau, W. 1963. *Etymological Dictionary of Harari.* Berkeley and Los Angeles.

Leslau, W. 1979. *Etymological Dictionary of Gurage (Ethiopic).* 3 vols. Wiesbaden.

Leslau, W. 1997. *Ethiopic documents: Argobba. Grammar and Dictionary.* Wiesbaden.

EPIGRAPHIC SOUTH ARABIAN

Avanzini, A. 1977–1980. *Glossaire des inscriptions de l'Arabie du Sud, 1950–1973.* 2 vols. (Quaderni di Semitistica, 3). Firenze.

Beeston, A.F.L., M.A. Ghul, W.W. Müller, J. Ryckmans. 1982. *Sabaic Dictionary (English-French-Arabic).* Louvain-la-Neuve, Beyrouth.

Biella, J.C. 1982. *Dictionary of Old South Arabic. Sabaean dialect.* Harvard Semitic Studies.

Conti Rossini, K. 1931. *Chrestomathia arabica meridionalis epigraphica,* Glossarium pp. 99–261. Roma [Latin glosses; with comparison to other Semitic languages].

Ricks, S.D. 1989. *Lexicon of Inscriptional Qatabanian.* Roma.

MODERN SOUTH ARABIAN

Johnstone, T.M. 1977. *Ḥarsusi Lexicon, and English-Ḥarsusi Word-list.* London.

Johnstone, T.M. 1981. *Jibbāli Lexicon.* Oxford.

Johnstone, T.M. 1987. *Mehri Lexicon and English-Mehri Word-list.* London.

Leslau, W. 1938. *Lexique soqoṭri (sudarabique moderne) avec comparaisons et explications étymologiques* (Collection de la Société de Linguistique de Paris, 41). Paris.

Nakano, Aki'o. 1986. *Comparative Vocabulary of Southern Arabic: Mahri, Gibbali, and Soqotri.* (Studia Culturae Islamicae, 29.) Tokyo.

NORTHWEST SEMITIC

Hoftijzer, J., K. Jongeling. 1995. *Dictionary of the Northwest Semitic Inscriptions.* 2 vols. Leiden [a revised and expanded version of the next item].

Jean, Ch.F., J. Hoftijzer. 1960. *Dictionnaire des inscriptions sémitiques de l'Ouest.* Leiden [refers to Phoenician and Punic, other Canaanite, and Aramaic inscriptions].

HEBREW

CLASSICAL

Brown, F., S.R. Driver, & Ch.A. Briggs. 1907. *A Hebrew and English Lexicon of the Old Testament.* Oxford [several reprints].

Clines, David J. A., John Elwolde et al. (eds.). 1993–. *Dictionary of Classical Hebrew.* Sheffield [vol. I 1993, II 1995, III 1996, IV 1998).

Gesenius, W. 1915. *Hebräisches und aramäisches Handwörterbuch über das Alte Testament.* Bearbeitet von Dr. Frants Buhl. Berlin [17th edition; numerous reprints; translated into English].

Koehler, L. & W. Baumgartner. 1967–96. *Hebräisches und Aramäisches Lexicon zum Alten Testament.* Leiden.

Koehler, L. & W. Baumgartner. 1994–2000. *The Hebrew and Aramaic Lexicon of the Old Testament.* Leiden-New York-Köln.

Reymond, Phillipe. 1991. *Dictionnaire d'hébreu et d'araméen bibliques.* Paris.

Alonso Schökel, Luis, et al. 1994. *Diccionario bíblico hebreo-español.* Madrid.

MODERN

Ben Yehuda, E. 1909–1958. *Thesaurus totius hebraitatis = Milon ha-lašon ha-'ivrit.* 17 volumes. Jerusalem-Tel Aviv [in Hebrew].

Choueka, Y. 1997. *Rav-Milim. A Comprehensive Dictionary of Modern Hebrew*. 6 vols. [in Hebrew]
Even-Shoshan, A. 1969. *Ha-Milon He-Ḥadaš*. Jerusalem [several editions in one, four, and seven volumes]. [in Hebrew]
Klein, E. 1987. *A Comprehensive Etymological Dictionary of the Hebrew Language for Readers of English*. Jerusalem-Hafia.

PHOENICIAN

Estañol, J. F. 1980. *Vocabulario Fenicio*. Barcelona.
Krahmalkov, Ch.R. 2000. *Phoenician-Punic Dictionary*. Leuven.
Tomback, R.S. 1978. *A Comparative Semitic Lexicon of the Phoenician and Punic Languages*. Missoula, Montana.

UGARITIC

Aistleitner, J. 1963. *Wörterbuch des ugaritischen Sprache*. Berlin [several reprints; comparisons with other languages].
Gordon. C.H. 1965. *Ugaritic Textbook*. Rome. Glossary pp. 347–507 [2nd ed. 1967] [previously published as *Ugaritic Handbook* 1947, *Ugaritic Manual* 1955; with comparisons to other Semitic languages].
Olmo Lete, G. del & J. Sanmartín. 1996–2000. *Diccionario de la lengua ugarítica*. 2 vols. Aula Orientalis Supplement 7–8. Barcelona.

ARAMAIC

Dalman, G.H. 1922 [2nd ed.]. *Aramäisch-neuhebräisches Handwörterbuch*. Frankfurt a. Main [reprint 1938].
Jasrow, M. 1926. *A Dictionary of the Targumim, the Talmud Babli and Yerushalmi, and the Midrashic Literature*. New York — Berlin.
Krauss, S. 1899. *Griechische und lateinische Lehnwörter im Talmud, Midrasch und Targum*. 2 vols. [reprint Hildesheim 1964].
Levy, J. 1876–89. *Chaldäisches Wörterbuch über die Targumim und Midraschim*. 4 vols. [reprinted in one volume, Köln 1959].
Sokoloff, M. 1990. *A Dictionary of Jewish Palestinian Aramaic of the Byzantine Period*. Ramat-Gan.
Vogt, Ernestus. 1971. *Lexicon linguae aramaicae Veteris Testamenti documentis antiquis illustratum*. Roma.

SYRIAC

Bar Baḥlul, H. 1901. *Lexicon Syriacum*. 3 vols. Paris [2nd ed. 1940].

Brockelmann, C. 1928. *Lexicon Syriacum*. [2nd ed.] Halle.

Costaz, L. 1963. *Dictionnaire syriaque*. Beyrouth.

Dogan, Hatune. 1997 (2nd ed. 1998). *Wörterbuch Syrisch (Aramäisch)-Deutsch, Deutsch-Syrisch (Aramäisch)*. Warburg.

Murad, Mikha'il. 1994. *Arabic-Syriac Dictionary*. Aleppo.

Payne Smith, R. 1879–1901. *Thesaurus Syriacus*. 2 vols. Oxonii.

Payne Smith, J. 1903. *A Compendious Syriac Dictionary*. Oxford.

Al-Qardahi, Jibra'il. 1994. *Qāmūs Suryānī-ʿArabī* [Syriac-Arabic dictionary]. Aleppo.

NEO-ARAMAIC

MANDAIC

Drower, E.S., Macuch, R. 1963. *A Mandaic Dictionary*. Oxford.

Macuch, R. 1965. *Handbook of Classical and Modern Mandaic*. Berlin [contains an English-Modern Mandaic vocabulary as well as additions and corrections to *Mandaic Dictionary*].

NENA

Ashitha, O.M. 1997. *Ḥilqā de Leššānā: Assyrian-Arabic Dictionary*. Baghdad.

Hozaya, Younan & Anderios Youkhana. 1999. *Arabic-Assyrian Dictionary*. Arbil.

Maclean, A.J. 1901. *A Dictionary of the Dialects of Vernacular Syriac*. Oxford [reprint Amsterdam 1972].

Oraham, A.J. 1943. *Oraham's Dictionary of the Stabilized and Enriched Assyrian and English*. Chicago.

Shilo, Varda. 1995. *Hebrew-Assyrian Dictionary* [Zakho dialect]. 2 vols. Jerusalem.

Yona, M. 1999. *Neo-Aramaic — Hebrew, Hebrew — Neo-Aramaic Dictionary* [Zakho dialect]. 2 vols. Jerusalem.

MAʻLULA

Bergsträsser, G. 1921. *Glossar des neuaramäischen Dialektes von Maʻlula*, in *Abhandlungen für die Kunde des Morgenlandes*, 14/4 [reprint 1966].

TUROYO

Ritter, Helmut. 1979. *Ṭūrōyo. B. Wörterbuch*. Beirut. [A facsimile edition of the author's typescript; does not contain verbs.]
Svensk-turabdinskt lexikon — Leksiqon Swedoyo-Suryoyo. Stockholm, 1988 [a small Swedish-Turoyo dictionary, in Roman script].

Beyond the Semitic Sphere

INTRODUCTION

The two papers that go beyond the Semitic family are offered in chronological order: first the relationship between Semitic and Egyptian, then the relationship between Semitic and Hamito-Semitic (or Semitohamitic, as is preferred by Voigt; see below).

Following a bibliographical survey, Helmut Satzinger mentions the factors that should be taken into consideration when trying to evaluate the close relationship between Egyptian and the Semitic family as compared with the larger sphere of Hamito-Semitics: the factor of time, the historico-cultural factor, and possible areal affects. Then Satzinger explores, one by one, the various domains in language where this connection of Egyptian to the Semitic language family can be shown: lexicon, phonology, morphology (stems, case, number and gender, TMA, the old perfective, pronoun conjugation), verbal morphosyntax and syntax (status, rhematic vs. clausal), and finally the adverbial sentence and its role for verbal expression. He concludes his exposition by listing some differences between Egyptian and Semitic, touching upon the larger sphere of Hamito-Semitic in this regard, and even beyond.

Rainer Voigt surveys the relationship between the languages of the Semitic family within the broader Semitohamitic phylum. Voigt prefers the term Semitohamitic over Hamito-Semitic, and states that "new terms are only justified through new ideas". While not explicitly referring to the now widely used term Afroasiatic, his statement also serves as an argument for avoiding this term as well. After a short survey of the history of the discipline, a methodological note on the reconstruction of the sound system of a proto-language, and some reference to comparative Semitohamitic dictionaries, the author goes on to detail his view of the state of the art in the description and analysis of the phonological system of Semitohamitic. This is followed by a discussion of the Semitic root structure and noun classes as compared to the reconstructed Proto-Semitohamitic structures, and finally a discussion of the reconstruction of the Proto-Semitohamitic verbal system.

THE EGYPTIAN CONNECTION: EGYPTIAN AND THE SEMITIC LANGUAGES

HELMUT SATZINGER

THE EMERGENCE OF MODERN EGYPTIAN GRAMMAR

The past hundred years have seen a good deal of progress in studies of Egyptian and also in Comparative Egypto-Semitic Studies. It must be admitted, though, that by the end of the nineteenth century the practical knowledge of Egyptian was already extraordinarily great. The members of the "Berlin school," Adolf Erman, Georg Steindorff and Kurt Sethe, accomplished the pioneering phase which had begun with François Champollion and continued with Richard Lepsius, Samuel Birch, Heinrich Brugsch and others. At the end of the 19th century the great lexicographic venture of the Berlin Academy of Sciences was inaugurated (the last of the five main volumes appeared in 1931). From 1880 onward, through the twentieth century, various stages and idioms of the Egyptian language were documented in reference grammars and textbooks.

Middle Egyptian: Erman (1894, 2 1902, 3 1911, 4 1928); Gardiner (1927, 2 1950, 3 1957); Lefebvre (1940); de Buck (1941, 2 1944); Westendorf (1962; language of medical texts); Sander-Hansen (1963), and several more textbooks, even in Arabic: Bakir 1954, 2 1955; Nur el-Din 1998).

Old Egyptian: Edel (1955/64).

Late Egyptian: Erman (1880, 2 1933); Korostovtsev (1973); Černý & Groll (1978); Neveu (1996); Junge (1996).

Demotic: Spiegelberg (1925); Lexa (1940–1951); Johnson (1986, 2 1991); Simpson (1996).

Coptic: Steindorff (1894, 2 1904; 1951); Mallon (1904, 2 1907); Till (1928; 1931; 1955, 2 1961); Chaîne (1933); Jelanskaja (1964); Vergote (1973–1983); Polotsky (1987/1990); Shisha-Halevy (1988b) and other textbooks; a modern and comprehensive grammar by Bentley Layton is in the press.

Some scholars attempted a delineation of the Egyptian language and grammar not so much for Egyptologists as for general linguists and/or Semitists; e.g. Callender (1975a; 1975b), Schenkel (1990), Loprieno (1995).

The basis for much of this work was laid in partly large-scale grammatical analyses, starting with Sethe's (1899–1903) monumental work on the verb and his (Sethe 1916) monograph on the nominal sentence, both dealing with the evidence from all periods of the language. In the following the most important additional works on particular topics are listed (especially studies that are still of value and not outdated by later research; with minor exceptions, monographs only).

Dealing with all periods: Polotsky (1944, main focus on Coptic: the *finalis* conjugation; the "second tenses"); Fecht (1960, accent and syllable structure); Osing (1976, derivation of nouns); Schenkel (1983a, transcription; plural formation; 1983b, derivation of nouns).

On particular idioms and topics:

Middle Egyptian: Gunn (1923, negative constructions; prospective tense; etc.); Polotsky (1965, the tenses; 1976, nominal and adverbial "transpositions" of the verb); Doret (1986, verbal system of late Old and early Middle Egyptian), etc.

Old Egyptian: Sander-Hansen (1941; 1956); Allen (1984, Pyramid Texts: verbal morphology)

Late Egyptian: Hintze (1950–1952); Groll (1967; 1970); Frandsen (1974); Satzinger (1976).

Demotic: Johnson (1976); articles by Janet R. Johnson, Richard A. Parker, Ronald J. Williams and others.

Coptic: Polotsky (e.g., 1960; 1962); Wilson (1970); Shisha-Halevy (1988a; 1989); articles by Alexander Böhlig, Wolf-Peter Funk, A. I. Jelanskaja, P. V. Jernstedt, L. Th. Lefort, Peter Nagel, Hans Jakob Polotsky, Hans Quecke, Ariel Shisha-Halevy, W. D. Young and others.

Phonetics: Czermak (1931–1934); Albright (1934); Vergote (1945); Rössler (1971); various articles by these authors and many others (cf. Beinlich-Seeber 1999: III 510–511 for publications before 1947).

Lexicography: The Berlin *Wörterbuch*; Faulkner (1962); Meeks (1980–1982); Hannig (1995); for Late Egyptian: Lesko (1982–1990); for Hieroglyphic texts of the Ptolemaic period: Wilson (1997); for Demotic: Erichsen (1954); a Demotic Dictionary project is in progress at the Oriental Institute, Chicago University; for Coptic: Crum (1939); Westendorf (1965–1977); Coptic etymological dictionaries: Černý (1976); Vycichl (1983). Special fields: v. Deines & Westendorf (1961–1962: medical texts); Hoch (1994: Semitic loans).

Bibliography: Pratt (1925; 1942); the Annual Egyptological Bibliography at Leiden was begun since 1947. The time before 1947 is now covered by Beinlich-Seeber (1998); Coptic bibliography: Kammerer (1950). Later contributions in journals, in particular in *Aegyptus* and in *Archiv für Orientforschung*.

EGYPTIAN AND SEMITIC

Generally speaking, the works mentioned above would indicate correspondences with Semitic, though sporadically, as they occurred in the course of the investigation or presentation. There are, however, also contributions that focus on the (genetic) relationship between Egyptian and Semitic. The first comprehensive study is by Erman (1892) who deals with phonetics, stem formation and morphology of pronouns, nouns and verbs, and syntax, as well as with lexical comparisons and sound correspondences.

Since its initial appearance in the 1870's, the concept of Hamitic languages — as a sister family of Semitic — included Egyptian (for an overview cf., e.g., Jungraithmayr 1983; Satzinger 1999b). Nevertheless, many held that the place of Egyptian was somewhere between Semitic and Hamitic (cf., e.g., Brockelmann 1908: 9). Some scholars claimed — even in more recent times — that it was downright Semitic (cf. Vergote 1965; Rössler 1971), though they conceded that it must have separated from the main stream before all other Semitic ramification (cf., e.g., Vycichl 1958: 368; 1959). However, for a considerable time most researchers have accepted Greenberg's concept of Hamito-Semitic or Afroasiatic being a macro-phylum that constitutes of several branches or families — among them Semitic and Egyptian — of more or less equal standing. Accordingly, the node of descent that connects Egyptian and Semitic is not — at any rate not essentially — lower than the other nodes.

Even before Greenberg, the African relations were taken into account up to a certain extent. In particular those scholars who were trained by Hermann Junker and Wilhelm Czermak, in the tradition of Leo Reinisch, in the *Institut für Ägyptologie und Afrikanistik* of Vienna University also included Berber (especially Zyhlarz, Vycichl, Rössler), Chadic (especially Vycichl 1934) and Cushitic. Zyhlarz (1932–1933) expressly attempts to counterbalance the predominance of Semitic in comparison with Egyptian by investigating various aspects of Egyptian and "Hamitic" (Berber and Cushitic; Hausa — being what he termed "Niggerhamitisch" — is not included): morphology and stem and theme derivation of the verb, phonetics and lexicon in comparison with Egyptian.

Apart from making numerous suggestions of his own, Calice (1936) presented a critical evaluation of all etymologies that had been proposed — e.g., by Erman (1892), Albright (1917–1918; 1927), Ember (especially 1930), Brockelmann (1932), Littmann (1932). More etymologies are proposed by, e.g., Yeivin (1936), Cohen (1947), Leslau (1962), Conti (1978).

Rössler (1950) analyses verbal stem derivation and conjugations of

Akkadian, Berber, Egyptian (with an excursus on Hausa), Bedauye, Mehri and Ge'ez (in his eyes, the verbal systems of languages like Arabic, Canaanite and Aramaic represent a younger type and are not subjected to the analysis). The suffix conjugation appears as the conjugation of predicative nouns, in particular adjectives, as attested by Akkadian, Kabyle and Bedauye in particular. From these, the perfect forms with $a-i$ and $a-u$ vocalism of the "younger Semitic languages" are derived. The dynamic perfect (including the Egyptian old perfective of action verbs) developed from suffix-conjugated perfective participles, viz. *qatil–*. This new perfect superseded the old *iprVs* type perfect in Hebrew, Aramaic and Arabic.

Vycichl (1958) seems to assume that all Egyptian words with a Semitic etymology are loans from (Proto-)Semitic. He documents phonetic correspondences with some 160 etymologies that he regards as certain, and he discusses 76 etymologies (partly those dealt with in the first part, partly new).

Thacker (1954) deals with the *Relationship of the Semitic and Egyptian verbal systems*. He meticulously analyses the vocalisation of the Egyptian verb forms and derives his theory: "The Semitic and Egyptian verbal systems are offshoots of the same parent system. They parted at an early and incomplete stage of development and continued their growth each along its own lines" (p. 335). Semitic and Egyptian developed their verbal systems independently, from the same starting point (three verbal bases: (a) $qVtl$; (b) $qtVl$; (c) $qVttVl$. / (a) $sV\underline{d}m$; (b) $s\underline{d}Vm$; (c) $sV\underline{d}Vmm$[sic]), but arrived partly at different points. So Semitic developed the prefix conjugation by inversion of the suffix conjugation: *qatl–* + *ta* > *ta-qatil*. The Egyptian pronoun conjugation (i.e., the "suffix conjugation" of Egyptological terminology), on the other hand, is reached by conceiving the subject as genitival. Thacker is not willing to accept that Egyptian has, in contrast to Semitic, many two-radical verbs; he interprets them as hollow verbs, so numerous in Semitic and so rare in Egyptian. It is still worth while to pursue Thacker's crucial idea that all conjugations of Semitic and Egyptian have (the same) verbal nouns as their verbal basis. To be exact: we are dealing in Egyptian with two verbal nouns, an unmarked form *CaCVC*, and a marked form with gemination or reduplication and "pluralic" meaning, as we would say today.

Vergote (1965) presented a study of the Egyptian nominal stems, including infinitives and old perfectives, trying to establish their relation to the corresponding Semitic stems.

Janssens (1972) distinguished three basic verb forms for both Egyptian and Semitic: preterite (perfective $s\underline{d}m=f$ and *iprus*, etc., respectively); jussive (subjunctive $s\underline{d}m=f$ and Sem. jussive, respectively); imperfect (imperfective *sḏm=f* and *iparras*, etc., respectively). His reconstruction of the vocalisation of the Egyptian verb must be considered outdated.

Loprieno (1986) proceeds from a common Egypto-Semitic ("Afroasiatic") verbal system on the basis of a tripartite aspectual system: *zero*, perfective (marked), imperfective (unmarked). The second co-ordinate is "±realized." This ambitious work suffers from various theoretic shortcomings (cf. Satzinger 1989).

Of course, there are also Semitists that take Egyptian into consideration. Apart from those already mentioned, there are, e.g., Diakonoff (1965); Aspesi (1977); Belova (1980; 1989); Petráček (1988).

Egyptian has much in common with Semitic, as compared with most Cushitic (including Omotic; cf. Lamberti 1999) and all Chadic languages. But when evaluating similarities between individual branches of Afroasiatic it is crucial to take into account (1) the factor of time, (2) the historico-cultural factor, and (3) possible areal effects.

(*The factor of time.*) Egyptian and Akkadian are attested in the third millennium BC, other Semitic languages somewhat later. The other branches of Afroasiatic are attested only recently (with the exception of the rather meagre evidence of ancient Libyan), and often enough not to a satisfactory extent. This means that comparisons must allow for a further development of several thousand years on the side of the other branches.

(*The historico-cultural factor.*) The Afroasiatic relationship dates back to Mesolithic times. Many important cultural achievements, such as agriculture and cattle-breeding, are later. The social structure and the forms of rule have changed drastically. This is of particular importance for lexical comparison. Many terms that appear basic to us cannot be expected to be part of the inherited common vocabulary. (Characteristic examples are terms like *ḥsb* "to reckon" and *ḫtm* "to seal": the meaning is the same, the transcription is identical for Egyptian and Arabic, there is obviously a close relationship, but it must be other than genetic.)

(*Areal effects.*) The prehistory of the speakers of the individual branches of Afroasiatic is controversial, as is the question of the original Afroasiatic homeland, and consequently the reconstruction of the migrations from there to their present locations. It is usually very hard to say who in the course of time used to be the neighbours of the individual groups.

Historical Egypt is constituted of two populations: that of the Delta, and that of the Nile Valley. Most probably, these groups had different languages, and it is only one of them that is the ancestor of historical Egyptian. At present, many assume that Proto-Egyptian is the language of the Southerners (Naqâda culture; cf. Helck 1984; Helck, 1990). We know nothing at all about the other language.

The Valley population is not indigenous. It has immigrated either from the south or from the south-west. The implications of this question concern the languages with which Egyptian may have had contact before it entered the light of history. In the south, we may expect Cushitic (including Omotic) languages, and apart from Afroasiatic, various Eastern Sudanic languages (of the Nilo-Saharan macro-phylum), and Kordofanian languages (Niger-Kordofanian macro-phylum). In the south-west, the presumable neighbours would probably have spoken either Chadic languages, or Saharan languages (again, Nilo-Saharan). But these assumptions are, of course, based on the present distribution.

In fact, Egyptian has much in common with Semitic. It has virtually the same principles of word order (leaving out of consideration on the Semitic side the end position of the verb in Akkadian, as also in Amharic). The verbal predicate (and also the nominal predicate, though not the adverbial predicate) comes first, subject and complements follow. Phrases have their nucleus in head position — the modified precedes the modifier: verb — complements, noun — attribute, noun — genitival expansion (regens — rectum), preposition — complement. There are prepositions and no postpositions (a seeming exception is the rare and archaic *js* "like"; it is, however, to be related to the Akkadian "dative" ending *-iš*, cf. below, for "case"). The relation between the preposition and its complement resembles the genitival relation in so far as in both cases the same set of personal pronouns is used, viz. the suffix pronoun. Attributive adjectives come after the substantive. In the earliest phase of the language, attributive demonstrative pronouns also follow the substantive (*pr pn* "this house"), whereas Middle Egyptian sees the emergence of new sets that precede the substantive (from one of these the definite article develops: *p3-pr* "the house"). Numerals, however, are nuclear: they precede the noun except for number "two."

There are, on the other hand, more or less conspicuous divergences in vital areas. The Egyptian and Semitic personal pronouns vary both in paradigmatic structure (since Egyptian has also an enclitic pronoun, intermediary between absolute and suffix pronoun) and partly in substance — at least at first glance. The demonstrative pronoun is totally different, both in structure and in substance.

Several features of Egyptian are briefly presented here in order to give an impression of the degree of its relationship to Semitic. (NB: Loprieno 1995 is an excellent exhaustive and up-to-date reference for the Egyptian language in general. As may be expected, there are, however, minor points here and there where the present author would disagree. In the following, this is not always expressly mentioned.)

LEXICON

In comparative works of Afroasiatic lexicon (e.g., Calice 1936; Cohen 1947; Vycichl 1958; Diakonoff 1965; Diakonoff et alii 1993–1997; Orel & Stolbova 1994; Ehret 1995) Egyptian items are not very conspicuous among those of the other branches. We have to consider that Egyptian is a single language whereas the other branches are — with the exception of Berber — groups of numerous languages. On the other hand, the attested Egyptian lexicon with its approximately seventeen thousand entries presents much more material than what is recorded in the average Chadic and Cushitic languages. It has, however, long been noted with astonishment (cf. Erman 1892: 105) that Egyptian displays only few Semitic roots in those semantic fields where clear correspondences would be expected, like, e.g., terms of family relationship, the lower numbers, verbs of a basic meaning, like "to do," "to come," etc. The "basic word-lists" of one hundred, or two hundred, or two hundred twenty items, which Swadesh has developed for the purpose of mass comparison, furnish us with an instrument to objectify the degree of lexical relationship. In the one hundred word list we find a small number of long-established comparisons:

		Semitic	Egyptian
17	to die	*m-w-t	mwt (Copt. infinitive mū' < *māwVt)
39	to hear	*š̠-m-'	sḏm (Copt. infinitive sōtm < *sādem < *sāḏVm; metathesis; with Egn. ḏ [i.e. č̠] as palatalized ', or ḡ, as in Egn. nḏm ~ Sem. na'im– "pleasant" and Egn. pVsīd– ~ Sem. tiš'– "nine")
40	heart	*libb–	jb (*jib)
42	I	*'anāku	jnk (*janák; Copt. anók)
62	not	*lā	nj (Copt. n–)
89	tongue	*lišān–	ns (*nis; Copt. las)
92	two	*tn-āni (dual)	snw(j) (Copt. snau)
94	warm	*ḫāmm–	šm(m), var. ḥm(m̂) (Copt. infinitive hmom: xmom < *ḥVmám)
95	water	*mā'–	mw (*maw; Copt. mou)
97	what	*mā	mj
99	who	*man	mj

Other equations are only possible on the basis of the "new" phonetics by Rössler (1971) (for which see below):

| 30 | fly (noun) | *ḏub(V)b | 'ff (Sem. ḏ ~ Egn. '; Copt. af, aaf < *'í/úffVf [?]); but cf. |

Sem. *'-w-f* "to fly"!
35   green   **w-r-q*   *w3ḏ* (with Egn. *ḏ* [i.e. *č̣*]
                                 as palatalized *ḳ*; Copt. infinitive *u̯ōt*)
37   hand   **yad–*   ' (Sem. *d* ~ Egn. '), var. *d* (Copt. *–tá=*)

Dto., with seemingly irregular sound correspondences:

54   moon   **war(i)ḫ–*   *j'ḥ* (**jā'Vḥ*; Copt. *ooh*, dialectally *i̯oh*;
                                 irregular: Sem. *r* ~ Egn. ')
71   sand   **ḥāl–* (Heb.) *š'j* (with Egn. *š* as palatalized *ḫ*; irregular:
                                 Sem. *l* ~ Egn. ')
64   one   **'aḥVd-/waḥVd–* *w'jw* **wí'jVw* (defended by Schenkel 1990:
                                 55, in the assumed form *w'"w*;
                                 however, Sem. *ḥ* ~ Egn. ' is not
                                 regular.)

Indirect evidence (all non-"Rösslerian" phonetics: according to Rössler,
Egn. {d} is *ṯ*, not *d/ḏ*):

21   ear   **'ud̲in–*   the hieroglyphic ear sign, ⌀, has
                                 the phonetic value *jd̲(n)*
37   hand   **yad–*   the hieroglyphic hand sign, ⟅, has
                                 the phonetic value *d*

PHONOLOGY

Consonants: a characteristic of Afroasiatic languages is the existence
of "emphatic" consonants in addition to (non-emphatic) voiceless and
voiced plosives and fricatives. For a long time it was held that Egyptian
is the only branch that does not have them, except for *ḳ (q)* (cf. Diakonoff
1965: 19). But Rössler (1971) and Schenkel (1988) were able to show
that — at least in principle — "*ḏ*" and "*d̲*" are emphatic, viz. *ṯ* and *č̣*
respectively, at least until the first millennium BC (cf. Satzinger 1997).
But still more spectacular is Rössler's discovery that Egyptian ' behaves
like a dental occlusive in respect to co-occurrence restraints, and not at
all like a laryngeal.

On the other hand, comparatists continue to claim that a regular
correspondence between Semitic ' (and *ḡ*) and Egyptian ' is beyond any
doubt. This has inspired further studies that attempt to find more reliable
and more detailed evidence (cf. Zeidler 1992; Schenkel 1993; Satzinger
1999a; 1999b). Obviously, the Semitic–Egyptian sound correspondences
are far more complicated than has been thought before. In particular, there
seems to be much alternation between emphatic and voiced occlusives,

both on the Afroasiatic level and in (Proto-)Egyptian. With this *caveat*, the following chart may be set up (it takes some inspiration from Kammerzell 1998 without, however, resuming several hypothetical details).

Voiceless			Emphatic			Voiced			Varia
fricative	affricate	plosive	fricative	affricate	plosive	fricative	affricate	plosive	
p̄ [φ] "f" (or p̄?)		P							*b m w*
s	c "z"	t			ṭ "d"			d "ꜥ "	*n r* "ꜣ" *l* "r"
š	č "t"			č̣ "d"			j?		*y* "j"
x "h"		k	x̱ "h"		ḳ	g [ɣ] "h"		g	ꜥ ꜣ "ꜣ" h

Note that the phonemes of line 3 have originated in those of line 4 in the course of a partial palatalization of Proto-Egyptian.

Vowels: There is no evidence that Egyptian did not have the same basic set of vowels as Semitic, viz. *a – i – u*. As for vowel length, the "Palaeo-Coptic" (Edgerton 1947) syllable laws caused a drastic change. Vowels cannot be but long in an open stressed syllable, and they must be short in closed stressed syllables and, in addition, in all unstressed syllables. Stress is usually on the penult, in rarer cases on the last syllable. (Some modifications of these syllable laws are assumed by Schenkel 1983a.)

An important source for the investigation of Egyptian phonetics are renderings of Egyptian names and words in cuneiform and, vice versa, renderings of Semitic words and Near Eastern names in Egyptian script. But these transcriptions have also an impact on Semitic phonetics. The original sound value of the Semitic sibilant that is realized in Hebrew as *samekh* has been assumed to be [s]; among the arguments for assuming an original sound value [ts], at least until the second millennium BC, is its correspondence with Egyptian *t̠* [c] in the transcriptions (cf. Hoch 1994: 408 + n. 34).

FORMATION OF STEMS

Analysis of Egyptian roots, stems and forms is hampered by transmission in a medium that does not render vowels and syllable structure. Still, it is clear that the role the consonants play in roots and stems is as important as it is in Semitic (this is ultimately the reason why the Egyptians developed a consonantal script for their language). Egyptian nominal stems are derived in similar ways as in Semitic. Of the external modifications of Afroasiatic stems (cf., e.g., Diakonoff 1965: 38), Egyptian has the *m*– prefix (with conditioned variants *n*–, *mn*–) for forming nomina loci and instrumenti, nomina agentis and patientis (though participles are not formed with *m*– prefix; for these, cf. Osing 1987) as well as collectives (Vergote 1965; id., 1973/1983, Ia: 155 § 89; Osing 1976: 119, 206, 209, 211, 256).

There are two classes of adjectives: those that are derived from verbs of quality (at least some being their participles), and those derived from nouns or prepositions by means of the "nisba" ending –*j* (earlier also –*w* [**-Vwi?*]).

Verbal stems may have two to five radicals (stems with six radicals — formed by total reduplication of three radical roots: ABCABC — are quite exceptional), though verbs with three radicals are by far the most typical. Four-radical verbs are often formed by reduplication of two-radical roots (ABAB); all five-radical stems display a reduplication of the second and third radicals (ABCBC). The forms of two-radical verbs seem to have the vocalization of the second syllable of the pertinent forms of three-radical verbs; cf. **win* "opening" vs. **wānim* "eating" (active participles; see Osing 1987). Verbs whose last radical is *j* ("weak verbs") behave differently from "strong verbs"; cf. *sdm=f* "that he hears" (aorist, clausal form), with no modification being apparent in the consonantal skeleton, but *ḥzz=f* "that he praises" (of root *ḥzj*), with a reduplication of the second radical and loss of the weak third radical; infinitives **sā́dVm* (Coptic *sōtm*) "to hear," **ḥī́z-at* (Coptic *hī́se*) "to praise."

There seem to be a few *pi"el* forms, though this is doubted by some (cf. Coptic *mū'* < **mā́wVt* "to die," *mout* < **máwwVt* "to kill"). The causative stem prefix **sV*– (e.g., *'nḫ* [inf. **>* *ắnVḫ*, Coptic *ōnh*] "to live," *s-'nḫ* [inf. **sá'naḫ*, Coptic *sá'ₐnš*] "to make live") is much more conspicuous. It is, however, no longer operative.

NOMINAL MORPHOLOGY (1): CASE

In some Semitic languages there is a nominative in –*u*, an accusative in –*a* and a genitive in –*i*, viz. in Akkadian and in Arabic; in Ge'ez, the phonetic development has caused the merging of nominative and genitive (Moscati 1964, ²1969: 94). The case in –*a* is used for the objects of transitive verbs, but also as adverbial case (such as Arabic *al-yawm-a* "today," *barr-an wa-baḥr-an* "on land and on sea," *ǧidd-an* "very" — literally, "with zeal *or* effort" —, *'akbaru 'ilm-an* "greater in respect to knowledge"), for the predicative noun after some verbs of *being* or *becoming* (Arabic: *kāna* and its "sisters", Ge'ez: *kōna*), for the predicative noun in the "absolute negation," Arabic *lā 'ilāh-a* "there is no god," and, in Arabic, under certain conditions for the vocative (e.g., *yā 'abd-a llāhi*). These usages and, in addition, the traces of a case in *–a* in Berber and Cushitic lead to the assumption that it was not originally the case of the object of the verb (accusative), but rather an absolute case. Its realms were the absolute noun, the predicate and the address (vocative). Its later use as an accusative and as an adverbialis can be plausible under the assumption that it marked the predicative phrase as a whole. If the nucleus of the predicate is a verb the predicate phrase may also comprise an object and/or an adverbial complement which then received the predicate marker *–a*. In this way it became primarily associated with the object (cf. Satzinger forthcoming (b)). This amounts to the eventual development of an accusative case system (viz., with a nominative as subject case and an accusative as object case). Akkadian, however, seems to have split the Afroasiatic absolute case into an accusative in *–a* (object, adverbs) and an absolute case in *–Ø* (called *absolute state*; in particular for the absolute noun and as vocative). — Apart from the cases mentioned there is a dative/adverbialis in *–iš* (Akkadian; rudiments in **-ah* in Ugaritic and Hebrew, *–s* in Epigraphic South Arabian; *js* in Egyptian, and perhaps *–s* in Central Cushitic and in Omotic/West Cushitic; cf. Diakonoff 1965: 58 note 8) and a locative that is homonymous (and ultimately identical) with the nominative, viz. in *–u*.

Historical Egyptian certainly has no case endings. However, traces of case endings can be seen: absolute case in *–a*, nominative in *–u*, genitive in *–i*, and an adverbialis/dative in **-is* (cf. Zeidler 1992: 210–212; for the absolute case see Satzinger 1991: 130; 1997: 35–36). There is no reason to assume that Proto-Egyptian — as also Berber and Cushitic — ever had the Semitic accusative system, with accusative in *–a* (*pace* Callender 1975a; Loprieno 1995: 55), but rather an absolute case system, with an absolute case in *–a* (in a paradigm with the absolute personal pronoun, for which cf. below), and a case in *–u*, agentive (nominative) and locative: as also in some ergative languages it was probably the locative that served as an agentive case. (The corresponding personal pronoun is the suffix pronoun, which also encompasses the genitival function.) The assumption of an ergative system (for which see the following) would imply that there was originally also a case for the subject of intransitive verbs that was identical with the case of the object of transitive verbs. (The corresponding personal pronoun is in Egyptian the enclitic pronoun.)

The characteristic feature of ergativity is that the objects of transitive verbs are in the same case (viz. the absolutive) as the subjects of intransitive verbs, whereas the subjects / agents of transitive verbs are in a particular case, the ergative. By way of contrast, an accusative system implies that the subjects of transitive and intransitive verbs are in the same case, viz. the nominative, whereas the objects of transitive verbs are in the accusative. In Egyptology, the ergative issue has been raised in recent publications (cf., e.g., Zeidler 1992: 210–212; Loprieno 1995: 83–85; Roccati 1997; Reintges 1998: 458; cf. for Semitic: Müller 1995; for Berber: Aikhenvald 1995; for Chadic: Frajzyngier 1984). Actually, there is no Afroasiatic language that has an ergative system, whether fully fledged or a "split ergative" (the arguments of Aikhenvald 1995 are not convincing; the evidence of Berber is better accounted for by an absolute case model, cf. Sasse 1984). Nevertheless, Egyptian can add some evidence, in addition to Diakonoff's (1965: 58) arguments, that points to the possibility that originally Afroasiatic did have an ergative system. This concerns the personal pronouns and the stative form of the old perfective (suffix conjugation).

In historical Egyptian the paradigms of the personal pronoun do not correspond to distinct case functions. The absolute pronoun is both used as an absolute case (e.g., for nominal predicates) and (with restrictions) for the subject of the nominal sentence; this is in a measure comparable with Semitic. The enclitic pronoun expresses both the object of transitive verbs and the subject of the adjectival sentence (which also encompasses participles: *jrj sw* "he (is one who) does," *ḥ'j sw* "he (is one who) rejoices"). The function of the suffix pronoun is similar to the genitival function of its Semitic counterpart, but in addition it expresses the pronominal subject in what is here called the "pronoun conjugation." It may be assumed that the pronominal paradigms are a testimony of an older case system: absolute pronoun ~ absolute case (predicates, etc.); enclitic pronoun ~ absolutive case (originally, subject of intransitives [?], patient expression with transitives); suffix pronoun ~ genitive and ergative (originally, agent expression with transitive verbs [?]). Cf. Table 1.

The old perfective in its stative form has perhaps developed from an ergative construction: its pronominal element denotes the subject of intransitive verbs and the object of transitive verbs, equalling thus to the absolutive case of the pronoun. A delimitation from the enclitic pronoun just mentioned has yet to be drawn.

NOMINAL MORPHOLOGY (2): NUMBER, GENDER

Like Semitic, Egyptian originally distinguishes three numbers, viz. singular, plural and dual. The latter tends to be given up rather early, a phenomenon that is familiar from other languages (Semitic, Indo-European).

Like Afroasiatic in general, Egyptian has two genders, masculine and feminine. In the personal and demonstrative pronouns, third person, a further form exists that is used for facts rather than objects, or for quantities (enclitic pronoun *st*; demonstratives with *n–* base, viz. *nn*, *nw*, *nf*, etc.). These forms tend to be used as plurals, thus replacing the original plural forms. Whereas the gender of nouns is distinguished by their endings (see below), the pronouns have particular forms for each gender. The demonstratives, however, use different bases: *p–* (masculine), *t–* (feminine) and *n–*. To these, the deictic elements are attached: *–w* (< *–j*) and *–n* (proximity), *–f* (distance).

Like Afroasiatic in general, Egyptian distinguishes gender not only in the third, but also in the second person of the personal pronoun (in writing, though, in the singular only; the plural forms may either have merged or be distinguished by different vowels: e.g., **kumu > *tun, **kina > *tin).

The morphemes of gender/number discrimination can be compared with some of those of other branches, including Semitic. But Egyptian gender/number formation is — in particular in the traditional view (cf. Satzinger 1997: 36–37; 1999d) — of a uniformity that stands in marked contrast to the other Afroasiatic branches. All feminine nouns have the ending *–t* (which is mostly **–at*, but cf. monosyllabic words like **pu·t* "sky," and the *nisba* adjectives, masc. **jamíniy* "western," fem. **jamíni·t*). The masculine plural is in *–w*, the dual in *–wj*; the feminine plural is in *–wt*, the dual in *–tj*. It has been shown, however, that the masculine plural may be formed from a base different from the singular. As a kind of broken plural, there is a pattern **CaCúC–*, to which form the plural ending is attached: **nátar* (or **nátir*) "god," plur. **natúr-uw*; **san* "brother," plur. **sanúw-uw* (Schenkel 1983 (a): 177–178; Satzinger 1999d).

If the Semitic plural endings **–ū*, **–ī* are modifications of case endings (nominative and oblique case, respectively), the same should be true of the Egyptian plural ending *–w*. It is, then, an indirect vestige of the common case ending *–u* (absolutive > nominative).

In Egyptian there are no traces of mimation or nunation, neither in the singular, nor in the plural or dual.

VERBAL MORPHOLOGY (1): TENSES, ASPECTS, MOODS

A tentative sketch of TAM reconstruction in Proto-Semitic may assume a present perfect category that is expressed by the suffix conjugation. It may originally have been a "pseudo-conjugation" for the predicative adjective (Tropper 1995), though its use with other verbs (both static and dynamic) cannot be overlooked. The dynamic expression of events is the prefix conjugation which is attested in two basic aspectual forms: an unmarked short form (cf. Akk. *iprVs*) and an imperfective fuller form (cf. Akk. *iparrVs*). (We may presently disregard assumptions of a third stem.) From this material, the individual languages have developed their tense systems in various ways. The present perfect was preserved in Akkadian. In Hebrew the use of the suffix conjugation was extended to the preterite tense, while in Arabic and Ethiosemitic the category of the present perfect lost even more ground, the suffix conjugation becoming primarily the form of the preterite. The main realm of the unmarked prefix form (i.e., the form of the *iprVs* type) came to be the present (and future) and the subjunctive and (or) modal forms. The marked form (i.e., the form of the *iparrVs* type) was lost, except for Akkadian and South Semitic. To a certain measure the prefix conjugation forms of the *iprVs* type are now in Hebrew, Biblical Aramaic and Arabic an imperfective counterpart to the suffix conjugation, whereas originally the *iparrVs* type forms were the imperfective counterpart to the *iprVs* type forms.

Berber has an amalgam of the prefix and suffix conjugations for forming all tense paradigms, with clear vestiges of the *iparrVs* type, in addition to the *iprVs* type stem. The suffix conjugation, in its true form, is preserved as a present perfect in Kabyle only (Rössler 1950: 478–486). Vestiges of the original suffix conjugation in Cushitic and Chadic are — for different reasons — still controversial issues.

VERBAL MORPHOLOGY (2): THE OLD PERFECTIVE

Recent discoveries in the field of the Egyptian suffix conjugation (that is the *pseudo-participle* (Erman), the *old perfective* (Gardiner), or the *stative* (Polotsky); what Egyptology calls "suffix conjugation" is here called "pronoun conjugation") may shed new light on the Semitic facts. Functionally, two main uses of the Egyptian suffix conjugation may be discerned (Satzinger 1998).

1. the "Stative," a present perfect (static present of verbs of quality, static passive of transitive verbs). Like several other rhematic forms (i.e., forms that are neither clausal nor "contingent"), the old perfective tends early to be restricted to circumstantial status ("he being good," "he having been clad," etc.).

2. the "Perfect," a dynamic preterite. Attested in the Old Kingdom, this use is becoming obsolete in Middle Egyptian. It seems, however, that it survived with intransitive verbs of motion, and perhaps some other action verbs.

Schenkel (1994) has shown in a rather sophisticated way that there is a significant morphological difference between the two "uses" mentioned. Whereas the dynamic forms seem to be conjugated the way it has been imagined up till now (the conjugation ending being directly joined to the verbal base, e.g. *sadV́m-kVw*), the static verbs insert, in the first and second persons (Satzinger 1999c), a long vowel before the ending (e.g. *sadm-V̄-kVw*), which is of course reminiscent of the stative forms of Akkadian (e.g. *parsāku*). It is not very plausible to assume that the Egyptian stative and perfect developed independently of Semitic in such a similar way. Instead, it may suggest that the stative-perfect dichotomy is not an innovation of (Proto-)Semitic but an old Afroasiatic feature (Satzinger forthcoming (c)). Whereas the Semitic languages generalized one form for both uses (in Akkadian, the old perfective, otherwise the Perfect) Egyptian has preserved both.

An important feature connected with the use of the old perfective is the "suppletive system" (Polotsky 1984: 116) in the perfect of the Egyptian verbal system. In this, the old perfective is used for (most) intransitives and for the passive of the transitives. The active voice of the transitives, however, is conveyed by the *n*-form of the pronoun conjugation:

šm·w "he has gone" *rdj·n=f* "he has given" *rdj·w* "he has been given"

The tense connotations of the two forms, old perfective and *sdm·n=f*, developed in the same way. A present perfect originally, they began to be used as a preterite from the late Old Kingdom onward. The two forms are truly suppletive, just as *il est allé, il a donné,* and *er ist gegangen, er hat gegeben,* respectively. The suffix conjugation is in this way fully integrated into the tense system.

VERBAL MORPHOLOGY (3): THE EGYPTIAN PRONOUN CONJUGATION

Egyptian is the only branch of Afroasiatic that has no vestige whatsoever of the prefix conjugation. In its place, it has its peculiar pronoun conjugation (called "suffix conjugation" in Egyptology). Its structure is the following (cf. Satzinger 1997: 38):

1. verbal stem in one of various forms (interior or exterior modification): obviously, several vocalization and syllabication patterns; reduplication of the second of the 3 radicals; reduplication of the last radical; prefixation of *j–*; suffixation of *–y/w* (passive), of *–t* (resultative!?)
2. gender and number markers (with attributive forms only): *–Ø, –t*; *–w, –wt*

3. external tense markers: $-\emptyset$, $-n$ (present perfect > past tense), $-w/j$ (prospective tense); "contingent tenses" $-jn$ (past), $-k3$ (prospective), $-\underline{h}r$ (unmarked)
4. external voice markers: $-\emptyset$, $-tw$ ($< -tj$ or $-t$?)
5. subject expression: substantive, demonstrative, numeral, proper name etc.; suffix pronoun; $\emptyset$ (expressing an indefinite or impersonal subject)
    Some examples:

1.	2.	3.	4.	5.	translation	syntactic status	tense
jjj (root: *jwj*)	*w*	—	—	—	"who (plur.) have come"	attribute	perfect
ḥzjj (root: *ḥzj*)	*w*	—	—	—	"who (plur.) have been praised"	attribute	perfect passive
ḫpp (root: *ḫpj*)	*wt*	—	—	*3ḫw* (*ḥr-sn*)	"(the ways [fem. pl.] on) which the blessed use to walk"	attribute	aorist
rdj	*t*	*n*	—	*f*	"what (fem.) he gave"	attribute	perfect
'nḫ	*t*	*j*	—	*ntr* (*jm*)	"(on which) a god will live"	attribute	prospect.
gmm (root: *gmj*)		—	*tw*	*f*	"that it (masc.) is found"	substantival	aorist
gmj	—	*n*	—	*f*	"that he was found"	substantival	perfect
gmj	—	*n*	*tw*	*bw*	"that the place was found"	substantival	perfect passive
ḥzj	—	*j/w*	—	*nswt*	"that the king will praise"	substantival	prospect

1.	2.	3.	4.	5.	translation	syntactic status	tense
prj	—	—	—	*f*	"(they found him) going out"	rhematic (circumstantial)	aorist
gmjj (root: *gmj*)	—	—	—	*bw*	"the place having been found"	rhematic (circumstantial)	perfect passive
nḥm	—	—	—	Ø	"they (indef. meaning) took"	rhematic, impersonal	perfect
ḫpr	—	*(w)*	—	Ø	"it (indef. meaning) will become"	rhematic, impersonal	prospective
rdj	—	*jn*	—	Ø	"and they (indef. meaning) gave"	contingent, impersonal	perfect
jrj	—	*jn*	*tw*	Ø	"then one acted"	contingent, impersonal passive	perfect

In Gardiner's view, Egyptian verbs have two aspectual forms, comparable to the *iprVs* and the *iparrVs* types of Akkadian and Ethiosemitic. The discriminating feature is, however, not gemination (or lengthening) of the second of the three stem consonants, but rather its reduplication. This aspectual reduplication (wrongly called "gemination" in Egyptology) is, in the main, restricted to some forms of the majority of the ultimae infirmae verbs: *ḥzj* "to praise," but *ḥzz=f* "that he praises," the "imperfective participles" *ḥzzj(·t /*etc.) "who praise(s)" and *ḥzzw(·t /*etc.) "who is/are praised," and the "imperfective relative form," *ḥzzw(·t /*etc.)*=f* "whom/whose (etc.) ... he praises." Note, however, that — according to the Polotskyan scheme — one of the forms claimed by Gardiner for the "perfective" forms must be grouped with the "imperfective" forms. The so-called circumstantial *sḏm=f*, *ḥzj=f* "(he) praising," is — in terms of tense and aspect — probably on a par with the substantival form *ḥzz=f* "that he praises" and the other "imperfective" forms mentioned. It may be imagined that originally the rhematic/circumstantial forms (like *ḥzj=f*) displayed the characteristic reduplication but lost it by syncopation (*ḥVzzV–*) on account of a different syllable structure.

VERBAL MORPHOSYNTAX AND SYNTAX: SYNTACTICAL STATUS, RHEMATIC VS. CLAUSAL

Egyptian not only has participles of all three main tenses, viz. perfect, aorist (in the sense of Turkish) and prospective, in both voices, that serve as predicative nuclei of attribute clauses, but also conjugated forms, called *relative forms*. Whereas this has been recognized for a very long time, it was only Polotsky (1944, etc.) who discovered that there is a series of "that" forms, comparable to the relative forms:

w3w·t ḫpp·wt 3ḫ·w ḥr=sn "the ways on which the blessed walk" (relative form, aorist)

ḫpp 3ḫ·w ḥr w3·wt "that the blessed walk on the ways" ("that" form, aorist)

w3·t (fem.) "way," *ḫpj* "to walk," *3ḫ* (masc.) "blessed," *ḥr* "on," *=sn*, suffix personal pronoun, 3rd plural.

w3·t tw ḏsr·t ḫpj·t·n Ḏḥwtj ḥr=s "this exalted way on which Thoth walked" (relative form, perfect)

ḫpj·n Ḏḥwtj ḥr w3·t tw ḏsr·t "it is on this exalted way that Thoth walked" ("that" form, perfect)

tw, demonstrative, fem. sing.; *ḏsr* "exalted"

nn mr jrjj=k r=f "this injury which you were going to do against him" (relative form, prospective)

jrjj=k nn mr r=f "that you are going to do this injury against him" ("that" form, prospective)

nn, demonstrative, non-individual; *mr* "evil"; *jrj* "to do"; *=k*, suffix personal pronoun, 2nd masc. sing.; *r* "towards, against"; *=f*, suffix personal pronoun, 3rd masc. sing.

Recognition of the existence of substantival forms, or rather of nominal forms that can function both as substantives and as attributive adjectives, has an impact on the theories on the origin of the pronoun conjugation. The verbal element is most probably a verbal noun (Schenkel 1975), though its category is not equivalent to the verbal nouns preserved in Egyptian and Semitic. On the one hand, it existed in two aspectual variants: one simple form with perfective meaning (*ḥzj*), the other one a reduplicated imperfective form (*ḥzz(j)*). On the other, it was not confined to substantival function but had also that of a verbal adjective, as it could be used as an attribute. Adding an actor expression (noun or suffix pronoun) could yield both "that" forms and relative forms: *ḥzz=f* "his praising" = "that he praises"; *ḥzz·t=f* "the (female whom) his praising (concerns)" = "whom (fem.) he praises"; *ḥzj=f* "his having praised" = "that he (has) praised"; *ḥzj·t=f* "the (female whom) his having praised (concerns)" =

"whom (fem.) he (has) praised" (Satzinger 1997:39). Actually, there is a close parallel to this in a neighbouring, though unrelated language; cf. the Proto-Old Nubian conjugation system, as reconstructed by Browne (1982; 1988: 7–12; 1998: 23–26); also cf. Satzinger (1995: 157–158; 1997: 40; 2001: 262–263).

Some of the tense markers are probably verbs of saying used as auxiliaries. This feature is wide-spread in Eastern Africa, both in Afroasiatic and Nilo-Saharan languages. $s\underline{d}m \cdot \underline{h}r = f$ "then he hears" may be explained as "he says: listening," $s\underline{d}m \cdot jn = f$ "then he heard" is $*s\underline{d}m \cdot j \cdot n = f$ "he has said: listening." The auxiliary of $s\underline{d}m \cdot k\underline{3} = f$ "then he will hear" means "to think," "to plan"; hence $*$"he plans to listen." The tense marker n, on the other hand, is most probably derived from the homonymous preposition meaning "to," a most general expression of a possessive relation (akin to Semitic li–). Hence, $s\underline{d}m \cdot n = f$ can be compared with Syriac $šmī'$-leh "he has heard," but also with the perfect forms in Western European languages formed with "to have" as an auxiliary.

THE ADVERBIAL SENTENCE AND ITS ROLE FOR VERBAL EXPRESSION

Like the vast majority of African languages (and some Western European languages; see Satzinger 2000) Egyptian conspicuously distinguishes sentences with adverbial predicates (or predicatives) from sentences with nominal predicates.

1. Adverbial sentence:
Unmarked sequence: Subject — Predicate
Very often embedded into the *jw* construction or as subject of *m=k*, *m=t̲*, *m=t̲n* ("behold"), *js̲t* (yields a kind of parenthesis), *nn* ("... is not"; yields a negatived adverbial clause), *ntj* ("which is ..." ; yields a relative clause); *nt·t* ("that ... is ..." ; yields a noun clause); *wnn* ("to be"; allows to transpose an adverbial sentence into various tenses and/or nominal and adjectival statuses etc.).

—	*N.*	*h̲r=j*	"N. is with me" (with nominal subject only; with pronominal subject, the adverbial sentence must be embedded)
jw	*=f*	*h̲r=j*	"he is with me"
m=k	*sw*	*h̲r=j*	"behold, he is with me"
js̲t	*sw*	*h̲r=j*	"now, he was with me" (when in past context)
nn	*sw*	*h̲r=j*	"he is not with me"

nt·t	=*f*	*ḥr*=*s*	(1) "(the woman) with whom he is"; (2) "that he is with her"
wn·jn	=*f*	*ḥr*=*j*	"then he began to be with me"
wn	=*f*	*ḥr*=*j*	"he was with me"
wn·t	=*f*	*ḥr*=*s*	"(the woman) with whom he was"
wnn	=*f*	*ḥr*=*j*	(1) "that he is with me"; (2) "that he shall be with me"
wnn·t	=*f*	*ḥr*=*s*	"(the woman) with whom he (1) is wont to be, (2) shall be"

2. The nominal sentence (cf. Shisha-Halevy 1984; 1987; Doret 1989/1990/1992):

No embedding in constructions with *jw*, *wnn* etc.

Unmarked sequence: Predicate — Subject

Snbj rn=*j* "my name is *Snbj*"; usually, however, the nominal sentence with substantival subject is extended to a tripartite construction by using a demonstrative pronoun as a dummy subject; e.g. *zšw pw sn*=*k* "your brother is (the type of) a scribe (*zšw*)" (< "he is a scribe, viz. your brother").

In both the bipartite and the tripartite constructions the subject may be rhematized which yields "naming" constructions (cf. Shisha-Halevy 1984: 181; 1989:89–95), explicative or glossing utterances etc.; e.g., bipartite: *sn·t*=*f Spd·t*, *sšmw*=*f ntr dw3* "his sister is Sothis, his guide is the morning star."

With pronominal subject, first and second persons, this rhematization is neutralized. The sequence #absolute pronoun — noun# is here the natural one: *jnk sn*=*k* "I am your brother"; *jnn sn·w*=*k* "we are your brothers"; *ntk sn*=*j* "you are my brother"; *ntt sn·t*=*j* "you are my sister"; *nttn sn·w*=*j* "you (pl.) are my brothers." (The Coptic writing system allows to see that the absolute pronoun is prosodically weakened in these cases: *ang-pek-són* "I am your brother," as opposed to *anók-pe* "it is I.") In the third person, however, the structure is #noun — *pw*#: *sn*=*j pw* "he is my brother," *sn·t*=*k pw* "she is your sister," *sn·w*=*sn pw* "they are their brothers."

Egyptian verbal utterances are not, contrary to what may be surmised from the above, confined to verbal sentences of either kind, viz. the pronoun conjugation and the old perfective. Also in Semitic languages, nominal sentence conjugations may complement the system of the verbal conjugations. An analogous conjugation exists in Egyptian in the so-called adjectival sentence: *nfr sw* "he is good," *jrj sw* "he (is one who) does." Whereas this is a marginal feature for verbal expression (probably due to its static meaning), the adverbial sentence conjugations play here a paramount role. Their predicative element (of adverbial function) is either the old perfective or one of the adverbial forms that are built up of preposition plus infinitive. There are three of these "gerunds": the progressive gerund, *ḥr sḏm* "(on) listening," the suppletive form for intransitive verbs of motion, *m jj·t* "(in) coming," and the future gerund, *r sḏm* "to(wards) listen(ing)." They may be freely used, expanding a noun in a verbal phrase, as "he is seen *m jj·t* coming along," or *ḥr wn ꜥ3* "opening the door-wing." When, however, they function as predicates in adverbial sentences we have to do with the following Egyptian tenses:

Progressive: *jw=f ḥr sḏm* "he is listening"
Progressive, verbs of motion: *jw=f m jj·t* "he is coming along"
Future: *jw=f r sḏm* "he shall/will hear"

It has been mentioned above that the rhematic verb forms tended early to be primarily used as nuclei of clauses of circumstance. In particular, this applies to the following.

Rhematic aoristic *sḏm=f*, "(he) listening"
Rhematic *sḏm·n=f*, "(he) having heard"
Old perfective, e.g. *nfr·w* "(he) being good," or *stp·w* "(he) having been chosen"

In this adverbial function the verb forms in question can also fill the predicative slot in the adverbial sentence. The resulting conjugations are the true Middle Egyptian main sentence forms of their respective tenses.

Aorist: *jw=f sḏm=f* "he hears (by habit, nature etc.)"
Perfect: *jw sḏm·n=f* "he heard" (transitive verbs only)
Static present/present perfect: *jw=f* + old perfective, as *jw=f prj·w* "he has gone out," or *jw=f stp·w* "he has been chosen"
(At the same time, this latter is the perfect form of the dynamic intransitive verbs and the passive perfect form of the transitive verbs — see above, for this "suppletive system.")

In this way we arrive at the Polotskyan scheme of Middle Egyptian tenses as represented in the table on p. 248 (cf. Satzinger 1986).

It took Egyptology a long time to accept the results of the Polotskyan revolution. Even then, some made strange use of them (e.g., Junge 1978). By now, a sort of revisionist "counterrevolution" is under way which aims at restraining the "syntactic" (or "parts of speech") preponderance of what has unluckily been termed the *Standard Theory*, in favour of "pragmatic" issues or whatever. On closer inspection, though, the target is usually less Polotsky's results than rather what some have made of them (cf. Satzinger & Shisha-Halevy 1999). Some authors are not aware of the fact that basically diverging theoretical paradigms, as transformational or generative grammar or X-bar theory, are not apt to either verify or falsify a structuralistic analysis.

Main sentence	Clause or phrase of circumstance (adverbial)	noun clause (substantival)	attribute clause (adjectival; feminine singular examples)
Perfect: (1) *jw sḏm·n=f* (2) *jw=f* + ps.-part.	*sḏm·n=f* old perfective	(1+2) *sḏm·n=f*	*sḏm·t·n=f*
Aorist *jw=f sḏm=f*	*sḏm=f (ḥzj=f)*	*sḏm=f (ḥzz=f)*	*sḏm·t=f* *(ḥzz·t=f)*
Prospective *sḏm=f*	*sḏm=f*	*sḏm=f*	*sḏm·t·j=f*
Progressive *jw=f ḥr sḏm*	*ḥr sḏm*	(either constructions with "relative adjective" *ntj*, as *nt·t=f ḥr sḏm*, etc., or with auxiliary *wnn*, as *wnn=f ḥr sḏm*, *wnn·t=f ḥr sḏm*, etc.)	
Dto., verbs of motion *jw=f m jj·t*	*m jj·t*		
Future *jw=f r sḏm*	*r sḏm*		

A main point of attack is what is conceived as the "non-verbalistic" character of the Polotskyan scheme (with no autonomous Middle Egyptian verb forms other than the imperative, the prospective *sḏm=f* and the obsolescent perfective *sḏm=f*). This appears to be a profound misunderstanding. As soon as the adequate rendering of an utterance "he uses to hear" is *jw=f sḏm=f* this has become a paradigmatic verbal form, not less so than, e.g., the prospective *sḏm=f*. Still, we have every right to analyse it as consisting of an *jw* construction (#*jw* plus subject# "there/here is...") into which an adverbial sentence is embedded, viz. #subject plus adverbially used aoristic *sḏm=f*#. Although these *jw* forms have become grammaticalized in Middle Egyptian, each and every element of what they are composed of can be found in free adverbial use, with virtually the same tense function as in the respective *jw* form.

Similar arguments, both contra and pro, apply to the concept of the Afroasiatic conjugated verb forms being ultimately based on verbal nouns / verbal adjectives. Feeling discomfort about such a "non-verbalistic" approach attests to an Indo-European (plus Semitic) ethnocentric attitude. The Indo-European and the Semitic language types dispose of person, gender (in Semitic) and number discriminating conjugations as grammatical features that are peculiar to the verb and alien to the noun. Yet there are numerous types of documented languages that do not have these features, the "isolating" language type being the most extreme example. Schenkel (1975: 72–73) has rightly drawn attention to the Altaic languages where the verbal noun generally seems to be the basis of conjugated verb forms (note that "there is a recurrent parallelism between the personal possessive markers and the verbal personal endings" [Campbell 1991: 49]). Hungarian, a Uralic language, has in the "definite conjugation" endings that are near-identical with the possessive endings (e.g., *köszön-ö-m*, *–ö-d* "I/you thank (for)" vs. *köszönt-ö-m*, *–ö-d* "my/your thanks"; *nevet-e-m*, *–e-d* "I/you laugh (at...)" vs. *nevetés-e-m*, *–e-d* "my/your laughter").

CONCLUSION

Egyptian and Semitic are related languages, with astounding resemblances and disturbing dissimilarities. Their high age of attestation brings the two Afroasiatic branches closer together. But they still are separated by a prehistory of several thousand years, and it was only a comparatively short time-span, beginning with the fourth millennium, that brought them together in areal contact. Some points of diversity:

• Unlike all other branches, Egyptian does not dispose of a prefix conjugation. In its place, Egyptian has its peculiar pronoun conjugation. Some Semitic languages have secondarily (i.e., much later than the suffix and prefix conjugations) developed comparable structures. In Ge'ez, verbal nouns in the adverbial accusative (as *qatīl-a* "while/when killing," or the like) may be conjugated by means of the suffix pronoun: *qatīlō* (< **qatīl-a-hū*) "when he killed." A further comparable feature are the circumstantial expressions formed by adjectives that are in concord with their referent: ("you [nominative], or your, or of you [genitive] ..." *tekūz-e-ka* "being sad"; "you [accusative] ..." *tekūz-a-ka* "being sad" (Satzinger 1968; Kapeliuk 1998)). In Syriac, the suffix pronouns are employed in the new perfect *qtīl-leh* which has been compared with the

Egyptian $sdm·n=f$ form; note, however, two important differences: first, the passive participle is in concord with the object of the construction (it is only in Neo-Aramaic that this concord may be absent); second, the suffix pronoun functions as a copy pronoun for a substantival subject: *N. qtīlā-leh* "N. has killed (her)" = Egyptian *sm3·n N.* (this latter argument also applies to the Ethiosemitic constructions mentioned).

• In contrast to Semitic, Egyptian has a particular pattern for the sentence with adverbial predicate. Egyptian is here in concord not only with the other Afroasiatic branches, but rather with the vast majority of African languages (cf. Satzinger 1997: 40–41; 2000). Many of them also have a progressive construction of the pattern of this sentence with adverbial predicate, like English *he is* (*preposition > *a–) *listening* (and its Celtic equivalents) and Egyptian *jw=f hr sdm* (cf. Shisha-Halevy 1995; 1998).

• Not Semitic, but at least Egyptian and Chadic have a category of clause conjugations, which are typically employed in rhematizing constructions. It can also be found in some Cushitic languages and in non-Afroasiatic languages of Africa, such as Old Nubian, Igbo, Fulani, etc. (cf. Jungraithmayr 1994; Satzinger 1997; 2000; 2001; forthcoming (a)).

• Unlike all other branches, the Semitic case system has shifted from an absolute — nominative opposition to a nominative — accusative opposition (Sasse 1984).

BIBLIOGRAPHY

Aikhenvald, Alexandra Yu. 1995. Split ergativity in Berber languages. *St. Petersburg Journal of African Studies* 4: 39–68.

Albright, William Foxwell. 1917–1918. Notes on Egypto-Semitic etymology. *American Journal for Semitic Languages and Literatures* 34: 81–98; 215–255.

Albright, William Foxwell. 1927. Notes on Egypto-Semitic etymology. *Journal of the American Oriental Society* 47: 198–237.

Albright, William Foxwell. 1934. *The Vocalization of the Egyptian Syllabic Orthography.* (American Oriental Series, 5.) New Haven.

Allen, James P. 1984. *The Inflection of the Verb in the Pyramid Texts.* (Bibliotheca Aegyptia 2.) Malibu.

Aspesi, Francesco. 1977. *La distinzione dei generi nel nome antico-egiziano e semitico.* (Pubblicazioni delle Facoltà di Lettere e Filosofia dell'Università di Milano 80.) Firenze.

Aspesi, Francesco. 1990. Genre des noms et genre des morphèmes personnels en chamito-sémitique. In: Hans G. Mukarovsky (ed.). *Proceedings of the Fifth International Hamito-Semitic Congress* I. (Veröffentlichungen der Institute für Afrikanistik und Ägyptologie der Universität Wien 56. Beiträge zur Afrikanistik Band 40.) Wien, 11- 28.

(Bakir:) *'Abdu-l-muḥsin Bakīr*. 1954, ²1955. *Qawā'idu l-luġati l-Miṣriyyati fī 'aṣrihā d-dahabiyy. Miṣr*.

Beinlich-Seeber, Christine. 1998. *Bibliographie Altägypten 1822–1946*. Teil I–III. (Ägyptologische Abhandlungen, Band 61.) Wiesbaden.

Belova, A. G. 1980. Struktura kornja v drevneegipetskom i semitskix jazykax. In: *Tezisy dokladov sovetskoj delegacii na 2-oj simpozium učenyx socialističeskix stran na temu "Teoretičeskie problemy jazykov Azii i Afriki."* Moskva, 5–9

Belova, A. G. 1989. Refleksy semitskix sibiljantov v drevneegipetskom. *Meroè* 4: 9–21.

Brockelmann, Carl. 1908. *Kurzgefasste vergleichende Grammatik der semitischen Sprachen*. (Porta Linguarum Orientalium 21.) Berlin.

Brockelmann, Carl. 1932. Ägyptisch-semitische Etymologien. *Zeitschrtift für Semitistik und verwandte Gebiete* 8: 97– 117.

Browne, Gerald M. 1982. The Old Nubian Verbal System. *Bulletin of the American Society of Papyrologists* 19: 9–38.

Browne, Gerald M. 1988. *Studies in Old Nubian*. (Beiträge zur Sudanforschung, Beiheft 3.) Wien — Mödling.

Browne, Gerald M. 1989. *Introduction to Old Nubian*. (Meroitica 11.) Berlin.

Buccellati, Giorgio. 1968. An interpretation of the Akkadian Stative as a Nominal Sentence. *Journal of Near Eastern Studies* 27: 1–12.

Buck, Adriaan de. 1941, ²1944. *Egyptische grammatica*. Leiden.

Calice, Franz †. 1936. *Grundlagen der ägyptisch-semitischen Wortvergleichung; eine kritische Diskussion des bisherigen Vergleichsmaterials*. (Wiener Zeitschrift für die Kunde des Morgenlandes. Beiheft 1.) Herausgegeben von Heinrich Balcz. Wien.

Callender, John B. 1975a. Afroasiatic cases and the formation of Ancient Egyptian constructions with possessive suffixes. *Afroasiatic Linguistics* 2.6: 1–18.

Callender, John B. 1975b. *Middle Egyptian*. (Afroasiatic Dialects 2.) Malibu.

Campbell, G. L. 1991. *Compendium of the World's Languages*. London–New York.

Castellino, G. R. 1962. *The Akkadian Personal Pronoun and Verbal System in the Light of Semitic and Hamitic*. Leiden.

Černý, Jaroslav† — Sarah Israelit Groll, assisted by Christopher Eyre. 1975, ²1978, ³1984. *A Late Egyptian Grammar.* (Studia Pohl: Series Maior 4.) Rome.

Chaîne, Marius. 1933. *Éléments de grammaire dialectale copte; bohaïrique, sahidique, achmimique, fayoumique.* Paris.

Cohen, Marcel. 1947. *Essai comparatif sur le vocabulaire et la phonétique du chamito-sémitique.* (Bibliothèque de l'École des Hautes Études. Sciences historiques et philologiques, 291e fascicule.). Paris.

Cohen, Marcel. 1968. Les langues chamito-sémitiques. In: A. Martinet (ed.). *Le Langage.* (Encyclopédie de la Pléïade 25.) Paris, 57–63.

Cohen, Marcel. 1969. Vue générale du verbe chamito-sémitique. In: *Proceedings of the International Conference on Semitic Studies held in Jerusalem.* Jerusalem, 45–48.

Collier, Mark A. 1992. Predication and the Circumstantial $s\underline{dm}(=f)/s\underline{dm}.n(=f)$. *Lingua Aegyptia* 2: 17–65.

Collier, Mark. 1994. Grounding, Cognition and Metaphor in the Grammar of Middle Egyptian. *Lingua Aegyptia* 4: 57– 87.

Conti, Giovanni. 1978. *Rapporto fra egiziano e semitico nel lessico egiziano dell'agricoltura.* (Quaderni di Semitistica, 6.) Firenze.

Deines, Hildegard von, & Wolfhart Westendorf. 1961–1962. *Wörterbuch der medizinischen Texte.* (Grundriss der Medizin der alten Ägypter VII.1–2.) Berlin.

Diakonoff, Igor M. 1965. *Semito-Hamitic Languages. An Essay in Classification.* Moscow.

Diakonov (Head of Team), Igor M., Anna G. Belova, (Alexander S. Chetverukhin,) Alexander Ju. Militarev, Victor Ja. Porkhomovsky (and Olga G. Stolbova). 1993–1997: Historical Comparative Vocabulary of Afrasian. *St. Petersburg Journal of African Studies* 2: 5–28; 3: 5–26; 4: 7–38; 5: 4–32; 6: 12–35.

Dolgopolsky, Aron. 1990. On Chadic correspondences of Semitic š. In: Hans G. Mukarovsky (ed.). *Proceedings of the Fifth International Hamito-Semitic Congress* I. (Veröffentlichungen der Institute für Afrikanistik und Ägyptologie der Universität Wien 56. Beiträge zur Afrikanistik Band 40.) Wien, 213–225.

Doret, Eric. 1986. *The Narrative Verbal System of Old and Middle Egyptian.* (Cahiers d'Orientalisme 12.) Genève.

Edel, Elmar. 1955/1964. *Altägyptische Grammatik.* (Analecta Orientalia 34/39.) Roma.

Edgerton, William F. 1947. Stress, vowel quantity, and syllable division in Egyptian. *Journal of Near Eastern Studies* 6: 1–17.

Ehret, Christopher. 1995. *Reconstructing Proto-Afroasiatic (Proto-Afrasian).* (Linguistics 126.). Berkeley — Los Angeles — London.

Ember, Aaron. 1930. *Egypto-Semitic Studies* (ed. Frida Behnk). (Veröffentlichungen der Alexander Kohout Memorial Foundation: Philologische Reihe 2.) Leipzig.

Erichsen, Wolja. 1954. *Demotisches Glossar*. Kopenhagen.

Erman, Adolf. 1880. ²1933. *Neuägyptische Grammatik*. Leipzig.

Erman, Adolf. 1892. Das Verhältnis des Ägyptischen zu den semitischen Sprachen. *Zeitschrift der Deutschen Morgenländischen Gesellschaft* 46: 93–129.

Erman, Adolf. 1894, ²1902, ³1911, ⁴1928. *Ägyptische Grammatik*. (Porta linguarum orientalium 15.) Berlin.

Faulkner, Raymond O. 1962. *A Concise Dictionary of Middle Egyptian*. Oxford.

Fecht, Gerhard. 1960. *Wortakzent und Silbenstruktur*. Untersuchungen zur Geschichte der ägyptischen Sprache. (Ägyptologische Forschungen 21.) Glückstadt.

Frajzyngier, Zygmunt. 1984. On the Proto-Chadic Syntactic Pattern. In: *Current Progress in Afro-asiatic Linguistics. Papers of the Third International Hamito-Semitic Congress*. Amsterdam/Philadelphia, 139–159.

Frandsen, Paul John. 1974. *An Outline of the Late Egyptian Verbal System*. Copenhagen.

Gardiner, Sir Alan H. 1927, ²1950, ³1957. *Egyptian Grammar*. Oxford.

Groll, Sarah Israelit. 1967. *Non-Verbal Sentence Patterns in Late Egyptian*. London.

Groll, Sarah Israelit. 1970. *The Negative Verbal System of Late Egyptian*. London — New York.

Gunn, Battiscombe. 1924. *Studies in Egyptian Syntax*. Paris.

Hannig, Rainer. 1995. *Grosses Handwörterbuch Ägyptisch — Deutsch*. Die Sprache der Pharaonen (2800–950 v.Chr.). (Kulturgeschichte der Antiken Welt, 64.) Mainz.

Helck, Wolfgang. 1984. Der König von Ober- und Unterägypten. In: *Studien zu Sprache und Religion Ägyptens. Zu Ehren von Wolfhart Westendorf*. Vol. I. Göttingen, 251–256.

Helck, Wolfgang. 1990. Gedanken zur Entstehung des altägyptischen Staates. In: *Festschrift Jürgen von Beckerath*. (Hildesheimer Ägyptologische Beiträge 30.) 97–117.

Hintze, F. *Untersuchungen zu Stil und Sprache neuägyptischer Erzählungen*. 2 vols. (Insitut für Orientforschung, Veröffentlichung 2/6). Berlin, 1950–1952.

Hoch, James E. 1994. *Semitic Words in Egyptian Texts of the New Kingdom and Third Intermediate Period*. Princeton.

Huehnergard, John. 1987. "Stative," predicative form, pseudo-verb. In: *Journal of the American Research Center in Egypt* 47: 215–232.

Janssens, Gerard. 1972. *Contribution to the Verbal System in Old Egyptian.* A new approach to the reconstruction of the Hamito-Semitic Verbal System. (Orientalia Gandensia 6.) Leuven.

Jelanskaja, A. I. 1964. *Koptskij jazyk.* (Jazyki narodov Azii i Afriki.) Moskva.

Johnson, Janet H. 1976. *The Demotic Verbal System.* (Studies in Ancient Oriental Civilization 38.) Chicago.

Johnson, Janet H. 1986, 21991. *Thus Wrote 'Onchsheshonqy.* An Introductory Grammar of Demotic. (Studies in Ancient Oriental Civilization 45.) Chicago.

Junge, Friedrich. 1978. *Syntax der mittelägyptischen Literatursprache.* Mainz.

Junge, Friedrich. 1996. *Einführung in die Grammatik des Neuägyptischen.* Wiesbaden.

Jungraithmayr, Herrmann. 1983. Hamitosemitisch. In: Herrmann Jungraithmayr & Wilhelm J. G. Möhlig (eds.). *Lexikon der Afrikanistik.* Berlin, 103–104.

Jungraithmayr, Herrmann. 1994. "Zweite Tempora" in afrikanischen Sprachen — ägyptisch-tschadische Gemeinsamkeiten? In: M. Bietak et alii (eds.). *Zwischen den beiden Ewigkeiten.* Festschrift Gertrud Thausing. Wien, 102–122.

Kammerer, Winifred. 1950. *A Coptic Bibliography.* Ann Arbor.

Kammerzell, Frank. 1998. The sounds of a dead language. Reconstructing Egyptian phonology. *Göttinger Beiträge zur Sprachwissenschaft* 1: 21–41.

Kapeliuk, Olga. 1998. The Ethio-Semitic possessive pronouns as predicalizers in historical perspective. *Aethiopica* 1: 148–163.

Korostovtsev, M. 1973. *Grammaire du néo-égyptien.* Moscou.

Layton, Bentley. Forthcoming. *A Coptic Grammar. Sahidic Dialect. With a chrestomathy and glossary.* (Porta Linguarum Orientalium.) Wiesbaden.

Lefebvre, Gustave. 1940. *Grammaire de l'égyptien classique.* (Bibliothèque d'Etudes, 12.) Le Caire.

Leslau, Wolf. 1962. Semitic and Egyptian Comparisons. *Journal of Near Eastern Studies* 21: 44–49.

Lexa, František. 1940–1951. *Grammaire démotique.* 7 vols. Prague.

Lipiński, Edward. 1999. *Semitic Languages — Outline of a Comparative Grammar.* (Orientalia Lovaniensia Analecta 80.) Leuven.

Littmann, Enno. 1932. Bemerkungen zur ägyptisch-semitschen

Sprachvergleichung. *Zeitschrift für ägyptische Sprache und Altertumskunde* 67: 63–68.

Loprieno, Antonio. 1986. *Das Verbalsystem im Ägyptischen und im Semitischen.* Zur Grundlegung einer Aspekttheorie. (Göttinger Orientforschungen. IV. Reihe: Aegypten 17.) Wiesbaden.

Loprieno, Antonio. 1995. *Ancient Egyptian.* A Linguistic Introduction. Cambridge.

Mallon, Alexis. 1904, ²1907, ⁴1956. *Grammaire copte, avec bibliographie, chrestomathie et vocabulaire.* Beyrouth.

Meeks, Dimitri. 1980–1982. *L'Année Lexicographique* I–III. Paris.

Moscati, Sabatino. 1964, ²1967. *An Introduction to the Comparative Grammar of the Semitic Languages.* (Porta Linguarum Orientalium, Neue Serie 6.) Wiesbaden.

Müller, Hans-Peter. 1995. Ergative Constructions in Early Semitic Languages. *Journal of Near Eastern Studies* 54: 261–271.

Neveu, François. 1996. *La langue des Ramsès. Grammaire du néo-égyptien.* Paris.

(Nur el-din:) 'Abd al-ḥalīm Nūr-al-dīn. 1998. *Al-luġatu l-miṣrīyatu l-qadīma. Al-Qāhira.*

Orel, Vladimir E. and Olga V. Stolbova. 1994. *Hamito-Semitic Etymological Dictionary: Materials for a Reconstruction.* (Handbuch der Orientalistik I, 18.) Leiden — New York — Köln.

Osing, Jürgen. 1976. *Die Nominalbildung des Ägyptischen.* 2 vols. Mainz/Rhein.

Osing, Jürgen. 1987. Die Partizipien im Ägyptischen und in den semitischen Sprachen. In: Jürgen Osing & Günter Dreyer (eds.). *Form und Mass.* Festschrift für Gerhard Fecht. (Ägypten und Altes Testament 12.): 337–360.

Parker, Richard. 1961. The durative tenses in P. Ryland IX. *Journal of Near Eastern Studies* 20: 180–187.

Petráček, Karel. 1988. *Altägyptisch, Hamitosemitisch und ihre Beziehungen zu einigen Sprachfamilien in Afrika und Asien. Vergleichende Studien.* (Acta Universitatis Carolinae Philologica. Monographica 10). Praha.

Polotsky, Hans Jakob. 1944. *Études de syntaxe copte.* (Publications de la Société d'Archéologie Copte [textes et documents, 9].) Le Caire. [= Polotsky 1971: 102–207]

Polotsky, Hans Jakob. 1965. *Egyptian Tenses.* (The Israel Academy of Sciences and Humanities. Proeedings 2.5.) Jerusalem. [= Polotsky 1971: 71–96]

Polotsky, Hans Jakob. 1971. *Collected Papers.* Jerusalem.

Polotsky, Hans Jakob. 1976. Les transpositions du verbe en égyptien classique. *Israel Oriental Studies* 6: 1–50.

Polotsky, Hans Jakob. 1984. Randbemerkungen. In: Friedrich Junge (ed.). *Studien zu Sprache und Religion Ägyptens.* Zu Ehren von Wolfhart Westendorf. I: Sprache, 113–123.

Polotsky, Hans Jakob. 1987/1990. *Grundlagen des koptischen Satzbaus.* (American Studies in Papyrology 28/29.) Decatur/Atlanta, Georgia.

Ray, John D. 1999. The vocalisation of adjectives in Egyptian. *Lingua Aegyptia* 6: 119–140.

Reintges, C. H. 1998. Ancient Egyptian in 3D: Synchrony, Diachrony and Typology of a Dead Language. *Orientalia* 67, 447–476. [Revue of Loprieno 1995.]

Roccati, Alessandro. 1997. Studi tipologici. I. Sull'ergatività dell'egiziano. In: A. Bausi / M. Tosco (eds.). *Afroasiatica Neapolitana.* Contributi presentati all' 8⁰ Incontro di Linguistica Afroasiatica (Camito-Semitica) (Studi Africanistici. Serie Etiopica 6.) Napoli, 113–122.

Rössler, Otto. 1950. Verbalbau und Verbalflexion in den semitohamitischen Sprachen. Vorstudien zu einer vergleichenden semitohamitischen Grammatik. *Zeitschrift der Deutschen Morgenländischen Gesellschaft* 100: 460–514. *English version*: Rössler, Otto. 1981. The structure and inflection of the verb in the Semito-Hamitic languages. Preliminary studies for a Comparative Semito-Hamitic grammar. Translated by Yoël Arbeitman. In: Yoël Arbeitman & Alland R. Bomhard (eds.). *Bono Homini Donum. Essays in Historical Linguistics in Memory of J. Alexander Kerns.* (Amsterdam Studies in the Theory and History of Linguistic Science. Series IV — Current Issues in Linguistic Theory 16.) Amsterdam, 679–748.

Rössler, Otto. 1971. Das Ägyptische als semitische Sprache. In: Franz Altheim / Ruth Stiehl. *Christentum am Roten Meer I.* Berlin — New York, 263–326.

Ruhlen, Merritt. 1987. *A Guide to the World's Languages.* Vol. I. Stanford University Press. [Victoria (Australia).]

Sander-Hansen, C. E. 1941. *Über die Bildung der Modi im Altägyptischen.* (Det Kongelige Danske Videnskabernes Selskab. Historisk-filisofiske Skrifter 1.3.) København.

Sander-Hansen, C. E. 1956. *Studien zur Grammatik der Pyramidentexte.* (Analecta Aegyptiaca 6.) København.

Sander-Hansen, C. E. 1963. *Ägyptische Grammatik.* Wiesbaden.

Sasse, Hans-Jürgen. 1981. Afroasiatisch. In.: Heine, Bernd / Schadeberg, Thilo C. / Wolff, Ekkehard (eds.). *Die Sprachen Afrikas.* Hamburg.

Sasse, Hans-Jürgen. 1984. Case in Cushitic, Semitic and Berber. In: James Bynon (ed.). *Current Progress in Afro-asiatic Linguistics. Papers of the Third International Hamito-Semitic Congress.* Amsterdam/Philadelphia, 111–126.

Satzinger, Helmut. 1976. *Neuägyptische Studien.* Die Partikel *ír.* Das Tempussystem. (Wiener Zeitschrift für die Kunde des Morgenlandes. Beiheft 6.) Wien.

Satzinger, Helmut. 1986. On tense and aspect in Middle Egyptian. In: G. Englund & P. J. Frandsen (eds.). *Crossroads — Chaos or the Beginning of a New Paradigm.* Papers from the Conference on Egyptian grammar, Helsingør. København, 297–313.

Satzinger, Helmut. 1989. Bemerkungen zum ägyptischen Verbalsystem gelegentlich zweier Neuerscheinungen. *Wiener Zeitschrift für die Kunde des Morgenlandes* 79: 197–220.

Satzinger, Helmut. 1991. Structural analysis of the Egyptian independent personal pronoun. In: Hans G. Mukarovsky (ed.). *Proceedings of the Fifth International Hamito-Semitic Congress* 1987, volume 2. (Veröffentlichungen der Institute für Afrikanistik und Ägyptologie der Universität Wien. Beiträge zur Afrikanistik 41.) 121–135.

Satzinger, Helmut. 1995. (Review of:) Gerald M. Browne, Introduction to Old Nubian. *Orientalia* 64: 156–158.

Satzinger, Helmut. 1997. Egyptian in the Afroasiatic frame: recent Egyptological issues with an impact on comparative studies. In: A. Bausi / M. Tosco (eds.). *Afroasiatica Neapolitana.* Contributi presentati all' 8º Incontro di Linguistica Afroasiatica (Camito-Semitica). (Studi Africanistici. Serie Etiopica 6. Napoli 1997.) 27–48.

Satzinger, Helmut. 1998. Varieties of the Old Perfective in Old Egyptian. In: C. J. Eyre (ed.). *Proceedings of the Seventh International Congress of Egyptologists, Cambridge, 3–9 September 1995.* (Orientalia Lovaniensia Analecta 82.) Leuven, 1021–1028.

Satzinger, Helmut. 1999a. Egyptian 'Ayin in variation with *D. Lingua Aegyptia* 6: 141–151.

Satzinger, Helmut. 1999b. Afroasiatischer Sprachvergleich. In: Stefan Grunert & Ingelore Hafemann (eds.). *Textcorpus und Wörterbuch. Aspekte zur ägyptischen Lexikographie.* (Probleme der Ägyptologie 14.) Leiden —- Boston — Köln, 367–386.

Satzinger, Helmut. 1999c. Observations in the field of the Afoasiatic suffix conjugation. In: Marcello Lamberti & Livia Tonelli (eds.). *Afroasiatica Tergestina.* Papers of the 9th Italian Meeting of Afro-Asiatic (Hamito-Semitic) Linguistics. Trieste, April 23–24, 1998

/ Contributi presentati al 9º Incontro di Linguistica Afroasiatica (Camito-Semitica). Trieste, 23–24 Aprile 1998. Padova, 23–33.

Satzinger, Helmut. 1999d. Koptische Vokalphoneme und ägyptische Pluralformation. In: *Ägypten und Nubien in spätantiker und christlicher Zeit.* Akten des 6. Internationalen Koptologenkongresses, Münster, 20.–26. Juli 1996. Band 2, 365–274.

Satzinger, Helmut. 2000. Egyptian as an African Language. In: C. Basile-A. Di Natale (eds.). *Atti del IV Convegno Nazionale di Egittologia e Papirologia, Siracusa, 5–7 Dicembre 1997.* Quaderni del Museo del Papiro IX, Siracusa, 31–43.

Satzinger, Helmut. 2001. Ancient Egyptian in the Context of African Languages. In: Josep Cervelló Autuori (ed.). *África antigua. El antiguo Egipto, una civilización africana.* Actas de la IX Semana de Estudios Africanos del Centre d'Estudis Africans de Barcelona (18–22 Marzo de 1996). Barcelona (Aula Ægyptiaca — Studia 1.), 257–265.

Satzinger, Helmut. (Forthcoming a). Relativformen, emphatische Formen und Zweite Tempora: Gliedsatzformen im Ägyptischen und im Tschadischen. In: *Festschrift Herrmann Jungraithmayr.*

Satzinger, Helmut. (Forthcoming b). On ergativity in Egyptian. In: Hetzron memorial volume, ed. Andrzej Zaborski.

Satzinger, Helmut & Ariel Shisha-Halevy. 1999. The Snark is dead. *Lingua Aegyptia* 6: 167–176.

Schenkel, Wolfgang. 1975. *Die altägyptische Suffixkonjugation.* (Ägyptologische Abhandlungen 32.) Wiesbaden.

Schenkel, Wolfgang. 1983a. *Aus der Arbeit an einer Konkordanz zu den altägyptischen Sargtexten.* Teil I: Zur Transkription des Hieroglyphisch-Ägyptischen (unter Mitarbeit von Rainer Hannig). Teil II: Zur Pluralbildung des Ägyptischen. (Göttinger Orientforschungen. IV. Reihe: Ägypten 12.) Wiesbaden.

Schenkel, Wolfgang. 1983b. *Zur Rekonstruktion der deverbalen Nominalbildung des Ägyptischen.* (Göttinger Orientforschungen. IV. Reihe: Ägypten 13.) Wiesbaden.

Schenkel, Wolfgang. 1988. Erkundungen zur Reihenfolge der Zeichen im ägyptologischen Transkriptionsalphabet. *Chronique d'Égypte* 63: 5–35.

Schenkel, Wolfgang. 1990. *Einführung in die altägyptische Sprachwissenschaft.* Darmstadt.

Schenkel, Wolfgang. 1993. Zu den Verschluß- und Reibelauten im Ägyptischen und (Hamito)Semitischen. Ein Versuch zur Synthese der Lehrmeinungen. *Lingua Aegyptia* 3: 137–149.

Schenkel, Wolfgang. 1994. *sčm.t*-Perfekt und *sčm.tí*-Stativ. Die beiden Pseudopartizipien des Ägyptischen nach dem Zeugnis der Sargtexte. In: H. Behlmer (ed.). ...*Quaerentes scientiam*. Festgabe für Wolfhart Westendorf zu seinem 70. Geburtstag. Göttingen, 157–182.

Schneider, Thomas. 1997. Beiträge zur sogenannten 'Neueren Komparatistik'. *Lingua Aegyptia* 5: 189–209.

Sethe, Kurt. 1899/1902. *Das aegyptische Verbum im Altaegyptischen, Neuägyptischen und Koptischen.* Leipzig.

Sethe, Kurt. 1916. *Der Nominalsatz im Ägyptischen und Koptischen.* (Abhandlungen der philosophisch-historischen Klasse der Königlichen Sächsischen Gesellschaft der Wissenschaften 33.3.) Leipzig.

Shisha-Halevy, Ariel. 1984. Notes on some Coptic nominal sentence patterns. In: *Studien zu Sprache und Religion Ägyptens. Zu Ehren von Wolfhart Westendorf.* Vol. I. Göttingen, 175–189.

Shisha-Halevy, Ariel. 1987. Grammatical discovery procedure and the Egyptian-Coptic nominal sentence. *Orientalia*, 56: 147-175.

Shisha-Halevy, Ariel. 1988a. *Coptic Grammatical Categories.* Structural Studies in the Syntax of Shenoutean Sahidic. (Analecta Orientalia 53.) Roma.

Shisha-Halevy, Ariel. 1988b. *Coptic Grammatical Chrestomathy.* (Orientalia Lovaniensia Analecta 30.) Leuven.

Shisha-Halevy, Ariel. 1989. *The Proper Name: Structural Prolegomena to its Syntax.* A Case Study in Coptic. (Wiener Zeitschrift für die Kunde des Morgenlandes. Beiheft 15.) Wien.

Shisha-Halevy, Ariel. 1995. Structural sketches of Middle Welsh syntax, I: The Converter Systems. *Studia Celtica* 29: 127–223.

Shisha-Halevy, Ariel. 1998. *Structural Studies in Modern Welsh Syntax: Aspects of the grammar of Kate Roberts.* Münster.

Simpson, R.S. 1996. *Demotic Grammar in the Ptolemaic Sacerdotal Decrees.* (Griffith Institute Monographs.) Oxford.

Spiegelberg, Wilhelm. 1925. *Demotische Grammatik.* Heidelberg.

Steindorff, Georg. 1894, ²1904. *Koptische Grammatik mit Chrestomathie, Wörterverzeichnis und Literatur.* (Porta Linguarum Orientalium 14.) Berlin.

Steindorff, Georg. 1951. *Lehrbuch der koptischen Grammatik.* Chicago.

Stern, Ludwig. 1880. *Koptische Grammatik.* Leipzig (reprint Osnabrück 1971).

Till, Walter. 1928. *Achmîmisch-koptische Grammatik mit Chrestomathie und Wörterbuch.* Leipzig.

Till, Walter. 1931. *Koptische Dialektgrammatik mit Lesestücken und Wörterbuch.* München.

Till, Walter C. 1955, ²1961. *Koptische Grammatik (saïdischer Dialekt) mit Bibliographie, Lesestücken und Wörterverzeichnissen.* (Lehrbücher für das Studium der orientalischen und afrikanischen Sprachen I.) Leipzig.

Tropper, Josef. 1995. Die semitische "Suffixkonjugation" im Wandel. Von der Prädikativform zum Perfekt. In: *Vom Alten Orient zum Alten Testament.* Festschrift für Wolfram Freiherrn von Soden zum 85. Geburtstag am 19. Juni 1993: 491–516.

Vergote, Jozef. 1945. *Phonétique historique de l'Égyptien: les consonnes.* (Bibliothèque du Muséon 19.) Louvain.

Vergote, Jozef. 1965. *De verhouding van het Egyptisch tot de semietische talen.* (With French translat.) Brussel.

Vergote, Jozef. 1973/1983. *Grammaire copte.* Tome Ia & Ib, IIa & IIb. Leuven.

Voigt, Rainer. 1990. The Tense-Aspect System of Biblical Hebrew. In: *Proceedings of the Tenth World Congress of Jewish Studies.* Division D, vol. I: The Hebrew Language, Jewish Languages, Jerusalem, 1–8.

Vycichl, Werner. 1934. Hausa und Ägyptisch. Ein Beitrag zur historischen Hamitistik. *Mitteilungen des Seminars für orientalische Sprachen* 37.3: 36–116.

Vycichl, Werner. 1958. Grundlagen der ägyptisch-semitischen Wortvergleichung. *Mitteilungen des Deutschen Archäologischen Instituts Abteilung Kairo* 16: 367–405.

Vycichl, Werner. 1959. Is Egyptian a Semitic language? *Kush* 7: 27–44.

Vycichl, Werner. 1983. *Dictionnaire Étymologique de la Langue Copte.* Leuven.

Vycichl, Werner. 1990. *La vocalisation de la langue égyptienne.* Vol. 1: La phonétique. (Bibliothèque d'Études 16.) Le Caire.

Westendorf, Wolfhart. 1962. *Grammatik der medizinischen Texte.* (Grundriß der Medizin der Alten Ägypter VIII.) Berlin.

Westendorf, Wolfhart. 1965–1977. *Koptisches Handwörterbuch.* Heidelberg.

Williams, Ronald J. 1948. On certain verbal forms in Demotic. *Journal of Near Eastern Studies* 7: 223–235.

Wilson, Marvin R. 1970. *Coptic Future Tenses: Syntactical Studies in Sahidic.* (Janua Linguarum, series practica 64.) The Hague — Paris.

Wilson, Penelope. 1997. *A Ptolemaic Lexicon. A Lexicographical Study in the Texts in the Temple of Edfu.* (Orientalia Lovaniensia Analecta 80.) Leuven.

Yeivin, Shmuel. 1936. Studies in comparative Egypto-Semitics. *Kêmi* 6: 63–80.

Zeidler, Jürgen. 1992. Altägyptisch und Hamitosemitisch. Bemerkungen zu den *Vergleichenden Studien* von Karel Petráček. *Lingua Aegyptia* 2: 189–222.

Zyhlarz, Ernst. 1932-33. Ursprung und Sprachcharakter des Altägyptischen. *Zeitschrift für Eingeborenen-Sprachen* 23: 25–45; 81–110; 161–194; 241–254.

Akkadian

| | Absolute (predicate, extraposition). | | | | Suffixes/prefixes. | | | |
	Acc./Prep.	Dative	Gen. abs. (sm).	Nomin.; subject.	Object.	Agent (+subject).	Genitive.	Subject (+ agent); patient.
1s	*y-ā-ti*	*y-ā-šim*	*y-ā-'um*	*'an-ā-ku*	*-nī*	*'a–*	*-i*	*-ā-ku*
1p	*niy-ā-ti*	*niy-ā-šim*	*niy-ā-'um*	**(')a)n-Vḥ-nu*	*-niy-ā-ti*	*na–*	*-nV*	*-ā-nu*
2sm	*kuw-ā-ti*	*kuw-ā-šim*	*kuw-ā-'um*	**'an-ta*	*-ka*	*ta–*	*-ka*	*-ā-ta*
2sf	*kiy-ā-ti*	*kiy-ā-šim*	*kiy-ā-'um*	**'an-ti*	*-ki*	*ta–...-í*	*-ki*	*-ā-ti*
2pm	*kunū-ti*	*kunū-šim*	*kunū-m*	**'an-tunu*	*-kunū-ti*	*ta–...-ū*	*-kunu*	*-ā-tumu*
2pf	*kinā-ti*	*kinā-šim*	...	**'an-tina*	*-kinā-ti*	...	*-kina*	*-ā-tina*
3sm	*suw-ā-ti*	*suw-ā-šim*	*suw-ā-'um*	*sū*	*-su*	**ya–*	*-su*	*-Ø*
3sf	*siy-ā-ti*	*siy-ā-šim*	*siy-ā-'um*	*sī*	*-sa*	*ta–*	*-sa*	*-at*
3pm	*sunū-ti*	*sunū-šim*	*sunū-m*	*sunu*	*-sunū-ti*	**ya–...-ū*	*-sunu*	*-ū*
3pf	*sinā-ti*	*sinā-šim*	...	*sina*	*-sinā-ti*	...	*-sina*	*-ā*

Table 1. The personal pronouns and the conjugational elements in Akkadian and Egyptian in confrontation.

Egyptian

	Absolute (predicate, extraposition; pron. topic > subject).	Subject.	Object.	Agent (+ subject).	Genitive.	Subject; patient.	Agent (+ subject).
1s	jnk *jan-**á**-k		ʔjw > wj	–j		–*ā̆-kj	–kj
1p	jnn *jan-**á**-n		n	–n		–*ā̆-nwj	–nwj > –wjn
2sm	t̠w-t *tuw-**á̆**-t, nt-k *jan(i)t-**á**-k		kw > t̠w	–k (<*ka)		–*ā̆-tj	–tj
2sf	t̠m-t *tim-**á̆**-t, nt-t̠ *jan(i)t-**á**-t̠		t̠m > t̠n	–t̠ (<*ki)		–*ā̆-tj	–tj
2p	? nt-t̠n *jan(i)t-**á̆**-tVn		t̠n	–tn (<*kun)		–*a-twnj	–twnj
3sm	sw-t *suw-**á̆**-t, nt-f *jan(i)t-**á**-f		sw	–f		–j	–j
3sf	st-t *sit-**á̆**-t, nt-s *jan(i)t-**á**-s sj		(3sn: st)	–s		–tj	–tj
3p	? nt-sn *jan(i)t-**á**-sVn		sn	–sn		3pm –*V̄wj 3pf –*V̄tj	–*V̄wj –*V̄tj

Table 2. The tense system of Old Egyptian

status:	independent and/or circumstantial		substantival	attributive (e.g., fem. sing.)	
	pronominal subject	substantival subject	("that" forms)	participles	relative forms
perfect (> preterite) intransitive	old perfective I*)	old perfective I*)	sḏm·n=f	—	sḏm·t-n=f (ḥzj)
transitive active	sḏm·n=f	sḏm·n=f	sḏm·n=f	—	sḏm·t-n=f (ḥzj)
transitive passive	old perfective I*)	sḏmw N.**) (ḥzjj)	sḏmw=f (> sḏm·n·tw=f)	sḏmw·t (ḥzjj)	sḏmw·t=f (ḥzjj)
old preterite intr., trans. active	old perfective II*)	sḏm N.**) (ḥzj)	sḏm=f (ḥzj)	sḏm·t (ḥzj)	sḏmw·t=f (ḥzj)
transitive passive	sḏm·tj=f (ḥzj)	sḏm·tj N. (ḥzj)	sḏm·tj=f (ḥzj)	—	—
present (> aorist) intr., trans. active	sḏm=f (ḥzj)		sḏm=f (ḥzz)	sḏmj·t (ḥzz)	sḏmw·t=f (ḥzzw)
passive	sḏm·tj=f (ḥzj)		sḏm·tj=f (ḥzz)	***)	—
prospective intr., trans. active	sḏm=f (ḥzjw/ḥzjj)		sḏm·w=f (ḥzjw/ḥzjj)	sḏm·tj (ḥzz) ***)	sḏm·t·j=f (ḥz)
passive	sḏm·tj=f (ḥzjw/ḥzjj)		sḏm·tj=f (ḥzjw/ḥzjj)	***)	—

In parentheses: stem forms of IIIae infirmae verb ḥzj "to praise."

*) Old perfective I: "stative" *saḏmá·kVj, old perfective II: "perfect" *saḏVm·kVj.

**) #N. + old perfective# is neither perfect nor preterite, but rather a static present (Satzinger 1989: 216).

***) Instead of a passive participle, aorist and prospective (and preterite?), the relative form is used, with zero subject: m33w·t=∅ "whom one sees" = "who is seen"; m33·t·j=∅ "whom one will/shall/can see" = "who will/shall/can be seen"; sḏdw=∅ sw ḥr·f "over (ḥr) whom one reads it (sw)" = "over whom it is read" (Satzinger 1984: 141–144).

THE HAMITIC CONNECTION: SEMITIC AND SEMITOHAMITIC

RAINER VOIGT

1. HISTORY OF THE DISCIPLINE

The notion that Near Eastern and North African languages belong to one big language family dates from the very beginning of research on them. It was not the similarity of specific language traits that led to the positing of such a language group, but the reverse. The idea was inspired by the genealogy of Shem, Ham and Japheth as sons of Noah in Genesis 10, which led to a "Völkertafel," a very early attempt to classify peoples in a genealogical way. Accordingly, in the research so far three trends have to be distinguished: (a) research on specific Semitic or "Hamitic" languages including their reconstruction within these language groups, (b) language comparisons between Semitic and "Hamitic" languages and reconstructions that comprise more than one language group, and (c) Nostratic comparisons between all three groups of the "Noachische Völkerfamilie," as Lepsius (1880:xxv) called it. The main promoters of a Semitohamitic genetic relationship in the nineteenth and twentieth centuries are, in the field of grammar, Friedrich Müller (*Die Sprachen der lockenhaarigen Rasse*, II. *Die Sprachen der mittelländischen Rassen*, Wien 1887), Leo Reinisch (e.g., *Das persönliche Fürwort und die Verbalflexion in den chamito-semitischen Sprachen*, Wien 1909), Carl Meinhof (*Die Sprachen der Hamiten*, Hamburg 1912), Igor M. Diakonoff (e.g., *Семитохамитские языки, Москва 1965, Semito-Hamitic languages*, Moscow 1965, and *Afrasian languages*, Moscow 1988), and Otto Rössler (e.g., his important article "Verbalbau und Verbalflexion in den semitohamitischen Sprachen" (1950), which was translated into English by Y. Arbeitman (1981)).

Incidentally, I follow the example of the last two authors, Diakonoff (before inventing the term Afrasian) and Rössler, who use the term "Semitohamitic" (without a hyphen), instead of "Hamito-Semitic" (with a hyphen), not to speak of more modern terms that do not add anything new to the idea of a macrofamily that consists of (at least) five language groups in Africa and Asia. In my view, new terms are only justified through new ideas. I use the term "Hamitic" simply in the sense of the "non-Semitic branches of the Semitohamitic language phylum."[1]

2. RECONSTRUCTION OF THE SOUND SYSTEM OF THE PROTO-LANGUAGE

According to the methodology of comparative historical linguistics, two languages are cognate if elements of the core vocabulary can be related to each other via a reconstructed node through recurrent sound correspondences. The cognate forms allow the reconstruction of a proto-form from which the current forms can be derived through regular sound laws. Most scholars will regard this procedure as sufficient to posit a relationship between languages — provided that the correspondences are valid and occur in a sufficient number. However, another procedure is necessary for establishing the ultimate proof of a genetic relationship. The sound laws relating the existing forms to the reconstructed forms ought to be investigated with respect to their phonetic and phonological properties and systematic features. The sound systems of the proto-language as well as of the documented languages ought to be established. The claim that phonemes of a language must be related to the proto-language through sound laws should be replaced by the claim that the sound system of a language must be related to the sound system of the proto-language through a set of sound laws. It is to be expected that these sound laws will show a certain degree of internal structuring. Whether or not the languages involved can be considered as cognate will depend on the sound systems posited and on the character of the sound developments assumed.

These considerations have a bearing on the much disputed relationship of Semitic to Egyptian and will be of vital concern in future comparisons between all Semitohamitic language groups.

3. COMPARATIVE SEMITOHAMITIC DICTIONARIES

For a long time, the *Essai comparatif sur le vocabulaire et la phonétique du chamito-sémitique* of Marcel Cohen (Paris 1947) was the only comparative dictionary in this field. This situation has changed completely with the publication of the *Сравнительно-исторический словарь афразийских языков* by a group of Russian scholars (A. Belova, A.

---

[1]   I am grateful to Dr. Y. Arbeitman for comments on a previous version of this article.

Militarëv, V. Porchomovskij, O. Stolbova) under the guidance of Igor' M. D'jakonov (Moscow 1981–1986), translated into English as "Historical comparative vocabulary of Afrasian" (*St. Petersburg Journal of African Studies*, vol. 2 (1993) ff.; = *HCVA*) and of the two dictionaries published in 1995, i.e., Vladimir Orel — Olga V. Stolbova's *Hamito-Semitic Etymological Dictionary* (Leiden [etc.], = *HSED*) and Christopher Ehret's *Reconstructing Proto-Afroasiatic* (Berkeley [etc.]).

4. THE PHONOLOGICAL SYSTEM OF SEMITOHAMITIC

The fundamental idea for structuring the sounds of Proto-Semitic (not to speak of the individual Semitic languages), to start with this language group, is their liability to the features of voice or "emphaticness." According to this principle, we get the following subdivisions:

I. triple phonemes that are identical except for voice or "emphaticness":

t	:	$ṭ$	:	d
$\theta\,(\underline{t})$	:	$\theta\,(\underline{t})$	:	δ
$s\,(s^3)$	:	$ṣ$	:	z
k	:	$ḳ(q)$	:	g

II. pairs of phonemes that are identical except for voice:

p	:	b
$x(\underline{h})$	:	$\gamma(\dot{g})$
$ħ\,(h)$	:	$\Upsilon\,(^c)$

III. pairs of phonemes that are identical except for "emphaticness":

$$ś\,(s^2) \quad : \quad ṣ́\,(ṣ^2)$$

IV. phonemes that have neither a voiced nor an "emphatic" counterpart:

$$s^1\ (\text{or}\ š),\ h,\ ʔ$$

V. If the glottal stop is considered as bearing the relevant distinctive feature of the "emphatic" (originally glottalized) series, it will form its own class.

Each of these sounds can be considered as representations of the respective archiphonemes. The following distinctive features are to be added to the respective archiphonemes:

I.	[– voice] [–emph]	:	[–voice] [+ emph]	:	[+ voice] [– emph]
II.	[– voice] [– emph]	:	ø	:	[+ voice] [– emph]

III.	[– voice] [– emph]	:	[– voice] [+ emph]		∅
IV.	[– voice] [– emph]	:	∅	:	∅
V.	∅	:	[– voice] [+ glott]	:	∅

The phonemes included in groups I–IV are characterized by the voiceless nature of their most unmarked members. Accordingly, the intrinsically voiced segments, i.e., the nasals *m* and *n* and the liquids *l* and *r* — not to speak of the semivowels *w* and *y* and the vowels — are not considered here. In conformity with the given scheme they may be represented as follows:

	∅	:	∅	: *m, n* *l, r*

The result of these deliberations is a consonant block that consists of the segments of the groups I–III. These consonants could be arranged in an array of three columns and nine rows:

		[– voice] [– glott]	[+ glott] [– voice]	[+ voice] [– glott]
	(1)	p	$<\dot{p}\ [p^{\textrm{?}}]>$	b
	(2)	t	$\underline{t}\ [t^{\textrm{?}}]$	d
	(3)	$\theta\ (\underline{t})$	$\theta\ (\underline{t})\ [{}^{t}\theta^{\textrm{?}}]$ [1]	$\eth$
$s^1\ (\check{s})$	(4)	$s\ (s^3)\ [{}^{t}s]$	$\underline{s}\ [{}^{t}s^{\textrm{?}}]$	$z\ [{}^{d}z]$
	(5)	$\acute{s}\ (s^2)\ [{}^{t}ł]$	$\underline{\acute{s}}\ (\underline{s}^2)\ [{}^{tł^{\textrm{?}}}]$[2]	$<\acute{z}\ [{}^{dł}]>$
	(6)	k	$\underline{k}\ (q)\ [k^{\textrm{?}}]$	g

(7)	x ($\underline{h}$)	$<\underline{x}[x^{?}]>$[3]	γ ($\dot{g}$)
(8)	$\hbar$ ($\d{h}$)	$<\hbar\ [\hbar^{?}]>$	Υ(^{c})
	h	$?$	–

1 In Arabic, this phoneme is realized as $\d{\d{o}}$.
2 In Arabic, this phoneme became a voiced emphatic dental ($\d{d}$).
3 Such a sound exists in Tigrinya as a postvocalic variant of $/k^{?}/$, as in $/\d{s}\partial bbu\d{k}/$
   $[^{t}s^{?}\breve{u}b{:}u^{(k)}x^{?}]$ 'good, nice'.

There are four gaps in this scheme which are marked by $< >$. The
consonants of group IV–V which do not belong to the consonant block,
are allocated to a specific row (as to s^{1}) or to specific columns (as to h
and $?$).

The comparison of Semitic with "Hamitic" languages, especially
Egyptian, has a long tradition, a survey of which is given in Voigt
[1999]. Here, it must suffice to mention only the most important works.
The Egypto-Semitic comparisons started as early as 1844 with Th.
Benfey (*Ueber das Verhältniss der ägyptischen Sprache zum semitischen
Sprachstamm*), see A. Erman (1892) and W. M. Müller (1905). In the
thirties we note the appearance of A. Ember: *Egypto-Semitic Studies*, ed.
by Fr. Behnk (Leipzig 1930), W. Czermak: *Die Laute der ägyptischen
Sprache: Eine phonetische Untersuchung* (Part 1–2, Wien 1931–1934),
and Fr. Calice: *Grundlagen der ägyptisch-semitischen Wortvergleichung*,
ed. by H. Balcz (Wien 1936). Several post-war publications, such
as J. Vergote: *Phonétique historique de l'égyptien: Les consonnes*
(Leuven 1945) and W. Vycichl "Grundlagen der ägyptisch-semitischen
Wortvergleichung" (1958), gave the impression that the ground for a
comparison between the two language groups had already been founded
and that only some details of that comparison were open to discussion.

The insight that isolated correspondences without systematic
considerations will not yield reliable results led Otto Rössler to a totally
different set of sound correspondences. The fundamental ideas underlying
the new system are:
  1) The incompatibility rules of a language have to be discovered.
  2) The respective sound systems have to be set up.

3) The sound systems of the two language groups have to be related to each other by using word correspondences and their sound correlations.

4) A third sound system (most probably one with a full consonant inventory) has to be posited as the common proto-system from which both systems are to be derived.

At the beginning, this could not meet with the approval of the Egyptologists, who are accustomed to their usual interpretation of the notational signs (*d* taken as voiced dental, *c*[*ain*] taken as laryngeal) as well as to a reduced sound system such as that, e.g., given in the *Lexikon der Ägyptologie*, vol. 3 (1980: 945):

[+ voic] [+ occl]	[− voic] [+ occl]	[− voic] [− occl]	[+ voic] [− occl]
b *d*	*p* *t*	*f* *s*	*z*
d̠ *g*	*t̠* *k̠*	*š* *ḫ*	
q		*ḥ* *ḥ*	*c*

This system is characterized by a fricative sub-system that accompanies the occlusive part. Emphatic consonants do not occur. As O. Rössler has shown convincingly, the traditional comparative work is based on a multitude of "Ungleichungen," such as Eg. *d̠* ≠ Sem. *d̠*, Eg. *z* ≠ Sem. *z*, Eg. *c* ≠ Sem. *c*, Eg. *f* ≠ Sem. *p/f*, etc., that led to a failure in establishing a system of valid sound correspondences.

The fundamental step was to base the comparisons on a sound system that is essentially that of Proto-Semitic. This becomes evident in the title of the revolutionary article "Das Ägyptische als semitische Sprache" (1971), which was not properly understood at first. It was not the illegitimate infringement of a Semitist into the field of Egyptian, as W. A. Ward had expressed it by saying: "There is nothing which requires us to measure Egyptian by a Semitic norm" (1985:240), but the first principled reconstruction of the Egypto-Semitic sound system. The Egyptian sound system, which is more reduced than the Semitic one, clearly shows traces of an internal development such as palatalization which reduces the number of phonemes to be reconstructed on a purely internal basis. Instead, in the Proto-Semitic sound system, so far no traces of an internal development have been detected. The attempts of G. Garbini to reduce the great variety of Semitic sounds as they are retained in Old South Arabian and in Arabic (as well as partly in other Semitic languages) to a small set of Proto-Semitic consonants are hardly to be followed. In fact, no arguments in favor of this theory are offered except for the merger of several sounds in some Semitic languages.

There is, for example, no argument for deriving the Proto-Semitic interdentals from plosive dentals through an internal process of spirantization. On the other hand, Egyptian did contribute to the Proto-Egypto-Semitic sound system by giving evidence for filling the four gaps in the Proto-Semitic system. The existence of an emphatic bilabial seems to be generally accepted. The voiced lateral, too, may be added to the phoneme inventory (see Voigt 1992). The emphatic uvular and the emphatic pharyngeal have to be added to the proto-system, too.

I should like to give a comparison between the Proto-Egyptian-Semitic sound system, that is the Proto-Semitic sound system plus the four additional phonemes, and the Egyptian sound system:

	*Eg.-Sem.				Eg.			
(1)	p	$<\dot{p}>$	b		p	f	b	
(2)	t	$\underdot{t}$	d		t	$\underdot{t}$	c	
(3)	$^{t}\theta$	$^{t}\underdot{\theta}$	$^{d}ð$		$s, \acute{s}$	$\underdot{t}$	c	
(4)	^{t}s	$^{t}\underdot{s}$	^{d}z		s	$\underdot{t}$	c	
(5)	$^{t}\acute{s}$	$^{t}\underdot{\acute{s}}$	$<^{d}\acute{z}>$		$\acute{s}$	$\underdot{t}$	c	
					[$\check{c}$	$\underdot{\check{c}}$	$\it{i}$	palat.]
(6)	k	$\underdot{k}$	g		k	$\underdot{k}$	g	
(7)	x	$<\underdot{x}>$	γ		[$\check{s}$	$\underdot{\check{c}}$	$\it{i}$	palat.]
(8)	$\hbar$	$<\underdot{\hbar}>$	Υ		$\underline{h}$	$\underdot{h}$	$\dot{g}(\underline{h})$	

The most important matters in the Egyptian system as compared to the proto-system are:

— the merger of the four voiceless dentals and affricates ($*^{t}t\it{?}$, $*^{t}\theta\it{?}$, $*^{t}s\it{?}$, $*^{t}\acute{s}\it{?}$ (in traditional Arabistic notation $\underdot{t}$, $\underdot{z}$, $\underdot{s}$, $\underdot{d}$) in Eg. $\underdot{t}$ ("$\underdot{d}$"),

— the reduction of the four voiced dentals and affricates *d, *dð, *dz, *dʐ to Eg. c, which only later became similar to the Semitic cain,
— the lack of a voiced sibilant ("z").

A first Berber-Semitic comparison as undertaken by Rössler (1964) is based on the same assumption that the Proto-Semitic sound system is more archaic than the Berber one.

The comparison of Semitic with Cushitic as contained in the *Сравнительно-историческая фонетика кушитских языков* by A. Dolgopolsky (1973) also presupposes a full phoneme inventory. The same is true for the Chadic reconstruction done by O. Stolbova in her *Studies in Chadic Comparative Phonology* (1996). Contrary to these first attempts of a Chadic reconstruction based on a full-fledged sound system of the proto-language, the reconstructions of H. Jungraithmayr and D. Ibriszimow in their two-volume *Chadic Lexical Roots* (1994) are less venturesome (or — as others would say — more realistic) in this respect.

5. DIFFERENT PHONOLOGICAL SYSTEMS

The sound system of O. Rössler, which is based on J. Cantineau (1951/52) and A. Martinet (1953), could be further developed by interpreting the phonemes phonetically in a more detailed way than before. It appears necessary to determine the differences between our consonant block and the sound system as given by Diakonoff (e.g., 1965:20, 1988:34, 1991:16, 1992:6). The slightly different transcription signs of 1993ff. (see 1995:8) are given in parentheses. The distinctive features added will help to understand the set-up of the system.

	[− occl] [− voice] [− glott]	[+ occl] [− voice] [− glott]	[+ occl] [− voice] [+ glott]	[+ occl] [+ voice] [− glott]	
(1)	−	*p*	*ṗ*	*b*	cf. 1
(2)	*f*				
(3)	−	*t*	*ṭ*	*d*	cf. 2

	[− occl] [− voice] [− glott]	[+ occl] [− voice] [− glott]	[+ occl] [− voice] [+ glott]	[+ occl] [+ voice] [− glott]	
(4)	s	c	$\c{c}$	3	cf. 4
(5)	$\check{s}$	$\check{c}$	$\check{\c{c}}$	$\check{3}$	cf. 3
(6)	$\hat{s}$	$\hat{c}$	$\hat{\c{c}}$	$?(\lambda)$	cf. 5
(7)	–	k	$\underset{.}{k}$	g	cf. 6
(8)	–	k^w	$\underset{.}{k}^w$	g^w	
(9)	$x(\underset{.}{h})$	$X\ (x)$	$\underset{.}{X}\ (x)$	9	cf. 7
(10)	$x^w\ (\underset{.}{h}^w)$	$X^w\ (x^w)$	$\underset{.}{X}^w\ (x^w)$	9^w	
(11)	$\underset{.}{h}/\underset{.}{h}^w$?				cf. 8
(12)			?		
(13)	h/h^w ?				

These are thirteen rows above. Eight of them correspond more or less to the eight rows of our consonant block. The main differences are:

1. A fricative row is added to the three column system. I see no real justification for positing f, $\check{s}$, $\hat{s}$, x (= $\underset{.}{h}$) *and* x^w (= $\underset{.}{h}^w$) as different from the corresponding occlusive phonemes p, $\check{c}$, $\hat{c}$, X (= x) and X^w (= x^w) respectively. But it must be admitted that it might be possible to prove the existence of one or another proto-phoneme of this kind. So far, however, the idea of fricatives besides the occlusive system can be proved only in the case of s (i.e. trad. "$\check{s}$", which corresponds to our s^1), i.e., the fricative sibilant associated with a sibilant affricate series, and h (which is not attached to any series).

At all events, it is strange to regard $\check{s}$ (formerly also transcribed as $\underline{s}$ by Diakonoff) as a proto-phoneme as it is posited only to account for the development of the causative morpheme and the third person pronouns in

Semitic (cf. Akkadian *šuu(-ʔaa-)* with Arabic *huu-a* 'he'). Indeed, these specific sound developments can be explained by (mor)phonological rules (see Voigt 1994). If we are going to posit proto-phonemes for all specific sound developments, the number of proto-phonemes would increase. And then why not posit a specific *l*-phoneme for the Arabic article that shows an assimilation not found elsewhere in the language?

The *ḥ* phoneme does not belong to the fricative column since it has a voiced counterpart (ʕ) therewith belonging to the kernel sound system.

2. The voiced lateral affricate *ǯ* (= our *ź*) whose existence is doubted should be posited for the proto-language (Voigt 1992).

3. The two labialized series (i.e., 8 and 10) — seven phonemes including the fricative labiovelar — appear to be unnecessary. I do not see the usefulness of a concept that transmits the labiality of a vowel onto an adjacent consonant. What is the advantage, e.g., of positing *x^wəç* 'leaf' instead of *xuç* (= *ḫuṣ* or better *ḫuuṣ-*, cf. Arab., Aram. *ḥuuṣ-* 'palm leaf')? Or, is there truly something to be gained by positing the following Proto-Semitic rules (as in Diakonoff 1992:79)?

$$g^wə- > gu-$$
$$ḳ^wə- > qu-$$
$$k^wə- > ku-$$

In reconstructing labiovelars as primitive sounds, one should not overlook that the origin of these sounds is a corollary to the process of vowel reduction as can be seen in Ethiosemitic languages as well as in Arabic dialects of the Maghreb. The normal historical development of vowel reduction is inverted, as in *$ḳ^wə$l-* 'call, voice' (cf. Hebr. *qôl*), which, on the other hand, is said to have become *$ḳ^wul$-* already in the proto-language (p. 24). The connection between labialization and vowel reduction seems to be accepted, as we predominantly find *shwâ*s among the words with labiovelar. The phoneme ə is regarded as necessary in order to account for the vowel variations as in Akkad. *libb^u, Hebr. lẹb̠ (< *libb-)*, Syriac *lebbâ* : Arab. *lubb^un* 'heart'. In my view this variation of a vowel before a labial can easily be explained by vowel assimilation. In this case the *shwâ* in the protoform *ləbb-* is said to lead to the vowels in the respective Semitic languages. It is hardly to be understood that *i* and *u* should be regarded as free alternations which led later on to their "secondary differentiation" (p. 77). This *shwâ semitohamiticum*, as it may be called, seems to be borrowed from Indo-European studies where the *shwâ indogermanicum* has been posited to account for an *i* in Indo-Iranian vs. an *a* in the rest of IE languages, e.g., Skr. *pitar*, Lat. *pater* < *pətēr* 'father'. Such vowel variations in Semitohamitic languages, otherwise not to be explained, are not covered by the *shwâ semitohamiticum*. They are simply cases of vowel assimilation (as *i/___ /b, m > u*), e.g.:

dəbas- 'honey' > *dibas-*, *dubas-*: Hebr. *dəḇaš*, Arab. *dibs^{un}*, Aram. *debšâ, dubšâ* (p. 81), better *dibas-*.

səm- 'name' > *sim-, sum-*: Hebr. *šęm*, Akk. *šum^u* (p. 33), better *s^1əm-*.

There are also cases where the *i* reflexes in all Semitic languages would lead to an *i* but nevertheless *ə* is posited as proto-phoneme. The reason for this is that the two universal vowels *i* and *u* are said not to have existed in the proto-language; both vowels are "vacillating" (p. 81). Whereas *i* in Semitic languages is derived from *shwâ*, *u* goes back to a word with a labiovelar (which, in fact, has the labiality taken over from the *u* vowel) or is derived from *shwâ* by assuming vowel variation (which does not explain anything).

Thus we have the strange situation that the vowel system of the proto-language knows only the two vowels *ə* and *a*. Since *ə* is dispensable in most cases (as in *dbas-* 'honey' and *sm-* 'name'), we would arrive finally at a one-vowel system of the proto-language. By the way, this is precisely what A. Kuipers did for Kabardian, a Northwest Caucasian language, see the critique by O. Szemerényi (1967:75ff.) who contests both the right analysis of Kabardian itself and its being an analogue for Proto-Indo-European.

4. According to Diakonoff, a system of "sonorants," altogether 15 proto-phonemes, accompany the occlusive and fricative consonant system given above.

m	*m̥*	
n	*n̥*	
r	*r̥*	
l	*l̥*	
y	*i̥*	
w	*u̥*	
ʕ	–	
Ḥ, Ḥ^w	–	= (?) *h^w* (Diakonoff 1993ff., see 1995:8)

In this system, only the well-known sounds *m, n, r, l, y* and *w* are to be accepted. The voiced laryngeal ʕ does belong — together with its counterpart *ḥ* (= ħ) — to the kernel system of sounds.

The status of the eight syllabic sonorants (*m̥, n̥, r̥, l̥, i̥, u̥, H̥* and *H̥ʷ*) is not clear. It appears to me that they have been introduced in order to get rid of traditional *a* and *u* vowels since they are said to yield -*am*-, -*an*-, -*ar*-, -*al*-, -*ay*-, -*aw*-, -*aʔ*- and -*uʔ-/-uw*- respectively. Again this technique has been taken over from IE linguistics, specifically Greek. There, syllabic nasals and liquids are reconstructed in order to account for specific vowel variations in contact with them. In IE *wl̥kʷos* > Skr. *vrka-*, Lith. *vilkas*, Got. *wulfs* 'wolf' the sound law *l̥ > Skr. *r̥*, Lith. *il/ul* Germanic *ul* is operative (Szemerényi 1989:49). I do not see a parallel to a Semitohamitic reconstruction *m̥s* besides *məs* 'night, late evening' (p. 33). We do have a vowel preceding *m* in various languages, as Hebr. *ʔemeš* 'evening' and Arab. *ʔamsi* 'yesterday', but these forms do not show a development that would differ from that with other consonants (cf. Hebr. *ʕeṣem* 'bone' with Arab. *ʕaḏ̣mun*). According to Diakonoff, in the proto-form *m̥s*- a prothetic vowel has arisen that brought about a prefixed initial glottal stop: *m̥s*- > *ams*- > *ʔams*-. I regard this as an unsuitable trick in order to shorten the word form to be reconstructed. Forms as *r̥ĉ*- 'earth' (p. 21) and *n̥f*- 'nose' (p. 33), as misleading as they are, do not contain less information than the fuller forms *ʔarĉ*- and *ʔanf*-.

In Semitohamitic, syllabic sonorants should only be reconstructed if, e.g., an *r* is represented in Arabic as *r*, but in Hebrew as *ar* and *ra* and in Ethiopic as *ər* (cf. the real case in IE), i.e., in those cases where a straight reconstruction (*ir* or *ar*) is not feasible.

In the same way, a reconstruction *mut̥*- 'death' does not make sense. One has to apply the rule *u̥ > au̥* (*mut̥*- > *maut̥*-). But what is gained by this procedure if one segment is simply replaced by another? Besides, if *maut*- is represented by *mut̥*- and *bait*- 'house' by *bit̥*- and *kalb*- 'dog' by *kl̥b*- (or *kl̥-b*-, p. 85), what would be the representation of other nouns of the *faʕl*- class? To some extent, the *ʕf̥ʕl*-class with syllabic second radical is expanded by applying the features of syllabicity to other segments as ʕ, e.g., *bʕ̥l* 'lord, husband' (p. 86); this technique is, however, not applied automatically, cf. *baʕl* besides *bʕ̥l* and *čaʕl-ab*- (?) 'fox' (p. 86). Apart from these cases, there are some nouns of the *faʕl* vocalization class, as *ragl*- 'foot', *nasr*- 'vulture' (p. 86), *ʔax(x)*- 'brother' (I reconstruct here *ʔahu*-) and *ʕamm*- 'uncle' (why not *ʕm̥*:- ?, p. 85). Through this procedure the unity of the *faʕl* noun class is broken up. I would consider this a disadvantage whereas the Diakonoff school would probably argue that we can follow up how such a noun class came into existence. We have seen, however, that the replacement of *aS* (= sonant) in the noun class *faSl-* (a phonetically determined sub-class of *faʕl-*) by *Ṣ̥*, which leads to *fṢ̥l-*, does not change very much. It obscures, indeed, the traditional noun class system (see below).

Among the many sonorants reconstructed by Diakonoff, there are two strange segments, i.e., **H̥* and **H̥ʷ*, which are said to be the sonorant equivalents to the plosive glottal stop **ʔ* (without or with labialization). They are "peculiar" sounds "developed from correptive stress, like the Danish *Stø̜d*tone" (p. 5). All three proto-phonemes would flow into Semitic *ʔ*. **H̥* is responsible for the vowel *a* followed by the glottal stop (i.e., **H̥ > aʔ*) whereas **H̥ʷ* should yield *uʔ / uw*. Four examples, somehow inspired by the most radical form of Indo-European laryngeal theory, may illustrate this.

*H̥ʷn̥č- ("**H̥ʷn̥č-*") 'woman' with the variant *ʔn̥č-* (p. 85) is given as the reconstruction for the etymon of Arab. *ʔunθaaᶡ*, OSA *ʔnθt*, Hebr. *ʔiššāʰ* (according to the rules given, however, **H̥ʷn̥č-* should yield Sem. **uʔ/wanč-*).

*rHs- (?) 'head' does not add anything new to the traditional reconstruction **raʔs-* since it is derived from this form through replacing *aʔ* by *H̥*.

*ĉH̥-n- 'goats and sheep' (p. 84) corresponds to **ṣ́aʔn- >* Hebr. *ṣoʔn*.

*bH̥-bH̥- > *baʔ-baʔ- > ba:b- 'door' (p. 84).

I must confess that I cannot follow this kind of reconstruction.

5. The so-called "bifocal," "groove-alveolar (or palatalized)" or post-alveolar sibilant affricates (i.e., series 5 / *č* : *ç̌* : *ǯ* /) correspond to what is generally regarded as interdental series (i.e., our series 3). This series has the traditional form / *t̠* : *t̠* : *d̠* / or / *θ* : *θ̣* : *ð* /.

I should like to characterize this series as an affricate series, i.e., *T* (the dental archiphoneme) + *θ, θ̣, ð* (with the development *T + θ = ᵗθ*, etc.):

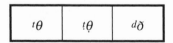

This interpretation differs from that of Diakonoff, who assumes a different kind of affricates where the phoneme *š* is added to the dental series / *t ṭ d* / (with the development *t + š > č*, etc.). With this phonetic interpretation of the proto-phonemes it is difficult to explain the sound development to the Semitic interdentals (*č > ᵗθ* with the *š > θ* sound change included). The argument is that it is easier to think of a sibilantization of the proto-Semitohamitic interdentals (a development that we can observe within Semitic as well as in Semitic loans in non-Semitic languages)

than the other way round, *viz.* the evolution of the specific interdental pronunciation in Semitic. But Diakonoff suggests a different development. He connects the rare sound development of *š* (= s^1) > *h* to the development of **č* (= *tš*) to Semitic *θ* as if **tʰ* (< **tš*) would have shifted to the Semitic interdental. With such an assumption (**(č* =) *tš* > *th* > *tʰ* > *θ*) the sound change s^1 > *h* is strongly misunderstood since the aspiration of the sibilant is morphologically conditioned in Semitic (personal pronouns and causative stem morpheme). It is strange that a sibilant should have reduced its friction in contact with occlusives. The language history of Greek demonstrates that IE **s* is retained in positions before and after an occlusive (as in *ἕσπερος* (< **uesperos*) 'evening', *ἐστί* (< **h₁esti*) 'is', and *δίσκος* (< **dik-skos*) 'quoit'. The sound change 'tenuis + sibilant' > 'tenuis + *h*' > 'tenuis aspirata' > 'fricative', which inspired Diakonoff when reconstructing the Proto-Semitohamitic 'inter-dentals,' does occur in Greek: **ks* > *kh* > *kʰ* > [*x*]. However, this specific development of the sibilant is restricted to its position between consonants, e.g., **eks-tros* > **ekhtros* > **ekʰtʰros* > *ἐχθρός* 'hated' (see Rix 1976: 76ff.) with the later spirantization of the aspirate (as in *kʰ* > [*x*]). Thus, this sound change is intended to reduce the consonant cluster; another device is to elide the first consonant of such a cluster (as in **dik-skos* > *δίσκος*).

In Semitic, an occlusive has a stabilizing influence on the sibilant as can be recognized in those languages in which the causative stem formative s_1 has become *h* or *∅/ʔ*, as in Arabic (IV. perf. *ʔafʕal=a*, impf. *i=ufʕil=u*). Here the sibilant s_1 is retained in the causative reflexive stem formation (X. perf. (*ʔi*)*stafʕal=a*, impf. *i=astafʕil=u*). Other examples from the modern South Arabian languages could be given here.

Assuming the sound development **th* > **tʰ* > *θ*, the interdentals could not have been originally affricated (**tθ*) in Semitic. Their affrication, however, is proved by their merger with the phonemes of the sibilant affricate series. Although the voiceless interdental **tθ* was early deaffricated, as we know from its merger with Hebrew *š* (< s_1), e.g. (**tθala: tθ-* >) **θala:θ-* > *šålô/oš* 'three', in the case of the emphatic *tθ* the affrication was maintained longer as is demonstrated by its merger with *ṭṣ* (< **ṭṣ*), e.g. **tθabi-* > *ṭṣəbî* 'gazelle'.

At the end of the century, we have basically two different approaches (not including that of Ehret 1995) for the etymological set-up of the Semitohamitic proto-language and its evolution to the different branches. The Rösslerian concept of the consonant block appears to be nearer to the languages attested and relies more on incompatibilities and languages' specific sound laws, whereas the Diakonoff school shows a greater fantasy and daring in reconstruction. There is a tendency to assign language (group) specific developments to the proto-language. We have already seen that the Semitic sound change s^1 (= Diakonoff's $š$) > h has been attributed to a new phoneme that has the sole purpose of explaining this specific Semitic sound weakening. There are other examples of sound laws transferred to the proto-language, as *bətm-, var. *bətn- 'pistachio nut' (p. 86) where the variant with *n* represents a secondary development. The same applies to the "variants" *pu̯ĉ, *pi̯ĉ 'egg' (p. 11), *xʷər, *xər 'hole, to dig' (p. 26) showing delabialization, *bVtn, *bVnVt 'navel, belly' (p. 12) with metathesis, *dm, *dam 'blood' (p. 14) showing vowel reduction, *čət, *čHt 'to smell' (p. 17, not clear to me), etc.

These remarks on Diakonoff's procedure do not apply in every respect to Orel and Stolbova's *HSED*. Here we do not find so huge a consonantal phoneme inventory. Nor do we find extremely few vowels (tending towards monovocalism) or many phonetically conditioned root variants — all characteristics of Diakonoff's system. Instead, nearly a Rösslerian consonant set and six vowels are posited for the proto-language. Among the vowels, however, one would hesitate to acknowledge the Proto-Semitohamitic status of such vowels as *e*, *o* and *ü*. Especially in the case of *ü*, it could be argued that the weakening process *u* > *i* responsible for this sound is very common in languages. Although the verification of *e and *o cannot be excluded, it seems that — in line with the Diakonoff school — individual language developments have been attributed to the proto-language. By comparing both Russian dictionaries, I should like to guess that Orel–Stolbova's work will serve more properly as a basis for future research, although the Egyptian comparisons are all to be abandoned in favor of comparisons based on Rössler's system of sound correspondences.

What is needed here is a discussion of the different concepts in general and the specific rules in particular. The present paper is intended to be a small contribution to this discussion.

6. SEMITIC ROOT STRUCTURE AND NOUN CLASSES

In his comparative work, Diakonoff argues for a different word structure in Semitohamitic and Proto-Semitic. A great deal of all triradical roots are reduced to biradical roots. This is a very strong claim that should be made more plausible than it has been so far by the partisans of this far-reaching theory. As to its methodological status, one can say: (1.) It will work under all circumstances. The neglect of one radical will raise the probability of a (pseudo-)fitting comparison. (2.) It will work more easily. (3.) It will work forever. If this kind of comparison becomes the norm, no one will return to a more difficult method of comparison that would necessarily yield less examples.

There are, however, some triradical roots accepted by Diakonoff, as *pVtVḥ* 'to open (wide)' (*HCVA*), *paḫʷVd*, *ṗaḫʷVd* 'thigh, hip', *pᶜl* 'to make, to do', *baɂʷḷ* 'mule, bastard' (*9 = γ*).

In this system, most triradical roots are derived from biradicals. The following expansion processes are said to have worked (according to *HCVA*):

— the addition of a glottal stop as second radical, e.g.: *pVd* > *p'd* 'to go out, to run (away)', *dm̥ I* > *d'm I* 'blood > red',

— the addition of a glottal stop as third radical, e.g.: *pVk̲* > *pk̲'* 'to peel, to scratch', *bVd* > *bd'* 'stick',

— the addition of a semi-vowel (*u* and *i*) as second radical, e.g.: *pəg II* > *pu̯g* 'to smell, to blow' (cf. *pəg I* 'to stretch, to draw' > *pgg*, Arab. *fǧǧ*), *fVl I* > *fu̯/il*, *fli/'* 'fortune-telling, magic speech',

— the addition of a semi-vowel (*u* and *i*) as third radical, e.g.: *pVg* > *pg'/u̯* 'to open', *paĉ* > *pĉu̯/i*, var. *pu̯ĉ* 'to stretch, to spread',

— the lengthening or reduplication of the second radical, e.g.: *pVk* 'to open' > *pkk*, Arab. *fkk*, *tm̥* 'completion, completeness' > *tmm*, Arab. *tamm-*,

— the reduplication of the two radicals, e.g.: *tak⁽ʷ⁾ I* 'to tread upon, to press, to strike' > *tktk*, Arab. *tktk* 'to crush, to tremble under foot',

— the addition of consonants (other than ', *u*, *i*) as third radical, e.g.: *pVŝ* > *pŝ-r*, Akk. *pšr* 'to loosen, to untie'; in the case of the proto-root *pr-* all kinds of consonants are allowed as the third radical added as *s*, *k*, *k̲*, *s*, *c*, *ç*, *g*, *m*, *d*, *h*, *ḫ*; nearly the same with the proto-root *pl-*, *dp-* and many other cases,

— the addition of *n*, ', *u* as first radical, e.g.: *pVŝ* > *n-pŝ*, Arab. *nfš* 'to comb, to card', *pḷ II* 'stone, to crush stone' > *n-pl*, Arab. *nabal-* 'big stone', *bit* 'house, to spend the night' > *'-bt*, *u-bt*,

— the addition of other consonants (*ᶜ*, *i*) as first radical, e.g.: *pḷ II* 'stone, to crush stone' > *ᶜ-pl*, Arab. *'a-ᶜbal* 'white rock', *dad* > *u̯/i-dd*, Hebr. *i̯ādîd* 'beloved, friend' (*i* > *u̯*); here, the possibilities seem to be restricted.

Some of these techniques do, indeed, occur in Semitohamitic languages, but not all of them together and not all in the manner depicted by Diakonoff (and in a more fanciful way by Ehret 1995). I cannot imagine a development of a language in which a consonant may be added as first, second or third radical to a biradical root. The same methodological mistake as noted above occurs here too, that is the assignment of language-specific traits and developments to the proto-language. I think it is methodologically wrong to extrapolate from the synchronic variation of a consonant (or segment) to its irrelevance in a diachronic reconstruction. From the existence of roots such as Classical Ethiopic √tf? 'to spit' and Arab. √tff, √tfl 'to spit' it does not follow necessarily that the 'oscillating' consonants ?, *f* and *l* are segments secondarily added. The similarity between Arabic *?anuθa* 'be female' and *ḥaniθa* 'be effeminated' cannot be explained by declaring *?* and *ḥ* to be prefixes (cf. German *verweiblichen / verweichlichen* with a similar meaning, which differ only in *b* vs. *ch*, thus coming to a proto-form *verwei-lichen* + "infix").

Without any rules or detailed concepts behind the development assumed, it will be very hard to accept such root expansions. The numerous root extensions with their functional characteristics as given by Ehret, i.e., **h* amplificative, **y* inchoative/denominative, γ^w complementive, *kw'* andative, ʕ partitive, *r* diffusive, *b* extendative, etc., i.e., all the other consonants of the sound inventory (1995:29ff.), do not fit the requirement of a solid linguistic theory. I cannot imagine a language in which all consonants of the phoneme inventory occur as functional elements. Comparison with well-studied languages leads us to conclude that the quantity has to be more limited. Compare the situation in Semitic and in most other Semitohamitic languages where we have mainly *y*, *t*, *?*, *n*, s^1, *h*, *m* as inflectional elements.

The system of noun classes is obscured by the recognition of such noun types as:

    type *CVC-*: **qas-t* 'bow' (p. 84, its "variant" Arab. *qaws-* demonstrates its origin from **qaws-t)*, **?ab(b)-* (?) 'father' (p. 85, with a "class marker of kinship terms -*u*" in Semitic; I would prefer to reconstruct **?abu-*), **gam-(a)l-* 'camel' (p. 84),

    type *CSC̥-*: **yum-* 'day', **ḳus-* 'bow', **ḳmḥ-* 'flour' (p. 85).

There is a tendency to monoconsonantal reconstructions, as in

    type *CS-*: **ʕ̥i-r* 'ass-foal', **kl̥-b-* 'dog', **ĉH̥-n-* 'goats and sheep' (p. 84), **dm̥-*, **dam-* 'blood' (p. 76, the difference between the two "variants" is not clear).

The problem of bi- vs. triradicality appears to be the central question of Semitohamitic comparative work (see Voigt 1988a). It remains a topic to be discussed in the next century.

7. RECONSTRUCTION OF THE MORPHOLOGICAL SYSTEM OF THE PROTO-LANGUAGE: THE PROTO-SEMITOHAMITIC VERBAL SYSTEM

A comparison of languages based exclusively on their vocabulary may not yield an unambiguous result if the common ancestor has to be dated too far back in history or if a language has undergone a very heavy lexical influence. The existence of a similar morphology — especially in the domain of the verb — is always an undoubtable proof of a genetic relationship. In the case of Semitohamitic we are in a good position to reconstruct parts of its morphology.

In all Semitohamitic languages and hence in their proto-language, the verbal system is the most important part. It is the part of a language that changes most slowly. Nevertheless, because of the time-depth of the proto-language, many languages have developed verbal systems quite different from those of the old languages, including the proto-language. In my conceptualization, the reconstruction has to be based on the most archaic languages. It is quite clear that Akkadian, Twareg and Beḍauye represent the most archaic languages of the respective language groups, i.e., Semitic, Berber, and Cushitic. When looking at these languages, one detects one suffix conjugation and three prefix conjugations — a situation that I dared to posit for the proto-language. There have been several objections to this reconstruction and in general against the view that such languages as Twareg, Beḍauye and Akkadian should have priority over so many other Semitohamitic languages.

(a) Some Egyptologists do not like the nearly total disregard of their language in morphological reconstructions, among them that of the verbal system. Loprieno could be mentioned here; his idea that the order of the morphemes in a proto-language morpheme complex was not yet fixed — he speaks about "labile morphologische Strukturen" (1986:16) — is very strange. This is reminiscent of the theories of former centuries that the proto-language must be "primitive" in one way or another.

The existence of the old suffix conjugation in Egyptian, the so-called pseudo-participle, is a strong argument for a Semitohamitic affiliation of Egyptian. On the other hand, the lack of all three prefix conjugations in such an old language is a remarkable fact that has led some scholars to doubt their relevance for a reconstruction of the proto-language. It is very doubtful whether one could regard Egyptian forms with a reduplicated consonant (as $mrr=f$) as reflexes of the old conjugation with a lengthened consonant.

(b) Many Chadicists do not like the exclusion of their huge language family in Semitohamitic reconstructive work. P. Newman is a representative scholar of this notion. He speaks of "Methodological pitfalls in Chadic-Afroasiatic comparisons" (1984) in the case of the root 'to drink,' which was reconstructed by H. Jungraithmayr (1994 I:51) with two or three radicals ($*s_2w(?/h?)$-) and by Newman with only one radical ($*s$- or $*sa$-). He argues that a reconstruction with more than one radical (as in the cognate Egyptian root $swr/\acute{s}wj$, which indeed opens the door to detecting reflexes in Chadic with more than one consonant) was done "to fit a pre-determined target" thus yielding to an "exercise in circularity." In fact, it is not justified to exclude strictly external evidence in a reconstruction. It is the weakness of a thoroughly internal reconstruction that it fails to recognize archaic elements in a language.

This becomes evident in the internal -*a*- apophony in Chadic verbs, as in Ron short stem *šoh* versus long stem *šwaáh* 'drink'. This type of alternation (see Jungraithmayr 1974, 1975) has been connected with the *a* ablaut in the Akkadian verb (cf. G stem of the strong verb pret. [*y*]*iprVs* : pres. [*y*]*iparrVs*, or of the weak II *u* verb class pret. *idūk* : pres. *idūak*[*k*] 'kill').

I would maintain this historic connection although some Chadicists would declare this *a* as an old suffix that entered the root. Indeed, for those who reconstruct only internally it is not difficult to account for an unexpected and undesired phenomenon in an internal way.

(c) Most Cushitists do not like to reconstruct more than one prefix conjugation for their proto-language. In fact, we do have two prefix conjugations in various East Cushitic languages (see Voigt 1985, 1987a) and three morphologically different prefix conjugations in Beḍauye (Reinisch 1895), e.g.:

root	stem	aorist	present	perfect	
delib	$O_{trans.}$	*adlib*	*adanliib,* *adalliib*	*iidlib*	'tauschen, kaufen'
	O_2	*adaalib*	*eedli(i)b*	*iidlab*	'Händler sein'
	T_1	*addalaab*	*addaliib*	*iddelib*	'(pass.)'
	S_1	*asdalib*	*asdaliib*	*esdileb*	'(caus.)'
	S_2	*asdaalib*	*asdaaliib*	*esdiileb*	'zum Händler ausbilden'
	M_1	*amdalaab*	*amdaliib*	*imdelib*	'bei einem (Ver-) Kauf mitwirken'

Nevertheless, only the aorist (or preterite) is widely accepted, e.g., by A. Zaborski (1975), as Semitohamitic inheritance corresponding to Akk. [*y*]*iprus* (= Hebr. *i̯ipros*). The shape of the Beḍauye present form that I compare with Akk. [*y*]*iparrVs* (= Old Eth. *yəfärrəs*, Mehri *yəfōrəs*) is said to have developed secondarily out of a periphrastic construction with an auxiliary verb *an*. The main problem with this solution is the fact that a nasal that is said to be the remnant of this auxiliary verb occurs only in (the singular forms of) one verb class in the basic stem (and not in the plural forms, the other verb classes of the basic stem, or in the many derived verb stems). So far, this problem has not been solved by adherents of the auxiliary verb hypothesis (see Voigt 1986, 1988b).

Finally, the third prefix conjugation of Beḏauye, i.e., the perfect (or past), should not be overlooked as is usually done. I regard this too as an element of the proto-language.

(d) The situation in Semitic linguistics is somewhat similar to that in Cushitic. Some Semitists have denied the proto-Semitic character of the [y]iparrVs / yǝfärrǝs / yǝfōrǝs present formation by hinting at the possibility of independent developments. It seems that this discussion has been settled now in favor of its Proto-Semitic recognition.

The third prefix conjugation, which is retained only in the Akkadian perfect form (i.e., [y]iptarVs), is currently accepted as Proto-Semitic only by myself, but I think the evidence from Berber and Cushitic is strong enough to support this theory. There are aspectual forms in Berber and Beḏauye that exhibit a dental. In Beḏauye the intransitive verb class of the basic stem, labeled reflexive by Reinisch (1895), is characterized by a dental. However, this dental (which is underlined in the following scheme) does not occur only in the present form, but also in the perfect (labelled plusquamperfect by Reinisch), e.g.:

root	aorist	present	perfect	
ʔaam	aʔaam	eetʔiim, eedʔiim	iitʔam, iidʔam	'aufsteigen, reiten'
baʔar	abaʔaar	atbeʔiir	itbeʔir	'erwachen, aufw.'
genaaf	agnaaf	adganiif	edgenif	'sich beugen, niederknien'
hadaaʔ	ahadaaʔ	adhadiiʔ	edhadiʔ	'alt werden'

This verbal class has been treated by Hudson (1974) as "(T)-forms" distinct from the "T-forms." Indeed, this represents the intransitive verb class and thus belongs to the basic stem.

In Berber, we have numerous conjugations in which the present form (however, not the perfect form) is characterized by a dental (underlined in the scheme), as in the Tayǝrt dialect of Twareg (Prasse/Ghubǎyd/Ghǎbdǝwan 1998):

imperative	aorist ('imparfait')	present ('imparfait intensive')	perfect ('parfait')	
agrək	*yagrək*	*yətagrăk*	*yogrăk*	'roter'
iɣwas	*iɣwas*	*itiɣwas*	*iɣwis*	'crier'
ămmăt	*yămmăt*	*yətamăttat*	*yəmmut*	'mourir'

The distribution of the dental element as a feature of verb classes or conjugations in the three language groups is as follows:

	aorist	present	perfect
Beḍauye	–	*t*	*t*
Twareg	–	*t*	–
Akkadian	–	–	*t*

The arguments for the specific spread of the dental element as given in Voigt (1987b) will need further elaboration.

The current theory that the Akkadian perfect has developed out of the (passive-reflexive) T stem is a short circuit argument. The possible connection between these two and even the possible derivation of the former from the latter (as maintained in Voigt 1987b) do not imply that this happened during the development of the language in which the similar morphemes occur.

If thus *all* Semitists at the present would agree only on reconstructing the [*y*]*iprVs* form — apart from the *parVs-* suffix conjugation, the nominal non-verbal character of which has sometimes been stressed, as in Huehnergard 1987 — the common stock of Semitohamitic features in the realm of the verb morphology would be very meager. It would be nearly inconceivable that the great variety of three prefix conjugations in different languages could have developed from this single prefix conjugation in a parallel way.

Indeed, one task of comparative linguistics in the next century is to discuss the morphological similarities between the archaic Semitohamitic

languages and the development of the innovative Semitohamitic languages
in more detail and with more linguistic arguments.

8. SUMMARY

In this contribution, there is no reference to the progress made in describing
the individual Semitohamitic languages, particularly in the area of the
Cushitic and Chadic language families. Instead, emphasis was placed
on the progress made by the end of the century in understanding the
phonological and morphological structure of the Semitohamitic language
phylum. The Proto-Semitohamitic phonological system as based on the
Egypto-Semitic sound comparisons (according to O. Rössler) is presented
and critically compared with that of I. Diakonoff. Several aspects of that
system, as the labialized series, the palatalized affricate (i.e., interdental)
series, the system of sonorants and the vowel system, have been criticized
strongly and in a detailed manner. The structure of the Semitohamitic
root and its expansion with several elements as posited by Diakonoff
is rejected as methodologically questionable. Among the morphological
traits to be reconstructed for the proto-language, the tripartite organization
of the aspectual forms (aorist: present: perfect) is treated with reference
to Beḍauye, Berber, and Akkadian.

While this paper does not include a survey of the comparative work
done in this century, reference will be made to the six *International
Hamito-Semitic Congresses* so far held: 1-A. Paris 1969 (see A. Caquot
— D. Cohen 1974), 1-B. (see J. — Th. Bynon 1975), 2. Firenze 1974 (see P.
Fronzaroli 1978), 3. London 1978 (see J. Bynon 1984), 4. Marburg/Lahn
1983 (see H. Jungraithmayr — W.W. Müller), 5. Wien 1987 (see H.
Mukarovsky 1990), 6. Moscow 1994 (unpublished to date). There is
another series of Semitohamitic conferences held in the U.S. and in Italy
(see V. Brugnatelli 1994, and A. Bausi — M. Tosco 1997). All these
congresses demonstrate a renewed interest in Semitohamitic studies. One
should hope that this will continue in the coming century.

REFERENCES

Alojaly, Gh.: see Prasse, Karl-G. — Gh. Alojaly — Gh. Mohamed [2]1998.
Balcz, H.: see Calice, Fr. 1936.
Behnk, Fr.: see Ember, A. 1930.
Bausi, A. — Tosco, M. (ed.). 1997. *Afroasiatica Neapolitana: Contributi*

presentati all'8° Incontro di Linguistica Afroasiatica (Camito-Semitica) (Napoli 1996). Napoli.

Benfey, Th. 1844. *Ueber das Verhältniss der ägyptischen Sprache zum semitischen Sprachstamm.* Leipzig.

Brugnatelli, V. (ed.). 1994. *Sem Cam Iafet: Atti dell 7ª Giornata di studi camito-semitici e indoeuropei (Milano 1993).* Milano.

Bynon, J. (ed.). 1984. *Current Progress in Afro-Asiatic Linguistics: Papers of the third international Hamito-Semitic congress (London 1978).* Amsterdam — Philadelphia.

Bynon, J. — Bynon, Th. (eds.). 1975. *Hamito-Semitica: Proceedings from a colloquium ... (London 1970).* The Hague — Paris.

Calice, Fr. 1936. *Grundlagen der ägyptisch-semitischen Wortvergleichung,* hrsg. v. H. Balcz. Wien.

Cantineau, J. 1951/52. Le consonantisme du sémitique. *Semitica* 4: 79–94.

Caquot, A. — D. Cohen (eds.). 1974. *Actes du premier congrès international de linguistique sémitique et chamito-sémitique (Paris 1969).* The Hague — Paris.

Cohen, David (ed.) 1988. (Les langues dans le monde ancien et moderne, 3) *Les langues chamito-sémitiques.* Paris.

Cohen, Marcel. 1947. *Essai comparatif sur le vocabulaire et la phonétique du chamito-sémitique.* Paris.

Czermak, W. 1931–1934. *Die Laute der ägyptischen Sprache: Eine phonetische Untersuchung.* Part I–II. Wien.

Diakonoff, Igor M. 1965. *Semito-Hamitic languages.* Moscow.

Diakonoff, Igor M. 1988. *Afrasian languages.* Moscow.

Diakonoff, Igor M. 1992. Proto-Afrasian and Old Akkadian: A study in historical phonetics. *JAAL* 4: 1–133.

Дьяконов, Игорь М. 1965. *Семитохамитские языки.* Москва.

—. [и другие]: *Сравнительно-исторический словарь афразийских языков.* Москва: выпуск 1 (1981), 2 (1982), 3 (1983).

—. (Введение) 1991. *Афразийские языки.* In: *Афразийские языки,* Кн. 1. *Семитские языки.* Москва (*Языки Азии и Африки,* 4), pp. 5–69.

D'jakonov, Igor' M. [et alii] 1993ff. Historical comparative vocabulary of Afrasian. *St. Petersburg Journal of African Studies* 2 (1993) 5–28; 3 (1994), 5–26; 4 (1995), 7–38; 5 (1995), 4–32; 6 (1997), 12–35. [not yet finished = *HCVA*]

Долгопольский, А.Б. 1973. *Сравнительно-историческая фонетика кушитских языков.* Москва.

Ehret, Chr. 1995. *Reconstructing Proto-Afroasiatic.* Berkeley.

Ember, A. 1930. *Egypto-Semitic Studies,* hrsg. v. Fr. Behnk. Leipzig.

Erman, Adolf. 1892. Das Verhältnis des Aegyptischen zu den semitischen Sprachen. *ZDMG* 46: 93–129.

Fronzaroli, P. (ed.). 1978. *Atti del secondo congresso internazionale di linguistica camito-semitica (Firenze 1974).* Firenze.

Hudson, R.A. 1974. A structural sketch of Beja. *African Language Studies* 15: 111–142.

Huehnergard, John. 1987. "Stative", predicative form, pseudo-verb. *JNES* 47: 215–232.

Ibriszimow, D.: see Jungraithmayr, H. 1994.

Jungraithmayr, Herrmann. 1974. Perfektiv-(Kurz-) und Imperfektiv-(Lang-) Stamm im Aspektsystem osttschadohamitischer Sprachen. *XVIII. Deutscher Orientalistentag ... in Lübeck 1972: Vorträge,* ed. by W. Voigt. Wiesbaden, 583–595.

Jungraithmayr, H. 1975. Types of conjugational forms in Chadic. *Hamito-Semitica ...,* ed. by J. and Th. Bynon. The Hague — Paris, 399–409.

Jungraithmayr, H. — Dymitr Ibriszimow. 1994. *Chadic Lexical Roots,* vol. 1. *Tentative reconstruction, grading, distribution and comments,* vol. 2. *Documentation.* Berlin.

Jungraithmayr, H. — W. W. Müller (eds.). 1987. *Proceedings of the Fourth International Hamito-Semitic Congresss (Marburg 1983).* Amsterdam — Philadelphia.

Klimov, G. A. 1986. *Einführung in die kaukasische Sprachwissenschaft.* Hamburg.

Lepsius, R. 1880. *Nubische Grammatik mit einer Einleitung über die Völker und Sprachen Afrikas.* Berlin.

Loprieno, A. 1986. *Das Verbalsystem im Ägyptischen und im Semitischen.* Wiesbaden.

Майзель, С.С. 1983. *Пути развития корневого фонда семитских языков.* Москва.

Martinet, A. 1953. Remarques sur le consonantisme sémitique. *BSL* 49: 67–78.

Meinhof, Carl. 1912. *Die Sprachen der Hamiten.* Hamburg.

Mohamed, Gh.: see Prasse, Karl-G. — Gh. Alojaly — Gh. Mohamed ²1998.

Mukarovsky, H.G. (ed.). 1990. *Proceedings of the Fifth International Hamito-Semitic Congress (Wien 1987).* Vol. 1–2. Wien.

Müller, Friedrich. 1887. *Die Sprachen der lockenhaarigen Rasse.* Band II. *Die Sprachen der mittelländischen Rassen.* Wien.

Müller, W. Max. 1905. Lautsystem und Umschrift des Altägyptischen. *OLZ* 8: 313–323, 361–371, 413–423.

Newman, P. 1984. Methodological pitfalls in Chadic-Afroasiatic comparisons. *Current Progress in Afro-Asiatic Linguistics*, ed. by J. Bynon, Amsterdam (etc.), 161–166.

Orel, Vladimir, Olga V. Stolbova. 1995. *Hamito-Semitic Etymological Dictionary*. Leiden. [= *HSED*]

Osing, J. 1980. Lautsystem. *Lexikon der Ägyptologie*. Bd 3. Wiesbaden, 944–949.

Petráček, Karel. 1989. *Úvod do hamitosemitské (afroasijské) jazykovědy*, k vydání připravil P. Zemánek. Praha.

Prasse, Karl-G. — Gh. Alojaly — Gh. Mohamed. ²1998. *Lexique touareg — français*. Copenhagen.

Reinisch, Leo. 1890. Das Zahlwort vier und neun in den chamitisch-semitischen Sprachen. *Sitzungsberichte der kaiserlichen Akademie der Wissenschaften (Wien), phil.-hist. Cl.*, 121, 1–40.

Reinisch, Leo. 1895. *Wörterbuch der Beḏauye-Sprache*. Wien.

Reinisch, Leo. 1909. *Das persönliche Fürwort und die Verbalflexion in den chamito-semitischen Sprachen*. Wien.

Rix, H. 1976. *Historische Grammatik des Griechischen — Laut- und Formenlehre*. Darmstadt.

Rössler, Otto. 1950. Verbalbau und Verbalflexion in den semito-hamitischen Sprachen. *ZDMG* 100: 461–514.

Rössler, Otto. 1964. Libysch — Hamitisch — Semitisch. *Oriens* 17: 199–216.

Rössler, Otto. 1971. Das Ägyptische als semitische Sprache. In: Fr. Altheim — R. Stiehl, *Christentum am Roten Meer*. Bd 1. Berlin — New York, 263–326.

Rössler, Otto. 1981. The structure and inflexion of the verb in the Semito-Hamitic languages. *Bono homini donum — Essays in historical linguistics in memory of J. A. Kerns*, ed. by. Y. L. Arbeitman and A. R. Bomhard. Amsterdam, 679–748. [Translation of Rössler 1950]

Satzinger, H. 1997. Egyptian in the Afroasiatic frame: Recent Egyptological issues with an impact on comparative studies. *Afroasiatica Neapolitana: Contributi presentati all' 8⁰ Incontro di Linguistica Afroasiatica (Camito-Semitica)*, ed. by A. Bausi and M. Tosco. Napoli, pp. 27–48.

Столбова, О.В. 1986. *Реконструкция консонантной системы западночадских языков*. In: *Сравнительно-исторический словарь афразийских языков*, вып. 3, Москва, 80–115.

Stolbova, O. V. 1996. *Studies in Chadic Comparative Phonology*. Moscow.

Stolbova, O. V.: see Orel, V. — O. Stolbova 1995.

Szemerényi, O. 1967. The new look of Indo-European: Reconstruction and typology. *Phonetica* 17: 65–99.

290   *Rainer Voigt*

Szemerényi, O. ³1989. *Einführung in die vergleichende* [i.e., indogermanische, R.V.] *Sprachwissenschaft.* Darmstadt. [The 4th (corrected reprint of the 3rd) edition has been translated into English as: *Introduction to Indo-European Linguistics.* Oxford 1996.]

Vergote, J. 1945. *Phonétique historique de l'égyptien: Les consonnes.* Louvain.

Voigt, R. 1985. Die beiden Präfixkonjugationen des Ostkuschitischen. *Afrika und Übersee* 68: 87–104.

Voigt, R. 1986. Die Verbalklassen des Grundstammes im Bedauye. *Africana Marburgensia* 19, 2: 26–37.

Voigt, R. 1987a. The two prefix-conjugations in East Cushitic, East Semitic, and Chadic. *BSOAS* 50: 330–345.

Voigt, R. 1987b. Derivatives und flektives t im Semitohamitischen. *Proceedings of the Fourth International Hamito-Semitic Congress (Marburg 1983)*, ed. by H. Jungraithmayr and W. W. Müller. Amsterdam — Philadelphia, 86–107.

Voigt, R. 1988a. *Die infirmen Verbaltypen des Arabischen und das Biradikalismus-Problem.* Stuttgart.

Voigt, R. 1988b. Zur Bildung des Präsens im Beḍauye. *Cushitic — Omotic: Papers from the International Symposium on Cushitic and Omotic Languages.* Hamburg, 379–407.

Voigt, R. 1989. Verbal conjugation in Chadic. *Current Progress in Chadic Linguistics* ..., ed. by Z. Frajzyngier. Amsterdam — Philadelphia, 267–284.

Voigt, R. 1992. Die Lateralreihe / š ṣ ź / im Semitischen. *ZDMG* 142: 37–52.

Voigt, R. 1994. Der Lautwandel s¹ > h in wurzellosen Morphemen des Alt- und Neusüdarabischen. *Semitic and Cushitic Studies*, ed. by G. Goldenberg and Sh. Raz. Wiesbaden, 19–28.

Voigt, R. 1999. Ägyptosemitischer Sprachvergleich. *Aspekte zur ägyptischen Lexikographie* hrsg. v. St. Grunert u. I. Hafemann. Leiden — Köln, 345–366.

Vycichl, W. 1958. Grundlagen der ägyptisch-semitischen Wortvergleichung. *Mitteilungen des Deutschen Archäologischen Instituts (Abteilung Kairo)* 16: 367–405.

Ward, W. A. 1985. Reflections on methodology in Egypto-Semitic lexicography. *Palestine in the Bronze and Iron Ages: Papers in honour of Olga Tufnell*, ed. by J. N. Tubb. London, 231–248.

Zaborski, A. 1975. *The verb in Cushitic.* Cracow.

Zemánek, P.: see Petráček, K. 1989.

Languages in Contact

INTRODUCTION

As with other domains of inquiry, there has been a traditional resistance to giving serious attention to areal features and the significant impact language contact may have on the structure of language on the one hand, and on historical evaluation and comparative linguistics on the other. While the study of modern languages has been more open to pondering these aspects of linguistic change, this is generally not the case with regard to study of ancient Semitic languages. This statement may at first sound surprising. Accounts of bilingualism are as old as the oldest attestations of a Semitic language, viz., Akkadian and its relationship with Sumerian. An anecdotal story discovered in the ancient Mesopotamian site of Uruk (Modern Warka, biblical אֶרֶךְ) tells about a doctor who had succeeded in curing a resident of Uruk and went there by invitation of his patient. Upon arrival, he stops to ask directions of a woman referred to him by his patient. He addresses her by pronouncing her name:
— Ninlugalabzu?
— *anni lugalmu.*
— Why do you curse me?
— Why would I curse you? I said, "Yes, sir."
— Pray, give me directions to the house of Ninurtasagentarbizaemen, brother of Ninurtamizideshkiangani.
— *namtušmen.*
— Why do you curse me?
— Why would I curse you? I said, "Sir, he is not home."
— Where did he go?
— *edingirbi šuzianna sizkur gabari munbala.*
— Why do you curse me?
— Why would I curse you? I said, "He is making an offering in the temple of his god Shuzianna."
[Let] him [go] there,
so that [the students] will gather and throw him out of the Great Gate.
(Reiner 1986; Foster 1993: 835–6)
Akkadian has changed radically due to language contact, and these changes have indeed been noted time and again in the literature. So are foreign influences detected in other languages, such as Hebrew or Aramaic. Still, this vast recognition of the effects of language contact has usually not advanced beyond mere description, pointing out the possible

influences on explications, and setting forth hypotheses and theories (cf. also Huehnergard 1996: 268-271). One significant exception to this situation is Bauer's attempt to explain the emergence of (ancient) Hebrew as a mixed language (Bauer and Leander 1922: §2; cf. Sáenz-Badillos 1993: 54-5).

Stephen A. Kaufman was assigned to review studies of language contact in the Ancient Near East. At the beginning of his lecture, Kaufman expressed discomfort at the fact that he was tagged (only by Israeli scholars?) as a language contact person, a stamp obviously placed on him due to his famous work on the contact between Akkadian and Aramaic (Kaufman 1974). Yet, Kaufman testifies that he had accepted this task precisely because he was still interested in following developments in the study of language contact. The reason Kaufman was assigned to deal with contacts among the ancient Semitic languages was precisely his keen interest in and contribution to this field. The point is, as mentioned above, that the domain of language contact as an area that merits general and theoretical examination remains a desideratum.

The paper opens with some remarks about the possible origins of Semitic languages or Afro-Asiatic in a contact situation proto-stratum. Kaufman then proceeds to survey research done in the various branches of Semitic, starting with contact situations between Semitic and non-Semitic languages, mainly Sumerian-Akkadian, Greek on Aramaic and Hebrew, Persian on Aramaic. He then proceeds to inner-Semitic contact situations: Ugarit-Akkadian, Amarna Akkadian, Akkadian Aramaic, Aramaic on Hebrew, possible Canaanite influences on literary Old Aramaic, Aramaic on the Arabic lexicon. Kaufman ends his discussion with some notes on inner-language situations, i.e., diglossia and the contact between formal and colloquial speech. Kaufman was unable to expand on his talk for this publication and asked that it be included in the basically oral format it was given. For this reason, coverage of work done in this field has unfortunately remained somewhat incomplete. For example, his view regarding the prehistory of Afro-Asiatic and Semitic requires more elaboration, and it is hoped that Kaufman will publish a treatise on this intriguing subject. Also, we would like to hear why Kaufman feels "discomfited with the presuppositions underlying the study of the linguistic code used in West Semitizing Amarna tablets." I must express frustration at the fact that a methodological paper of mine has not yet been published, 14(!) years after its conception (Izre'el forthcoming); still, I can refer the interested reader to my concise grammar of Canaano-Akkadian published recently (Izre'el 1998), a description based upon these methodological premises.

The situation is quite different with research in language contact in the modern Semitic languages. This is the topic of Olga Kapeliuk's paper, divided into four parts: Ethio-Semitic, Neo-Aramaic, Israeli Hebrew and spoken Arabic. As Kapeliuk notes, there are hardly any general or theoretical works on language contact in the Modern Semitic world, but the issue of language contact has been dealt with quite extensively with regard to the individual language or language clusters, which do lean on theoretical premises. During the discussion that followed Kapeliuk's presentation at the conference, a rather heated debate came up regarding theories of the emergence of Israeli Hebrew, and whether the changes it suffered justify a change in its definition as a Semitic language. As Gideon Goldenberg has reiterated, long-standing arguments defining a language as Semitic lean not on a statistical measurement of old and new features, but on its genetic relationships. The latter are recognizable mainly via morphological traits and core vocabulary. As Meillet wisely suggested long ago, genetic origins can be traced as long as morphology remains unchanged. Once all morphological traits change, the original proto-language can no longer be demonstrated (Meillet 1914 = 1975: 76–109).

REFERENCES

Bauer, H. and P. Leander. 1922. *Historische Grammatik der hebräischen Sprache*. Halle.

Foster, Benjamin R. 1993. *Before the Muses: An Anthology of Akkadian Literature*. Two volumes. Bethesda, Maryland.

Huehnergard, John. 1996. New Directions in the Study of Semitic Linguistics. In: Jerrold S. Cooper and Glenn M. Schwartz. *The Study of the Ancient Near East in the Twenty-First Century: The William Foxwell Albright Centennial Conference*. Winona Lake, Indiana. 251–272.

Izre'el, Shlomo. 1998. *Canaano-Akkadian*. (Languages of the World / Materials, 82.) München.

Izre'el, Shlomo. Forthcoming. Some Methodological Requisites for the Study of the Amarna Jargon: Notes on the Essence of That Language. In: Barry J. Beitzel and Gordon D. Young (eds.). *Amarna in Retrospect: A Centennial Celebration*. Winona Lake, Indiana.

Kaufman, Stephen A. 1974. *The Akkadian Influences on Aramaic*. (Assyriological Studies, 19.) Chicago.

Meillet, Antoine. 1914. Le problème de la parenté des languages. *Scientia (Rivista di scienza)*, vol. XV, no. XXXV-3.

Meillet, Antoine. 1975. *Linguistique historique et linguistique générale*.

(Collection linguistique publié par La Société de Linguistique de Paris, 8.) Paris. (Originally published: 1921–1938.)

Reiner, Erica. 1986. "Why Do You Cuss Me?" *Proceedings of the American Philosophical Society* 130: 1–6.

Sáenz-Badillos, Angel. 1993. *A History of the Hebrew Language.* Translated by John Elwolde. Cambridge.

LANGUAGES IN CONTACT:
THE ANCIENT NEAR EAST

STEPHEN A. KAUFMAN

I have long noticed that once Israeli colleagues type-cast you as a specialist in a certain field, you can never escape the label. Hence my role today, based on research I did almost thirty years ago (see Kaufman 1974). Permit me before I begin, then, since I am not currently actively involved in this particular area of research, to apologize in advance for any serious omissions or oversights. I do maintain a speculative interest in this field, though. So many of my remarks today will reflect issues that I have been thinking about for a rather long time.

The twentieth century has been a very productive one in the area of the study of languages in contact. Indeed it is a field that scarcely existed prior to this century. We have already heard from Prof. Kapeliuk how the modern Semitic languages have fared in this study. What I would like to deal with here is not "what has the twentieth century wrought" in this field but rather where we stand now and what do Semitic linguists have the potential to learn from and contribute to the study of "languages in contact" for the next century?

As usual in historical linguistics, there are three different directions from which to approach our subject: typological, chronological, and geographic. I shall attempt to combine them here into an "outside → in" sequence, i.e. starting from the most distant connections and moving to the closest.

PREHISTORY

One of the most important periods in the history of the Semitic languages — and one deserving of a substantial increase in our awareness of the possibilities of language contact at that time — is in the proto-stratum. As is surely the case with most language phyla and families, we should no longer imagine them to be descended from a single, limited common proto-language, but rather languages and dialects in contact within an area. Substrate languages, borrowing, and creolization all have a role to play in the development of language whenever peoples and their languages move from place to place and have contact with one another over generations and centuries. The latter two — borrowing and creolization — of course, have generated an explosion of interest among linguists during the last generation (see especially Sebba 1997). Nonetheless, the current, generally-accepted understanding of the nature of Afro-Asiatic ignores this uncomfortable but central contribution to our knowledge provided by real-world languages.

My imaginary picture of the early history of the languages we commonly refer to as Afro-Asiatic is this: a core linguistic area of proto-Afro-Asiatic (itself almost certainly a cousin to proto-Indo-European) — probably centered in or near the Nile Delta — from which a central core of Egyptian per se advanced typologically in one direction while Berber and Semitic, western and eastern peripheral dialects respectively, moved as peripherals together in another typological direction. Chadic and Cushitic/Omotic resulted from contact situations (undoubtedly often repeated in both cases) with various African language groups. Semitic for its part was early on in close contact, presumably along the north-eastern Mediterranean littoral, with primitive Indo-European and was particularly strongly influenced by the latter in the area of vocabulary. Again, determining whether, at each stage and in each area, substrates, simple borrowing, or complete creolization were involved will never be achievable, but I would not be surprised to learn that Semitic resulted from a rather intense instance of language contact.

(As the reader can tell, by and large I tend to be highly sympathetic to the kind of new approach to the history of Semitic advocated by L. Edzard in his recent monograph [Edzard 1998] but unknown to me at the time of the lecture).

Let us now turn to specific and more demonstrable instances of language contact.

PRE-SUMERIAN MESOPOTAMIAN

I have nothing to report in this area. Isolated attempts to relate Sumerian to other language isolates (such as Ural-Altaic, Japanese or Korean) cannot be said to have born any edible fruit, although the Ural-Altaic hypothesis is still widely discussed, especially, it seems, on the WWW! (See the bibliography.)

Sumerian-Akkadian

This area is particularly ripe for research. Although it is widely recognized that there was a great deal of (undoubtedly mutual) influence in the areas of lexicon and syntax in particular, even the study of these phenomena has been less thorough than we would like. But the study of the impact of Sumerian on the morphology of the verbal system of Akkadian is just in its infancy. It took its first steps in the 1960's but is not yet close to hitting its stride. Moreover, the discovery of Eblaic as a sister language of Akkadian — if not a dialect thereof — adds a whole new layer of complexity to the fascinating subject of the interrelationship of Akkadian and Sumerian.

Steve Lieberman's complicated work on Sumerian Loanwords in Old Babylonian Akkadian (Lieberman 1977) was cut short by his untimely death — before he could elaborate on the complexities of his work to us. The plethora of Sumerian realia loanwords is evident on nearly every page of the modern Akkadian dictionaries, however.

Everyone admits that the verb-final word order of standard Akkadian is due to the influence of the Sumerian substratum, a type of influence more recently attested in the case of many of the modern Ethiopian languages due to Cushitic influence. But whereas, in the case of Ethiopian, scholars readily recognize the presence of other Cushitic features (beyond that of word order) in Semitic speech, in the case of Akkadian, the overwhelming influence of Sumerian on its grammar has yet to be appreciated. Undoubtedly this is due in no small part to our relatively poor understanding of Sumerian. Only in the past couple of decades has our understanding of the grammar of the Sumerian verbal system reached a relatively sophisticated level, and it is precisely in the area of the verbal system where that influence was strongest. In particular, most of these phenomena involve "grammaticalization" one way or another, a particularly "hot" topic of linguistics over the past decade (Bybee 1994, Diewald 1997, Heine 1991, Pagliuca 1994, Traugott 1991).

Perfect

A peculiar feature of the Akkadian verbal system as compared to the rest of the Semitic languages is the "perfect," *iptaras* form — originally a relative tense/aspect that developed into a simple past tense in late Akkadian dialects. This is obviously a case of grammaticalization of the lexical *-ta-* infix of the reflexive/reciprocal stem, yet comparative Semitic grammarians have been remarkably silent on this topic, so that this is thus a case of grammaticalization not widely known to general linguists. Though such grammaticalization can happen in any language — and the movement from passive/reflexive constructions to perfect aspect to past tense is a widely known development in language, of course — it seems certain that the impetus in this case was the similar bifunctionality of the Sumerian verbal prefix *ba-*.

Bisyllabic present

The bisyllabic present tense form of Akkadian — *iparras* — is widely regarded as a survival from proto-Semitic, in light of similar forms in South Arabian/Ethiopic and, supposedly, in Libyco-Berber. Space prohibits a detailed discussion of this material at this juncture, but I believe that this is not a Proto-Semitic phenomenon at all, but yet another example of grammaticalization of a lexical stem under Sumerian influence; i.e. the D-stem — its common Semitic function indicating multiplicity/repetition of action for active verbs — grammaticalized into an aspect form connoting repetition. The Sumerian parallel is in the use of the reduplicated verbal stem of many verbs to form the present tense and, more importantly, to form transitive forms from intransitive ones, precisely the major other function of the Semitic D-stem.

Ventive

Another peculiarity of Akkadian grammar is the ventive verbal ending — *am* in the singular — indicating movement toward. Though often sought after in other Semitic languages (see Fassberg 1994), no suggestions for its identification there have been at all compelling. Morphologically this ending consists of the dative pronominal suffix of the first person singular, alone when the direction is toward the speaker or the indirect object is not a pronoun, prefixed to other pronominal endings when the direction is toward another pronominal indirect object. Directionality, of course, is a central concern of the ergative Sumerian verbal system, the Sumerian conjugational prefix *mu-* indicating involvement by or beneficence to the speaker. The key here again is the identity between this morpheme and the first person pronominal suffix, as in Akkadian.

Greek on Aramaic and Hebrew

Recent decades have seen some direct contributions to this area of interest, but much more remains to be done. One thing that has provoked my interest in particular — due to the pioneering lexicographic work of

Michael Sokoloff on Jewish Palestinian Aramaic and my own involvement with the Comprehensive Aramaic Lexicon Project — has been a new appreciation for the date of the overwhelming majority of Greek loanwords and foreign words in Aramaic texts. As a student I naturally assumed — and this seems to be the general assumption of most scholars and scholarly works (applying to the subject the same lack of thought that I did as a graduate student) — that the bulk of such loans occurred in Hellenistic or Roman times. In fact, it now appears rather that it is not until the Byzantine Period that this kind of extreme linguistic interference is to be found. This is a datum of no little import for the dating of many classic Jewish texts in particular.

Other

The Late Bronze Age: Hittite/Hurrian/Mitannian/Egyptian etc. vocabulary in Akkadian and other Semitic languages.

Long overdue is a new assessment of the phonology and typology of Ancient Near Eastern culture words of foreign origin in Late Bronze Age Semitic, and how the linguistic evidence all ties in with the textual and archaeological sources to extend our picture of the history of trade, culture, technology, and the like.

Persian on Aramaic

Formal Achaemenid Aramaic (Reichsaramäisch or Official Aramaic) was strongly influenced by the Persian dialects of the empire that it served. Since this type of Aramaic in turn served as the model for all of subsequent literary Aramaic (Standard Literary Aramaic), it is important to understand its underpinnings. But the most recent book on Achaemenid Aramaic (Folmer 1995) does not deal with lexical interference at all and hardly touches on grammatical interference in any significant way.

In addition to Persian, we also are in need of a more focused study on the foreign elements in Egyptian Aramaic materials in general — including Egyptian, Greek, and Akkadian. A new concordance/prosopography to these materials by B. Porten and J. Lund (in press, Comprehensive Aramaic Lexicon Project) should help facilitate such work.

INNER-SEMITIC

Inter-language

Levantine North-West Semitic and Akkadian during the Late Bronze Age.

Ugarito-Akkadian

The Akkadian of Ugarit has been thoroughly published and heavily analyzed during the past generation — primarily by the students of Moran and Rainey — some of whom are in this room (Sivan 1984, Huehnergard 1989).

Amarna Akkadian

The Amarna material, published much earlier, however, is a lot more interesting but perhaps a lot less satisfying in terms of the treatment it has received. Beginning with Moran (Moran 1950) and ending with Rainey's massive study of the subject (Rainey 1996), much of both the theory and the specifics of the study of this data leaves me with a sour aftertaste. I am uneasy with the direction the study of the volitive modality has taken and equally discomfited with the presuppositions underlying the study of the system of linguistic code used in the West Semitizing Amarna tablets.

Akkadian Aramaic

Since my own work on the influences of Akkadian on Aramaic (Kaufman 1974), there has been relatively little new of import to report on — except for the fascinating bilingual inscription from Tell Fekheriyeh (see Kaufman 1982), which has given us a more direct view of the kind of mutual interrelationship I examined in that volume — specifically, detailed evidence for mutual interdependence in the areas of syntax, lexicon, and literary style.

Aramaic on Hebrew

The relationship between Hebrew and Aramaic is an extremely complex one — surely one of the most complex of all of the Semitic languages. Up to the first third of the 20th century our knowledge of Aramaic came from texts and dialects having undergone profound changes in the East — quite different looking from Hebrew in many respects. New finds of older texts have demonstrated beyond a doubt what we should have assumed anyway: that in fact "Aramaic" was just a part of a North-West Semitic speech continuum (Garr 1985).

Deir 'Alla: The Balaam inscription serves as a kind of counter-example to the overuse of "contact" to explain things. The several volumes of studies devoted to the issue of whether this text is in Aramaic, Hebrew, or Canaanite (in particular cf. the conference volume [Hoftijzer and van der Kooij 1991]) demonstrate — unfortunately — that there is still a strong tradition of outmoded linguistic categorization pervading the field of Ancient Near Eastern philology. The language of Deir 'Alla is what it is; it is what it should be, something in between Hebrew, Aramaic, and Ammonite. What it is not is an example of linguistic interference.

"Canaanite" Aramaic

On the literary level, in the middle decades of the 20th century it was commonplace to talk about the "Canaanite" influences on Old Aramaic literary language and style as a way of accounting for the fact that such Aramaic texts tend to be more similar in many ways to Phoenician and/or Hebrew than they are to later Aramaic. I think that it is fair to say that this view has finally and appropriately passed from the scene. Canaanite is definable only in terms of something else, i.e., Aramaic, and the Canaanite-Aramaic dichotomy — (if one ever existed) — could hardly have been valid in the second millennium; so neither Ugaritic nor Eblaitic can justifiably be classified as Canaanite.

Aramaic on the Arabic lexicon

Given the advances that have occurred in each lexical area independently during the 20th century, this is an area that is undoubtedly ready for some new studies (but I cannot speak knowledgeably about it).

INNER-LANGUAGE

Diglossia and the contact between formal and colloquial speech

There has been rather fruitful research in this area during the last few decades both in the area of Hebrew (Rendsburg 1990, 1990a) and Aramaic, and, of course, continuing studies on the situation in Arabic that began the entire discussion (see the general overview in Fernández 1993). In Hebrew and Aramaic the discussion has often concentrated on the relationship between synchronic diglossic situations and the development of the later formal dialects, i.e. Late Biblical Hebrew and its relationship to earlier dialects and the development of the various types of standard literary Aramaic.

A very interesting topic for research in this area would be to study what is the time "lag" between formal and spoken language in the ancient Near Eastern world. My guess is that it is usually around two centuries. Also, just how does the formal language infuse into the spoken? This has clearly happened repeatedly throughout the history of the Near East. Undoubtedly there are many paths of diffusion, but they need to be delineated more carefully.

Another related area on the front burner of research is the awareness of language "contact" by ancient authors and its reflection in their literary compositions. The solution to many of the problems of difficult biblical books such as Job lies in this direction (see the articles of Kaufman 1988 and Rendsburg 1990a, 1995), not — as was common in the middle of the century — in the adduction of Ugaritic or Phoenician parallels.

I hope that I have demonstrated that the area of ancient Semitic languages in contact is a very fertile one. It is a field not only worthy of cultivation, but one whose produce must be widely shared with students of general linguistics.

REFERENCE LIST

Web page. URL: http://www2.4dcomm.com/millenia/uaetymbx.html.

Autran, Charles. 1925. *Sumérien et Indo-Européen: L'aspect morphologique de la question*. Paris.

Ball, Charles James. 1913. *Chinese and Sumerian*. London.

Bobula, Ida Miriam. 1982. *Origin of the Hungarian Nation*. Problems Behind the Iron Curtain Series, No. 3. Astor, FL.

Bouda, Karl. 1938. *Die Beziehungen des Sumerischen zum Baskischen, Westkaukasichen und Tibetischen*. Neudruck der Ausgabe 1938 ed. Assyriology Monographs. Leipzig.

Bybee, Joan L., Revere D. Perkins, and William Pagliuca. 1994. *The Evolution of Grammar: Tense, Aspect, and Modality in the Languages of the World*. Chicago.

Csoke, Sándor. 1970. *Szumer-Magyar Egyeztető Szótár Kézirat Helyett*. Buenos Aires.

Diewald, Gabriele. 1997. *Grammatikalisierung: Eine Einführung in Sein und Werden Grammatischer Formen*. Germanistische Arbeitshefte 36. Tübingen.

Edzard, Lutz. 1998. *Polygenesis, Convergence, and Entropy: an Alternative Model of Linguistic Evolution Applied to Semitic Linguistics*. Wiesbaden.

Fassberg, Steven Ellis. 1994. *Sugyot Be-Taḥbir Ha-Miqra*. Sidrat Sefarim Le-Ḥeqer Ha-Miqra Mi-Yesodo Shel S. Sh. Peri. Jerusalem.

Fernández, Mauro. 1993. *Diglossia: a Comprehensive Bibliography, 1960–1990 and Supplements*. Amsterdam Studies in the Theory and History of Linguistic Science. Series V, Library & Information Sources in Linguistics, v. 23. Amsterdam, Philadelphia.

Folmer, M. L. 1995. *The Aramaic Language in the Achaemenid Period: a Study in Linguistic Variation.* Orientalia Lovaniensia Analecta 68. Leuven.

Garr, W. Randall. 1985. *Dialect Geography of Syria-Palestine, 1000–586 B.C.E.* Philadelphia.

Heine, Bernd, Ulrike Claudi, and Friederike Hünnemeyer. 1991. *Grammaticalization a Conceptual Framework.* Chicago.

Hoftijzer, J., and G. van der Kooij. 1991. *The Balaam Text From Deir 'Alla Re-Evaluated. Proceedings of the International Symposium Held at Leiden, 21–24 August 1989.* Leiden, New York.

Hopper, Paul J., and Elizabeth Closs Traugott. 1993. *Grammaticalization.* Cambridge Textbooks in Linguistics. Cambridge (England), New York.

Huehnergard, John. 1989. *The Akkadian of Ugarit.* Harvard Semitic Studies no. 34. Atlanta.

Jarvi, Pentti K. 1978. *Where Did the Sumerians Go? and Their Relationship With Suomians (Finns).* S.l.

Kaufman, Stephen A. 1974. *The Akkadian Influences on Aramaic.* The Oriental Institute of the University of Chicago. Assyriological Studies no. 19. Chicago.

Kaufman, Stephen A. 1988. The Classification of the Northwest Semitic Dialects of the Biblical Period and some Implications Thereof. *Proc. of the Ninth World Congress of Jewish Studies. D. Panel Sessions.* Jerusalem, 41–57.

Kaufman, Stephen A. 1992. Reflections on the Assyrian Aramaic Bilingual From Tell Fakhariyah. *MAARAV* 3: 137ff.

Kaulins, Andis. 1977. *The Baltic Origin of the Indo-European Languages and Peoples: an Inquiry into the History of Mankind and Its Languages.* 1st ed. S.l

Lessau, Donald A. 1994. *A Dictionary of Grammaticalization.* Bochum-Essener Beiträge zur Sprachwandelforschung Bd. 21. Bochum.

Lieberman, Stephen J. 1977. *The Sumerian Loanwords in Old-Babylonian Akkadian.* Harvard Semitic Series v. 22. Missoula, Mont.

Moran, William L. 1950. *A Syntactical Study of the Dialect of Byblos as Reflected in the Amarna Tablets.* Ph.D. dissertation, Johns Hopkins University. To be published in William L. Moran, *Amarna Studies: Collected Writings.* Harvard Semitic Studies 49. Winona Lake.

Nagy, Sándor. 1973. *The Forgotten Cradle of the Hungarian Culture.* Toronto.

Pagliuca, William. 1994. *Perspectives on Grammaticalization.*

Amsterdam Studies in the Theory and History of Linguistic Science v. 109. Amsterdam, Philadelphia.

Rainey, Anson F. 1996. *Canaanite in the Amarna Tablets: a Linguistic Analysis of the Mixed Dialect Used by Scribes From Canaan.* Handbuch der Orientalistik. Erste Abteilung, Der Nahe und Mittlere Osten 25. Bd. Leiden, New York.

Rendsburg, Gary. 1990. *Diglossia in Ancient Hebrew.* American Oriental Series v. 72. New Haven, Conn.

Rendsburg, Gary. 1990a. *Linguistic Evidence for the Northern Origin of Selected Psalms.* Monograph Series (Society of Biblical Literature) no. 43. Atlanta.

Rendsburg, Gorg. 1995. Linguistic variation and the "foreign" factor in the Hebrew Bible. *Israel Oriental Studies* XV: 177–190.

Sebba, Mark. 1997. *Contact Languages, Pidgins and Creoles.* Modern Linguistics Series. New York.

Sivan, Daniel. 1984. *Grammatical Analysis and Glossary of the Northwest Semitic Vocables in Akkadian Texts of the 15th–13th C. b.C. from Canaan and Syria.* Alter Orient und Altes Testament Bd. 214. Neukirchen-Vluyn.

Traugott, Elizabeth Closs, and Bernd Heine. 1991. *Approaches to Grammaticalization.* Typological Studies in Language v. 19. Amsterdam, Philadelphia.

LANGUAGES IN CONTACT:
THE CONTEMPORARY SEMITIC WORLD

OLGA KAPELIUK

In his contribution on mono- and multilingualism to the encyclopedic volume *Le Langage* published under the supervision of A. Martinet (1968: 648), Uriel Weinreich writes "En dépit de l'importance et de la fréquence des situations plurilingues, il y a une tendance courante, parmi les linguistes même, à considérer l'unilinguisme comme la règle et le plurilinguisme comme quelque chose d'exceptionnel." And, as a matter of fact, the dominant schools of modern linguistics — the historical and comparative school in the 19th century, and the structural and generative disciplines in the 20th century — allow very little room or none at all to the effects of language contacts on the evolution of languages or on their structure on the synchronic level. Contact-induced language change should be of particular interest to historical linguists, but the latter have traditionally been prejudiced in favor of internal explanations and resorted to external explanations only when all efforts to find internal motivations failed (Thomason & Kaufman 1988: 57). Like all dogmas that aspire to provide a uniform explanation of all concrete facts and, at the same time, provide a strict *modus operandi* for their analysis, the modern linguistic doctrines tend to disregard motivations and mechanisms which can be triggered by causes of a more diversified and accidental character and distort the ideal image. Such, however, happen to be the historical, sociological, economic and cultural facts which, together with the extreme diversity of encounters between different languages, produce what is defined as contact-induced language change.

However, since the beginning of this century, growing interest in unwritten languages from the American, African and Australian continents has led to attempts to produce genetic classifications without the possibility of resorting to written records from earlier stages of the languages under investigation. This created an imperative need to distinguish between what was inherited and what was acquired from other languages in contact situations. The constantly increasing quantity of new data about tens or even hundreds of hitherto uninvestigated languages and about most diversified linguistic situations, together with new fields of interest such

307

as immigrant language behavior, pidgins and creoles, areal linguistics, multilingualism and bilingualism, dialect contacts, second language acquisition etc. lead to systematization and crystallization of a theoretical framework for the exploration of the effects of language contacts. The best known work on this subject is U. Weinreich's book *Languages in Contact* (1953) but many other linguists, especially in the United States, contributed immensely in providing tools for a systematic analysis of language contacts. A recent work, *Language Contact, Creolization and Genetic Linguistics* by S. G. Thomason and T. Kaufman (1988), provides useful guidelines and unanmbiguous terminology that, when used with a certain degree of flexibility, may also be applied to language contacts in modern Semitic, as they are reflected in the relevant linguistic literature of the 20th century.

During the last hundred years, three main factors have considerably facilitated the study of the impact of foreign speech on living Semitic. The first of these was a better knowledge of ancient written records of what may be considered the ancestor, or a close variant of the ancestor, of every Semitic language that has survived until today. This made it possible to compare different stages of the language and identify changes which could be attributed to foreign language interference. Normally, convergent developments in all the sub-groups of the family, or in most of them, could be interpreted as regular evolution, whereas deviations from common evolutionary patterns are more readily examined in the language contact perspective. Second: since the history of the Middle East is relatively well known since most ancient times, and the African regions with the best historical documentation are those inhabited by speakers of Semitic languages, situations conducive to language interference could be deduced from historical material. The third factor consists of the restricted number of living Semitic languages and the relative ease with which they may be identified as belonging to one genetic group. Even in extreme cases of language intereference at the periphery of the Semitic area, like in the case of the Gurage dialects in southern Ethiopia, the Jewish Neo-Aramaic dialects of Azerbaijan, or an Arabic pidgin in southern Sahara, linguists with some experience could unravel the basic Semitic elements behind any foreign disguise. It was also from the periphery that such 19th century scholars as F. Praetorius for Ethio-Semitic and Cushitic[1] and Th. Nöldeke for Neo-Aramaic and Iranian[2] initiated the study of language interference in Semitic. Foreign interference figures in all the

---

[1]   For bibliographical references see Leslau 1988a note 2.

[2]   Nöldeke, Theodor. *Grammatik der neusyrischen Sprache am Urmia-See und in Kurdistan.* Leipzig. 1868, XVII–XXXVIII.

other Semitic languages as well. It ranges from restricted borrowing due to casual contacts, through heavy lexical borrowing and deep structural change as a result of language shift of whole segments of population, and up to some examples of pidginization and creolization. Surprisingly enough, the language that has most often been described as an extreme case of language interference, namely Modern Hebrew, is actually one of the least affected by the action of foreign substrates or adstrates, as far as its grammatical structure is concerned.

The present survey is divided into chapters on Ethio-Semitic, Neo-Aramaic, Israeli Hebrew and spoken Arabic. There are almost no major works on language contacts in contemporary Semitic, but there are many articles on this subject and many grammars discuss it in special paragraphs. Not all these numerous publications could be cited, but an effort was made to mention at least one publication per author.[3] The reader may easily complete the information by consulting the extensive bibliographical lists that accompany most of the articles quoted. We may add that language contacts in the domain of Semitic continue to be investigated by individual linguists while the Johannes Gutenberg University in Mainz recently started an ambitious research project under the title "Kulturelle und sprachliche Kontakte in Nordostafrika/Westasien" which, without any doubt, will carry this branch of linguistic investigation well into the twenty-first century. Also certain recently created bodies such as the JIDA or the CIIL continue to manifest special interest in language contacts.

ETHIO-SEMITIC

Of all the sub-families of Semitic that are still spoken, Ethio-Semitic is the one in which the effects of language contacts were the most thoroughly investigated by linguists during this century. This is not surprising, as this group underwent quite spectacular changes under the impact of the Cushitic languages, which were spoken in the Horn of Africa at the time of the Semitic immigration and continue to be spoken to this day in adjacent territories or in enclaves inside the Semitic speaking areas in Ethiopia. Arabic and European languages also influenced Ethio-Semitic, but only the vocabulary. They did not affect the structure of the language, as did Cushitic. Semitists exploring Cushitic language intereference in the modern languages of Ethiopia gained considerably from the growing interest in the Cushitic and Nilo-Saharan languages

---

[3]   Publications that have appeared between the time of the submission of this paper and the time of proofreading could have been incorporated only at random.

during the last decades. The amount of information on these languages increased significantly, allowing a better understanding of their impact on Semitic. The exploration of the non-Semitic languages of Ethiopia is probably the most active branch of Ethiopian linguistics today and is conducted both by western linguists and Ethiopian graduates of the Institute of Languages of the Addis Ababa University. Extensive study of the Ethiopian languages and the contribution of young Ethiopians to the research owe much to the efforts, as initiator and organizer, of Lionel M. Bender, who edited three basic collective works: *Language in Ethiopia* (1976 — with several collaborators), *The Non-Semitic Languages of Ethiopia* (1976) and *Nilo-Saharan Language Studies* (1983). In these volumes the issue of language contact received special attention. There is no doubt that the study of contacts between Semitic and Cushitic was favored by the longstanding tradition established nearly a century and a half ago by F. Praetorius[4] according to which many of the linguists working on the languages of Ethiopia divide their time between Semitic and Cushitic. On the other hand, study of contacts between Semitic and Cushitic produced some descriptions of the influence of Semitic on Cushitic (Zaborski 1976: 81–84; id. 1975: 171–172 for bibliography).

Significant traces of Cushitic influence had already been detected in Ge'ez vocabulary (Appleyard 1978), phonology and syntax. In W. Leslau's *Comparative Dictionary of Ge'ez* (1987; id. 1988a) every entry with a possible relationship to a Cushitic lexeme includes a note to that effect and a distinction may be established between words belonging to the common Hamito-Semitic stock and those which have to be considered as more recent borrowings. These loanwords refer mainly to the flora and fauna and artifacts characteristic of Ethiopia (Gragg 1991). Certain structural changes in Ge'ez phonology and syntax have also been attributed to early Cushitic influence. These include the introduction of labio-velar phonemes (Leslau 1988a: 61); certain changes in word order and the possibility of preposing the relative clause to its head noun; the frequent use of the gerund (Kapeliuk 1997a); and the extremely important role played by the relative verb, especially in cleft-sentences (Kapeliuk 1985). Later, with more and more Cushitic speaking segments of population shifting to the language of the Semitic settlers, and with an abrupt decrease in Semitic immigration following the rise of Islam, the impact of the local languages was considerably strengthened, resulting in the cushiticizing "allure générale" of modern Ethio-Semitic (Cohen M. 1931: 45).

It is generally admitted that the Cushitic languages which influenced Ethio-Semitic both as substrates and as adstrates are Bilin, Bedja, the

---

[4]   In his frequent brief notices in *ZDMG* and *BA* during the 1880's and 1890's.

Agaw group and Afar-Saho in the northern domain of Geʻez, Tigre and Tigrinya, and the Agaw and Sidamo groups, as well as Oromo and Somali as adstrates in the domain of Amharic, Gurage, Harari as well as in Argobba and Gafat, now extinct (Leslau 1945a; id. 1952; id. 1959a; id. 1962; Plazikowsky — Brauner 1950–1951; Appleyard 1977; Hudson 1994). Cushitic language interference was stronger in the south than in the north. Regarding vocabulary, the part of Cushitic is manifest in all the modern languages. Thus, for instance, proceeding from his *Etymological Dictionary of Gurage* (1979), W. Leslau identified 1300 Cushitic loanwords out of a total of 6500 roots, that is, 20% of the lexicon (id. 1986). The overwhelming majority of the loanwords were nouns, with only 130 verbs, including verbal compounds with the verb "to say," one of the most conspicuous common features of the Ethiopian area (Ferguson 1976). Semantically, the borrowings from Cushitic refer mainly to the physical environment, to the local flora and fauna and to such cultural subjects as agricultural products, breeding, food, clothes and habitation. Specific Cushitic terms for patterns of social organization as well as beliefs and superstitions also entered the Semitic languages unchanged.

The structural imprint of Cushitic on Ethio-Semitic is equally significant. It is discussed in some detail in Thomason & Kaufman (1988: 129–135) as an example of what they classify as "Moderate to heavy interference," which may be attributed to the effects of language shift but in which enough inherited grammatical patterns remain to show that genetic continuity has not been clearly disrupted. It seems that most changes in the structure of modern Ethio-Semitic occurred long ago, because they are already documented in the most ancient text preserved in any of these languages, namely in an Amharic text from the 13/14th century (Richter 1999). In phonology, Cushitic influence has been associated with the incorporation in Ethio-Semitic of new phonemes such as the labio-velars k^w, q^w, g^w, x^w, the prepalatals č, ǧ, ž, š, č̣, ň, and *y* as the palatalization of *l*, and with the ejective pronunciation of the Semitic emphatic consonants (Leslau 1945a; id. 1959a; id. 1962), though the latter has been considered by some as an original feature of ancient Hamito-Semitic (Dolgopolsky 1977). In the domain of morphology, despite an exaggerated tendency to attribute to Cushitic certain suffixes that may easily be included among Semitic innovations (Leslau 1945a; Moreno 1948), there are such features as consonant reduplication in nouns, adjectives and verbs for marking multiplicity or fragmentation, which definitely represent an areal feature. But the most significant and interesting changes, which Cushitic speakers shifting in masses to the dominant language must have introduced into Semitic, belong to syntax. In his article "The Ethiopian language area," Ch.

Ferguson (1976: 75) enumerates eighteen common features characteristic of Ethio-Semitic and Cushitic but absent from a Nilo-Saharan language, chosen for comparison's sake, and from English. These features include SOV word order, subordinate clause preceding the main clause, the use of converbs and of postpositions, "quoting clauses," etc. Other important similarities, such as the nominal status of the relative verb (Cerulli 1934–37) or the diffusion of cleft-sentences in the whole area (Appleyard 1989; Kapeliuk 1985: 191–194; id. 1988: 103–109) also belong to this category. The connection to Cushitic is perhaps less evident at first sight in such cases as the creation of a future tense in some Gurage dialects (Raz 1991) or the use of the conjunction of coordination in main verb negation and in the relative particle used before the imperfect in Amharic, but these too have been interpreted as Cushitic calques that penetrated the Semitic system (Hetzron 1973; id. 1975). It should, however, be stressed that some authors, such as R. Hetzron, are not entirely clear on whether similar structural phenomena in Ethio-Semitic and Cushitic should be considered as a common Hamito-Semitic heritage or as the result of language borrowing between two coterritorial living language groups.

Another language that has left an indelible imprint on Ethio-Semitic, but only as far as the lexicon is concerned, is Arabic. Borrowing words from Arabic goes back as far as Ge'ez. Throughout its long history as a spoken and as a literary language, Ge'ez was exposed to the influence of Arabic. Arabic speakers constantly migrated to Ethiopia. They found commercial opportunities, established political entities and converted local inhabitants to Islam. Moreover, from the 13th century onwards, religious Ethiopian writings, though all of them Christian, were translated from Arabic (Leslau 1958). When the translators had a problem finding a Ge'ez equivalent for an Arabic word, one possible solution was to borrow the term as it was, sometimes explaining it in glosses (Kropp 1986). The Arabic loanwords often refer to religious subjects as well as to superstitions. Arabic words and expressions are often used in magical texts (Cohen D. 1985; Kane 1983).

In modern Ethio-Semitic, Arabic loanwords are even more numerous because part of the speakers of Ethio-Semitic were converted to Islam. Another reason is that since time immemorial most of the merchants and peddlers in the region were of Arab origin. We are particularly well informed about the contribution of Arabic to modern Ethiopic thanks to W. Leslau's special interest in this subject. In his series of articles on Arabic loanwords, he dedicated at least one full study to each Ethio-Semitic language, namely Tigre (1956a; 1981), Tigrinya (1956b), Amharic (1957a; 1988b; also Brzuski 1983), Harari (1956c), Gurage (1956d) and Argobba (1957b). These articles were later gathered in one volume (Leslau 1990). Leslau also provides a full list of Arabic loanwords in the indices to his *Etymological Dictionary of Harari* (1963: 176–186) and to the *Etymological Dictionary of Gurage* (1979: 757–761) and he further explores these loanwords in his analysis of Harari (1959b) and Amharic vocabularies (1964). The Arabic origin of loanwords is also indicated in Thomas Kane's masterly dictionaries of Amharic (1990) and of Tigrinya (2000). While the presence of Arabic loanwords is particularly conspicuous in the languages spoken by Muslims, the Arabic element is quite considerable and well integrated in the predominantly Christian languages (Amharic, Tigrinya) (Titov 1991). In the Amharic dialect of Wollo, whose speakers are predominantly Muslims, words and expressions borrowed from Arabic replace several common terms used by Christians, e.g.: *kähadi* "infidel" is replaced by *zindiq* etc. (Amsalu 1991). The highest proportion of borrowings from Arabic is to be found in Harari, a language spoken exclusively by Muslims in a city which for many centuries served as an important center of Muslim learning. A vocabulary count showed that out of 2200 Harari roots, 607 were borrowed from Arabic, that is, about 27.5% (Leslau 1959b).

With the exception of purely religious and literary vocabulary, the Arabic loanwords entered the Ethio-Semitic languages from spoken dialects brought to Ethiopia from Egypt, Sudan and the Arabian Peninsula. Phonetically they were adapted to the local pronunciation (emphatics became ejectives, Arabic *ṣ* is rendered by *s* and Arabic *ḥ* by *k*). In morphology, both nouns and verbs were incorporated in the local system (e.g., Tigrinya *fənğal* "cup" — broken plural: *fənğawəlti*); the verbal roots act as bases for a full verbal derivation, frequentative stems included. Semantically, besides the religious vocabulary, many loanwords refer to various kinds of utilitarian products (such as textiles, food, tools and instruments, and weapons) as well as to commerce and money. In recent decades, during the Eritrean struggle for independence, because of special political circumstances, the vocabulary of Tigre and Tigrinya absorbed a large number of Arabic political and military terms. Thus, for instance, whereas Amharic resorted to the Geʻez root *'abaya* "to refuse" for creating the (incorrect) neologism *abyot* "revolution," Tigrinya simply borrowed the term *sawra* from Arabic (Kapeliuk 1979). To this day, when Amharas write or speak disparagingly about the present Eritrean government they use the word *šaabiya* "the popular" from *al-jabha al-ša'biyya* or the EPLF "Eritrean Popular Liberation Front" now in power.

However, most of the loanwords in the domain of politics come from European languages. Ethio-Semitic has a long tradition of borrowing from Indo-European, going back to the Greek words which entered Geʻez by the dozens (Grébaut 1923). In the modern languages, particularly in Amharic and in Tigrinya, which until recently were the only languages regularly used in writing on contemporary matters, many loanwords were introduced first from Italian and French and then almost exclusively from English. Many western and Ethiopian linguists studied the European loanwords. The studies were conducted both in connection with language interference (Beəmnet 1955:64–102; Fusella 1960; Abraham 1963) and in relation to the coining of modern terminology and the establishment of Language Academies (Assefa 1984; Amanuel 1984; Amsalu 1984).[5] Special attention was accorded to the Marxist-Leninist terminology introduced in the 1970s and 1980s in Amharic and Tigrinya (Fusella 1988; Richter 1988; Gankin 1988; Kapeliuk 1973-79; id. 1979; Abraham 1991). Numerous European loanwords, which entered modern Ethio-Semitic at a relatively early stage, were incorporated in the morphological system mainly as nouns, but some also as verbs, e.g., in Amharic from Italian *fabrica*: *fäbärräkä* "to fabricate," passive: *täfäbärräkä*, factitive: *asfäbärräkä*. More recent borrowings, especially those dealing with Marxist ideology, were promptly discarded after the change of regime in 1991.

In coining neologisms, Ge'ez often serves as a lending source of words and roots (Abraham 1991). The tendency to draw from a prestigious literary ancestor language is not limited to Ethio-Semitic. It is also a current procedure in Neo-Aramaic in relation to Old Syriac, and in spoken Arabic vis-à-vis literary Arabic, not to mention biblical and post-biblical Hebrew as the almost exclusive stock of roots for planned innovation of Hebrew. In Ethiopia, Amharic also serves as a lending source for the other Semitic languages. As the language of the royal court since the 13th century, it was used in decrees and royal edicts (Amanuel 1984). In modern times, it became the national and official language and the language of elementary education, leading to extensive bilingualism (Cooper 1976; Cooper & Horvath 1976; Mesfin 1974). In the last decade of the century, the language policy of the Ethiopian government changed from imposed amharization to ethnic pluralism (Daniel 1997), but Amharic still provides many loanwords and syntactical and stylistic calques to the other local languages. Language contacts in central and south-western Ethiopia are now thoroughly investigated by a research team from the University of Mainz (Richter 1998).

---

[5] There is an abundant literature on the sociolinguistic aspects of language contacts in Ethiopia. Additional bibliographical material may be found in any of the articles mentioned in the text.

NEO-ARAMAIC

Another branch of Semitic which underwent heavy foreign language interference is Neo-Aramaic, and in particular the peripheral dialects spoken on the northern and north-eastern extremity of the Semitic language area. Close cohabitation with Iranian-speaking nations since the most ancient times and a possible language shift to Aramaic by Christian speakers of Persian and Kurdish before and during the expansion of Islam caused profound changes in the vocabulary and the structure of Neo-Aramaic (Tsereteli 1978: 15–18; Murre-van den Berg 1999: 1–3, 90–91, 357–358; Chyet 1997: 219–233). These transformations do not, however, put in doubt the genetic filiation of the Neo-Aramaic dialects within the Semitic family, despite the term Kurdo-Aramaic applied to them by H. J. Polotsky (1960) and despite an early classification of a collection of words in the Jewish dialect of Sihne (Sanandaj) as a corrupt form of Kurdish (Morgan 1904), a misinterpretation which was promptly corrected by providing Semitic etymologies to most of the words on the list (Perles 1904). Later, contacts with Turkish and with Arabic and Persian (either directly or by the intermediary of Kurdish or Turkish) also left their imprint on the Neo-Aramaic lexicon. In the case of the Jewish dialects, Hebrew also served as a lending source. Due to their status as minorities, the speakers of Neo-Aramaic are subject to this day to heavy pressure from the neighboring dominant languages and many of them are bilingual or multilingual (Garbell 1965a: 15; Odisho 1993). One example is the Aramaic-speaking Jews of Zakho who still use Kurdish in their dirges long after their immigration to Israel (Blau 1985), while 33 out of 153 proverbs collected among them were in Kurdish (Sabar 1978).

Grammarians and lexicographers recognized the impact of Iranian on Neo-Aramaic from the beginning of scientific investigation of it in the 19th century. In the 20th century, after a long hiatus caused by political upheavals, we witness in the early 1960s a renewal of interest from western scholars in Neo-Aramaic (Poizat 1973–79: 350; Krotkoff 1989). The impact of foreign languages on Neo-Aramaic is often mentioned in works of a more general character (see, for instance, the etymologies in the glossary in Krotkoff 1982, or the description of Indo-European influence on the written variety of the Urmi dialect in Murre-van den Berg 1999:226–229). However, only few publications are devoted to the specific subject of language contact, with the notable exception of Yona Sabar's treatment of the Jewish dialects. Among the special publications dealing with language contacts proper, the most important contribution is represented by I. Garbell's study on the "Impact of Kurdish and Turkish on the Jewish Neo-Aramaic dialect of Persian Azerbaijan and the adjoining regions" (1965b) and in her other publications on that dialect (1965a in the glossary; id. 1964). The author explores various aspects of foreign influence on the structure and vocabulary of the dialect and provides etymologies for loanwords from K[urdish], T[urkish] and from what she somewhat misguidingly calls K/T but which in reality refers to Arabic or Persian material which entered the Neo-Aramaic dialect via one of these adstrates or through both.

M. Chyet provides an exhaustive review of linguistic and socio-cultural similarities between Neo-Aramaic and Kurdish and their speakers in his article "Neo-Aramaic and Kurdish: an interdisciplinary consideration of their influence on each other" (1995). A somewhat negative evaluation of the changes caused by foreign influence in the normalized written Urmi dialect may be found in J. Friedrich's article "Das Neusyrische als Typus einer entarteten semitischen Sprache" (1962), in which the evolution of Neo-Aramaic is described as degradation from the original Semitic system. It seems that the non-Semitic aspect of the dialects under investigation disturbed certain linguists. In the introduction to his book on the Jewish dialect of Zakho I. Avinery writes that it may be considered "the 'best' of all modern Aramaic dialects owing to its almost complete freedom from Persian, Arabic and Turkish influences, at least insofar as the conjugation of verbs, the declension of nouns and morphology in general is concerned. In certain areas, particularly in the field of syntax, the Zākhō dialect is also considered the 'purest'" (1988: v). This, of course, is an idealization, especially if compared with more balanced statements by J. B. Segal (1955: 253) and by Y. Sabar (1989: 273–274).

The language material speaks for itself. In the vocabulary of the Jewish dialect from Azerbaijan described by I. Garbell (1965b), 68.9% of the nouns, 23.57% of the adjectives, 59% of the prepositions, 28% of the verbal roots and 46% of the particles represented borrowings from Kurdish or Turkish or from both. The dialects spoken in Iraq, on the other hand, contain many borrowings from Kurdish and direct borrowings from Arabic, as may be seen, for instance, in the Christian dialect from Aradhin described by G. Krotkoff (1982). Even in the most ancient written texts known to date, namely in the Jewish manuscripts from the 17th century from Iraqi Kurdistan, in a sample of 1050 lexical entries from one typical text, 315 were of Arabic origin, borrowed either directly or by the intermediary of one of the local languages (Sabar 1984). A relatively recent case of Arabic contribution to Neo-Aramaic is represented by the loans from Palestinian Arabic in the speech of the first wave of Jewish immigrants from Kurdistan to Palestine in the 1920s (Sabar 1974b; Meehan & Alon 1979).

Foreign influence is not restricted to the lexicon. It permeates all the layers of the language causing sometimes profound structural changes. Thus in phonology, following massive lexical borrowing, new phonemes, such as the affricates *č* and *ǧ* and the fricative *ž*, were integrated in the phonemic system together with the spirantized variants of what remained from the *bgdkpt* series, a process similar to what is happening in Modern Hebrew, probably as a result of the loss of gemination under Indo-European influence (Kapeliuk 1999). The very peculiar transformation of the spirantized variants of *t* and *d* into *l* in the Jewish dialects from the region of Lake Urmia was compared with a similar phenomenon in the coterritorial Mukri dialect of Kurdish (Kapeliuk 1997b). As for the phenomenon of vowel harmony in the peripheral dialects, it was attributed either to Turkish or Kurdish influence (Polotsky 1961; Friedrich 1962; Garbell 1964; Younansardaroud 1998). In morphology the Semitic dialects absorbed many features from the substrates and adstrates, in particular from Iranian. The most significant and interesting among them is the overall reshaping of the Neo-Aramaic verbal system according to Kurdo-Persian verbal categories. This process was mentioned in connection with the passive participle constructed ergatively and used as the perfect in Old Syriac (Kutscher 1969; Friedrich 1957–58). Later the analysis was extended to the whole Neo-Aramaic verbal system and exhaustive comparisons were provided, first by F. Pennacchietti (1988; Pennacchietti & Orengo 1995) and then by a few others (Chyet 1995: 238–249; Kapeliuk 1996a; id. 2002 on the passive; Younansardaroud 1999). Another interesting problem concerns the gender of loanwords, considering that Neo-Aramaic distinguishes between masculine and feminine while some of the lending languages do not, or present a different distribution (Matveev 1968). Many question marks could have been avoided in this chapter with a little knowledge of Kurmanji Kurdish, which definitely prefers the feminine to the masculine. Therefore it should not be surprising that a word like *tarix* "history" is in the feminine, as in Kurdish, nor that the Hebrew loanwords *sefer* "book" and *siddur* "prayerbook" are also in the feminine by analogy to the Kurdish feminine substantive *kitêb* "book" (Garbell 1965b). Neo-Aramaic also borrowed a considerable number of affixes from other languages, including a few prefixes (Marogulov 1935: 34–35, 38–39), a procedure not very common in Semitic. Most of the prefixes come from Iranian, e.g., *behona* "stupid" from Kurdish *bê* "without" and Old Syriac *hona* "mind". According to Garbell (1965b), 73% of the derivational suffixes in the Jewish dialect investigated by her were of K[urdish] or T[urkish] or K/T origin. She also recorded many syntactical similarities to Turkish and Kurdish as well as lexical calques in this dialect.

In the normalized Christian dialect of Urmia, on the other hand, beside the usual borrowings (Odisho 1988: 20), certain effects of syntactical influence from European languages have been detected, such as, for instance, the frequent use of gerundial constructions. The latter was attributed to the English background of the American Presbyterian missionaries, who were the first to put this dialect into writing and produced many translations (Murre-van den Berg 1999), and later to Russian, in the numerous texts published in the former Soviet Union until World War II (Friedrich 1962; Kapeliuk 1996b). Neo-Aramaic also absorbed European words either as loans of long date or as neologisms, in particular from the international Marxist-Leninist lexicon in the texts from the Soviet Union. The latter have been defined as a special category because they did not submit to the rules of vowel harmony (Marogulov 1935: 36–37), and they benefited from a special mention in the law on orthography from 1934.[6]

Neo-Aramaic also draws from two prestigious lending sources. These are Old Syriac for the Christians and Hebrew for the Jews. As in the case of Ge'ez mentioned above, Old Syriac serves as a source of words and roots for replenishing the vocabulary and coining modern terminology. Like Ge'ez, Old Syriac and Biblical Hebrew were not only the languages of cult known to the learned clergy and rabbis, they also served as the languages of all written activity until the introduction of writing in the spoken language. The knowledge of Old Syriac was particularly appreciated among the Chaldeans (Oussani 1901), and today we even witness attempts among speakers of Ṭuroyo to revive the ancient language following the model of Modern Hebrew (Brock 1989). All the Christian denominations still consider Old Syriac as an endless lending stock (see, for example, in Oraham 1943) and as a model for orthography (Polotsky 1961; Murre-van den Berg 1999). As for the influence of Hebrew on the Jewish dialects, it is of two different kinds. On the one hand, there is the Hebrew religious vocabulary integrated in the speech of the Jews in the diaspora from the prayers and study of the Bible, and on the other hand, there are the loans from Israeli Hebrew which penetrated the speech of the immigrants from Kurdistan after their massive immigration to Israel in 1951–52. The influence of the spoken Hebrew is very strong, and it is gradually replacing the former Aramaic speech (Sabar 1974a; id. 1974b; id. 1975; Khan 1999: 9–12).

---

[6]   Published in the Neo-Aramaic newspaper *Koxva d Madinxa* [The Eastern Star] from 5.9.1934 (Tbilisi).

ISRAELI HEBREW

The terms Israeli Hebrew, Modern Hebrew or General Hebrew are applied by all the authors, with the notable exception of H. Blanc, only to the Ashkenazi variant of modern Hebrew. H. Blanc has shown that there is also an "Arabicized Israeli Hebrew" standard (1954; id. 1964) which is spoken by those Israelis of oriental origin whose speech does not conform to the Ashkenazi variant, but who were not necessarily born as speakers of Arabic. Thus, for instance, he recorded the characteristic pronounciation of *ḥ* and ' in the speech of an informant born in Palestine, whose mother tongue was Judeo-Spanish. The author of these lines has observed correct use of *ḥ* and ' in the speech of persons of Iranian origin as well as among some Amharic-speaking Ethiopian youngsters who were educated in religious boarding schools with an overwhelming majority of oriental students, despite the fact that these sounds do not exist in the mother tongues of either group. To my knowledge, with the exception of H. Blanc, no linguist has referred to Arabicized Israeli Hebrew as a second standard of this language and as a model of imitation (for oriental Jews, whatever their language of origin) and not merely as a dialect or a communal variant (Bentolila 1983: 93; Devens 1978: VIII). Consequently the survey which follows refers exclusively to the Ashkenazi variant.

The issue of language contact, as far as Israeli Hebrew is concerned, differs considerably from what we have seen regarding Ethio-Semitic and Neo-Aramaic. Although in all three groups the main problem is that of substrate action and language shift, in the two groups discussed above the process was a natural one, extending over long periods of time, and uncontrolled. In Israeli Hebrew, on the other hand, the shift from the substrate to the target language is, in agreement with immigrant language behavior, extremely abrupt and is accompanied by an intensive normative and levelling action of the Israeli educational system and of the media. As a result of this activity, foreign anomalies are eliminated within one or two generations of native speakers, as may be seen, for instance, in the examples quoted by B. Podolsky in his article on recent mass immigration from Russia and its linguistic impact (1995). Nevertheless, from the beginning of study of the revival of Hebrew, exaggerated attention was accorded to the impact of both Yiddish and Slavic on the speech of the inhabitants of Palestine and later of Israel. The details of this impact were extensively documented both in monographic studies and in works of a more general character dealing with the revival of Hebrew and its actual nature (Blau 1981; Fellman 1973). The abundance of this kind of studies may be seen in bibliographies (Weinberg 1965) and in bibliographical lists in such works as H. Rosén's *Contemporary Hebrew*

(1977), and more recently in P. Wexler's book on the *Schizoid Nature of Modern Hebrew* (1990).

The pioneering study on the subject of Hebrew language contacts is due again to I. Garbell, who in 1930 presented in Berlin her doctoral thesis on *Foreign Influences on Israeli Hebrew* [in German] providing "a rather comprehensive survey of features that set current Hebrew off from classical layers, attributing, of course, all the differences to foreign influences" (Rosén 1977: 34). The exploration of the European elements in Israeli Hebrew continued, in particular during the 1950s and the 1960s. Linguists with a European background dealt with questions of lexical borrowing, loan translations and calques (Tubielewicz 1956); with the yiddishized rendering of the consonantal and suprasegmental phonemes in Israeli Hebrew (Zand 1965); with borrowed morphemes such as -*nik* that, although of Slavic origin, probably entered Hebrew from Yiddish (Masson 1969–70); or with suffixes of endearment and diminutives as well as place names (Altbauer 1949; id. 1956). M. Masson (1973–79a; id. 1976) documented exhaustively the morphological treatment of loanwords from Slavic and Yiddish. He also discussed the behavior of international words, which, according to him, also penetrated Israeli Hebrew via Yiddish-German or Slavic (1973–79b). An interesting structuralist attempt to classify foreign, viz. western borrowings on a formal basis, without etymological considerations, reduced considerably the dimensions of this phenomenon (Weiman 1950). It should be stressed that the majority of these works were published several decades ago and since then many loans were replaced by their Hebrew equivalents. Thus, for instance, nobody says *revolucioni* for *mahapxani* anymore, and *civilizacija* is regularly replaced by *tarbut*. The same applies to the host of Aramaic words and expressions which were introduced into literary modern Hebrew at its beginnings (Klausner 1949). Now the most important lending language is English, with some borrowings from Arabic. Loanwords from Arabic are mainly found in the informal speech of native speakers of Israeli Hebrew; they have been described by H. Blanc (1955) and classified into such semantic categories as food, realities of Eretz Israel, children's games, exclamations, curses and blessings, etc.

From the abundant factual material on foreign influences in Israeli Hebrew provided by various authors, it may be concluded that only a few phenomena may unequivocally be singled out as real structural changes, and certainly none of them can be compared to what occurred in Ethio-Semitic or in Neo-Aramaic. Besides the undeniable yiddishized pronunciation of the Israeli Hebrew consonants (which, by the way, is almost identical to that of Eastern Neo-Aramaic) and a few borrowed suffixes, only a timid attempt at distinguishing between aspectual features in a number of verbs may be defined as a true grammatical innovation, inspired by Yiddish or Slavic, or by both. Thus the opposition between *laxac* and *natan lexica*, *yašav* and *hityašev*, *zaxar* and *nizkar* and *yašan* versus *nirdam* (Blanc 1965) is probably an answer to the need of speakers of East European background to render the category of aspect, so vital in their mother tongues (Podolsky 1995). Other syntactical and morphological phenomena, such as the passage to the SVO word order, the dissolution of the possessive complex based on the construct state and the disappearance of gender distinction in the plural of verbs, are already attested not only in post-Biblical Hebrew, but also in so a 'pure' Semitic language as, for instance, the Palestinian urban dialect of Arabic (Kapeliuk 1989).

It seems that the tendency among many linguists to view Israeli Hebrew as a kind of mixed language in which Hebrew lexical elements, together with an infinite number of loans, were forced upon a basically Indo-European, or more precisely Germano-Yiddish or Slavic structure (or *innere Form*) did not always result from an objective linguistic analysis of the factual data. In certain cases it might have been due to a pessimistic and patronizing attitude of scholars from the diaspora who, during the first half of the 20th century, considered with suspicion the "unscientific" efforts made by members of the Yishuv to revive a dead language (Bergsträsser 1983: 64; Mainz 1948–51). On another occasion, language structure was confused with what it was supposed to convey, and the mainly western nature of topics dealt with by means of Israeli Hebrew was projected onto the structure of the language itself, which was described as basically Indo-European (Rosén 1955: ch. 2 reviewed in Blanc 1956a; Rosén 1977: 24–25, 86–98). More recently, in the spirit of the theories elaborated in connection with pidgins and creoles, Sh. Izre'el (1986) pointed out the interest in testing Israeli Hebrew with tools applied to the study of pidgins and creoles. However, referring to Israeli Hebrew as a pidgin or creole would mean that it is non-genetic (Thomason & Kaufman 1988). Consequently there would be no point in dealing with it within the framework of Semitic linguistics and it should be included in the special category of pidgins or creoles just as, for instance, French creoles, which are never included in the grammar of French nor in studies on Romance languages. As to P. Wexler's conclusion that Israeli Hebrew is just a kind of Yiddish which, in turn, is a kind of Slavic, it seems to be no more than a provocative prank "pour épater le bourgeois" personified for the occasion by more traditional grammarians.

Extremist views may easily be refuted with two basic arguments. First: Israeli Hebrew morphology is by far the most conservative of all the living Semitic languages (Goldenberg 1997), Arabic dialects included and, contrary to all the pidgins, it has been only slightly simplifed. Second: a statement that modern Hebrew is a *Mischsprache* may be proffered only by those who completely disregard what has happened in all other living Semitic languages during their evolution and, in particular, in Ethio-Semitic and Neo-Aramaic. If these two are normal Semitic languages, certainly so is Israeli Hebrew. Compared with them it may be considered an ideal model of a living Semitic language (Kapeliuk 1996a).[7]

ARABIC

In spoken Arabic the effects of language contact oscillate between two poles. On the one hand is the bulk of the Arabic dialects, stretching from the Middle East to the Atlantic Ocean. In these foreign influence is relatively light, as is often the case with a superstrate imposed on local populations by invading masses, though it increases towards the extremes. On the other hand, on the fringes of the Arabic speaking area there are some cases of heavy language interference, bordering on language mixture and pidginization (Kaye & Rosenhouse 1997: 263–266). The latter have received considerable attention from linguists during the last decades. First and foremost among them is Maltese, an offshoot of Western spoken Arabic which was brought to the island by Arab and Berber invaders who remained there for four centuries. The language underwent substantial influence from medieval Sicilian and from Italian, especially after it was cut off from other Arabic dialects and from literary Arabic as source of renovation (Comrie 1991). Documental remnants of romanicized Arabic from the neighboring island of Sicily go back as far as the early twelfth century in notarial documents containing Romance lexical borrowings (Agius 1994). During the last two centuries English has exerted a strong influence on Maltese lexicon and it still serves today, together with Maltese, as the official language of the Republic of Malta. English is extensively used in writing and partly in education and represents the main source of borrowings (Camilleri 1994; Borg 1994).

In the study of Maltese in the past, heavy stress was placed on the perenniality of the Semitic base and on its conservative character in spite of many centuries of isolation from Arabic and heavy pressure from Romance. Both J. Aquilina in his famous grammar (1959) and A. Borg in his doctoral thesis on Maltese phonology and morphology (1978) treat

---

[7]   Editorial comment: for a recent reassessment of theories regarding the emergence of Israeli Hebrew see Kuzar 2001: Chapter 2, especially section 4.

in separate chapters the Semitic and Romance components, stressing on many occasions the Semitic character of the language. According to A. Borg (1978: 352), "The greatest impact made by Italian is in the area of phonology ... the great influx of Romance lexicon that has invaded Maltese, has ... left almost intact the morphological signalling system inherited from Arabic" (also Krier 1976). In recent years interest has increased in the Romance component of the language and scholars now call for a less normative and more realistic approach to the Romance elements (Tosco 1993; Misfud 1995). In Maltese the main issue of language contact is in the domain of morphology, or how to adapt massive Indo-European material to the rules of Semitic noun and verb patterns. Basically the Romance nominal material is well integrated (Misfud 1994) while verbs are conjugated with Arabic endings, sometimes with slight changes. It is interesting to note that English verbs are italianized before integrating in the local conjugation (Tosco 1993; Misfud 1995). European influence is strongly felt in all layers of the vocabulary as well as in phraseology (Fenech 1978).

Among other Arabic dialects which evolved in isolation there is the interesting case of the Cypriote Maronite dialect of the village of Kormakiti. Brought to Cyprus in the 12th century, the Turkish occupation in 1571 severed it from speakers of Arabic (Borg 1985; id. 1994). The dialect underwent heavy interference from Greek and, to a lesser degree, from Turkish, but this interference is restricted only to the vocabulary, which contains about 30% Greek words. These, however, were excluded from the study of the dialect by M. Tsiapera (1969), probably with good reason as many of them seem completely inadaptable to Semitic (Roth 1985). Also, in Arabic dialects spoken in a few pockets in south-eastern Turkey, the influence of the adstrates — Kurdish, Turkish and Neo-Aramaic — is pertinent. Thus phonemic velarization of whole words and consequent vowel harmony were attributed either to Turkish or Kurdish or to both (Jastrow 1969; id. 1978–81: 47–52; Sasse 1971). During the centuries-old cohabitation with speakers of Neo-Aramaic in south-eastern Anatolia, the Arabic dialects have also borrowed from them (Jastrow in print).

Enclaves of Arabic speakers exist also in Uzbekistan and in Afghanistan (Blanc 1963: 381–382; Jastrow 1997; id. 1998; Kapeliuk in print). In Uzbekistan Arabic is spoken in a few villages and it was influenced mainly by Tajiki-Persian and also by Turkic (Uzbek and Turkmen), especially because all the speakers are bilingual or trilingual. The foreign impact is easily identified in the pronunciation, especially in the loss of emphatics. Some interesting structural changes took place in morphology: the Persian prefix *mi-* has been adopted for marking the imperfective aspect together with the Semitic imperfect. The infinitive is created with the Iranian suffix -an, e.g., ǧajan "to come" (Fischer 1961). In the domain of syntax, Turkic contributed an interesting use of nominal verb forms (Jastrow 1995).[8] In the Arabic dialect spoken in four villages in Afghanistan, some similar structural changes took place. Under Tajiki influence the verb is relegated to the end of the sentence (but see Versteegh 1984–86) and the direct object directly precedes the verb. Distinction of gender in nouns and verbs as well as the definite article have not been retained, as in the coterritorial languages (Sīrat & Knudsen 1973; Ingham 1994).

On the African continent there are also some specimens of isolated Arabic dialects but only in a few was foreign influence strong enough to alter their basic Arabic structure (Blanc 1971; Roth 1979; Owens 1993; Kaye 1976; Heine 1982; Versteegh 1984; id. 1994). Most interesting among them are the pidginized varieties, combining Arabic vocabularies with grammatical base formed from mixed elements from local languages. The Arabic pidgins and creoles received much attention in the last two decades from linguists who try to unravel their different components, both in the perspective of Arabic and in the more theoretical perspective of pidgin and creole studies (Kaye 1991 and the bibliography there; Prokosch 1986; Avram 1993; Owens 1985; id. 1989; id. 1991; Tosco & Owens 1993). It is possible that the existence of a pidginized form of Arabic goes back as far as the Middle Ages. Thomason & Elgibali (1986) published a short text in a pidginized form of Arabic from the eleventh century from western Sahara whose population was primarily composed of speakers of Niger-Congo languages and who may have acquired their rudimentary knowledge of Arabic from Berbers whose Arabic was non-native and incorrect.

As to the main body of the Arabic dialects, the effect of language contact on them and on the literary language was relatively light compared to the other branches of Semitic, and restricted mainly to the vocabulary. It resulted from the action of the substrates with which the speakers of Arabic came in contact during their expansion, from subsequent cohabitation with speakers of different languages and from superstrate pressure following foreign occupation and colonization. The subject of the substrates of Arabic has been exhaustively treated by W. Diem (1979), who also summarized the extant literature. Some works are devoted to the impact of Aramaic. In 1918 M. Feghali published an essay on the Syriac words in the Lebanese dialects, pointing out the great number of

[8]   The Proceedings of *JIDA* 2 from 1995 have not been published but there exists a Collection of the papers presented by the participants which was kindly put at my disposition by Prof. Arieh Levin from the Hebrew University in Jerusalem who also helped with bibliographical information on Arabic.

lexical borrowings in the domain of agriculture, commerce, intellectual life, family and religion. The loans have generally preserved the Old Syriac consonants but the vowels were adapted to Arabic. The subject of the Aramaic substrate continues to preoccupy the Semitists (Contini in print), while the intensive research activity of German scholars during the last two or three decades in Neo-Aramaic and the Arabic dialects of the *Mašriq*, or in both, as in the case of O. Jastrow, also produced some important studies on the reciprocal influences of the two groups (Arnold & Behnstedt 1993; Jastrow in print). On the African continent, substrate contribution concerns mainly Coptic and Berber. Egyptian Arabic has acquired numerous lexical items from practically all the languages with which it has come in contact. Coptic was among these languages and it contributed to the vocabulary of Egyptian Arabic, in particular as spoken in Upper Egypt, some 109 sure items in the domain of flora and fauna, environment, climate and certain ustensils not used in Arabia (Bishai 1964; Sobhy 1950). Further to the west the influence of Berber is discernible in phonetics and in vocabulary, mainly on rural topics (Brunot 1950: 20, 24; Ghazi 1957–60).

The action of superstrates on Arabic, both spoken and written, concerns mainly lexical influence exerted by Turkish during many centuries and by the languages of the colonizing Western powers since the 19th century. Turkish left a great number of loanwords, especially in the domains of administration, law and warfare in all the Arabic dialects and in particular in Egypt where Turkish-speaking mercenaries seized power as early as the 13th century, well before the Ottoman conquest. In a study on Turkish loanwords in Egyptian Arabic, their list and explanations cover one hundred pages (Prokosch 1983). Foreign influence on the Palestinian Arabic dialect has also been investigated (Shivtiel 1995). Western languages have left a particularly strong imprint on the vocabulary of the North African dialects. Romance borrowings in Arabic go back as far as the Muslim occupation of Spain and later cohabitation between speakers of the two groups in certain settlements in North Africa and Egypt (Ghazi 1957-60; Cifoletti 1994), but most loans belong to the colonial period. Thus, for instance, a list of 1500 lexical items from Spanish has been established for the Moroccan dialect of the former Spanish protectorate; these are now systematically replaced by borrowings from literary Arabic (Ibn Azzuz 1953). A detailed study of language interference in the Moroccan dialect from French as well as from classical Arabic is due to J. Heath (1989), who also provides morphological rules for the integration of the loanwords and their full lists. The book is conceived as a study in general linguistics on language contact and code switching, with the Moroccan dialect providing a rich and diversified illustration. The same author examined the effects of foreign influence on Moroccan phonology (1999).

Literary Arabic also absorbed loanwords and calques from foreign languages (Blau 1981). Whereas in the remote past the lending languages were mainly Greek, Syriac and Persian, in modern times the main lending language is English, especially as far as technology and science are concerned (Wehr 1934; Sa'id 1967). Contrary to the spoken language, the part of the loanwords in the literary language is limited. The imperviousness of literary Arabic to foreign interference has been attributed to nationalistic and religious reasons and to the great attachment of arabophones to their linguistic culture. But even a study of a huge fictional corpus by Nagib Maḥfuz, containing many dialogues imitating the speech of different social classes in Egypt between 1918 and 1936, showed only 0.23% foreign vocabulary, the dominant lending languages being Italian, then French and, far behind them, English (Issawi 1966–67).

Special attention was devoted to Hebrew elements in Judeo-Arabic. As far as the written material from the Middle Ages is concerned there has been, according to B. Hary (1995), a longstanding debate over the status of Judeo-Arabic: is it a language in its own right, or is it merely Arabic with some special religious and cultural vocabulary? He considers Judeo-Arabic as an ethnolect and a meeting point of classical and dialectal Arabic, of Hebrew and of Aramaic. The part of Hebrew in the spoken Jewish dialects is also very important, as was demonstrated in 1912 by M. Cohen who devoted a whole chapter to Hebrew loans in his study on the Jewish dialect of Algiers. This subject was thoroughly investigated for the North African Jewish dialects (Brunot & Malka 1939; Leslau 1945b; Zafarani 1967) in particular in Israel by M. Bar-Asher (1993; id. 1991 — see bibliography there), Bentolila (1983: 50–70), J. Chetrit (1989) and others. All the North African countries (Morocco, Tunisia, Algeria and Libya) were covered and much material was collected from written and oral sources. The dialect of the Yemenite Jews was also investigated in this perspective by S. D. Goitein (1931; Blanc 1956b) who also provided some phonetic and morphological rules for these Hebrew loans. Similarly, a list of Hebrew words and the rules for their pronunciation were provided for the Baghdadi Jewish dialect (Mansour 1991), while Sh. Moreh (1993) discussed the interesting case of the Shi'ite satirical Baghdadi poet Mulla 'Abbud al-Karkhi (1861–1946) who used Hebrew words and expressions in his poems about Jews. O. Jastrow described some Jewish dialects from Iraq and Syria (1989; id. 1990; id. 1992) and pointed out the existence of many Hebrew loans, in particular in the domain of religion, as well as many loans from modern Hebrew in the speech of immigrants in Israel who have a good knowledge of Hebrew.

An interesting case, but entirely different from what occurred in the Judeo-Arabic dialects, is represented by the speech of the Arab citizens of Israel, many of whom have a good knowledge of spoken (and often also written) Israeli Hebrew and tend to introduce Hebrew words and expressions into their Arabic speech, in particular when discussing Israeli matters. This phenomenon has been investigated quite intensively both in the sedentary (Koplewitz 1990; Amara 1995; Amara & Spolsky[9]) and in the bedouin dialects (Henkin 1995).

ABBREVIATIONS

AAL	Afroasiatic Linguistics
AE	Annales d'Ethiopie
AfO	Archiv für Orientforschung
AION	Annali dell'Istituto Orientale di Napoli
AL	Anthropological Linguistics
AO	Acta Orientalia
AuÜ	Afrika and Übersee
BA	Beiträge zur Assyriologie
BSOAS	Bulletin of the School of Oriental and African Studies
CIIL	cf. Aguade, Yordi 1994
DOT	Deutscher Orientalistentag
EVO	Egitto e Vicino Oriente
GLECS	Groupe Linguistique d'Etudes Chamito-Sémitiques
HA	Hebrew Abstracts
ICML	International Conference on Minority Languages
ILAA	Incontri di Linguistica Afroasiatica
IJMES	International Journal of Middle East Studies
IOS	Israel Oriental Studies
JAAS	Journal of Assyrian Academic Studies
JAOS	Journal of the American Oriental Society
JES	Journal of Ethiopian Studies
JIDA	Journées Internationales de Dialectologie Arabe
JMMD	Journal of Multilingual and Multicultural Development
JNES	Journal of Near Eastern Studies
JQR	Jewish Quarterly Review
JSAI	Jerusalem Studies in Arabic and Islam
JSS	Journal of Semitic Studies

---

[9]   I am indebted for this information to Prof. J. Rosenhouse from the Technion Institute of Technology in Haifa.

LW   Languages of the World
MEA   Middle Eastern Affairs
MES   Middle Eastern Studies
NEAS   Northeast African Studies
NES   Near Eastern Studies
OLZ   Orientalische Literaturzeitung
OS   Orientalia Suecana
PICES   Proceedings of the International Conference of Ethiopian
          Studies
PIOC   Proceedings of the International Orientalists' Congress
ROMM   Revue de l'Occident Musulman et de la Méditerranée
RRL   Revue Roumaine de Linguistique
RSE   Rassegna di Studi Etiopici
SGA   Sprache und Geschichte in Afrika
STUF   Sprachtypologie und Universalienforschung
ZDMG   Zeitschrift der Deutschen Morgenländischen Gesellschaft

BIBLIOGRAPHY

Abraham Demoz. 1963. European loanwords in an Amharic daily
    newspaper. In J. Spencer (ed.). *Language in Africa.* Cambridge,
    116–122.
Abraham Demoz. 1991. Lexical innovation in contemporary Amharic.
    In A.S. Kaye (ed.). *Semitic Studies in Honor of Wolf Leslau.*
    Wiesbaden, 1–27.
Agius, Dionisus A. 1994. Siculo-Arabic: interferences, deletions, and
    additions. *JIDA* 1, I: 345–359.
Aguade, Yordi et alii. 1994. *Actas del Congreso Internacional sobre
    Interferencias Linguisticas Arabo-Romances y Paralelos Extra-
    Iberos. Madrid 10–14.12.1990.* Zaragoza (quoted as *CIIL*).
Altbauer, Mojżesz. 1949. O technice zdrobnień we współczesnej
    hebrajszczyźnie [On the technique of creating the diminutive in
    contemporary Hebrew]. *Lingua Posnaniensis* 1: 189–198.
Altbauer, Mojżesz. 1956. Elementy słowiańskie w hebrajskiej toponimii
    Izraela [Slavic elements in Hebrew toponymy]. *Onomastica* 2:
    64–68.
Amanuel Sahle. 1984. Tigrigna: recent history and development. *PICES*
    7: 79–90.
Amara, M.H. 1995. Hebrew and lexical reflections of sociopolitical
    changes in Palestinian Arabic. *JMMD* 16/3: 165–172.
Amara, N. G. & Spolsky, B. 1986. The diffusion of Hebrew and English

lexical items in the spoken Arabic of an Israeli village. *AL* 28: 43–54.

Amsalu Aklilu. 1984. The Ethiopian Languages Academy: history and current development. *PICES* 7: 11–15.

Amsalu Aklilu. 1991. The influence of Arabic on Wollo Amharic. In A.S. Kaye (ed.). *Semitic Studies in Honor of Wolf Leslau.* Wiesbaden, 72–81.

Appleyard, David L. 1977. A comparative approach to the Amharic lexicon. *AAL* 5: 43–109.

Appleyard, David L. 1978. Linguistic evidence of non-Semitic influence in the history of Ethiopian Semitic. *Abbay* 9: 49–56.

Appleyard, David L. 1989. The relative verb in focus constructions: an Ethiopian areal feature. *JSS* 34: 294–305.

Aquilina, Joseph. 1959. *The Structure of Maltese — a Study in Mixed Grammar and Vocabulary.* Malta.

Arnold, Werner & Behnstedt, Peter. 1993. *Arabisch-aramäische Sprachbeziehungen in Qalamūn (Syrien).* (Semitica Viva, 8) Wiesbaden.

Assefa Gebre-Mariam Tesemma. 1984. Technical terms in Amharic: problems and solutions. *PICES* 7: 91–101.

Avinery, Iddo. 1988. *The Aramaic Dialect of the Jews of Zākhō* [in Hebrew]. Jerusalem.

Avram, Andrei. 1993. On the phonology of Arabic pidgins and creoles. *RRL* 38/5: 403–412.

Bar-Asher, Moshe. 1991. Hebrew elements in North African Judeo-Arabic: alternations in meaning and form. In A. S. Kaye (ed.). *Semitic Studies in Honor of Wolf Leslau.* Wiesbaden, 128–149.

Bar-Asher, Moshe. 1993. The Hebrew component in the Judeo-Arabic dialect of Algeria [in Hebrew]. *Hebrew and Arabic Studies in Honour of Joshua Blau.* Tel Aviv, 135–191.

Beəmnet Gebre Amlak. 1995. *The Growth of a Language or how Amharic evolved* [in Amharic]. Addis Ababa.

Bender, Lionel M. 1976. *The Non-Semitic Languages of Ethiopia.* East Lansing.

Bender, Lionel M. 1983. *Nilo-Saharan Language Studies.* (Committee on Northeast African Studies, 13) East Lansing.

Bender, Lionel M. et alii. 1976. *Language in Ethiopia.* London.

Bentolila, Yaakov. 1983. *The Sociophonology of Hebrew as Spoken in a Rural Settlement of Moroccan Jews in the Negev* [Ph. D. thesis, in Hebrew]. Jerusalem.

Bergsträsser, Gotthelf. 1983. *Introduction to the Semitic Languages,* translated by P.T. Daniels. Winona Lake (originally published in German in 1928).

Bishai, Wilson B. 1964. Coptic influences on Egyptian Arabic. *JNES* 23: 39–47.

Blanc, Haim. 1954. The growth of Israeli Hebrew. *MEA* 5: 385–392.

Blanc, Haim. 1955. The Arabic element in the Hebrew speech [in Hebrew]. *Lešonenu La'am* 6/1–4: 6–14, 27–32, 20–26.

Blanc, Haim. 1956a. Review of H. Rosén, *Our Hebrew as Seen by the Methods of Linguistics* (Tel Aviv 1955, in Hebrew). *Language* 32: 794–802.

Blanc, Haim. 1956b. Dialect research in Israel. *Orbis* 5: 185–190.

Blanc, Haim. 1963. Soviet and East European Linguistics — Semitic. In Th. A. Sebeok (ed.). *Current Trends in Linguistics* 1. The Hague, 374–391.

Blanc, Haim. 1964. Israeli Hebrew texts. In *Studies in Egyptology and Linguistcs in Honour of H.J. Polotsky*. Jerusalem, 132–152.

Blanc, Haim. 1965. Some Yiddish influences in Israeli Hebrew. In U. Weinreich (ed.). *The Field of Yiddish — Second Collection*. The Hague, 185–201.

Blanc, Haim. 1971. Linguistics in Sub-Saharan Africa — Arabic. In Th. Sebeok (ed.). *Current Trends in Linguistics* 7. The Hague, 501–509.

Blau, Joshua. 1981. *The Renaissance of Modern Hebrew and Modern Standard Arabic*. (Near Eastern Studies, 18) Berkeley — Los Angeles.

Blau, Joyce. 1985. Les Juifs du Kurdistan. In Ch. Robin (ed.). *Mélanges Linguistiques Offerts à Maxime Rodinson*. Paris, 123–132.

Borg, Alexander. 1978. *A Historical and Comparative Phonology and Morphology of Maltese* [Ph.D. thesis]. Jerusalem.

Borg, Alexander. 1985. *Cypriot Arabic*. Stuttgart.

Borg, Alexander. 1994. Observations on some evolutionary parallels and divergences in Cypriot Arabic and Maltese. *CIIL*:21–40.

Brock, Sebastian. 1989. Some observations on the use of classical Syriac in the late twentieth century. *JSS* 34: 363–375.

Brunot, Louis. 1950. *Introduction à l'Arabe Marocain*. Paris.

Brunot, Louis & Malka, Elie. 1939. *Textes Judeo-Arabes de Fès*. (Institut des Hautes Etudes Marocaines, 33) Rabat.

Brzuski, Witold. 1983. *Arabic loans in ancient and contemporary Amharic* [in Polish]. (Dissertationes Universitatis Varsoviensis 82) Warsaw.

Camilleri, Antoinette. 1994. Language contact between Maltese and English: codeswitching and crosslinguistic influence. *JIDA* 1, I: 431–449.

Cerulli, Enrico. 1934–37. Le mode relatif dans les langues couchitiques. *GLECS* 2: 61–63.

Chetrit, Joseph. 1989. The Hebrew-Aramaic component of the Moroccan Judeo-Arabic. [in Hebrew] *Massorot* 3–4: 203–284.

Chyet, Michael. L. 1995. Neo-Aramaic and Kurdish: an interdisciplinary consideration of their influence on each other. *IOS* 15: 219–249.

Chyet, Michael L. 1997. A preliminary list of Aramaic loanwords in Kurdish. In A. Ashrafuddin & Zahniser A. H. M. (eds.). *Humanism, Culture and Language in the East — Studies in Honor of Georg Krotkoff.* Winona Lake, 283–300.

Cifoletti, Guido. 1994. Italianismi del dialetto di Tunisi. *JIDA* 1, I: 451–458.

Cohen, David. 1985. Paroles et charmes éthiopiens — hypothèses à propos du langage médico-magique. In Ch. Robin (ed.). *Mélanges Linguistiques Offerts à Maxime Rodinson.* Paris, 148–159.

Cohen, Marcel. 1912. *Le Parler Arabe des Juifs d'Alger.* (Société Linguistique de Paris, 4) Paris.

Cohen Marcel. 1931. *Etudes d'Ethiopien Méridional.* Paris.

Comrie, Bernard. 1991. Towards a history of Arabic Maltese. In A. S. Kaye (ed.). *Semitic Studies in Honor of Wolf Leslau.* Wiesbaden, 234–244.

Contini, Ricardo. in print. Le substrat araméen en néo-arabe libanais. *ILAA* 9 (forthcoming).

Cooper, Robert L. 1976. Government language policy. In M.L. Bender et alii (eds.). *Language in Etiopia.* London, 187–190.

Cooper, Robert L. & Horvath, Ronald J. 1976. Language migration and urbanization. In M.L. Bender et alii (eds.). *Language in Ethiopia.* London, 191–212.

Daniel Aberra. 1997. Language situations in Ethiopia in the 1990's. *PICES* 13, I: 431–440.

Devens, Monica. 1978. *Phonetics of Israeli Hebrew: "Oriental" versus "General" Israeli Hebrew* [Ph.D. thesis]. Los Angeles.

Diem, Werner. 1979. Studien zur Frage des Substrats im Arabischen. *Der Islam* 56: 12–79.

Dolgopolsky, Aharon B. 1977. Emphatic consonants in Semitic. *IOS* 7: 1–13.

Feghali, Michel F. 1918. *Etudes sur les Emprunts Syriaques dans les Parlers Arabes du Liban.* Paris.

Fenech, Edward. 1978. *Contemporary Journalistic Maltese.* Leiden.

Ferguson, Charles A. 1974. The role of Arabic in Ethiopia. In J.B.Pride & J. Holmes. *Sociolinguistics*2. London, 112–124.

Ferguson, Charles A. 1976. The Ethiopian language area. In M.L. Bender et alii (eds). *Language in Ethiopia*. London, 63–76.

Fischer, Wolfdietrich. 1961. Die Sprache der arabischen Sprachinsel in Uzbekistan. *Der Islam* 36: 232–263.

Friedrich, Johannes. 1957-58. Zur passivischen Ausdruckweise im Aramäischen. *AfO* 18: 124–125.

Friedrich, Johannes. 1962. Das Neusyrische als Typus einer entarteten semitischen Sprache. *AION* 4: 95–106.

Fusella, Luigi. 1960. Osservazioni linguistiche sull'amarico moderno. *PICES* 1: 81–88.

Fusella, Luigi. 1988. The draft constitution of the People's Democratic Republic of Ethiopia. *PICES* 9, V: 49–57.

Gankin, Emmanuel B. 1988. Vocabulary replenishment in the Amharic language and topical problems of the Amharic-Russian lexicography. *PICES* 9, V: 58–64.

Garbell, Irene. 1964. 'Flat' words and syllables in Jewish East New Aramaic of Persian Azerbaijan and the contiguous districts. In *Studies in Egyptology and Linguistics in Honour of H.J. Polotsky*. Jerusalem, 86–103.

Garbell, Irene. 1965a. *The Jewish Neo-Aramaic Dialect of Persian Azerbaijan*. The Hague.

Garbell, Irene. 1965b. The impact of Kurdish and Turkish on the Jewish Neo-Aramaic dialect of Persian Azerbaijan and the adjoining regions. *JAOS* 85: 159–177.

Ghazi, M.F. 1957-60. Les emprunts dans les parlers arabes de Tunisie. *GLECS* 8: 17–19.

Goitein, Shlomo D. 1931. Hebrew elements in the colloquial of the Jews of Yemen [in Hebrew]. *Lěšonénu* 3: 356–380.

Goldenberg, Gideon. 1997. Conservative and innovative features in Semitic languages. *ILAA* 8: 3–21.

Gragg, Gene. 1991. 'Also in Cushitic': how to account for the complexity of Ge'ez-Cushitic lexical interactions? In A.S. Kaye (ed.). *Semitic Studies in Honor of Wolf Leslau*. Wiesbaden, 570–576.

Grébaut, Sylvain. 1923. Vocables étrangers. *Aethiops* 2: 59–60.

Hary, Benjamin. 1995. Judeo-Arabic in its sociolinguistic setting. *IOS* 15: 73–95.

Heath, Jeffrey. 1989. *From Code-Switching to Borrowing: Foreign and Diglossic Mixing in Moroccan Arabic*. (Library of Arabic Linguistics, 9) London.

Heath, Jeffrey. 1999. Sino-Moroccan citrus: borrowing as a natural linguistic experiment. In L. Edzard & M. Nekroumi, *Tradition and Innovation*. Wiesbaden, 168–176.

Heine, Bernd. 1982. *The Nubi Language of Kibera — an Arabic Creole*. (Language and dialect Atlas of Kenya, 3) Berlin.

Henkin, Roni. 1995. Code mixing in the Negev Bedouin city of Rahat. *JIDA* 2: 59–68.

Hetzron, Robert. 1973. The element *-mm* in the Amharic tense system. *AION* 33 (n.s. 23): 1–10.

Hetzron, Robert. 1975. Genetic classification and Ethiopian Semitic. In J. Bynon & Th. Bynon (eds.). *Hamito-Semitica*. The Hague, 105–123.

Hudson, Grover. 1994. Agaw words in South Ethiopian Semitic? *PICES* 12: 1261–1269.

Ibn Azzuz, Mohammad. 1953. *Glosario de Mil Quinientes Voces Españolas Usadas entre los Marroquies en el Árabe Vulgar*. Madrid.

Ingham, Bruce. 1994. The effect of language contact on the Arabic dialect of Afghanistan. *CIIL*:105–117.

Issawi, Charles. 1966–67. European loanwords in contemporary Arabic writing: a case study of modernization. *MES* 3: 110–133.

Izre'el, Shlomo. 1986. Was the revival of Hebrew a miracle? [in Hebrew]. *Ninth World Congress of Jewish Studies*. Division D — I: 77–84. Revised English version: <http://spinoza.tau.ac.il/humanities/semitic/emergence.html>.

Jastrow, Otto. 1969. Arabische Textproben aus Mardin und Āzex. *ZDMG* 119: 29–59.

Jastrow, Otto. 1978–81. *Mesopotamisch-arabische qəltu-Dialekte*. Wiesbaden.

Jastrow, Otto. 1989. The Judeo-Aramaic dialect of Nusaybin/Qāmešli. In P. Wexler et alii (eds.). *Studia Linguistica et Orientalia Memoriae Haim Blanc Dedicata* (Mediterranean Language and Culture Monograph Series, 6) Wiesbaden, 156–169.

Jastrow, Otto. 1990. *Der arabische Dialekt der Juden von 'Aqra und Arbîl*. Wiesbaden.

Jastrow, Otto. 1992. Der arabische Dialekt der Juden von Kirkuk. *JSAI* 15: 240–254.

Jastrow, Otto. 1995. Towards a reassessment of Uzbekistan Arabic. *JIDA* 2: 95–103.

Jastrow, Otto. 1997. Wie arabisch ist Uzbekistan-Arabisch? In Wardini, E. (ed.). *Built on Solid Rock — Studies in Honour of Prof. Ebbe Egde Knudsen*. Oslo.

Jastrow, Otto. 1998. Zur Position des Uzbekistan-Arabischen. *DOT* 26: 173–184.

Jastrow, Otto. in print. Aramaic loanwords in the Arabic dialects of southeastern Turkey. *DOT* 27 (forthcoming).

Kane, Thomas L. 1983. An unpublished Ge'ez-Amharic magic

manuscript. In S. Segert & A.J.E. Bodrogligeti (eds.). *Ethiopian Studies Dedicated to Wolf Leslau*. Wiesbaden, 243–256.

Kane, Thomas L. 1990. *Amharic — English Dictionary*. Wiesbaden.

Kane, Thomas L. 2000. *Tigrinya — English Dictionary*. Springfield.

Kapeliuk, Olga. 1973–79. Les néologismes éthiopiens. *GLECS* 18–23: 321–323.

Kapeliuk, Olga. 1979. Marxist-leninist terminology in Amharic and Tigrinya. *NEAS* 1/2: 23–30.

Kapeliuk, Olga. 1985. La phrase coupée en guèze. In Ch. Robin (ed.). *Mélanges Linguistiques Offerts à Maxime Rodinson*. Paris, 191–204.

Kapeliuk, Olga. 1988. *Nominalization in Amharic*. (Aethiopistische Forschungen, 23) Wiesbaden.

Kapeliuk, Olga. 1989. Some common traits in the evolution of Neo-Syriac and of Neo-Ethiopian. *JSAI* 12: 294–320.

Kapeliuk, Olga. 1996a. Is modern Hebrew the only 'indo-europeanized' Semitic language? And what about Neo-Aramaic? *IOS* 16: 59–70.

Kapeliuk, Olga. 1996b. The gerund and gerundial participle in Eastern Neo-Aramaic. *STUF* 51: 276–288.

Kapeliuk, Olga. 1997a. Reflections on the Ethio-Semitic gerund. *PICES* 13: 492–498.

Kapeliuk, Olga. 1997b. Spirantization of t and d in Neo-Aramaic [in Hebrew]. *Massorot* 9–11: 527–544.

Kapeliuk, Olga. 1999. Regularity and deviation in peripheral Neo-Semitic. In L. Edzard & M. Nekroumi (eds.) *Tradition and Innovation*. Wiesbaden, 11–21.

Kapeliuk, Olga. In print. Iranian and Turkic Interference in Arabic and Aramaic dialects. *JSAI* (forthcoming).

Kaye, Alan S. 1976. *Chadian and Sudanese Arabic in the Light of Comparative Arabic Dialectology*. The Hague.

Kaye, Alan S. 1991. Peripheral Arabic dialectology and Arabic pidgins and creoles. *LW* 2: 4–16, and CIIL: 125–137.

Kaye, Alan S. & Rosenhouse, Judith. 1997. Arabic dialects and Maltese, in R. Hetzron (ed.) *The Semitic Languages*. London, 263–311.

Khan, Geoffrey. 1999. *A Grammar of Neo-Aramaic — the Dialect of the Jews of Arbel*. Leiden.

Klausner, Joseph. 1949. The aramisms in our language [in Hebrew]. *Lěšonénu* 16: 192–195.

Koplewitz, Immanuel. 1990. The use and integration of Hebrew lexemes in Israeli Spoken Arabic. *ICML* 4, II: 181–195.

Krier, Fernande. 1976. *Le Maltais au Contact de l'Italien*. (Forum Phoneticum, 15) Hamburg.

Kropp, Manfred. 1986. Arabisch-äthiopische Übersetzungstechnik am Beispiel der *Zena Ayhud (Yosippon)* und das *Tarikä Wäldä-'Amid.* *ZDMG* 136: 314–346.

Krotkoff, Georg A. 1982. *A Neo-Aramaic Dialect of Kurdistan.* (American Oriental Series, 64). New Haven.

Krotkoff, Georg. 1985. Studies in Neo-Aramaic lexicology. In A. Kort & S. Morschauser (eds.). *Biblical and Related Studies Presented to Samuel Iwry.* Winona Lake, 123–134.

Krotkoff, Georg. 1989. An annotated bibliography of Neo-Aramaic. In W. Heinrichs (ed.). *Studies in Neo-Aramaic.* (Harvard Semitic Studies) Atlanta, 3–26.

Kutscher, Ezekiel Y. 1969. Two 'passive' constructions in Aramaic in the light of Persian. *Proceedings of the International Conference on Semitic Studies — Jerusalem, 1965.* Jerusalem, 132–151.

Kuzar, Ron. 2001. *Hebrew and Zionism: A Discourse Analytic Cultural Study.* (Language, Power and Social Process, 5.) Berlin.

Leslau, Wolf. 1945a. The influence of Cushitic on the Semitic languages of Ethiopia — a problem of substratum. *Word* 1: 59:82.

Leslau, Wolf. 1945b. Hebrew elements in the Judeo-Arabic dialect of Fez. *JQR* 36: 61–78.

Leslau, Wolf. 1952 The influence of Sidamo on the Ethiopic languages of Gurage. *Language* 28:63–81.

Leslau, Wolf. 1956a. Arabic loanwords in Tigre. *Word* 12: 125–141.

Leslau, Wolf. 1956b. Arabic loanwords in Tigrinya. *JAOS* 76: 204–213.

Leslau, Wolf. 1956c. Arabic loanwords in Harari. In *Studi Orientalistici in Onore di Giorgio Levi della Vida.* Rome, II: 14–35.

Leslau, Wolf. 1956d. Arabic loanwords in Gurage. *Arabica* 3: 266–284.

Leslau, Wolf. 1957a. Arabic loanwords in Amharic. *BSOAS* 19: 221–244.

Leslau, Wolf. 1957b. Arabic loanwords in Argobba. *JAOS* 77: 36–39.

Leslau, Wolf. 1958. Arabic loanwords in Ge'ez. *JSS* 3: 146–168.

Leslau, Wolf. 1959a. Sidamo features in the South Ethiopic phonology. *JAOS* 79: 1–7.

Leslau, Wolf. 1959b. An analysis of the Harari vocabulary. *AE* 3: 275–298.

Leslau, Wolf. 1962. The influence of the Cushitic substratum on Semitic reexamined. *PIOC* 25, I: 387–390.

Leslau, Wolf. 1963. *Etymological Dictionary of Harari.* Berkeley and Los Angeles.

Leslau, Wolf. 1964. Toward a history of the Amharic vocabulary. *JES* 2: 12–20.

Leslau, Wolf. 1979. *Etymological Dictionary of Gurage.* Wiesbaden.

Leslau, Wolf. 1981. Additional Arabic loanwords in Tigre. In R.G.

Stiegner (ed.). *Festschrift Maria Höfner zum 80. Geburtstag.* Graz, 171–198.

Leslau, Wolf. 1986. Cushitic loanwords in Gurage. *PICES* 6 A: 373–387.

Leslau, Wolf. 1987. *Comparative Dictionary of Ge'ez.* Wiesbaden.

Leslau, Wolf. 1988a. Analysis of the Ge'ez vocabulary: Ge'ez and Cushitic. *RSE* 32: 59–109.

Leslau, Wolf. 1988b. Additional Arabic loanwords in Amharic. In S. Uhlig & Bairu Tafla. *Collectanea Aethiopica.* Wiesbaden, 87–109.

Leslau, Wolf. 1990. *Arabic Loanwords in Ethiopian Semitic.* Wiesbaden.

Mainz, Ernest. 1948–51. Quelques tendances dans le développement de l'hébreu moderne. *GLECS* 5: 68–70.

Marogulov, Qonstantin I. 1935. *A Grammar for Adult Education* [in Neo-Aramaic]. Moscow.

Mansour, Jacob. 1991. *The Jewish Baghdadi Dialect.* Or-Yehuda.

Martinet, André. 1968. *Le Langage — Encyclopédie de la Pléiade* (sous la direction d'A. Martinet). Paris.

Masson, Michel. 1969–70. A propos de l'origine du suffixe -*nik* en hébreu israélien. *GLECS* 14: 79–87.

Masson, Michel. 1973–79a. L'emprunt en hébreu moderne: le filtrage des éléments verbaux. *GLECS* 18–23: 479–493.

Masson, Michel. 1973–79b. Le traitement formel des éléments paneuropéens en hébreu moderne. *GLECS* 18–23: 611–630.

Masson, Michel. 1976. *Les mots nouveaux en hébreu moderne.* Paris.

Matveev, K.P. 1965. The category of gender of borrowed substantives in contemporary Assyrian [in Russian]. *Semitskije Jazyki*[2]. Moscow II/1: 162–167.

Meehan, Charles & Alon, Jacqueline. 1979. 'The boy whose tunic stuck to him', a folktale in the Jewish Neo-Aramaic dialect of Zakho (Iraqi Kurdistan). *IOS* 9: 174–203.

Mesfin Wolde-Mariam. 1974. The relative distribution of the major linguistic and religious groups in urban areas. *PICES* 4: 193–221.

Misfud, Manwel. 1994. Internal pluralization in Maltese: continuity and innovation. *JIDA* 1, I: 91–105.

Misfud, Manwel. 1995. *Loanwords in Maltese — a descriptive and comparative study.* Leiden.

Moreh, Shmuel. 1993. Hebrew words and Baghdadi Judeo-Arabic in the poetry of the Iraqi poet Mulla 'Abbūd al-Karkhī. In *Hebrew and Arabic Studies in Honour of Joshua Blau.* Tel Aviv, 351–373.

Moreno, Mario M. 1948. L'azione del cuscitico sul sistema morfologico delle lingue semitiche dell'Etiopia. *RSE* 7: 121–130.

Morgan, Jacques J. 1904. Le dialecte israélite de Sihneh. In *Mission Scientifique en Perse.* Paris V — *Etudes Linguistiques,* 312–322.

Murre-van den Berg, Helen. 1999. *From a Spoken to a Written Language — the Introduction and Development of Literary Urmia Aramaic in the 19th century.* Leiden.

Odisho, Edward Y. 1988. *The Sound System of Modern Assyrian (Neo-Aramaic).* (Semitica Viva, 2) Wiesbaden.

Odisho, Edward Y. 1993. Bilingualism and multilingualism among Assyrians, a case of language erosion and demise. In R. Contini et alii (eds.). *Semitica — Serta Philologica Constantino Tsereteli Dicata.* Torino, 189–200.

Oraham, Alexander J. 1943. *Oraham's Dictionary of the Stabilized and Enriched Assyrian Language and English.* Chicago.

Oussani, Gabriel. 1901. The modern Chaldeans and Nestorians and the study of Syriac among them. *JAOS* 22: 79–96.

Owens, Jonathan. 1985. The origin of East African Nubi. *AL* 27: 229–271.

Owens, Jonathan. 1989. Zur Pidginisierung und Kreolisierung in Arabischen. *AuÜ* 72: 91–107.

Owens, Jonathan. 1991. Local and universal sources of a creole verbal construction. In A.S. Kaye (ed.). *Semitic Studies in Honor of Wolf Leslau.* Wiesbaden, 1169–1179.

Owens, Jonathan. 1993. *A Grammar of Nigerian Arabic.* Wiesbaden.

Pennacchietti, Fabrizio A. 1988. Verbo neo-aramaico e verbo neo-iranico. *Tipologie della Convergenza Linguistica — Atti del Convegno della Società Italiana di Glottologia.* Pisa, 93–101.

Pennacchietti, Fabrizio A. & A. Orengo. 1995. Neo-aramaico, curdo e armeno: lingue a contatto. *EVO* 19: 221–233.

Perles, Felix. 1904. Über das Semitische im jüdischen Dialekt von Sihneh. *OLZ* 12: 483–486.

Plazikowsky-Brauner, Hermine. 1950–1951. Review of C. Brockelmann. *Abessinische Studien* (Berlin 1950). In *ZDMG* 100: 663, 101: 385–397.

Podolsky, Baruch. 1995. Mass immigration and its possible impact on the linguistic situation in Israel. *IOS* 15: 253–263.

Poizat, Bruno. 1973–79. Une bibliographie commentée pour le néo-araméen. *GLECS* 18–23: 347–414.

Polotsky, Hans Jakob 1960. The Targum Jews and their language. [in Hebrew]. *Gešer* 6: 180–181.

Polotsky, Hans Jakob 1961. Studies in Modern Syriac. *JSS* 1: 1–32.

Prokosch, Erich. 1983. *Osmanisches Wortgut im Ägyptisch-Arabischen.* Berlin.

Prokosch, Erich. 1986. *Arabische Kontaktsprachen (Pidgin und Kreolsprachen) in Afrika.* (Grazer Linguistische Monographien, 2) Graz.

Raz, Shlomo. 1991. Semitic South Ethiopic: the definite future revisited. In A.S. Kaye (ed.). *Semitic Studies in Honor of Wolf Leslau.* Wiesbaden, 1248–1264.

Richter, Renate. 1988. Modern terminology in Ethiopian languages. *PICES* 9, V:104–113.

[Richter, Renate]. 1998. *Preliminary Report — Linguistic Contacts in Central and South-West Ethiopia* (Cultural and Linguistic Contacts — Research Project, 295). Mainz.

Richter, Renate. 1999. Sprachentwicklung und Sprachkontakt in Aethiopien. Unpublished paper presented at a meeting of the Research Project: *Kulturelle und sprachliche Kontakte in Nordostafrika/Westasien* of the Johannes Gutenberg University in Mainz. 9 pp.

Rosén, Haim B. 1955. *Our Hebrew as Seen by the Methods of Linguistics.* [in Hebrew]. Tel-Aviv.

Rosén, Haim B. 1977. *Contemporary Hebrew.* The Hague.

Roth, Arlette. 1979. *Esquisse Grammaticale du Parler Arabe d'Abbéché (Tchad).* (GLECS — Supplément 8) Paris.

Roth, Arlette. 1985. Quelques observations sur le vocabulaire de la cuisine dans le parler arabe de Kormakiti (Chypre). Ch. Robin (ed.). *Mélanges Linguistiques Offerts à Maxime Rodinson.* Paris, 320–334.

Sabar, Yona. 1974a. The Hebrew elements in the Neo-Aramaic dialect of the Jews of Zakho in Kurdistan [in Hebrew]. *Lĕšonénu* 38: 206–216.

Sabar, Yona. 1974b. The socio-linguistic aspects of the bilingual Hebrew Neo-Aramaic contact in Israel. *HA* 15: 44–47.

Sabar, Yona. 1975. The Hebrew elements in the Aramaic dialect of the Jews of Azerbaijan [in Hebrew]. *Lĕšonénu* 39: 272–294.

Sabar, Yona. 1978. Multilingual proverbs in the Neo-Aramaic speech of Jews of Zakho — Iraqi Kurdistan. *IJMES* 9: 215–235.

Sabar, Yona. 1984. The Arabic elements in the Jewish Neo-Aramaic texts of Nerwa and Amādīya, Iraqi Kurdistan. *JAOS* 104: 201–211.

Sabar, Yona. 1989. Substratal and adstratal elements in Jewish Neo-Aramaic. In P. Wexler et alii (eds.). *Studia Linguistica Memoriae Haim Blanc Dedicata.* (Mediterranean Language and Culture Monograph Series, 6) Wiesbaden, 264–276.

Sabar, Yona. 1990. General European loanwords in the Jewish Neo-Aramaic dialect of Zakho, Iraqi Kurdistan. In W. Heinrichs (ed.). *Studies in Neo-Aramaic.* (Harvard Semitic Studies) Atlanta, 53–66.

Sa'id, Majed F. 1967. *Lexical Innovation through Borrowing in Modern Standard Arabic.* (Princeton Near East Papers, 6) Princeton.

Sasse, Jürgen H. 1971. *Linguistische Analyse des arabischen Dialekts der Mallamīye in der Provinz Mardin* [Ph. D. thesis]. Munich.

Segal, J.B. 1955. Neo-Aramaic proverbs of the Jews of Zakho. *NES* 14: 251–270.

Shivtiel, Avihai. 1995. Foreign influence on the Palestinian Arabic dialect. *JIDA* 2[7]: 217–226.

Sīrat, Abdul-Sattar & Knudsen, Ebbe E. 1973. Notes on the Arabic dialect spoken in the Balkh region of Afghanistan. *AO* 35: 89–101.

Sobhy, George P. 1950. *Common Words in the Spoken Arabic of Egypt of Greek or Coptic Origin*. Cairo.

Thomason, Sarah G. & Elgibali, Alaa. 1986. Before the Lingua Franca: pidginized Arabic in the eleventh century A.D. *Lingua* 68: 317–349.

Thomason, Sarah G. & Kaufman, Terrence. 1988. *Language Contact, Creolization and Genetic Linguistics*. Berkeley — Los Angeles.

Titov, E.G. 1991. Morphological and semantic peculiarities of Arabic loanwords in contemporary Amharic [in Russian]. In *Irano-Afrazijskije Jazykovyje Kontakty*. Moscow 2: 92–97.

Tosco, Mauro. 1993. Morfologia italiana in maltese. In R. Contini et alii (eds.). *Semitica — Serta Philologica Constantino Tsereteli Dicata*. Torino, 319–322.

Tosco, Mauro & Owens, Jonathan. 1993. Turku, a descriptive and comparative study. *SGA* 14: 177–267.

Tsereteli, Konstantin G. 1978. *The Modern Assyrian Language*. Moscow.

Tsiapera, Maria. 1969. *A Descriptive Analysis of Cypriot Maronite Arabic*. (Janua Linguarum — Series Practica, 66) The Hague.

Tubielewicz, Władysław. 1956. Vom Einfluss europäischer Sprachen auf die Gestaltung des modernen Hebräisch. *Rocznik Orientalistyczny* 20: 337–351.

Versteegh, Kees. 1984. *Pidginization and Crealization: the Case of Arabic*. (Current Issues in Linguistic Theory, 33) Amsterdam.

Versteegh, Kees. 1984–86. Word order in Uzbekistan Arabic and universal grammar. *OS* 33–35: 443–453.

Wehr, Hans 1934. *Die Besonderheiten des heutigen Hocharabischen mit Berücksichtigung der Einwirkung der europäischen Sprachen*. Berlin.

Weiman, Ralph W. 1950. *Native and Foreign Elements in a Language: a Study in General Linguistics Applied to Modern Hebrew*. Philadelphia.

Weinberg, W. 1956. A bibliography of spoken Israeli Hebrew. *HA* 10: 3–16.

Weinreich, Uriel. 1953. *Languages in Contact*. (Linguistic Circle of New York, 1) New York.

Wexler, Paul. 1990. *The Schizoid Nature of Modern Hebrew: a Slavic Language in Search of a Semitic Past.* Wiesbaden.

Younansardaroud, Helen. 1998. Synharmonism in the Särdä:rid dialect. *JAAS* 12/1: 77–82.

Younansardaroud, Helen. 1999. The influence of Persian on the Särda:rid dialect. *JAAS* 13/1: 65–68.

Zaborski, Andrzej. 1975. *The Verb in Cushitic — Studies in Hamito-Semitic I* (Zeszyty Naukowe Uniwersytetu Jagiellońskiego — Prace Językoznawcze, 48). Kraków.

Zaborski, Andrzej. 1976. Cushitic overview. In Bender, Lionel M. *The Non-Semitic Languages of Ethiopia.* East Lansing, 67–84.

Zand, Michael I. 1965. Yiddish as the substrate of contemporary Hebrew [in Russian]. *Semitskije Jazyki*2. Moscow I/2: 221–245.

New Finds and Dialectology
in the Modern Semitic World

INTRODUCTION

Special attention was given at the conference to the evaluation of new finds in the twentieth century. Two papers dealt with this issue: Appleyard's paper on the South Semitic languages and Zuckerman's paper on the ancient world (see below, p. 435). Simeon-Senelle's paper on the Modern South Arabian languages, which could not be read at the conference, was also devoted to describing new finds in this field. New discoveries in the modern languages of other branches of the Semitic family, namely Arabic and Neo-Aramaic, were discussed, following the author's suggestion, in Jasrow's papers on dialectology, which find their proper place in this section of our volume. This change in scope, which has affected the distribution of the other two papers in the respective sections, is a direct result of the state of the art in dialectology in Semitic Linguistics.

Much the same as in the case of language contact, general and theoretical interest in dialectology has been rather scant in Semitic linguistics. With regard to the Semitic languages of the ancient world, the term "dialect" has even appeared as a misnomer, as in the case of Akkadian. As I will discuss briefly in my review of Hetzron's book, (below, pp. 503–504) it seems rather absurd to me to regard two and a half millennia and a wide geographic spread, as attested in ancient Mesopotamia, as consisting of a single language with dialects. While one cannot really speak of dialectological studies in Semitic languages of the ancient world, one must nevertheless mention two significant contributions to the field: Harris 1939 and Garr 1985 (mentioned also by Greenstein, below, p. 442), both dealing with the continuum of language varieties of the Northwest Semitic family (see further Garbini 1960, 1988; cf. Kaufman 1988). Still, a pioneering study in introducing synchronic geographical linguistics into the field is Israel 1984 (cf. Izre'el 1988). The use of the term "dialects" in the study of modern Semitic languages is no less problematic, and the traditional term "Arabic dialects" will confirm this assessment. Admittedly, the definition of dialect vs. language has been a moot question in linguistics, and criteria for defining a language variety as a dialect or as a separate language are not readily available. Some would insist on leaving aside linguistic criteria entirely in favor of political and social ones, a concept that has much to recommend it. This is definitely the case with regard to the Arabic varieties. The history of research in individual areas has also contributed to terminological blurring, as in the case of both Arabic and Neo-Aramaic.

The theoretical study of dialectology is a recent development in general linguistics. It has incorporated not only geographical varieties, but also social, ethnic and other varieties of which the demographic characteristics of the speakers are used to define them (Chambers and Trudgill 1998). Semitic linguistics has only very recently started to supply materials for serious dialectological studies, and as the four contributions in this section demonstrate, references to dialects in the Semitic world are usually confined to the notion of geographical dialects. (It will therefore be noted that this section of our volume is the only one where papers deal with specific groups of Semitic languages instead of being arranged according to theoretical orientation.) Still, as Appleyard shows, some early buds of Ethiopian sociolinguistic dialectology are already present. Intensive field studies in recent times, notably handled by two of the contributors to this volume, Otto Jastrow (peripheral Arabic dialects and Neo-Aramaic) and Marie-Claude Simeone-Senelle (the Modern South Arabian languages), have resulted in a good amount of data being collected. These accumulated data will now enable us to start serious dialectological studies, especially with regard to geographical varieties, but also beyond, given accessibility to the appropriate tools and further data.

In his survey of the state of the art in Arabic dialectology, Otto Jastrow emphasizes the possible profit students may gain from their Semitic studies if they begin by studying Arabic dialectology. Arabic is the largest linguistic continuum of the Semitic world, comprising hundreds of dialects. The paper presents some basic issues of Arabic dialectology and discusses the progress, or lack of progress, in their study. After some notes on the spread of Arabic and the emergence of several zones of Arabic dialects, including language islands, Jastrow reviews the research in each of these areas. Then he discusses briefly the notion of Arabic diglossia (or multiglossia) and the dichotomy between sedentary and Bedouin dialects. As against the flourishing research of the past, the study of Arabic dialectology seems to the author to be in decline. Jastrow calls attention to the need for more field studies, which suffer especially from the lack of access to areas where some of these varieties are spoken.

Jastrow's survey of the state of the art in Neo-Aramaic dialectology opens with a brief description of the extant Neo-Aramaic language varieties. He groups them and then proceeds to review the work done on each of the groups: Western Neo-Aramaic, Turoyo, Neo-Mandaic, and the NENA (Northeastern Neo-Aramaic) group. Jastrow confines his review to the study of the spoken varieties. Compared to the study of Arabic language varieties, the study of Neo-Aramaic languages and dialects is thriving. Still, most Neo-Aramaic languages are doomed to become extinct in the near future, and more field research is needed in order to document them. Jastrow ends his survey with a rather austere remark, calling on scholars of the older Aramaic languages to show more interest in Neo-Aramaic, as they have much to gain from the study of these languages.

Marie-Claude Simeone-Senelle's evaluation of the state of the art of the Modern South Arabian languages draws mainly from her own intimate acquaintance with these languages. As in the case of many Arabic and Neo-Aramaic dialects, the emphasis here is on the fact that the Modern South Arabian languages are primarily used in speech. The Modern South Arabian languages were practically unknown to the scientific world until the first half of the nineteenth century. After a brief account of the discovery of these languages (including Hobyot) and of the new approach to their study in the second half of the twentieth century, there follows a brief account of their description, detailing phonology and phonetics, morphology, syntax and the lexicon. From there, the way is open for some comments on the study of geographical dialects. The paper concludes with comments on oral literature and classification.

The last paper in this section is David Appleyard's survey of the state of the art in the study of the South Semitic languages. Appleyard reviews the finds in Ethio-Semitic languages and in Modern South Arabian languages in the larger framework of the Semitic family, since these languages, among the modern Semitic languages, "have the most to contribute to the picture of the Semitic language family." Following a discussion of this premise, Appleyard reviews the umbrella term "South Semitic" with regard to classification within this subfamily and the relationships of its members to other languages of the Semitic family, notably Arabic. This review also includes the Epigraphic South Arabian material. Then Appleyard surveys the twentieth century finds in Epigraphic South Arabian, Modern South Arabian and Ethiopian Semitic languages, which leads to a detailed linguistic assessment of the present state of knowledge.

Following this study, Appleyard briefly reviews the state of the art in South Semitic dialectology, a task originally assigned to Shlomo Raz. The rich data stemming from the South Semitic languages is a fertile ground for dialectological studies, and thus Appleyard's paper concludes with some desiderata.

REFERENCES

Chambers, J. K. and Peter Trudgill. 1998. *Dialectology.* (Cambridge Textbooks in Linguistics.) Second edition. Cambridge.

Garbini, Giovanni. 1960. *Il semitico di nord-ovest.* (Istituto universitario orientale di Napoli, Quaderni della sezione linguistica degli annali, 1.) Napoli.

Garbini, Giovanni. 1988. *Il semitico nordoccidentale: Studi di storia linguistica.* (Studi Semitici — Nuova Serie, 5.) Roma.

Garr, W. Randall. 1985. *Dialect Geography of Syria-Palestine, 1000–586 B.C.E.* Philadelphia.

Harris, Zellig S. 1939. *Development of the Canaanite Dialects.* (American Oriental Series, 16.) New Haven.

Israel, Felice. 1984. Geographic Linguistics and Canaanite Dialects. In: James Bynon (ed.). *Current Progress in Afro-Asiatic Linguistics: Papers of the Third International Hamito-Semitic Congress (London, 1978).* (Amsterdam Studies in the Theory and History of Linguistic Science, Series IV; Current Issues in Linguistic Theory, 28.) Amsterdam, 363–387.

Izre'el, Shlomo. 1988. Review of Garr 1985. *Bulletin of the Schools of Oriental Research* 270: 94–97.

Kaufman, Stephen A. 1988. The Classification of the North West Semitic Dialects of the Biblical Period and Some Implications Thereof. In: *Proceedings of the Ninth World Congress of Jewish Studies (Jerusalem, August 4–12, 1985).* Panel Sessions: Hebrew and Aramaic. (Publications of the Perry Foundation for Biblical Research in the Hebrew University of Jerusalem.) Jerusalem, 41–57.

ARABIC DIALECTOLOGY
THE STATE OF THE ART

OTTO JASTROW

In the present paper I should like to review the state of the art in Arabic dialectology. This is not an easy task, because Arabic is by far the largest Semitic language, not only of today but of all times. No other Semitic language has ever occupied an area of similar dimensions or been spoken by so many millions of people. Trying to determine how many dialects of Arabic exist is futile. There are hundreds of them if you define dialects as differing significantly in structure; if you define them as varieties just recognizably different from each other, there are tens of thousands.

Studying Arabic dialectology is the perfect introduction for anybody intending to work in Semitic linguistics or philology. Here you can watch sound changes and morphological changes, syntactic and semantic developments almost as if in a laboratory. It is in fact difficult to think of any diachronic development that does not actually happen in some Arabic dialect somewhere.

These two facts — the importance of the Arabic language area and the abundance of different dialects — have made Arabic dialectology a flourishing discipline over the last century and a half. It is impossible to cite the many important contributions that have been made to this field or to give a detailed outline of the history of the discipline. What I shall try to do, in the limited space available, is to present some of the basic issues in Arabic dialectology — as I see them — and discuss the progress — or lack of progress — that has been made in tackling them.

The rise of Islam in the 7th century A.D. provided the impetus by which the Arabic language area was enlarged to its present impressive dimensions. Before that decisive event, Arabic was confined to the centre and north of the Arabian peninsula and some adjoining areas of the Fertile Crescent. With the Islamic conquests the language area expanded very rapidly. In the north, Palestine and Syria were conquered; in the east, Iraq, Iran and Transoxiana; in the west, Egypt, North Africa up to the Atlantic and, eventually, the larger part of Spain (including Majorca), Sicily and Malta. Not all of these areas were won over permanently to Arabic. In the east, Iranian and later on Turkic languages asserted themselves, but to

347

this day there are Arabic language enclaves all over the eastern borders of Iran, in Afghanistan and even in Uzbekistan.

Add to these the better known Arabic dialect islands of southeastern Turkey and the dialect of Kormakiti in Cyprus. In the west, Spain, Majorca and Sicily were lost to Arabic, but Malta has remained Arabic-speaking to this day. Whereas the progress of Arabic seems to have been halted permanently in the east, the west and the north, it has been progressing steadily southward, namely in North Africa and into Equatorial Africa. Many varieties of Arabic are encountered today as linguistic enclaves in a large expanse of territory stretching from Sudan through Chad, Cameroon, Niger, Nigeria and Mali to Mauretania.

If we keep in mind these facts of the external history of Arabic we can divide the present-day language area into three different zones. **Zone I** is the area taken up by Arabic before the rise of Islam, **Zone II** comprises the vast expanse of territory that became Arabicized due to the Islamic conquests, and **Zone III** comprises the Arabic enclaves or *Sprachinseln* situated outside the continuous Arabic language area. It should be obvious that the varieties of Arabic encountered in these three zones have a very different historical status as well as synchronic structure.

The Arabic dialects spoken in **Zone I**, i.e. the Arabian peninsula, have a time depth that cannot be estimated in absolute terms. They reach down into the prehistory of the language, sometimes displaying features that are plainly more archaic than the respective Classical Arabic forms. It is tempting to view some of these dialects as going back to the formative age when Arabic slowly took shape and detached itself from the Semitic continuum in which it originated. But even without indulging in such diachronic romanticism, we can state unequivocally that it is in the Arabian peninsula that we can find the most archaic Arabic dialects of today. They were preserved because immediately after the Islamic conquests the centre of gravity moved to the new Islamic territories, allowing the peninsula to slip back into a primordial timelessness from which it was torn only a half century ago, with the advent of the age of oil production. Since then, however, an enormous amount of cultural destruction has already been wrought, and more is to come.

The dialects of **Zone II**, on the other hand, could be called colonial Arabic. Their linguistic history starts at the moment when Arabic is implanted in the newly conquered territories. The historical dates are for the most part quite well-known; the *terminus post quem*, obviously, is the rise of Islam in the early 7th century. Therefore the main interest of the dialects of Zone II does not lie in their archaisms but rather in their innovative features. The view already taken by the Arab grammarians, that Arabic was corrupted at the moment when it was adopted by large foreign populations, can be accepted as basically true, except of course for the fact that it is couched in terms of a value judgement from which scholars should abstain. But there can be no denying the fact that the evolution of Arabic dialects became more pronounced with the growing distance from the heartland, i.e. from Zone I, and that the substratal influences of the conquered peoples, be it Aramaic in the north, Iranian and Turkic in the east or Coptic and Berber in the west, asserted themselves in the shaping of new types of dialects. At the same time, the overarching classical language imposed a kind of barrier that prevented these dialects from deviating too much from a common structural pattern. The influence of Standard Arabic is more strongly felt in big cities than in the countryside, but even the rural dialects have never been free to develop entirely on their own. Nevertheless, I cannot accept the widely publicized thesis of Kees Versteegh (1984), according to which the Arabic dialects are a product of pigdinization with subsequent stages of creolization and decreolization (or classicization). This theory is a blatant overstatement that does not capture the essence of the linguistic development of Arabic. It was created on the evidence of some Central African varieties that might be rightly called Pidgin Arabic, but certainly this model is not applicable to all Arabic language islands (called here Zone III), let alone the dialects of Zone II and I.

The Arabic language islands that are here lumped together as **Zone III** all share the fact of being separated from the continuum of the Arabic language area by stretches of territory where other languages are spoken. The minority Arabophone populations of Zone III usually also speak one or several majority languages. Likewise, the medium of education is not Arabic but some other official language, and therefore there is less influence of Classical Arabic to restrain the dialects in their development. The impact of adstrate or superstrate languages is strongest in these dialects and contributes to their exotic character. However, the fact that we have to deal with an Arabic language enclave does not tell us anything about its age. It might be an ancient survival, as in the case of Uzbekistan Arabic, or a product of the recent past like many Central African varieties.

Just which of these three zones should be most important for the study of Arabic dialects is a matter open to debate. I personally would be inclined to give equal importance to all three. As a matter of fact, however, it is Zone II that so far has got the greatest amount of attention. This of course is mainly due to the external history of the Arab world and its interaction with Western powers. The Arabic dialects that were the first objects of scholarly study were those spoken around the Mediterranean. The monumental books that mark the beginnings of our profession, like:

Spitta-Bey (1880) on Cairo
Stumme (1896) on Tunis
W. Marçais (1902) on Tlemcen
W. Marçais (1911) on Tangiers
M. Cohen (1912) on Jewish Algiers
Féghali (1919) on Kfar 'Abīda

describe the dialects of coastal or near coastal towns of the Mediterranean, from Morocco to Lebanon, via Algeria, Tunisia and Egypt. The hinterlands remained unexplored much longer and are still largely so today.

Thus the term 'Egyptian Arabic' for many decades was synonymous with Cairene Arabic, until the joint work of P. Behnstedt and M. Woidich, starting from the late 1970s, gradually unearthed a very rich and variegated dialect landscape. The work of these two scholars culminated in the five volumes of *Die ägyptisch-arabischen Dialekte*, published between 1985 and 1994. They comprised an introductory volume, a dialect atlas, two volumes of texts from all major dialect groups (Delta, Nile Valley, Oases) and an Arabic-German glossary. With the publication of the reverse glossary, German-Arabic, this monumental work was completed in 1999.

A different situation obtained for Greater Syria (i.e. Syria, Lebanon and Palestine). The older literature was more evenly spread over the whole area and included the first dialect atlas, namely G. Bergsträßer's *Sprachatlas von Syrien und Palästina* of 1915, L. Bauer's *Das palästinische Arabisch* of 1910, Barthélemy's monumental *Dictionnaire arabe-français*, published between 1939 and 1965, J. Cantineau's *Le dialecte arabe de Palmyre* (2 vols., 1934) and finally the same author's regional study *Les parlers arabes du Ḥōrān*, published in two volumes in 1940 and 1946; the first volume is a detailed atlas. Research on Syrian Arabic gained a new momentum with the studies done on Damascus Arabic. They were initiated by Hans Wehr, who was the first German Arabist to use a tape recorder (preceded only by Haim Blanc for his 1953 study of the Druze dialects of northern Israel). The texts recorded by Hans Wehr in Damascus were published by Ariel Bloch and Heinz Grotzfeld in 1964, followed by two grammars by Heinz Grotzfeld (1964 and 1965) and a syntactical study by Ariel Bloch (1965). Also in 1964, another very detailed grammar of Damascus Arabic was published by Mark Cowan. In the late 1980s Peter Behnstedt settled down in Aleppo for a couple of years. He published several papers on Aleppo, a two volume study of the oasis dialect of Soukhne (1994) and finally, in 1997, his *magnum opus* 'Sprachatlas von Syrien'.

Let us now turn to Iraq. This country, which is of oustanding importance for Arabic dialectology, was still largely a *terra inognita* until 1964. In that year Haim Blanc published his masterful *Communal Dialects in Baghdad*. A concise book of only 200 pages, it nevertheless marked a turning point in the dialectology of Iraq. Haim Blanc not only described the three divergent dialects spoken by Jews, Christians and Muslims in Baghdad, but also outlined the so-called Mesopotamian Arabic dialect area with its fundamental concept of *qəltu* and *gələt* dialects. The work on Jewish Baghdadi was later continued by a scholar from Haifa, Jacob Mansour, with a detailed grammar, additional texts and an — as yet — unfinished glossary (Mansour 1991 and earlier versions in Hebrew). Christian Arabic of Baghdad was the subject of a study by Farida Abu Haidar in 1991. The present author received his inspiration from Blanc's book and started to work on the northernmost fringes of the Mesopotamian area, namely in southeastern Turkey. He published extensively on the so-called Anatolian *qəltu* dialects (Jastrow 1973, 1978, 1981). Later he shifted his attention further inland and published, in 1990, a book on the Arabic dialects spoken by the Jews of Arbil and 'Aqra in northern Iraq. He also worked on the Jewish and Muslim varieties of Mossul Arabic (Jastrow 1979, 1989, 1991). Until today, Iraq constitutes the unique case of an Arab country whose minority dialects have been investigated much more extensively than the dialects spoken by the Muslim majority. The following, predominantly Muslim areas are still awaiting detailed dialectological research: the Euphrates valley from Falluja up to the Syrian border, the Tigris valley between Samarra and Mossul, the central area around Baghdad and, finally, the Shi'i south including the city of Basra.

Contrary to Iraq, North Africa was covered rather extensively and at a much earlier date. Most of the important early work on Maghrebine Arabic is due to French scholars, especially Marcel Cohen (1912) and William Marçais (1902, 1911), but there are also important contributions by Hans Stumme (1896, 1898). Around the middle of the century there was another upsurge in French fieldwork on North African Arabic, resulting in important studies by Gilbert Boris (1958), Louis Brunot (1939, 1940, 1931-52), William Marçais (1925 and 1958–61), Philippe Marçais (1956) and David Cohen (1963, 1964–1975). Among the most recent French contributions to the field one should mention Dominique Caubet (1993) and the multi-volume dictionary of Ḥassānīya by Cathérine Taine-Cheikh (1988 ff.)

When I talk to linguist colleagues working in other fields I sometimes find it difficult to explain that in Arabic dialectology we often have to investigate not what we would like to but what is accessible to us. This situation is particularly acute when it comes to Zone I, the area comprising the Arabian peninsula. This area is occupied by several independent states, but in the order of importance for dialectology Saudi Arabia comes first, followed by Oman and Yemen; the remaining states, i.e. Kuwait, Bahrain, Qatar and the Emirates, are of much lesser importance. The possibility of fieldwork in this area, especially in Saudi Arabia, has always been restricted, in fact more often than not research was carried out by persons who went there on some other assignment. Nevertheless one could not call the country nowadays a *terra inognita*. There even exists a country-wide survey by Theodore Prochazka Jr. (*Saudi Arabian Dialects*, 1988). The individual areas, however, are very unevenly covered. Best known are the Bedouin dialects of the center (often referred to as Najdi Arabic). Among the most important descriptions one might mention Abboud (1979), Ingham (1982, 1986, 1994) and Johnstone (1967). Important oral traditions of the Najdi tribes have been collected and published by Sowayan (1992) and Kurpershoek (1994, 1995). In contrast, the whole western part of the country, comprising the Ḥijāz, Najrān, 'Asīr and the Saudi Tihāma remains practically uninvestigated, with the notable exception of Mecca (Schreiber 1971). Fieldwork in western Saudi Arabia remains one of the most urgent tasks in Arabic dialectology.

To conclude this short survey, let us now turn to the Arabic language enclaves or *Sprachinseln* — our Zone III. The amount of attention given to the different language islands varies a great deal. The most fascinating one — in my view — namely Uzbekistan Arabic, has been covered quite well by the Soviet scholars Vinnikov (1962, 1969) and G. Tsereteli (1956) in the years before World War II, but their many publications, including several books, have been little studied in the West because they are in Russian. The main desideratum that remains is a phonetic study of this still surviving variety. A kind of dialect continuum, or rather a continuum of language islands, stretches from Uzbekistan via Afghanistan to the eastern borders of Iran where we find many enclaves in the area between Birjand and Sarakhs. These dialects are more or less akin to Uzbekistan Arabic, but so far have been hardly investigated. There is even some affinity between Uzbekistan Arabic and the Anatolian *qəltu* dialects. While many of the latter have been described by the present writer, there still remains a large area in the mountains of Kozluk and Sasson where some intriguingly divergent dialects are awaiting closer investigation.

The Arabic dialect enclave in Cyprus came to the attention of Arabists as late as 1951. This variety, called Cypriot Arabic (Borg 1985), was spoken by a community of Maronite Christians in the village of Kormakiti in the north of Cyprus, but subsequently the community was torn apart by the Turkish invasion of the island in 1974.

A unique case in Arabic dialectology is Maltese, the official language of the state of Malta. Linguistically it originated from an Arabic dialect of predominantly North African (Maghrebine) type, but was considerably enriched by Italian and English vocabulary. Being the language of a Christian nation, Maltese has been completely disconnected from the Arabic-speaking world since the Middle Ages and has developped its own orthography in Latin characters (Puech 1994). In contrast to the Arab states Malta has an interest in promoting the study of its spoken language, and there is an impressive indigenous scholarship in Maltese grammar and lexicography (Aquilina 1959, 1987–90).

Of the many Arabic enclaves in Central Africa we may single out two that have, in recent years, received particular scholarly attention, i.e. Nigeria (Kaye 1976, 1982, 1986, Owens 1993) and Chad (Jullien de Pomerol 1999 a and b).

When the Islamic armies carried the Arabic language from its pre-Islamic territory to the wider Islamic world, they also exported two phenomena apparently connected with Arabic from the beginning, namely the so-called diglossia and the dichotomy of Bedouin vs. sedentary dialects. The term 'diglossia' describes a situation in which two cognate but largely divergent linguistic varieties coexist in a speech community, a 'high variety' (i.e., Classical Arabic or, at present, Modern Standard Arabic) and a 'low variety' (i.e., an Arabic dialect). The two varieties have different social functions that hardly overlap (Ferguson 1959, Diem 1974; — for more elaborate models assuming a number of levels — *mustawayāt* — or using the concept of 'multiglossia' see Badawi 1973 and Hary 1992, respectively). While being absent from most language enclaves (Zone III) where the 'high variety' is usually an official language unrelated to Arabic, diglossia is today, as it was in the past, a stable factor in the Arab countries. Unfortunately the 'low variety', although constituting the basis of everyday speech, is held in contempt by Arab academia, which means that Arabic dialectology as a discipline exists mainly outside the Arab world.

Another feature inherited from the remote past is the dichotomy of Bedouin versus sedentary dialects. In almost every Arab country today we find a clear-cut difference between Bedouin and sedentary dialects even if the speakers of Bedouin dialects may no longer be nomads but have become sedentarized. There is a stereotype, likewise inherited from olden times, that Bedouin Arabic is 'purer' and closer to Literary Arabic than the speech of townspeople. If we take a look at some present-day Bedouin dialects, however, there is not much to corroborate this stereotype, at least not on the phonological level where we find innovations not shared by the sedentary dialects, e.g.

a) Old Arabic *kāf* has become an affricate *č* in the vicinity of front vowels, e.g. **kaff* > *čaff* 'palm of hand', **kabīr* > *čibīr* 'big', **kān* > *čān* 'he was'. In the Central Arabian (Najdi) dialects, the reflex is *c* [ts] instead.

b) Old Arabic *qāf* is represented by a voiced post-velar stop *g* which again, like *k*, has become an affricate *ǧ* in the vicinity of front vowels, e.g., **qidr* > *ǧidir* 'pot', **qarīb* >*ǧirīb* 'close', **sīqān* > *sīǧān* 'legs'. In the Central Arabian (Najdi) dialects, the reflex is *ǧ* [dz] instead.

c) In the sequence *aXC*, where *X* is a 'guttural' (i.e. a post-velar, pharyngal or glottal consonant) and *C* any consonant, a vowel *a* was inserted between *X* and C, e.g. **qahwah* > **gahawah* 'coffee'. This process is called '*gahawah* syndrome'.

d) The vowel *a* in an open syllable (unless in the vicinity of a 'guttural') was raised to *i*, e.g. **katab* > *kitab* 'he wrote', **katabat* > **kitibat* 'she wrote'.

e) In a sequence of two open syllables word stress was shifted to the second open syllable and the vowel of the first was elided. This rule was applied to syllables resulting from the changes described in c) and d) above. Thus, e.g.: **kitibat* > **kitíbat* > *ktibat* 'she wrote', *gahawah* > *gaháwah* > *ghawah* 'coffee'.

Compared to many of the more conservative sedentary dialects that don't have those features, present-day Bedouin dialects thus look progressive rather than conservative. The question is, however, just when did those phonological changes take place? For the internal chronology of the Bedouin dialects it is important to note that some of them do not display the affrication of **k* and **g* (< **q*), i.e. features a) and b) above. Among the dialects that reflect an older stage prior to the affrication are the dialects of the Negev Bedouin (Blanc 1970) and of some Bedouin tribes in southern Najd, e.g. the 'Ajmān and the Āl Murrah (Ingham 1986).

On the morphological level, on the other hand, Central Arabian Bedouin dialects in general are more conservative than the sedentary dialects of the surrounding countries (Zone II). They preserve some archaic features, e.g. the 'internal passive' and the nunation or *tanwīn*. Both features can be exemplified by the Shammar phrase (taken from Sowayan 1992, p. 96) *kill ixīditin tūxad* 'every booty that is being taken'. The only sedentary dialects that display similar morphological features are encountered in Zone I, in the southwestern corner of Saudi Arabia ('Asīr, Najrān) and in Oman. In those regions we find very archaic dialects in which the opposition between the Bedouin and the sedentary type, so clear-cut elsewhere in the Arabic-speaking world, is almost neutralized. Clive Holes, discussing these features in a 1996 article, comes to a similar conclusion: "'Bedouin' and 'sedentary' as categories are not so clearly demarcated in southern Arabia as they are in the Fertile Crescent."

What we need most, in Arabic dialectology, is thus what we are least likely to achieve, namely extensive fieldwork in Saudi Arabia, especially in 'Asīr, Najrān and Tihāma, as well as in Yemen and Oman, that is, in the most conservative areas of Zone I. We also need continued fieldwork on the language islands (Zone III) and on the dialects of the religious minorities.

What happens at present, however, is more or less the opposite. I may be too pessimistic, but sometimes I have the feeling that Arabic dialectology as a discipline is on the decline. It is true that there are still spectacular achievements, like the publication of Behnstedt's *Sprachatlas von Syrien* in 1997, but on the whole, the number of people who take an active interest in Arabic dialectology, either as teachers or as investigators, seems to be decreasing. There are several reasons for this decline. First and foremost is the official attitude in the Arab world, which ranges from indifference to hostility, including denial of the existence of dialects. This attitude, in the long run, tends to diminish the acceptance of the discipline also in the West. Another problem is the inaccessibility of many areas, in fact whole countries, to fieldworkers. Thirdly, the North American continent has more or less given up fieldwork on Arabic dialects. This stands in sharp contrast with the 1960s when, for example, the famous Georgetown series (later renamed the Richard Slade Harrell Arabic Series) was published: based on a contract with the United States Office of Education, a number of excellent textbooks, grammars and dictionaries of four major varieties of Arabic — Urban Moroccan, Cairene, Damascene and Muslim Baghdadi — were produced within just a few years — see, e.g., Clarity et al. 1964, Cowell 1964, Erwin 1963, 1969, Harrell 1962, 1965, 1966, Sobelmann and Harrell 1963, Stowasser and Ani 1964, Woodhead and Beene 1967. Nowadays, however, the United States contributes very little to the field. Although probably the country with the largest number of Arabists in the world, it ranges far behind places like Sweden or Finland in its contribution to Arabic dialectology. The new paradigm in North American linguistics — which reached Arabic studies with some delay — is theory-oriented. New publications are expected to conform to the latest terminology, not to make new data available. Predominant interest in theory, however, very soon brings about a decline in descriptive technique, including transcription. In recent years I have seen many manuscripts on Arabic linguistics that displayed a considerable ignorance of transcription, not only of dialects — any dialects — but also of Standard Arabic.

Germany, in contrast, still remains the strongest country of all in this field. But in German universities the traditional discipline of *Orientalistik* is now being gradually narrowed down to Islamic studies, more precisely to contemporary Islamic studies. Arabic linguistics in general or dialectology in particular have no place in this new concept.

In a larger perspective, and this is my concluding remark, it seems to me that the current academic trend, whether in Arabic, in Semitics or in general linguistics, is slowly disengaging itself from the world of living languages and retreating to a kind of global chatroom where no informants and no fieldwork are needed. During the next century, most of today's languages will become extinct. In anticipation, some linguistic disciplines have started to treat today's living languages as if they were extinct already.

Note: I am endebted to Simon Hopkins for reading an earlier version of this paper and suggesting a number of important improvements both in content and form, not all of which were actually observed. The responsibility for all the remaining imperfections is entirely mine.

BIBLIOGRAPHY

Abboud, P. F. 1979. The Verb in Northern Najdi Arabic. *BSOAS* 42: 467–499.

Abu-Haidar, Farida. 1979. *A Study of the Spoken Arabic of Baskinta*. Leiden-London.

Abu-Haidar, Farida. 1991. *Christian Arabic of Baghdad*. Wiesbaden (Semitica Viva 7).

Agius, Dionisius A. 1996. *Siculo Arabic*. London (Library of Arabic Linguistics 12).

Ambros, Arne A. 1977. *Damascus Arabic*. Malibu.

Aquilina, Joseph. 1959. *The Structure of Maltese*. A Study in Mixed Grammar and Vocabulary. Valetta.

Aquilina, Joseph. *Maltese-English Dictionary*. Vol. 1, 1987; vol. 2, 1990. Malta.

Arnold, Werner. 1998. *Die arabischen Dialekte Antiochiens*. Wiesbaden (Semitica Viva 19).

Badawī, Saʿīd. 1973. *Mustawayāt al-ʿarabiyya al-muʿāṣira fī Miṣr*. Cairo.

Barthélemy, A. 1935–1969. *Dictionnaire Arabe-Français*. Dialectes de Syrie: Alep, Damas, Liban, Jérusalem. Paris.

Bauer, Leonhard. 1910. *Das palästinische Arabisch*. Die Dialekte des Städters und des Fellachen. Leipzig 2nd ed. (reprint 1970).

Behnstedt, Peter. *Die nordjemenitischen Dialekte*. Teil 1: Atlas. Wiesbaden 1985. Teil 2: Glossar. I. Alif-Dāl. Wiesbaden 1992. II. Ḏāl-Ġayn. Wiesbaden 1996 (Jemen-Studien 3).

Behnstedt, Peter. 1987. *Die Dialekte der Gegend von Ṣaʿdah (Nord-Jemen)*. Wiesbaden (Semitica Viva 1).

Behnstedt, Peter. 1989. Christlich-Aleppinische Texte. *ZAL* 20, 43–96.

Behnstedt, Peter. 1994. *Der arabische Dialekt von Soukhne (Syrien)*. Teil 1: Volkstümliche Texte. Teil 2: Phonologie, Morphologie, Syntax. Teil 3: Glossar. 2 vols. Wiesbaden (Semitica Viva 15).

Behnstedt, Peter. 1997–2000. *Sprachatlas von Syrien*. 1. Kartenband, Beiheft. II. Volkskundliche Texte. Wiesbaden (Semitica Viva 17).

Behnstedt, Peter and Manfred Woidich. 1985–94. *Die ägyptisch-arabischen Dialekte*. Bd. 1: Einleitung und Anmerkungen zu den Karten. Bd. 2: Dialektatlas von Ägypten. Bd. 3: Texte (2 vols.). I. Delta-Dialekte. II. Niltaldialekte. III. Oasendialekte. Bd. 4: Glossar Arabisch— Deutsch. Bd. 5: Glossar Deutsch-Arabisch. Wiesbaden (Beihefte zum Tübinger Atlas des Vorderen Orients. Reihe B, Nr. 50, 1–5).

Bergsträßer, Gustav. 1915. Sprachatlas von Syrien und Palästina. *ZDPV* 38 (1969–222).

Blanc, Haim. 1953. *Studies in North Palestinian Arabic*. Linguistic Inquiries among the Druzes of Western Galilee and Mt. Carmel. Jerusalem (Oriental Notes and Studies published by the Israel Oriental Society 4).

Blanc, Haim. 1964. *Communal Dialects in Baghdad*. Cambridge, Mass. (Harvard Middle Eastern Monographs 10).

Blanc, Haim. 1970. The Arabic Dialect of the Negev Bedouins. *Proceedings of the Israel Academy of Sciences and Humanities* IV, 7: 112–150.

Blau, Joshua. 1960. *Syntax des palästinensischen Bauerndialekts von Bīr Zēt*. Walldorf-Hessen.

Bloch, Ariel und Heinz Grotzfeld. 1965. *Damaszenisch-arabische Texte mit Übersetzung, Anmerkungen und Glossar*. Wiesbaden (Abhandlungen für die Kunde des Morgenlandes 35,2).

Bloch, Ariel. 1965. *Die Hypotaxe im Damaszenisch-Arabischen mit Vergleichen zur Hypotaxe im Klassisch-Arabischen*. Wiesbaden (Abhandlungen für die Kunde des Morgenlandes 35,4).

Borg, Alexander. 1985. *Cypriot Arabic*. Stuttgart (Abhandlungen für die Kunde des Morgenlandes 47,4).

Boris, Gilbert. 1958. *Lexique du parler arabe des Marāzîg*. Paris (Études arabes et islamiques. Série 3: Études et documents 1).

Brunot, Louis. 1950. *Introduction à l'arabe marocain*. Paris.

Brunot, Louis et Elie Malka. 1939. *Textes Judéo-arabes de Fès*. Rabat.

Brunot, Louis et Elie Malka. 1940. *Glossaire Judéo-arabe de Fès*. Rabat.

Brunot, Louis. *Textes arabes de Rabat*. I. Textes, transcription et traduction annotée. Paris 1931. II. Glossaire. Paris 1952.

Cantineau, Jean. 1934. *Le dialecte arabe de Palmyre*. I. Grammaire. II. Vocabulaire et textes. Beirut (Mémoires de l'Institut Français de Damas).

Cantineau, Jean. Études sur quelques parlers de nomades d'Orient. *AIEO* 2 (1936) 1–118; 3 (1937) 119–237.

Cantineau, Jean. *Les parlers arabes du Ḥōrān*. I. Notes Générales — Grammaire. Paris 1940. II. Atlas. Paris 1946 (Collections Linguistiques de la Société Linguistique de Paris).

Cantineau, Jean. 1960. *Études de linguistique arabe*. Paris.

Caubet, Dominique. 1993. *L'arabe marocain*. I. Phonologie et Morphosyntaxe. II. Syntaxe et Catégories Grammaticales, Textes. Paris.

Cesàro, Antonio. 1939. *L'arabo parlato a Tripoli*. Roma.

Clarity, Beverly E., Karl Stowasser and Ronald Wolfe. 1964. *A Dictionary of Iraqi Arabic*. English-Arabic. Washington, D.C. (Georgetown University Arabic Series 6).

Cleveland, R.L. 1963. A Classification for the Arabic Dialects of Jordan. *Bulletin of the American Society of Oriental Research* 167: 56–63.

Cohen, David. 1963. *Le dialecte arabe Ḥassānīya de Mauritanie (parler de la Gəbla)*. Paris.

Cohen, David. *Le parler arabe des Juifs de Tunis*. I. Textes et documents linguistiques et ethnographiques. La Haye-Paris 1964. II. Étude linguistique. La Haye-Paris 1975.

Cohen, Marcel. 1912. *Le parler des Juifs d'Algers*. Paris (Collection linguistique publiée par la Société de Linguistique de Paris).

Corriente, Federico. 1977. *A Grammatical Sketch of the Spanish Arabic Dialect Bundle*. Madrid.

Corriente, Federico. 1997. *A Dictionary of Andalusi Arabic*. Leiden (Handbuch der Orientalistik, Erste Abt., 29. Band).

Cowell, Marc W. 1964. *A Reference Grammar of Syrian Arabic (based on the Dialect of Damascus)*. Washington, D.C. (Richard Slade Harrell Arabic Series 7).

Denizeau, Claude. 1960. *Dictionnaire des parlers arabes de Syrie, Liban et Palestine*. (Supplément au dictionnaire arabe-français de A. Barthélemy) Paris. (Études Arabes et Islamiques. Études et Documents 3).

Diem, Werner. 1973. *Skizzen jemenitischer Dialekte*. Wiesbaden (Beiruter Texte und Studien 13).

Diem, Werner. 1974. *Hochsprache und Dialekt im Arabischen*. Untersuchungen zur heutigen arabischen Zweisprachigkeit.

Wiesbaden (Abhandlungen für die Kunde des Morgenlandes XLI, 1).

El-Hajjé, Hassan. 1954. *Le parler arabe de Tripoli (Liban)*.

Erwin, Wallace M. 1963. *A Short Reference Grammar of Iraqi Arabic*. Washington, D.C. (Georgetown University Arabic Series 4).

Erwin, Wallace M. 1969. *A Basic Course in Iraqi Arabic*. Washington, D.C. (The Richard Slade Harrell Arabic Series 11).

Féghali, Michel T. 1919. *Le parler arabe de Kfar 'Abīda (Liban-Syrie)*. Paris.

Ferguson, Charles A. 1959. The Arabic Koinè. *Language* 35: 616–630.

Ferguson, Charles A. 1959. Diglossia. *Word* 15: 325–340.

Fischer, Wolfdietrich. 1959. *Die demonstrativen Bildungen der neuarabischen Dialekte*. Ein Beitrag zur historischen Grammatik des Arabischen. s'Gravenhage (Dissertation Erlangen 1953).

Fischer, Wolfdietrich. 1961. Die Sprache der arabischen Sprachinsel in Uzbekistan. *Der Islam* 36: 232–263.

Fischer, Wolfdietrich und Otto Jastrow (Hsg.). 1980. *Handbuch der arabischen Dialekte*. Wiesbaden (Porta Linguarum Orientalium, N.S. 16).

Fleisch, Henri. 1974. *Études d'arabe dialectal*. Beirut.

Gairdner, William H.T. 1927. *The Phonetics of Arabic*. A Phonetic Inquiry and Practical Manual for the Pronunciation of Classical Arabic and of one Colloquial (the Egyptian). London (The American University of Cairo. Oriental Studies).

Grotzfeld, Heinz 1964. *Laut- und Formenlehre des Damaszenisch-Arabischen*. Wiesbaden (Abhandlungen für die Kunde des Morgenlandes 35,3).

Grotzfeld, Heinz. 1965. *Syrisch-arabische Grammatik (Dialekt von Damaskus)*. Wiesbaden (Porta Linguarum Orientalium, N.S. 8).

Harning, Kerstin Eksell. 1980. *The Analytical Genitive in the Modern Arabic Dialects*. Göteborg (Orientalia Gothoburgensia 5).

Harrell, Richard S. 1957. *The Phonology of Egyptian Colloquial Arabic*. New York.

Harrell, Richard S. 1962. *A Short Reference Grammar of Moroccan Arabic*. Washington, D.C. (Georgetown University Arabic Series 1).

Harrell, Richard S. 1965. *A Basic Course in Moroccan Arabic*. Washington, D.C. (The Richard Slade Harrell Arabic Series 8).

Harrell, Richard S. (ed.). 1966. *A Dictionary of Moroccan Arabic*. Arabic-English. Compiled by Thomas Fox and Mohammed Abu Talib. Washington, D.C. (The Richard Slade Harrell Arabic Series 9).

Hary, Benjamin H. 1992. *Multiglossia in Judeo-Arabic*. With an Edition,

Translation and Grammatical Study of the Cairene Purim Scroll. Leiden.

Heath, Jeffrey and Moshe Bar-Asher. 1982. A Judaeo-Arabic Dialect of Tafilalt (Southeastern Morocco). *ZAL* 9: 32–78.

Hillelson, S. 1935. *Sudan Arabic Texts with Translation and Glossary.* Cambridge.

Hinds, Martin and El-Said Badawi. 1986. *A Dictionary of Egyptian Arabic.* Arabic-English. Beirut.

Holes, Clive. 1989. Towards a Dialect Geography of Oman. *BSOAS* 52: 446–462.

Holes, Clive 1996. The Arabic Dialects of South Eastern Arabia in a Socio-Historical Perspective. *ZAL* 31: 34–56.

Ingham, Bruce. 1982. *North East Arabian Dialects.* London (Library of Arabic Linguistics, Monograph No. 3).

Ingham, Bruce. 1986. Notes on the Dialect of Āl Murrah of Eastern and Southern Arabia. *BSOAS* 49: 271–291.

Ingham, Bruce. 1994. *Najdi Arabic. Central Arabian.* Amsterdam (London Oriental and African Language Library 1).

Jastrow, Otto. 1973. *Daragözü — eine arabische Mundart der Kozluk-Sason-Gruppe (Südostanatolien).* Nürnberg (Erlanger Beiträge zur Sprach- und Kunstwissenschaft 46).

Jastrow, Otto. *Die mesopotamisch-arabischen qəltu-Dialekte.* Bd. I: Phonologie und Morphologie. Wiesbaden 1978. Bd. II: Volkskundliche Texte in elf Dialekten. Wiesbaden 1981 (Abhandlungen für die Kunde des Morgenlandes 43,1 und 46,1).

Jastrow, Otto. 1979. Zur arabischen Mundart von Mossul. *ZAL* 2: 36–75.

Jastrow, Otto. 1989. Notes on Jewish Maṣlāwi. *Jerusalem Studies in Arabic and Islam* 12. *Haim Blanc (1929–1984) in memoriam,* 282–293.

Jastrow, Otto. 1991. Brotbacken. Ein Text im arabischen Dialekt der Juden von Mossul. In memoriam Ezra Laniado. *ZAL* 23: 7–13.

Jastrow, Otto. 1990. *Der arabische Dialekt der Juden von 'Aqra und Arbīl.* Wiesbaden (Semitica Viva 5).

Jastrow, Otto. 1998. Zur Position des Uzbekistan-Arabischen. In: Preissler, Holger und Heidi Stein (Hsg.). *Annäherung an das Fremde.* XXVI. Deutscher Orientalistentag vom 25. bis 29. 9. 1995 in Leipzig. Stuttgart (ZDMG-Suppl. 11), 173–184.

Jiha, Michel. 1964. *Der arabische Dialekt von Bišmizzīn.* Beirut (Beiruter Texte und Studien 1).

Johnstone, Thomas M. 1967. *Eastern Arabian Dialect Studies.* London (London Oriental Studies 17).

Jullien de Pomerol, Patrice. 1999. *Grammaire pratique de l'arabe tchadien*. Paris.

Jullien de Pomerol, Patrice. 1999. *Dictionnaire arabe tchadien-français*. Paris.

Kaye, Alan S. 1976. *Chadian and Sudanese Arabic in the Light of Comparative Arabic Dialectology*. The Hague.

Kaye, Alan S. *A Dictionary of Nigerian Arabic*. Vol. I, Malibu 1982. Vol II, Malibu 1986.

Kurpershoek, P. Marcel. *Oral Poetry and Narratives from Central Arabia*. I. The Poetry of Dindān. A Bedouin Bard in Southern Najd. Leiden 1994. II. The Story of a Desert Knight. The Legend of Šlēwīḥ al-'Aṭāwi and other 'Utayba Heroes. Leiden 1995.

Mansour, Jacob. 1991. *The Jewish Baghdadi Dialect*. Or-Yehuda (Studies in the History and Culture of Iraqi Jewry 7).

Marçais, Philippe. 1956. *Le parler arabe de Djidjelli (Nord Constantinois, Algérie)*. Paris (Publications de l'Institut d'Études Orientales d'Alger 16).

Marçais, Philippe. 1977. *Esquisse grammaticale de l'arabe maghrébin*. Paris.

Marçais, William. 1902. *Le dialecte arabe parlé à Tlemcen*. Grammaire, textes et glossaire. Paris (Publications de l'École des Lettres d'Alger 26).

Marçais, William. 1911. *Textes arabes de Tanger*. Transcription, traduction annotée et glossaire. Paris.

Marçais, William et Abderrahman Guîga. *Textes arabes de Takroûna*. I. Textes, transcription et traduction annotée. Paris 1925. II. Glossaire. Contribution à l'étude du vocabulaire arabe (8 vols.). Paris 1958–61. (Bibliothèque des langues orientales vivantes).

Mitchell, T.F. 1962. *Colloquial Arabic. The Living Language of Egypt*. London.

Owens, Jonathan. 1984. *A Short Reference Grammar of Eastern Libyan Arabic*. Wiesbaden.

Owens, Jonathan. 1993. *A Grammar of Nigerian Arabic*. Wiesbaden (Semitica Viva 10).

Palva, Heikki. 1965. *Lower Galilean Arabic*. An Analysis of its Anaptycic and Prothetic Vowels with Sample Texts. Helsinki (Studia Orientalia Ed. Societas Orientalis Fennica 32).

Panetta, Ester. 1943. *L'arabo parlato a Bengasi*. Roma.

Piamenta, Moshe. 1990–1991. *Dictionary of Post-Classical Yemeni Arabic*. Vol. 1–2. Leiden.

Puech, Gilbert. 1994. *Ethnotextes maltais*. Wiesbaden (Studia Melitensia 1).

Prochazka, Jr., Theodore. 1988. *Saudi Arabian Dialects.* London-New York (Library of Arabic Linguistics. Monograph Nr. 8).

Reichmut, Stefan. 1983. *Der arabische Dialekt der Šukriyya im Sudan.* Hildesheim.

Reinhardt, C. 1894. *Ein arabischer Dialekt gesprochen in 'Oman und Zanzibar.* Stuttgart-Berlin (Lehrbücher des Seminars für Orientalische Sprachen zu Berlin 13).

Rosenhouse, Judith. 1984. *The Bedouin Arabic Dialects.* General Problems and a Close Analysis of North Israel Bedouin Dialects. Wiesbaden.

Rossi, Ettore. 1939. *L'arabo parlato a Ṣan'ā'.* Grammatica — Testi — Lessico. Roma (Pubblicazioni dell' Istituto per l'Oriente).

Sabuni, Abdulghafur. 1980. *Laut- und Formenlehre des arabischen Dialekts von Aleppo.* Frankfurt/M. (Heidelberger Orientalistische Studien 2).

Schabert, Peter. 1976. *Laut- und Formenlehre des Maltesischen anhand zweier Mundarten.* Erlangen (Erlanger Studien 16).

Schmidt, H. und Paul Kahle. 1918, 1930. *Volkserzählungen aus Palästina.* I–II. Göttingen (Forschungen zur Religion und Literatur des Alten und Neuen Testaments I: 17. 18).

Schreiber, Giselher. 1971. *Der arabische Dialekt von Mekka.* Abriß der Grammatik mit Texten und Glossar. Freiburg i.Br. (Islamkundliche Untersuchungen 9) (Dissertation Münster/Westf. 1970).

Singer, Hans-Rudolf. 1984. *Grammatik der arabischen Mundart der Medina von Tunis.* Berlin.

Sobelman, Harvey and Richard S. Harrell (eds.). 1963. *A Dictionary of Moroccan Arabic.* English-Arabic. Washington, D.C. (Georgetown University Arabic Series 3).

Socin, Albert. Der arabische Dialekt von Mosul und Mardin. *ZDMG* 36 (1882) 1–53, 238–277; 37 (1883) 293–318.

Sowayan, Saad A. 1992. *The Arabian Oral Historical Narrative. An Ethnographic and Linguistic Analysis.* Wiesbaden (Semitica Viva 6).

Spiro, Socrates. 1923. *Arabic-English Dictionary of the Modern Arabic of Egypt.* 2nd ed. Cairo.

Spitta-Bey, Wilhelm. 1880. *Grammatik des arabischen Vulgärdialects von Ägypten.* Leipzig.

Stowasser, Karl and Moukhtar Ani. 1964. *A Dictionary of Syrian Arabic (Dialect of Damascus).* English-Arabic. Washington, D.C. (Georgetown University Arabic Series 5).

Stumme, Hans. 1896. *Grammatik des tunisischen Arabisch nebst Glossar.* Leipzig.

Stumme, Hans. 1898. *Märchen und Gedichte aus der Stadt Tripolis in Nordafrika.* Leipzig.

Stumme, Hans. 1904. *Maltesische Studien.* Leipzig.

Sutcliffe, Edmund F. 1936. *A Grammar of the Maltese Language, with Chrestomathy and Vocabulary.* Oxford.

Taine-Cheikh, Cathérine. 1988 ff. *Dictionnaire Ḥassānīya-Français.* Paris.

Talay, Shabo. 1999. *Der arabische Dialekt der Khawētna.* I. Grammatik. Wiesbaden Semitica Viva 21,1).

Talmoudi, Fathi. 1980. *The Arabic Dialect of Sūsa (Tunisia).* Göteborg (Orientalia Gothoburgensia 6).

Trombetti, Alfredo. 1912. *Manuale dell'arabo parlato a Tripoli.* Bologna.

Tsereteli, G.V. 1956. *Arabskie Dialekty Srednej Azii.* Tom I: Bucharskij arabskij dialekt. Tbilisi.

Vanhove, Martine. 1993. *La langue maltaise.* Études syntaxiques d'un dialecte arabe 'périphérique'. Wiesbaden (Semitica Viva 11).

Versteegh, Cornelis (Kees) H.M. 1984. *Pidginisation and Creolisation: The Case of Arabic.* Amsterdam/Philadelphia (Amsterdam Studies in the Theory and History of Linguistic Science. Series IV vol. 33).

Vinnikov, I. N. 1962. *Slovar' dialekta bucharskich arabov.* Moskva (Palestinskij Sbornik. Vypusk 10 [73]).

Vinnikov, I. N. 1969. *Jazyk i fol'klor bucharskich arabov.* Moskva (Akademija Nauk SSSR).

Watson, Janet. 1993. *A Syntax of Ṣanʿānī Arabic.* Wiesbaden (Semitica Viva 13).

Weissbach, F.H. 1930. *Beiträge zur Kunde des Irak-Arabischen.* Leipzig (Leipziger Semitistische Studien 4).

Woodhead, D. R. and W. Beene. 1967. *A Dictionary of Iraqi Arabic.* Arabic-English. Washington, D.C. (The Richard Slade Harrell Arabic Series 10).

NEO-ARAMAIC DIALECTOLOGY
THE STATE OF THE ART

OTTO JASTROW

Aramaic was one of the great languages of antiquity and for many centuries functioned as the *lingua franca* of most of the Near East. Its decline started with the rise of Islam, when it was superseded, in a comparatively short period of time, by a closely related Semitic language, Arabic. Since then Aramaic has been reduced to a bundle of scattered dialects. Once a literary language of great importance, it is now mostly represented by unwritten vernaculars used by marginal populations. So complete was the eclipse of this once pre-eminent language that Orientalists for a long time believed Aramaic to have become extinct altogether. It was only in the second part of the 19th century that the scholarly world became aware of the continued existence of Aramaic as a spoken vernacular. Only gradually were the various Neo-Aramaic idioms discovered and investigated, but quite from the beginning of this new discipline in Aramaic studies the disappearance of Neo-Aramaic varieties proceeded at a greater speed than their scholarly investigation and documentation. The speakers of Neo-Aramaic idioms, all belonging to religious minorities, were subjected to almost continuous persecutions, which in some cases took the character of genocide. As a result, most Neo-Aramaic speakers today are refugees scattered over five continents, and the chances of survival for Neo-Aramaic are bleak indeed. It is therefore certainly very appropriate to try to define the state of the art in Neo-Aramaic studies and to ask ourselves what has been achieved, what should be done and what we can realistically hope to achieve in the near future.

Neo-Aramaic today exists in the following four groups:

(1) Western Neo-Aramaic (WNA) is spoken only in three villages in the Qalamun mountains in Syria, some 60 kms northwest of Damascus, namely Ma'lūla, Bax'a and Ǧubb'adīn. The population is in part still Christian, but in part became islamicized about two or three centuries ago. Only these three villages, with an estimated 5,000 speakers, today represent the western branch of Aramaic. The three following groups all belong to the eastern branch or Eastern Neo-Aramaic. They are:

(2) Ṭuroyo, a cluster of closely related dialects spoken in the province

of Mardin in southeastern Turkey by Syrian Orthodox Christians. I think
it appropriate to call Ṭuroyo a language because it is internally uniform
and at the same time sharply different from the neighbouring varieties.
The variety most closely related to Ṭuroyo was the language of Mlaḥsô,
formerly spoken in two villages in Diyarbakır province (Jastrow 1994). It
became extinct in 1998 when the presumably last speaker died in Qāmišli
in Syria.

(3) Northeastern Neo-Aramaic or NENA. Here we have to deal with
a large group of different languages and dialects that are scattered over
an enormous territory comprising southeastern Turkey, northern Iraq and
northwestern Iran. Of course we are dealing only with language enclaves
or language islands (*Sprachinseln*) surviving in a predominantly Kurdish
and, in the case of Azerbaijan, Turkic language area. The NENA languages
are spoken by Christian and Jewish communities.

We shall presently return to this group, which is oustanding for the
number of varieties it comprises. Before that, however, let us mention the
last of the four main groups, namely Neo-Mandaic.

(4) Neo-Mandaic was spoken until recently — and hopefully still is
on a modest scope — by the so-called Mandeans, followers of a gnostic
religion which survived in southern Mesopotamia in the Šaṭṭ el-'Arab
region, both in Iraq and the neighbouring Iranian province of Khuzistan.
The Mandeans were particularly afflicted by the First Gulf War, when
their habitat became a war zone. Most of them have left the area and
sought refuge in the West. Reportedly, thousands of them are now living
in Australia, in the Sydney area.

When we look at the geographical distribution of the surviving four
Neo-Aramaic language groups and at the distances separating them —
from the mountains north of Damascus to the marshes of the Šaṭṭ el-'Arab
— we can still feel the size of the original Aramaic language area, of
which they are the last remains. The area where Neo-Aramaic survived
best, however, is the area of Kurdistan, home of the many NENA varieties.

At this point it may be useful to say a word about the degree of linguistic
differentiation obtaining between the Neo-Aramaic varieties. There can
be no doubt that the four main groups are mutually incomprehensible.
Among the NENA group again there may be at least a dozen language
profiles different enough to be mutually incomprehensible. Let us remain
on the macro-level of the four main groups and give just two linguistic
examples illustrating the structural differences, one taken from phonology,
and one taken from morphology.

The example taken from phonology illustrates in a single word two
characteristic sound shifts, one concerning the O(ld) A(ramaic) long vowel

ā, the other the OA pharyngal fricative *ḥ*. They are both represented in the same Aramaic word, namely *ḥmārā* 'donkey'. Here is what we get:

Maʿlūla	Ṭuroyo	NENA	N-Mandaic
ḥmōra	*ḥmōro*	*xmāra*	*(hmāra)*

The Neo-Mandaic word is not actually documented, perhaps non-existing, but it would have the shape indicated in brackets. The sample word shows the shift of long *ā* to *ō* in the two westernmost varieties, Maʿlūla and Ṭuroyo. While in Ṭuroyo the change is unconditional, in Maʿlūla it takes place only in a stressed syllable. The OA pharyngal *ḥ* is preserved in the two westernmost varieties, in NENA it is predominantly shifted to *x*, in Mandaic to *h*.

Now comes our morphological example. OA has a prefix conjugation — *yiqṭul* — and a suffix conjugation — *q(ə)ṭal*. Both survived in Western Neo-Aramaic (Maʿlūla); in Mandaic only the suffix conjugation survived. In the two more central groups, Ṭuroyo and NENA, neither survived and instead a construction based on the older participles was introduced. The examples use the root for 'to open' and 'to kill', respectively.

Maʿlūla	Ṭuroyo	NENA	N-Mandaic	(< former)
ifθaḥ	*ftiḥ-le*	*ptix-le*	*gəṭal*	(suffix conjug.)
yifθuḥ	*fōtiḥ*	*pātix*	*gāṭel*	(prefix conjug.)

Note that in Maʿlūla *ifθaḥ* the *i* vowel, although carrying the word stress, is originally an anaptyctic vowel, not a prefix as in *yifθuḥ*. The meaning of the above forms is still close to the original functions of suffix and prefix conjugation, thus the first line denotes the past, meaning 'he opened' and 'he killed', respectively; the second line denotes future or subjunctive, thus, e.g.

Maʿlūla	Ṭuroyo	
batte yifθuḥ	*kōbiʿ fōtiḥ*	he wants to open/will open

We are now ready to cast a second glance on the largest existing Neo-Aramaic group, namely NENA. As pointed out, NENA is just a blanket term under which an amazing variety of languages and dialects are lumped together. The NENA area begins in southeastern Turkey where it borders upon Ṭuroyo. The river Tigris here acts as a borderline dividing the two groups. Formerly the NENA territory in Turkey was very important because it comprised a large area in the Hakkari mountains, the home of the Nestorian Christians. The Nestorians were organized in tribes living in the various valleys of the high mountains; their paramount chief was the Nestorian patriarch. During World War I the Nestorians were attacked by the Turkish army and forced to flee from their country. They took refuge with the British in Iraq, but a few years later, thousands of them were able to cross the Tigris into northeastern Syria, where they settled along the Khabour river. There are almost 40 Nestorian — or, as they now call themselves, Assyrian — villages on the Khabour. The villages were settled according to the original tribal affiliations and therefore it is possible until today to retrieve most of the original Hakkari dialects, although in a somewhat diluted form, from among the Khabour Assyrians. In recent years, however, a severe and permanent water shortage has forced most of the Khabour people into exile. Many of them are now to be found in the USA or Australia.

The NENA area continues from the Turkish border into Iraq. It covers the whole of northern Iraq and the adjoining regions of northwestern Iran, more precisely Iranian Azerbaijan and Iranian Kurdistan. Of course we always have to bear in mind that we are talking only of a number of small language islands scattered over a very large territory, which is predominantly Kurdish- or Azeri-speaking. The Aramaic dialects in this large area are divided according to two concurrent principles: one is the geographical distribution, the other the religious affiliation. Thus while it may be only natural that a Jewish dialect in Iranian Azerbaijan is completely different from a Jewish dialect in Iranian Kurdistan, given the considerable geographic distance, it is less commonplace but highly characteristic for NENA that a Jewish and a Christian dialect coexisting in the same town may be completely different as well. Take for instance the town of Urmia on the shore of lake Urmia in Azerbaijan, which had both a Christian and a Jewish Aramaic-speaking minority. To the Christians, however, the speech of the smaller Jewish community was quite incomprehensible and they did not consider it Aramaic at all. In order to communicate with each other Christians and Jews would resort to the majority languages Azeri and Persian.

It is certainly not possible, in the short space available, to convey more than the most fleeting impression of the far-reaching linguistic divergences obtaining among the NENA varieties. I shall try to illustrate them with a sound change involving the interdentals $\underline{t}$ an $\underline{d}$ of Middle Aramaic, as presented by the words *baitā/bētā* 'house' and **īdā* 'hand'.

	'house'	'hand'
Hakkari —Tkhuma tribe (Christ.)	*bḗθa*	*íða*
Hakkari — Tiari tribe (Christ.)	*bḗša*	*ída*
Hakkari — Jilu tribe (Christ.)	*bíya*	*ída*
N Iraq — Christians	*bḗθa*	*íða*
NW Iraq — Jews (e.g., Zākho)	*bḗsa*	*íza*

NE Iraq — Jews (e.g., Amediya)	*bḗθa*	*íða*
Iran. Azerbaijan — Christians	*bḗta*	*ída*
Iran. Azerbaijan — Jews	*bēlá*	*īdá*
Iran. Kurdistan — Christians	*bḗsa*	*ída*
Iran. Kurdistan — Jews	*bēlá*	*īlá*

Without going into too much detail, we can make the following observations. In the Middle Aramaic period a sound change dubbed Spirantization of *Begadkefat* took place, by which stops were shifted to fricatives in postvocalic and intervocalic position. The Old Aramaic words *baitā* and *īdā* thus became *baitā* and *īdā*. The two newly created interdentals have been preserved in a good many NENA varieties, as can be seen from the above list, but there were also various sound shifts. Sometimes they involved both *t* and *d* in a symmetrical way, yielding for instance two dental stops — *t* and *d* — or two sibilants — *s* and *z*. Sometimes the sound change was asymmetrical, yielding for instance a sibilant and a stop — *s* and *d*. On Iranian territory apparently there are no instances of dialects preserving the interdentals. On the other hand there is a unique lateral reflex that appears in two degrees. In the northern area of Azerbaijan only the voiceless interdental yields a lateral reflex, while the voiced interdental is represented by *d*; in the Kurdistan area, however, both older *t* and *d* are represented by the lateral *l*, yielding *bēlá* 'house' and *īlá* 'hand'. Incidentally, these dialects also preserve an older stress pattern, with nouns stressed on the last syllable, whereas in the remaining dialects stress has shifted to the penultimate. (The fact that in the surrounding Turkish and Iranian languages stress usually falls on the last syllable may have contributed to this preservation.)

After this short survey of the surviving Neo-Aramaic varieties, let us now turn to an assessment of the actual state of the art, again divided according to the four main groups.

WESTERN NEO-ARAMAIC (NWA)

This has for a long time been the smallest variety involved, being spoken only by the people of three villages (Ma'lūla, Bax'a and Ǧubb'adīn) totalling some 5,000 speakers. Moreover, there is a longstanding bilingualism, with Syrian Arabic functioning as a second language. A few decades ago scholars therefore were wont to predict that WNA would be the first Neo-Aramaic language to become extinct, while some NENA varieties, especially the Christian ones, with many thousands of speakers at the time, were considered much safer. But history took a different, unfortunately much harsher direction, and today WNA is the only variety that is still spoken, unthreatened, on its traditional territory. The inhabitants of the three villages are in fact the only speakers of Neo-Aramaic who have not seen any persecution at all. Since there are still children growing up speaking Aramaic as a first language, there is no fear for WNA in the immediate future. Likewise the state of scholarly investigation of this language is rather satisfactory. Werner Arnold, continuing the work of his predecessors Prym and Socin (ed. by Bergsträsser 1915), Bergsträsser (1915, 1919, 1921), Reich (1937), Spitaler (1938) and Correll (1978), has in recent years produced six books (Arnold 1989–91) which make WNA the best-known of all Neo-Aramaic languages. His books comprise four volumes of newly recorded texts (two from Ma'lūla and one each from the other two villages), a comparative grammar of the three dialects and an introductory language course to be used in the classroom. Arnold is now working on a comprehensive dictionary, the last major tool still wanting in WNA studies.

ṬUROYO

Until the year 1970 Ṭuroyo was still spoken by approximately 20,000 people in its original homeland, the so-called Ṭūr 'Abdīn in southeastern Turkey. As pointed out earlier, the language area was compact and the dialect differences only minor. The main dialect cleavage separated the dialect of the only town of very modest proportions, Midyat, from the village dialects, spoken in some 30 villages. Since 1970, however, the situation has changed much for the worse, because a large majority of Ṭuroyo speakers have fled from religious persecution and are today scattered over central Europe and the USA. In Germany alone there are now an estimated 40,000 Syrian-Orthodox Christians from Ṭūr 'Abdīn. Even if we take into consideration that only the older people among them who still grew up in the old country can serve as fullfledged informants, there are virtually hundreds of persons in Germany who could be used in a linguistic investigation.

The Ṭuroyo language first became known through a volume of texts published by Eugen Prym and Albert Socin in 1881, but subsequently research stopped for 80 years. In 1960 the late Hellmut Ritter became interested in Ṭuroyo and started to collect tape recordings and grammatical data. Between 1967 and 1971 he published three volumes of new texts, more than 2,000 pages in total. He had planned to continue with a grammar and a dictionary, but he died before he could complete his projects. He left behind, however, two bulky manuscripts, one entitled "Wörterbuch", the other "Grammatik". Both manuscripts were in a very unfinished state, but Rudolf Sellheim, who was responsible for Ritter's manuscripts, decided to publish them in facsimile in order to make the data accessible to the scholarly world. The so-called "Wörterbuch" was published in 1979. It contains Ritter's lexical material excluding the verbs. All lexical data on the verbs are contained in the second volume, the so-called "Grammatik", published in 1990. This grammar mainly deals with the Ṭuroyo verb and gives a very detailed and accurate description of its complex morphology, complete with many paradigms and all the lexical material.

The present author took a different approach to Ṭuroyo studies. He concentrated on a single dialect, the one spoken in the easternmost village of Midin, and, for his dissertation, wrote a grammatical description of that particular dialect (Jastrow 1967, 4th edition 1993). Years later, Jastrow had a suitable doctoral student who was himself a native Ṭuroyo speaker from Midin, Shabo Talay. With his assistance, Jastrow was able to publish a Ṭuroyo language course in 20 lessons, called *Lehrbuch der Ṭuroyo-Sprache* (Jastrow 1992).

There are several important issues in Ṭuroyo studies that so far have not been taken up. First of all, more work should be done on the actual dialectology of Ṭuroyo because most of the 30-odd dialects have not yet been described as varieties in their own right. This is especially true for the urban dialect of Midyat, which would be a very rewarding subject for a monograph. The absence of a dictionary is a severe lack too. The two postumously published works by Ritter (1979, 1990) can by no means fill this gap. Since a full-fledged dictionary of Ṭuroyo at this time is nowhere in sight, I have decided to publish my own files of the verb — basically an ordered wordlist of Ritter's material — as a Ṭuroyo verb glossary. This is a limited project that I should be able to complete within a forseeable length of time.

NEO-MANDAIC

What we know about Neo-Mandaic we owe to a single person, the late Rudolf Macuch. He is the one who discovered Neo-Mandaic during his stay in Iran in the 1950s, and to date he has been the only scholar to publish on the subject. His last book, *Neumandäische Texte im Dialekt von Ahwāz* (Macuch 1993), is also his best. It contains a grammatical sketch (100 pages), texts (260 pages) and a glossary (80 pages). Unfortunately, however, Macuch had a pre-phonological approach to language studies; therefore his description of the sound system and the morphology of this important variety is far from transparent.

Neo-Mandaic, however, is a good example of a language that is hard to investigate because it is not accessible. The original language area in the Šaṭṭ al-'Arab hardly invites fieldwork, and in any case not too many Mandaeans are left there. There are, of course, many refugees in a place both very remote and quite accessible, namely Australia. But there is another problem even more difficult to overcome: most Mandaeans of today do not speak Mandaic any longer. Thus it seems doubtful whether there will be any new research at all.

THE NENA GROUP

What remains to discuss now is the state of the art in NENA research. NENA, short for Northeastern Neo-Aramaic, is the largest and most complex group of Neo-Aramaic, as I pointed out in the previous discussion. Consequently, although it has attracted more research than the smaller groups, the overall results are far from satisfactory. Let us shortly discuss the main subgroups one by one.

HAKKARI DIALECTS (SOUTHEASTERN TURKEY)

Suprisingly, the research situation for the Hakkari dialects is not as gloomy as one would expect, given the fact that the speakers, the so-called Hakkari Nestorians, were driven out of their country more than 80 years ago. Due to the secondary settlements in the Khabour area, many of the original Hakkari dialects have survived. My former doctoral student, Shabo Talay, spent half a year in the Khabour region in 1997 and is at present working on a comparative description of all remaining dialects. Another young scholar in Neo-Aramaic studies, Hezy Mutzafi from Tel Aviv University, has, besides his fieldwork on the Jewish NENA varieties, collected very interesting material on the Hakkari dialects during a stay in Australia. Besides Australia, there is of course the USA, which is today home to a large number of speakers not only of Hakkari varieties but of all Christian NENA dialects. Sam Fox, working in Chicago, recently published a monograph on one of the rarer Hakkari dialects, namely Jilu (Fox 1997).

CHRISTIAN NENA DIALECTS OF IRAQ AND IRAN

During the last decades, the large Aramaic-speaking Christian communities in Iraq and Iran have been more or less dissolved, and speakers are now to be found almost everywhere on the globe.

This is an opportunity for research, but a bad omen for the future because no language is likely to survive under these conditions for long. Unfortunately this situation has not been matched by a surge of renewed interest in the Christian NENA varieties. One notable exception is Helen Younansardaroud of Berlin, who has just completed a dissertation on her native dialect of Sardaroud, a village in the vicinity of Urmia (Younansardaroud 1999). Whoever sofar has studied the Christian Urmi or Urmia dialect must have been both amazed by the complexity of its phonological system and exasperated by the rather inadequate descriptions given thereof. The dissertation of Younansardaroud presents a very clear and convincing outline of the phonology and phonetics that goes far beyond the earlier studies.

JEWISH NENA DIALECTS OF IRAQ AND IRAN

The fate of the Jewish communities speaking NENA dialects was somewhat different from the Christian ones. When in 1950–51 the whole Jewish population of Iraq was removed to Israel in a spectacular airlift later to be called "Operation Ezra and Nehemia" there were among them speakers of dozens of Jewish NENA varieties, none of which had been previously investigated. Material was collected on some of them, but others were neglected for a long time. One of the dialects that first attracted scholarly attention was that of the Jews of Zākho, at the same time the dialect with the largest number of speakers. The late Professor H.J. Polotsky collected very valuable material on Zākho, but published only part of it (Polotsky 1961, 1979, 1986). More recently, Bob Hobermann published a book on the verb in the dialect of Amediya (Hoberman 1990). Both Bob Hoberman and Hezy Mutzafi collected data on the Jewish dialect of Koy Sandjaq, a very intriguing variety, but so far their data have not been published.

The Jewish NENA dialects of Iran had a similar fate. Although the majority of the speakers left Iran for Israel at the same time as the Iraqi Jews, some stayed on until the outbreak of Khomeini's Islamic revolution in 1979, when they were forced to leave. Again, some of their dialects have since been studied while others are still neglected. Whereas for the Azerbaijani subgroup there existed an earlier book by Irene Garbell (1964), the Jewish dialects of Iranian Kurdistan remained virtually unknown until the beginning of the 1980s. According to Simon Hopkins, one of the best specialists of this subgroup, these dialects are "quite exotic and unlike anything else in NENA." That was perhaps the reason why Hopkins did extensive fieldwork especially for these dialects. He collected an impressive amount of first-rate tape recordings and linguistic data and, some years ago, set himself to write a comprehensive study of Kerend, the southernmost dialect of this subgroup and, incidentally, of the whole NENA group. Unfortunately the publication of this major work was hampered by many technical problems, but I am hopeful that it will soon see the light. Meanwhile, under the supervision of Gideon Goldenberg, Yaffa Israeli wrote a dissertation on Saqqiz, another dialect of the Iranian Kurdistan subgroup (Israeli 1998).

When we compare the state of the art in Arabic dialectology with that in Neo-Aramaic, we have no reason to complain. For a discipline so extravagant and exotic, the number of people engaged in serious research is quite amazing. Our main problem is that time is running out for Neo-Aramaic, for some varieties faster than for others, but the *ineluctabile tempus* is drawing closer for all of them. For this reason fieldwork must be given absolute priority, at the expense of other fascinating approaches like diachronic and comparative studies or the study of the written Neo-Aramaic varieties, a subject upon which I could not touch in this short paper.

To end on a somewhat bitter note: If Arabic dialectology suffers from the indifference and sometimes even hostility manifested toward it by the official Arab world, Neo-Aramaic linguistics is no less bedeviled by the contempt of scholars of the classical Aramaic varieties, who for the most part do not care at all about the modern languages. For them Neo-Aramaic seems to be a subject more akin to Bantu studies than to their own field. I daresay, however, that all students of the classical Aramaic varieties could greatly benefit from delving into the intricate grammatical structures of Neo-Aramaic, and a course in one Neo-Aramaic language should become mandatory for all of them.

Note: I am indebted to Simon Hopkins for reading an earlier version of this paper and suggesting a number of important improvements both in content and form, not all of which were actually observed. The responsibility for all the remaining imperfections is entirely mine.

BIBLIOGRAPHY

Arnold, Werner. *Das Neuwestaramäische*. I. Texte aus Bax'a. Wiesbaden 1989. II. Texte aus Ǧubb'adīn. Wiesbaden 1990. III: Volkskundliche Texte aus Ma'lūla. Wiesbaden 1991. IV: Orale Literatur aus Ma'lūla. Wiesbaden 1991. V. Grammatik. Wiesbaden 1990. VI: Wörterbuch (in preparation). (Semitica Viva 4, I–VI).

Arnold, Werner. 1989. *Lehrbuch des Neuwestaramäischen*. (Semitica Viva, series didactica 1). Wiesbaden.

Avinery, Iddo. 1988. *The Aramaic Dialect of the Jews of Zākhō* (in Hebrew). Jerusalem.

Bergsträsser, Gustav (ed.). 1915. *Neuaramäische Märchen und andere Texte aus Maʿlūla*, hauptsächlich aus der Sammlung E. Pryms und A. Socins. Leipzig.

Bergsträsser, Gustav. 1919. Neue Texte im aramäischen Dialekt von Maʿlūla. *Zeitschrift für Assyriologie* 32: 103–163.

Bergsträsser, Gustav. 1921. *Glossar des neuaramäischen Dialekts von Maʿlūla*. Leipzig.

Correll, Christoph. 1978. *Untersuchungen zur Syntax der neuwestaramäischen Dialekte des Antilibanon*. (Abhandlungen für die Kunde des Morgenlandes XLIV,4). Wiesbaden.

Fox, Samuel Ethan. 1997. *The Neo-Aramaic Dialect of Jilu*. (Semitica Viva 16). Wiesbaden.

Friedrich, Johannes. 1959. Neusyrisches in Lateinschrift aus der Sowjetunion. *ZDMG* 109: 50–81.

Friedrich, Johannes. 1960. *Zwei russische Novellen in neusyrischer Übersetzung und Lateinschrift*. (Abhandlungen für die Kunde des Morgenlandes XXXIII,4). Wiesbaden.

Garbell, Irene. 1964. Flat Words and Syllables in Jewish East New Aramaic of Persian Azerbaijan and the Contiguous Districts (A Problem in Multilingualism). In: H. B. Rosén (ed.): *Studies in Egyptology and Linguistics in Honor of H. J. Polotsky*. Jerusalem.

Garbell, Irene. 1965. *The Jewish Neo-Aramaic Dialect of Persian Azerbaijan*. The Hague.

Goldenberg, Gideon. 1992. Aramaic Perfects. *Israel Oriental Studies* XII: 113–137.

Heinrichs, Wolfhart (ed.). 1990. *Studies in Neo-Aramaic* (Harvard Semitic Studies 36). Atlanta.

Hetzron, Robert. 1969. The Morphology of the Verb in Modern Syriac (Christian Colloquial of Urmi). *JAOS* 89: 112–127.

Hoberman, Robert D. 1985. The Phonology of Pharyngeals and Pharyngealization in Pre-Modern Aramaic. *JAOS* 104: 221–231.

Hoberman, Robert D. 1988. The History of the Modern Aramaic Pronouns and Pronominal Suffixes. *JAOS* 108,4: 557–575.

Hoberman, Robert D. 1989. *The Syntax and Semantics of Verb Morphology in Modern Aramaic*. A Jewish Dialect of Iraqi Kurdistan. New Haven.

Hoberman, Robert D. 1990. Reconstructing Pre-Modern Aramaic Morphology: The Independent Pronouns. In: Heinrichs, Wolfhart (ed.): *Studies in Neo-Aramaic* (Harvard Semitic Studies 36). Atlanta, 79–88.

Hopkins, Simon. 1989. Neo-Aramaic Dialects and the Formation of the Preterite. *JSS* 34,2: 413–432.

Hopkins, Simon. (in preparation). *The Jewish Neo-Aramaic Dialect of Kerend (Iranian Kurdistan).* I. Texts, Translations and Notes. II. Grammar, Glossary.

Israeli, Yaffa. 1998. *The Jewish Neo-Aramaic Language of Saqqiz (Southern Kurdistan)* (in Hebrew). Jerusalem (PhD Dissertation, The Hebrew University).

Jacobi, Heidi. 1973. *Grammatik des thumischen Neuaramäisch (Nordostsyrien).* (Abhandlungen für die Kunde des Morgenlandes XL,3). Wiesbaden.

Jastrow, Otto. 1993. *Laut- und Formenlehre des neuaramäischen Dialekts von Mīdin im Ṭūr 'Abdīn.* 4th edition (Semitica Viva 9) Wiesbaden (Dissertation, Universität des Saarlandes, 1967).

Jastrow, Otto. 1988. *Der neuaramäische Dialekt von Hertevin (Provinz Siirt).* (Semitica Viva 3). Wiesbaden.

Jastrow, Otto. 1990. Personal and Demonstrative Pronouns in Central Neo-Aramaic. In: Heinrichs, Wolfhart (ed.): *Studies in Neo-Aramaic* (Harvard Semitic Studies 36). Atlanta, 89–103.

Jastrow, Otto. 1992. *Lehrbuch der Ṭuroyo-Sprache.* (Semitica Viva, Series Didactica 2). Wiesbaden.

Jastrow, Otto. 1994. *Der neuaramäische Dialekt von Mlaḥsô.* (Semitica Viva 14). Wiesbaden.

Krotkoff, Georg. 1982. *A Neo-Aramaic Dialect of Kurdistan.* Texts, Grammar, and Vocabulary. New Haven.

Krotkoff, Georg. 1990. An Annotated Bibliography of Neo-Aramaic. In: Heinrichs, Wolfhart (ed.): *Studies in Neo-Aramaic* (Harvard Semitic Studies 36). Atlanta, 3–26.

Maclean, Arthur John. 1895. *Grammar of the Dialects of Vernacular Syriac.* Cambridge.

Maclean, Arthur John. 1901. *Dictionary of the Dialects of Vernacular Syriac.* Oxford.

Macuch, Rudolf. 1965. *Handbook of Classical and Modern Mandaic.* Berlin.

Macuch, Rudolf. 1989. *Neumandäische Chrestomathie mit grammatischer Skizze, kommentierter Übersetzung und Glossar.* (Porta Linguarum Orientalium, Neue Serie XVIII). Wiesbaden.

Macuch, Rudolf. 1993. *Neumandäische Texte im Dialekt von Ahwāz.* (Semitica Viva 10). Wiesbaden.

Marogulov, Q. I. 1976. *Grammaire néo-syriaque pour écoles d'adultes* (dialecte d'Urmiah), traduit par Olga Kapeliuk (GLECS Suppl. 5). Paris.

Nakano, Aki'o. 1973. *Conversational Texts in Eastern Neo-Aramaic (Gzira Dialect).* (Study of Languages and Cultures of Asia and Africa, A Series, No. 4) Tokyo.

Nöldeke, Theodor. 1868. *Grammatik der neusyrischen Sprache am Urmia-See und in Kurdistan.* Leipzig.

Odisho, Edward Y. 1988. *The Sound System of Modern Assyrian (Neo-Aramaic).* (Semitica Viva 2). Wiesbaden.

Pennacchietti, Fabrizio A. and Mauro Tosco. 1991. *Testi Neo-Aramaici dell' Unione Sovietica raccolti da Enrico Cerulli.* (Istituto Universitario Orientale, Dipartimento di Studi Asiatici, series minor XXXV). Napoli.

Polotsky, H. J. 1961. Studies in Modern Syriac. *JSS* 6: 1–13.

Polotsky, H. J. 1979. Verbs with two objects in Modern Syriac (Urmi). *Israel Oriental Studies* 9: 204–227.

Polotsky, H. J. 1986. Neusyrische Konjugation. In: *On the Dignity of Man. Oriental and Classical Studies in Honour of Frithiof Rundgren,* edd. Tryggve Kronholm and Eva Riad (Orientalia Suecana 33–35). Stockholm.

Prym, Eugen und Albert Socin. 1881. *Der neuaramäische Dialekt des Ṭūr 'Abdīn.* 2 vols. Göttingen.

Reich, S. 1937. *Études sur les villages araméens de l'Anti-Liban.* (Documents d'Études Orientales, Tome VII). Damascus.

Ritter, Hellmut. *Ṭūrōyo. Die Volkssprache der syrischen Christen des Ṭūr 'Abdīn.* A: Texte. Band I–III. Beirut 1967–1971. B: Wörterbuch. Beirut 1979. C: Grammatik. Stuttgart 1990.

Sachau, Eduard. 1895. *Skizze des Fellichi-Dialekts von Mosul.* Berlin.

Sara, Salomon I. 1974. *A Description of Modern Chaldean.* The Hague.

Spitaler, Anton. 1938. *Grammatik des neuaramäischen Dialekts von Ma'lūla (Antilibanon).* (Abhandlungen für die Kunde des Morgenlandes XXIII,1). Leipzig.

Tsereteli, Konstantin. 1978. *Grammatik der modernen assyrischen Sprache (Neuostaramäisch).* Übersetzt von Peter Nagel. Leipzig.

Younansardaroud, Helen. 1999. *Der neuaramäische Dialekt von Sardaroud (Urmia-Gebiet).* (Dissertation, Freie Universität Berlin).

LES LANGUES SUDARABIQUES MODERNES A L'AUBE DE L'AN 2000
EVALUATION DES CONNAISSANCES

MARIE-CLAUDE SIMEONE-SENELLE[*]

INTRODUCTION

Sous l'appellation générique de "sudarabique moderne" (= SAM) sont regroupées actuellement six langues: *mehri, hobyot, harsusi, bathari, jibbali, soqotri.* L'aire de répartition de ces langues est restreinte et assez homogène; sur le continent, elle comprend la province du Mahra, à l'est du Yémen, et à l'ouest d'Oman, la région du Dhofar, la baie et les îles de Kurya Murya ainsi que le Jiddat al-Harâsis; les îles yéménites de Soqotra, Abd-al-Kuri et Samha, dans le golfe d'Aden, représentent un prolongement excentré de cette zone sudarabophone. Le nombre de citoyens yéménites et omanais qui ont pour langue maternelle une langue sudarabique est difficile à évaluer précisément, l'estimation varie entre 100.000 et 140.000 locuteurs.

Ces langues sémitiques, qui appartiennent à la branche méridionale du sémitique occidental, sont restées inconnues jusqu'au milieu du dix-neuvième siècle.

L'existence, dans le sud de la Péninsule arabique, de langues *parlées*, différentes de l'arabe, est mentionnée dès le dixième siècle de l'ère chrétienne, donc peu de temps après les dernières inscriptions en sudarabique ancien; mais il faut attendre la fin de la première moitié du dix-neuvième siècle pour apprendre que ces langues sont encore parlées et, en même temps, avoir un aperçu de leur structure linguistique. D'abord par le biais de la publication de listes lexicales (Wellsted 1835a, 1835b, 1840), puis grâce à une approche descriptive, plus linguistique (Fresnel 1938). La paternité des études sudarabiques modernes revient aux savants viennois qui, à partir de 1898, se rendirent en Arabie dans le cadre de la *Südarabische Expedition* ou dans son sillage. Les très

[*]   The author of this article, submitted in 1999, requested its withdrawal in April 2002. For technical reasons, her request could not be satisfied.

nombreux textes relevés représentent plus de mille pages imprimées entre 1902 et 1909, ils constituent les seules archives, dans les trois langues jusqu'alors découvertes (soqotri, mehri et une variété de jibbali), et ils portent témoignage d'une culture de tradition orale dont les racines sont ancrées dans l'Antiquité de la péninsule Arabique.[1] Ces textes mettent aussi à la disposition des savants sémitisants de l'époque une masse de données originales qui élargit considérablement la famille sud-sémitique et permet une meilleure connaissance de l'ensemble du sémitique.

Les travaux de A. Jahn, D.-H. Müller et W. Hein sont à la base des études grammaticales de M. Bittner et de E. Wagner. Le seul dictionnaire de soqotri qui existe à ce jour est celui qu'a établi W. Leslau, à partir des textes de Müller (*cf.* la bibliographie).

On peut suivre l'histoire de ces découvertes et l'état des études sudarabiques modernes jusqu'en 1945 à travers la bibliographie thématique commentée de Leslau (1946), je m'attacherai donc plutôt, ici, à présenter les avancées qui ont marqué la deuxième moitié du vingtième siècle, siècle qui est sans conteste celui de la fondation des études de sudarabique moderne.

BREF HISTORIQUE DE LA DECOUVERTE DES SIX LANGUES

Avant d'aborder le développement de la linguistique sudarabique proprement dite, il nous faut rappeler les différentes étapes de la découverte des langues.

Le soqotri [sḳaṭri], le mehri [mehri] et le jibbali [jibbāli], sous ses variétés eḥkīli et šawri, sont les trois premières langues à avoir été découvertes par des non-spécialistes puis étudiées par des sémitisants. Elles sont parlées dans ce qui est actuellement la République du Yémen (soqotri et mehri) et le sultanat d'Oman (mehri et jibbali). Dans les années qui suivent les travaux des Viennois, B. Thomas découvre en 1929 deux nouvelles langues, parlées en Oman, le harsusi [ḥarsūsi] et le bathari [baṭḥari]; il porte ainsi à cinq le nombre de langues connues (Thomas 1937).

Il faut attendre la fin des années 60 pour que les recherches linguistiques reprennent leur essor, grâce aux travaux de T.M. Johnstone qui étudie essentiellement les langues d'Oman: harsusi, jibbali et mehri du Dhofar. C'est lui qui va faire adopter le nom de jibbali pour une langue connue sous des appellations diverses (*cf. infra*); c'est lui aussi qui, le premier, mentionne le nom de ce qu'il présente alors comme un dialecte du jibbali, le hobyot (hobyōt), parlé à la frontière entre le Yémen et le Dhofar

---

[1]   *Cf.* Fresnel (1838, V/janvier: 63) qui définit ainsi le Mahra: "où sont les restes de la tribu [...] qui parle, comme vous le savez, une autre langue que l'arabe, une langue qui du temps d'Abraham était celle de l'Arabie Heureuse".

(Johnstone 1981: xii). Les recherches sur le hobyot parlé au Yémen sont menées à partir de 1985 par la *Mission Française d'Enquête sur les Langues Sudarabiques du Yémen.*[2] C'est en 1982, que cette mission a été créée, à l'instigation des autorités yéménites, et plus précisément de l'Université d'Aden, elle travaille sur les trois langues parlées au Yémen: mehri, hobyot et soqotri.

NOUVELLE APPROCHE DES LANGUES SUDARABIQUES MODERNES DANS LA DEUXIEME MOITIE DU XXe SIECLE

Exceptée la présentation de B. Thomas, les recherches linguistiques sur le SAM, jusque dans les années 70, se fondent sur les seules sources alors existantes: les textes recueillis par Müller, Jahn et Hein. Il faut attendre 1969 et les premiers séjours en Oman et à Soqotra de T.M. Johnstone pour qu'à nouveau les enquêtes de terrain aient lieu; elles vont donner un nouvel élan aux études sudarabiques modernes. Pratiquant la linguistique de terrain, les linguistes vont orienter leurs recherches, non seulement en fonction de ce que leurs prédecesseurs ont découvert, mais ils vont aussi baser leur analyse sur des données relevées par eux-mêmes *in situ.* La méthode d'approche et l'optique changent: on n'établit plus une théorie à partir de textes qui, bien que constituant un corpus riche et diversifié, restent figés dans le temps, mais la théorie et l'enquête vont de paire; l'enquête alimente la théorie et permet de la confronter à la réalité linguistique dans son quotidien et telle qu'elle se manifeste dans toutes les activités humaines.

L'exploration plus poussée des langues déjà connues comme le mehri, le soqotri et le jibbali, la découverte des trois autres langues ont permis de discerner des sous-groupes à l'intérieur du sudarabique moderne. Les enquêtes extensives et intensives ont mis à jour l'existence d'une dialectologie très diversifiée pour certaines de ces langues. C'est à partir de là que se développe l'étude dialectologique des langues SAM.

La présence sur le terrain, tout en permettant de mieux délimiter les frontières linguistiques et dialectologiques, laisse appréhender la situation sociolinguistique de ces langues. Il a été possible d'évaluer plus précisément la place occupée par les langues SAM, langues maternelles de locuteurs musulmans dans des pays dont la langue officielle est

---

[2] La *MFELSY* est devenue en 1989 *Mission Française d'Enquête sur les langues du Yémen* (quand elle s'est élargie à l'arabe). Pour le sudarabique moderne, la *Mission* a compris entre 1982 et 1993 deux chercheurs, A. Lonnet et M.-Cl. Simeone-Senelle. Depuis 1994, les missions sur le terrain (Mahra et Soqotra) effectuées dans ce cadre le sont par M.-Cl. Simeone-Senelle.

l'arabe, langues de minorités linguistiques dans un environnement social et politique en pleine évolution (Simeone-Senelle 1998c).

Le relevé de littérature orale s'est poursuivi tout au long de ce siècle, il a enrichi la "bibliothèque" constituée par les savants viennois et il porte témoignage de la pérennité de cette culture sudarabique.

DECOUVERTE DU HOBYOT

Les locuteurs désignent leur langue par le nom de hobyot [həwbyōt], les arabophones connaissant son existence ont "arabisé" le nom en *hūbiyya*. La langue est parlée dans les montagnes du Dhofar, à la frontière entre le Yémen et l'Oman, par une population de quelques centaines de personnes, pasteurs qui quittent leurs habitations à la saison des pluies pour aller vivre plus haut dans la montagne, dans des grottes. Ils sont en contact avec les Mahra de langue mehri et avec les locuteurs de jibbali. Au Yémen, ces contacts se font essentiellement sur la côte, dans les deux villages de Jadib et Hawf où les bédouins descendent pour commercer et les enfants pour être scolarisés. La jeune génération est trilingue, parfois quadrilingue (hobyot, mehri et/ou jibbali, arabe).

Quand il a découvert son existence, Johnstone a vu dans le hobyot, d'abord une variante dialectale originale du jibbali de l'ouest, très mêlée de mehri (1981: xii), puis plus tard l'a rapprochée du mehri, même si certains aspects de la phonologie et de nombreux termes lexicaux le lient au jibbali (1988: xi). Morris a commencé dans les années 80 à travailler sur le hobyot du Dhofar, mais les seules données publiées à ce jour sont les termes qui illustrent, à titre de comparaison, le *Mehri Lexicon* de Johnstone. Les recherches sur le hobyot du Yémen, menées par la *Mission Française* puis par Simeone-Senelle, mettent en évidence plusieurs facteurs qui semblent décisifs pour l'identification de cette langue. Arnold (1993: 24), à la suite d'une brève enquête en Jordanie auprès de locuteurs de hobyot originaires du Dhofar, conclut aussi à l'originalité du hobyot.

La conscience des locuteurs (de hobyot et de mehri), l'histoire des populations de la région, telle que l'a conservée la tradition orale, sont autant de faits qui, combinés à des phénomènes linguistiques, permettent d'identifier le hobyot comme une langue à part entière.

Au Yémen, les locuteurs de hobyot se définissent comme Mahra de langue hobyot, présents dans la région avant que les Mahra de langue mehri n'arrivent. La langue porte les marques de contacts réguliers, d'une part avec le mehri au Yémen, d'autre part avec le jibbali en Oman. Citons pour exemples: la présence de réalisations rétroflexes, comme en mehri du Yémen; l'articulation occlusive uvulaire sourde [q] de la fricative uvulaire /ġ/, comme dans certains dialectes mehri (et arabes) du Yémen; le maintien, à l'état vestigiel d'une conjugaison particulière (en –n) pour le conditionnel de quelques rares verbes, comme en mehri du Dhofar et en jibbali (Simeone-Senelle 1997: 403); certains pluriels externes en –te, comme en jibbali, et non –ten comme en mehri (*id.*: 392); une construction de la négation qui oscille entre un système à morphème discontinu, comme en mehri d'Oman et en jibbali, et un morphème unique postposé, comme en mehri du Yémen (Simeone-Senelle,1994a: 201–2, 1997b: 413–4); l'absence d'article défini comme en mehri du Yémen (et contrairement au mehri d'Oman et au jibbali).

D'autres traits distinguent le hobyot:

— les fricatives dento-alvéolaires et la pharyngale sonore sont toujours attestées (contrairement au mehri où le système est instable de ce point de vue).

— Le hobyot a, pour correspondant du *š sémitique, un **h**, comme en mehri, et non un š comme en jibbali: **hēmac** "il a entendu" (*cf.* mehri **hīma**, **hōma** et jibbali **šícc**). Cela permet de considérer comme caractéristique de cette langue les pronoms personnels indépendants 2m.pl. et 3m.pl. **tum** et **hum**; *cf.* mehri **hēm** et jibbali **šum** (Simeone-Senelle 1997b: 387).

— La construction du futur à l'aide de la particule **med** est aussi originale par rapport aux autres langues sudarabiques modernes (Simeone-Senelle 1993: 264–5, Simeone-Senelle et Vanhove 1997: 88–9).

La description plus approfondie du hobyot fera apparaître des faits de ressemblance et de divergence qui devraient permettre de mieux comprendre certains phénomènes d'évolution subis par les langues SAM. Ces recherches revêtent un caractère d'urgence quand on sait que la langue est parmi les six langues SAM, la plus menacée, à la fois par le petit nombre de ses locuteurs (environ une centaine) et par leur mode de vie traditionnel qui ne résistera pas longtemps à la modernité véhiculée par l'arabe.

LA DESCRIPTION DES LANGUES ET LEUR DIALECTOLOGIE

L'enquête sur les langues nouvelles et le développement de l'étude dialectologique ont permis de revoir les présentations qui avaient, par manque de données, généraliser des faits dialectaux, ou particulariser des faits qui vont se révéler plus généraux. La connaissance interne au groupe s'est accompagnée d'une meilleure différenciation des langues. Les traits originaux que présentent certains dialectes doivent permettre de mieux comprendre l'évolution des langues.

PHONOLOGIE ET PHONETIQUE

Consonnes

La découverte par les savants viennois de l'existence en SAM des fricatives latérales, attestées dans l'écriture de certaines langues sémitiques (hébreu, sudarabique antique, guèze), a distingué ces langues comme conservatrices d'un système consonantique que l'on peut faire remonter à un stade très proche de celui qui est reconstruit pour le sémitique commun.

La mise à jour, pour toutes ces langues, d'un système consonantique comprenant des phonèmes éjectifs, qu'on ne pouvait plus interpréter comme des variantes phonétiques des emphatiques vélarisées (Johnstone 1975c, Simeone-Senelle 1991), est importante. L'existence de tels phonèmes dans des langues sémitiques parlées en Arabie, permet de revoir l'hypothèse qui attribuait l'existence des éjectives en éthio-sémitique à un phénomène de substrat ou de contact avec des langues africaines non sémitiques. Leur présence en SAM tend à conforter l'hypothèse de la primauté de l'articulation éjective des emphatiques sur la prononciation vélarisée, qui est celle attestée en arabe (Cantineau 1951–52: 93).

Ces traits mettent en évidence le caractère plus conservateur des langues sémitiques périphériques par rapport aux langues centrales comme l'arabe.

La découverte, par Johnstone, de l'existence de la palato-alvéolaire glottalisée /ṣ̌/, comme phonème et non comme variante, dans les langues d'Oman a été confirmée dans les langues du Yémen (Lonnet et Simeone-Senelle 1997: 350). Cette consonne, qui peut provenir de la phonologisation d'une variante phonétique, apparaît, dans les six langues, comme un phonème surnuméraire par rapport au système que l'on peut envisager de reconstruire pour le sémitique commun (Cohen 1988: 35).

L'enquête extensive sur le soqotri a permis de revoir la thèse selon laquelle le soqotri ne possédait pas de fricatives vélaires, excepté dans des termes empruntés à l'arabe. Les recherches effectuées par les chercheurs français, à partir de 1985, sur un dialecte occidental de Soqotra, jusqu'alors jamais décrit, permettent de démentir l'affirmation de la non existence de ce phonème en soqotri (*cf.* Cantineau (1951–52: 88): "Cette consonne [ġ] a disparu ... en soqotri"). Le dialecte en question possède en effet les deux fricatives (sourde et sonore) dans des termes qui ne peuvent être des emprunts (Simeone-Senelle 1997b: 382) et l'absence du phonème ne se vérifie que dans un certain nombre de dialectes soqotri, non dans le système de la langue (Lonnet et Simeone-Senelle 1997: 366). Ce phénomène peut éclairer différemment l'hypothèse de l'existence d'un seul phonème /ᶜ/, *qui se serait dédoublé en un* ġ, phonologisé dans certaines langues sémitiques.

La présence du **h** *parasite*, résultat d'une évolution phonétique qui s'est phonologisée, est désormais attestée dans tous les dialectes connus du soqotri.

La réalisation rétroflexe, du groupe consonantique formé par une sonante vibrante suivie d'une apico-alvéolaire, a été découverte dans certains parlers mehri du Yémen ainsi que dans le hobyot du Yémen; elle permet d'expliquer l'évolution de certains mots (*cf.* **kōn** "corne") en SAM.

Il est acquis désormais que, parmi ces langues, seul le soqotri ne possède pas dans le système consonantique de fricatives dento-alvéolaires. En mehri du Yémen, la confusion des interdentales avec les dentales correspondantes est un phénomène dialectal et sociolectal. Ce fait, ajouté à celui de l'existence du **ᶜ**, même si son statut est instable dans beaucoup de dialectes mehri du Yémen, permet de tempérer l'affirmation du caractère innovateur du mehri du Yémen comparé au mehri du Dhofar, plus conservateur (Johnstone 1988: xi).

Voyelles

Le système vocalique varie selon les langues: le mehri a, selon les dialectes, deux ou trois phonèmes vocaliques brefs mais six voyelles longues. Le soqotri et le jibbali présentent le système le plus riche (avec huit voyelles brèves (Johnstone 1975b: 103; 1981: xv). L'opposition de quantité n'existe pas en jibbali, elle paraît peu productive en soqotri (Lonnet et Simeone-Senelle, 1997: 364, 367).

Syllabe et accentuation

Nous n'attirerons l'attention que sur quelques faits relevés après les années 60.[3]

— Certaines des langues SAM admettent une initiale vocalique; les groupes consonantiques, rares en soqotri, se rencontrent en mehri et sont plus fréquents en jibbali: **íkkféf** "il va à l'aveuglette".

— Pour ce qui est de la gémination consonantique, il a été mis en valeur que, contrairement à ce qui a parfois été avancé, la gémination consonantique existe en SAM, mais elle n'a jamais de valeur dérivationnelle. Son apparition est liée à des règles morpho-phonétiques et accentuelles, elle présente comme particularité celle de se déplacer

---

[3] Pour une description plus complète, voir Lonnet et Simeone-Senelle 1997: 354–60.

dans le mot en fonction du paradigme (voir aussi Simeone-Senelle 1997b: 387).

— Les règles d'accentuation des langues SAM ont pu être définies et Johnstone a démontré la place particulière qu'occupe le jibbali de ce point de vue, puisque la langue accepte pour un même terme plusieurs syllabes accentuées (Johnstone 1975b: 104).

MORPHOLOGIE[4]

Les faits les plus pertinents sont:

— La confirmation de l'absence, en mehri et en hobyot du Yémen, de l'article défini, présent dans les autres langues SAM du continent, y compris en mehri d'Oman.

— La confirmation de la vitalité du duel nominal, excepté en jibbali où son apparition et l'accord sont instables, et l'existence d'un duel verbal (y compris pour la première personne) dans toutes les langues. Seuls les dialectes mehri de l'ouest du Yémen n'ont pas gardé trace de ce duel verbal.

— La morphologie verbale a donné lieu à de nombreuses recherches (*cf.* Bibliographie). Les faits relevés les plus remarquables sont:

    — L'existence d'une conjugaison particulière pour le conditionnel (base du subjonctif comportant à toutes les personnes du paradigme un suffixe **–n**, dans les hypothétiques irréelles). Décrite pour la première fois par Johnstone (1975: 110) pour le mehri du Dhofar et le jibbali, cette conjugaison n'est pas attestée en mehri du Yémen et n'apparaît que dans de très rares verbes en hobyot, toujours dans un type particulier d'hypothétique.

    — L'existence d'une classe de verbes "moyens" (ceux que Johnstone qualifie de verbes de type B), opposés aux verbes actifs (de type A) et au passif. Ils ont un schème particulier de conjugaison et parfois de dérivation.

    — La grande vitalité du passif vocalique en soqotri, avec souvent une valeur d'impersonnel.

    — Des conjugaisons préfixales particulières au jibbali et au soqotri où l'indice personnel peut ne pas être marqué à certaines personnes du paradigme (Johnstone 1968 ;1980a).

    — Les constructions verbo-nominales ou l'emploi de périphrases verbales pour le futur, différentes selon les langues.

---

4   Voir aussi Simeone-Senelle 1997b: 387–411.

SYNTAXE

La syntaxe très complète, établie par Wagner (1953), remonte au milieu du vingtième siècle et se fonde sur les textes relevés par les Viennois, elle ne porte donc que sur les trois langues alors connues. Johnstone a surtout recueilli des matériaux portant sur la morphologie, le lexique (et la littérature orale) et sa contribution à la syntaxe dans sa présentation générale des cinq langues SAM est réduite à quelques notes (Johnstone 1975: 120). La brève étude qui est parue en 1997, permet d'avoir un aperçu un peu plus détaillé sur les six langues (Simeone-Senelle 1997b: 411–419). D'autre part, à l'occasion de la présentation de certaines langues ou d'études de textes de littérature orale, des remarques syntaxiques sont faites et des articles traitent de points particuliers de la syntaxe (*cf.* Bibliographie), mais force est de constater que, depuis Wagner (1953), aucun ouvrage traitant exclusivement de syntaxe sudarabique n'a paru.

LEXIQUE

C'est un domaine qui a fait l'objet de l'attention de beaucoup de chercheurs, mais le seul dictionnaire de soqotri existant à nos jours reste celui de Leslau (1938), élaboré à partir du dépouillement des textes de Müller. La dialectologie soqotri au fur et à mesure des recherches apparaît comme particulièrement riche et un dictionnaire insérant les termes dialectaux serait de la plus haute utilité. Les relevés de vocabulaire, effectués sur le terrain et portant sur des domaines très diversifiés (*cf.* Bibliographie), mettent en valeur cette diversité et présentent des termes non recueillis par Müller, mais ils ne représentent qu'une part infime du lexique soqotri.

En mehri, excepté pour le mehri d'Oman (Johnstone 1988), aucun ouvrage ne vient compléter le dictionnaire de Jahn. Quelques données de hobyot et un nombre plus conséquent de termes en bathari, relevés par Morris, ont été intégrés dans le *Mehri Lexicon*. Un dictionnaire de mehri du Yémen en cours d'élaboration devrait être publié prochainement (par l'auteur de cet article).

Le jibbali et le harsusi ont chacun un dictionnaire (Johnstone 1977, 1981).

DIALECTOLOGIE

Les études dialectologiques plus poussées, faites sur la base d'enquêtes de terrain extensives, à partir des années 70, ont amené à une délimitation linguistique et géographique des dialectes d'une même langue. Les langues concernées sont essentiellement le mehri, le jibbali et le soqotri. Le harsusi et le bathari restent peu explorés, le hobyot, de ce point de vue, est aussi très peu connu.

Le mehri

Le mehri comprend deux grands groupes dialectaux:

— le mehri du Dhofar en Oman (mehri oriental), circonscrit aux montagnes du Dhofar où les Mahra sont en contact avec les locuteurs de langue jibbali et avec ceux de hobyot;

— le mehri "méridional" ou mehri occidental, parlé au Yémen, dans le Mahra. La limite ouest des dialectes mehri du Yémen peut être posée au wâdi Masîla (Simeone-Senelle 1998c: 4–5). L'aire s'est restreinte depuis les années 70 où Johnstone l'étendait jusqu'aux environs de Mukalla (Johnstone 1975: 94); la frontière nord-ouest est, elle, par contre, difficile à déterminer: aux marches du désert, le village de Thamud était encore en 1987 fréquenté par des Mahra de langue mehri, mais on ne possède pas de données sur les territoires au-delà.

Les Viennois ont travaillé essentiellement sur le mehri du Yémen. Johnstone est le spécialiste du mehri du Dhofar; les dialectes de toute la partie côtière du Yémen (entre le wâdi Masîla et la frontière), avec quelques incursions dans l'arrière pays de Qishn et de al-Ghayda, ont été étudiés par les chercheurs français.

Le nom mehri de la langue reflète la morphologie des dialectes qui la désignent: au Yémen, *mehrīyet* à l'ouest, *mehriyōt* à l'est, et en Oman, *mehrayyet*.

A l'intérieur du mehri du Yémen, on distingue les parlers orientaux des parlers occidentaux, la limite semblant être la région d'al-Ghayda. Parmi chacun de ces deux groupes, il est aussi possible de différencier d'une part, à l'intérieur du Mahra, les dialectes paysans, parlers des bédouins pasteurs semi-nomades dans la steppe désertique, ou cultivateurs de palmeraies dans certaines vallées (comme celles du wâdi Masîla ou du wâdi Jiza'); d'autre part, sur la côte, les dialectes villageois ou citadins, ceux des locuteurs exerçant diverses activités liées au commerce ou à la vie maritime. A en juger par les changements survenus entre 1989 et 1998 (entre la mission la plus ancienne dans la région et la plus récente) il faut accorder une attention particulière à al-Ghayda, centre administratif de la province, devenu depuis 1991 une véritable capitale régionale. Le dialecte mehri de la ville a énormément évolué en très peu de temps, suite en particulier à la présence de beaucoup de sudarabophones, venant de tout le Mahra et même d'Oman, ainsi que des arabophones de tout le pays qui s'y installent, pour des périodes plus ou moins longues. Le dialecte de Qishn, l'ancienne capitale dont le rayonnement historique et culturel est important, est toujours très valorisé.

Le soqotri

La diversité dialectale du soqotri est enregistrée dans le *Lexique soqotri* et abordée dans les études de syntaxe de Wagner (Müller a en effet relevé de nombreux textes en soqotri de Soqotra et un conte en dialecte de Abd-al-Kûri). C'est Naumkin (1988: 271–31) qui, le premier, a constaté les divergences dialectales très importantes entre les parlers de l'île principale et celui de Abd-al-Kûri. Johnstone a annoté son exemplaire personnel du *Lexique* de Leslau en l'illustrant d'exemples de différences lexicales entre des dialectes de la côte nord (essentiellement Hadibo et Qadhub) qu'il avait relevées à Soqotra. Les enquêtes menées par la *Mission Française*, depuis 1985, dans différents points de l'île ont permis de revoir le tableau que l'on pouvait jusqu'alors brossé de la dialectologie du soqotri. Des différences notables (phonétiques, morphologiques et lexicales) y ont été relevées qui permettent de distinguer selon les deux axes, sociologique et géographique:

— sur la côte nord, trois secteurs dialectologiques:

— au centre, Hadibo, la capitale, a un parler de citadins, en contact permanent avec l'arabe et les autres dialectes soqotri, et qui évolue très vite. Il présente des différences avec les parlers de deux localités proches 'Elha (à l'est) et Qadhub (à l'ouest), où vivent des petits cultivateurs (de palmiers dattiers essentiellement) et des pêcheurs.

— A l'est, à Momi, le dialecte, peu étudié, de paysans agriculteurs (millet, palmiers dattiers) ou fabricants de chaux.

— A l'ouest, le dialecte de Qalansiyya qui présente des traits que l'on ne soupçonnait pas en soqotri (*cf.* ci-dessus "Phonologie — Consonnes").

— Sur la côte sud: au centre la région de Noged, très peu peuplée par des pêcheurs et où les données relevées n'ont pas encore été suffisamment exploitées.

— Dans le centre de l'île: dans la chaîne des Hagher, les parlers les plus conservateurs qui sont ceux de bédouins pasteurs vivant dans des endroits difficilement accessibles (des grottes aménagées à flanc de montagne) et réputés incompréhensibles par les autres Soqotri. Seuls les hommes sont en contact avec la côte et, parmi les gens âgés et les femmes, beaucoup parlent très peu arabe.

Les habitants de l'île d'Abd-al-Kûri, ont une variété de soqotri très influencée par l'arabe hadrami de la région de Qusa'ir (Naumkin 1993: 359 n. 2), avec laquelle les pêcheurs de l'île sont en contacts fréquents. Le seul texte publié dans ce dialecte au début du siècle (Müller 1902: 92–111), en pendant avec une version en soqotri de Soqotra, laissait apparaître des variantes assez importantes. C'est aussi ce que confirment les données relevées en 1991, par les chercheurs français avec la collaboration de Aydaroos, auprès de pêcheurs de Abd-al-Kûri séjournant sur la côte du Hadramawt.

La dialectologie du soqotri a de quoi surprendre par sa diversité surtout si on prend en compte l'aire et le nombre d'habitants. Ses caractéristiques dialectales restent à étudier et à évaluer en termes d'archaïsmes, d'innovations et d'influences. L'isolement de l'île jusqu'à cette fin de siècle explique en grande partie le particularisme linguistique du soqotri à l'intérieur du SAM, mais la situation risque d'évoluer très vite maintenant que l'île possède un port (depuis 1996) et un aéroport pour les avions de lignes (1999).

Le jibbali

Le nom de la langue en jibbali est *geblēt* (Johnstone 1981: xi). C'est Johnstone (1975b) qui, après avoir désigné la langue par le terme *śḥeri* ou *śheri*, "montagnard, campagnard" (*śheri* en est le correspondant arabisé), adopte le terme de *jibbāli* qu'il juge moins connoté socialement que le premier. Avant lui, le jibbali était le plus souvent désigné par le nom du dialecte décrit: *śxawri*, repris par Müller à son informateur (1907: vi), puis par ceux qui ont travaillé sur ses textes, ou encore *əḥkili* (Fresnel), ou *qarāwi* (nom arabe du dialecte — *qarauwi (grauwi)*) (Müller, 1907: vi, n.1). L'appellation de jibbali sera finalement adopté par la communauté des chercheurs travaillant sur les langues SAM. Trois groupes dialectaux sont distingués (Johnstone 1981: xii):

— à l'est, le jibbali oriental parlé dans les villes côtières comme Mirbât et Sidh et leur arrière pays. Le parler des îles Kuria Muria en est une variété, objet de dérision de la part des locuteurs du continent qui le qualifient de "langage enfantin".

— Les dialectes du centre, qui diffèrent peu entre eux et qui sont les plus prisés.

— Et enfin, les dialectes occidentaux, les plus dévalorisés, sur lesquels les données sont insuffisantes; Johnstone mentionne seulement que l'emploi des diminutifs dans ce parler est "excessif" (1981: xii).

Les différences entre les dialectes du centre et de l'est sont relevées du point de vue lexical, phonologique et morphologique dans le *Jibbāli Lexicon*.

Le hobyot

La comparaison des données en hobyot du Yémen avec celles relevées par Arnold (1991) en hobyot d'Oman laisse apparaître des différences dialectales dans tous les domaines (phonétiques, morphologiques et syntaxiques). Nous avons vu ci-dessus (*cf.* Découverte du hobyot) que les variantes dialectologiques sont fonction du degré de contact avec les deux autres langues de la région: le jibbali et le mehri du Dhofar ou du Yémen, dans sa variété *mehriyōt*). Une étude détaillée reste à faire.

Le harsusi

Le harsusi est désigné par *ḥersīyet* en sudarabique. Nous ne savons pas s'il existe une dialectologie harsusi. La langue est parlée par une toute petite communauté dont la population mâle émigrait massivement dans les années 70 vers les champs de pétrole. Leur parler était alors très marqué par les contacts permanents avec l'arabe dialectal, seule variété à être utilisée sur les lieux de travail. Les femmes, les vieillards et les enfants, restés dans la région d'origine, perpétuaient l'usage de la langue, gravement menacée à brève échéance. Le changement économique qu'a connu la région dans les années 80 (implantation dans Jiddat al-Harâsis d'un parc national employant les Harâsis comme gardiens) peut avoir eu des conséquences sur la situation linguistique. Des enquêtes restent à faire dans ce domaine.

Le bathari [*baṭḥāri*]

Les seules données publiées par Thomas (1937) et par Morris (1983) ne permettent pas de savoir s'il existe une dialectologie de cette langue parlée par la communauté des Batâhira, sur la bande côtière de la baie de Kuria Muria. Dans ce domaine aussi les recherches revêtent un caractère d'urgence.

LITTERATURE ORALE

Tous les chercheurs qui se sont intéressés à ces langues et à la culture qu'elles véhiculent se sont préoccupés de recueillir de la littérature orale. Parmi celle-ci, les contes et la poésie semblent tenir la première place. Les genres du proverbe et de la devinette ne semblent plus très vivants. Si la récolte est moins abondante que celle des savants viennois, cela ne tient qu'en partie au fait que cette littérature est en déperdition; les linguistes de la deuxième moitié du XXe siècle n'ont pas basé leurs recherches sur l'étude de textes, les matériaux sur lesquels ils travaillent sont plus diversifiés. Le recueil de textes continue cependant à enrichir la bibliothèque édifiée par nos illustres prédécesseurs.

Johnstone avait recueilli 106 textes (essentiellement des textes en prose, avec quelques poésies) en mehri du Dhofar, c'est H. Stroomer qui en est l'éditeur (Stroomer 1996, 1999). Ces textes revêtent une très grande importance puisque ce sont les premiers et les seuls textes en mehri du Dhofar. Des contes et des poésies incantatoires en mehri du Yémen ont été publiés depuis 1984 (Simeone-Senelle, Lonnet et Mohammed-Bakheit; Lonnet et Simeone-Senelle 1987; Lonnet, Simeone-Senelle et Mohammed-Bakheit; Simeone-Senelle 1995). Un autre ouvrage verra le jour en 2001, avec des textes (prose et poésie) en mehri du Yémen, dans les deux variétés *mehriyet* et *mehriyōt* (Simeone-Senelle à paraître).

Johnstone (1974) a traité de la langue de la poésie en jibbali, en l'illustrant de courts exemples; les nombreux textes en prose et en poésie qu'il a recueillis de son vivant n'ont pas encore été publiés. Un poème jibbali a été édité par Morris (1985) qui a aussi présenté des échantillons de la poésie en bathari (1983).

En soqotri, Naumkin et Porkhomovskij (1981) ont édité des textes de régions différentes de Soqotra et (Naumkin 1988) en dialecte de Abd-al-Kûri, quatre petites pièces poétiques, dont le sens reste hermétique.

La poésie est un genre extrêmement vivant, peut-être encore plus dans l'île de Soqotra que dans le Mahra. Lors d'une mission en 1998, en plus d'anecdotes humoristiques, j'ai en effet enregistré et commenté 15 poésies qui sont échangées à l'occasion de joutes, par cassettes audio interposées, entre des poètes vivant à Soqotra et leurs partenaires en poésie, émigrés dans des Emirats du Golfe. Ces textes et leurs commentaires seront prochainement publiés.

Le degré de connaissance atteint à la fin du XXe siècle permet désormais une classification plus fiable de ces langues et une meilleure appréciation de leur place à l'intérieur du groupe sudarabique, à l'intérieur du sémitique méridional et enfin à l'intérieur de la famille sémitique.

CLASSIFICATION

A l'intérieur du sudarabique moderne

Johnstone présente le bathari et le harsusi comme des dialectes très évolués du mehri, on a vu que le hobyot peut, lui aussi, être rapproché du mehri oriental (du moins pour ce qui est du hobyot parlé au Yémen).

Il est possible de distinguer trois sous-groupes au sein des langues sudarabiques modernes. Le premier englobe le mehri, le hobyot, le bathari et le harsusi. Le deuxième est composé du jibbali et enfin le troisième du soqotri. Il n'y a pas d'intercompréhension entre les locuteurs de langues appartenant à des sous-groupes différents. A l'intérieur du premier sous-groupe l'intercompréhension est parfois difficile à évaluer, des facteurs linguistiques, géographiques mais aussi psychologiques sont à prendre en compte: un locuteur d'un parler plus prestigieux a plus de mal à comprendre le locuteur d'un parler "mineur" que le contraire. Ainsi un Mehri de langue hobyot avoue-t-il mieux comprendre un Mehri de langue mehri (à condition qu'il ait un parler oriental) que celui-ci ne le comprend.

A l'intérieur du sudarabique: relation entre les langues anciennes et modernes

En ce qui concerne les liens, à l'intérieur du sudarabique, entre les langues anciennes et les langues modernes, l'avancée des études en SAM met en évidence l'absence de filiation directe entre les deux groupes, contrairement à ce qu'auraient pu laisser croire les premières hypothèses. Les langues modernes qui n'ont vraisemblablement pas eu de tradition d'écriture, sont les seuls vestiges vivants, produits de l'évolution de langues parlées dans tout le sud de la péninsule Arabique, bien avant la pénétration de l'arabe, venu du nord. Alors que les recherches ont permis de mieux délimiter le groupe sudarabique moderne et sa place originale à l'intérieur du sémitique méridional, elles ne permettent pas encore de déterminer le degré exact de relation entre les langues antiques (les seules dont on ait des traces écrites) et les langues modernes parlées (dont on n'a pas de traces écrites).

A l'intérieur du sémitique

Les premières hypothèses de classification sont élaborées sur la base des maigres données disponibles jusqu'en 1902 et qui ne portent que sur trois langues (soqotri, jibbali, mehri): certains rattachent alors le SAM à l'éthiopien (relié au copte (Renan), parfois au phénicien (Glaser)), d'autres à l'hébreu et au phénicien, ou à l'arabe du nord, ou à l'araméen (*cf.* Leslau 1946: 19–22). Il ne fait désormais aucun doute que le SAM appartient au groupe méridional du sémitique de l'ouest, comme les langues sudarabiques anciennes et comme les langues éthio-sémitiques parlées en Ethiopie et en Erythrée.

Elles ont été le substrat de l'arabe dans cette région, leur connaissance peut permettre d'expliquer certains traits dialectaux arabes au Yémen (comme la conjugaison de l'accompli en **–k**), mais aussi dans toutes les régions qui ont été arabisées lors de la conquête arabe (à partir du 7e–8e s.) avec le concours de soldats originaires de ces provinces, en même temps qu'elle peut apporter de précieuses indications sur la façon dont s'est faite cette arabisation. Ces langues parlées ont pu aussi jouer un rôle dans la "sémitisation" de la Corne de l'Afrique. L'intérêt considérable que présentent ces six langues pour une meilleure connaissance des langues sémitiques et de leur évolution est encore augmenté par le fait qu'elles ont conservé des traits disparus de toutes les autres langues sémitiques modernes.

CONCLUSION

La présentation du développement et de l'avancée des études sudarabiques tout au long du 20me siècle, si elle constitue un bilan n'en demeure pas moins orientée vers l'avenir. En effet, le terrain est immense et un siècle d'études ne suffit pas à une connaissance exhaustive: il reste encore de vastes secteurs non défrichés, ou insuffisamment explorés, dans le domaine de la linguistique sudarabique. Ils touchent aussi bien à la dialectologie, la syntaxe, la comparaison que la reconstruction. Ce sont autant de perspectives qui s'offrent aux jeunes sémitisants du vingt et unième siècle.

BIBLIOGRAPHIE COMPLEMENTAIRE

Parmi les ouvrages parus avant 1945, tous répertoriés par Leslau (1946), seuls ceux qui sont cités dans le présent article apparaissent ici.

Cette bibliographie ne se prétend pas exhaustive; elle ne prend pas en compte par exemple tous les ouvrages et articles parus sur les relations à l'intérieur du sud sémitique, ni les études d'ethnologie.

Al-Aidaroos, Mustafa Zein. 1996. An Introduction to the Mehri Tongues. *Journal of Social Sciences and Humanities*, Vol. 1. Nr. 1 (June 1996). Aden.

Arnold, Werner. 1993. Zur Position des Hóbyót in den neusüdarabischen Sprachen. *ZAL* 25: 17–24.

Cantineau, Jean. 1951–52. Le consonantisme du sémitique. *Semitica IV*: 79–94.

Cohen, David. 1974. La forme verbale à marques personnelles préfixées en sudarabique moderne. *IV Congresso Internazionale di Studi Etiopici — Roma, 10–15 aprile 1972, Parte II*. Rome, 63–70.

— 1984. *La phrase nominale et l'évolution du système verbal en sémitique. Etudes de syntaxe historique*. Paris.

— 1988. Le sudarabique moderne. In *Les langues dans le monde ancien et moderne. Les langues chamito-sémitiques*, éd. par J. Perrot. Paris, 127–131.

Fresnel, Fulgence. 1938. Quatrième lettre sur l'Histoire des Arabes avant l'Islamisme; Note sur la langue hhymiarite — Cinquième lettre sur l'Histoire des Arabes avant l'Islamisme. *Journal Asiatique* V / janvier: 45–66, / juin: 497–544 ; VI / juillet: 79–84, / décembre: 529–570.

Hayward, K.M., R.J. Hayward & Sālim Bakhīt Al-Tabūki. 1988. Vowels in Jibbâli Verbs. *BSOAS* 51/2: 240–250.

Goldenberg, Gideon. 1979. The modern South Arabian prefix-conjugation: addendum to *BSOAS* XL.3, 1977. *BSOAS* XLII, 3: 541–546.

Johnstone, Thomas Muir. 1968. The non-occurence of a *t–* prefix in certain Socotri verbal forms. *BSOAS* 31/3: 515–525.

— 1970a. A definite article in the Modern South Arabian languages. *BSOAS* 33/2: 295–307.

— 1970b. Dual forms in Mehri and Harsūsi. *BSOAS* 33/3: 501–512.

— 1972. The language of Poetry in Dhofar. *BSOAS* 35/1: 1–17.

- 1973. Diminutive patterns in the Modern South Arabian languages. *Journal of Semitic Studies* 18/1: 98–107.

— 1974. Folklore and folk literature in Oman and Socotra. *Arabian Studies* 1: 7–24.

— 1975a. Oath-talking and vows in Oman. *Arabian Studies* 2: 7–17.

— 1975b. The Modern South Arabian languages. *Afro-Asiatic Linguistics* 1/5: 93–121.

— 1975c. Contrasting articulations in the Modern South Arabian languages. In *Hamito-Semitica*, ed. by James and Theodora Bynon. The Hague, Paris, 155–159.

— 1976. Knots and Curses. *Arabian Studies* 3: 79–83.

— 1977. *Harsūsi Lexicon and English-Harsūsi Word-List*. London.

— 1978. A St. George of Dhofar. *Arabian Studies* 4: 59–65.

— 1980a. Gemination in the Jibbāli language of Dhofar. *ZAL* 4: 61–71.

— 1980b. The Non-occurence of a *t–* prefix in certain Jibbāli verbal forms. *BSOAS* 43/3: 466–470.

— 1981. *Jibbāli Lexicon*. London.

— 1982a. Haḍramawt, iii Language and dialects. In *Encyclopaedia of Islam*, n.e. fasc. 5–6: 339–340. Leiden. (*Encyclopédie de l'Islam*: 339).

— 1982b. Language and Society in Dhofar. *Ur, the International Magazine of Arab Culture* II–III: 81–83.

— 1982c. The system of enumeration in the South Arabian Languages. In *Arabian and Islamic Studies. Articles presented to R.B. Serjeant*, ed. by R.L. Bidwell and G.R. Smith. London — New York, 225–228.

— 1984. New sibilant phonemes in the Modern South Arabian languages of Dhofar. In *Current Progress in Afro-Asiatic Linguistics, The Third International Hamito-Semitic Congress*, ed. by J. Bynon. Amsterdam-Philadelphia, 389–390.

1986. Mahrī. In *Encyclopédie de l'Islam*, n.e. Leiden, 82–83.

— 1987. *Mehri Lexicon and English-Mehri Word-List, with Index of the English Definitions in the Jibbāli Lexicon*, compiled by G. Rex Smith. London.

Leslau, Wolf. 1946. Modern South Arabic languages. A Bibliography. *Bulletin of the New York Library* 50/8: 607–633.

Lonnet, Antoine. 1985. The Modern South Arabian languages in the RDP of Yemen. *Proceedings of the Seminar for Arabian Studies* 15: 49–55.

— 1991. La découverte du sudarabique moderne: le *Ehhkili* de Fresnel (1838). *Matériaux Arabes et Sudarabiques*, n.s. 3: 15–89.

— 1993. Quelques résultats en linguistique sudarabique moderne. *Quaderni di Studi Arabi* 11: 37–82.

— 1994. Le verbe sudarabique moderne: hypothèses sur des tendances. *Matériaux Arabes et Sudarabiques*, n.s. 5: 213–255.

— 1998. The Soqotri language: past, present and future. In *Soqotra. Proceedings of the First International Symposium on Soqotra Island: Present & Future*, ed. by H. Dumont. Vol. 1: 297–308. New York.

Lonnet, Antoine et Marie-Claude Simeone-Senelle. 1984. Observations phonétiques et phonologiques sur les consonnes d'un dialecte mehri. *Matériaux Arabes et Sudarabiques* 1: 187–218.

— 1987. *Râbût*: Trance and incantations in Mehri folk medicine. *Proceedings of the Seminar for Arabian Studies* 17: 107–115.

— 1997. La phonologie des langues sudarabiques modernes. In *Phonologies of Asia and Africa (Including the Caucasus)*, ed. by Alan S. Kaye. Vol. 1: 337–372. Winona Lake.

Lonnet, A., Simeone-Senelle M.-Cl. et Sabri Mohamed-Bakheit. 1988. Un avatar sudarabique d'Abû Nuwâs. In *Cahiers de Littérature orale, La tradition au présent* (Monde arabe): 219–231.

Matthews, Charles D. 1967–1970. On the Borders of the Sands. *University of South Florida Language Quarterly* 6/1–2: 39–47; 6/3–4: 7–12; 7/1–2: 41–48; 7/3–4: 43–48; 8/1–2: 43–47; 8/3–4: 11–19.

— 1969. Modern South Arabian determination. A clue thereto from Shahri. *JAOS* 89: 22–27.

Morris, Miranda. 1983. Some preliminary remarks on a collection of poems and songs of the Baṭāḥirah. *Journal of Oman Studies* 6/1: 129–144.

— 1985. A poem in Jibbāli. *Journal of Oman Studies* 7: 121–130.

Müller, Dav. Heinr. 1902. *Die Mehri- und Soqoṭri-Sprache. I. Texte.* Wien.

— 1907. *Die Mehri- und Soqoṭri-Sprache. III. Shauri-Texte.* Wien.

Müller, Walter. 1993. Zum Wortschatz des neusüdarabischen Mehri. *ZAL* 25: 225–232.

Nakano, Aki'o. 1986. *Comparative Vocabulary of Southern Arabic — Mahri, Gibbali and Soqotri.* Tokyo.

Naumkin, V.V. 1988. *Sokotrijcy, istoriko-etnografičeskij očerk* [*The Socotrans: A Historical and Ethnographical Study*]. Moscou.

— 1993. *Island of the Phoenix. An Ethnographic Study of the People of Socotra.* Reading.

Naumkin, V.V. et V. Ja. Porkhomovskij. 1981. *Očerki po etnolingvistike Sokotry* [*Essays on Ethnolinguistics of Socotra*]. Moscou.

Pennacchietti, Fabrizio. 1969. Un articolo prepositivo in neosudarabico. *RSO* 44: 285–293.

Petráček, Karel. 1968. Das Problem des ġain in Südsemitischen. *Wiss. Z. Univ. Halle*, XVII'68 G, 2/3: 139–145.

— 1986. Pour une stratigraphie linguistique de la péninsule Arabique. *Šulmu. International Conference of Socialist Countries. Prague, Sept. 30–Oct. 3, 1986*, ed. by Petr Soucek & Vladimir Vavousek. Prague, 257–271.

— 1988. The South Arabian language periphery. In *A Miscellany of Middle Eastern Articles. In Memoriam Thomas Muir Johnstone 1924–83*, ed. by A.K. Irvin, R.B. Serjeant & G.R. Smith. Harlow, 216–225.

Rodgers, J. 1991. The subgrouping of the South Semitic languages. In *Semitic Studies in Honor of Wolf Leslau on the Occasion of his 85th Birthday*, ed. by Alan S. Kaye. Vol. 2: 1323–1336. Wiesbaden.

Schneider, R. 1954–1957. Les noms de parenté en sudarabique moderne. *GLECS* VII: 27–31.

Simeone-Senelle, Marie-Claude. 1991a. Notes sur le premier vocabulaire soqotri: le Mémoire de Wellsted (1835). Première partie. *Matériaux Arabes et Sudarabiques*, n.s. 3: 91–135.

— 1991b. Récents développements des recherches sur les langues sudarabiques modernes. In *Fifth International Hamito-Semitic Congress, 1987*, ed. by Hans G. Mukarovsky. Vol. 2: 321–337. Wien.

— 1992. Notes sur le premier vocabulaire soqotri: le Mémoire de Wellsted (1835). Deuxième partie. *Matériaux Arabes et Sudarabiques*, n.s. 4: 13–82.

— 1993. L'expression du futur dans les langues sudarabiques modernes. *Matériaux Arabes et Sudarabiques*, n.s. 5: 249–278.

— 1994a. La négation dans les langues sudarabiques modernes. *Matériaux Arabes et Sudarabiques*, n.s. 6: 249–278.

— 1994b. Suqutra: parfums, sucs et résines. *Saba* 2: 9–17.

— 1994c. Aloe and Dragon's Blood, some medicinal and traditional uses on the Island of Socotra. *New Arabian Studies* 2: 186–198.

— 1995a. Magie et pratiques thérapeutiques dans l'île de Soqotra; le médecin-guérisseur. *Proceedings of the Seminar for Arabian Studies* 25: 117–126.

— 1995b. Incantations thérapeutiques dans la médecine traditionnelle des Mahra du Yémen. *Quaderni di Studi Arabi* 13: 131–157.

— 1997a. Suḳutra. 3. Language. In *Encyclopaedia of Islam*, 809–811. Leiden [version française: Suḳutra. Langue. In *Encyclopédie de l'Islam*: 844–845].

— 1997b. The Modern South Arabian Languages. In *The Semitic Languages*, ed. by R. Hetzron. London, 379–423.

— 1998a. La dérivation verbale dans les langues sudarabiques modernes. *Journal of Semitic Studies* XLIII/1: 71–88.

— 1998b. The Soqoṭri Language. In *Soqotra. Proceedings of the First International Symposium on Soqotra Island: Present & Future*, ed by H. Dumont. Vol. 1: 309–321. New York.

— 1998c. Les langues sudarabiques modernes: des langues sémitiques en danger? In *16th International Congress of Linguistics 20–25 July 1997*, ed. by B. Caron, Elsevier: CDRom Paper n°044.

— 1999. Les langues sudarabiques modernes. Bilan et perspectives. In *Chroniques yéménites*. 1998/99: 87–94. Sanaa.

— à paraître. De quelques fonctions de *d–* dans les langues sudarabiques modernes. In *La transcatégorialité: la grammaticalisation en synchronie*, éd. par Stéphane Robert. Louvain.

— avec la collaboration de Sabri Mohammed Bakheit. A paraître. *Textes en mehri du Yémen, avec commentaires linguistiques*. [Semitica Viva] Wiesbaden.

— 2001 [sous presse]. Une version soqotri de la légende de Abu Shawârib. In *Studies in the History of Arabia* (Miscellanies in the Honor of Professor Rex G. Smith), supplement to the *Journal of Semitic Studies*. Venetia Porter and John Healey (eds.)

Simeone-Senelle, Marie-Claude et Antoine Lonnet. 1985–86. Lexique des noms des parties du corps dans les langues sudarabiques modernes.

Première partie: la tête. *Matériaux Arabes et Sudarabiques* 3: 259–304.

1988–89. Lexique des noms des parties du corps dans les langues sudarabiques modernes. Deuxième partie: les membres. *Matériaux Arabes et Sudarabiques*, n.s. 2: 191–255.

1991. Lexique soqotri: les noms des parties du corps. In *Semitic Studies in Honor of Wolf Leslau on the Occasion of his 85th Birthday, November 14th, 1991*, ed. by Alan S. Kaye. Vol. II: 1443–1487. Wiesbaden.

— 1992. Compléments à *Lexique soqoṭri*: les noms des parties du corps. *Matériaux Arabes et Sudarabiques*, n.s. 4: 85–108.

Simeone-Senelle, M.-Cl., Lonnet A. et Sabri Mohamed-Bakheit. 1984. Histoire de Said, Saida, la méchante femme et l'ange. *Matériaux Arabes et Sudarabiques* 3: 237–268.

Simeone-Senelle, Marie-Claude et Martine Vanhove. 1997. La formation et l'évolution d'auxiliaires dans des langues sémitiques (langues sudarabiques modernes et maltais). In *Grammaticalisation et reconstruction. Mémoires de la Société Linguistique de Paris*. Tome V: 85–102. Paris.

Stroomer, Harry. 1996. Mehri texts collected by the late Professor T.M. Johnstone. *Israel Oriental Studies* XVI. Studies in Modern Semitic Languages, ed. by S. Izre'el and S. Raz. Leiden, New York, Köln, 271–288.

— (ed.). 1999. *Mehri Texts from Oman. Based on the Field Materiales of T.M. Johnstone*. Wiesbaden.

Swiggers, P. 1981. A phonological analysis of the Harsūsi consonants. *Arabica XXVIII, fasc. 2–3*: 358–361.

Testen, David. 1992. The Loss of the Person-marker *t–* in Jibbali and Socotri. *BSOAS* LV, 3: 445–450.

Thomas, Bertram. 1937. Four Strange Tongues from South Arabia. The Hadara Group. *Proceedings of the British Academy* 23: 239–331.

Voigt, Rainer. 1994. Der Lautwandel S[1] > H in wurzellosen Morphemen des Alt- und Neusüdarabischen. In *Semitic and Cushitic Studies*, ed. by Gideon Goldenberg & Shlomo Raz. Wiesbaden, 19–28.

Wagner, Edwald. 1953. *Syntax der Mehri-Sprache unter Berücksichtigung auch der anderen neusüdarabischen Sprachen*. Berlin.

— 1959. Der Dialekt von ᶜAbd-el-Kūrī. *Anthropos* 54, 2/3: 475–486.

— 1993. Gedanken zum Verb des Mehri aufgrund der neuen Materialen von T.M. Johnstone. *ZAL* 25: 316–339.

Wellsted, James Raimond. 1835a. Report on the Island of Socotra. *The Journal of the Asiatic Society of Bengal* IV / 39, March 1835: 138–166.

— 1835b. Memoir on the Island of Socotra. *The Journal of the Royal Geographical Society of London* V: 129–229.
— 1840. *Travels to the City of the Caliphs.* London.
Zaborski, Andrzej. 1994. Arcaismi ed innovazioni nei pronomi personali del sudarabo moderno. In *Sem Cam Iafet. Atti della 7a Giornata di Studi Camito-Semitici e Indoeuropei (Milano, 1 giugno 1993)*, ed. by Vermondo Brugnatelli. 251–262.

NEW FINDS IN THE 20TH CENTURY:
THE SOUTH SEMITIC LANGUAGES

DAVID APPLEYARD

1. PRELIMINARIES

Alongside the discoveries made in the field of Semitic languages of the Ancient Near East, the "new finds" in the 20th century in the languages of the southern extent of the traditional range of Semitic languages have probably had the most to contribute to the picture of the Semitic language family. In the first place, the sheer body of linguistic data that has been added to the corpus available to the Semitist is considerable, most particularly from the almost 30 modern languages that comprise the Modern South Arabian and Ethiopian branches. Almost all of these were either unknown to linguistic science in the 19th century, or at least very little known, and even then, with rare exceptions, were ignored or under-utilised in the general Semitic scholarship of the period — and have even been under-utilised if not actually ignored in much of the 20th century. In the second place, the contribution that South Semitic languages have made to linguistic science in general, and to Comparative Semitic linguistics, in particular, is significant and unique, and has in many ways redefined older views, informed as they were by an attitude of reverence for the "classical" languages. Traditional Comparative Semitics was driven by such classical languages and often only made secondary reference to modern materials — and as the majority of the South Semitic languages have only been recorded in modern times, this means that South Semitic is *de facto* typically under-represented in traditional Comparative Semitics. In this connection, I can only repeat what Hetzron said (Hetzron, 1977: 9) when speaking of Ethiopian Semitic, but the same applies equally to South Arabian:

'This branch has been, overtly or by implication, represented as a deformed, even degenerate outgrowth of Semitic, of anecdotal interest. Yet, on the one hand, it should be recognised that Ethiopian Semitic has given up less of some of the "typical" traditional Semitic features than, say, Modern East Aramaic (Modern Syriac). But even

401

departure from the traditional pattern would not justify neglect. ......
On the other hand, more importantly, the modern Semitic languages
of Ethiopia have been shown to provide new evidence and insights
for a reconstruction of proto-Semitic.'

Of course, it is natural that a general comparative grammar should focus
initially on the oldest attestations, where these are extensive enough to
provide a sound basis for the work in hand. After all, no comparative
grammar of Indo-European that I know of focuses on, say, Italian, Modern
Greek, English, Modern Russian, Modern Armenian, Hindi, or whatever,
rather than Latin, Ancient Greek, Gothic, Old Church Slavonic, and so on.
None the less, older attested data is likely to take priority in a comparative
grammar of a language family, and thus in the reconstruction of proto-
forms (something, by the way, that Comparative Semiticists have curiously
been reluctant to do, unlike Comparative Indo-Europeanists). However,
modern linguistic data, from obviously later stages of development within
the family, are, I would say, equally important:

- Modern languages may preserve archaisms that corroborate or
  add to what the older, "classical" languages show.
- Modern languages may exhibit features that help to explain,
  or cast a different light on elements occurring in the classical
  languages — there are two instances of this, where some
  modern Ethiopian Semitic languages were thought to illuminate
  "classical" forms elsewhere in Semitic, to which I shall return
  later.
- Modern languages can, of course, also provide information on
  areas of linguistic form that written, "dead" languages rarely,
  if ever, can: phonetics, questions of prosody, stress, pitch, etc.
- Last but not least, modern languages are just as valid pieces of
  linguistic evidence as classical languages with the weight of
  traditional reverence and scholarship behind them. All Semitic
  languages should be and are of interest to the general Semitist.

It is odd, therefore, that at a time when a good part of what we
now know of modern South Semitic languages had been described in
some initial way at least, the comparative grammar of Moscati, Spitaler,
Ullendorff and von Soden (1969) chose virtually to exclude citations
from modern languages, and, it seems to me, modern South Semitic
languages, in particular, which have so much to offer the comparativist.
Thankfully, this situation has begun to be reversed. The two most recent
surveys, the collection of descriptions of both ancient and modern
Semitic languages edited by Hetzron (*The Semitic Languages*, 1997),

and Lipiński's self-designated comparative work (*Semitic Languages: Outline of a Comparative Grammar*, 1997), both pay full and due recognition to modern Semitic languages, including, of course, South Semitic languages.[1]

In this paper I would like to look not only at the new linguistic data that have come to light this century — and their importance to Semitic linguistics and, indeed, linguistic science in general — but also at how scholars have assessed those data, especially in the area of identifying and classifying the South Semitic languages within the Semitic family.

2. WHAT COMPRISES "SOUTH SEMITIC"

To extend, therefore, the meaning of the term "new finds" what is new in South Semitic is not only the raw linguistic data itself, but also the developing understanding of where the South Semitic languages are to be placed within the family as whole. Similarly, the question of what comprises South Semitic has developed during the past century. The way that question has been answered is increasingly informed by developments in the general linguistic understanding of how languages may be related, of the mechanisms of language change, and most specifically of the effects of language contact and linguistic diffusion. For much of the last hundred years, the standard descriptions of Semitic followed the line of grouping Arabic, Epigraphic South Arabian, Modern South Arabian and Ethiopian together as one branch of the Semitic family. The idea, I believe, goes back to Ewald, but, as is well known, was taken up with little change relevant to the genealogical question, and repeated by Nöldeke in his *Encyclopaedia Britannica* article:

> 'One thing at least is certain, that Arabic (with Sabaean, Mahri and Socotri) and Ethiopic stand in a comparatively close relationship to one another, and compose a group by themselves, as contrasted with the other Semitic languages.'

(1911: 621)

Much the same wording was repeated by Driver in his 1932 *Encyclopaedia Britannica* article, and again in a host of other general surveys from Marcel Cohen's remarks in his section of Hamito-Semitic in *Les langues du monde* to Rabin's article in the *Encyclopaedia Judaica*. A slight modification in the classification, really no more than a cautious tampering, was made by Leslau in his *Encyclopaedia Britannica* article, where he says:

[1]   See the reviews of these two books in this volume.

'South Semitic is divided into Southeast Semitic, including South Arabic and Ethiopic, and into Southwest Semitic, with Arabic as its representative.'

(1961: 314)

Ullendorff, in his article on Semitics for the *Current Trends in Linguistics* series, is patently aware of Leslau's classification in so far as he employs the same odd nomenclature, but still prefers to cling to the familiar model:

'In speaking — as we customarily do — of ... South-West Semitic (the languages of Arabia and Ethiopia) we are simply reflecting the geographical facts, without drawing any genetic or typological inferences. Schemes of classification which identify and distinguish groupings within the Semitic area on the basis of specific bundles of isoglosses may derive support from structural, functional and genetic criteria ... [and] it may be claimed that the rough geographical division indicated above corresponds tolerably well to the distribution of gross linguistic features.'

(1970: 264)

This is not the place to go on at length on this topic, and a full account is given by Hetzron in Part A of his book on *Gunnän-Gurage* (1977: 8–24). It is indeed to Hetzron that we owe the first and clearest statement of the classification of South Semitic with which I think most scholars would now agree. In his contribution to the First International Congress of Semitic and Hamito-Semitic Linguistics (Hetzron, 1974: 181–94), he first consolidated suggestions that had been circulating for some time, originating with Christian's observations regarding similarities between the two Akkadian and South Arabian-Ethiopian prefix conjugations, and finding an echo later in Diakonoff's pioneering book on Hamito-Semitic (or Semito-Hamitic as he called it then) (1965). Hetzron followed Diakonoff and placed Arabic clearly with the Central Semitic languages (Hebrew, Canaanite, Aramaic). He repeated this classification, accompanied by some morphological arguments, in his monograph *Ethiopian Semitic* (1972: 15–16) and again in his book on Gunnän-Gurage, cited above.

Another good summary of the history of and arguments for the removal of Arabic from the South Semitic branch may be found in Alice Faber's chapter on "Genetic Subgrouping of the Semitic Languages" in Hetzron's edited volume on Semitic (1997: 3–15). It will be, nonetheless, a good idea to remind the reader of the major isoglosses that have at times been called upon to define South Semitic, both incorporating and excluding Arabic:

to include Arabic:
unconditional sound change PSem $*p > *f$

extensive use of broken plurals, e.g. *faras : ʔafrās*
verb stems with long first vowel *kātaba, takātaba*

to exclude Arabic:
maintenance of glottalised articulation of emphatics, as against innovated pharyngealisation/velarisation
personal endings in the perfect 1st, 2nd sg, 2nd pl. in *-k-* (innovation in the 2nd persons)
maintenance of **yVkattVb* imperfect indicative, as against innovated **yVktVb-u*

On the premise that classificational grouping of languages should be made on the basis of shared innovation (and especially morphological and lexical innovation), rather than shared retention, only the second of the latter set, namely the 1st and 2nd person sing. endings of the perfect in *-k-*, can properly distinguish the South Semitic branch comprising Epigraphic South Arabian (ESA), Modern South Arabian (MSA) and Ethiopian. On this question of innovations as the prime criterion for classificational grouping, it is worth remembering that Arabic has many innovations that incontrovertibly point to its membership of the Central Semitic branch, along with Northwest Semitic (Ugaritic, Canaanite, Aramaic, etc.).

Interestingly, probably the most widely quoted isogloss is the third one — the **yVkattVb* imperfect indication, a supposedly shared retention of the Semitic "periphery", also of course maintained in Akkadian, and incidentally now generally seen as an Afroasiatic inheritance (or, at least, common to Berber, Cushitic and Semitic as a prefix conjugated paradigm). Yet, opinions have varied whether ESA had such an imperfect form ever since Beeston queried whether variations in mediae infirmae verbs such as *ymwtn* as against *ymtn* might correlate with indicative as against subjunctive/jussive functions. He was forced to conclude, however, that no such correlation could be established and that "the differences in weak root imperfects are purely graphic and not morphological" (1984: 16). Others, most notably Avanzini (1991) and Nebes (1994) have re-examined the question, and Nebes has now quite convincingly demonstrated that only *yVktVb-* can be established for the imperfect base-stems in Sabaean and in the other ESA languages where there are adequate data.

D. Cohen (1974) even questioned whether MSA forms really derived from **yVkattVb*, as the Ethiopian so evidently do: e.g. Mehri 3msg. *yəro:kəz*, 3mpl. *yə'rakzəm*, as against subjunctive *yər'ke:z, yər'ke:zəm*, etc. I believe, on the other hand, that the MSA forms are exactly parallel to the Ethiopian (Appleyard 1996: 209–214). Voigt (1994b) has also published a reasoned account of the relationship between the MSA and Ethiopian verbal systems. The evidence, comparing MSA and Ethiopian (represented here by Geʻez), may be summarised in the following table; the Proto-MSA reconstructions are tentative:

verb type 1A	perfect	imperfect (3msg/3mpl)	subjunctive (3msg/3mpl)
Mehri	rə'ko:z	yə'ro:kəz, yə'rakzəm	yər'ke:z, yər'ke:zəm
Jibbāli	rə'fɔs	yə'rɔfəs, yə'rɔfəs	'yɔrfəs, yər'fɔs
Soqoṭri	'k'əfɔd k'ə'bɔr	i'k'ɔfəd, i'k'ofəd yə'k'abər, yə'k'obər	lə'k'afəd, lə'k'afid lik''bɛr, lik''bər
Proto-MSA	*qə'tal	*yə'qatəl, *yə'qatəlu	*yəq'tIl, *yəq'tIlu
Geʻez	k'ä'tälä	yə'k'ättəl, yək'ä'ttəlu	'yək'təl, yək''təlu

So, even this cherished isogloss is of weaker significance than hitherto believed. Obviously, the actual linguistic situation is far more complex than the familiar "tree with branches" model can reflect. It has long been recognised that the "wave" model of language divergence and convergence has special relevance to the Semitic family, where for most of the supposed history of the family the constituent members remained in a defined geographical region and contiguous to one another — hence the notion of the innovating centre of diffusion and, for instance, Garbini's theory of "amorrisation", regarding which he says with respect to ESA:

> 'L'amorreizzazione del sudarabico epigrafico si revela, in definitiva, piuttosto consistente, sì che è stato possibile sostenere un'affinità del sudarabico epigrafico più stretta con il nordarabico che con l'etiopico.'
>
> (1984: 148)

I think there is much to be said in favour of ESA, and especially Sabaean, being heavily subjected to North Arabian[2] linguistic innovations: such an

---

2   I use the term in a geographical sense, i.e. referring to linguistic innovations radiating from or through the language(s) of the northern part of the Arabian peninsula.

argument may be used, for instance, to explain the apparent absence, and presumed loss of the **yVkattVb* imperfect. The same argument may of course be progressed to exclude ESA from South Semitic altogether: the replacement of older **yVkattVb-* by **yVktVb-u* in the function of imperfect (indicative) is an innovation linking ESA with Central Semitic, but then we are still left with the equally important South Semitic isogloss of innovating 2nd person perfect suffixes in **-k-*, ESA evidence of which has now turned up in the recently discovered cursive texts on wood. The same argument may also be used to explain the form of the 3rd person pronouns in **h-* alongside more archaic forms in **š-* in non-Sabaean ESA [s₁] and MSA, though such an explanation would presuppose an assumption that the **s->*h-* development is a Central Semitic innovation, which is not necessarily exclusively the case. A similar change obviously happened independently in MSA affecting a proto-MSA **š*, not only in the pronouns and other "heavily worked" morphemes, but also in some lexical items, as Voigt (1994a) has elegantly demonstrated. The evidence of the pronouns may be summarised as follows:

independent pronoun	3msg	3fsg	3mpl	3fpl	3dl
Mehri	*heh*	*seh*	*he:m*	*se:n*	*hi:*
Jibbāli	*šε*	*sε*	*šum*	*sεn*	*ši*
Soqotri	*yʰeh* *yʰe*	*seʰ* *se*	*yʰan* *yʰən*	*san* *sεn*	*heʰi, hi* *yʰi*
Proto-MSA	**ší*	**sí*	**ším*	**sín*	**šəy*
Sabaic	*h[w]ʔ*	*h[y]ʔ*	*hmw*	*hn*	*hmy*
Qatabanic	*s₁w*	*s₁y-t*	*s₁m*	*-s₁n*	*s₁my-t*

Though there has recently been discussion whether ESA belongs more with Central Semitic than with a reduced South Semitic comprising just MSA and Ethiopian (Porkhomovsky 1997), for practical reasons in the discussion that follows in the second part of this paper I will include ESA alongside MSA and Ethiopian under the heading of South Semitic. First, however, it would be as well to reiterate the linguistic inventory.

3. SOUTH SEMITIC LANGUAGES — INVENTORIES

EPIGRAPHIC SOUTH ARABIAN

Epigraphic South Arabian, which is also referred to in the literature as Sayhadic, a term coined by Beeston to avoid the chance of confusion with Arabic or an assumed genetic and temporal affiliation with Modern South Arabian, is usually described as comprising 4 languages: Sabaic, Qatabanic, Hadramitic and Minaic, all of which are preserved only in inscriptional material dating from the beginning of the 1st millennium BCE through to the 6th century CE. To monumental inscriptions on durable materials such as stone and metal, there have now been added somewhere in the region of 1,000 documents written in a cursive script and concerning everyday matters, written on palm ribs and only discovered in 1973. Only a fraction of these has been published to date (Ryckmans et al. 1994), though what little is available already provides some linguistic data that is not found in the monumental texts. The best documented ESA language is Sabaic. ESA inscriptions have been found in Egypt, in the Aegean and in Ethiopia, wherever trade took the Ancient South Arabians, but the home of the ESA languages, where the overwhelming majority of the inscriptions is found, is in the south-west corner of the Arabian peninsula, essentially in what is now the western half of Yemen.

The consonantal nature of the script in which all of the ESA languages are written obviously obscures much that would be of interest and may in itself contribute to the general sense that the languages are "relatively close to each other", something to which the influence and prestige of Sabaic over the other languages may also have contributed. The apparently significant isogloss of 3rd person pronouns in *h-* which separates Sabaic from the other languages with s_1- might suggest a major rift, yet other isoglosses equally seem to bind all four languages together, e.g. determinate state or suffixed article in -[*h*]*n*.

MODERN SOUTH ARABIAN

The most recent survey of MSA (Simeone-Senelle in Hetzron 1997) speaks of 6 languages: Mehri, Ḥarsusi, Baṭhari, Hobyōt, Jibbāli and Soqoṭri, of which Mehri is the most widespread with about half of the total number of 200,000 MSA speakers. The MSA languages are spoken in eastern Yemen and western Oman, along the coast and in the hinterland, and on the island of Soqoṭra. Mehri, Jibbāli and Soqoṭri were first extensively described in the publications of the Austrian Südarabische Expedition, which started collecting material at the very end of the 19th century and published its results in the early years of the 20th century. Hobyōt, on the other hand, was only "discovered" in 1985, and together with Ḥarsusi and Baṭḥari would seem to form a closely related cluster with Mehri. To the work on the emerging complex picture of MSA dialectology first carried out by Johnstone in the 1970s and '80s we are now fortunate to be able to add the recent studies of the CNRS team and especially Simeone-Senelle. Nonetheless, MSA remains the least studied area of modern Semitic, but the signs for continuing and future scholarship into the next century are extremely promising.

ETHIOPIAN SEMITIC

Ethiopian is the largest member of the South Semitic branch both in terms of number of speakers and number of languages. The question, just how many Ethiopian Semitic languages there are is, however, contentious. Hetzron's list (1972) comprises 22 languages and mentions a few other "varieties" or dialects, yet even the list of 22 is probably a little over-ambitious as several of the languages he lists separately under one or other of the "Gurage" headings are described as "exhibiting such a great deal of similarity that they may be considered one unit." (1977: 4) — so Enär and Indägäñ in the list, or Wälane and Soddo. The question of the "Gurage" languages will be taken up in the section on Ethiopian dialectology later in this paper. Incidentally, one thing that emerges clearly from Hetzron's work, which he repeats in several places, and which would do no harm to repeat once more, is that the term "Gurage" does not encompass a single language, cluster of dialects, or even a genetic unit; it only has currency in a geographical sense. The languages subsumed under this name fall into 3 distinct genetic groups, one of which (East Gurage) is in classificational terms closer to languages such as Amharic and Harari than to the other so-called Gurage languages. The only really methodologically sound and indeed the definitive internal classification of Ethiopian is that carried out by Hetzron (1972), which may be summarised in diagrammatic form as follows:

1. *North Ethiopic*
   Ge'ez, Tigre, Tigrinya
2. *South Ethiopic*
2A. *Transversal South Ethiopic*
   Amharic, Argobba, Harari
   Silt'i, Wälane, Zway   [together = *East Gurage*]

2B. Outer South Ethiopic
   Gafat
   Soddo, Goggot, Muhir   [together = *North Gurage*]

   Mäsqän
Izha, Chäha, Gura, Gumär
         [together = *Central Western Gurage*]   [= *Western Gurage*]
         Innämor, Gyeto, Indägäñ, Enär
         [together = *Peripheral Western Gurage*]

Ethiopian Semitic has been fortunate in the outstanding scholars that it has attracted. No discussion of Ethiopian Semitic would be complete, or even possible, without recourse to the manifold published research of Wolf Leslau; the most complete, and indeed in several cases the only descriptions of several Ethiopian Semitic languages are owed to him. A great deal of what we know about the languages subsumed under the term "Gurage" was collected and published by him, and in addition he has produced sizeable descriptive studies on Tigre, Tigrinya, Amharic, Argobba, Harari, Gafat ... indeed, I do not think there is an Ethiopian Semitic language that has not received his attention. We should also not forget here either H.J. Polotsky or Gideon Goldenberg, whose analytical studies have provided not only a large amount of data but also brilliant insights, as, of course, have those of Robert Hetzron.

The field of Ethiopian Semitic is "inexhaustible and exceptionally fascinating" (Goldenberg 1977: 461), and provides a wealth of exciting linguistic structures to keep the general linguist occupied for a lifetime. For the Semitist, I think, the Ethiopian field provides not only an "inexhaustible" body of data, but also a living laboratory of the close interaction of Semitic languages with one (or more) different language families over a long period of time. It is something of a truism to say that in Ethiopia and Eritrea the Semitic *'Sprachtypus'* has been influenced by Cushitic languages, and certainly a lot of what might seem unfamiliar about Ethiopian to a general Semitist is probably attributable to such interaction; for instance, syntax is always the first example to be cited, where the modern Ethiopian languages, but not of course Ge'ez, all have an SOV sentence structure with much that that entails typologically. However, in specific cases it is sometimes difficult to disentangle the countless threads of influence and identify the direction in which it has operated. It is all too easy to ascribe a seemingly "un-Semitic" looking feature to Cushitic. On the other hand, whilst not ignoring the possibility of Cushitic influence, it is sometimes possible to look for a "Semitic" explanation for certain perhaps unexpected or unfamiliar features. This is what Hetzron did, for instance, when attempting to explain the morphemes of main verb marking in several Outer South

Ethiopic languages as survivals, in part, of a Proto-Semitic morpheme set. This question together with Hetzron's analysis will be examined later in this paper.

4. SOUTH SEMITIC LANGUAGES — LINGUISTICS

As a preliminary to detailed discussion, however, the question needs to be asked, what have the members of South Semitic offered the field of Semitics as a whole, and linguistics in general, by way of especially interesting linguistic forms? Here I shall restrict myself to the modern languages, especially Ethiopian Semitic, with which I am more familiar.

MODERN SOUTH ARABIAN

The most outstanding feature of the Modern South Arabian languages, at least on initial acquaintance, is the extraordinary phonemic systems and complex sets of morphophonemic rules that they all exhibit. Phonemically, the MSA languages have the most complex systems, especially consonantal systems, of any modern Semitic languages. They are the only modern languages to preserve three distinct sibilant (alveolar fricative) series, such as are now generally reconstructed for Proto-Semitic: denti-alveolar /s/ and /z/, palato-alveolar /š/, and lateral-alveolar /ś/ (Simeone-Senelle 1997: 382). All except Soqotri also have an interdental fricative series: /θ/ and /ð/. A phonetic feature that is also seen as significant for Comparative Semitics is the realisation of the "emphatic" phonemes as glottalised, as in Ethiopian, rather than velarised, as in Arabic. The process of palatalisation, and, in Jibbāli, the loss of intervocalic labial consonants and the effect of guttural obstruents (*h*, *x*, *γ*, *ʕ* and *ħ*) particularly in the inflexion of verbs, all make for extremely complex morphophonemic processes (see Hayward 1988).

In the area of morphology, MSA languages are unique amongst modern Semitic languages in maintaining a fully functioning category of the dual in nouns, pronouns and verb inflection, though the forms themselves may well be restructured using the vowel -*i* (from *-əy* and thence *-ay*) as the almost ubiquitous dual marker — only challenged by the vowel -*o* / -*ɔ* (from original verbal ending *-a:* of some persons of the perfect and imperfect) in part of the verbal system. (Johnstone 1970b)

Another morphological feature of interest to the comparativist that one might mention is the creation of a definite article in MSA (excluding Soqotri) which differs in form and somewhat in distribution from definite markers in other Semitic languages, and especially other South Semitic languages. In Omani Mehri and Ḥarsūsi the definite marker has the form *a*-, and in Jibbāli ɛ-, before voiced or glottalised (emphatic) consonants, Ø before other consonants, and in Jibbāli triggers lengthening of the initial syllable vowel in nouns beginning with *ʔ*: *ʔerʹni* 'hare' : *ʔeːrʹni* 'the hare'. Johnstone records a variant *ħ[a]*- and *h[a]*- in Mehri and Ḥarsūsi, which has become fixed in such items as *ħayd* 'hand', *ħəʹyawm* 'sun' and *ħaam* 'mother'. In Soqoṭri there are traces of probably the same prefixed marker in the "mimetic prosthetic vowel" (Johnstone 1970a: 301–2) found before nouns originally beginning in *ʔ*, *w* or *y*: *ʔəʔəd* 'hand', *ʔəʔərəh* 'moon', *ʔoʔoz* 'ewe', *ʔeʔərʹbiyoh* 'locust', etc. Unusually for Semitic, the definite marker is required with nouns followed by the pronominal possessive suffixes: Jib. ɛ-ʹbritš 'his daughter', M. *a-ʹbətk* 'your house'. It would be natural to connect this prefixed definite marker to the proclitic article *hn-* found in Liḥyānite, *ʔam-* / *ʔan-* in ancient Yemeni colloquial Arabic (Ḥimyarite), and even Standard Arabic *ʔal-*, and so on. It is significant, however, that it is different from the systems of definite marker that were developed in ESA with a suffixed -*[h]n*, and independently in different varieties of Ethiopian. Simply put, definite marking was developed independently in ESA and MSA, and again independently within various individual languages in Ethiopian. The form of the MSA marker, however, is almost certainly due to the influence of some form of Arabic, or better North Arabian diffusion. Voigt also suggests (1998: 248) that the MSA article represents the result of diffusion of a *ha*-form of the article from the centre, and is not a direct outcome of what he reconstructs as an ancient Common Semitic article, such as is still seen in the ESA form.

Mehri	indefinite	definite	
	gɛːd	*aʹgɛːd*	'skin'
	kʹaːb	*aʹkʹaːb*	'heart'
	kawb		'wolf'
	moh / *ħəʹmoh* *rəbʹyeːt* / *ħarəbʹyeːt*		'water' 'locust'
	ħayd *ħaam* *ħəʹyawm*		'hand' 'mother' 'sun'

ETHIOPIAN SEMITIC

When we turn to Ethiopian Semitic there is such a wealth of interesting linguistic topics that have been discussed in the literature that it is difficult, in a general paper like this, to make a choice. Quite at random, we can mention, from phonology, topics such as the phonemic status of the 6th order vowel [ə] in Amharic and Ge'ez, the nature of the vocalic systems in other Ethiopian languages (Tigre, "Gurage", etc.), and stress in Amharic; and from morphophonemics, the matter of prosodic labialisation and palatalisation in Western Gurage; from morphology, pronominal systems and pronominal marking in various languages, and of course a whole range of topics relating to the verbal system such as tense and aspect, derived stem patterns, consonantal gemination in the verb, and so on; and in the field of syntax, which perhaps holds more remaining challenges and exciting issues than other levels of linguistic analysis, relative clause structures (especially in Amharic), concatenating structures and the use of various clitics (again, especially in Amharic), as well as the role of gerund or converb constructions, and copula constructions.

Here, I would like to focus on just two morphological topics that I find particularly interesting in relation to the question where they can lead, or mislead, the comparativist. The first of these is the question of Main Verb Markers which occur in South Ethiopic, and the second concerns 'heavy' and 'light' pronoun object suffixes in Outer South Ethiopic.

Main Verb Markers

Most (and maybe all) South Ethiopic languages make a formal distinction in at least one tense between verbs that occur in main clauses and those that occur in (some) subordinate clauses. Where this feature is found, the main clause verb form is typically distinguished and derived from the subordinate by means of an added element. In languages of the group called Transversal South Ethiopic (TSE) by Hetzron the added element derives from an auxiliary use of the root *hlw 'be', and the distinction between main and subordinate is found only in the non-past (imperfect) tense. Hetzron (1972: 37) compared this function of the *hlw auxiliary to the Main Verb Markers (MVMs) of North Gurage, which have quite a different form and traces of which also occur in Western Gurage. Compound tenses with *hlw, of course, occur in North Ethiopic as well, including a handful of rare instances in Ge'ez, but the function of these compounds is not syntactic in the way that has developed in TSE, but rather aspectual. For example, a form such as Tigrinya *ʔəkäyyəd ʔalloku* 'I go/am going (now)' is distinguished from simple *ʔəkäyyəd* in that it variously indicates an immediate present and a continuous or rather on-going action, whilst the exact formal equivalents in Amharic, *əhedallähu* and *əhed*, do not mark any kind of aspectual contrast but are differentiated syntactically: main verb v. subordinate verb (see Voigt 1977: 336ff). In any event, as Goldenberg (1977) pointed out in his review article of Hetzron 1972, it was rather disingenuous of Hetzron to suggest that this use of **hlw* in TSE "replaced ... original Main Verb Markers" still found in North Gurage. The innovation of formally contrasting main and subordinate verbs has distinct realisations in TSE and North Gurage, and no one realisation can be assumed to be the original one. The formal distinction of main verb from subordinate verb forms is, of course, found in many Cushitic languages, especially those, such as Agaw (Central Cushitic) and Highland East Cushitic, which are believed to have formed the substratum beneath Ethiopian Semitic. The TSE forms are shown in the following table:

	tense	main	subordinate	relative
Amharic	non-past	*yəsäbr-all*	*yəsäbər*	*yämm-isäbər* (Old Amh. *Ø-yəsäbər*)
	past	*säbbärä, säbro-all*	*säbbärä*	*yä-säbbärä*
Argobba	non-past	*yəsäbr-äl*	*yəsäbər*	*yämmi-säbər*
	past	*säbbära, säbrədu-l*	*säbbära*	*yä-säbbära*
Harari	non-past	*yisabr-a:l*	*yisabri*	*yisabri-z-a:l* (Old Har. *Ø-yisabri*)
	past	*sabara*	*sabara*	*zi-sabara*
Silt'i	non-past	*imask-a:n*	*imask*	*imask-Ø-a:n*
	past	*masaka, masak[a]-a:n*	*masaka*	*ya-masaka*

In North Gurage, the equivalent MVMs have a quite different form: *-u/-i/-n/-t*, the distribution of which may be summarised as *-u* after a consonant or short vowel except in certain persons where *-i* occurs (primarily 3sg fem — but with some other occurrences including where object pronouns are involved), and *-n* or *-t* according to language after original long vowels. This distribution led Hetzron to equate *-u ~ -n/-t*, at least, formally with the *-u:-n[a/i]* suffix of Central Semitic (or Proto-Semitic as he would have it) added to form the imperfect indicative (i.e. Arabic *yaqtul-u* but *yaqtulu:-na*). To explain the *-t* forms in Ethiopian (in fact Outer South Ethiopic – OSE) he proposed an additional **-t* suffix: **-ut > -u, *-nt > -n ~ -t*. Whilst the processes variously reducing a hypothetical **-nt* to *-n* or *-t* are not inconceivable within the historical phonetics of Ethiopian Semitic, the loss of the final consonant from a putative **-ut* is less convincing. Traces of these MVMs, especially *-n* and *-t*, occur in other OSE languages, though only in North Gurage do they occur widely. The following tables illustrate the principal occurrences in Muhir and in Goggot.

Muhir	non-past main	non-past subordinate
1 sg	*äsäbru*	*äsäbər*
2 sg masc	*təsäbru*	*təsäbər*
2 sg fem	*təsäbrət*	*təsäbir < təsäbri*
3 sg masc	*yəsäbru*	*yəsäbər*
3 sg fem	*təsäbri*	*təsäbər*
1 pl	*nəsäbrəno < nəsäbrənä+u*	*nəsäbrənä*
2 pl masc	*təsäbrəmʷət*	*təsäbrəmʷ*
2 pl fem	*təsäbrəmat*	*təsäbrəma*
3 pl masc	*yəsäbrəmʷət*	*yəsäbrəmʷ*
3 pl fem	*yəsäbrəmat*	*təsäbrəma*
MVM	*-u / ...C, ...Cä; -i* (3 sg fem) *-t / ...CV:*	—

Goggot	non-past main	past main
1 sg	*äsäbru*	*säbbärkʷi < säbbärku + i*
2 sg masc	*təsäbru*	*säbbärko < säbbärkä + u*
2 sg fem	*təsäbrən*	*säbbäršən < säbbärši + n*
3 sg masc	*yəsäbru*	*säbbäro < säbbärä + u*
3 sg fem	*təsäbri*	*säbbärätti*
1 pl	*nəsäbrəno < nəsäbrənä+u*	*säbbärno < säbbärnä + u*
2 pl masc	*təsäbrəmun*	*säbbärkəmun*
2 pl fem	*təsäbrəman*	*säbbärkəman*
3 pl masc	*yəsäbrəmun*	*säbbärmun*
3 pl fem	*yəsäbrəman*	*säbbärman*
MVM	*-u /...C* (except 3 sg fem), *...Cä* *-i* (3 sg fem) *-n /...CV:*	*-i* (1 sg, 3 sg fem) *-u /...Cä* *-n /...CV:* (except 1 sg)

One major difference, that can hardly be without significance, between the morphology of the Central Semitic and the OSE elements is that in the latter the MVMs are placed finally in the verb complex, i.e. after any pronoun complement suffix: contrast Arabic *yaqtul-u-ni:* 'he kills me' but *yaqtulu:-Ø-ni:* (i.e. *-na* deleted before the pronoun object) 'they kill me' with Muhir *yəsäbr-e-w* 'he breaks me', *yəsäbərrat* [= *yəsäbər+:a+t*] 'he breaks her' and *yudmʷ-i-t* 'they tell him'. Hetzron was thus forced to propose a transposition of {Verb + MVM + Pron. Complement} (as in Arabic and presumably Proto-Semitic) to {Verb + Pron. Complement + MVM} (as in OSE). This means, of course, that the MVM in OSE occupies the same position in the morpheme sequence as the MVM in TSE originating in the verb **hlw*: cf. Amharic *yəgädl-äññ-all*, *yəgädlu-ññ-all*, which also can hardly be without significance. A further point the relevance of which Goldenberg (1977: 479) first highlighted, I believe, is that in the OSE languages the same phonemes — *n, t* and *u* — also constitute the base of the copula, as they also do in various other Ethiopian languages. The details are carefully laid out in tabular form by Goldenberg, to which may be added the copula in *ta-* in Harari and the 3rd person copula *tu, ta,* etc., in Tigre. In this connection, it is doubtless also significant that in North Gurage, where these MVMs still occur intact, compound tenses and the copula (not always both past and non-past, though) do not take the MVMs. If the MVMs in OSE were thus copular in origin, then it would be understandable why the copula itself and compound forms do not add MVMs. I would therefore concur with Goldenberg's suggestion and say that the origin of these MVMs is indeed to be sought in the copula, and their resemblance to the indicative suffix in Central Semitic is entirely fortuitous. It would indeed be exceptional, to my mind, if a group of modern Semitic languages, as radically modified by contact with neighbouring non-Semitic languages as OSE is, were to preserve such an archaic feature. What is more, even the form of the *-u/-i* and *-t* copular elements, at least, are most likely of Cushitic rather than Semitic origin. In Highland East Cushitic, with which the OSE languages have long been in contact, the feminine copula has the common form **-t[t]V*, and optionally in Hadiyya (i.e. *-tte*) and partially in Sidamo (after proper names, nouns denoting humans, and pronouns) the same (i.e. *-ti*) is used with masculine subjects. In other contexts in Sidamo the copula has the form *-ho* (strictly speaking, not just *-u* as noted by Goldenberg based on Cerulli), which may nonetheless be the origin of the Ethiopian MVM and copula in *-u*. The vowels *-u* and *-i* are also typically associated with masculine and feminine gender marking, respectively, in pronominal, deictic and hence copular morphemes across Cushitic including in Highland East Cushitic — the *-i* MVM, it will be recalled, is typically associated with the 3sg fem (where not attributed to dissimilation of labials as in the Goggot 1sg past *säbbärkʷi* < *säbbärku* + *i* < **säbbärku* + *u*).

'Heavy' and 'Light' Pronoun Complements

Another feature of OSE morphology which Hetzron saw as in part preserving what he reconstructed as a Proto-Semitic feature concerns the opposition between what Polotsky first called 'heavy' and 'light' object and mediate pronoun suffixes added to verbs. Here, I wish to refer only to the object pronoun suffixes. Essentially, 'heavy' suffixes are added to verb forms that originally ended in a long vowel, whilst 'light' suffixes are added to those that ended in a consonant. Verb forms that originally ended in a short vowel, or a vowel of putative variable length, have a mixed set, sometimes 'heavy', sometimes 'light'. The actual situation in the various languages concerned is far more complicated, however, than I have space to do justice here, and details may be found both in Hetzron (1972: 46–54, 1977: 60–68) and Polotsky (1951: 30–33), as well as in other sources cited especially by Hetzron. The principle that the initial consonant of the object suffix should vary in relation to the preceding verb-final is not in itself anything out of the ordinary — so, 2 sg masc. *-kkä* after an original long vowel with compensatory lengthening of the consonant when vocalic length was lost, versus -*xä* elsewhere. Fluctuation in the length of the initial consonant of object pronoun suffixes occurs in Ge'ez as traditionally pronounced, though apparently not always in accord with the principle just outlined: *k'ätä'läkkä* with consonant length following a short vowel, versus *k'ätäl'nakä* without a lengthened consonant of the suffix following an originally long or fluctuating ("anceps") vowel. In some Tigrinya dialects, a similar fluctuation has been recorded: *fälät'kukka* but *k'ätälkuxa*, with object pronoun suffixes reminiscent of both 'heavy' and 'light' after the supposedly "anceps" ending -*ku*.

What is interesting, something from which Hetzron draws particular inference for Comparative Semitics, is the presence of the element -*nn*- in the 'light' suffixes. He suggests that the distribution of -*nn*- or -*:*- (consonant lengthening) suffixes in the 3rd person 'light' suffixes derives directly from Proto-Semitic, where for 3 sg masc. and fem. he would reconstruct object suffixes *-*nnu:* and *-*nna:*, respectively, after short vowels ("-*u* of the indicative and -*a* of the cohortative/jussive") alongside the more familiar *-*hu:* and *-*ha:* elsewhere. (Hetzron 1969, repeated in 1972, 1977). He saw a similar (but not identical) situation in the 1st sing. object suffix, where he suggested both *-*i:* / *-*ya* and *-*nni:* could be reconstructed for Proto-Semitic, reflected, for instance, in the -*e* versus -*ññ* endings in Muhir. However, in all ancient Semitic languages the verbal complement of the 1st sing. is indicated by -*ni:*, with the sole exception of Old Assyrian -*ī* as a variant of -*ni* in accusative function. It is only in OSE that -*e* occurs in the function of (light) verbal complement alongside (heavy) -*ñ*). The -*nn*- element occurs in OSE in other persons, too, in the 2nd persons and the 3rd person plural of the 'light' suffixes after perfect tense verbs, which according to Hetzron would be due to analogy with the 3rd person singular forms.

Muhir	heavy	light — imperfect	light — perfect
1 sg	-ññ	-e	-e
2 sg masc	-kkä	-xä	-nnaxä
2 sg fem	-kkʸ	-hʸ	-nnahʸ
3 sg masc	-w, -y	ʷ-:, -nn	-nn
3 sg fem	-wa, -ya	-:a, -nna	-nna
1 pl	-nnä	-änä	-nä
2 pl masc	-kkəmʷ	-xəmʷ	-nnaxmʷ
2 pl fem	-kkəma	-xma	-nnaxma
3 pl masc	-wämʷ, -yämʷ	-:ämʷ, -nnämʷ	-nnämʷ
3 pl fem	-wäma, -yäma	-:äma, -nnäma	-nnäma

where ʷ- = internal labialisation, and : = consonant lengthening

The problem with all of this, ingenious as it is, is rather similar to that of the Main Verb Markers. Aside from the fact that most would now reconstruct the Proto-Semitic 3rd person sing. object pronouns as *-šu:, *-ša:, respectively, I am not sure whether there would be any agreement on proposing a distributional variant *-nnu: in spite of what Hetzron called the "neat distinction" (1972: 46) in Biblical Hebrew between yišmərennu: 'he guards him' and yišmərɛhu: 'let him guard him', and other *n forms in Ugaritic — sg. -nh, -n, -nn, and in the Phoenician of Cyprus and in Punic — 3pl. -nm. Certainly, other explanations have been proposed for these. Whatever the opinion may be on these older Semitic forms, however, I would again repeat, would it not indeed be exceptional, if a group of modern Semitic languages, as radically modified by contact with neighbouring non-Semitic languages as OSE is, were to have preserved such a feature? — supposing it were Proto-Semitic and not an innovation of Canaanite.

DIALECTOLOGY IN ETHIOPIAN SEMITIC

(Our late, much lamented colleague, Prof. Shlomo Raz, was to have presented a paper on dialectology in Ethiopian Semitic at the conference that underlies the present collection of papers, and subsequently submitted a written article to this volume. Following his untimely death in April 1999, the editor invited me to include a section on the topic in my discussion of new finds and developments in South Semitic linguistics in the 20th century. I was greatly flattered by this invitation, and out of respect and homage to a fine scholar, who was also a close friend, willingly agreed to append the following remarks on Ethiopian dialectology. It should be emphasised, however, that the observations that follow are entirely my own thoughts on the subject, but I would like to think that they would not offend Prof. Raz's academic and scholarly sensibilities, or be outside the spirit of what he might have wished to say.)

The range of Ethiopian Semitic languages has provided, and continues to provide linguists with an extensive field of data upon which to work, supplying many interesting and challenging linguistic forms and structures for analysis, and contributing greatly to typological studies of human language that have become so much more prominent in general linguistics in the last couple of decades. Ethiopian dialect studies, in the strictest sense of the phrase, have however hardly begun. It is, of course, true that in various descriptive studies the question, for instance, has been raised whether Argobba is a dialect of Amharic (see especially Leslau 1997: 130–1), or whether all the "Gurage" varieties are necessarily independent languages (Hetzron 1977: 4), though I doubt that everyone would now wish to go so far as Leslau and speak of all of "Gurage" as a dialect cluster (1969b), or propose a common "Gurage" node in the Ethiopian Semitic family tree (see Leslau 1969a). These are more terminological questions, whether a certain speech form is a dialect of another or a separate language, and the criteria that are used to define a dialect will very much influence the question and its answer. Thus, mutual intelligibility is probably the most usually employed defining criterion. Even defining what constitutes mutual intelligibility leads on to further need for close definition: does mutual intelligibility necessarily require complete comprehension of what speaker of dialect A says by speaker of dialect B? This question is particularly relevant in the case of Argobba: an Argobba utterance such as *nägärun wägär mäññədah satto:nk' attəwažž* 'do not speak before you know the matter well' (Leslau 1997: 113) would almost certainly not be comprehensible to an Amharic speaker, where the equivalent would be *nägärun t'əru adrəgäh sattawk' attənnagär*, in which only the first word is identical, whereas Argobba *yalmät't'a əndähona bəččayän əhedalluh* 'if he does not come, I shall go alone' (Leslau 1997: 107) is virtually identical to its Amharic equivalent. Researchers who have worked on Argobba generally conclude that it is a dialect of Amharic in that there is a high percentage of common vocabulary (S.L.L.E. 74%, Leslau 87%) and morphology (S.L.L.E. 85%). On impressionistic grounds, Zelealem Leyew writing in the 1994 S.L.L.E. Report says of Argobba speakers that it seemed to him that they spoke

Amharic "but in a different fashion," and the Argobba speakers of the Shewa-Robit area, most of whom use Amharic as their first language, "are not usually aware of a language called 'Argobba' which is supposed to be different from Amharic," but use it whenever they are together and wish to identify themselves as distinct from Amharas. These statements show how difficult and complex the question is of determining what constitutes a separate language or a dialect.

As regards the linguistic study of dialectology properly speaking, there has also appeared a tantalisingly brief outline of Amharic dialects (Habte Mariam Marcos 1973, together with a somewhat more polished version of the same in Cowley et al. 1976), which in themselves serve to show how much more there is to be done in the dialect geography of the largest of the Ethiopian Semitic languages. Fieldwork for this study was carried out in one or two locations only within the three regions of Wollo, Mänz and Gojjam, and thus cannot begin to be deemed a proper survey. Some prominent phonetic, morphological and lexical variations are listed for the three dialect areas. Leslau's recent reference grammar of Amharic (1995) also contains scattered references to dialect variation, again focusing on the principal dialect regions and using what can be described as a developing "Standard (educated and literary) Amharic", which is essentially educated Addis Ababa Amharic, as a control. The impression gained from the data that has been published suggests that dialect differentiation in Amharic is not inhibitive to mutual comprehension between dialects, but that there are cross-cutting isoglosses that prevent the clear subgrouping of dialects. Thus, Cowley et al. suggest that phonologically the dialects of Addis Ababa and Gondar form a separate cluster, whilst Mänz and Wollo form another close group, whereas syntactic isoglosses set Addis Ababa, Mänz and Wollo apart as a group from each of Gojjam and Gondar. However, the Amharic dialect data does yield one or two morphological features that are perhaps not without significance for the understanding of the history of Amharic as a whole. Firstly, in the dialect of Gojjam, the gerund form of the verb, which in other dialects of Amharic is restricted to subordinate position dependent on a verb head, can be used both as a main verb form with past meaning and in headless relative clauses: (a) *ammämäñ bəlo täññəto* 'he went to bed saying, I'm sick', where other dialects would use a main verb form *täñña* or *täññətwal* in final position; (b) *yätäsärk'o-tu altägäññäm* 'what was stolen has not been found', equivalent to other dialects *yätäsärräk'ä-w altägäññäm*. The use of the gerund, which in origin is a nominal form of the verb used in adverbial (i.e. subordinate) function as a main verb is, of course, also seen in Tigrinya. In so far as Gojjam and the Tigrinya-speaking regions are not adjacent, I doubt whether this could be attributed to an areal feature, but may simply be a parallel development, and Gojjami usage of the gerund goes far beyond what is usual in Tigrinya in that the former may also regularly generate a negative form, e.g. *albältom* 'he hasn't eaten', whilst negative gerunds are seemingly rare and unusual in Tigrinya.

Perhaps of somewhat more concrete significance for the interpretation of the history of Amharic is the Gojjami usage of the prefix *yä-* in the functions (a) of indirect object (dative) and even (b) of direct object marker: (a) *yäläǧu sät't'ähut* 'I gave it to the child'; (b) *yäbet lək'äbbaw* 'so that I paint the house'. The interesting point about this is that whilst the prefix *yä-* with possessive-attributive (genitive) and relative-clause marking functions, which is common to all dialects, would generally be derived from earlier *zä-* (thus in Ge'ez), the prefix *yä-* with the extra functions in Gojjami would presumably be derived from *lä-*, which is of course the usual "dative" prefix in other dialects. Palatalisation of *l* to *y* is a regular morphophonemic process in Amharic under closely defined conditions, and sporadic palatalisation of *z* to *y* can be observed in a few instances, such as in the demonstratives *yəh* (allomorph *-zzih*) and *ya* (allomorph *-zziya*, *-zza*) from **zikä* and **ziʔa*, respectively. There would therefore be no problem in deriving Gojjami *yä-* from two different sources. Interestingly, if this is the case, the particle *yä-* with "dative" and object marking functions would seem again to parallel Tigrinya, where *nə-* (*nä-* in combination with the article: *nätu, näta*, etc.) is both the marker of indirect objects and, optionally, direct objects: *saʔri nätu färäs habəwo* 'give some grass to the horse', *nəhawu harimuwo* 'he struck his brother'. In the Tigrinya dialects of Agame and Enderta *nə-* is replaced by *lə-*, which further suggests a formal connection with Gojjami *yä-*. One isogloss connecting the two may easily be a coincidence, but two isoglosses look more interesting.

Similarly, the existence of dialect variation in Tigrinya has been noted, if somewhat impressionistically (Ullendorff 1955: 22, 1985: 17), though details are mostly lacking in the literature (but see Leslau 1939). Much needs to be done in this area, too.

As with dialect geography, the sociolinguistic aspects of Ethiopian dialectology have barely been explored, or indeed hardly begun. One interesting sociolinguistic interpretation of a phonemic feature that is usually described as pertaining to geographically defined dialects, the interchange between *s'* and *t'*, is provided by Takkele Taddese (1992). In regional dialect terms, the occurrence of the glottalised fricative *s'* in uneducated speech is generally a feature of the Gondar and Gojjami dialect, replaced in the Amharic of Shoa, Mänz and Wollo by the glottalised stop *t'*. Takkele notes, however, that the careful differentiation of *s'* and *t'* by educated speakers, including speakers whom he describes as "urban dwellers", some of whom might be described as semi-educated at least in so far as a knowledge of the correct origin of words containing one or other of these phonemes is concerned, has given rise to a class or social dimension to the use of *s'*: to use *s'* indicates that the speaker is educated. He records cases of hypercorrection, where an "unjustified" *s'* is used instead of *t'*. He also notes the development of new pairs of words in speech, sometimes with a semantic bifurcation according to whether one or other phoneme is used: *k'ärräs'ä* 'carve' but *k'ärrät'ä* 'levy tax'; *as'änna* 'confirm, strengthen' but *at'änna* 'study'; or *anat'i* 'carpenter' but *həns'a* 'building' (but the dictionaries also record a written variety *ənt'a*), where in the last example the two lexemes derive from the same Amharicised Ge'ez root, which is not, however "fully Amharicised", as the agent form *anat'i* instead of **anač'* shows.

Another notable, if highly specialised exception to the study of the sociolinguistic aspect of dialectology is Leslau's study of Ethiopian argots, or speech forms of specific trade, craft or "caste" groups (1964). Four argots are briefly described, two specific to occupational groups (Gojjami merchants, and minstrels), one current to practitioners of the *zar* spirit-possession cult, and one used by a "Gurage secret society".) All these argots use common methods to disguise normal speech, such as the use of loan vocabulary, descriptive or tangential terminology (e.g. merchant's argot *makkalämya* 'mouth' lit. 'speaker'), root modification, and so on. Perhaps the most interesting feature emerging from these, that has a distinct relevance to understanding the operation of deep-level linguistic features relevant to the Semitic family as a whole, is the transposition of consonant radicals in verbal and even nominal forms. There seems even within one and the same argot to be no predictability of transposition. Thus, the minstrel's argot form *däwwäk'ä* 'fall' represents a $C_2C_1C_3$ transposition of regular *wäddäk'ä*, whilst *närräbä* 'was' is $C_1C_3C_2$ of *näbbärä*, and *tä-läk'k'äbä* 'receive' is $C_3C_1C_2$ for *tä-k'äbbälä*, and so on. Nominal forms and even particles show similar transposition of consonant radicals: *raga* 'with' for *gara*, *ərt'u* 'good' for *t'əru* (also showing the Amharic syllabification preference of *ərC*... over *rəC*...), *čubbo* 'dog' to which Silt'i *bučo* may be compared. Another strategy employed by this argot is the insertion of an augment, or additional radical into the radical sequence: *wärrädä* 'descend' becomes *wärännädä*, but *räggämä* 'curse' becomes *ränäggämä*, i.e. $C_1C_2nC_3$ and $C_1nC_2C_3$, respectively. Similarly, *t'äffa* 'disappear' become *t'äräffa*, and *käffätä* 'open' becomes *käräffätä*. Leslau records other consonantal augments used to disguise verbal roots. This clearly suggests that there is a deep level recognition of root structure in the mind of the speaker. It is not a simple insertion of an extra syllable, because the rules of morphology operate with the new consonantal string in the normal way, making an originally triliteral root like *wärrädä* into a quadriliteral root *wärännädä*, which inflects just like an orginal quadriliteral such as *märämmärä*.

CONCLUDING REMARKS — DESIDERATA

To conclude, I cannot do better than to repeat that the variety and complexity of linguistic form and structures to be found in the modern South Semitic languages, MSA and Ethiopian, is very rich indeed, yet has only begun to be researched. There are still many obstacles to be overcome in our understanding of these languages — not the least, fuller, in-depth descriptions building on the pioneering work of Bittner et al. and Johnstone in MSA, and Leslau, Goldenberg and Hetzron, especially, in Ethiopian. This work is going on now, and the future for South Semitic linguistics in the 21st century promises to be bright and productive. Nor should I forget to mention ESA — we know very well how chance archaeological discovery can revolutionise our field of Semitic linguistics, and the real significance of the recently discovered later Sabaean texts on palm ribs from Nashān has perhaps yet to be fully appreciated.

Specifically from Ethiopia, we need sound descriptions of the dialects of the largest South Semitic languages,Tigrinya and Amharic, which have become languages of literacy and bureaucracy in the modern states of Eritrea and Ethiopia and which are thus now engaged in establishing standard forms. Dialect studies should not focus only on regional variation, but also on special languages associated with different registers, different social groups, and the implications of these two larger languages used as lingua francas where they are most open to influence from other Ethiopian languages. The power that Amharic especially has in the last century exerted over other modern Ethiopian Semitic languages is not inconsiderable, and in recent decades with the growth of mass media in Ethiopia this influence cannot have diminished. The 20th century has already seen the death of one Ethiopian Semitic language, Gafat, and the situation of Argobba suggests that it is moribund and will not be far behind. Leslau's recent (1997) book on Argobba and the 1994 report of the Survey of Little Known Languages of Ethiopia (SLLE) on Argobba go some way towards recording what will soon be lost. What, though, is the situation of the smaller "Gurage" varieties at the end of the 20th century? Of the larger languages Silt'i has now been adopted as an official regional language of literacy and a novel in Chäha has already been published. Languages are inevitably being changed by the demands of standardisation and the effects of widening use in the modern communications and educational environment. The increasing pace of change requires an increased intensity of activity from scholars to record these languages, to compile full-scale dictionaries, to collect oral literature, to study the subtleties of language use in a multilingual society where multingualism is the norm and not the exception.

BIBLIOGRAPHY

Appleyard, David L. 1996. Ethiopian Semitic and South Arabian: towards a Re-examination of a Relationship. *Israel Oriental Studies* XVI: 203–28.

Avanzini, Alessandra. 1991. Linguistic data and historical reconstruction: between Semitic and Epigraphic South Arabian. In *Semitic Studies in Honor of Wolf Leslau*, ed. by Alan S. Kaye. Vol. I: 107–18. Harrassowitz: Wiesbaden.

Beeston, A.F.L. 1984. *Sabaic Grammar*. Journal of Semitic Studies Monograph, 6. Manchester. [Revised edition of *A Descriptive Grammar of Epigraphic South Arabian*. 1962. London].

Bender, M.L., J.D. Bowen, R.L. Cooper & C.A. Ferguson (eds). 1976. *Language in Ethiopia*. London.

Cohen, David. 1974. La forme verbale à marques personnelles préfixées en sudarabique moderne. In *IV Congresso Internazionale di Studi Etiopici (Roma 1972)*, Vol II: 63–70.

Cohen, Marcel. 1931. *Études d'éthiopien méridional*. Société Asiatique, Collection d'ouvrages orientaux. Paris.

—. 1939. *Nouvelles études d'éthiopien méridional*. Bibliothèque de l'École des Hautes Études, 275. Paris.

Cowley, Roger, Marvin L. Bender, Charles A. Ferguson, Hailu Fulass & Getatchew Haile. 1976. The Amharic Language. In *Language in Ethiopia*, ed. M.L. Bender et al., 77–98. London.

Diakonoff, I.M. 1965. *Semito-Hamitic Languages. An Essay in Classification*. Moscow.

—. 1988. *Afrasian Languages*. Moscow.

Faber, Alice. 1997. Genetic subgrouping of the Semitic Languages. In *The Semitic Languages*, ed. by Robert Hetzron, 3–15. London & New York.

Garbini, G. 1984. *Le lingue semitiche* (Seconda edizione riveduta ed ampliata). Napoli.

Goldenberg, Gideon. 1968. *Kəstanəñña*. Studies in a Northern Gurage language of Christians. *Orientalia Suecana* 17: 61–102.

— 1977. The Semitic languages of Ethiopia and their classification. *Bulletin of the School of Oriental and African Studies* XL 3: 461–507.

Gragg, Gene. 1997. Ge'ez (Ethiopic). In *The Semitic Languages*, ed. by Robert Hetzron, 242–60. London & New York.

Gruntfest, Y.B. 1974. The problem of classifying Southern Semitic languages. In *IV Congresso Internazionale di Studi Etiopici (Roma, 10–15 aprile 1972)*. Vol. II, 105–14. Accademia Nazionale dei Lincei, anno CCCLXXI (1974), quaderno n. 191. Problemi attuali di scienza e di cultura. Roma.

Gutt, Eeva & Hussein Mohammed. 1997. *Silt'e–Amharic–English Dictionary (with Concise Grammar by Ernst-August Gutt)*. Addis Ababa.

Gutt, Ernst-August. 1997. The Silte Group (East Gurage). In *The Semitic Languages*, ed. by Robert Hetzron, 509–34. London & New York.

Habte Mariam Marcos (ed). 1973. Regional variations in Amharic. *Journal of Ethiopian Studies* XI, 2: 113–29.

Hayward, R.J., K.M. Hayward & Sālim Bakht Al-Tabīki. 1988. Vowels in Jibbāli verbs. *Bulletin of the School of Oriental and African Studies* LI 2: 240–50.

Hetzron, Robert. 1968. Main Verb-Markers in Northern Gurage. *Africa* 38: 156–72.

—. 1972. *Ethiopian Semitic: Studies in Classification*. Journal of Semitic Studies Monograph, 2. Manchester.

—. 1974. La division des langues sémitiques. In *Actes du Premier Congrès International de Linguistique Sémitique et Chamito-Sémitique*, ed. by A. Caquot & D. Cohen, 181–94. The Hague.

—. 1975. Genetic classification and Ethiopian Semitic. In *Hamito–Semitica*, ed. by James & Theodora Bynon, 103–21. The Hague.

—. 1977. *The Gunnän-Gurage Languages*. Ricerche di Semitistica e del Vicino Oriente Antico, XII. Napoli.

Hetzron, Robert (ed). 1997. *The Semitic Languages*. London & New York.

Hudson, Grover. 1997. Amharic and Argobba. In *The Semitic Languages*, ed. by Robert Hetzron, 457–85. London & New York.

Johnstone, T.M. 1970a. A definite article in the Modern South Arabian languages. *Bulletin of the School of Oriental and African Studies* XXXIII 2: 295–307.

—. 1970b. Dual forms in Mehri and Ḥarsūsi. *Bulletin of the School of Oriental and African Studies* XXXIII 3: 501–12.

—. 1975. The Modern South Arabian languages. *Afroasiatic Linguistics* 1/5 = 1: 93–121.

—. 1977. *Ḥarsūsi Lexicon and English-Ḥarsūsi Index*. London.

—. 1981. *Jibbāli Lexicon*. London.

—. 1987. *Mehri Lexicon and English-Mehri Word-List*. London.

Kaye, Alan S. (ed). 1991. *Semitic Studies in Honor of Wolf Leslau. On the Occasion of his Eighty-fifth Birthday, November 14th 1991*. 2 Vols. Wiesbaden.

Kogan, Leonid E. 1997. Tigrinya. In *The Semitic Languages*, ed. by Robert Hetzron, 424–45. London & New York.

Kogan, Leonid E. & Andrey V. Korotayev. 1997. Sayhadic (Epigraphic South Arabian). In *The Semitic Languages*, ed. by Robert Hetzron, 220–41. London & New York.

Leslau, Wolf. 1938. *Lexique soqoṭri (sudarabique moderne) avec comparaisons et explications étymologiques*. Collection linguistique publieé par la Société Linguistique de Paris, 41. Paris.

—. 1939. Observations sur quelques dialectes du tigrigna. (Dialectes d'Akkele Gouzay, d'Adoua et du Hamasen.) *Journal Asiatique* 231: 61–115.

—. 1943. South-East Semitic. (Ethiopic and South Arabic). *Journal of the American Oriental Society* 63: 4–14.

—. 1945a. *Gafat Documents. Records of a South-Ethiopic Language*. American Oriental Series, Vol. 28. New Haven.

—. 1945b. Short Grammar of Tigre. *Journal of the American Oriental Society* 65, 1: 1–26 and 65, 3: 164–203.

—. 1950. *Ethiopic Documents: Gurage*. Viking Fund Publications in Anthropology, 14. New York.

—. 1956. *Étude descriptive et comparative du gafat (Éthiopien méridional)*. Collection linguistique publieé par la Société Linguistique de Paris, 57. Paris.

—. 1961. Semitic Languages. In *Encyclopaedia Britannica*. Vol. 20: 314–17. Chicago, London & Toronto.

—. 1963. *Etymological Dictionary of Harari*. University of California Publications Near Eastern Studies, 1. Berkeley & Los Angeles.

—. 1964. *Ethiopian Argots*. Janua Linguaram, Series Practica 17. The Hague.

—. 1965. *Ethiopians Speak. Studies in Cultural Background. I. Harari*. University of California Publications Near Eastern Studies, 7. Berkeley & Los Angeles.

—. 1966. *Ethiopians Speak. Studies in Cultural Background. II. Chaha*. University of California Publications Near Eastern Studies, 9. Berkeley & Los Angeles.

—. 1968. *Ethiopians Speak. Studies in Cultural Background. III. Soddo.* University of California Publications Near Eastern Studies, 11. Berkeley & Los Angeles.

—. 1969a. Is there a proto-Gurage? In *Proceedings of the International Conference on Semitic Studies held in Jerusalem, 19–23 July 1965,* 152–71. Jerusalem.

—. 1969b. Towards a classification of the Gurage dialects. *Journal of Semitic Studies* 14: 96–109.

—. 1970. Ethiopic and South Arabian. In *Current Trends in Linguistics, VI.* ed. by Thomas A. Sebeok, 467–527. The Hague.

—. 1979. *Etymological Dictionary of Gurage (Ethiopic).* 3 vols. Wiesbaden.

—. 1981. *Ethiopians Speak. Studies in Cultural Background. IV. Muher.* Aethiopistische Forschungen, 11. Wiesbaden.

—. 1991. *Comparative Dictionary of Geʻez. Geʻez-English / English-Geʻez with an Index of the Semitic Roots.* Wiesbaden.

—. 1992. *Gurage Studies. Collected Articles.* Wiesbaden.

—. 1995. *Reference Grammar of Amharic.* Wiesbaden.

—. 1997. *Ethiopic Documents: Argobba. Grammar and Dictionary.* Aethiopistische Forschungen, 47. Wiesbaden.

Lipiński, Edward. 1997. *Semitic Languages. Outline of a Comparative Grammar.* Orientalia Lovaniensia Analecta 80. Leuven.

Marrassini, Paolo. 1991. Some observations on South Semitic. In *Semitic Studies in Honour of Wolf Leslau,* ed. by Alan S. Kaye. Vol. II: 1016–23. Wiesbaden.

Moscati, Sabbatino, Anton Spitaler, Edward Ullendorff & Wolfram von Soden. 1969. *An Introduction to the Comparative Grammar of the Semitic Languages. Phonology and Morphology.* Porta Linguarum Orientalium, Neue Serie VI. Wiesbaden.

Nebes, Norbert. 1994. Zur Form des Imperfektbasis des unvermehrten Grundstammes im Altsüdarabischen. In *Festschrift Ewald Wagner zum 65. Geburtstag,* ed. by Wolfhart Heinrichs & Gregor Schoeller. Vol. I: 59–81. Beirut.

Nöldeke, Theodor. 1911. Semitic Languages. In *Encyclopaedia Britannica.* Vol. XXIV. Cambridge.

Petráček, Karel. 1988. The South Arabian language periphery. In *A Miscellany of Middle Eastern Articles. In Memoriam Thomas Muir Johnstone 1924–1983,* ed. by A.K. Irvine, R.B. Serjeant & G. Rex Smith, 216–25. Harlow.

Polotsky, H.J. 1938. Études de grammaire gouragué. *Bulletin de la Société de Linguistique de Paris* 39: 137–75.

—. 1951. *Notes on Gurage Grammar*. Notes and Studies Published by the Israel Oriental Society, No. 2. Jerusalem.

Porkhomovsky, Victor. 1997. Modern South Arabian languages from a Semitic and Hamito-Semitic perspective. *Proceedings of the Seminar for Arabian Studies* 27: 219–23.

Raz, Shlomo. 1983. *Tigre Grammar and Texts*. Afroasiatic Dialects Vol. 4. Malibu.

—. 1997. Tigré. In *The Semitic Languages*, ed. by Robert Hetzron, 446–56. London & New York.

Rodgers, Jonathan. 1991. The subgrouping of the South Semitic languages. In *Semitic Studies in Honour of Wolf Leslau*, ed. by Alan S. Kaye. Vol. II: 1323–36. Wiesbaden.

Ryckmans, Jacques, Walter Müller & Yusuf M. Abdallah. 1994. *Textes du Yémen Antique Inscrits sur Bois*. Publications de l'Institut Orientaliste de Louvain, 43. Louvain.

Simeone-Senelle, Marie-Claude. 1997. The Modern South Arabian Languages. In *The Semitic Languages*, ed. by Robert Hetzron, 378–423. London & New York.

Survey of Little-known Languages of Ethiopia (S.L.L.E.). 1994. *Linguistic Report no. 22 (November/December 1994). Argobba — The People and the Language*. (Zelealem Leyew & Ralph Siebert). Addis Ababa.

Takkele Taddese. 1992. Are s' and t' variants of an Amharic variable? A sociolinguistic analysis. *Journal of Ethiopian Languages and Literature* 2: 104–21.

Ullendorff, Edward. 1955. *The Semitic Languages of Ethiopia*. London.

—. 1971. Comparative Semitics. In *Current Trends in Linguistics 6. Linguistics in South West Asia and North Africa*, 261–73. The Hague.

—. 1985. *A Tigrinya (Təgrəñña) Chrestomathy*. Äthiopistische Forschungen 19. Stuttgart.

Voigt, Rainer. 1977. *Das tigrinische Verbalsystem*. Marburger Studien zur Afrika- und Asienkunde. Serie A: Afrika Bd. 10. Berlin.

—. 1994a. Der Lautwandel S^1 > H in Wurzellosen Morphemen des Alt- und Neusüdarabischen. In *Semitic and Cushitic Studies*, ed. by Gideon Goldenberg & Shlomo Raz, 19–28. Wiesbaden.

—. 1994b. Neusüdarabisch und Äthiopisch. In *Arabia Felix. Beiträge zur Sprache und Kultur des vorislamischen Arabien. Festschrift Walter W. Müller zum 60. Geburtstag*, ed. by Norbert Nebes, 291–307. Wiesbaden.

—. 1998. Der Artikel im Semitischen. *Journal of Semitic Studies* 43: 221–258.

Wagner, Ewald. 1997. Harari. In *The Semitic Languages*, ed. by Robert Hetzron, 486–508. London & New York.
Zaborski, Andrzej. 1994. Arcaismi ed innovazioni nei pronomi personali del sudarabo moderno. In *Sem Cam Iafet*. Atti della 7ª Giornata di Studi Camito-Semitici e Indoeuropei (Milano, 1º giugno 1993), ed. by Vermondo Brugnatelli, 251–62. Milano.

Broadening Our Horizons

INTRODUCTION
WITH SOME NOTES ON PSYCHO- AND NEURO-LINGUISTICS AND WITH SOME COMMENTS ON THE POTENTIAL USE OF COMPUTERS IN LINGUISTIC STUDIES

The sixth and last substantive section of our disposition of the state of the art in Semitic linguistics concerns areas that are, in some ways, beyond the immediate scope of our field. Some of these areas are tangential to linguistics or philology; some are those that traditional Semitics has shown little concern with; others are related to new and promising techniques of study.

Simeone-Senelle mentioned briefly the issue of oral literature in Modern South Arabian languages. This rich field of exploration is but one of many areas where linguistics can contribute to other disciplines. For many fields of inquiry, including anthropology, cultural studies and many others, a linguistic study is a prerequisite. Theoretical approaches to all these fields of study can be found only rarely and in a haphazard manner with regard to the cultures where modern Semitic languages are spoken. Attempts to elicit a general overview of this aspect (or should I say aspects?) of linguistic studies in the modern Semitic world have failed, and I am reluctant to try to give even a brief conspectus of what has been done or what can be done with linguistics as an aid to other disciplines in the modern world. This must be marked a desideratum.

Edward L. Greenstein did undertake to review advances in linguistic study as an aid to other disciplines in the ancient Semitic world. As it turns out, the paper focuses on implications for the interpretation of ancient texts and cultures that new developments in linguistic study entail. Greenstein starts by stating the often neglected recognition that further interpretation of practically all aspects of ancient texts can only be based on solid prior linguistic research. Then he takes the reader to a survey based on some theoretical premises that will lead him to deal with the more textual aspects of language study. Greenstein's theoretical premises are offshoots of the fundamental concept that language is a reflection of the way its users see the world, and therefore linguistics is to be taken as the point of departure when philology is to be applied. Following these premises, Greenstein goes on to explore the work done in linguistics when it becomes entangled in diverse fields, such as discourse analysis, poetics, anthropology, psychoanalysis, literacy and finally, intertextuality.

His examples are drawn in many cases from the study of Biblical Hebrew, since it is in biblical research that linguistics and philology have been exploited to the utmost for extra-linguistic applications (cf. O'Connor's paper). Greenstein ends his expressive survey by reminding us of the often ignored truism that the meanings of the texts we read result from the kind of training we have, from the theories and methods we tend to employ, and from the models and parallels we adduce in order to gain the leverage of understanding. Language does not mean by itself; we make sense of it. And so one of the important objects of our study should be our own assumptions about language and our own habits of thought.

A recently developed discipline related to linguistics is cognitive studies. In fact, linguistics is now regarded by some as a branch of cognitive sciences. While this is yet almost entirely a *terra incognita* in Semitic linguistics, one domain intimately related to linguistics in this rich new world is the study of first language acquisition. Ruth Berman and Dorit Ravid spoke at the conference about the state of the art in this area when Semitic languages are the subject of observation. A paper based on this lecture was published in *Hebrew Studies* (Berman and Ravid 2000). The authors' frame of reference is developmental psycholinguistics, a field of research that became established in the 1960s as a result of developments in cognitive psychology and linguistic theory. As such, the article considers the impact of literacy on register distinctions and metalinguistic awareness in child language acquisition in general, and in Israeli Hebrew and Palestinian Arabic in particular. In fact, most of the research in child language and first language acquisition has been conducted on Israeli Hebrew, and only some in contemporary Arabic dialects (p. 85 and notes 4–5). Berman and Ravid further discuss empirical studies of children's developing knowledge of the consonantal root as the basis of new word formation, a topic of special interest to Semitic linguistics and the study of Semitic morphology in particular. Studies in this domain are reviewed as evidence for the interaction between universally shared common features and trends defined as "universals" and the typological specific and language-particular tasks faced by children acquiring a Semitic language.

Looking at language in order to learn about cognition has a lot more to offer. Cognitive sciences are a huge cluster of research fields. Among other directions of study that have begun to use data from Semitic languages, one can mention the study of speech pathologies (Grodzinsky 1990, especially chapter 3; Friedmann and Grodzinsky 1997; Grodzinsky 2000; Friedmann and Grodzinsky forthcoming). This is not the place to deal with possible developments in cognitive sciences. Still, there is one interesting topic of research that I have found intriguing from the point of view of Semitic linguistics, a topic that may at first look quite esoteric, even eccentric. This is the study of slips of the tongue. I first became acquainted with research on slips of the tongue through an article in *Scientific American* (Motley 1985; cf. also Cutler 1982). This article reports on research on elicitation of slips of the tongue, claiming that "analysis of natural slips of the tongue ... reveals a good deal about the mental organization of linguistic components" (p. 116). The details are not important. However, one significant feature that has emerged in this research did strike me. It is well known that slips of the tongue, at least one type of them ("spoonerism"), tend to switch between phonemes of adjacent words or between similar words even if not collocated. Humoristic changes of phonemes between adjacent words also tend to operate in very similar ways, and Uri Horesh reminded me of one very frequent in Israeli Hebrew: *zarax mipirxoni* for *parax mizixroni*, i.e., it "escaped my mind" (literally: "flew away from my memory"). This is very similar to English examples that have been found in the elicitation research, like *fast passion* for *past fashion*, or brought there from natural speech, like *flute fry* for *fruit fly*.

While reading through this paper and looking at the examples, I recalled the so-often redefined and rejected apparent truism that every beginner in Semitics learns, namely that Semitic languages treat consonants differently from vowels, and that consonants carry the lexico-semantic component while vowels serve to form the grammatical component of a word. While I know that I am putting myself into the cross fire by raising this issue, let me risk my neck by asking whether research into slips of the tongue can teach us anything about Semitic languages, or perhaps from a different angle: can Semitic linguistics add anything to the study of human cognition and language generation from insights gained in research of slips of the tongue? This may make sense in the context of findings in reported research, viz., that slips of the tongue are not random, but are largely explicable by reference to certain basic constraints (Crystal 1997: 264).

Bruce Zuckerman was asked to contribute a paper dealing with new finds related to the Semitic languages of the ancient world during the twentieth century. Trying to deal with this very issue has resulted in a switch to technical means of dealing with these new finds, a switch that I have found favorable and gratifying. Zuckerman opens by explaining the title of his paper, which makes us refer to Hackett's review of the methodologies used while working with little data. He continues by listing some of the most important new Northwest-Semitic inscriptional discoveries of the twentieth century, and by reviewing some of the linguistic tools used at the end of that century. Zuckerman reminds us that the texts we usually read in academic publications are not the data as they appear in their original form. Also, as we all know, the interpretation of inscriptions may be affected by their physical shape and condition. He then goes on to describe some new photographic techniques, developed by Zuckerman and his team, which may serve the linguist and philologist in extracting better and more complete data from the find. He further discusses the impact such new techniques may have on research.

New techniques of elucidating linguistic data and exploiting them was also the subject of a lecture by Yaacov Choueka, who spoke about Natural Language Processing (NLP) and Semitic languages. Choueka, who is a computer scientist, has been involved in computerized linguistic projects for decades: corpora of Hebrew texts, a dictionary of Modern Hebrew, and software for morphological analysis of Hebrew and punctuation. As a written version of Choueka's lecture could not be incorporated into this volume, I would like to present a few highlights from his lecture.

While NLP implies the computational processing of living languages, the techniques involved can also be applied to dead languages. After all, says Choueka, for a computer every language is a dead language. In spite of much effort invested at the beginning of the computer era, there was not much progress in making computers understand human language until the mid 1980s. Computers actually taught computer scientists that human language is too complex a phenomenon. In the mid 1980s, due to advances in computer technologies, mainly storage capacity and rapid processing power, the need to have large textual corpora on computers was eased. Texts started to be published via electronic means, and OCR (Optical Character Reading) was introduced, which made corpus compilation even swifter. The introduction of the WWW also contributed to the availability of a huge amount of written materials in electronic form, and brought with it more awareness of the need for text processing. Finally, changes in commercial trends and the global open market have made products in this area less constricted in use and distribution; e.g., there is much more demand for translation. All this further entailed a growth in funding resources. A shift from linguists to computer scientists in the field of language processing has resulted in a methodological shift, in that the linguists' striving for building ideal models of language was replaced by computer scientists' striving for practical problem solving, which no longer included a demand for full satisfaction.

The existence of large electronic corpora has enhanced remarkably the ways in which language can be researched, as large corpora are like laboratories, where linguistic rules can be extrapolated and linguistic theories can be tested. It further enhanced the use of probabilistic and statistical methods, with some interesting results for our understanding of linguistic structures. In contrast to Chomskian concepts (and Chomsky's own objection to using corpora), which focused on syntax and elicited data via introspection, statistical and probabilistic methods introduced a renewed interest in words, in the lexicon and in phraseology, and enabled us to look further into morphology and other aspects of language.

Statistical techniques are used by programs that manipulate textual data without any prior knowledge of linguistic features, either lexical or grammatical. These programs extract from the corpus its lexical and grammatical features via statistical, probabilistic methods. This extrapolation of lexicon and grammar is valid only if we have a very large corpus to process.

Language-intelligent computer assistance has many applications; many of them have become a matter of daily use for many of us, as some technology for exploiting such assistance already exists. Among these applications Choueka mentioned extracting information from search engines or using computers for textual output of non-linguistic data. With regard to linguistic applications, an already developed strategy is the study of collocations, or, more generally, studying words in their environment. This strategy, or methodology, is at its best when used with large corpora, and it is here that dictionary building and the study of the lexicon and its relation to grammar can be shown to be most fruitful. A short list of corpus applications with special attention to (Hebrew) linguistics can be found in <http://spinoza.tau.ac.il/humanities/semitic/cosih.html>. For new developments in lexical studies and the new area of lexicogrammar I would refer the interested reader to the work of John Sinclair, founder of the COBUILD corpus (The Bank of English); e.g. Sinclair 1991, 1996, 1998. Useful, concise, yet comprehensive are four complementary books on corpus linguistics: McEnery and Wilson 1996; Kennedy 1998; Biber, Conrad and Reppen 1998; Tognini Bonelli 2001.

Of course, research into lexica and grammars of dead languages can benefit from corpora as well, given that we have a large corpus of data. As suggested by Choueka, the study of collocations can be especially fruitful in all types of textual data, dead languages included. Dictionary making can profit quite a lot by using these newly developed techniques. Lexicogrammar is a new area of studies that can be developed into many directions, including, inter alia, the disambiguation of homonyms and homographs, which is especially difficult in the type of scripts in which Semitic languages are written, and given the complex morphology of these languages. These two features, the type of deficient writing and the complex Semitic morphology, make a significant difference for computer analysis between, say, English and Hebrew. Choueka made a comparison between the numbers of legitimate strings of letters in English and Hebrew texts, which is one million in English as compared with seventy million such strings in Hebrew. Disambiguation of character strings should be achieved prior to any further processing of a text.

Needless to say, computer work is becoming a major tool in processing both texts and linguistic data, and the twenty-first century will doubtless see an immeasurably increased use of computers in already developed and new, unimaginable directions. Corpus linguistics is a fast expanding methodology, and development of computational strategies for all areas in linguistics is in the process of rapid growth. Listing of achievements and desiderata in these domains in a book seems to me an anachronism. Any such report would, of course, be quite outdated by the time of publication. Therefore, I should like to mention only two electronic references that may aid readers in their search for further development in the vast field of Semitic linguistics and beyond: (1) A comprehensive tool for information on all kinds of linguistic work, including Semitic linguistics, is the LINGUIST List <http://linguistlist.org/>, from where other useful lists can also be accessed (e.g., The Corpora List; lists on Arabic, etc.). (2) Web pages dealing with work done on ancient Semitic languages can be searched at <http://www-oi.uchicago.edu/OI/DEPT/RA/ABZU/ABZU.HTML>. (See also Hackett's paper, pp. 57–8.)

REFERENCES

Berman, Ruth A. and Dorit D. Ravid. 2000. Research in Acquisition of Israeli Hebrew and Palestinian Arabic. *Hebrew Studies* 41: 83–98.

Biber, Douglas, Susan Conrad and Randi Reppen. 1998. *Corpus Linguistics: Investigating Language Structure and Use.* (Cambridge Approaches to Linguistics.). Cambridge.

Crystal, David. 1997. *The Cambridge Encyclopedia of Language.* Second edition. Cambridge.

Cutler, Anne (ed.). 1982. *Slips of the Tongue and Language Production.* Berlin. (=Linguistics 19 (7/8): 561–847.)

Friedmann, Na'ama and Yosef Grodzinsky. 1997. Tense and Agreement in Agrammatic Production: Pruning the Syntactic Tree. *Brain and Language* 56: 397–425.

Friedmann, Na'ama and Yosef Grodzinsky. Forthcoming. Neurolinguistic Evidence for Split Inflection. In: M. A. Friedemann & L. Rizzi (eds.). *The Acquisition of Syntax: Issues in Comparative Developmental Linguistics.* Oxford.

Grodzinsky, Yosef. 1990. *Theoretical Perspectives on Language Deficits.* Cambridge, MA.

Grodzinsky, Y. 2000. The Neurology of Syntax: Language Use without Broca's Area. *Behavioral and Brain Sciences* 23: 1–71.

Kennedy, Graeme. 1998. *An Introduction to Corpus Linguistics.* (Studies in Language and Linguistics.) London.

McEnery, Tony and Andrew Wilson. 1996. *Corpus Linguistics.* (Edinburgh Textbooks in Empirical Linguistics. Edinburgh.

Motley, Michael T. 1985. Slips of the Tongue. *Scientific American.* Sept. 1985: 116–123, 144.

Sinclair, John McH. 1991. *Corpus, Concordance, Collocation.* Oxford.

Sinclair, John McH. 1996. The Search for Units of Meaning. *Textus* 9: 75–106.

Sinclair, John McH. 1998. The Lexical Item. In: Edda Weigand (ed.). *Contrastive Lexical Semantics.* (Current Issues in Linguistic Theory, 171.) Amsterdam, 1–24.

Tognini Bonelli, Elena. 2001. *Corpus Linguistics at Work.* (Studies in Corpus Linguistics, 6.) Amsterdam.

SOME DEVELOPMENTS IN THE STUDY OF LANGUAGE AND SOME IMPLICATIONS FOR INTERPRETING ANCIENT TEXTS AND CULTURES

Edward L. Greenstein

The discipline of linguistics has often been characterized by trends toward the attainment of a certain purity, by analyzing the components of language in splendid isolation from socio-historical realities and from the other academic disciplines. Notable exceptions are psycholinguistics, sociolinguistics, anthropological linguistics, and — relatively recently — text linguistics. Semitic linguistics has shown impressive growth in sophistication in the last generation or two, but this maturation has been largely confined to the "purer" areas of historical and structural analysis. This is especially true of the linguistic analysis of the ancient Semitic languages, where the areas of phonology, morphology, syntax, semantics, dialectology, and historical reconstruction continue to receive the most attention. The traditional focus of Semitic linguistics on the conventional areas of language study can largely be explained by the nature of the available data. One does not have native informants to examine psychologically, sociologically, and — except by inference — anthropologically. One has texts of various genres and types, which are still our major source of historical reality as well as our exclusive source of language.

While Semitic linguistics has continually benefited from developments in general linguistics, the philological and historical study of the ancient Near East have paid only limited attention to linguistics, be it general or Semitic. The emergence of competing linguistic theories, as well as the tendency of some of them to formalism and technical obscurity, has not made the effort easy or appealing.

Nevertheless, if one were to assess the potential contribution of the academic discipline of linguistics *per se* toward the illumination of the ancient world and its cultures, it is my impression that the contribution would be somewhat modest. An increase in linguistic sophistication of the traditional kinds — phonology, morphology, syntax — would not make dramatic improvements in philology or historiography (for some exceptions, see below), although such sophistication surely enhances the sensitivity of readers to the rhetoric and poetics of the texts they read as well as providing critics with a more precise vocabulary for describing what they and other readers find.[1] Traditional linguistics either brings sophistication (read: systematization and technique) to the analysis of individual languages or it connects the features of individual languages to the features of other languages in an attempt to produce a theory of language in general and to formulate linguistic universals.

A possible exception might be semantics — the study of meaning. There is still relatively little work in ancient Semitic semantics that appears to be conversant with contemporary linguistic theory. The proper study of semantics involves a description of how the lexicon of a language is made to interact with the various components of grammar in the process of making meaning (cf., e.g., Katz & Fodor 1964; Scanlin 1992). Little Semitic lexicography analyzes this interaction. Some notable exceptions are the studies in Biblical Hebrew in Kaddari (1976), Muraoka (1998), and Rubinstein (1998). Although I will not be devoting here an extended discussion to the area of semantics, I will touch on some aspects of it in several of the sections below.

Another exception to my assessment that the value of traditional linguistics to the study of ancient cultures is limited, might be dialectology, or more precisely, linguistic geography. The mapping of languages and dialects ought to reveal historical movements and influences. Garr's 1985 volume *Dialect Geography of Syria-Palestine, 1000–586 B.C.E.*, for example, presents a fairly complete picture, except that it confines itself to the traditional components of grammar and neglects lexical isoglosses.[2] Garr prefers to describe a linguistic continuum among the ancient Northwest Semitic languages and dialects; but it may be more precise and historically revealing to identify a number of language centers surrounded by peripheries, where the effects of linguistic contact are more pronounced (cf. Izre'el 1988). In his concluding chapter Garr does remark on some historical and cultural implications of his study. But it is for the historian who has become familiar with Garr's book and with the critical academic discussion of it to draw conclusions in the light of other types of historical evidence (cf. the discussion in Huehnergard 1996: 268).

Yet another exception is the diachronic study of Biblical Hebrew that maps out stages in the development of the language. Systematic contrast

---

[1]   See, e.g., the linguistically informed studies of Biblical Hebrew poetics enumerated in Bodine (1992: 303–304); and for Akkadian poetics, e.g., Hecker (1974), Reiner (1985) and Vogelzang & Vanstiphout (1996).

[2]   For a similar neglect of lexical isoglosses in a recent discussion of Ugaritic's linguistic affinities, see Greenstein (1998: 405–406).

of lexical and syntactic usages can often distinguish earlier from later Hebrew, corresponding quite neatly to the historical boundary between monarchic Israel and Judah (prior to the sixth century B.C.E.) and so-called post-Exilic or Persian dominated Judah (following the sixth century B.C.E.). This distinction is crucial for the relative dating of Biblical texts, which have not survived in contemporary manuscript form but only in late copies from the Roman period and later. The existence of the "classical" (pre-sixth century) era of Biblical Hebrew, which has been doubted and denied in some recent publications, dovetails with the conventionally assumed historical background of certain Biblical texts, making both political and literary history viable academic endeavors (see esp. Hurvitz 1997; 1999; and see further section 5 below).

In a similar vein, numerous philological and linguistic studies of ancient Semitic texts serve the specific functions of establishing date and provenience. For example, Moran (1975) has shown that the Jerusalem scribe of the El Amarna letters was trained in Syria, and Izre'el (Izre'el & Singer 1990: 51–84) has confirmed a fourteenth century B.C.E. date for the so-called "General's Letter" from Ugarit.

Now although the payoff of traditional linguistics for the interpretation of ancient Semitic texts and cultures may have been limited, there are what strike me as some very significant developments in the study of language in general outside the conventional areas of linguistics, and these may have important implications for our attempts to understand the ancient world and its cultures. I shall address some of these insights about language, many if not most of which are by now commonplace, and I shall bring some illustrations of how each has affected or can affect our philological endeavors. The topics I shall touch on are:

1. that language is contextual, that it is known to us as discourse;

2. the fact that the language in the texts we study is often artificially structured, that it has a poetics;

3. that language is social and cultural, that it may reveal patterns of thought or cultural conceptions, that it may be revealing anthropologically;

4. the fact that the language we know through texts is not *langue* but *parole*, and that linguistic performance is always affected by the speaker's or writer's psychology;

5. that language takes both spoken and written form, that these forms are different, that literacy makes a difference; and

6. that we have learned through philosophy and through postmodern criticism that meaning is not inherent in language but is constructed by the interpreter, so that, as a consequence, all textual sense is intertextual in character.

1. DISCOURSE ANALYSIS

For decades linguistics dealt mainly with units of speech smaller than the sentence, primarily the word. During the succeeding decades linguistics began treating the sentence as the key unit of sense. Over the past few decades some linguists and philosophers of language have begun to realize that even a thoroughgoing analysis of a sentence is not sufficient to determine its meaning (cf. Bodine 1995: 1–18).[3] Each utterance occurs within a context, whose nature is essential to understanding it (see, e.g., Green 1989). Spoken language — discourse — can be descriptive or informative; it can be exhortative; it can be fraught with implication; it can be ironic; and so on (see, e.g., Austin 1962; Searle 1969, 1979, 1983). All language whose discursive situation is known has purposes or functions that are integral to its meaning. In postmodern thought, the boundary dividing discourse from all other text can be broken down, since in the act of interpretation we attribute motive and function to all texts in which we inscribe sense (see, e.g., Fish 1980). Without context, the statement "Let there be light!" could mean: "Please ignite the lamp," or "I wish there were light," or "By my word will light come into being."

A study of the Old Babylonian verb and its tenses must consider not only paradigms and syntax but also the discourse functions of verb forms in context. As is well known, the last verb in the protasis of a law in the so-called Code of Hammurapi occurs in the infixed *-t* form. Such a usage is in most instances not a tense or aspect function but a discourse function, a rhetorical indicator that the case has been described and that the law in such a case will follow (cf. Goetze 1936; Huehnergard 1997: 157–158).[4]

Studies of the Hebrew verb, such as the 1986 book by Alviero Niccacci, translated as *The Syntax of the Verb in Classical Hebrew Prose* (Niccacci 1990),[5] as well as the work of Robert Longacre (e.g., 1989, 1992, 1995), show that different verb forms have different functions depending on the genre or discourse-type in which they are employed. In prose narrative the *waw-* consecutive plus short prefixed form (*wayyiqtol*) is the primary form. In direct discourse, the free standing verb forms, both prefixed and suffixed, are primary. In dialogue, the imperative is used to express

---

[3]   For a fairly comprehensive survey of discourse analysis in its various forms, see van Dijk (1997).

[4]   Huehnergard (1996: 267) does well to call attention to Khan's discourse perspective on the syntactic functions of the casus pendens (Khan 1988), although he expresses some skepticism concerning the utility of discourse analysis in general.

[5]   See also Niccacci (1994), a discourse analysis of verb forms and their rhetorical functions in the Moabite inscription of King Mesha.

commands; but in ritual instructions, the *waw-* consecutive plus suffixed form (*weqātaltā*)[6] is often used. Attention to discourse functions leads to the conclusion that Biblical Hebrew verb forms do not have an inherent tense or aspect; tense and aspect are conditioned by discourse functions, where verb forms derive their meaning from contrast with other forms (cf. Greenstein 1988).[7]

My own recent work has suggested that the much discussed difference between the use of the *yaqtulu* as a present-future tense in Ugaritic epic narrative as opposed to the *wayyiqtol* preterite of Biblical prose narrative is most straightforwardly explained by reference to discourse function (Greenstein 1998a: 408–413; 2000: 38–39).[8] Ugaritic epic relates events outside any evident historical context; there is no indication of which story takes place before or after any other story. Ugaritic narration is accordingly oriented to the present; it is a dramatic form of presentation for which the *yaqtulu*, which contrasts with the *qatala* for introducing background and other secondary functions, is the most appropriate verbal vehicle. Biblical prose narrative, on the other hand, is historically oriented; it is placed within an explicit chronological framework in which the past time of the narrative is distinguished from the present time of the narrator by the use of phrases such as "then" (e.g., Gen. 12: 6), "formerly" (e.g., 1 Sam. 9: 9), and "up until this day" (e.g., Josh. 7: 26) as well as other devices. Different arrays of verbs serve the narrator's different discourse functions.

Discourse functions can be fulfilled not only by morphology and syntax but even by words, when they are employed formulaically or rhetorically. Garr (2000) has shown that in the Aramaic part of the bilingual inscription from Tell Fakhariyeh, the statue itself is denoted by two different terms, דמותא "likeness," and צלמא "image." Although the terms are coreferential and virtually synonymous (cf. Zadok 1982:118), they are used to make a rhetorical, or more technically a "pragmatic," distinction between two discrete sections of the text: the presentation of the ruler as petitioner vis-à-vis the gods (lines 1ff.) and the representation of the ruler to his people (lines 12ff.).

It has been noted as well that the fairly common Biblical Hebrew verb וילך "he went," may be virtually void of semantic content when it serves simply to indicate, as it sometimes does, the beginning of a new

---

6   The vocalization here is not that of Tiberian, Massoretic Hebrew (for which see esp. Malone 1993; cf. Greenstein 1992) but a kind of reconstruction of the Hebrew of the Persian period, when classical Hebrew literature was first consolidated.

7   For a relativist theory of tense in general, see, e.g., Ogihara (1996).

8   By contrast, Segert (1984: 88–90) distinguishes *yaqtulu* and *qatala* not with respect to discourse function but by reference to aspect and tense. In poetry, he writes, the two forms represent the imperfect vs. the perfect, in prose, the non-past vs. the past.

episode (so, e.g., Naḥmanides at Exod. 2: 1 [Chavel 1959: 282]; Dillmann 1880: 12; cf. Houtman 1993: 270); e.g., "Reuben went and he lay down with Bilha, his father's concubine..." (Gen. 35: 22); "A man from the house of Levi went and he took a daughter of Levi" (Exod. 2: 1).[9] Some commentators become exercised over the question of where the character went; but from a discourse perspective, the question is beside the point. The place to which the character "went" is irrelevant and unmentioned; going from one place to another is a way of indicating the inception of a narrative. The meaning lies in the discourse function and not in any supposed semantic content.

2. POETICS

Linguists, the most prominent of whom was Roman Jakobson, have been trying to formalize the rules by which language is made into art, into literature (e.g., Jakobson 1981).[10] The endeavor is founded on the assumption — an assumption that, like most things, is challenged in poststructuralist thought — that there are features that distinguish poetic language from ordinary language and literary texts from other texts (see, e.g., Derrida 1992; cf., e.g., Eagleton 1982: 1–16; Attridge 1992).

It has been suggested, for example, that parallelism in West Semitic poetry consists essentially of formulating a proposition binarily, in couplet form, such that the second line "restates" (cf. Geller 1979: 16) or "echoes" (cf. Alonso Schökel 1988: 48) the first line. Parallelism is often understood to involve the use of virtually synonymous terms that are brought together by virtue of their similarity in sense and in spite of their differences in sense (cf., e.g., Gevirtz 1973). We would have, then, what William Whallon (1983: 82–97) describes as a luxuriation in language, a redoubling of expression in which nuances of difference are to be disregarded. The Ugaritic and Hebrew poets combined "wine" and "honey" (cf. Dahood 1972: 209) just as the poet of *Beowulf* combined "wine" and "mead,"

---

9   Most commentators overlook the phenomenon. Another example is Josh. 23: 16. Although Dillmann (1880: 12) and others compare Deut. 31: 1, the Septuagint and a Qumran fragment support an emendation there of וילך "He went," to ויכל "He completed (speaking)" (cf., e.g., Tigay 1996: 400 n. 4). Naḥmanides and Van Seters (1994: 26–27) compare the instance of וילך ויקח "he went and he took," in Hos. 1: 3; but there, as Van Seters observes, we have the performance of the command לך קח "Go, take!" where the phrase "he went" is conditioned by the imperative and not a matter of simple narration.

10 Particularly pertinent to the study of ancient Semitic poetry is Jakobson (1966). For an exemplary comparative and contrastive analysis of poetics in diverse cultures, see Miner (1990).

because they had been coupled in the literary tradition, not because it makes a real difference if one drinks or serves to a god wine or honey. The courageous Yael in the Song of Deborah takes an instrument in her "hand" (יד), a different instrument in her "right hand" (ימין), in order to bash in the head of the Canaanite general Sisera (Judges 5: 26).[11] For Whallon, as for numerous Bible scholars, only one weapon and one motion was involved (cf., e.g., Halpern 1983: 46–48). The two propositions have the same poetic sense.

The ancient prose narrator of Judges 4: 21 reads it differently. For him, Yael took a tentpin in her left hand and rammed it into Sisera's skull with a mallet held in her right hand. Whallon and the others think the ancient Israelite author of Judges 4 misunderstood the sense of the parallelism. But did he? Should not the reading of Judges 4 be taken as evidence of how the parallelism should be understood? Are terms juxtaposed in parallelism meant to be homogenized, as Whallon suggests and as Stanley Gevirtz (1973) has argued in his book on early Hebrew poetry? Or are they to be appreciated for their differences, as James Kugel (1981) and Robert Alter (1985) would have it (cf. O'Connor 1980: 51–52; Berlin 1985: 14–15)?

When Job opens his mouth to speak and invokes a curse on the day of his birth and the night of his conception (Job 3: 3), he is referring to two related but distinct events, as the lines that follow, which elaborate separately on the day (vv. 4–5) and then on the night (vv. 6–9), make clear. In the couplet in Job 3: 3 and in many others, the terms that are brought together in parallelism are significant on account of their difference in sense.

A poetics assumes that there is a fixed system of conventions that all competent poets and their audiences would know. But the existence of a one-to-one correspondence between so-called poetic features and their function or sense is questionable. Readers read against and not only with conventions (cf., e.g., Culler 1975; Rabinowitz 1987). Parallel terms may here be compared, there contrasted. The value of poetics, and of linguistics in general, may lie not in providing fixed rules of interpretation but in calling attention to diverse linguistic phenomena that may be utilized by the interpreter in making sense of a work. The Hebrew verb ברא, "create," may have been chosen for use in Genesis chapter 1 as much for its alliteration with the opening word בראשית, "at the beginning of," as for its semantic nuances (cf., e.g., Bar-Efrat 1989: 203; Sasson 1992: 186 n. 13; Robinson 1999: 93). The fact that the opening couplet of the Babylonian myth *Enūma eliš* uses the idiom "to

---

[11] Even if two different hands are meant, it is by no means implied that the word יד alone can denote "left hand"; cf., e.g., Greenstein 1983: 65 n. 58; Berlin 1985: 15–16; contrast, e.g., Kugel 1981: 43.

be called by name" to refer to the coming into being of the sky and the earth need not be interpreted only in terms of its ideational significance. Since the myth concludes with the recitation of the fifty names of the divine hero Marduk and their midrashic interpretation, beginning the text with reference to naming forms a literary inclusio, framing the work (cf., e.g., Foster 1995: 10). Philologists need to be alert to poetic possibilities because the language in the texts we study occurs not in isolation but as part of a literary structure. And even if the literary structures to which we relate are themselves the product of our hermeneutical moves (e.g., Fish 1980; Greenstein 1998b), in order to understand a text as well as we can, we must investigate potential poetic functions no less than lexicographical meaning and syntax.

On account of poetics, meaning may even be at odds with ordinary sense. Thus Job in his opening utterance refers to himself at birth as an adult, a man — גבר. That would be nonsense ordinarily, but in the poetics of the discourse as a whole, Job refuses to acknowledge the human circumstances of his birth — he avoids any mention of his father and mother, for example; it is therefore logical in this poetic context of seeking to obliterate the conditions of his birth that he suppress the infant he once was and relate to himself only as he is (and wishes he weren't) now — a "man." In addition, by referring to himself as a "man" he connects himself to the "man" (גבר) mentioned later in the poem, the man whose life is ignored by the deity (cf., e.g., Greenstein 1995a; Fokkelman 1998: 171).

Poetics, as was said at the outset of this section, is only a specialized use of language. Concepts associated primarily with the poetic may sometimes apply equally to language as such. A well-known case is figurative expression, which may characterize ordinary discourse as well as literature (e.g., Lakoff & Johnson 1980). In a highly useful but nonetheless conventional manner, Streck (1999) isolates for study those metaphors and similes that occur in Akkadian epic poetry. However, such figurative expressions as one finds there are not exclusive to the poetic corpus. The expression "to rage like a lion," for example (see Marcus 1977: 87; cf. Held 1970: 52 with n. 35), is employed no less in Assyrian royal inscriptions and annals, which, though not exactly in the realm of ordinary discourse, are composed in a literary prose and not in epic verse. The same metaphor of the raging lion lies behind a Babylonian lexical commentary that glosses *nadāru*, "to rage," by citing an incantation that employs the figure of the "raging lion" (*labbu nadru*; Geller 1987: x–xi). Letters, as well as poems, may employ poetic figures and tropes (cf., e.g., Cochavi-Rainey 1997).[12]

---

12   For an examination of Mesopotamian figurative language that is not restricted by

Not only poetically used terms but all terms may be related either metaphorically (paradigmatically) or metonymically (syntagmatically). These functions are contrastive and should not be confused. Philologists, no less than literary critics, need to be sensitive to the difference.

A case in point: Hurowitz (1997) proposes that the familiar and wide-ranging Hebrew word *nepeš*, most basically "throat," can refer to "food" in Isa. 58: 10. The semantic range of *nepeš* extends metonymically on two separate tracks, so to speak. In the sense of "organ of breathing" (note that Hebrew נפש and Akkadian *napāšu* both mean "to open the throat, to breathe"), *nepeš* comes to mean "breath," "life," "living being" (i.e., a person). In the sense of "organ of eating" (note that one ingests food through the gullet), *nepeš* comes to mean "appetite" or, more generally, "desire." In some Biblical contexts, *nepeš* appears to mean "sustenance" (that which sustains life) but it would seem that this meaning is connected metonymically not to "track two" — the appetite — but rather to "track one" — breath and life. Tracking the metonymic development in reverse, one finds the sequence: sustenance-life-breath-organ of breathing. Hurowitz's suggestion is based on the close semantic relationship between "sustenance" and "food"; but that is a metaphorical relation (one term stands in the paradigmatic place of the other), not a metonymic one.[13]

Theoretically, word meanings can be extended by metaphorical processes as well as metonymic ones (e.g., Anderson 1973: 182). However, the Hebrew word *nepeš*, as we have seen, typically takes on newer meanings through metonymy not metaphor. If Hurowitz's interpretation still be cogent, he might argue more in keeping with the overall metonymic pattern of the semantic development of *nepeš* that the meaning "food" is derived on "track two," as the object of appetite, and not as a near synonym of the notion of "sustenance," which is almost certainly derived on "track one."

3. ANTHROPOLOGY

As Edward Sapir had written in his 1921 book *Language*, "language does not exist apart from culture, that is, from the socially inherited assemblage

---

genre and is more in keeping with Lakoff & Johnson's (1980) relation of metaphors to the concepts by which we think, see Lambert (1987), a survey of figures connected to love and love-making. In the field of Biblical studies there are several extended and sophisticated studies of metaphors, such as: Brettler (1989), Stienstra (1993), Kowalski (1996), Vall (1993); and see also Camp & Fontaine (1993).

13   In Jakobson's parlance (1960: 358), Hurowitz's derivation is from the "axis of selection" rather than from the "axis of combination."

of practices and beliefs that determines the texture of our lives" (Sapir 1968: 207). At the same time, Sapir asserted that language does not reflect culture in a unique and direct manner. Different languages may share in the same culture (ibid.: 208–214). In this book, written prior to a later essay of his that would be developed influentially by Benjamin Lee Whorf (Whorf 1956), Sapir underscored the universality of thought. "The latent content of all languages is the same," he wrote (ibid.: 218). This belief became a commonplace for many linguists and anthropologists. Consider this typical assertion from a textbook in anthropology: "With sufficient effort, it is possible to say anything in any language" (Gumperz 1973: 155a). One should therefore be very cautious in drawing any cultural conclusions from the fact that different languages express themselves differently.

Mesopotamian royal inscriptions tend to begin with the name of the king who is memorializing his achievements (e.g., ^{d}AG-ku-$dúr$-ri-$ù$-RU, "Nebuchadrezzar," in Frame 1995: 13) or the god to whom the inscription is dedicated (e.g., ^{d}en-$líl$-$lá$, "Enlil," in ibid.: 15; both Nebuchadrezzar I, 1125–1104 B.C.E.). West Semitic royal inscriptions tend to begin with the name of the object that is dedicated or with the pronoun "I"; e.g., *'nk . klmw . br .hy[']*, "I am Kilamuwa, son of Hayya" (Gibson 1982: 33; Zenjirli, ca. 825 B.C.E.). One would surely hesitate to conclude from this difference that names and gods were more important to Mesopotamians than to West Semitic peoples; or that West Semitic rulers were more materialist and egocentric than their Mesopotamian counterparts. The differences in rhetoric would seem to derive from different literary traditions, not from different patterns of thought.

On the other hand, it is widely known, or claimed, that the ancients in general, and the Semitic speaking peoples among them, did not make the same dichotomy that we do between a signifier and its referent, between a name and the thing it denominates (cf., e.g., Kristeva 1989: 50–51; Bottéro 1992: 98–100).[14] Naming and being are closely intertwined, so that, as mentioned above, the Akkadian expression "to be named" can have the sense of being created, of coming into being. In the great Akkadian Epic of Gilgamesh it is said that the wild man Enkidu, who was specially fashioned in order to restrain the king Gilgamesh, was created as *zikru ša* $^{d}Anim$, literally "the name of (the high god) Anu" (Gilgamesh I 83; Parpola 1997: 72). The Chicago *Assyrian Dictionary* has difficulty in accounting for this usage, differentiating this term *zikru* from the more common word *zikru*, meaning "name" (Oppenheim 1961: 112–116). But the concept

---

[14] Bottéro (1977) develops his views on the close identification of signifier and referent on the basis of a detailed analysis of the midrash on the fifty names of Marduk in the last section of the myth *Enūma eliš*.

that name and thing are closely identified in ancient thought goes a long way in explaining the usage (see, e.g., Rabinowitz 1993: 1–25). The name is the being; and so the "name of Anu" is a replica of Anu. The dictionary proposes the same sense, but it does not venture to account for it anthropologically.

There is indeed a tension between the inclination of linguists who believe that all human beings have similar patterns of thought and linguists who believe that differences in languages reflect differences of thought (see, e.g., Bloom 1981). Semanticists of the generative school and of other schools have sought to identify universal concepts or meanings that should be expressed in every culture, although not necessarily by means of lexemes alone.[15] Anna Wierzbicka, for example, has developed the seventeenth century philosophical theory that proposes the existence of what she calls "semantic primitives" — fundamental concepts such as "I," "you," "this," "want," "think," "become," and "world," whose meanings are so basic that they cannot be defined; it is they that serve as the basis for defining all other concepts (Wierzbicka 1972; 1991). Although she acknowledges that "every language is a self-contained system and [that], in a sense, no words or constructions of one language can have absolute equivalents in another," she nevertheless seeks to establish a high degree of overlap between what she determines are the most fundamental concept-words of languages (Wierzbicka 1991: 10). By virtue of near universal semantic and syntactic structures, à la Chomsky (1957; cf. now 1995), she posits a foundation for "cross-cultural understanding" (Wierzbicka 1991: 14–15). At the same time, she differentiates the ethnically diverse *meanings* of words from the virtually universal uses of words — semantics from pragmatics, à la Wittgenstein (ibid.: 17).

John Myhill (1997) has tried to refine Wierzbicka's theory by testing the senses of hypothetically universal emotion words in Biblical Hebrew in order to distinguish what is actually universal and what is apparently language-specific. He contends, for example, that the verb *yāre'*, with respect to the deity, has the positive sense of "fearing" God, while the verb *pāḥad* which he defines as the fear of something bad happening because God is displeased, must have the negative sense of "fearing" rather than revering God. I have found several exceptions to this claim, such as Hosea 3: 5: "In the end will the Israelites repent, they will seek YHWH their God as well as David their king; they will revere (וּפָחֲדוּ) YHWH and his presence in the end of days" (cf. also Mic. 7: 17; Ps. 36: 2; 119: 161; Prov. 28: 14).[16]

---

[15] For diverse forms of generative semantics, see Fodor (1977).

[16] The divine epithet פַּחַד יִצְחָק (Gen. 31: 42, 53), often rendered as "Fear of Jacob," may well be another instance the usage of פחד denoting reverence or, more precisely in this

Myhill is supposed to be testing for universals, but actually he is assuming them. He sets out with the view that has long been in fashion among linguists but which has been increasingly debunked by anthropologists, holding that languages work in essentially the same way and express essentially the same things (see above). Anthropologist James Boon (1982: 23) speaks for many in asserting the contrary: "To construe diversity as a secondary, surface aspect of universal language is to short-circuit studies in language and culture." Boon goes on to cite the distinguished line of linguists from Wilhelm von Humboldt through the successors of Sapir and Whorf (cf. Steiner 1975; 1978), who have maintained that languages are fundamentally different in the ways they construct reality (cf. Grace 1987). It is in fact only Myhill's presupposition that Hebrew expresses the basic emotions such as fear and compassion in an abstract fashion.

My own sense has always been that Hebrew, like other ancient Semitic languages, does not express the abstract lexically but rather expresses abstract reasoning implicitly, by indirection, as in figuration (cf., e.g., Talmon 1987), forming analogies, and making deductions (cf., e.g., Geller 1989: 72). Thus Jacobs (1971: 367) has shown that the Bible implicitly uses *a fortiori* (קל וחומר) reasoning; e.g., Moses tells the Israelites in Deut. 31: 27 that if they dare to behave rebelliously under his revered leadership, all the more likely are they to rebel following his death.[17] And Herzog (1991) has demonstrated that many multiple rhetorical questions in the prophetic literature assume a syllogistic type of argument. An example is Jeremiah 31: 19a:

> Is Ephraim a truly precious son to me? [Answer: No.]
> A child in whom I take delight? [Answer: No again.]
> How is it, then, that ever since I have disowned him,
>   I still keep calling him to mind?[18]

The implicit syllogism[19] is as follows:

instance, an object of veneration. However, the interpretation of the epithet has long been controversial; see, e.g., Malul (1985), who reviews the issues and for contextual reasons favors the interpretation "thigh" in the euphemistic sense of genitals.

17   For other proposed instances, see, e.g., Gen. 44: 8; Exod. 6: 12; Num. 12: 14; 1 Sam. 23: 3; Jer. 12: 5; Ezek. 15: 5; Prov. 11: 31; Est. 9: 12.

18   For a proper rendering of this verse, see Held (1969: 79); cf. van Selms (1971–72). For formulaic parallels, see, e.g., Num. 11: 12; Job 7: 12. Most translations and commentaries misconstrue the rhetorical function of *kī* in the third line and fail to comprehend the logical argument; e.g., Bright (1965: 275, 282); Holladay (1989: 154); McKane (1996: 796, 801–02). Carroll (1986: 595, 600) mistranslates but gives a proper understanding of the logical point in his commentary.

19   The syllogism is implicit because, as Herzog (1991) points out, one of the three

a. Parents will keep calling to mind a favored/delightful child.
b. Ephraim is a far cry from being a favored/delightful child.
c. God the Parent keeps thinking of/is inclined to recognize Ephraim!

[A reversal of logic, which is the ironic point of the question.][20]

Abstract reasoning is implicit as well in systems of classification. This, of course, is the thesis of the classic anthropological essay by Lévi-Strauss, *The Savage Mind* (1973). Lists and other forms of categorization do not serve merely pragmatic functions but express conceptualization, stemming perhaps from a penchant to put some order to reality (ibid.: 1–33). Classification, like poetics (see section 2 above) and like language in general, operates either syntagmatically or paradigmatically (ibid.: 149–150). While Lévi-Strauss may often tend to the positing of universal structures, he underscores in this study that cultures will develop diverse taxonomic systems in relation to the ways that their worldviews and experiences are structured (ibid.: 35–74).

Although the scribal cultures of the ancient Near East proliferated lists of writing signs, words, and, indeed, all manner of phenomena (cf., e.g, Oppenheim 1964: 245-248; Civil 1995), the lists have not been adequately mined for the anthropological insights into ancient conceptualization that is embodied in them. The large Babylonian series ḪAR-ra (ur₅-ra) = ḫubullu, for example, combines syntagmatic and paradigmatic associations, beginning with the implements of the scribe, moving syntagmatically to materials used for the manufacture of writing tools, then paradigmatically to other raw materials, and so forth. A more thorough analysis, relating to other lists as well as to other cultural phenomena and factors — an ethnography of the society — can shed invaluable light on ancient habits of thinking, at least within scribal circles (cf. Larsen 1987; and see section 5 below). Thus, for example, the separate lexical list called "Proto-Izi" (Veldhuis 1997: 56) contains fifteen items that can be analyzed into five sets of three, in which one

propositions — in this instance, proposition (a) — is not articulated but understood. The fact that such a logical step can be skipped in the prophetic discourse would seem to be a direct consequence of the oral situation of the rhetorical context, in which certain assumptions that are shared by speaker and audience are, as in conversation, left unsaid (cf., e.g., Tannen 1982). See section 5 below.

[20] Vanstiphout (1998: 403) has pointed out an implicit syllogism in the Sumerian Dream of Lugalbanda (for a provisional edition and translation see ibid.: 405–412). The underlying propositions are as follows:

a. A specially endowed person can perform task X.
b. Lugalbanda is a specially endowed person.
c. Lugalbanda can perform task X.

item represents fire or a metaphorical substitute, such as flame or ashes; another item represents metonymically a container of the fire, such as a kiln or torch; and a third item also metonymically represents a product of fire, such as charcoal or heat.[21]

However, the full-length study of one part of ḪAR-ra = *ḫubullu* by Veldhuis (1997), which is a substantial textological treatment with the major aim of drawing historical conclusions concerning ancient scribal schooling, shows almost no acquaintance with anthropological perspectives. His topical schematization of the large lexical series overlooks the underlying conceptual level of the list's organization. Veldhuis (1997: 91) sees the most general level of arrangement in the concrete categories of which the series is constructed — "trees and wooden objects"-"reed"-"fish" etc. A simple attempt to seek a more abstract level would reveal that most of the series is organized into diverse natural elements: "wood"-"reed"-"fish"-etc. On the next, lower level of organization one would find the concrete objects "wood," "reed," "fish," etc., and on the next lower level such concrete manifestations of "wood," "reed," "fish," etc., as types of wood/trees, reeds, fish, etc. Then, by metonymy, one finds the levels of objects made from wood, reed, fish, etc., and then various paradigmatically related classes. The recurrence of paradigmatic/metaphorically-related classes down the list of each category — which is predictable from an inspection of other lists (see immediately above), where the metaphorical and metonymic intermix — can explain the "anomalies" in the lists that are difficult for Veldhuis (1997: 92) to fathom. A "ferry-boat" occurs in the middle of a listing of boat parts, for example, because it functions as a paradigmatic substitute for "boat." The recurrence of an item representing a conceptually higher node on the list provides a degree of cognitive coherence to the list as the principle of organization is made explicit again.

Moreover, if one understands that the lexical series is organized most abstractly by natural elements, one can explain, as Veldhuis does not, what brick molds are doing in the middle of a list that he labels "agricultural tools" (Veldhuis 1997: 95–98). In accordance with the anthropological expectation that the highest node in the list should represent the "realm" in which objects are found or from which they derive (cf. Hallpike 1979: 203), the overall category in which the agricultural implements are listed should be redefined conceptually as

---

[21]   The hypothesis that the list is organized according to recursive conceptual patterns can be supported by the fact that such sequences are quite transparent in other lists. In an Old Babylonian Sumerian grammatical list one finds, for example, a sequence like "he gave"-"he gave to him"-"they gave to him" followed by the sequence "he paid"-"he paid him"-"they paid him" etc. (Veldhuis 1997: 59).

"the ground." The categories of "agricultural tools" and "brick molds" will then represent paradigmatically-related classes of tools for working in/with the ground.[22]

A unique, anthropologically attuned study of classification within a semantic field in ancient Semitic is Brenner's (1982) comprehensive analysis of Hebrew color terms. Brenner finds a certain degree of correlation with the so-called universal semantic principles for color categorization proposed by Berlin & Kay (1969). Berlin and Kay's study holds, for example, that from a developmental point of view, terms for "black" and "white" evolve from more general terms conveying "darkness" and "brightness." The fact that neither Hebrew *šāḥōr* "black," nor any synonym in the sense of "dark" appears in relatively early (monarchic) Hebrew does not jibe with the theory, but Brenner (1982: 57) suggests that this may result from the fact that the data base is limited. Landsberger's (1967) study of color terms in Sumerian and Akkadian would appear to bear out the independent findings of Berlin and Kay. In fact, one may adduce Berlin & Kay (1969) in order to support the hypothesis that the Sumerian terms babbar and gi$_6$ and the Akkadian terms *peṣû* and *ṣalmu* meant "bright" and "dark," respectively, before they came to mean "white" and "black" as well.

Lakoff (1987) enters the debate about conceptual universals through a study of metaphor. Building on Lakoff & Johnson (1980), Lakoff eschews the notion of universal conceptions but relates metaphors to certain concepts that are known and used within a culture. These concepts result from human experience and observation so that they may occur across different cultures; e.g., people's body heat and blood pressure rise when they are angry, so that the conceptions of anger as heat and pressure can become expressed, as they are in English, in arrays of metaphors by which anger is articulated in relation to heat and pressure (Lakoff 1987: 380–415). Such conceptions cannot predictably occur in any other language, but, as they are claimed to rest on physiological phenomena, they should not be contradicted by other languages, by representing anger, for example, as cold (ibid.: 407). In any event, figurative language is not merely a literary trope — it is a window on thinking. Consider this typical assessment from a large reference book on psycholinguistics:

> Metaphor, metonymy, irony, oxymora, and so on do not merely provide a way for us to talk about the way we think, reason,

---

22 One should only remark that the Mesopotamian lists reflect a stage of development more sophisticated than the "primitive" one discussed by Hallpike (1979: 203), in which objects in the various "realms" — such as forest, village, sea, etc. — "are not ordered hierarchically."

and imagine; these figures are also constitutive of our experience. Speakers cannot help but employ figurative discourse because they conceptualize much of their experience in figurative terms. Listeners find figurative speech easy to understand precisely because much of their thinking is constrained by figurative processes (Gibbs 1994: 413; cf. Cacciari & Glucksberg 1994: 448).

Hebrew and the other ancient Semitic languages tend to concrete rather than abstract expression (cf. in general, e.g., Ullmann 1966; and for Semitic, e.g., Malamat 1990). Thus, while Hebrew has a number of words and expressions for conveying a sense of "anger" — especially in the pre-Persian periods before the verb כעס comes to predominate (Hurvitz 1972: 174 n. 303; Rooker 1990: 147–148) — not one of them is, in my judgment, abstract; each has a concrete connotation, each suggests a physical manifestation, whether it is "getting a hot (or wrinkled) nose" (חרון אף),[23] "shaking" (רגז), "foaming at the mouth" (קצף; Cohen 1978:

---

[23] Conventionally, the idiom *ḥārā 'ap* is interpreted to mean "the nose (or anger) burned," even though the putative Arabic etymology of Hebrew *ḥārā* does not hold water. The Arabic etymon is *ḥarra*; cf. Ethiopic *ḥarara*, Akkadian *erēru*, and Ugaritic *ḥrr*; cf., e.g., Aistleitner (1974: 107). Based on the fact that the antonymous expression is *he'erīk 'ap*, "lengthened the nose," Ehrlich (1899: 83–84) proposed that *ḥārā 'ap* be understood to have the basic sense of "cringing the nose," a facial gesture opposite to that of lengthening the nose. He pointed to a likely etymon in Arabic *ḥariya*, "to diminish, narrow," whose root matches that of Hebrew חרי precisely.

Gruber (1980: 491–510) admits that there is no etymological basis for rendering *ḥārōn* as "burning" but he adduces such verses as Exod. 15: 7 and Ps. 58: 10 to support his view. However, in the former verse חרון can be, and is usually understood to be, an abbreviation of the full expression, חרון אף, in the sense of "anger." The fact that this anger is said to cause burning reveals nothing about the idiom's original meaning. Heating up and burning are two very widely attested metaphors for anger, not only in Hebrew and Semitic but in English and other languages as well; cf., e.g., Lakoff (1987: 380–415). Similarly, in Ps. 58: 10, a particularly difficult verse (cf. Tate 1990: 84), חרון would seem to denote "anger" (cf., e.g., Jewish Publication Society 1982: 74). Although Gruber's rendering can find support in, e.g., Weiser (1962: 429), I would follow the more scrupulous philological analysis of Hakham (1970: 339–340): Before the wicked's briars mature into thornbushes, God will sweep them away in anger while they are fresh (i.e., God will undermine the schemes of the wicked before they can manage to execute them).

Myhill (1997) fails to make proper use of the fact that neither חרון nor אף has a primary meaning that denotes anger; each term expresses the sense of "anger" by way of abbreviating the full idiom. The distinction is important. Consider the fact that Biblical Hebrew טפש means "to be fat" (cf. Akkadian *ṭapāšu*, "be fat") and that in later Hebrew טפש comes to mean "stupid." Looking only at the word טפש, one might conclude that in ancient Semitic, or in Hebrew at least, being fat and being stupid are related ideas. However, the sense of "stupid" is clearly derived from the idiom טפש לב "the heart grew fat" (see Ps. 119: 70 and cf. the expression השמין לב "to cause the heart to grow fat/thick," i.e., impervious to understanding, in Isa. 6: 11). Compare such

24–25), "spitting venom" (חמה; ibid.: 25; Held 1985: 99 n. 11), etc. No term represents a pure, disembodied anger, contrary to the assumptions and arguments of Myhill, cited above.

A useful way of explaining the difference between ancient Semitic expression and that of modern industrial societies is presented in Denny (1991). Denny explains that ancient and so-called primitive societies tend toward contextualization, that is, expressing concepts in relation to concrete manifestations of them, while modern societies tend toward decontextualization, that is, expressing concepts in the abstract, disconnected from their concrete manifestations. A circular object is contextual, a circle is decontextual. The need for decontextualizing arises, according to Denny, when people begin relating things to people in different walks of life from themselves. One would not expect to find rampant decontextualization in the ancient Near East, and if I am correct that we don't, that anthropological perspective on language could shed further light on ancient Semitic thought. The question may be related to the effects of literacy, on which see section 5 below.

4. PSYCHOANALYSIS

One of the linguist's tasks is to try to abstract the forms and rules of language, to grasp the grammar of a language in its ideal form, as *langue*. But the philologist always meets the linguistic object of study in its actually occurring forms, as *parole*. *Parole* is by definition tainted by the dispositions and neuroses of the people who use language. Linguists may want to avert their eyes from the implications of this most human of all sides of language, but, as Kristeva (1989: 274) writes:

> Psychoanalysis renders impossible the habit commonly accepted by current linguistics of considering language outside its *realization* in *discourse*, that is, by forgetting that language does not exist outside the *discourse of a subject*, or by considering this subject as *implicit*, as equal to himself, as a fixed unit coinciding with his discourse. This Cartesian postulate...was shaken up by the Freudian discovery of the unconscious and its logic.

One may argue over what methods of psychoanalysis are more correct or more effective. But one can hardly gainsay the claim that a sensitivity

---

expressions as "thick-headed" in English. The sense of טפש as "stupid" is dependent on the full expression טפש לב.

to the unconscious and the ways it works is essential to gaining a full understanding of texts, including ancient ones.[24]

One finds evidence of proto-Freudian psychoanalysis in ancient Near Eastern texts. Gilgamesh dreams of an axe lying at the entrance of his marital chamber (Gilgamesh I 255–272; Parpola 1997: 74; translation in Kovacs 1989: 12). People gather round, and Gilgamesh embraces the axe like a wife. Upon awakening, he asks his divine mother what it means. She explains that the axe — a phallic symbol if there ever was one — is a man that he will love and embrace as a wife. The reference, of course, is to Gilgamesh's counterpart and partner, Enkidu (for some discussion, see Streck 1999: 214–215). In the light of such an unabashed usage of a phallic figure in a classic of Mesopotamian literature,[25] one can only wonder at the many translators of the Babylonian Dialogue between a Master and His Servant who render the negative characterization of a castrating woman as "a sharp iron dagger that cuts a man's throat" (Lambert 1960: 147, line 52; cf., e.g., Speiser 1967: 348; Biggs 1969: 601; Foster 1993: 816; Livingstone 1997: 496) without taking any note of the obvious Freudian irony.

A psychoanalytic approach to language was exploited by the critic Mieke Bal (1987: 66–88) when she homed in on the utterance of Boaz in the Biblical Book of Ruth (3: 10). Boaz is impressed with the attentions of the younger woman Ruth, remarking that she is performing an extraordinary kindness by going after him rather than after a younger man. Although few Biblical exegetes have paid much attention to this utterance, it rather clearly exhibits Boaz's sexual insecurity and indirectly expresses his gratefulness for the sexual invigoration that Ruth is about to bring him (cf. Greenstein 1998b: 222).

The episode of Moses' dialogue with God at the Burning Bush exemplifies the concepts of displacement and condensation that play so central a role in Freudian dream analysis (Freud 1953: 277–338). Moses is summoned in order to extricate Israel from its bondage in Egypt. By means of displacement, this crucial but intimidating mission is represented by a variety of symbols. First, the enslaved Israel is figured in the image of the bush that burns but is not consumed (see Philo 1966: 311; Midrash Exodus Rabbah 2: 5; and other references in Propp 1998: 222; cf., e.g., Sarna 1991: 14). The analogy between a fire threatening to

---

[24] For Freud's contributions to literary theory and textual interpretation, see Willbern (1989). For the post-Freudian developments of psychoanalytic criticism, see Straton (1987: 279–350). For a critical summary of psychoanalytic approaches to literary theory and interpretation, see Eagleton (1983: 151–193).

[25] Oppenheim (1956: 215) admits that "an erotic interest" between "the two heroes of the epic" is indicated here, but Butler (1998: 19), in a very recent study of Mesopotamian dreams, merely observes that Gilgamesh's dream is of the "symbolic message" type.

consume (אכל) the bush and a land — in this case Egypt — threatening to consume (אכל) a people is familiar from Numbers 13: 32, where the territory of Canaan is described as "a land that consumes its inhabitants." The image of preservation is also not unique in the Bible. The prophets Amos (4: 11) and Zechariah (3: 2) both use the image of a firebrand removed from the fire as a figure of rescue and salvation.

In addition to the figure of the burning bush representing the rescue of the Israelites, the three signs given to Moses by God also symbolize the rescue. Each of the signs symbolizes the transformation of something safe or healthy into something dangerous or unhealthy, and then back to safety and health again — a recapitulation of the story of Israel in Egypt as a whole.[26] Moses' rod is turned into a snake and then back to a rod. Moses' hand is turned leprous and then back again. Moses tosses water on the ground, and it is turned to blood. The symbolism should be evident: Israel was enslaved in Egypt, but will be brought out intact (cf. the classical interpretations cited by Houtman 1993: 393, 398–399). The connection between Egypt and the dangerous or unhealthy place is even suggested by a play on words, another dream mechanism pointed out by Freud (1953: 204–207, 421–425, etc.) and known from ancient Egyptian (e.g., Wilson 1969), Mesopotamian (e.g., Oppenheim 1956: 241),[27] and rabbinic dream interpretations (e.g., S. Lieberman 1962: 71; cf. Niehoff 1992). The leprous hand of Moses is מצורעת, whose similarity to the name of Egypt, מצרים, requires no further comment.

Dream language not only displaces, it also condenses; that is, the symbols of dreams often carry more than one meaning; they are, in Freud's terminology, "overdetermined" (e.g., Freud 1953: 283–284, 306–308). Thus, the water Moses turns to blood by tossing it on the ground prefigures the first of the ten plagues, wherein the Nile River and all the other water of Egypt is turned into blood (cf., e.g., Childs 1974: 78). More poignantly, the turning of Moses' stiff rod into a limp snake symbolizes Moses' temporary loss of virility (cf., e.g., Zeligs 1986: 72–73).[28] The text

26 The literary figure by which a major theme of a work is represented within the work in miniature form is called "mise en abyme"; for bibliography and some instances in ancient Near Eastern and Biblical literature, see Greenstein (1998c).

27 There is an excellent example of wordplay in Gilgamesh's dream of the axe, mentioned above (cf. Cooper 1973: 40 with n. 6). Gilgamesh sees the axe by his side, and it is interpreted to refer to his comrade, his "brother," Enkidu. The Akkadian word for "side" and "brother" — *aḫu* — is homonymous, condensing both meanings. Further on, Gilgamesh will confirm the identification, referring to Enkidu as "the axe at my side" (*ḫaṣṣin aḫīya*; Gilg. VIII 45; Parpola 1997: 99; line 34 in the translation by Kovacs 1989: 70).

28 Zeligs (1986: 57–78 and passim) interprets the burning bush episode and other phenomena in the story of Moses as well in Freudian terms.

tells us that Moses was so afraid of the snake that he fled. Moses repeatedly expressed to God his anxieties about going on the mission to Egypt. In the end, God gave him no choice, and he went. God assured Moses he would be with him. Similarly, and symbolically, Moses' rod which had turned into a snake stiffened up into a rod, once Moses took hold of its tail.

To sum up, one may agree or disagree with a particular psychoanalytic interpretation. But in light of what we have learned about language as *parole*, one can hardly expect to understand any text without it.

5. SPOKEN AND WRITTEN

The study of ancient literacy and of literacy in general have taken on renewed momentum in the past thirty years. Old commonplaces have been overturned and exaggerated claims for the consequences of literacy have been nuanced. A tendency to focus on the impact of literacy has given way to a tendency to examine the functions of literacy. "What matters is what people do with literacy, not what literacy does to people" (Olson, Hildyard & Torrance 1985: 14).

Scholars have been acknowledging that in the ancient world writing was the province of a scribal class and certain other elites. Where once it was thought that alphabetic scripts like Hebrew and Greek would have made literacy available to the masses, more recent assessments find reading and writing to be the privilege of a few even in Jerusalem and Athens. The evidence of the Bible and of ancient Hebrew epigraphy shows writing to be of the social elites, like scribes, prophets, priests, military officers, and other officials (Young 1998; cf. Crenshaw 1998: 29–49; contrast Demsky 1995); and a fresh scrutiny of the Greek evidence shows that even in fifth century B.C.E. Athens only a small elite was literate (Harris 1989; Thomas 1992). The alphabet makes literacy easier, but to engage in reading and writing still requires motivation, an appropriate mindset, and extensive training.

The sociological fact that writing comes only with schooling has led scholars to rethink the claims that have been made to the effect that writing gave rise to reflection, abstraction, and logical thought (e.g., Goody 1977; Ong 1982; Havelock 1991; Narasimhan 1991). The idea that it is writing that has enabled the development of philosophy, science, and literature has turned out to be no more than our own "cultural mythology" (Brown & Yule 1983: 2). Refined cognition is a product of education, not of writing *per se* (e.g., Horowitz & Samuels 1987: 15; Thomas 1992: 25–26; Heath 1992: 337; Cole & Nicolopoulou 1992: 345). Both thinking and writing are learned in school; that is what they have in common. Indeed, we have shown some examples of "logical thinking" in ancient Mesopotamia and Israel in section 3 above. Neither Israel nor any other ancient Near Eastern culture created a philosophical mode of discourse, as did the Greeks. But Israel was apparently no less literate than Athens; the express articulation of abstract reasoning was simply not isolated in ancient Semitic cultures as a discipline in and of itself.

The fact that writing is essentially a scribal activity in the ancient Near East draws our attention to scribal literary phenomena. In Mesopotamia and Egypt, for example, scribes developed a special literary language (cf., e.g., Lambert 1968: 123–124; Lichtheim 1973: 211). The literary language that we refer to as Standard Babylonian is distinguished by lexical, syntactic, morphological, and phonological features (von Soden 1932–33; Hecker 1974). Although certain of these features characterized the oral poetry from which the literary scribal language in part derived, other scribal phenomena — like orthographic jokes (Civil 1972; Foster 1974: 82–83), coded writing (cf., e.g., S. J. Lieberman 1987: 164–167; Tov 1995), or the inscription of a sentence or a scribe's name as an acrostic in a text (Brug 1990; Soll 1992) — are clearly the consequences of writing. Indeed, Michalowski (1996: 191) speaks of the scribes evolving a separate culture and ideology. Writing, textuality, became, at least for some scribes, a conceptual framework by which to experience the world. The array of phenomena in the heavens were accordingly metaphorized as "sky writing" (*šiṭir šamē*; Reiner 1992: 146a; cf. Michalowski 1990: 396).

Writing surely enabled the ancient scribes to collect and systematize their knowledge (see, e.g., Larsen 1987; Vanstiphout 1995). An important implication for all of us who read ancient Near Eastern texts is that we should bear in mind that the texts we read are, so far as we ordinarily can know, elite creations that may be entirely atypical of the popular literature. The literary canon that evolved within scribal circles was the literature of the elite, not the public (e.g., Alster 1992: 26; Hurowitz 1999: 9*).[29] Ancient texts are by and for scribes. The themes and issues that exercise ancient literary works, then, reflect the worldview of a small class, and not necessarily of the society at large.

Writing as an esoteric phenomenon lends it a peculiar mystique. In the ancient world texts could have an ontological significance of their own, possessing magical powers or serving as monuments (e.g., Gelb 1963: 230–235; Thomas 1992: 74–100; Rabinowitz 1993; Niditch 1996: 54–57). Greco-Roman curse tablets and Aramaic magic bowls of the

---

[29]   For the nature of "canon" in Mesopotamian literature, see the diverse views expressed, e.g., in Rochberg-Halton (1984); S. J. Lieberman (1990); Hallo (1991); Hurowitz (1999).

first millennium C.E., for example, incorporate letter-like symbols many
of which are patent imitations of cuneiform writing, which was by then
long in disuse, in an apparent effort to add a mystical element.[30] The
mystical aspect of writing needs to be appreciated in order to account for the
transformation of certain texts into scripture (cf. Goody 1982: 211; Demsky
1995: 367).

The emergence of written language alongside oral language does not
in general lead to a detachment of the former from the latter. Studies of
literacy repeatedly stress the interdependency of written and oral modes
of communication (e.g., Tannen 1982; 1992). This is especially true of the
ancient world (e.g., Thomas 1992; Vogelzang & Vanstiphout 1992; Niditch
1996). Even though some matters would be recorded in writing, the daily
business of government and commerce would still be conducted orally
(e.g., Havelock 1991: 21). Literary texts were written either for scholastic
reasons — to serve as curriculum in the schools — or as an aid for oral
performance (e.g., Gitay 1980; Cooper 1992: 111–114; Westenholz 1992:
147–153). By and large, written literature does not differ in essentials
from its oral counterparts (e.g., Finnegan 1992: 126–133). Thus, the
presence of formulaic language and conventional literary structures in
ancient Semitic literatures such as those of Mesopotamia (see Vogelzang
& Vanstiphout 1992 in general and Izre'el 1992 in particular) or of the
Hebrew Bible (see, e.g., Watters 1976; Polak 1989), does not in and of
itself bespeak a background in oral performance. Features of originally
orally composed texts are incorporated into written literature as well.

Nevertheless, writing does make a difference in the linguistic character
of discourse. The slow and deliberate nature of writing allows for
the integration of presuppositions and propositions that is reflected in
connected prose (e.g., Chafe 1982: 37–38; Brown & Yule 1983: 12;
Chafe & Danielewicz 1987). From a historical perspective, prose, which
was developed in ancient Egypt and is perhaps best known from the
Hebrew Bible, is a product of writing. But one should be chary of
concluding that prior to writing there was no prose. Oral storytelling is in
general typically in prose. What distinguishes oral from written prose is
that the former employs diverse linguistic and paralinguistic techniques
— such as intonation and gesturing — to convey focus and train of
thought, while written discourse, which lacks contextual cues, must make
logical connections and presuppositions explicit (e.g., Halliday 1987;
Tannen 1992). Spoken discourse as an extemporaneous activity, tends to

---

30 For illustrations, see, e.g., Gager (1992: 8, fig. 1; 56, fig. 7); Naveh & Shaked (1993:
    108, fig. 17). For brief discussion, see Gager (1992: 10–11); Scholem (1971: 635).
    These characters are developed in medieval Kabbalah as the so-called "Alphabet of
    Metatron," as I have learned from David Moss.

be weak in vocabulary, but complex in its syntax, in which clauses are intricately strung together in sequence. "Written language tends to be lexically dense, but grammatically simple" in this respect (Halliday 1987: 71).

Writing typically differs from oral discourse in the syntactic structures that it favors, such as nominalization, the use of attributive (as opposed to predicate) adjectives, conjoined phrases, relative clauses, and the passive voice (e.g., Chafe 1982: 40–46; Brown & Yule 1983: 15–17). Basing himself on the research of Chafe and others, Polak (1998) has found that later Biblical Hebrew, of the Persian period, exhibits signs of a distinctly written style, including embedded clauses, long noun strings, and "explicit syntactic constituents" like the relative pronoun.[31] It is hardly coincidental that in the Persian period we encounter the writerly activity of the Chronicler, rewriting sources from an earlier period (Niditch 1996: 127–129). Vanstiphout (1995: 2193) regards such an intertextual use of one text by another as a distinctively literate phenomenon, but we shall see that intertextuality is generally understood nowadays in much broader terms.

6. INTERTEXTUALITY

One of the salient features of postmodern literary theory is what Roland Barthes (1986) has called "the death of the author" (see further, e.g., Leitch 1992: 19–38). Authors may have had something in mind when they wrote up their texts, but their intentions, to the extent that they are relevant, are inaccessible to us, and any efforts of ours to get at their meaning are uncorroborable. Texts get their meaning from the interpretations that we give to them (cf., e.g., Fish 1980: 174–180, 322–337; 1989: 68–86).[32] The constructor of sense who is known to us and whose activities and thoughts can be examined is the reader. Now what we know about readers is that when we read, we associate what we read with other texts we have read.[33] We cannot help understanding and interpreting the present text according to frameworks of comparison and contrast that come to mind from somewhere in our previous experience. We don't read anything cold; if we were to try,

---

[31] Deutscher (2000) shows increased syntactic complexity over time in Akkadian; the phenomenon would apparently derive from similar conditions, to wit, the evolution of a written style.

[32] For further bibliography and discussion, see, e.g., Greenstein (1998b). For a nuanced critique of this perspective, see, e.g., Shusterman (1991).

[33] Writing, of course, is no less intertextual, written under the influence of and largely composed of previously encountered language, tropes, genres, and texts.

we would make out nothing. All reading is in this broad sense intertextual (cf., e.g., Clayton & Rothstein 1991).

As scholars working in a discipline, we try to discipline ourselves in choosing the texts we bring to bear in the interpretation of a given text, the intertexts of our text. The intertexts we choose will determine the meaning we find or construct. The Hittite text known as the Apology of Hattushilish III (Otten 1981; cf. van den Hout 1997), for example, in which Hattushilish relates the background of the coup in which he overthrew his nephew with the support of the main goddess, will mean something different if it is read alongside autobiographical texts (cf., e.g., Greenstein 1995b), or other works of political propaganda like the story of David (cf., e.g., Wolf 1967), or other stories of usurpers of the throne (cf., e.g., Hoffner 1975), or other religious texts describing devotion to a god or goddess (cf., e.g., van den Hout 1995: 1107–12). An ancient epic will mean one thing to a political historian, another thing to a historian of religion, another to a mythographer, and yet another thing to a lover of literature who comes across it in an anthology, where it is juxtaposed with other compositions which had nothing to do with it in ancient times.[34]

Because intertextual reading brings two or more texts into association, the features and meanings of one may, like languages in contact (e.g., Weinreich 1974: 109; Lehiste 1988: 28), interpenetrate with the features and meanings of the other. The flow of sense-making is bidirectional. An intertextual reading of the Ugaritic epic of Kirta (see now Greenstein 1997) and the Biblical story of David can enhance the interpretation of each. Both Kirta and David enjoy the special patronage of their gods, El and YHWH, respectively (cf., e.g., Lichtenstein 1987: 3 with 15 nn. 21–22). Both marry the daughter of a king. Both become ill, at which point their eldest son makes a claim on their throne (Kirta III vi; Greenstein 1997: 40–42; 1 Kings 1; for discussion, see Rummel 1981: 295–306; Parker 1989: 198–199). In view of the Kirta epic, where the king is nursed back to health by a magical female creature made especially for him by his god El (Kirta III v–vi; Greenstein 1997: 38–39), one may appreciate the unpropitious character of David's ailment. He is tended not by a divine creature but by a nubile woman who can do no more than try unsuccessfully to warm him. By contrast with Kirta, David will not get well. Reading in the other direction, so to speak, in view of the David story, the Kirta epic, which is probably missing its proper ending (see, e.g., Parker 1989: 203–205), is likely to have concluded with the

---

[34] For intertextuality in ancient Egyptian literature, see the brief but pointed remarks of Loprieno (1996: 222–225).

destruction of Kirta's eldest son and the succession of one of his younger children.

We can never remind ourselves too often that the meanings of the texts we read result from the kind of training we have, from the theories and methods we tend to employ, and from the models and parallels we adduce in order to gain the leverage of understanding. Language does not mean by itself; we make sense of it. And so one of the important objects of our study should be our own assumptions about language and our own habits of thought. This conference is one of those excellent occasions when we have an opportunity of doing just that.

BIBLIOGRAPHY

Aistleitner, Joseph. 1974. *Wörterbuch der ugaritischen Sprache*. 4th ed. Berlin.

Alonso Schökel, Luis. 1988. *A Manual of Hebrew Poetics*. Subsidia Biblica 11. Rome.

Alster, Bendt. 1992. Interaction of Oral and Written Poetry in Early Mesopotamian Literature. In Vogelzang & Vanstiphout (1992), 23–69.

Alter, Robert. 1985. *The Art of Biblical Poetry*. New York.

Anderson, James M. 1973. *Structural Aspects of Language Change*. London.

Attridge, Derek. 1992. Derrida and the question of literature. In Derrida (1992), 1–29.

Austin, J. L. 1962. *How to Do Things with Words*. Oxford.

Bal, Mieke. 1987. *Lethal Love: Feminist Literary Readings of Biblical Love Stories*. Bloomington.

Bar-Efrat, Shimon. 1989. *Narrative Art in the Bible*. Trans. D. Shefer-Vanson. Sheffield.

Barthes, Roland. 1986. The Death of the Author. *The Rustle of Language*. Trans. Richard Howard. New York. [First published: 1968.]

Berlin, Adele. 1985. *The Dynamics of Biblical Parallelism*. Bloomington.

Berlin, Brent, and Kay, Paul. 1969. *Basic Color Terms: Their Universality and Evolution*. Berkeley.

Biggs, Robert D. 1969. Akkadian didactic and wisdom literature. In *Ancient Near Eastern Texts Relating to the Old Testament*. James B. Pritchard (ed.). Princeton, 592–607.

Bloom, Alfred H. 1981. *The Linguistic Shaping of Thought: A Study in the Impact of Language on Thinking in China and the West*. Hillsdale.

Bodine, Walter R. (ed.). 1992. *Linguistics and Biblical Hebrew*. Winona Lake.

Bodine, Walter R. 1995. Introduction: Discourse Analysis of Biblical Literature: What It Is and What It Offers. In *Discourse Analysis of Biblical Literature*. Walter R. Bodine (ed.). SBL Semeia Studies. Atlanta, 1–18.

Boon, James A. 1982. *Other Tribes, Other Scribes: Symbolic Anthropology in the Comparative Study of Cultures, Histories, Religions, and Texts*. Cambridge.

Bottéro, Jean. 1977. Les noms de Marduk, l'écriture et la "logique" en Mésopotamie ancienne. In *Essays on the Ancient Near East in Memory of Jacob Joel Finkelstein*. Maria de Jong Ellis (ed.). Memoirs of the Connecticut Academy of Arts and Sciences 19. Hamden, 5–28.

Bottéro, Jean. 1992. *Mesopotamia: Writing, Reasoning, and the Gods*. Trans. Zainab Bahrani and Marc van de Mieroop. Chicago and London.

Brenner, Athalya. 1982. *Colour Terms in the Old Testament*. Journal for the Study of the Old Testament Supplement 21. Sheffield.

Brettler, Marc. 1989. *God Is King: Understanding a Biblical Metaphor*. Journal for the Study of the Old Testament Supplement 76. Sheffield.

Bright, John. 1965. *Jeremiah*. Anchor Bible. Garden City, NY.

Brown, Gillian, and Yule, George. 1983. *Discourse Analysis*. Cambridge.

Brug, John F. 1990. Biblical acrostics and their relationship to other ancient Near Eastern acrostics. In *The Bible in the Light of Cuneiform Literature*. Scripture in Context III. William W. Hallo, Bruce William Jones & Gerald L. Mattingly (eds.). Lewiston, 283–304.

Butler, S. A. L. 1998. *Mesopotamian Conceptions of Dreams and Dream Rituals*. Alter Orient und Altes Testament 258. Münster.

Cacciari, Cristina, and Glucksberg, Sam. 1994. Understanding Figurative Language. In *Handbook of Psycholinguistics*. Morton Ann Gernsbacher (ed.). San Diego, 447–477.

Camp, Claudia V., and Fontaine, Carole R. (eds.). 1993. *Women, War, and Metaphor: Language and Society in the Study of the Hebrew Bible = Semeia* 61. Atlanta.

Carroll, Robert P. 1986. *The Book of Jeremiah*. Old Testament Library. London.

Chafe, Wallace L. 1982. Integration and involvement in speaking, writing, and oral literature. In *Spoken and Written Language: Exploring Orality and Literacy*. Deborah Tannen (ed.). Norwood, 35–53.

Chafe, Wallace, and Danielewicz, Jane. 1987. Properties of written and spoken language. In *Comprehending Oral and Written Language.* Rosalind Horowitz & S. Jay Samuels (eds.). San Diego, 83–113.

Chavel, Ḥayyim David. 1959. *Commentary of Ramban [Naḥmanides] on the Torah.* Vol. 1. Jerusalem (in Hebrew).

Childs, Brevard S. 1974. *The Book of Exodus: A Critical, Theological Commentary.* Old Testament Library. Philadelphia.

Chomsky, Noam. 1957. *Syntactic Structures.* Janua Linguarum. The Hague.

Chomsky, Noam. 1995. *The Minimalist Program.* Current Studies in Linguistics. Cambridge, Mass.

Civil, Miguel. 1972. Scribal Whimsies. *Journal of the American Oriental Society* 92: 271.

Civil, Miguel. 1995. Ancient Mesopotamian lexicography. In *Civilizations of the Ancient Near East.* Jack M. Sasson (ed.). New York. 4: 2305–2314.

Clayton, Jay, and Rothstein, Eric. 1991. Figures in the corpus: theories of influence and intertextuality. In *Influence and Intertextuality in Literary History.* Jay Clayton & Eric Rothstein (eds.). Madison, 3–36.

Cochavi-Rainey, Zipora. 1997. Selected similes, descriptions, and figures of speech from the El-Amarna letters and their Biblical parallels. *Lěšonénu* 60: 165–179 (in Hebrew).

Cohen, Harold R. (Chaim). 1978. *Biblical Hapax Legomena in the Light of Akkadian and Ugaritic.* SBL Dissertation Series 37. Missoula, Montana.

Cooper, Jerrold S. 1977. Gilgamesh dreams of Enkidu: The evolution and dilution of narrative. In *Essays on the Ancient Near East in Memory of Jacob Joel Finkelstein.* Maria de Jong Ellis (ed.). Memoirs of the Connecticut Academy of Arts and Sciences 19. Hamden, 39–44.

Cooper, Jerrold S. 1992. Babbling on: recovering Mesopotamian orality. In Vogelzang & Vanstiphout (1992), 103–122.

Crenshaw, James L. 1998. *Education in Ancient Israel.* New York.

Culler, Jonathan. 1975. *Structuralist Poetics: Structuralism, Linguistics, and the Study of Literature.* Ithaca.

Dahood, Mitchell. 1972. Ugaritic-Hebrew parallel pairs. In *Ras Shamra Parallels, Volume I.* Loren R. Fisher (ed.). Analecta Orientalia 49. Rome, 71–382.

Demsky, Aaron. 1995. Literacy. *The Oxford Encyclopaedia of Archaeology in the Near East.* Eric Meyers (ed.). New York. 3: 362–369.

Denny, J. Peter. 1991. Rational thought in oral culture. In *Literacy and*

Orality. David R. Olson & Nancy Torrance (eds.). Cambridge, 66–89.

Derrida, Jacques. 1992. *Acts of Literature*. Derek Attridge (ed.). Routledge.

Deutscher, Guy. 2000. *Syntactic Change in Akkadian: The Evolution of Sentential Complementation*. New York.

Dijk, Teun A. van (ed.). 1997. *Discourse Studies*. 2 vols. London.

Dillmann, August. 1880. *Die Bücher Exodus und Leviticus*. Kurzgefasstes exegetisches Handbuch zum Alten Testament. Leipzig.

Eagleton, Terry. 1982. *Literary Theory: An Introduction*. Minneapolis.

Ehrlich, Arnold B. 1899. *Mikra Ki-Pheschuto*. Vol. 1. Berlin. [Reprint: New York 1969.]

Finnegan, Ruth. 1992. *Oral Poetry: Its Nature, Significance, and Social Context*. Bloominton and London.

Fish, Stanley. 1980. *Is There a Text in This Class?* Cambridge, Mass.

Fish, Stanley. 1989. *Doing What Comes Naturally: Change, Rhetoric, and the Practice of Theory in Literary and Legal Studies*. Durham and London.

Fodor, Janet Dean. 1977. *Semantics: Theories of Meaning in Generative Grammar*. Cambridge, Mass.

Fokkelman, Jan P. 1998. *Major Poems of the Hebrew Bible at the Interface of Hermeneutics and Structural Analysis. Volume 1: Exodus 15, Deuteronomy 32, and Job 3*. Studia Semitica Neerlandica. Assen.

Foster, Benjamin R. 1974. Humor and cuneiform literature. *Journal of the Ancient Near Eastern Society of Columbia University* 6: 69–85.

Foster, Benjamin R. 1993. *Before the Muses: An Anthology of Akkadian Literature*. Bethesda.

Foster, Benjamin R. 1995. *From Distant Days: Myths, Tales, and Poetry of Ancient Mesopotamia*. Bethesda.

Frame, Grant. 1995. *Rulers of Babylonia from the Second Dynasty of Isin to the End of Assyrian Domination (1157–612 BC)*. Royal Inscriptions of Mesopotamia, Babylonian Periods, 2. Toronto.

Freud, Sigmund. 1953. *The Interpretation of Dreams. The Standard Edition of the Complete Psychological Works of Sigmund Freud*. James Strachey with Anna Freud (trans. & ed.). Vols. 4–5. London. [First published: 1900–1901.]

Gager, John G. (1992). *Curse Tablets and Binding Spells from the Ancient World*. New York & Oxford.

Garr, W. Randall. 1985. *Dialect Geography of Syria-Palestine 1000–586 B.C.E.* Philadelphia.

Garr, W. Randall. 2000. "Image" and "Likeness" in the Inscription from Tell Fakhariyeh." *Israel Exploration Journal* 50: 227–234.

Gelb, I. J. 1963. *A Study of Writing*. Rev. ed. Chicago.

Geller, M. J. 1987. Introduction. In *Figurative Language in the Ancient Near East*. M. Mindlin, M. J. Geller & J. E. Wansbrough (eds.). London, ix–xiii.

Geller, Stephen A. 1979. *Parallelism in Early Hebrew Poetry*. Harvard Semitic Monographs 20. Missoula, Mont.

Geller, Stephen A. 1989. Textual juxtaposition and the comparative study of Biblical and Ancient Near Eastern literature. In *Approaches to Teaching the Hebrew Bible as Literature in Translation*. Barry N. Olshen & Yael S. Feldman (eds.). New York, 72–77.

Gevirtz, Stanley. 1973. *Patterns in the Early Poetry of Israel*. 2nd ed. Studies in Ancient Oriental Civilization 32. Chicago.

Gibbs, Raymond W., Jr. 1994. Figurative thought and figurative language. In *Handbook of Psycholinguistics*. Morton Ann Gernsbacher (ed.). San Diego, 411–446.

Gibson, John C. L. 1982. *Textbook of Syrian Semitic Inscriptions, Volume III: Phoenician Inscriptions*. Oxford.

Gitay, Yehoshua. 1980. Deutero-Isaiah: oral or written? *Journal of Biblical Literature* 99: 185–197.

Goetze, Albrecht. 1936. The t-form of the Old Babylonian verb. *Journal of the American Oriental Society* 56: 297–334.

Goody, Jack. 1977. *The Domestication of the Savage Mind*. Cambridge.

Goody, Jack. 1982. Alternative paths to knowledge in oral and literate cultures. In *Spoken and Written Language: Exploring Orality and Literacy*. Deborah Tannen (ed.). Norwood, 201–215.

Grace, George W. 1987. *The Linguistic Construction of Reality*. Kent.

Green, Georgia M. 1989. *Pragmatics and Natural Language Understanding*. Hillsdale, New Jersey.

Greenstein, Edward L. 1983. How does parallelism mean? In Stephen A. Geller, Edward L. Greenstein & Adele Berlin. *A Sense of Text: The Art of Language in the Study of Biblical Literature*. Jewish Quarterly Review Supplement 1982. Winona Lake, 41–70.

Greenstein, Edward L. 1988. On the prefixed preterite in Biblical Hebrew. *Hebrew Studies* 29: 7–17.

Greenstein, Edward L. 1992. An Introduction to a generative phonology of Biblical Hebrew. In Bodine (1992), 29–40.

Greenstein, Edward L. 1995a. The loneliness of Job. In *The Book of Job in Scripture, Thought, and Art*. Lea Mazor (ed.). Jerusalem, 43–53 (in Hebrew).

Greenstein, Edward L. 1995b. Autobiographies in Ancient Western Asia. In *Civilizations of the Ancient Near*. Jack M. Sasson (ed.). New York. 4: 2421–32.

Greenstein, Edward L. 1997. Kirta. In *Ugaritic Narrative Poetry*. Simon B. Parker (ed.). Writings from the Ancient World. Atlanta, 9–48.

Greenstein, Edward L. 1998a. On a new grammar of Ugaritic. *Israel Oriental Studies* 18: 397–420.

Greenstein, Edward L. 1998b. Reading strategies and the story of Ruth. In *Women in the Hebrew Bible: A Reader*. Alice Bach (ed.). New York and London, 211–231.

Greenstein, Edward L. 1998c. The retelling of the flood story in the Gilgamesh epic. In *Hesed ve-Emet: Studies in Honor of Ernest S. Frerichs*. Jodi Magness and Seymour Gitin (eds.). Atlanta, 197–204.

Greenstein, Edward L. 2000. Direct discourse and parallelism. In *Studies in Bible and Exegesis 5, Presented to Uriel Simon*. Shmuel Vargon et al. (eds.). Ramat-Gan, 33–40 (in Hebrew).

Gruber, Mayer I. 1980. *Aspects of Nonverbal Communication in the Ancient Near East*. Studia Pohl. 2 vols. Rome.

Gumperz, John J. 1973. Language and communication. In *Explorations in Anthropology: Readings in Culture, Man, and Nature*. Morton H. Fried (ed.). New York, 150–161.

Hakham, Amos. 1970. *The Book of Psalms. Da'at Miqra'*. 2 vols. Jerusalem (in Hebrew).

Halliday, M. A. K. 1987. Spoken and written modes of meaning. In *Comprehending Oral and Written Language*. Rosalind Horowitz & S. Jay Samuels (eds.). San Diego, 55–82.

Hallo, William W. 1991. The concept of canonicity in cuneiform and Biblical literature: A comparative appraisal. In *The Biblical Canon in Comparative Perspective*. Scripture in Context IV. K. Lawson Younder, Jr., William W. Hallo & Bernard F. Batto (eds.). Lewiston, 1–19.

Hallpike, C. R. 1979. Classification. *The Foundations of Primitive Thought*. Oxford, 169–235.

Halpern, Baruch, 1983. Doctrine by misadventure: between the Israelite source and the Biblical historian. In *The Poet and the Historian: Essays in Literary and Historical Biblical Criticism*. Richard E. Friedman (ed.). Harvard Semitic Studies 26. Chico, Cal., 41–73.

Harris, William V. 1989. *Ancient Literacy*. Cambridge, Mass.

Havelock, Eric. 1991. The oral-literate equation: A formula for the modern mind. In *Literacy and Orality*. David R. Olson & Nancy Torrance (eds.). Cambridge, 11–27.

Heath, Shirley Brice. 1992. Literacy: An Overview. *International Encyclopedia of Linguistics*. William Bright (ed.). New York. 2: 337–340.

Hecker, Karl. 1974. *Untersuchungen zur akkadischen Epik.* Alter Orient und Altes Testament Sonderreihe 8. Neukirchen-Vluyn.

Held, Moshe. 1969. Rhetorical questions in Ugaritic and Biblical Hebrew. *Eretz-Israel* 9: 71–79.

Held, Moshe, 1970. Studies in Biblical homonyms in the light of Akkadian. *Journal of the Ancient Near Eastern Society of Columbia University* 3: 46–55.

Held, Moshe, 1985. Marginal notes to the Hebrew lexicon. In *Biblical and Related Studies Presented to Samuel Iwry.* Ann Kort & Scott Morschauser (eds.). Winona Lake, 93–103.

Herzog, Eliezra. 1991. *The Triple Rhetorical Argument in the Latter Prophets.* Ph.D. diss., Jewish Theological Seminary, New York.

Hoffner, Harry A., Jr. 1975. Propaganda and political justification in Hittite historiography. In *Unity and Diversity: Essays in the History, Literature, and Religion of the Ancient Near East.* Hans Goedicke & J. J. M. Roberts (eds.). Baltimore, 49–62.

Holladay, William L. 1989. *Jeremiah 2: A Commentary on the Book of the Prophet Jeremiah 26–52.* Hermeneia. Minneapolis.

Horowitz, Rosalind, and Samuels, S. Jay. 1987. Comprehending oral and written language: critical contrasts for literacy and schooling. In *Comprehending Oral and Written Language.* Rosalind Horowitz & S. Jay Samuels (eds.). San Diego, 1–52.

Hout, Theo P. J. van den. 1995. Khattushili III, King of the Hittites. In *Civilizations of the Ancient Near East.* Jack M. Sasson (ed.). New York. 2: 1107–1120.

Hout, T. P. J. van den. 1997. Apology of Hattušili III. In *The Context of Scripture, 1: Canonical Compositions.* William W. Hallo & K. Lawson Younger, Jr. (eds.). Leiden, 199–204.

Houtman, Cornelis. 1993. *Exodus.* Vol. 1. Historical Commentary on the Old Testament. Kampen.

Huehnergard, John. 1996. New directions in the study of Semitic languages. In *The Study of the Ancient Near East in the 21st Century: The William Foxwell Albright Centennial Conference.* Jerrold S. Cooper & Glenn M. Schwartz (eds.). Winona Lake, Indiana, 251–272.

Huehnergard, John. 1997. *A Grammar of Akkadian.* Harvard Semitic Museum Studies 45. Atlanta.

Hurowitz, Victor Avidgor. 1997. A forgotten meaning of *nepeš* in Isaiah LVIII 10. *Vetus Testamentum* 47: 43–52.

Hurowitz, Victor Avigdor. 1999. Canon and canonization in Mesopotamia: Assyriological models or ancient realities? In *Proceedings of the*

Twelfth World Congress of Jewish Studies. Division A: The Bible and Its World. Ron Margolin (ed.). Jerusalem, 1*–12*.

Hurvitz, Avi. 1972. *The Transition Period in Biblical Hebrew: A Study in Post-Exilic Hebrew and Its Implications for the Dating of the Psalms*. Jerusalem (in Hebrew).

Hurvitz, Avi. 1997. The Historical Quest for "Ancient Israel" and the Linguistic Evidence of the Hebrew Bible: Some Methodological Observations. *Vetus Testamentum* 47: 301–315.

Hurvitz, Avi. 1999. The Relevance of Biblical Hebrew Linguistics for the Historical Study of Ancient Israel. *Proceedings of the Twelfth World Congress of Jewish Studies*. Jerusalem. Division A: The Bible and Its World. 21*–33*.

Izre'el, Shlomo. 1988. Review of Garr, *Dialect Geography of Syria-Palestine, 1000–586 B.C.E. Bulletin of the Schools of Oriental Research* 270: 94–97.

Izre'el, Shlomo. 1992. The study of oral poetry: reflections of a neophyte. Can we learn anything on orality from the study of Akkadian poetry, especially in Akhetaton? In Vogelzang & Vanstiphout (1992). 155–225.

Izre'el, Shlomo, and Singer, Itamar. 1990. *The General's Letter from Ugarit: A Linguistic and Historical Reevaluation of RS 20.33* (Ugaritica V, *No. 20*) Tel Aviv.

Jacobs, Louis. 1971. Hermeneutics. *Encyclopaedia Judaica*. Jerusalem, 8: 366–372.

Jakobson, Roman. 1960. Linguistics and Poetics. In *Style in Language*. Thomas A. Sebeok (ed.). Cambridge, Mass., 350–377.

Jakobson, Roman. 1966. Grammatical parallelism and its Russian facet. *Language* 42: 399–429.

Jakobson, Roman, 1981. *Selected Writings, 3: Poetry of Grammar and Grammar of Poetry*. The Hague.

Jewish Publication Society. 1982. *The Writings* כתובים. Philadelphia.

Josephus Flavius. 1978. *Jewish Antiquities, Books I–IV*. Vol. 4. H. St. J. Thackeray (trans.). Loeb Classical Library. Cambridge, Mass./London.

Kaddari, Menahem Z. 1976. *Studies in Biblical Hebrew Syntax*. Ramat-Gan (in Hebrew).

Katz, Jerrold J., and Fodor, Jerry A. 1964. The structure of a semantic theory. In *The Structure of Language: Readings in The Philosophy of Language*. Jerry A. Fodor & Jerrold J. Katz (eds.). Englewood Cliffs, 479–518.

Khan, Geoffrey, 1988. *Studies in Semitic Syntax*. Oxford.

Kovacs, Maureen Gallery. 1989. *The Epic of Gilgamesh*. Stanford.

Kowalski, Vesta M. H. 1996. *Rock of Ages: A Theological Study of the Word* צור *as a Metaphor for Israel's God*. Unpublished Ph.D. diss., Jewish Theological Seminary, New York.

Kristeva, Julia. 1989. *Language — The Unknown: An Initiation into Linguistics*. Trans. Anne M. Menke. New York.

Kugel, James L. 1981. *The Idea of Biblical Poetry: Parallelism and Its History*. New Haven.

Lakoff, George. 1987. *Women, Fire, and Dangerous Things: What Categories Reveal about the Mind*. Chicago.

Lakoff, George, and Johnson, Mark. 1980. *Metaphors We Live By*. Chicago and London.

Lambert, W. G. 1960. *Babylonian Wisdom Literature*. Oxford.

Lambert, W. G. 1968. Literary style in first millennium Mesopotamia. *Journal of the American Oriental Society* 88: 123–132.

Lambert, W. G. 1987. Devotion: The languages of religion and love. In *Figurative Language in the Ancient Near East*. M. Mindlin, M. J. Geller & J. E. Wansbrough (eds.). London, 25–39.

Landsberger, Benno. 1967. Über Farben im Sumerisch-akkadischen. *Journal of Cuneiform Studies* 21: 139–173.

Lehiste, Ilse. 1988. *Lectures on Language Contact*. Cambridge, Mass.

Leitch, Vincent B. 1992. *Cultural Criticism, Literary Theory, Poststructuralism*. New York.

Lichtheim, Miriam. 1973. *Ancient Egyptian Literature, Volume 1: The Old and Middle Kingdoms*. Berkeley.

Lieberman, Saul. 1962. *Hellenism in Jewish Palestine*. New York.

Lieberman, Stephen J. 1987. A Mesopotamian background for the so-called *Aggadic* "measures" of Biblical hermeneutics? *Hebrew Union College Annual* 58: 157–225.

Lieberman, Stephen J. 1990. Canonical and official cuneiform texts: Towards an understanding of Assurbanipal's personal tablet collection. In *Lingering over Words: Studies in Ancient Near Eastern Literature in Honor of William L. Moran*. Tzvi Abusch, John Huehnergard & Piotr Steinkeller (eds.). Harvard Semitic Studies 37. Atlanta, 305–336.

Lichtenstein, Murray H. 1987. Rite and Writ in an Ugaritic Legend: Ritual and Literary Elements in the Curing of King Keret. Unpublished ms.

Livingstone, Alasdair. 1997. Dialogue of pessimism or the Obliging slave. In *The Context of Scripture, Volume 1: Canonical Compositions from the Biblical World*. William W. Hallo & K. Lawson Younger, Jr. (eds.). Leiden, 495–496.

Longacre, Robert E. 1989. *Joseph, A Story of Divine Providence: A Text*

Theoretical and Textlinguistic Analysis of Genesis 37 and 39–48. Winona Lake.

Longacre, Robert E. 1992. Discourse perspective on the Hebrew verb: Affirmation and restatement. In Bodine (1992), 177–189.

Longacre, Robert E. 1995. Building for the worship of God: Exodus 25: 1–30: 10. In *Discourse Analysis of Biblical Literature*. Walter R. Bodine (ed.). SBL Semeia Studies. Atlanta, 21–49.

Loprieno, Antonio. 1996. Defining Egyptian literature. In *The Study of the Ancient Near East in the 21st Century: The William Foxwell Albright Centennial Conference*. Jerrold S. Cooper & Glenn M. Schwartz (eds.). Winona Lake, Indiana, 209–232.

Malamat, Abraham. 1990. "You Shall Love Your Neighbor as Yourself": A case of misinterpretation? In *Die Hebräische Bibel und ihre zweifache Nachgeschichte: Festschrift für Rolf Rendtorff zum 65. Geburstag*. Erhard Blum, Christian Macholz & Ekkehard W. Stegemann (eds.). Neukirchen-Vluyn, 111–115.

Malone, Joseph L. 1993. *Tiberian Hebrew Phonology*. Winona Lake.

Malul, Meir. 1985. More on *paḥad yiṣḥāq* (Genesis XXXI 42, 53) and the Oath by the Thigh. *Vetus Testamentum* 35: 192–200.

Marcus, David. 1977. Animal similes in Assyrian royal inscriptions. *Orientalia* 40: 86–106.

McKane, William. 1996. *A Critical and Exegetical Commentary on Jeremiah*. 2 vols. International Critical Commentary. Edinburgh.

Michalowski, Piotr. 1990. Presence at the Creation. In *Lingering over Words: Studies in Ancient Near Eastern Literature in Honor of William L. Moran*. Tzvi Abusch, John Huehnergard & Piotr Steinkeller (eds.). Harvard Semitic Studies 37. Atlanta, 381–396.

Michalowski, Piotr. 1996. Sailing to Babylon, Reading the Dark Side of the Moon. In *The Study of the Ancient Near East in the Twenty-First Century: The William Foxwell Albright Centennial Conference*. Jerrold S. Cooper & Glenn M. Schwartz (eds.). Winona Lake, 177–193.

Miner, Earl. 1990. *Comparative Poetics: An Intercultural Essay on Theories of Literature*. Princeton.

Moran, William L. 1975. The Syrian scribe of the Jerusalem Amarna letters. In *Unity and Diversity: Essays in the History, Literature, and Religion of the Ancient Near East*. Hans Goedicke & J. J. M. Roberts (eds.). Baltimore & London, 146–166.

Muraoka, T. (ed.). 1998. *Semantics of Ancient Hebrew*. Abr-Nahrain Supplement 6. Louvain.

Myhill, John. 1997. What is universal and what is language-specific in emotion words? Evidence from Biblical Hebrew. *Pragmatics & Cognition* 5: 79–129.

Naḥmanides, Moses. 1959. *Commentary on the Torah*. Vol. 1. Charles D. Chavel (ed.). Jerusalem (in Hebrew).

Narasimhan, R. 1991. Literacy: its characterization and implications. In *Literacy and Orality*. David R. Olson & Nancy Torrance (eds.). Cambridge, 177–197.

Niccacci, Alviero. 1990. *The Syntax of the Verb in Classical Hebrew Prose*. W. G. E. Watson (trans.). Journal for the Study of the Old Testament Supplement. Sheffield.

Niccacci, Alviero. 1994. The Stele of Mesha and the Bible: verbal system and narrativity. *Orientalia* 63: 226–248.

Niditch, Susan. 1996. *Oral World and Written Word: Ancient Israelite Literature*. Louisville.

Niehoff, Maren. 1992. "A Dream Which Is Not Interpreted Is Like a Letter Which Is Not Read". *Journal of Jewish Studies* 43: 58–84.

O'Connor, M. 1980. *Hebrew Verse Structure*. Winona Lake.

Ogihara, Toshiyuki. 1996. *Tense, Attitude, and Scope*. Studies in Linguistics and Philosophy 58. Dordrecht.

Olson, David R., Hildyard, A., and Torrance, Nancy. 1985. *Literacy, Language, and Learning: The Nature and Consequences of Reading and Writing*. Cambridge.

Ong, Walter J. 1982. *Orality and Literacy: The Technologizing of the Word*. London and New York.

Oppenheim, A. Leo. 1956. *The Interpretation of Dreams in the Ancient Near East with a Translation of an Assyrian Dream-Book*. Transactions of the American Philosophical Society 46/3. Philadelphia, 177–373.

Oppenheim, A. Leo (ed.). 1961. *The Assyrian Dictionary*. Vol. 21 (Z). Chicago.

Oppenheim, A. Leo. 1964. *Ancient Mesopotamia*. Chicago.

Otten, Heinrich. 1981. *Die Apologie Hattušilis III: Das Bild der Überlieferung*. Wiesbaden.

Parker, Simon B. 1989. *The Pre-Biblical Narrative Tradition: Essays on the Ugaritic Poems* Keret *and* Aqhat. Society of Biblical Literature Resources for Biblical Study 24. Atlanta.

Parpola, Simo. 1997. *The Standard Babylonian Epic of Gilgamesh*. State Archives of Assyria Cuneiform Texts 1. Helsinki.

Philo of Alexandria. 1966. *Philo with an English Translation*. Vol. 6. F. H. Colson (trans.). Loeb Classical Library. London & Cambridge, Mass.

Polak, Frank H. 1989. Epic formulas in Biblical narrative — frequency and distribution. *Les actes du second colloque international "Bible et informatique: méthodes, outils, résultats."* Genève, 435–488.

Polak, Frank H. 1998. The Oral and the Written: syntax, stylistics, and the development of Biblical prose narrative. *Journal of the Ancient Near Eastern Society* 26: 59–105.

Propp, William H. C. 1998. *Exodus 1–18.* Anchor Bible. New York.

Rabinowitz, Isaac. 1993. *A Witness Forever: Ancient Israel's Perception of Literature and the Resultant Hebrew Bible.* Bethesda.

Rabinowitz, Peter J. 1987. *Before Reading: Narrative Conventions and the Politics of Interpretation.* Ithaca & London.

Reiner, Erica. 1985. *Your thwarts in pieces, Your mooring rope cut: Poetry from Babylonia and Assyria.* Michigan Studies in the Humanites 5. Ann Arbor.

Reiner, Erica (ed.). 1992. *The Assyrian Dictionary.* Volume 17: Š III. Chicago, Glückstadt.

Robinson, Robert B. 1999. "Sing Us One of the Songs of Zion": Poetry and Theology in the Hebrew Bible. In *The Labour of Reading: Desire, Alienation, and Biblical Interpretation.* Fiona C. Black, Roland Boer, & Erin Runions (eds.). SBL Semeia Studies. Atlanta, 87–106.

Rochberg-Halton, Francesca. 1984. Canonicity in cuneiform texts. *Journal of Cuneiform Studies* 36: 127–144.

Rooker, Mark F. 1990. *Biblical Hebrew in Transition: The Language of the Book of Ezekiel.* Journal for the Study of the Old Testament Supplement 90. Sheffield.

Rubinstein, Eliezer. 1998. *Syntax and Semantics: Studies in Biblical and Modern Hebrew.* Tel Aviv (in English and Hebrew).

Rummel, Stan. 1981. Narrative structures in the Ugaritic texts. In *Ras Shamra Parallels Volume III.* Stan Rummel (ed.). Analecta Orientalia 51. Rome, 221–332.

Sapir, Edward. 1968 [1921]. *Language: An Introduction to the Study of Speech.* New York.

Sarna, Nahum M. 1991. *The JPS Torah Commentary: Exodus* שמות. Philadelphia.

Sasson, Jack M. 1992. Time...to Begin. In *"Sha'arei Talmon": Studies in the Bible, Qumran, and the Ancient Near East Presented to Shemaryahu Talmon.* Michael Fishbane, Emanuel Tov with Weston W. Fields (eds.). Winona Lake, 183–194.

Scanlin, Harold P. 1992. The Study of Semantics in General Linguistics. In Bodine (1992), 125–136.

Scholem, Gershom. 1971. Kabbalah. In *Encyclopedia Judaica.* Jerusalem. 10: 489–653.

Searle, John R. 1969. *Speech Acts.* London.

Searle, John R. 1979. *Expression and Meaning.* Cambridge.

Searle, John R. 1983. *Intentionality.* Cambridge.

Segert, Stanislav. 1984. *A Basic Grammar of the Ugaritic Language.* Berkeley.

Selms, A. van. 1971–72. Motivated interrogative sentences in Biblical Hebrew. *Semitics* 2: 143–149.

Shusterman, Richard. 1991. Beneath interpretation. In *The Interpretive Turn: Philosophy, Science, Culture.* David R. Hiley, James F. Bohman & Richard Shusterman (eds.). Ithaca and London, 102–128.

Soden, Wolfram von. 1932–33. Der hymnisch-epische Dialekt des Akkadischen. *Zeitschrift für die Assyriologie* 40: 163–227; 41: 90–183.

Soll, Will. 1992. Acrostic. In *Anchor Bible Dictionary.* David Noel Freedman (ed.). New York, 1: 58–60.

Speiser, E. A. 1967. The Case of the Obliging Servant. In *Oriental and Biblical Studies: Collected Writings of E. A. Speiser.* J. J. Finkelstein & Moshe Greenberg (eds.). Philadelphia, 344–366.

Steiner, George. 1975. *After Babel: Aspects of Language and Translation.* London.

Steiner, George. 1978. Whorf, Chomsky, and the Student of Literature. *On Difficulty and Other Essays.* New York and Oxford, 137–163.

Stienstra, Nelly. 1993. *YHWH is the Husband of His People: Analysis of a Biblical Metaphor with Special Reference to Translation.* Kampen.

Straton, Shirley F. (ed.). 1987. *Literary Theories in Praxis.* Philadelphia.

Talmon, Shemaryahu. 1987. *Har and Midbār:* An antithetical pair of Biblical motifs. In *Figurative Language in the Ancient Near East.* M. Mindlin, M. J. Geller & J. E. Wansbrough (eds.). London, 117–142.

Tannen, Deborah. 1982. The oral/literate continuum in discourse. In *Spoken and Written Language: Exploring Orality and Literacy.* Deborah Tannen (ed.). Norwood, 1–16.

Tannen, Deborah. 1992. Literacy: sociolinguistic aspects. *International Encyclopedia of Linguistics.* William Bright (ed.). New York. 2: 346–349.

Tate, Marvin E. 1990. *Psalms 51–100.* Word Biblical Commentary. Dallas.

Thomas, Rosalind. 1992. *Literacy and Orality in Ancient Greece.* Cambridge.

Tigay, Jeffrey H. 1996. *The JPS Torah Commentary: Deuteronomy* דברים. Philadelphia.

Tov, Emanuel. 1995. Letters of the cryptic A script and paleo-Hebrew letters used as scribal marks in some Qumran scrolls. *Dead Sea Discoveries* 2: 330–339.

Ullmann, Stephen. 1966. Semantic Universals. In *Universals of Language*. 2nd ed. Joseph H. Greenberg (ed.). Cambridge, Mass., 217–262.

Vall, Gregory. 1993. *From Womb to Tomb: Poetic Imagery and the Book of Job*. Unpublished Ph.D. diss., Catholic University of America, Washington, D.C.

Van Seters, John. 1994. *The Life of Moses: The Yahwist as Historian in Exodus-Numbers*. Louisville.

Vanstiphout, Herman. 1995. Memory and literacy in Ancient Western Asia. In *Civilizations of the Ancient Near East*. Jack M. Sasson (ed.). New York. 4: 2181–2196.

Vanstiphout, Herman L. J. 1998. Reflections on the dream of Lugalbanda (A typological and interpretive analysis of LH 322–365). In *Intellectual Life of the Ancient Near East. Papers Presented at the 43rd Recontre assyriologique internationale, Prague, July 1–5, 1996*. Jiří Prosecky (ed.). Prague, 397–412.

Vogelzang, Marianna E., and Vanstiphout, Herman L. J. (eds.). 1992. *Mesopotamian Epic Literature: Oral or Aural?* Lewiston.

Vogelzang, M. E., and Vanstiphout, H. L. J. (eds.). 1996. *Mesopotamian Poetic Language: Sumerian and Akkadian*. Cuneiform Monographs 6. Groningen.

Watters, William R. 1976. *Formula Criticism and the Poetry of the Old Testament*. Beiheft zur Zeitschrift für die alttestamentliche Wissenschaft 138. Berlin.

Weinreich, Uriel. 1974. *Languages in Contact: Findings and Problems*. The Hague and Paris.

Weiser, Artur. 1962. *The Psalms: A Commentary*. Trans. Herbert Hartwell. Old Testament Library. London.

Westenholz, Joan Goodnick. 1992. Oral traditions and written texts in the Cycle of Akkade. In Vogelzang & Vanstiphout (1992), 123–154.

Whallon, William. 1983. *Inconsistencies: Studies in the New Testament, the* Inferno, Othello, *and* Beowulf. Cambridge/Totowa, N.J.

Whorf, Benjamin Lee. 1956. *Language, Thought, and Reality: Selected Writings of Benjamin Lee Whorf*. John B. Carroll (ed.). Cambridge, Mass.

Wierzbicka, Anna. 1972. *Semantic Primitives*. Linguistische Forschungen 22. Frankfurt.

Wierzbicka, Anna. 1991. *Cross-Cultural Pragmatics: The Semantics of Human Interaction*. Trends in Linguistics Studies and Monographs 53. Berlin & New York.

Willbern, David. 1989. Reading after Freud. In *Contemporary Literary Theory*. G. Douglas Atkins & Laura Morrow (eds.). Amherst, 158–179.

Wilson, John A. 1969. The Interpretation of Dreams. In *Ancient Near Eastern Texts Relating to the Old Testament*. James B. Pritchard (ed.). 3rd ed. Princeton, 495.

Wolf, Herbert M. 1967. *The Apology of Hattušiliš Compared with Other Political Self-Justifications of the Ancient Near East*. Ph.D. diss., Brandeis University.

Young, I. M. 1998. Israelite literacy: interpreting the evidence. *Vetus Testamentum* 48: 239–253, 408–422.

Zadok, Ran. 1982. Remarks on the Inscription of *HDYSʕY* from Tall Fakhariya. *Tel Aviv* 9: 117–129.

Zeligs, Dorothy F. 1986. *Moses: A Psychodynamic Study*. New York.

WORKING WITH A LITTLE MORE DATA
NEW FINDS IN THE TWENTIETH CENTURY:
THE SEMITIC LANGUAGES OF THE ANCIENT WORLD

BRUCE ZUCKERMAN

It's a well known and oft-told anecdote, especially among students who received their education in Semitic studies in the Near Eastern Languages and Cultures Department at Harvard University, including the occasional interloper there, such as myself. The story involves one of the central, creative figures in the study of Comparative Semitics of the Twentieth Century, Thomas O. Lambdin. The story goes that he was teaching his class in Comparative Semitics to a group of 20 or so graduate students. As usual, these novitiates were scribbling briskly to keep up with the pace of Lambdin's lecture. Then he stopped rather suddenly and peered over the rims of the half-glasses he normally wore. This brought everything to a grinding halt as 20 pairs of eyes looked up from their notes with an expression of mild surprise. His statement, long remembered, came almost as a rebuke: "I don't know if you've noticed it," he declared sharply, "but *we work with no data in this field."*

I think this remark made a deep and lasting impression for two reasons. First, it epitomized the mindset of certainly one of the keenest linguistic thinkers of our time, as he tried to make some relational sense among the collection of languages we still rather quaintly persist in naming after Noah's more sedentary son. It is also a remark of profound humility, a *caveat* to all who would endeavor to explain the ancient written *corpora* from the Near Eastern world and use them further to understand the civilizations and cultures from which they emerged. Perhaps it is not quite of the proportion of Dante's motto upon entry into the Inferno — "Abandon hope, all ye who enter here" — but it is a warning to tread rather softly, since the theoretical structures underfoot may be as slight as a house of cards. No surprise, then, that when his students produced a *Festschrift* in Lambdin's honor, they memorialized this endeavor to explain the world of ancient Semitic Linguistics with the title *"Working with No Data"* (Golomb and Hollis 1987).

The second reason why Lambdin's remark has made a lasting impression is also the most obvious: because it is just so fundamentally *true* — a point that, had it not been called to our attention by so eminent a figure, we might desire conveniently to forget. After all, one likes to think of the pursuit of knowledge in the most positive, optimistic terms. In our particular case, we like to think that not only are ancient textual puzzles set before our eyes in order for us to solve them; but we also want to believe that given enough time, enough ingenuity, the right insights, the right approaches, these puzzles are not only solvable but, ultimately, they *will be* solved. Alas, what Lambdin's dictum reminds us is that all this just *might* be so, except for one insurmountable problem: *we work with no data in this field.* Or to put this another way: the data that we have are statistically insignificant and, by-and-large, uncontrollable.

You do not have to be a professional in the modern study of linguistics to grasp the problem. If you wish to understand the phonological, morphological and syntactical structure of languages, their dialectology, how they interact or any other aspect of this field of study, you not only need a large data base but you also need to be able to classify your data with a fair degree of precision: for example, who said what? how did they say it? where did they come from? when did they say it? But in the field of ancient Semitic studies, we are hardly ever able to answer these questions to a degree that a modern linguist would find satisfactory. Even where the data are fullest, in Assyriological studies, for example, we never seem to have a genuine control of the texts; we never can quite answer questions such as those posed above to a sufficient degree so we can state: *now* we control the data. And when one turns to a field such as Northwest Semitic studies, the problems involved in working with statistically insignificant data in an uncontrolled context become enormous.

Nonetheless, it would be unfair to paint the overall picture solely in such gloomy terms. Over the last century the picture has changed dramatically and much to the better. If we *still* basically work with no data in this field, at least there is a *little more* data than we had before; indeed, more, I imagine, than anyone at the beginning of the 20th century might have dreamed possible.

There are a number of means by which we can assess the increase in data over the last century. If I may confine myself to my own area of expertise, the Northwest Semitic languages and literatures, we can simply tick off the extraordinary discoveries that have altered and augmented the data in such profound ways. We might begin with the Elephantine discoveries that happened near the turn of the 19th century; note as well the Ugaritic corpus — perhaps the single greatest boon to biblical and Northwest Semitic studies of the century — add, of course, the various additions to First Temple Hebrew that come from Lachish, Arad, Beer Sheva and so many other sites; the various epigraphic discoveries that have allowed us to develop our knowledge of other West Semitic languages, at least to a limited degree, in Phoenician, Aramaic, Ammonite, Moabite, Trans-Jordanian (that is, Deir Alla) and Edomite; we also had better include the Dead Sea Scroll discoveries in all their shapes and forms as well and, to some degree, the corpus of tablets from Ebla. It is an extraordinary list in the Northwest Semitic field *alone*, and there are undoubtedly some that I have neglected to name that ought to be added to this "hit-parade" of discoveries. One could just as easily compile an equally impressive a list of such discoveries on the East Semitic and South Semitic fronts.

One could also look at the new discoveries of the 20th century in terms of the impact they have made on our tools for study. For example, the impact on lexicography has been profound — from the *Chicago Assyrian Dictionary* through the successive editions of *Koehler-Baumgartner* to the newest projects such as the *Dictionary of Classical Hebrew* and the *Complete Aramaic Lexicon*. In terms of morphological study, it need only be noted that substantial studies have been done on all the ancient Semitic languages because these were absolutely necessary in order to assess and assimilate the influx of new data. Indeed, major grammars have been written on languages that we did not even know existed a century ago.

Again, a small example from the field of Northwest Semitic studies may be allowed to illustrate the larger point. In the mid-1980s, W. Randall Garr published his study, *A Dialect Geography of Syria-Palestine, 1000–586 BCE*. To some degree this title is misleading and almost oxymoronic. Dialect Geography, as it is usually understood, should not have a significant historical dimension, let alone an historical dimension of four to five centuries. Rather, it should present a profile of languages and dialects in contact at a discrete, given period — ideally, the shorter the better. Of course, in the case of ancient Semitic languages, the state of the data is hardly ideal. Nor is it my intention to criticize Garr for his title or for the endeavor that he undertook in his work. Quite to the contrary. I have no doubt that he understood the issue raised above better than most.[1] The point he was trying to make, and which I wish to reemphasize here, is that by the mid-1980s we had accumulated enough data that we could actually begin to *think* seriously about dialectology in the Northwest Semitic languages. At the beginning of the 20th century, that would have been a more remote possibility. Today — however inadequately, however speculatively, we can actually, if tentatively, begin to think about the sorts of issues Garr raised in what might be characterized as a valid, academic fashion. Of course, one might note that Zelig Harris already began this sort of inquiry

---

[1] See, e.g., his comments, *ibid.* pp. 9–10.

decades earlier with his *Development of the Canaanite Dialects*; still, it is nonetheless striking how much more data Garr had to work with as we began to near the end of the century. Should he wish to revise his grammar now at the beginning of the Twenty-First Century, he would have a sizable amount of new data to examine that would help refine our admittedly hazy picture of Northwest Semitic dialects all the more.

I could go on like this for some time, but, to be blunt, there seems little point in belaboring the obvious — nor is it the best use of my time and expertise in trying to assess the nature and the impact of the new data we have for ancient Semitic languages from the Twentieth Century. We all understand the accomplishments of the past, but a salient concern that particularly remains of issue, at least in my view, is what do we do about all this acquired data today and into the Twenty-First Century? It is this concern, upon which I wish to focus our attention for the remainder of this discussion.

First of all, one might note that I have intentionally characterized the various written records uncovered in the Twentieth Century in terms of their data-content rather than simply labeling them as "texts." This distinction between "data" and "text" is, I believe, worth maintaining. In terms of "finds" of a written nature, we obviously begin with some manner of physical objects — clay tablets impressed with wedges, stone stelae incised with chiseled indentations or sculpted *bas reliefs*, papyri or animal skins overlaid with inks, for example. At the end point of the academic endeavor, the information derived from these physical objects are published as various, classified texts. The basis upon which scholars derive "texts" from physical objects are the data, that is, a depiction of those physical remains determined by analysis to convey linguistically significant information — as opposed to extraneous physical remains such as gouges, dents, chips, abrasions, flecked off surfaces, etc., that get in the way of this information. The data are the signal which must be separated from the noise so that they can subsequently be "decoded," as it were, into texts.

Note, I emphasized that the data are a *depiction* of the information. After all, as everyone who works on ancient inscriptions well understands, the data are in the eye of the beholder. There is inevitably a degree — usually an uncomfortably high degree — of subjectivity involved in demarcating the signal from the noise. Of course, this is the essence of the philological endeavor: a number of scholars lay out a variety of informed opinions assessing the data which are in turn judged by their peers. The ultimate aim, in the long term, is to build a consensus within the scholarly community as to what the texts we derive from the data can teach us about the ancient world.

That would basically be all that needs to be said about the data, except for one rather crucial point: those aforementioned physical objects, the greater and lesser finds of the Twentieth Century, are not immutable. This century has taught us a hard lesson: that ancient remains, especially once they have been recovered and brought into the modern world and its less than ideal environment, cannot be depended upon to stay the way they were at the time of their discovery. Even under the best conditions, the inks fade, the tablets break and chip, the skins dissolve, the stones abrade, the papyri fall apart and crumble. And the more these objects are handled, so that scholars can study and learn from the texts, the more likely it is that such mishaps will occur. Moreover, conditions all too frequently are far from the best: The decades of conflict that have torn apart Lebanon can hardly have boded well for the early alphabetic inscriptions that were the pride of National Museum in Beirut. One can only shudder to think what may be occurring now to the Assyriological collections (discovered and undiscovered) in Baghdad and elsewhere in Iraq.

Because the physical objects are not safe from harm, the time necessary for acquiring the data always tends to be running down and ultimately out. So this makes the data important, indeed crucial, since in many cases it is the existing data upon which we must depend more than the physical objects *themselves* for interpretation of ancient texts. The trouble is, the data *also* are not immutable, especially in the form in which they are most viable, namely as visual, usually photographic, images. Again the history of the 20th century has taught a hard lesson. The original negatives that are the basis for the pictures of the Elephantine corpus published by Sachau and Sayce have been lost, presumably destroyed during World War II. A number of negatives of the Dead Sea Scrolls are no longer traceable; others have been seriously damaged, often beyond repair or recovery. One can journey to many museums and libraries and encounter similar, unfortunate circumstances. In many instances, the biggest problem is not so much determining whether the original photographic images are in decent condition but whether they can actually be found at all.

I think the reason this is often so is because original photographic images are not well understood within the scholarly community nor among the librarians and curators who have responsibility for maintaining them — especially in terms of the vital role they play in preserving the data. Rather, the tendency is to look at these images more as a means to an end — namely, the publication of the texts — rather than as an intrinsically important end in themselves. There is a tendency to assume that, once the final publication of an edition has been achieved — transcription, commentary with the printed "plates" at the back — the role of the original images ceases to be particularly important. They can be relegated to wherever one relegates such things in museum or library storage (if, indeed, they are preserved at all). After all, if anyone wishes actually to look at the data, he or she can find it at the end of the given text-volume. In some cases, the data are conveniently recorded as microfilms or fiche, and now, more recently, as low resolution digital images. To most scholars these become the data — the point of reference for reading the texts — rather than the original pictures themselves.

As a general rule, rarely are the original images given the respect they deserve or are they kept as archivally pristine as they ought to be. And yet, to my mind, as we survey the finds of the Twentieth Century and our ongoing efforts to turn their data into texts, *nothing* is more crucial. The reason is simple: Images of the sort scholars usually rely upon for the data, be they plates printed in the back of volumes, microfilm or fiche frames or the typical digital images — *all* such data are largely inadequate for serious analysis. I have had occasion in the past to write about the technical reasons why this is so;[2] consequently, I will not restate the same points here. Let me simply summarize by noting that nothing thus far surpasses the high resolution and detail to be found in the original photographic negatives and transparencies made of various ancient, inscribed objects when they were newly discovered and in their best condition.

A quick example to illustrate the point. Almost everyone who has worked on the Ugaritic corpus has been forced, until relatively recently, to rely on the pictures printed in the back of A. Herdner's *Corpus des Tablettes en Cunéiformes Alphabétiques* (*CTA*) as the basic source for the primary, visual data. Nonetheless, anyone who has tried to read these texts sign-by-sign based on the *CTA* plates knows how inadequate they are as the foundation for serious philological work. In 1997 a team of scholars led by Wayne Pitard, went back to the Collège de France in Paris to examine and copy the original negatives made in the 1930s from which the *CTA* plates were printed, as part of a cooperative effort between the Mission de Ras Shamra, the Ugaritic Text Digital Edition Project of the University of Illinois and the University of Southern California (USC), and USC's West Semitic Research Project. Over the last several years those of us involved have begun to assess the results of this effort and can say without equivocation: the difference between the negatives and

---

2   See B. Zuckerman and K. Zuckerman, Bringing the Dead Sea Scrolls Back to Life; A New Evaluation of the Photographic and Electronic Imaging of the Dead Sea Scrolls, *Dead Sea Discoveries* 3 (1996), 178–207; *idem*, Photography of Manuscripts, *The Oxford Encyclopedia of Near Eastern Archaeology* (5 vols.; E. Meyers *et al.*, eds.; New York 1997), vol. 4: 336–347; *idem*, Photography and Computer Imaging, *Encyclopedia of the Dead Sea Scrolls* (L. Schiffman, *et al.*, eds.; New York 2000) 669–675.

the published renditions of same in *CTA* is like night-and-day. Instead of the somewhat murky, low contrast, poorly screened, hard-to-see images found in *CTA*, the original negatives are amazingly sharp and clear, containing, in terms of dynamic range and subtlety, easily double the visual data that one can see in the published versions. Moreover, there are a number of images that had never been published (and, alas, a few images documented in the *CTA* volume that were no longer in the Collège's files and which are presumably misplaced or lost). Indeed, when compared to images that either Pitard or I, myself, made of these same texts mostly in the 1990s, they hold up remarkably well. Granted, because the newer images were done with better films, at higher magnification and with more sophisticated lighting techniques than the earlier pictures, the latter often can show a detail of information missed in the images of a half a century ago. On the other hand, the tablets were in far better condition then than they are today; so there are a number of instances in which the older images preserve data that have been lost in the intervening time.[3] Of course, the point is not whether the older images or the newer images are better; they need to be used *together* in order to gain the best data from which to derive the best readings of the texts. The sum is greater than the parts.

This concept of bringing things together leads me to the next point for consideration. As we stand at the turning point of the millennium, it is my firm belief that the study of ancient documents — especially those ancient documents that are of central concern to the field of ancient Semitic linguistics and philology — also are at a turning point. The way we look at ancient inscriptions — the way we approach the data — is in the process of dramatic change. Already the next generation of scholars is beginning to visualize the data in a largely different manner than has been the case for nearly all of the last century; and as the new century begins, this change will only accelerate. The force behind this change is technological, reflecting especially the impact of digital imaging and enhancement tools that are now becoming routinely available at relatively low cost to virtually anyone who wishes to invest a little time into becoming minimally computer-literate.

Conceptually, the reason these new technologies offer such significant advantages is that they allow the scholar to use various types of data in combination with the result being, once again, a sum greater than the parts. The basic reason this is so can be summarized in one word: precision. The standard software packages available for analysis of image

---

[3]   For an illustration of this, see B. Zuckerman, M. Lundberg, L. Hunt, InscriptiFact: A Networked Database of Ancient Near Eastern Inscriptions; Project Overview, on the InscriptiFact Website (www.inscriptifact.com/information), fig. 3.

data allow one to make comparisons with a precision that proves to be vital but which previously was all but impossible to achieve.

Let us consider this issue of precision in terms of its impact on photographic documentation. As is well known, this has been my major area of interest for some time. One concern that has always been at the forefront of this work is methodology: the procedure of documentation; how one can most effectively record the visual data. Over the years, as our West Semitic Research Project teams have worked on various projects, we have evolved detailed methods of approach to achieve these ends. But, over the last several years, I must say that the impact of computer imaging technology has forced me and my colleagues to rethink what we do in rather profound ways; and from a methodological standpoint, this is only the beginning.

Where this has proven especially to be so is in terms of inscriptions that have a significant depth dimension, for example, cuneiform tablets, stone stelae, seals and seal impressions. In all such cases one positions the light in order to create shadow-detail that will in turn reveal the disposition of the signs. This is a subtle business, since different shadow-details will appear or disappear depending on where the light is placed. In the past our tendency had been to try various lighting angles and then choose the one that best seemed to convey the most information, the best depiction of the data. On occasion, we might choose more than one lighting angle, but this was never really done in a systematic manner. Why not? I think the reason is that we never really visualized the data in an inscription as emerging from a combination of images; rather, the tendency was to find the *best* angle (or maybe the one or two best) and look at the data from that perspective or those perspectives alone.

The impact of computer imaging techniques has changed the way we now look at such things because of our ability to make precise matches. That is, using standard algorithms in any imaging software package, we can take images shot from different light angles (also different levels of magnification) and put them at precisely the same scale. Then we can, in turn, look at individual signs in close coordination and see how they appear in these different lights. In this way, the signs can often be "pieced" together from the combination of images. Indeed, it often proves the case that a given sign is not at all clear as one superficially looks at the images with different lights, even when one places them side-by-side. It is only when one puts them at precisely the same scale on a computer screen — especially if they are superimposed — and looks at how the matched images coordinate that the subtleties of the patterns emerge. In fact, it is often now the case, particularly in areas where a text has significant damage, that one only sees the best depiction of the data after such close, coordinated comparisons are made. Naturally, that has changed the way we now document an inscription. The policy now is *always* to shoot at least two contrasting light angles (and, where necessary, more than that), since we really cannot be sure what there is to see until the data are brought together in combination.

More recently, technological advances have allowed researchers to make even more dramatic strides in the application of contrasting light angles. Thomas Malzbender and Daniel Gelb (the latter, coincidentally, the grandson of the illustrious Semitist, I. J. Gelb!) of Hewlett-Packard Imaging Laboratories have developed an imaging/lighting hardware/software package that allows one to view a given ancient inscription with dynamic light. The system has proven to be particularly effective on cuneiform tablets although the potential application of this imaging system to other sorts of three-dimensional inscriptions is most promising. Using a digital camera mounted on top of a domed structure, the device fires off a succession of digital pictures, each of which is illuminated by an individual strobe light source fixed on the dome at evenly spaced and distributed lighting angles — some 40 to 50 lighting angles in all. Then using these 40–50 data images as points of reference, their program amalgamates and extrapolates these images into a single, integrated view that allows one to see the target at any light angle — including angles that were not actually shot by the camera. As one moves a control device around, e.g., a computer mouse, the light also moves and plays at different angles across the surface. The result is the equivalent of having at one's command a very precise beam of light that can be placed at any angle at any given moment. As the virtual light moves, the play of shadows changes, making the subtle indentations on a clay surface appear in sharp relief in direct response to the precise lighting angles optimal for visualizing them. This process is particular effective for capturing signs on curved surfaces, (e.g., the typical obverse side of a cuneiform tablet), where no single lighting angle is best for visualizing all the indentations of the cuneiform wedges. Moreover, with a couple of clicks, Malzbender and Gelb can alter the reflectivity characteristics of the surface to startling effect. For example, they can make the dull matte finish of the clay surface become "super-shiny," as though it had been dipped in molten metal. Once again, with this lighting effect, nuanced details suddenly become clear that were not visible before. Although the system now exists only as a single prototype, it has been tested on a wide variety of three-dimensional inscriptions, including a significant sample of tablets from the Yale Babylonian Collection, with a great degree of success. Various other enhancements, e.g., move and zoom capabilities, are part of the soft imaging package with more being added all the time, as Malzbender and Gelb continue to develop and elaborate this imaging system.

It should be noted that such an imaging system is only practical due to the precision of computer imaging techniques. In this case some 50 separate images have been integrated into a larger whole, a process that can only be achieved if registration is precisely consistent from image to image. The degree of accuracy required for this sort of matching can only be achieved in the realm of digital imaging.[4]

This ability to make precise matches also has an impact on how one visualizes inscriptions of essentially two dimensions, for example, ostraca, scrolls and papyri inscribed with inks. In this case the ability to do fragment matching and alignments becomes especially significant. As we all know, fragments of a given inscription are often separated or simply get lost. Not infrequently, a given document needs to be pieced together from the holdings of more than one museum, library or private collection. Even when fragments have been matched by conservators and curators, the physical alignments are often imperfect, which can in turn skew proper coordination and therefore interpretation. Standard software algorithms allow one to collect images of individual fragments from any number of pictures in which they occur, put them all at a common scale and then move them around electronically like jigsaw puzzle pieces. By the same token, one can fine tune fragment alignments electronically, even make "repairs" in areas where documents have been torn, etc. Already a few articles have appeared that use this ability to repiece documents together;[5] I know of one major effort now under way to repiece an entire Coptic papyrus manuscript from numerous randomly placed fragments.[6] In so far as I am aware this will be the first sophisticated example of electronic papyrology, but, undoubtedly, it will not be the last.

Another technique that works in close concert with those noted above involves the ability to "cut out" individual, clearly read signs or groups of signs in combination and move them to areas of an inscription where

---

4   See further, M. Lundberg, Reading Ancient Inscriptions in Virtual Light, www.usc.edu/ dept/LAS/wsrp/information/article.html. An unsigned article discussing the process also appears on the Hewlett-Packard website, www.hpl.hp.com/news/2000/oct-dec/ 3dimaging.html. For an online demonstration that shows some of the aspects of this imaging system, see www.hpl.hp.com/news/2000/oct-dec/3dimaging_files/tablet_ demo.html.

5   See, e.g., B. Zuckerman and M. Lundberg, New Aramaic Fragments from Qumran Cave One, *Newsletter, The Comprehensive Aramaic Lexicon* 12 (Autumn 1996), 1–5. For a popular discussion of the process involved, see J. N. Wilford, Digitized Fragments Help Decipher Dead Sea Scrolls, *New York Times*, April 2, 1996, pp. B7–B9.

6   This work is being done by Gesina Robertson on a manuscript from the Staatliche Museen in Berlin, under the auspices of the Institute of Antiquity and Christianity.

a reading is unclear. By superimposing the clear signs over the areas in question, one can frequently make convincing determinations as to what the readings are. In most cases this is done by process of elimination. That is, it is not so much the case that one can determine, for certain, that this trace of a sign coincides with only this particular clear letter; more typically, one can simply eliminate a given group of signs from serious consideration because they cannot possibly match. This ability to narrow down the range of choices then allows the interpreter to bring in other means of discrimination more decisively — for example, phonological, morphological or contextual considerations — and thereby reach a more informed conclusion. This same ability to move around signs also allows one better to judge whether various proposed restorations can actually fit in the lacunae of a given inscription. Again, it is not so much a case of being able to determine for sure that a particular restoration should be made; rather, one uses this technique to determine which of the competing proposals can be excluded either because they overfill or underfill the available space.

I also want to make reference to the drawing of texts and the related concern of paleography. All standard software imaging packages contain highly effective drawing programs that can allow even the minimally skilled to compete on the same level with the best graphic artist. Furthermore, because these same programs allow one to do the work on discrete layers which can be made visible or invisible with a keystroke, the ability electronically to compare and quickly adapt one's drawings to the actual, physical evidence is extraordinary. Indeed, employing images with contrasting lights, one can begin drawing a letter in one picture, move the drawing to the other picture and finish it there. Drawings can be color-coded so the successive strokes (each on an individual layer) can be superimposed on one another in contrasting hues in order to make clearer just how a given sign or letter was put together. Finally, and most significantly, everything can be measured with precision — length and angles of strokes, for example — so that one may build a statistical profile of a given scribal hand, *ductus*, or, more broadly, the scribal typology.

I know of two dissertations that are exploring paleography of ancient *corpora*, employing these techniques — one focusing on the Ugaritic tablets,[7] the other on provenanced First Temple Hebrew ostraca (see C. Rollston). Sometimes I wonder whether these efforts will only succeed in "recreating the wheel," that is, rediscovering and reaffirming what the great paleographers who have worked in our field during the 20th century had

---

[7] A Harvard dissertation on the *ductus* of the Ugaritic scribes by John Ellison, under the supervision of Jo Ann Hackett, expected completion date, 2001.

already concluded. But even if this were to prove to be so, there would be a significant gain — since there would then be a statistical grounding for these conclusions rather than conclusions based, by and large, on connoisseurship. Still, I strongly suspect that new concepts will emerge from these dissertations and the studies that will follow after them — probably not so much undercutting what has been previously concluded, but allowing us to track the developments in paleography to a much more subtle degree: with the greater precision that these computer imaging techniques allow us to gain.

Stephen A. Kaufman may have put it best when he once declared to me in regard to the impact of the new computer-driven technologies on the study of ancient Near Eastern inscriptions: "You know what this means?" he said. "It means we have to do everything over." It's both a daunting and an exciting prospect. The new finds of Twentieth Century are *renewable* — there is every likelihood that new analyses of their data will open them up and significantly reformulate the way we read these texts. Moreover, inscriptions that previously seemed impossible to read may now be amenable to interpretation, utilizing the technological approaches mentioned above, not to mention other technological advances which time precludes discussing here. And who knows what new tools may be handed to us as the next century unfolds?

Still, before this paper dissolves into a frenzy of millennial anticipation, it may be appropriate to inject a note or two of caution. Computer imaging can — indeed, already has — been overused to reach questionable academic conclusions. The ability to work with precision is a double-edged sword — just as it allows one to examine the evidence with unprecedented precision, it can also allow one to skew the evidence with a subtlety that only the most sophisticated would recognize. I have had occasion to discuss this more problematic aspect of computer imaging in the past and what safeguards, in my view, are necessary to allow scholars the ability to judge the reliability of computer-imaged manipulations.[8] For our purposes here, it simply requires reemphasis that one cannot always judge an image by the final result. How the result was achieved, how the data were manipulated, must always be a concern to anyone who wishes to use these techniques in an appropriate, academic fashion.

Another, perhaps more subtle point: It seems that the more we advance in computer-imaging techniques, the more we encounter problems, often of an unexpectedly difficult nature that require a constant rethinking of methodology. Let me illustrate this point from a current project, the analysis of the data from the Incirli inscription which I am doing in

---

[8]   See Photography of Manuscripts, *op. cit.* (N 5) p. 346.

collaboration with Prof. Kaufman. We have taken many different pictures of this inscription, using various degrees of magnification as well as contrasting lighting angles along the lines discussed above. As noted, the aim has been to coordinate the data with precision so that everything matches up at a common scale. In general we can do this — but we have discovered that there are distinct limitations. Even when things are matched in scale, they do not perfectly match. The problem, we have begun to realize, is skew. When we took our original pictures of the stela, the film-camera could not be kept perfectly stable, it would move, often twist, if ever so slightly, as one advanced the film from shot to shot. It is this twist that throws things off, subtly, to be sure, but just enough so that when one draws the inscription electronically, the drawings will not perfectly match from picture-to-picture.

This raises interesting methodological issues. Should we try to make a single drawing that is not quite accurate for all pictures or a series of discrete drawings, accurate for each picture but not perfectly compatible with one another? Should we create a master drawing of the text based on one overall picture of the text, relying on the detailed pictures to guide this drawing but not using them for this drawing? Should we try to skew all the images to a common skew, as it were, so that each image is slightly distorted but the drawings based upon them will all match? Stay tuned. Frankly, I never dreamed we would encounter such technological problems when trying to work with the image data of this inscription! Of course, technology may ultimately overcome this particular difficulty. The use of a digital camera, which, in contrast to a film camera, has no moving parts, could eliminate the skew problem. The application of the Hewlett-Packard methodology could give one nuanced lighting of the text from virtually any lighting angle. In all probability, such techniques will allow significant gains, but — and this one can count on — as a given problem is solved, others will certainly turn up.

Before concluding, I want to consider one final point regarding the issue with which we began: what do we do with the data we have gained in the Twentieth Century? Our West Semitic Research Project[9] is trying to come to grips with this issue in a pragmatic manner, by beginning to build an image database of all the images in our archives — the project even has a working title: We call it the "InscriptiFact" relational image database.[10] Projects of this type, I believe, represent the model for the way we will deal with the data in the new century. The concept is simple: namely, to build an

---

9   See www.usc.edu/dept/LAS/wsrp.
10 Up-to-date information for the InscriptiFact Project can be found at the project's website, see N 6.

image data-base that will be available over the internet so that any scholar will have access to an array of high-resolution images at his or her fingertips from anywhere in the world.

The conceptual underpinning for this project comes from one already in existence at the University of Southern California, the "Information System for Los Angeles," called ISLA for short.[11] This is basically a highly sophisticated image base that maps Los Angeles by coordinating all existing mapping data on the city. Using this image base, one can go to any particular neighborhood in LA and see it in any map or cartographical photo (e.g., aerial and satellite imagery). In fact, one can take a trip back through time by examining maps and images of the city as far back as they go and thereby looking at how the city has changed over the years.

We realized that the program-architecture used for this project could serve as a model for an image base of ancient inscriptions, which are, after all, topographical maps in miniature. A prototype that shows how InscriptiFact will look and operate is already operational. What one will eventually see will be an image base that will allow one to go to any particular inscription within the archives of the West Semitic Research Project and, ultimately, other similar projects in an open-ended relational database. A given inscription will be mapped in terms of all existing images (both recent and early) in a coordinated fashion so that a given scholar can survey the data from a remote location.[12] Granted, there are currently technological limitations to how such an image base would work, particularly due to the inability of the Internet to move large blocs of data of the sort our images entail. But there can be little doubt that these are temporary problems that will soon be overcome as the Internet becomes more powerful as a conveyor of detailed data.

We are even talking about the concept of having "electronic-fellows" for InscriptiFact — that is, scholars who would be assigned data space and have access to an array of software packages, resident in the USC system which they could operate from a remote location. This would allow scholars to work with highly sophisticated algorithms without the necessity of having high-powered hardware and software on their own computers. All they would need is access — InscriptiFact would do the rest. It is projects like this[13] that will serve as models for future work on ancient inscriptions, and "the future," in this regard, is not very far away.

---

[11] See the ISLA website: www.usc.edu/isd/locations/cst/ISLA.

[12] See preliminarily, www.inscriptifact.com/prototype. We expect a fully operational prototype allowing access to around 5000 images of ancient Near Eastern texts to be available for public review and access some time in 2001.

[13] Another example is ETANA, "Electronic Tools and Ancient Near Eastern Archives"; see preliminarily, staffweb.library.vanderbilt.edu/etana.

So what do we need to be thinking about *now* as we await this future? There are two points I would wish to make. First, all museums and libraries that have early, archival images of ancient inscriptions should make them *high* priority items in their holdings. Efforts should be made to track all such images down, to catalogue them properly and precisely and to insure that they are kept in an archivally stable environment. Most especially, efforts should be made systematically to copy them both photographically and digitally so that optimal "use-copies" can be available for study using the types of computer-imaging techniques alluded to above. I want to emphasize, in passing, that, in my opinion, digital documentation *alone* is (at least at this stage of the game) unsatisfactory. We simply do not know enough about the long terms stability of digital data and the storage media for same to place all our "eggs" in that one basket. For the time being, photographic image data — a type of data well understood and with an archival history going back now more than a century — must also be maintained. Second, scholars, librarians and curators should place special emphasis on cooperation. It would be a fundamental error, if each museum or library with significant holdings in ancient texts should decide unilaterally to make its own discrete image base so that there develop a wide variety of separate and potentially incompatible data protocols: a digital Tower of Babel. Planning should begin now for the future in order to build a network of mutually compatible, easily accessible image bases — once again, the sum of such cooperative efforts will be far greater than the parts.

I began this paper with an anecdote and I have another with which to end it. Some years ago I had occasion to speak at another gathering of scholars — in that case, a gathering to assess the current state of Dead Sea Scroll research. Over breakfast, I happened to be sitting next to an eminent and highly skilled scholar, one of the official editors charged with publishing a particular scroll-manuscript. This manuscript, which was highly fragmentary, represented a formidable challenge because so little of it remained and even that which remained was in poor condition. As we sat talking, the scholar made a remark that made a great impression upon me. This is what that scholar said: "You know, when I edit a Dead Sea Scroll, I feel like I'm writing fiction."

I know how that scholar feels. Over the last several years, Prof. Kaufman and I have been working on a formidably difficult inscription, the aforementioned Incirli Stela — certainly the most difficult thing I have ever endeavored to analyze as I think Kaufman would concur. In order to do so, we have used every technological trick in the book. Indeed, I can state with fair confidence that the Incirli Stela is the most thoroughly photographed and digitally scanned and analyzed inscription of its kind.[14] And yet ... I think we both have a tremendous sense of uncertainty regarding how the inscription is to be read and some of that uncertainty is due to the amount of data we have to work with. What we have discovered is that, as the level and quality of the data increases, this does not always lead to clarity. Rather, it can lead to more and more potential choices. The more ways you have to look at a text seem to lead to more ways you can read it. Sometimes I feel as though we are drowning in the data, that all our technological techniques really do not cut down our subjectivity in interpreting the data but only increase it. And when that happens, I begin to wonder, is it the data we are reading or simply our *imaginings* of the data?

The trouble is the trouble with which we began — even with more data we still basically have *no* data. That is the curse of this field of study — but, I also think it is the blessing. For it teaches us that all the data are precious and that when new data emerge (as they undoubtedly will in the Twenty-First Century) our knowledge will undergo profound change — simply because any significant increase in data necessarily alters the picture in profound and unpredictable ways. That's what makes the field of Semitic studies frustrating; that's also what makes it ever-surprising and fascinating.

REFERENCES

CAD. 1956–. *The Assyrian Dictionary of the Oriental Institute of the University of Chicago*. Chicago.

Clines, David J. A., John Elwolde et al. (eds.). 1993–. *Dictionary of Classical Hebrew*. Sheffield [vol. I 1993, II 1995, III 1996, IV 1998).

Garr, W. Randall. 1985. *A Dialect Geography of Syria-Palestine, 1000–586 BCE*. Philadelphia.

Golomb, D. M. & S. T. Hollis, eds. 1987. *"Working with No Data": Semitic and Egyptian Studies Presented to Thomas O. Lambdin*. Winona Lake.

Harris, Zelig S. 1939. *Development of the Canaanite Dialects*. New Haven.

A. Herdner. 1963. *Corpus des Tablettes en Cunéiformes Alphabétiques*. Paris.

Koehler, L. & W. Baumgartner. 1967–96. *Hebräisches und Aramäisches Lexicon zum Alten Testament*. Leiden.

---

[14] See www.humnet.ucla.edu/humnet/nelc/stelasite/stelainfo.html.

Koehler, L. & W. Baumgartner. 1994–. *The Hebrew and Aramaic Lexicon of the Old Testament.* Leiden-New York-Köln.

Rollston, C. 1999. *The Script of Hebrew Ostraca of the Iron Age: 8th–6th Centuries BCE.* Johns Hopkins Univ. diss.

Reviews

Hetzron, Robert (ed.). *The Semitic Languages*. London: Routledge. 1997

Reviewed by Shlomo Izre'el

The Semitic Languages is one volume in a Routledge series dedicated to grammatical surveys of languages that constitute a single language family. Its editor, Robert Hetzron, has brought together eminent specialists in their respective areas and managed to set up a volume summarizing what we know of the Semitic languages toward the end of the twentieth century.

In a review of Daniels' edition of Bergsträsser's *Einführung in die Semitischen Sprachen* (Bergsträsser 1983), I expressed disagreement with the raison d'être for the English edition of this book as expressed by its editor as follows:

> Bersträsser's *Einführung*, published more than half a century ago [actually, in 1928] makes a wonderful monument for the achievements of Semitics of its time, yet also serves as a reminder of its stagnation in the past two generations. This, however, is not quite true as for the study of some of the languages in particular, especially the modern dialects, and also as for some developments in the methods of studying languages in general, especially during the most recent years. That is why I do not accept the *raison d'être* of this new edition, namely "that Bergsträsser's *Einführung* has not been superseded, and that is unlikely to be." (Izre'el 1984: 663)

In many ways the book under review fills the gap by bringing forward, in a single, handy volume, the accumulated knowledge and recently developed methodologies in the study of Semitic languages. It also serves us well in pinpointing what still needs to be done, especially in methodology.

The book is divided into three parts: Part I: Generalities; Part II: Old Semitic; Part III: Modern Semitic. There are four chapters in the first division: Genetic Subgrouping of the Semitic Languages by Alice Faber; Scripts of Semitic Languages by Peter T. Daniels; and two chapters on grammatical traditions: The Arabic Grammatical Tradition by Jonathan Owens and The Hebrew Grammatical Tradition by Arie Schippers. While these latter two chapters serve to show the origins of Semitic Linguistics, this volume of *IOS* is in a way complementary, in that it shows trends in research in modern times. This is important if one wishes to learn about both achievements and mishandlings of Semitic Linguistics. Some

501

notice of other grammatical traditions and perhaps even a mention of
the grammatical learning of the ancient Semitic scholars of Mesopotamia
(Black 1991; Dietel 1987) might help to complete the picture.

The second part, on old Semitic, includes chapters on Akkadian by
Giorgio Buccellati, Amorite and Eblaite by Cyrus H. Gordon, Aramaic
by Stephen A. Kaufman, Ugaritic by Dennis Pardee, Ancient Hebrew
by Richard C. Steiner, Phoenician and the Eastern Canaanite Dialects
by Stanislav Segert, Classical Arabic by Wolfdietrich Fischer, Sayhadic
(Epigraphic South Arabian) by Leonid E. Kogan and Andrey V. Korotayev,
and Geʻez by Gene Gragg. The third part, on Modern Semitic, includes
surveys of Arabic Dialects and Maltese by Alan S. Kaye and Judith
Rosenhouse, Modern Hebrew by Ruth A. Berman, The Neo-Aramaic
Languages by Otto Jastrow, The Modern South Arabian Languages by
Marie-Claude Simeone-Senelle, Tigrinya by Leonid E. Kogan, Tigré by
Shlomo Raz, Amharic and Argobba by Grover Hudson, Harari by Ewald
Wagner, The Silte Group (East Gurage) by Ernst-August Gutt and Outer
South Ethiopic by Robert Hetzron.

All of these chapters consist of concise grammatical overviews of
the respective languages or language clusters. Most of these papers
are excellent compilations and updates of the known facts that have
been accumulated in recent years, along with some original views either
in reconstructing deficiently-attested languages (e.g., Ugaritic), bringing
forth newly elicited linguistic field work (e.g., Neo-Aramaic, Modern
South Arabian), or suggesting new methodologies that can enrich our
view even of old beaten tracks (e.g., Ancient Hebrew).

If I may resort again to my review of Daniel's edition of Bergsträsser's
Einführung, I pleaded there for a new edition which would not start
with Proto-Semitic, but go the other way round: starting with accurate
descriptions of the individual languages and thus pave the way for a
description of Proto-Semitic. Hetzron's volume is aimed at a similar
goal, although a conspectus of a model of Proto-Semitic is — rightly
— not presented there. Instead, Faber's genetic overview, based on
Hetzron's (1976) principles of shared innovations, is presented following
the traditional model. The table on p. 6, listing the Semitic languages
according to their genetic grouping, shows some bias toward the Ethiopic
languages, Hetzron's own field of study. Taking a quick glance at the table
of contents of the book, one can see a similar bias, which is especially
overt when one gets into the modern world: There are six chapters
devoted to Ethiopic languages, and only four chapters to all the other
Semitic languages of our time (space is more generously allotted to the
other languages, but still injustice prevails). Fairly judged, this imbalance
is not only the result of the editor's preferences, but of what has been done

in the study of Semitic languages during the twentieth century, giving much more preference to the study of the African branch of this language family than to other branches.

Terminology is consistent with this trend. While varieties spoken in Ethiopia and Eritrea are regarded as separate languages, this is usually not so with regard to other modern linguistic continua, which are termed as dialects. The editor opens his preface as follows:

> This is the first general survey of Semitic that mentions all the languages of this family, doing justice to the modern tongues such as Arabic and Aramaic dialects and various languages of Ethiopia. (p. xv)

Of course, the question of distinction between dialects and languages is a moot question in linguistics in general and may well be regarded as a cultural rather than a linguistic issue. Still, linguists are expected to take a stand on this issue, at least in their own field of enquiry. Indeed, Otto Jastrow has titled his chapter on Neo-Aramaic The Neo-Aramaic Languages, and Kaye and Rosenhouse, after some deliberation, regard all Arabic languages as dialects (except for Maltese), as "[m]utual intelligibility remains ... the **most** important consideration in dialect recognition" (p. 263, emphasis in the original). I am not sure, however, whether other Arabists would endorse this claim.

In fact, this problem is not confined to modern languages, but also to terminology and thus concepts of treating linguistic clusters of the ancient world. To me it seems rather absurd to regard two and a half millennia and a wide geographic spread, as attested in ancient Mesopotamia, as consisting of a single language with dialects, namely Akkadian. Indeed, Assyrian and Babylonian are termed in the Semitistic literature as dialects of Akkadian, which causes misconceptions about the nature of these linguistic varieties, thus leading to unhappy consequences for their study. Can one conceive of a grammar of English which comprises all its geographical and historical varieties and describes them as a single model with variations? Indeed, Akkadian texts show significant variation in geographical terms, and drastic changes throughout its attested history, which makes it impossible to place all these under a single descriptive umbrella. Buccellati indeed understood this problem when he based his comprehensive Akkadian grammar on Old Babylonian (Buccellati 1996). Still, in his survey for this volume, based on the same data (but titled "Akkadian"), Buccellati speaks about Akkadian as "the oldest attested Semitic language" and of Old Babylonian as a dialect of Akkadian (p. 69). (In the case of Akkadian, serving as an example for the study of ancient languages, compilation of data consisting of texts written within a span of a few centuries and originating from a variety of geographical sites is understandable; sometimes even inevitable.) Faber, on her part, says that "until the discovery of the Eblaite texts, there was no reason to focus inquiry on the structure of East Semitic, since the only language assigned to that group was Akkadian, and Akkadian/East Semitic was what was left out of West Semitic" (p. 7). In other words: with no Eblaite at hand, there is no point in studying the relationships between the Akkadian languages (oops: dialects) ...

On the other hand, much space and time has been devoted to studying the relationships between Ugaritic and Canaanite. The reason is, of course, purely cultural, Ugaritic being the source of mythological texts closely related to ancient Hebrew mythology, with some very interesting lexical and structural proximities to biblical poetry and poetic language. This is further reflected in this volume by giving Ugaritic an almost identical amount of space to that given to old Aramaic with all its varieties. An almost identical space is also given to Amorite and Eblaite (which are put together for some obscure reason), of which knowledge is rather scanty (what is Amorite, anyway?).

In sum: the volume under review reflects not only the accumulated knowledge, but also the paths of interest which have shaped the study of Semitic languages in the past century. This is also reflected in the methodology behind the individual language descriptions. In order to enable easy comparison of features of the various Semitic languages, the editor has tried to make the presentations of the respective languages as uniform as possible. On the whole, this has turned out to be successful, and — given the limited space allotted for each presentation — some comparisons can indeed be made. This brings us to the question of the readership of this volume.

As stated by the short description of this volume in the publisher's Web site, the volume presents "a comprehensive survey of this language family ..., providing an essential source of reference for the specialist and the lay reader." The Routledge Language Family Descriptions series obviously aims at describing languages according to their genetic classification, so that comparative data can be adduced from reading these descriptions. However, the limited space allotted for each individual description makes the scope of this volume insufficient for thorough comparative research. Semitic linguists may make good use of this book for their needs for quick reference in fields outside the scope of their immediate research. While a lay reader may well be a potential reader of this series, I would assume that the majority of users are professional linguists. Still, I have found most of the individual language descriptions in this volume difficult for the uninitiated reader.

Thus, traditional transliterations are given for personal names in the chapter on Amorite and Eblaite (pp. 102ff.), and Barth's law serves as a point of departure for explaining some names (p. 103; also Ugaritic, p. 138). Moreover, Amorite is not really described, but given as a list of how the so-called Amorite names may reflect divergences from otherwise known (East-)Semitic structural affinities (again: what is Amorite, anyway?). Speaking about a morphological reflection of the opposition between active and stative verbs in thematic vowels (Aramaic, p. 125) can only be understood if one understands the basics of the Semitic verbal system. Having read Buccellati's structural detailed description of Akkadian, this gap may perhaps be filled by a skilled reader, yet I believe each language description should have been self-contained. Phoenician is supplied with a jussive form which cannot be recognized in the script (p. 183) and one is unable to know the origin of this assumption without some background in Biblical Hebrew (Garr [1985: 126] concludes that there was no distinction between indicative and jussive forms in Phoenician; cf. also Krahmalkov [2001: ch. 9]).[1] Similarly obscure for the uninitiated are references to a presupposed doubling of the second root radical (Sayhadic, p. 233; Harari, p. 487), the use of specific terminology, like the Ethiopic grammatological term n-order (Tigrinya, p. 427), and so forth. At this juncture I would ask the editor of the second edition of this volume to supply glosses for all translations given (as in the descriptions of the Arabic dialects and Maltese, Amharic and Argobba, or the Silte group), especially in the sections on syntax. This would greatly enhance the understanding of all cited examples.

This brings us to a more significant methodological issue, viz. the relationship between description and synchrony versus explanations and diachrony. Many writers place their points of departure toward language description at a former stage of the respective tongue, be it Proto-Semitic, a reconstructed phase of an individual branch, or an attested related language or language phase of the same branch. Semitic Linguistics has a long tradition of such a methodology, and the reviewed volume manifests this tradition. Every stage of a language is rooted in its past and contains starters for a new phase. Synchronic variation in language can at many points be regarded as a different view of diachronic change. Still, as so cleverly expressed by Paul Kiparsky (1970: 310), "the child learns his mother tongue in complete ignorance of its history. The child is the synchronic linguist *par excellence*." It follows that "a grammar, too, must be unprejudiced by historical considerations and built on the

---

[1] I wonder what one can deduce form the Byblos *tertiae yod* form *ymḥ* of the Aḥirom inscription.

synchronic facts of the language alone." Considering historical rules is justified only insofar as they have overt features that make them relevant to the synchronic description. Otherwise they have no descriptive value, but an explanative one. Some authors have come up with a pure description of their respective languages or language clusters, with only some resort to etymology or diachrony, e.g., Simeone-Senelle for the Modern South Arabian languages or Kogan on Tigrinya. Others resort more to historical explanations and comparisons, e.g., Berman on Modern Hebrew, Jastrow on Neo-Aramaic or Hetzron on Outer South Ethiopic. Others hold a midstream attitude, where comparison to an older, attested or reconstructed stage of the language is occasionally made, e.g., Buccellati on Akkadian, Pardee on Ugaritic (Ugaritic being largely the product of comparative Semitics, a synchronic description of Ugaritic is a significant achievement), or Gragg on Ge'ez.

Generally speaking, the majority of contributions give us good synchronic descriptions of the languages, dialects or language clusters involved, whereas diachrony is used for explanations only. Still, I find some contributions relying too heavily on history. For example, Berman's survey of Modern Hebrew tends to suggest the historical origin of many contemporary features, and makes occasional references to older stages of Hebrew: "Word stress follows the Sephardi reading tradition ... . As in classical usage, penultimate stress applies to the "segolate" class of derivative nouns, e.g., Biblical *mélex* 'king', Modern *méser* 'message', Mishnaic *nóhag* 'custom' ..." (p. 316). Would an uninitiated reader know that *mélex* and *nóhag* are common words in contemporary Hebrew very much like *méser*? In the following statement, history and synchrony are intertwined: "[T]he historical alternations neutralized in the past tense verb kara are manifested in other words derived from the same roots ..." (p. 315). Orthography serves as a meeting point of history and synchrony: "[T]he single surface phonetic string [kara] is past tense 3rd person masculine verb form which stands for five different lexemes *qrh* = 'happened', *qrʔ* = 'read', *qrʕ* = 'tore', *kry* (sic) [2] = 'mined', and *krʕ* = 'knelt'" (*loc. cit.*). Wagner practically bases his contribution on Harari on comparative-historical considerations: "The main changes in comparison with Geez are: Geez *ṣ*, *ḍ* became *ṭ* ..." (p. 487); "There exist polite forms for sg. 2 *axa:xu* and sg. 3 *azziyu* which seem to be the original forms of the plural ..." (p. 489). Occasionally he even resorts to arguing against or in favor of an explanative rule (e.g., pp. 489–90, 491, etc.).

Most notably, phonological descriptions tend to rely on history, and

---

[2]   While other items in this list seem to be represent orthographic variants (obviously, *h* in *qrh* is a *mater lectionis*), this item seems to reflect the root.

references to the loss of laryngeal and pharyngeal consonants are numerous, starting from Buccellati's Akkadian (p. 69) to Hetzron's Outer South Ethiopic (pp. 537, 543). This historical change usually entails a major alteration of the phonological and morphological systems of the languages involved. One outcome of the loss of laryngeal and pharyngeal consonants has been the introduction of (more) vocalic elements into the root. While occasional references to the origin of root radicals tend to be expressed, some scholars have absorbed a conceptual change and admit to vocalic root radicals (e.g., Outer South Ethiopic, p. 543; cf. Goldenberg 1997: 4). Others hold different strategies to handle what is usually called "weak" verbs (e.g., Akkadian, pp. 85–6).

Persistent tradition manifests itself mostly in the terms used for describing the tense, mood and aspect (TMA) systems. Hetzron has been well aware of this terminological crux:

> The most delicate case is the "tense vs. aspect" controversy: with which one of these categories do Semitic languages operate their verbal system, "tenses" like (a) "past", (b) "present-future" or "aspects" like (a) "completed" ~ "perfective" and (b) "noncompleted" ~ imperfect(ive)" (where the two (a)'s and (b)'s are respectively equivalent)? ... The majority of writers preferred aspectual terms. Yet this should not be taken at face value. For example, Professor Segert uses aspectual labels but calls the actual forms "tenses". Professor Steiner diplomatically speaks of "tense and/or aspect" without separating them. Dr. Gutt uses the term "aspect" for the basic stem forms of the verb (including a non-aspectual one), and the complete forms based on these are called "tenses". Professors Wagner and Hudson use plain "tense". What matters is that in each chapter the use of the author's preferred term is always clearly illustrated.
> The wisest statement I know about this controversy was uttered by Professor Chaim Rabin in a lecture: "Semitic has either aspects that express tenses or tenses that express aspects." (pp. xv–xvi)

TMA systems change in time, and the Semitic languages do not — in fact, they cannot — share a single system. Thus, different languages can and do manifest different systems, based on tense distinctions, aspectual distinctions, or both. Taking Rabin's statement at face value and not as a cynical remark, I would rather interpret it in Östen Dahl's terms, saying that there may be languages where the marked feature of a form would be aspectual, yet this form may have a regular implicature[3] of tense. This

---

[3] The term 'implicature' is used (after Dahl 1985: 11) to mean something that can be

is a common case in language, especially when a perfective form tends to be used for the past tense (Dahl 1985: 79).

As Hetzron notes, the issue is both terminological and conceptual, since terminology should reflect concepts. It occasionally happens, however, that terminology creates concepts. In the case of TMA terminology, I believe that aspectual terminology was coined to indicate a conceptual change (for a brief history of the concept see McFall 1982: 43ff.), but terminology has since tended to override the concepts behind it. As it has turned out, the aspectual terms "perfect" and "imperfect" usually tend to stand for morphological rather than semantic entities. As the collection under review shows, Semitic Linguistics is still struggling with the terminological tradition. Thus, while for Ugaritic the terms used are the modern, commonly used aspectual terms imperfective and perfective (p. 139), and thus a semantic statement is made, the description of Arabic dialects still uses the old morphological terminology "perfect" and "imperfect" (p. 292). At the beginning of the twenty-first century, Semitic Linguistics should transcend tradition in dealing with such a central feature of language.

One other comment on desiderata is due with regard to the weight given to syntax in Semitic studies. A brief statistical survey of the space allotted to syntax is illuminating: Seven contributions devote between 25% and 40% of their respective space to syntax (Akkadian, Ancient Hebrew, Ge'ez, Harari, Silte, Outer South Ethiopic, and Modern Hebrew occupying the leading position with 40%); five (Classical Arabic, Arabic Dialects, Modern South Arabian, Tigrinya and Amharic) 15%–25%; five (Aramaic, Ugaritic, Phoenician, Sayhadic and Tigré) 10%–15%; one contribution (Amorite and Eblaite) has only a few notes on syntax; and one (Neo-Aramaic) does not have a syntactic section at all. In many of the contributions syntactic descriptions are scattered in the morphological sections, e.g., when noting the word order of nouns and their modifiers (e.g., Tigré, p. 450) or when discussing annexation (e.g., Neo-Aramaic, p. 357).

The need to devote a large space to describing the rich morphology of Semitic languages will result in a bias toward morphological structures, but this tendency to deal with morphology should not cause the neglect of syntactic structures. Clearly, it is the history of research that has contributed to this neglect. As the statistics above show, attention to syntax has grown toward the end of the twentieth century, but much remains to be done (see Khan's contribution to this *IOS* volume, pp. 151–172).

inferred from the use of a certain linguistic category or type of expression, although it cannot be regarded as belonging to its proper meaning.

My last comment will address the publishers and future editors of the second edition of this volume: The reviewed edition is full of signs of careless editing, both technical and academic. There are typos, sloppy cross-references, and poor typography. Transcriptions declared to be IPA-based (Arabic dialects, p. 263) are not so. There is some observable carelessness in leaving repetitive passages or comments (e.g., the chapter on Tigré has two sections on prepositions, pp. 450 and 454). There are too many unclear statements that a good copy editor would have noticed; e.g., is the elative expressed morphologically or syntactically in Arabic dialects? (p. 285). Similarly, Modern Hebrew participial forms are not confined to the 3rd person (table, p. 318), and Neo-Aramaic dialects are occasionally mentioned in the respective chapter with no reference to their location or status beforehand (on pp. 347–8). The map on p. xiv is so full of mistakes that it should not have been used at all: there are no "Other Canaanite" languages spoken today; Akkadian languages had a much wider geographical spread, and so did Phoenician; Ugarit is located closer to the Mediterranean coast; Aramaic is attested much more to the west as well; Gelez is not a known Semitic tongue; and Soqotra is the bigger island of the two near the Horn of Africa (if in doubt, kindly check the wonderful maps supplied by Simeone-Senelle, pp. 380–1). Finally, the index is incomplete and reflects only a mechanical list of used terms: Are there no independent personal pronouns in Akkadian or in Ugaritic? Is there no conjugation in Ancient Hebrew or in Classical Arabic?

The Semitic Languages represents the state of the art in the study of the individual Semitic languages. It includes excellent descriptions of languages and language or dialect clusters. As such this volume is aimed at serving both initiated and uninitiated scholars as their main reference tool for a survey of the Semitic language family for many years to come. The second edition of the book should be clear of any problems of the sort mentioned.

REFERENCES

Bergsträsser, Gotthelf. 1983. *Introduction to the Semitic Languages. Text Specimens and Grammatical Sketches.* Translated with Notes and Bibliography and an Appendix on the Scripts by Peter T. Daniels. Winona Lake, Indiana.

Black, Jeremy A. 1991. *Sumerian Grammar in Babylonian Theory.* Second, revised edition. (Studia Pohl: Series Maior, 12.) Rome.

Dahl, Östen. 1985. *Tense and Aspect Systems.* Oxford.

Dietel, Robert G. 1987. *Ancient Akkadian Grammatical Concepts.*

PhD dissertation, University of Washington. University Microfilms International.

Garr, W. Randall. 1985. *Dialect Geography of Syria-Palestine, 1000–586 B.C.E.* Philadelphia.

Goldenberg, Gideon. 1997. Conservative and Innovative Features in Semitic Languages. In: *Afroasiatica Neapolitana.* (Studi Africanistici: Serie Etiopica, 6.) Napoli, 3–21.

Izre'el, Shlomo. 1984. Review of Bergsträsser 1983. *Bibliotheca Orientalis* 41: 663–671.

Krahmalkov, Charles R. 2001. *A Phoenician-Punic Grammar.* (Handbook of Oriental Studies: The Near and Middle East, 54.) Leiden.

Kiparsky, Paul. 1970. Historical Linguistics. In: John Lyons (ed.). *New Horizons in Linguistics.* Harmondsworth. (Repr. 1973.) 302–315.

McFall, Leslie. 1982. *The Enigma of the Hebrew Verbal System.* Sheffield.

Edward Lipiński. *Semitic Languages: Outline of a Comparative Grammar*. (Orientalia Lovaniensia Analecta 80) Leuven: Uitgeverij Peeters. 1997.

Reviewed by David Testen

Lipiński's *Semitic Languages: Outline of a Comparative Grammar* is destined to occupy an important place in comparative Semitic linguistics for a number of years to come. It has been conceived in response to the long-standing need for a comprehensive survey of the "state of the art" which encompasses the century of research which has passed since the days of Brockelmann. Previous surveys, such as Moscati et al. (1969), have managed to convey the wealth of new information which has accumulated over the course of the intervening decades, but have dedicated considerably less attention to the critical examination of the repercussions of this explosion of data for the task of reconstructing the hypothesized ancestral Semitic language.

The reader of *Semitic Languages: Outline of a Comparative Grammar* is immediately cautioned by the author, "To avoid an excessive overloading of the text, references are given, as a rule, only when they cannot be found easily in current grammars of the particular languages" (p. 18). This disclaimer notwithstanding, the task of using the *Outline* is greatly complicated by the fact that it contains virtually no references for either the data which it presents or the opinions which it propounds. This shortcoming proves particularly important because the discussion provided by the book is often somewhat one-dimensional, in that it allows virtually no insight into the author's processes of analysis and interpretation ("... we deemed it unwise to explain here at full length why the preference was given to certain theories to the exclusion of others, and thus to corroborate our views by quoting literature in extensive notes," ibid.) and the reader is left to rely on his or her knowledge of the literature to determine whether any given opinion expressed is common knowledge, an endorsement of one position or another in a long-standing controversy, or an idiosyncratic judgment on the author's part. The *Outline* should thus only be used with caution by the novice Semiticist, who is liable to fail to recognize that the picture which he or she is acquiring lacks the full richness (or, some might say, tendentiousness) of the field.

Lipiński's laconicity is particularly frustrating in the area of methodology. Since we are given little information concerning the grounds upon which he draws conclusions, we often come away with the impression that comparative Semitic linguistics is simply a matter of "eyeballing" the data — tallying up similar-looking forms whenever these show roughly comparable functions. Indeed, the notion of "superficial similarity" itself appears to be infinitely flexible, since it seems that one need only factor in a handful of familiar "randomizing factors" (palatalization, assimilation, dissimilation, syncopation, epenthesis, etc.) in order to relate virtually any set of forms that catches one's eye. However, the "appearance" of a set of forms is actually entirely irrelevant to the question of whether or not they are related, since that question can ultimately only be resolved on the basis of the systematicity of the chain of developments by which they are traced to a common source. In the course of his discussion, Lipiński frequently finds himself straying well beyond the range of the sound correspondences currently recognized as "regular" by the majority of the field, in part because he seems to avail himself of a somewhat opportunistic conception of sound change — the fact that a given change is documented for one Semitic language, for example, is felt to provide sufficient grounds for positing its effect in any other language, however far removed it might be in time, space, or genetic affiliation. Thus Lipiński adduces phonological phenomena encountered in southern Ethiopia in arguing that Proto-Semitic verbs of the I-*n* type should be reconstructed as originally biconsonantal.

"... It [the putative appearance of a secondary *n*] could be explained in two different ways. The Old Akkadian and Assyro-Babylonian imperative forms with a prosthetic vowel *u* or *i* (e.g., *uqur* 'break!'; *ikis* 'cut!') may suggest that the first radical of these monosyllabic verbs was originally long (e.g. **qqur*, **kkis*). The appearance of *n* in some of the inflected forms may then be interpreted as resulting from the dissimilation of the long phoneme in certain circumstances with a consequent generalization of the use of *n*. Another explanation may simply refer to the large number of roots in South Ethiopic, especially in Gurage (at least 120 examples), with a non-etymological *n* inserted in roots before velars (e.g., *əngər*, 'foot', vs. *ägər* < *ragl*), dentals (e.g. *əndät* 'mother', vs. *adot*), labials (e.g. *əmbərbäya*, 'butterfly', vs. Amharic *birrabirro*), sibilants (e.g. *ənzən*, 'ear', vs. *əzən* < *ʔudn*), palatals (e.g. *ənǧ*, 'hand', vs. *äǧ* < *yad*). This development still perceptible in Gurage dialects may have been operative in Proto-Semitic as well. In this hypothesis, the initial vowels of Old Akkadian and Assyro-Babylonian ought to be regarded as a secondary development, the more so that forms without prosthesis do occur." (p. 427)

Until we provide such rudimentary conceptions with adequate definitions in terms of the relevant time, space, and conditioning factors, and until we independently corroborate them with supporting evidence drawn specifically from the grammatical and lexical matrix of the language in question, they are simply the *ad hoc* nuclei of hypotheses. Lipiński is of course not the only Semiticist whose work is compromised by the casual conflation of "hypothesis" and "solution." Nevertheless, while it is clear that there are many details of the phonological history of the Semitic languages yet to be identified and clarified, abstract speculations about potential or imaginable developments contribute little of concrete value to the discussion.

In the realm of Semitic linguistics, the need for clarifying the methodological underpinnings of analysis grows ever more critical with the increased attention devoted to data originating in the other Afro-Asiatic language-groups. While there can be little doubt that these resources will ultimately prove to be of immense value for Semitic studies, we should remain aware that the field of Afro-Asiatic linguistics is still in its infancy. Using Afro-Asiatic material to resolve Semitic problems can be a very hazardous enterprise, particularly if the comparanda are adduced principally on the basis of superficial resemblance. Until the issue has been more fully investigated, for example, it is difficult to follow Lipiński when he argues that the "Libyco-Berber" verbal stem-affix *-t-* entitles us to trace the frequentative verbal formation in *-tan-*, which is attested clearly only in East Semitic (Akkadian *iptanarras* 'he frequently/iteratively decides'), back to Common Semitic (p. 403), despite the fact that the Berber affix differs from the marker of the Semitic *-tan-* verbs in that the Berber formant serves as a marker of imperfectivity rather than plurality/iterativity, and in that it operates on the inflectional level rather than on the derivational level. At the same time, Lipiński makes no mention of Speiser's (1955) more promising theory that traces of the West Semitic counterparts to the East Semitic *-tan-* verbs are to be found among the *hitpaʕel* verbs of Hebrew.

The reader of Lipiński's *Outline* must keep in mind the classification of the Semitic languages which the book employs, since Lipiński's views differ in significant details from those of most other researchers. Rather than seeing the primary division within the family tree in a bifurcation between "East Semitic" and "West Semitic," Lipiński posits a division into four branches, each labeled for one of the cardinal points ("North," "East," "West," and "South"), and each differing significantly from conventional usage. Lipiński's "North Semitic" branch is composed of "Palaeosyrian" (reflected in the Eblaite, Tell Beydar, and early Mari texts), Ugaritic, and Amorite, while the "East Semitic" branch consists solely of Akkadian, broken down by Lipiński into Old Akkadian, "Assyro-Babylonian," and "Late Babylonian" ("the written language of South Mesopotamia in the Persian, Seleucid, and Arsacid periods from 600 B.C. onwards," p. 55), the last of these somewhat unaccountably promoted to the status of a distinct subbranch within East Semitic. His "West Semitic" includes the Northwest Semitic languages along with Arabic, and thus roughly corresponds to what is frequently called "Central Semitic" (although Ugaritic and Amorite have been reassigned by Lipiński to "North Semitic"), and the remaining Semitic languages (Ethiopic, Epigraphic South Arabian, and Modern South Arabian) are dubbed "South Semitic," despite the fact that this term is more frequently employed by taxonomies in which these languages are connected with Arabic. It is important to keep track of Lipiński's terminology because very often the data which he cites are labeled at a disconcertingly abstract level — e.g., on p. 402 a verbal form *iš-ta-pá-ru* (read as *yištapparū* 'they sent continuously') is identified simply as "Palaeosyrian," and within the Modern Ethiopic data we encounter many forms labeled simply "Gurage."

The book suffers from a fair number of typographical errors, editorial slips, and non-English usages; there are enough errors among the cited forms and passages that the reader is cautioned not to use data from the book without checking against another source. Only rarely do the errors in English interfere seriously with the text's intelligibility —- it is fairly clear, for example, that the Ugaritic personal name *ʕn-qpʔt* (p. 447) was meant to be glossed as something on the order of "the spring is bubbling" (rather than as "the source is buoyant"), but I have not yet managed to decipher the paragraph introducing the summary table of verbal stems, where the reader is advised, "... The whole reconstruction is of course hypothetical. The thematic vowel of the prefix-conjugation is supposed to be *a*, regardless of the real *u*-class of the Arabic verb *qatala...*" (p. 414f.).

The preceding comments are intended to assist the potential reader in navigating this book, not to dissuade him or her from approaching it. Despite some problems with the structure and the editing of *Semitic Languages: Outline of a Comparative Grammar*, this book should be among the first consulted by anyone investigating a specific issue or problem in Semitic linguistic studies. It contains a great many ideas — notably in his discussion of the system of verbal categories — which the careful reader will find thought-provoking. In the long run, the *Outline* is best read, not as a panoramic survey of the field of comparative Semitic linguistics at the end of the twentieth century, but rather as an intellectual "diary" chronicling the reflections of a perceptive and thoughtful individual wending his way among the data and opinions which have accumulated over the history of this field. It is entirely possible that the reader will be left dissatisfied with certain of its habits of exposition, or unconvinced by certain of its modes of interpretation, but on almost every page he or she will find novel and interesting approaches to the complex issues with which comparative Semitic linguistics will continue to grapple for many years to come.

COMMENTS

I have added here a list of notes in the hope that they might be of value to the reader of this book. Please note that the list of corrections given here is not exhaustive.

p. 107 — In the chart of the Semitic consonants, the dental fricatives should be given as "s z ṣ" rather than "s z s".

p. 108 — The discussion of "phonemic split" and "phonemic merger" has confused the paradigmatic and syntagmatic levels of analysis. The term "split" does not normally refer to the development of a sequence of two sounds out of a single sound ("m > mb/p" or "ss > rs"), but rather to a change whereby a language's phonological inventory is augmented through the expansion of a single phoneme into two (or more) distinct elements in phonemic contrast to one another — e.g., the single phoneme *-k- of original *-ka 'you (masc. sg.)' and *-ki 'you (fem. sg.)' vs. the opposed phonemes seen in Amharic -h (masc.) and -š (fem.). Likewise, "merger" is normally used not of the simplification of a sequence of sounds into a single sound ("nt > tt" or "dt > dd") but rather of the loss of the distinctions by which opposed phonemes contrast with one another — e.g., the original Semitic three-way distinction between the phonemes *ṣ, *θ̣, and *ṣ́ giving way to a single phoneme ṣ in Hebrew and Akkadian.

p. 124 — "The fricative palatal [ç] is still attested nowadays in Śḥeri..." This presumably refers to the Jibbali phoneme s̃. According to Johnstone's description of the articulation of s̃ (Johnstone (1981): p. xiv), the point of articulation lies between the blade of the tongue and the palate, and the lips are rounded. This is quite different from the articulation of the canonical palatal continuant ç.

p. 144, p. 445 — "Assyro-Babylonian ḫ corresponds in general to [Proto-Semitic] ḥ or ġ..." Of the two examples of Akkadian ḫ reflecting Semitic *γ which Lipiński cites, the connection of ḫanāmu (glossed as "to grow rich") to the root of Arabic γanam-un 'small cattle' is not secure. Lipiński's source for this term was presumably the *Akkadisches Handwörterbuch* (ḫanāmum, "reichlich anwachsen," von Soden (1965): p. 320), which cites the Old Babylonian passage YOS 2 52:9 ("die Schafe auf 1500 iḫ-ni-ma"), but the *Chicago Assyrian Dictionary* reads this passage with a verb *ḫanû* 'plead' (*ana* 1500 U$_8$.UDU.ḪI.A [*wa-a*]*t-ra-ma aḫ-ni-ma* '(the flocks) have increased to 1500 sheep and I pleaded (with the city council) saying...' (Gelb et al. (1956): p. 76); the remaining attestations of the verb *ḫanāmu*, glossed 'to bloom' by the *CAD*, refer to aspects of feminine attractiveness. There are a number of puzzles associated with the Akkadian reflexes of Semitic **γ* (such as Lipiński's remaining example *ṣeḫēru* 'to be small,' which is surely related to Arabic *ṣaγīr-un* 'small'), but this does not justify leaving unmentioned the common opinion which relates Semitic **γ* not to Akkadian *ḫ* but to an "e-coloring aleph" — e.g., *erēbu* 'to enter' alongside Arabic *γaraba* 'he left.'

p. 205 — The form *šušš-*, glossed as 'sixty' (to be corrected to the fraction 'sixth'?), is evidently based upon the Babylonian hapax *šu-uš-šu* (in a lexical text). It is listed as the reflection of a Proto-Semitic geminate-stem pattern (**C$_1$uC$_2$C$_2$-*), but given the complexity of the forms representing the numeral "six" (Akkadian *šišš-*, Ugaritic *θθ*, Arabic *sitt-*, Amharic *səddəst*) and its various derivatives it is difficult to justify reconstructing a Proto-Semitic **šušš-*.

p. 207 — "When *-īm* is added in Hebrew, e.g., to *kalb-* to form *kalb-īm*..." The proper plural of Hebrew *kéleḇ* is *kəlåḇ-īm*; the correct forms are given in the paradigms in the summary section on p. 277. Oddly enough, I could find no mention in the book of the disyllabic plural stem of the segholate-pattern nouns, despite the importance ascribed to the extra vowel in many discussions of the history of the broken (stem-internal) plural formation.

p. 248 — In the table of Arabic broken plurals, the stem-type "*fʕial(un)*" as the plural of *fiʕlat(un)* should be corrected to *fiʕal(un)*.

p. 288 — "... another shift in Mehri and Soqotri where the numerals 'six' and 'seven' appear with an initial *h* or *yh* instead of the expected palato-alveolar *š*..." The reflection of Proto-Semitic **š* by *h* and *yh* in these languages is not a peculiarity of the numerals, as this passage unintentionally suggests, but rather a general development (the details of which are not as yet adequately understood) encompassing the phonological system as a whole (see p. 127).

p. 315 — "The equivalent of [Akkadian] *annium* in Mishnaic Hebrew is *hallā* and in Syriac *hānā* ..." While these forms may be functionally equivalent, it is not clear to what extent we should see a formal connection here as well, as Lipiński evidently intends: Syriac *hānā* 'this' cannot be separated from the *hā-dənā* found elsewhere in Aramaic, and has long been regarded as a reflection of the same construction (*hānā* < **hā(də)nā*).

p. 336f. — Lipiński takes the stem of the verbal adjective to be underlyingly monosyllabic (*pars-um*), ascribing the presence of the second vowel of the adjective's stative manifestation to anaptyxis (*paris* < **pars*). This view leaves unexplained, however, the qualitative distinctions evidenced by the putative anaptyxis (*damiq* 'he is good' vs. *rapaš* 'he is wide' vs. *qarub* 'he is near'). It seems far simpler to assume that the basic stem (for triconsonantal roots, at least) is underlyingly disyllabic (**CaCVC-um*), with the second vowel lost in open syllables in accordance with Akkadian's familiar rule of syncope.

    p. 338, p. 410 — Lipiński posits the existence of an early Semitic "perfective" form (corresponding to the "perfect" *i-ptaras* of Akkadian), said to indicate that "a state is produced in someone or in something, whether it be caused by another or by himself / itself," and finds evidence of this not only in Akkadian and Eblaite but also in Ugaritic (e.g., *lištbm tnn*, glossed as 'didn't I have muzzled the Dragon?') and Amorite. As he admits, it is difficult to draw a clear line of demarcation between the putative "perfective" and the Gt-stem. The ultimate proof will probably have to be more substantial than the mere presence or absence of a direct object, however, since few will find compelling the claim for Ugaritic that " ... *imtḫṣ ksp* with a direct object means 'I have seized / laid hands on silver', and obviously uses the perfective of the basic stem" (p. 338).

    p. 339, p. 410 — The evidence for the existence of present/imperfective stems of the Akkadian/Ethiopic type (*iparras, yəsabbər*) in Ugaritic and Andalusian Arabic is not convincing as it stands.

    p. 343, p. 351 — Lipiński follows Leslau (1967) and Hetzron (1968) in relating the ending *-u* found among Soddo, Gogot, and Muher main-clause present-tense verbs to the indicative ending *-u* of Arabic. See however Goldenberg (1974) for reservations about this equation, together with Hetzron's response (Hetzron 1976).

    p. 350 — "In [Amharic] main volitive and negative sentences, the jussive *yəngär* is used instead of [the imperfective]..." As the text stands, it is not clear that "negative" refers specifically to the negative counterparts to volitive constructions (i.e., to "prohibitive" sentences like *ayəngär*) rather than to main-clause negative sentences in general.

    p. 395 — In the table of the reflexes of the N-stem, the Arabic form is erroneously given as "*yunfaʕilu*" rather than *yanfaʕilu*.

    p. 401 — The cited Tunisian Arabic form *stʕāhid* 'he agreed with' is more likely to be related to Classical Arabic *ʕāhada* ('he promised, made an agreement') than to *waḥada* ('he was unique').

    p. 404 — It is not clear that the Ugaritic *tmtḫṣh* should be read as an infinitive (*wl šbʕt tmtḫṣh bʕmq* 'and she was not sated with her habit of fighting in the valley") rather than as a prefixed-conjugation verb; the case for a "tB/Gt" stem in Ugaritic thus stands in need of further supporting evidence.

p. 434 — "... Amharic *näkka* < **näkkäyä* 'he touched'..." Given Tigrinya *näk̲ʔe*, the most likely pre-Amharic reconstruction is **näkkäʔä*. The pre-form for the homonymous Amharic verb *näkka* in the sense 'he damaged' remains to be determined — Ge'ez *nakaya* and Tigrinya *näkkäyä* suggest that the lost radical of Amharic *näkka* was a **y*, but Ge'ez also has a verb *nakʕa* ('he injured'), indicating that the lost radical of the second *näkka* might have been a pharyngeal.

p. 452 — The inflected forms of the Ge'ez verb *samʕa* have been miscited. "*Samʕakəni, samʕakənāni, samʕakāni,* etc." ought to have been written *samāʕkəni, samāʕkənāni,* etc.

p. 454 — I am aware of no phonological reason to suspect that Ge'ez adverbs ending in *-u* might reflect an earlier **-əm*.

p. 462 — "Later, in the Neo-Assyrian period, a similar confusion seems to occur between *ana* and *ina*, both being indicated by the logogram AŠ..." See Parpola (1983): p. 47f. (note to r. 3 of text 39).

p. 472 — "... Arabic *ʔammā* , 'if'..." Unlike Arabic *ʔimmā*, composed of *ʔin* 'if' + the particle *mā* (the latter said by the grammarians to be *li-taʔkīd maʕnā l-šarṭ* "for the strengthening of the sense of the conditional"), *ʔammā* is not a conditional conjunction but an element in a topicalization construction (*ʔammā zaydan fa-raʔaytuhu ʔamsi* 'as for Zayd, I saw him yesterday'). Lipiński's simple gloss 'if' is misleading in that it reflects his assumptions about the source of the *ʔammā... fa-* formation. This becomes clear from his discussion of the latter in the section on syntax (cf. *fa-ʔammā l-yatīma fa-lā taqhar* (Sura 93:9), glossed as "and if it is an orphan, do not wrong!" and *ʔammā T̲amūdan fa-hadaynāhum* (Sura 41:16/17) "if it is Thamūd, we guided them aright" p. 537), where the conditional readings which Lipiński provides (rather than the expected "as for the orphan..." and "as for Thamūd...") seem contrived.

p. 479f. — "The semantic relation between **yatāwu* 'to be' and East Semitic *išū* 'to have'..." It is clear from early Old Akkadian renderings of the verb meaning "to have" (such as *la ti-su* 'you don't have' cited on p. 480) that the early Semitic phoneme underlying the sibilant of *išû* was either **š* or **ś*, but could not have been **θ*, which would have been spelled with the ŠU-series of characters rather than the SU-series (cf. p. 118). It is therefore improbable that there is any etymological connection between the verb *išû* 'have' and the West Semitic existential particles containing a reflex of **θ* (e.g., Hebrew *yeš*, Syriac *ʔīt*). For an alternate approach to the problem of Akkadian *išû*, see Testen (2000).

p. 486 — There is a negative missing from the Arabic passage "*kullu n-nāsi ʔaqdiru ʔurḍihim,*" judging by its translation "all people, I cannot satisfy them" (*lā ʔaqdiru ʔan ʔurḍiyahum*).

p. 513 — The "Arabic jussive *lā taqal*" should be spelled *lā taqul*.

p. 518 — In the translation for the Akkadian passage *ul qaqqaru qerbum-ma aḫūka isemmē-ma* (better: *išemmē-ma*) *šulma išapparakku*, *aḫūka* should be rendered as a singular ("... your brother will hear and send you greetings...").

p. 518 — "The preterite *īpuš*- is followed by the present-future *izakkar*- in the Old Babylonian sentence *pīšu īpušam-ma izakkaram ana* PN, 'he opened his mouth and he was speaking to PN'..." While a present-tense verb is not impossible in this context, one would more typically expect a verb in the perfect (*izzakar*-). It is therefore interesting to find what appears to be the same verb parsed by von Soden as a deviant perfect ("...Ähnlich wie bei manchen Nomina... unterbleibt die Elision schon in der aB Dichtung bisweilen, wenn *r* 3. Radikal ist; der 2. Radikal wird dann verdoppelt (z.B. *izzakkaram* 'er sagte' für *izzakram*..." von Soden (1952): p. 114 (§87i)).

p. 523 — The Arabic example "*marrat(u) bi-rağul(i) ʔabūh(u) nāʔim(un)*" should be corrected to *marartu bi-rajulin ʔabūhu nāʔimun* 'I passed by a man whose father was asleep.'

p. 525 — The Arabic passage "*ʔal-rağulu lladī šaʕru ʔabyaḍ* 'the man whose hair is white" is lacking the necessary resumptive pronoun (*al-rajulu llaðī šaʕru-hu ʔabyaḍu*). Since this would typically be expressed more simply as *al-rajulu l-ʔabyaḍu l-šaʕri*, it would have been more instructive if another sentence exemplifying the relative pronoun *allaðī* had been chosen.

p. 562 — It is surprising to find Tocharian singled out as the language through which the Indic term for sugar "probably" entered Arabic.

REFERENCES

Hetzron, Robert. 1968. Main Verb Markers in Northern Gurage. *Africa* 38: 152–172.

Hetzron, Robert. 1976. Response to Goldenberg (1974). *Afroasiatic Linguistics* 2/10: 199–201.

Gelb, Ignace J., et al., ed. 1956. *The Assyrian Dictionary of the Oriental Institute of the University of Chicago*. Chicago.

Goldenberg, Gideon. 1974. L'étude du gouragué et la comparaison chamito-sémitique. *Problemi Attuali di Scienza e di Cultura*, Quaderno n. 191 II. Rome, 235–249. Reprinted in *Studies in Semitic Linguistics: Selected Writings by Gideon Goldenberg* (Jerusalem 1998), 463–477.

Johnstone, T. M. 1981. *Jibbali Lexicon*. Oxford.

Leslau, Wolf. 1967. Hypothesis on a Proto-Semitic Marker of the Imperfect in Gurage. *Journal of Near Eastern Studies* 26: 121–125. Reprinted in *Gurage Studies: Collected Articles* (Wiesbaden 1992), 279–283.

Moscati, Sabatino, et al. 1964. *An Introduction to the Comparative Grammar of the Semitic Languages* (Porta Linguarum Orientalium, Neue Serie 6). Wiesbaden.

Parpola, Simo. 1983. *Letters from Assyrian Scholars to Kings Esarhaddon and Assurbanipal, Part II: Commentary and Appendices* (Alter Orient und Altes Testament 5/2). Kevelaer/NeukirchenVluyn.

von Soden, Wolfram. 1965. *Akkadisches Handwörterbuch (A–L)*. Wiesbaden.

von Soden, Wolfram. 1952. *Grundriss der akkadischen Grammatik* (Analecta Orientalia 33). Rome.

Speiser, E. A. 1955. The Durative Hithpacel: A tan-Form. *Journal of the American Oriental Society* 75: 118–121.

Testen, David. 2000. Conjugating the 'Prefixed Stative' Verbs of Akkadian. *Journal of Near Eastern Studies* 59: 81–92.

Bennett, Patrick R. *Comparative Semitic Linguistics: A Manual.* Winona Lake, Indiana: Eisenbrauns. 1998.

Reviewed by Shlomo Izre'el

While Robert Hetzron's *The Semitic Languages* summarizes the knowledge in Semitic languages accumulated towards the end of the century, Patrick R. Bennett's book takes advantage of this knowledge and of developed methodologies to offer a course book in Comparative Semitic Linguistics. This modest book, as it is described by its author, aims at giving students tools for Semitic reconstructions (p. 1). The book is certainly modest in size, but not in amount of knowledge, both that of the author and that provided to students. In 66 pages, enhanced by 182 pages of paradigms and wordlists to be used in exercises, the author gives uninitiated students answers to whatever questions they could possibly ask, but perhaps never knew they should be asking. There is a supplementary bibliography and a list of journals with their common abbreviations (pp. 119–126), an appendix on Semitic scripts (by Peter T. Daniels, pp. 251–260), and finally two indices, one of languages and one of glosses. An index of grammatical features would be useful as well.

This manual has seven parts: (1) Basics of Descriptive Linguistics; (2) A General Introduction to the Semitic Language Family; (3) An Outline of Comparative Linguistics; (4) Lexicostatistics: Some Alternatives; (5) Linguistic Reconstruction: Comparative and Internal; (6) Various Less Common Techniques; (7) Onward and Beyond.

The student starts by absorbing the basics of general linguistics. I found this chapter the best part of the manual and very useful indeed. In 16 pages, students learn everything they need to know about linguistics for this course and beyond. This is done by using Semitic data and a clear and illuminating method. It would take many hours to digest these 16 pages, but it is worth the effort. A teacher may be needed for guidance and occasional clarification, but this first chapter makes a very good basis for further studies. Teachers may want to suggest some modifications in this or that definition or state their own point of view regarding some individual topics. For example, as against the commonly noted tendency of inflectional morphemes to be affixed to a stem (p. 15), Semitic languages make a notable exception to this tendency in their nonconsecutive TMA (=Tense–Mood–Aspect) morphemes. I would also try to make a point of discussing the nature of the feminine marker as either an inflectional or a

521

derivational morpheme (same page). I would hesitate in transcribing the
first person suffix conjugation morpheme as *-tī* rather than *-ti* (p. 12 etc.),
and, in fact, I would insist that Biblical Hebrew be transliterated with
no length marking but with qualitative distinctions (cf. Steiner, Ancient
Hebrew, in Hetzron (ed.), *The Semitic Languages*, 172).

It seems to me that this is the first textbook in Semitic linguistics that
actually takes the students from linguistics to Semitics rather than asking
them to absorb (usually outdated) linguistic terminology and concepts
through the study of Semitic languages. This first chapter thus makes
Semitic Linguistics a branch of linguistics rather than treating linguistics
as an unfortunate necessity that one must swallow from time to time by
way of studying Semitic languages.

The second part is an extremely brief discussion of the nature of a
Semitic language as being a descendent of this family, and its relationship
with other languages. I am afraid that as much as brevity is needed and
sought, and as eloquent and concise the author of this book may be, at
times one should balance between the desire for brevity and the need
for comprehensiveness. This is not too much of a problem in the first
chapter, but it is from the second chapter on. As stated by the author, the
student who is to take this course is expected to have completed at least
one year's study of a Semitic language, and also possibly to have taken
a general course in comparative linguistics. The book is not aimed at the
"seasoned comparativist or the advanced Semitist" (p. 1). But the amount
of data, methodologies, different ways of looking at things, obstacles in
reconstructions, on the one hand — and an extremely compact, almost
laconic way of writing, on the other, makes it very difficult to absorb
the knowledge invested in this book. Take, for example, the following
paragraph:

> The Semitic Languages do, indeed, share many grammatical
> features; but Ghadamsi, a Berber language (Afroasiatic, but not
> Semitic) shares more of these features with classical Arabic
> (Semitic) than Chaha (an Ethiopic language) shares with Urmi
> (Neo-Aramaic). Chaha is linked with other Ethiopic languages by
> regular sound correspondences, by morphology, and by lexicon.
> Urmi is similarly linked with other Aramaic languages. Ghadamsi,
> on the other hand, is clearly part of Berber. Unless we choose
> to overlook the important differences which set Berber in general
> apart from Semitic in general, we cannot use features common to
> Ghadamsi and Arabic to define Semitic. Nor can features absent in
> Ghadamsi and Urmi be taken as diagnostic. (p. 20)

In order to digest this explanation, which seems clear indeed to the seasoned comparativist or the advanced Semitist, the poor student has first to familiarize himself with at least the names of all languages, to have heard about Afroasiatic, and to have some information on how genetic affiliations and relationships are decided upon. I am afraid that this is too much to ask of a beginner, especially since the reader will not find easy answers to all that is needed in this manual, certainly not before coming to this passage, but also not so easily after it.

Bennett leads the students towards their initial step in reconstruction by comparing vocabulary items, as we all do. He, however, makes them take this first step by using lexicostatistics. While most of us will find this unacceptable, Bennett chose this path "because it gives a logical progression for the learner from the simple cognacy judgments of lexicostatistics through the process of making reconstructions to the more complex logic necessary in internal reconstruction" (p. 25). The problem with such a start is not with its expressed logic, but with the human tendency to cherish whatever is learned first and to save it as a methodological basis. Getting rid of inherited early learning is like getting rid of some inherent feature of your personality. Most of us, who were given our initial education in Semitic studies through historical linguistics, found it hard to make a purely synchronic description of our respective field of study (see my remarks above regarding Hetzron's *The Semitic Languages*).

It is with the third part of the book that the real work indeed begins. Readers are now led through various ways of comparing words and their components, and try to figure out what is comparable and what is not. They are asked to go through lists of words and compare them in order to find reconstructional regularities. They are given explanations of the techniques and are asked to do exercises, to which plenty of data is supplied in the wordlists. The exercises are very useful, but are sometimes very difficult for the beginner, and require the help of a teacher in the first stages. I have found it almost useless to have students prepare ahead for a class meeting, since in many cases some basics need to be supplied orally. I believe this is the result of trying to encompass too much in too little space. For example, in order to try to solve Exercise 7 (Phonological Reconstruction A, p. 43), a student must be given some clue regarding the possibility of postulating a new element, in our case, the sibilant *ś*, which is not attested in any of the words in the list. None of the three languages represented in this exercise, Akkadian, Syriac and Arabic, have retained the original /*ś*/. If the students come to class looking perplexed, the teacher can show them his own skills, but to my taste, a frustrated student is not always a good one, and brilliant students who can come up with new theories are — alas! — too rare. Another example is the concept of skewing (pp. 30-33), which is given an overly prominent exposition. Moreover, it is explained much too early. Before getting entangled with irregularities, a student must be at home with regularities. One other example is Exercise 11 (Phonological Reconstruction, E, p. 46), where the student will find the following note: "The Syriac transcription is phonetic, not phonemic." I am not sure if the average student will know how to deal with this remark and the data in the list. In any case, I would suggest that a key to the exercises be supplied along with the manual.

Similarly overwhelming is the use of data — on the same level — from both ancient and modern languages and dialects. While I welcome the use of modern languages for any domain of Semitic studies, didactically, I myself would start with the ancient languages and only then introduce data from contemporary ones. This, I believe, would make for a gradual immersion into comparative work for the beginning student. After all, it is a well known fact that Proto-Semitic is much easier to reconstruct than Proto-Neo-Aramaic or Proto-Modern-South-Arabian, at least in the present state of affairs.

Bennett's reconstructions are interesting and appealing, and his methodologies are clearly presented (at least to teachers, which challenges us when we use this book for our courses). I am especially happy to notice Bennett's insistence on including areal linguistics aside from the genetic family-tree model, which enrich the student's perception of the processes involved in linguistic change. His insistence on exploitation of data (over using empty theories) is to be endorsed without hesitation, as well as his repeated warning against adhering to theories as truth. I am not capable of making sound judgments of all the data used in this book, but I did notice some slips (e.g., Akkadian has not only *paršaʔu* and *puršaʔu*, but also *peršaʔu* [p. 32]; Biblical Hebrew does not attest *rābab* but *rab*, and *ribrēb* is attested only from medieval texts with the meaning of "entitle as a Rabbi" < "make grow", whereas *hitrabreb*, attested from Mishnaic Hebrew, means "boast", [p. 52]). I believe that on the whole, the data seem to be used skillfully. Suggested reconstructions can be illuminating, e.g., the Arabic case and number marking (p. 51). Still, I wonder why the call for caution was not operative enough for use in verbal reconstruction. From the explanations given, and even more so from the list of forms (p. 54), one gets the impression that Akkadian data have not been taken seriously enough: The G imperfective form *iCaCCVC* is compared to Hebrew *CāCaC*, and the Akkadian stative is not listed at all. The result is a reconstructed system where G has two forms: *yCaCVCa* and *yVCCVu* (p. 55). Had I been the one to reconstruct this system, I would have taken out the final *a* from the first form and eliminated the final *-u* from the second. I would also add a third form: -*CaCCVC* (as well as refrain from adding personal affixes). While this procedure aims at reconstructing the Semitic derivational (stem) system, I am afraid that the students who are now asked to work on Exercise 16 and reconstruct the verbal inflection, will find it extremely difficult to do so, having absorbed this stem-system reconstruction as suggested.

In his conclusion, the author hopes to have made the (exhausted) student realize "that the techniques for reconstructing linguistic history are flawed" (p. 67). The reason for this statement is the conclusion that students must use more than one technique for reconstruction and, especially, that they must be cautious and learn much more. I couldn't agree more. In spite of all the difficulties described above, the textbook under review is definitely a good start for the potential researcher.

Gábor Takács. *Etymological Dictionary of Egyptian*. Vol. I: A Phonological Introduction. (= *Handbuch der Orientalistik*. Erste Abteilung: Der Nahe und Mittlere Osten. 47. Band). Leiden-Boston-Köln: Brill. 1999.

Reviewed by A. Dolgopolsky

Today we are witnessing a revival of comparative linguistics. After almost half a century of relative stagnation (apart from Indo-European, Finno-Ugric, Dravidian and partially Common Altaic very few fundamental studies, like etymological dictionaries or detailed comparative grammars, were published), comparative investigation of all kind of languages of Eurasia and Africa has begun to flourish. The Egyptian etymological dictionary under review is part of this revival. It is a breakthrough in Egyptian etymology. After 1912 (Calice) no attempt has been made to investigate the etymology of the Egyptian language on a large scale. The main interest of Egyptian linguistics was confined to the internal (synchronic and diachronic) description of the Egyptian language and of its Coptic descendant, while the comparativistic studies were restricted to morphology and only a small amount of lexemes. Today Gábor Takács has started an impressive and extremely important project of etymological investigation of the entire lexical stock of Egyptian in the framework of Hamito-Semitic (Afroasiatic) comparative linguistics.

The volume consists of eight chapters:

Chapter 1: "Periods of studying lexical affinities among Egyptian, Semitic, and other Afro-Asiatic languages" (a short history of Hamito-Semitic comparative linguistics).

Chapter 2: "Classification of Egyptian and the Afro-Asiatic language family" (dealing, among other problems, with lexical replacement of Proto-Egyptian words of Hamito-Semitic origin by words having no Semitic cognates).

Chapter 3: "Some problems of Egyptian's position within Afro-Asiatic and among African languages," including four sections: "Egyptian and Chadic," "Egyptian and Semitic," "Egyptian and the African language families" (dealing with lexical affinities between Egyptian and language families outside Hamito-Semitic: Nilotic and other Nilo-Saharan languages, Central Khoisan, subgroups of the Niger-Kongo family).

Chapter 4: "The Old Egyptian consonant system and Afro-Asiatic.

527

Regular correspondences between Egyptian and Afro-Asiatic." This is
the main chapter of the volume. It includes 29 sections, 22 of which
are each dedicated to a particular Egyptian consonant and its regular
cognates in Semitic and other Hamito-Semitic languages. Other sections
are: "Regular consonant correspondences between Egyptian, Semitic and
other Afro-Asiatic branches," "The Old Egyptian consonant system,"
"The problem of Egyptian ꜣ," "The problem of Old Egyptian *n* and **l*,"
and "Further questions."

Chapter 5: "Occasional, seemingly irregular consonant correspondences."

Chapter 6: "Incompatibility, assimilation, dissimilation."

Chapter 7: "The Egypto-Semitic consonant correspondences as set up
by Rössler and his followers" (a critical analysis of Otto Rössler's
suggestions concerning the phonetic value of Egyptian consonant
characters and of consonant correspondences between Egyptian and
Semitic).

Chaper 8: "The law of Belova" (analysis of Anna Belova's hypothesis
treating the initial Egyptian *w-* and *j-* as cognate with the Semitic *mediae
infirmae *w* and **y* and the vowels of Cushitic and Chadic roots; Takács
provides a list of 31 roots that confirm the validity of Belova's hypothesis).

The main text is folowed by a comprehensive bibliography (pp. 401–71)
covering the basic literature for all volumes of the dictionary.

The volume under review is not yet an etymological dictionary *stricto
sensu*. It is a phonological introduction to Egyptian etymology. G. Takács
is absolutely right in understanding that no serious etymological research
can be done before the sound correspondences between Egyptian and
Semitic (and as far as possible other Hamito-Semitic languages) have
been established on a large lexical basis. This is the scope of the volume
under review.

Actually the volume does not cover all words and roots of Egyptian.
It does not mention even some of the quite obvious basic cognates,
such as Eg. *jnk* 'I' — Semitic **ʔanāku* 'I'. This is the author's right,
because the scope of the volume is phonological. Nevertheless, for certain
phonemes it would be advisable to make a comprehensive list of cognates.
This is important for the cases when one Proto-Hamito-Semitic phoneme
yields several positionally conditioned sets of sound correspondences.
If we want to discover the positional rules governing the reflexes in
Eg., Sem., etc., we must see the distribution of these reflexes, which is
impossible without comprehensive lists of cognates. The first volume of
the dictionary does not fulfil this function. We do not find here even
some obvious cases of seemingly irregular (and hence interesting) sound
correspondences, such as Eg *kr.tj* 'horns' — Sem. **'ḳar(a)n-* 'horn' for

Eg. *k* ~ Sem. **ḳ*. Of course, this drawback will be overcome in the succeeding volumes of the dictionary. It is worth mentioning the fact that the positional conditions of multiple sound correspondences include the vocalic environment. Therefore, elucidating the sound correspondences presupposes the reconstruction of the Egyptian vowels and their history, which lies far beyond the scope of an Egyptian etymological dictionary. In my opinion, the publication of all volumes of Takács's dictionary will also contribute (albeit indirectly) to the study of Egyptian vowels.

Gábor Takács is in full command of the immense Egyptological literature concerning the meaning and history of Egyptian words. He has a sound professional acquaintance not only of Semitistic (historical phonology, lexicology, morphology), but also (unlike most of his predecessors) has good professional knowledge of Chadic and Cushitic linguistics.

For every proposed etymology, G. Takács provides exhaustive bibliographical references, especially those concerning comparison between branches of Hamito-Semitic. But here a critical remark is needed. When quoting Cushitic, Chadic and Berber cognates, Takács often does not indicate the names of scholars who recorded the forms in question. The references at the end of each entry and its parts are not sufficient: we must know the name of the scholar for every quoted form. Sometimes it is crucially important, because the level of reliability of Africanistic papers of the 19th and the early 20th centuries is much lower than that of modern scholarship. For instance, on pp. 226–27 (s.v. *dgj* 'to look at, see') Takács quotes Saho *ḍag, ḍig-* ~ *deg-*, Afar *ḍag, dag* 'erfahren, wissen,' most probably from Leo Reinisch's papers of the late 19th century. Today we have better and more reliable information about these languages. The variant with *d-* is not confirmed by modern sources and is probably due to inaccurate recording (in Reinisch's days phonology [in the modern sense of the word: phonemes, allophones, etc.] did not yet exist). Today we know that these verbs are prefix-conjugated, which may be helpful in solving the problem of the origin of the unexpected Saho-Afar *-ḍ-* (actually, retroflex *-ḍ-*) for the expected *d* (< Hamito-Semitic **d-*). Saho-Afar *-ḍ-* is likely to go back to the cluster **ʔ-* (prefix of 1 sg.) and the stem-initial **-d-*, just as in Awngi (emphatization of the initial consonant in 1 sg. of prefix-conjugated verbs). If we know the source of the data, we may judge the level of reliability of the quoted forms.

The etymological comparisons are almost always quite convincing and useful.

I shall quote here some of Takács's etymologies that have been helpful in improving my own long-range etymological comparisons (in my *Nostratic Dictionary*, now in progress):

On p. 76 Takács convincingly compared Eg. *st̠ɜ* 'weave, spin (yarn)' with Dahalo (Cushitic) *sakaʔ-* 'to plait.' This is very important, because it proves the presence of the laryngeal *ʔ* in the Proto-Hamito-Semitic etymon. In view of this etymological connection I have had to modify my Nostratic etymology: the ancient root, represented in Kartvelian **sk̲w-* 'to bind,' Agaw (Central Cushitic) **saɣ-/saq-* v. 'sew, weave,' West Chadic **sak̲-* 'weave,' Berber **√Hsɣ* 'joindre, unir, relier,' Finno-Ugrian **säku* 'to plait' and Tungusian **sakta-n*, **sakta-ma* 'wickerwork (mat, basket),' will now be reconstructed as **säk̲ᴸVᴶʔu* instead of my earlier reconstruction **säk̲u*. The emphatic **k̲* in Kartvelian and West Chadic and **-ɣ-* (> **-k̲-*) in Agaw and Berber will be now explained by contraction **kʔ* > **k̲*. But Takács's comparison with Sem. **√nsk* ~ **√skk* 'weave, plait' remains very questionable, because Semitic **s* goes back to an affricate and cannot correspond to Kartvelian, Agaw, Chadic, Finno-Ugrian and Tungusian **s-*, unless we admit secondary affricatization in the originally bi-morphemic Semitic root (with the prefix **n-*).

On p. 235 G. Takács found Chadic and Dullay (East Cushitic) cognates of Eg *jtj* (< **yky*) 'to take, seize, conduct, carry off': Angas-Sura **yak-* 'pick up,' Bole *yokk-* 'pluck,' proto-Dullay **akk- / *ekk-* 'take,' etc. I did not pay attention to them earlier. They fit very well in my Nostratic comparison (**yoK̂ᵀEˀ* 'to catch, seize' > Eg. *jtj* 'take, seize, Indo-European **eik̂-/*īk̂-* 'take possession, possess,' Dravidian **okk-* 'to trap', etc.).

The etymology of Eg. **ʕn* 'eye' is obvious and is known to many scholars (comparison with Semitic **ʕayn-* 'eye'). Takács adds here Dahalo *ʕēn-ād-* (*d̲* denoting gingival *d*) 'see from afar' and Jegu (East Chadic) *ʔinn-* 'können, kennen' (p. 125). This comparison (of a word for 'eye' with a word for 'see') may be confirmed by the fact that this root has the meaning 'to see' in other Hamito-Semitic and Nostratic languages as well: Berber (Tayert, East Tawellemmet *ənəy* 'to see,' Tashelhit *annäy*, present *y-ännäy* 'apercevoir quelque chose qui tombe sous les yeux', etc.), W[est] Ch[adic] (proto-WCh. **ʕayan-* v. 'see' > Bolewa *ʔinn-* id., etc.), Finno-Ugrian **oynā-* or **oyṅā-* 'to see' (> proto-Lappish **ōynē* v. 'see' > Lule-Lappish *åi'n-ēt*, etc.), Dravidian **unn-* v. 'think, look' (see Burrow-Emeneau 1984: #727), etc.

Takács (p. 259) convincingly compares Sem. **√ṣmd* 'join, bind, yoke' and Eg. *dmd̲* '(re)assemble, join, unite' (metathesis) with South Omotic: Ari *sud̲umt-* 'gather' (metathesis). This contribution will be taken into account in my *Nostratic Dictionary* s.v. **ĉ∇mᴸ∇ʃsˀ∇* 'to plait/tie together' (> Hamito-Semitic, Kartvelian, Uralic, Mongolian).

On p. 40 Takács convincingly proposes to compare Eg *hpɜ* 'navel' with Central Chadic: Musgu-Pus *hif-na* 'navel,' Masa *hif-dá* id., etc. This comparison is acceptable and will be included in my *Nostratic Dictionary* (*ḫUₗnₗpVꭹV* 'navel' > Eg. *ḫpꭹ*, Indo-European **Hʷembʰ-* / **Hʷnebʰ-*, Kartvelian **uₗmₗpe* or **uₗmₗpa*, 'navel', etc.).

Pages 203, 313–4: Takács found a solution for the problem of Eg. *wšb* 'answer.' It is traditionally compared with Semitic **-θūb-* 'return, answer,' though Eg. *š* is not the regular cognate of Sem. *θ*. Takács finds a better etymology by convincingly comparing Eg. *wšb* with Chadic **√śb* 'answer.'

Takács's etymology of Eg. *znzn.t* 'Feuerbrunst' (p. 128) is good and useful. He compares the Eg. word with Berber (Zwawa *zizən* 'se chauffer,' Zenaga *a-zzun* 'fire', etc.) and with Kirfi (West Chadic) *ꭓìŋꭓìŋì* 'charcoal.' It will be taken into account in the forthcoming *Nostratic Dictionary* in the entry **ꭓEnV* 'to burn (intr.), live coal (embers), fire' (> Tungusian **ꭓan-* 'burn,' Turkic **jan-* id., Finno-Ugric **śine* 'charcoal', Hamito-Semitic).

On p. 122 Takács (after Leslau and Hintze) compares Demotic Egyptian *mt* 'phallus' with Highland East Cushitic (Hadiyya, Sidamo *muta* 'penis') and with Omotic (Zala, Dache *mute* id.). This comparison has proved to be very useful for long-range linguistic etymology. Earlier I thought that this Eg. word belongs to Nostratic **mUtV* 'man,' but in the light of Takács's study I have changed my mind and found another etymology for this word (**moṭE* 'sprout' → 'penis' in Hamito-Semitic and Altaic).

I have not found any serious drawbacks in the volume under review. But some minor corrections are still necessary:

1. In the list of languages (p. 10) Moabite is not mentioned as *a language*: "?Moabite inscription (9th cent. B.C.): distinct from Hebrew." In fact, Moabite is a language, represented by two inscriptions and a few seals. It is generally considered different from Hebrew (pl. יר־, שת 'year', etc.). See Lipiński 1997: 60–61.

2. On p. 236 s.v. *snty* 'gründen, schaffen' Takács mentions Ahaggar Tuareg *əskən* 'squat on hind legs'. In fact it means 'stand on hind legs' (of quadrupeds) rather than 'squat' (cf. Foucauld 1951–2: 1814–5).

3. Takács does not try to find a solution to the problem of Eg *r* [*r*] that corresponds to Cushitic and Chadic **l*. He transcribes *jr.t* as [**ꭹl.t*] in spite of the Greek and Coptic evidence of **r*, namely the Greek transcription *ιρι* and the Cpt reflex (with *r* rather than *l*): *nomen actionis ieire* in the compound noun *banieire* 'qui a le mauvais œil' (Vycichl 1983: 60).

4. Somali *ʕan* means 'cheek' rather than 'chin' (as on p. 39), cf. Zorc-Osman 1993: 58, Abraham 1962: 13, DSI 1985: 87. Actually its stem is *ʕam-* (cf. pl. *ʕám-án*). Therefore (and because of the initial *ʕ-*) its comparison with Eg. *jnʕ* 'chin' (after Hodge 1968: 22) is to be rejected. As to Takács's comparison of Eg *jnʕ* with Chadic (Boghom *ŋa* 'chin', etc.), it is a good and quite reasonable idea.

5. Eg *hd* 'break stones' and Arabic *√hdd* 'break, crush' can hardly

be compared (as in Takács, p. 147) with Chadic *√ḥḏ 'break' [> Jimbin ḥaḍa 'push', Goemay ni hetni 'hit, strike'] because of the glottalized Chadic *ḍ and Chadic *h (which hardly corresponds to Sem. *h- and Eg. h-); the Chadic root is more likely to be cognate with Sem. *√ḫtt (> Biblical Hebrew נְחַת ni'ḥat̲ 'was broken,' Ugaritic ḫt 'broken', Tigre ḥatta 'was torn').

6. To pp. 44, 249: I do not accept Takács's etymology of Eg. ʕḏ 'huck up, hacken.' Takács compares it with Cushitic and Chadic words for 'dig': Saho -uʕug- v. 'dig', Angas ok 'dig', Lele yagi 'dig', etc. I prefer another etymology: Eg. ʕḏ is akin to West Semitic *√ʕṣ̌w 'divide, separate' > Arabic عضو‎ √ʕṣ̌w (impf. -ʕṣ̌ū) 'dépécer (un mouton, etc.), séparer par membres / parties, partager,' whence a derived noun: Semitic *ʕiṣ̌- 'piece, portion' > Arabic ʕiẓ̌-at- id., Geʿez ʕaṣ̌, ʕaṣ̌ā, Tigre ʕзč, Tigray ʕзča, ʕзča 'lot.'

7. Page 281 s.v. šʕd 'to cut.' Takács states that "it is commonly accepted that Eg. šʕd may go back prob. to *š₃d = Sem. *ṣ́rṭ 'to cut'" and remarks: "Not excluded, though different etymologies were also suggested." In my opinion, the comparison of šʕd with *ṣ́rṭ is hardly tenable (Eg ʕ is not cognate with Sem. *r), the Eg. verb šʕd is likely to go back to Nostratic *ẑaʕidᐁ or *ẑaɣidᐁ 'to cut' (> Indo-European *laidʰ- / *lidʰ- v. 'cut, wound', Finno-Ugrian *laδᐁ 'incision, notch' and Dravidian *naṭ- v. 'cut, tear').

8. On p. 125: "Semitic *naḥnu ~ *niḥnu 'we'". The variant *naḥnu does not exist. The vowel *a in Hebrew אֲנַחְנוּ ʔănaḥnū, Bibl. Aramaic אֲנַחְנָא ʔănaḥnā and Arabic naḥnu is due to positional factors (Philippi's law in Hebrew, influence of ḥ in Arabic). The right form is *niḥnu (whence Akkadian nīnu and Ethiopic nзḥna).

9. Arabic ḥaqira does not mean 'to be poor, wretched' (as in Takács, p. 211), but 'be mean, despicable, contemptible' (cf. Lane 1863–93: 611, Hava 1970: 134, Biberstein-Kazimirski 1860: I 466–7, Freytag 1830: I 407), which makes the comparison with Eg. ḫkr 'be hungry' rather questionable. Takács adduces here South Cushitic *√ḳʷr 'hunger' and Mupun (West Chadic) kȝr 'hunger', which is quite convincing. But he is hardly right in assuming that the initial *ḫ- is prefixal. It is preferable to suppose the loss of the initial laryngeal in South Cushitic and Angas-Sura (cf. Sura gʷoɣar 'girdle' ~ Semitic *√ḥgr 'belt' [see Dolgopolsky 1982, 33 and Stolbova 1987, 243] and Sura ḍugur 'to darn' ~ Eg. ḫtr 'bind together ~ Arabic ḥitār- 'corde principale de la tente'). This view is confirmed by external genetic comparison (Hamito-Semitic *√ḥḳr corresponds to Dravidian *akkar- 'necessity, want' [Burrow-Emeneau 1984: #21] < Nostratic *ḥAḲArᐁ 'need, want, be hungry', see my forthcoming Nostratic Dictionary s.v.).

10. Page 118: Eg. *ḥfʕ* 'fassen, packen' is compared with the [non-existent?] Arabic verb *ḥfʕ* 'to seize, packen' (mentioned in some Russian comparativistic papers, but not registered in Lane, Freytag, Biberstein-Kazimirsky, Belot, Dozy and other available dictionaries of Classical Arabic). The Eg. word should be compared with Iraqw *-húw-* v. 'take' and possibly with Dahalo *ḥap* 'snatch quickly' (Whiteley 1953; Ehret-Elderkin-Nurse 1989: 26).

11. Takács's comparison of Eg. *ḥmʕ* 'seize, grasp' with Hamer (South Omotic) *hʌm* 'hold, keep' (p. 123–4) is very good and new, but one misses here the obvious Semitic cognate, which is Akkadian *ḥamāmu* 'pluck and gather.' As to New Egyptian *ḥm* 'possess, gain mastery of', it should be kept apart, because it goes back to *ḥꜣm*.

12. P. 81: Eg *jdn* 'ear' is compared with East Chadic: Jegu *ʔúdúŋê* (pl. *ʔùdáŋ*), Birgit *ʔùdùŋgì* 'ear'. But the words of Jegu and Birgit are not genetic cognates, but loans from Chado-Sudanese Arabic: cp. Chado-Sudanese Arabic *uden* (dual *u'deyn*) 'ear' (see Roth-Laly 1965: I 24). Jegu and Birgit are spoken in a region adjacent to (and even surrounded by) an Arabic-speaking population, so that the borrowing is quite natural.

13. P. 258: Takács denotes Sem. *ṣ̂ (the emphatic lateral consonant yielding Arabic ض *ẓ̂* [traditionally transcribed as *ḍ*], Hebrew צ and Aramaic ע) with the sign *ḏ*, which is misleading, because *ḏ* is the traditional (and phonetically correct) sign for a different phoneme, namely for Arabic ظ *ẟ*.

14. On p. 324 Takács transcribes Hebrew יֵשַׁע *yešaʕ* 'Befreiung' with a long *ē*. This is a mistake: in the segolate nouns the vowel of the stressed syllable is always short (except for the pausal variant), while the Masoretic sign for closed *e* (*ṣere*) does not distinguish between long *ē* and short *e* (see Dolgopolsky 1999).

15. G. Takács does not take into account Karl Prasse's reconstruction of the Proto-Berber verbal morphology and the reflexes of ancient *w, *y and laryngeals that have influenced the verbal forms in modern Tuareg and other Berber languages (Prasse 1974). In my opinion, K. Prasse's theory is convincing and quite indispensable in dealing with Berber verbs.

Of course, the value of this magnificent study is not diminished by these few minor details that can be easily corrected in the forthcoming volumes.

We are looking forward to the subsequent volumes of this extremely important dictionary, which promises to open a new chapter in Egyptian and Hamito-Semitic comparative linguistics.

A note on symbols in reconstructions:

⌐ ⌐ — uncertainty brackets: ⌐a⌐ = a or similar.

∟ ⌐ — uncertainty brackets: ∟a⌐ = a or nothing.

∇ — unspecified vowel

Transcription signs:

Λ = as u in English *but*

ʕ = epiglottal approximant (like Arabic ع)

 c̣ = emphatic (glottalized) t͡s (IPA *ts'*)

č̣ = emphatic (glottalized) č (= IPA *t͡ʃ'*)

ĉ = glottalized lateral affricate

ḍ (in Saho, Afar, Somali) = IPA ɖ = postalveolar d

ḍ (in other Cushitic, Omotic and Chadic languages) = d' = preglottalized
   ("injective") d

δ = fricative d (English *th* in *that*)

з = central vowel

γ = voiced uvular fricative (Arabic غ)

H = unspecified laryngeal

Hʷ = labialized laryngeal

ħ (= Orientalistic ḥ) = Arabic ح

ḳ = emphatic (glottalized) k

Ḳ (in Nostratic reconstructions) = "ḳ or q̇" (when we cannot distinguish
   between ḳ and the emphatic uvular stop q̇)

ṅ = postalveolar n

ṉ = alveolar n (in Dravidian)

ω̃ = closed o (intermediate between o and u)

p̣ = emphatic (or glottalized) p

r̠ = dental (gingival) r (in Dravidian)

s̄ = palatal s

ŝ = voiceless lateral fricative (Welsh *ll*)

ṣ̂ = emphatic (glottalized) ŝ

ṭ = postalveolar t

ṭ = emphatic t

θ = fricative t (= t̠ of the Semitistic transcription), like English *th* in
   thin

ẑ = voiced fricative lateral

ẓ̂ (in Old Arabic) = emphatic (uvularized) lateral (Old Arabic and
   Dathina Arabic ض)

ǯ = affricate d͡z

ǰ = as j in English *joke*

ʒ́ = voiced palatal affricate

REFERENCES

Abraham, R. C. 1962. *Somali-English Dictionary.* 2nd ed. London.

Biberstein-Kazimirski, A. de 1860. *Dictionnaire arabe-français.* I–II. Paris.

Burrow, Thomas & M. B. Emeneau 1984. *A Dravidian Etymological Dictionary.* 2nd edition. Oxford.

Calice, F. 1936. *Grundlagen der ägyptisch-semitischen Wortvergleichung.* Wien.

DSI 1985 = *Dizionario somalo-italiano.* Realizzato sotto gli auspici accademici di Jaamacadda Ummadda Soomaaliyeed, Akademiyada Cilmiga Fanka iyo Suugaanta, Università degli studi di Roma "La Sapienza". Roma.

Dolgopolsky, A. 1982. Chadic — Semitic — Cushitic: Epenthetic -γ- in Sura in the light of Hamito-Semitic comparative linguistics. *The Chad Languages in the Hamitosemitic-Nigritic Border Area.* Ed. by H. Jungraithmayr. Berlin, 32–46.

Dolgopolsky, A. 1999. *The Nostratic Macro-Family and Linguistic Palaeontology.* Cambridge, England.

Dolgopolsky, A. 1999. *From Proto-Semitic to Hebrew: Phonology.* Milano.

Ehret, Christopher, E. D. Elderkin & D. Nurse. 1989. Dahalo lexis and its sources. *Afrikanistische Arbeitspapiere* (Köln) XVIII: 5–50.

Foucauld, p. Charles de. 1951–2. *Dictionnaire touareg-français.* I–IV. Paris.

Freytag, Georg W. 1830. *Lexicon Arabico-Latinum.* I–IV. Halle.

Hava, J. G. 1970. *Arabic-English Dictionary.* Beirut.

Hodge, C. T. 1968. Some Afroasiatic etymologies. *Anthropological Linguistics* XXII: 19–29.

Lane, E. W. 1863–93. *An Arabic-English Lexicon.* Book I, parts 1–8. London / Edinburgh.

Lipiński, Edward. 1997. *Semitic Languages.* Leuven.

Prasse, K.-G. 1974. *Manuel de grammaire touarègue (tăhăggart).* Vol. VI–VII. Copenhague.

Roth-Laly, Arlette 1965. *Lexique des parlers arabes tchado-soudanais.* Vol. I. Paris.

Stolbova, Olga 1987. Sravnitel'no-istoricheskaja fonetika i slovar' zapadnochadskix jazykov. In V. Porxomovskij (ed.), *Afrikanskoje istoricheskoje jazykoznanije.* Moscow.

Vycichl, Werner 1983. *Dictionnaire étymologique de la langue copte.* Leuven.

Whiteley, W. H. 1953. *Studies in Iraqw.* Kampala.

Zorc, R. David, and Madina M. Osman 1993. *Somali-English Dictionary with English Index.* 3rd ed. Kensington, MD.